MINDING THE LAW

MINDING THE LAW

ANTHONY G. AMSTERDAM

JEROME BRUNER

□

HARVARD UNIVERSITY PRESS

Cambridge, Massachusetts

London, England

2000

Library of Congress Cataloging-in-Publication Data

Amsterdam, Anthony G.
Minding the law / Anthony G. Amsterdam, Jerome Bruner.
p.   cm.
Includes bibliographical references and index.
ISBN 0-674-00289-X (alk. paper)
1. Law—United States—Interpretation and construction.
2. Law—United States—Methodology.
3. Judicial opinions—United States.
4. Culture and law.
I. Bruner, Jerome S. (Jerome Seymour)
KF425 .A48   2000
349.73—dc21   00-025428

Designed by Gwen Nefsky Frankfeldt

*To a decade of students and colleagues
in the Lawyering Theory Colloquium*

Contents

MINDING THE LAW

CHAPTER ONE

Invitation to a Journey

We need some briefing to start us on our way. For we propose to go about things in an unusual fashion. Unlike most books, this one will be less concerned with familiarizing what is strange than with making the already familiar strange again.

Our intention comes not out of some contrarian perversity, but out of a conviction that familiarity is dulling—that when our ways of conceiving of things become routine, they disappear from consciousness and we cease to know *that* we are thinking in a certain way or *why* we are doing so. Thus do enterprises of potential pith and moment stagnate, coming to be as thoughtless as the most mechanical routines of our daily folkways—like keeping a certain distance between us and an interlocutor while conversing—which we follow slavishly but without awareness. It requires either a breach of the spacing rule (which usually only takes us aback) or an astute anthropologist's account of "interpersonal distancing" to make the familiar strange again, to rescue the taken-for-granted and bring it back into mind.[1]

The practice of law is full of such dissociated routines, of canonical ways of proceeding "scarcely worth a moment's thought": the proper form for a brief, the right motion to file, the obvious line of precedent to cite, the correct way to advise a client. The substantive rules of the *corpus juris*, too, appear obvious for the most part, plainly discernible by skimming the headnotes of judicial decisions, with no need to worry through the text. Yet all of these appearances conceal pitfalls.

For although lawyers ordinarily fare better when they reduce both procedural matters and settled substantive rules to habit, following the Latin maxim *scientia dependit in mores,* this is so only when things hold steady. And the lawyer who assumes that things will always hold steady is in for some very ugly surprises—or for a life of missed opportunities through want of the capacity even to experience surprise.

One of us long ago discovered this fact through trial and error (mostly error), as a noncom in the attorneys' auxiliary corps trying to defend thousands of demonstrators against arrests and prosecutions, assaults and injunctions, during the civil rights protests of the 1960s. The survivors' lore on that bivouac was that you had to learn the ropes only as a way of figuring out how to untie them—that the most effective lawyers were those who quickly made sense of the local routines and even more quickly saw how much of them could be ignored or attacked as nonsense. It is the same in large matters of legal theory as in small matters of legal practice: familiarity insulates habitual ways of thinking from inspections that might find them senseless, needless, and unserviceable.

So we take as the agenda of this book to make some very familiar routines in law-thinking strange again. We want to concentrate especially on three commonplace processes of legal thought and practice, to target them for consciousness retrieval. They are processes without which lawyers, judges, and students of the law could not possibly make do for as much as one hour: categorizing, storytelling, and persuasion.

What distinguishes a contract from something "not worth the paper it's printed on"? That's legal categorizing. How do you describe to a court the circumstances surrounding the contract's alleged breach? That's legal storytelling. You tell the story differently—in a quite different tongue—depending upon whether you represent the plaintiff or the defendant in a breach-of-contract case. That's legal rhetorics. *Categorization, narrative,* and *rhetorics*—the stuff of everyday life in the law.

But life in the law is not lived in a vacuum. It is part of a pervasive world of *culture.* If law is to work for the people in a society, it must be (and must be seen to be) an extension or reflection of their culture. Therefore we shall have to explore as well what culture is, how it operates and through what instrumentalities.

Obviously, lawyers are not the only ones steeped in these processes: *nobody* could live without them. Yet the ways of lawyers and judges and students of the law are specialized ways, often so ostentatious in their specialization as to suggest the esoteric flimflam of a jealous guild. We will want to examine these specializations with particularity, but without assuming that they are as unique as they often appear and profess to be. So, we need to ask, how do *legal* categorizing, *legal* narrative, *legal* rhetorics, and *legal* culture differ from—and how do they resemble—similar doings outside the realm of law?

Here, good fortune smiles upon us. For much insightful study has recently delved these ubiquitous human doings in their general aspects, outside the law. We are in a position to draw upon these studies—in psychology, linguistics, anthropology, even in such seemingly remote disciplines as literary theory, neurology, and the computational sciences—for an enriched understanding of the general nature of the processes of categorizing, storytelling, and persuasion whose specialization makes up the life of law. And for a deeper appreciation, too, of how culture interfaces with these processes.

In speaking of the "general nature" of the processes, we do not overlook the vital point that everything that human beings do, including categorizing, narrating, and persuading, is in some sense specialized, reflecting the particular roles people are playing, the specific aims they are pursuing, the context-dependent position they occupy in their society. In that sense, one can give no *general* account of human pursuits. But we are not searching for some sort of "average" or benchmark account against which to compare what lawyers do. We seek, rather, a sense of the *possible* ways in which human pursuits can be carried out, and how the *legal* way fits into this picture. Doubtless, as many non-lawyers have learned to their grief, to "get into the hands of lawyers and the law" is to enter a different way of life. But in seeking to understand what way of life that is, we should consider the surrounding ways. And we should not imagine that law can ever be so specialized as to be altogether alien, foreign to life itself, *lebensfremd*. In this respect law must resemble literature a little. It will imitate life—or life will imitate it. Law that was totally alien to life would be as inconceivable as literature completely removed from the experience of its readers.

To be sure, law has special functions, institutional and cognitive. The law, we are told, saves us from forgetfulness of our most basic obligations to each other and the state, from endless cycles of revenge, from the tyrannies of public powers and the blindnesses of private passions, from fecklessness and faction. Yet if the law does any of these things at all well, it must do them by establishing continuities with the ways in which the people of a society conceive of it and of themselves, the ways in which they classify and comprehend, envision and dispute and puzzle out who they are and what they need and want, and why. For this reason also, we may have much to learn— even about those features of the law that are the most peculiar to it— by looking at them against the backdrop of what is known concerning other forms of ideation and imagination, controversy and discourse, within cultures. But to do this we must, once again, take off the blinders of familiarity.

There are many ways of making the familiar strange, if we are moved to use them. Juxtaposing the past and the present is surely one way— the historian's honored way of quickening consciousness. But it is no mythic whim that Clio, the Muse of History, has four sisters who are muses to poets of divers sorts. For poets, like historians, toil relentlessly to estrange the familiar, though they do it differently. Their tropes and metaphors, conceits and images and evocations cut across our daily, dulled perceptions of the world and lure us, even yank us, out of the banality of routine. In the chapters that follow, we will sometimes use both the historian and the poet to help us on our quest.

But our efforts to explore the processes of categorization, narrative, rhetorics, and culture will also lead us to use other techniques of estrangement. Perhaps the most powerful trick of the human sciences is to decontextualize the obvious and then recontextualize it in a new way. We will be about this constantly; and if some of the new vantage points from which we examine the familiar rituals of the law seem remote—as when we view the United States Supreme Court's 1992 opinion terminating the era of school-desegregation efforts in *Freeman v. Pitts* through the lenses of the dramaturgic structure classically used to write the quietus of Agamemnon and Julius Caesar—that will only be with the aim of getting far enough outside law's enclave to see afresh what appears to be going on unseen inside.

To some extent, this estranging methodology is the natural consequence of our collaboration. For, as our readers doubtless have remarked, the authors of this volume are an odd pair—a cultural psychologist and a litigator. That happy mismatch has required both of us to spend a good deal of effort over the last decade helping each other to "see" the world of the law differently—the cultural psychologist to see its inner workings as they look from up close; the litigator to see its larger features as they look from some distance. We cannot claim that this is a formula for keener vision, but we guarantee that it is one to make the sights of the legal universe constantly curiouser and curiouser.

Still, we would not have written this book in its present form, or at all, on the basis of that shared experience alone. We have come to write it as the consequence of a broader sharing—of a decade of teaching together, and with a small group of brilliant colleagues,[2] a seminar for second- and third-year law students of exceptional insight and perceptiveness. The nominal subject of the seminar is "lawyering theory": how to understand more richly the work that lawyers do in crafting arguments and cases and in counseling clients and negotiating, the work that judges do in deciding cases and crafting opinions, preserving and modifying the rules and traditions of the law. What we end up having done each year is to experience fresh ways of looking at these sorts of legal work as the ceaseless works-in-progress of a culture that, while binding its members in a common canon, leaves them free to some extent to visualize and even realize possible worlds beyond the canon.

And we have learned some lessons doing that—intriguing, rather humbling lessons. For example, though we and our students read quite a few Supreme Court opinions as well as a good deal of anthropology, it often turns out that neither of these provides our most vivid insights into the law. The insights are just as likely to come from, say, a close reading of a play by Aeschylus, a novella by Melville, a West African folktale, or even the memorable scene on Mt. Moriah in Genesis 22 where God commands Abraham to kill his only son, Isaac. All in the provinces of Clio's sisters. Reading these texts while reading law, we have found, has astonishing consciousness-retrieving effects.

We don't pretend to know why this is so—why, for instance, the dramatized conflict over the plea for asylum in Aeschylus' *The Suppliants* so vivifies the issues of interstate rendition procedure decided by the Supreme Court in the 1842 "fugitive slave case" of *Prigg v. Pennsylvania,* as well as today's most difficult "affirmative action" issues. Or why the Baila tale *The Child and the Eagle* freshens our students' and our own understanding of contemporary issues of deportation policy and capital-punishment law (and of potentially gendered perspectives on both). Perhaps these effects are the same stuff as the "estrangement" of the Russian Formalists (like Roman Jakobson and Viktor Shklovsky),[3] or of historical distance. But what has struck us repeatedly is that the combination of case law with Clio and her sisters not only opened the cases to a fuller range of possible readings but also readied our students for ideas in anthropology and linguistics, in psychology and even in Artificial Intelligence. And by the end of each year's trip, we had another crew of young lawyers who were so thoroughly liberated from the deadly habit of taking the law for granted that they could help us, in turn, to keep from lapsing back into the habit.

That, more than anything else, encouraged us to write this book.

But once launched on our task, we faced the occupational hazard shared by all who would reflect upon controversial doings—human scientists, law professors, lofty critics of all kinds. Can one rise above it all, *au delà de la bataille,* to achieve (as Thomas Nagel so aptly puts it) the "view from nowhere"?[4] Is that, indeed, our intention?

Hardly. After all, our concern is with the law as practiced, not with an abstract *corpus juris* and its commentaries. And as practiced, law has three related qualities that defy our best efforts to stand above it.

First, law is not simply a system of ideas but a series of consequences that human beings inscribe on the lives of other human beings through the medium of those ideas. However dispassionately one may seek to analyze the ideas, it is foolish to suppose that one's appraisal of the consequences will be dictated *exclusively* by that analysis. The analysis will help to expose the availability of choices and to elaborate some of the connections between ideas and consequences. But which consequences—and therefore which choices—one regards as tolerable or intolerable will necessarily depend in part upon one's values, faiths, and beliefs about the way in which human beings should be treated.

Second, law is adversarial. To take a position in relation to most legal subjects that have any interest at all is to occupy a position on a battlefield. One may join the battle more or less deliberately, provide support or cover more or less avowedly to one contending party or another, observe rules of combat that are fairer or unfairer; but neutrality is vouchsafed only to the dead—and to them involuntarily.

Third, all but the most trivial legal statements—in opinions from the bench, in advocate's arguments, in treatises and hornbooks and philosophies of law, even in connection with the judgment of what constitutes a relevant fact—are *interpretive* in nature. There are no logically unique solutions to the law's problems, though there are customary ones. The makers of legal arguments and rules and theories and their critics alike must constantly decide what they will talk about, and what they will say about it, guided by some vision of *what matters*. And so must we.

The aim of this book, as we have said, is to explore the ways in which human beings, including judges and lawyers, must inevitably rely upon culturally shaped processes of categorizing, storytelling, and persuasion in going about their business. Because these processes are ubiquitous in the law (as elsewhere), we might have chosen any of a wide variety of legal texts to illustrate them. The principal texts we chose are opinions of the Supreme Court of the United States in cases where the Court's results struck us as unjust. It was partly because their results seemed unjust (and partly because, as Supreme Court decisions, they had broad impact) that the cases *mattered* to us enough to deserve close study. Like everyone involved in the law, we have convictions about what is and what is not a just result. Those convictions are grounded in our views about how human beings should treat one another. Our views are debatable and are among the views that generate some of the fiercest political, moral, and legal debates in contemporary American culture. So be it. Despite their debatability, they make some legal subjects—and some Supreme Court opinions—far more interesting to us than others. We have chosen to study and to write about some of those that interest us the most.

But this does not mean that our purpose in writing about these cases is to criticize their results. We subject their *texts* to close reading; and where the reading shows that Supreme Court Justices have made undeclared categorial choices—or have chosen to take one narrative, rhetorical, or cultural direction rather than another without explaining why—we do not hesitate to say that the choices lack any justification *in the text*. To say this is not to say that the choices, let alone the results announced in the Justices' opinions, are unjustifiable. To criticize those choices and results would require normative analyses (including, conspicuously, a statement of our own values and the reasons for them) that constitute a wholly different subject than the subject of this book.

Thus, our answer to the question "shall we strive to stand above the battle?" is *no, but neither shall we seek to fight the battle here.* We will limit our efforts to examining the construction and the uses of some of the implements with which the battle is constantly fought. And that limitation entails two others, which we want to make explicit.

One: In examining how Supreme Court Justices construct the implements they use in battles, we do not intend to portray the Justices as either villains or heroes. Just as our purpose does not extend to criticizing the Justices' results, it does not extend to analyzing their motives. We have neither the information nor the competence to offer assessments in any of the dimensions that distinguish Goodies from Baddies—or to pretend to know what those dimensions might be.

Two: In examining particular Justices' opinions as illustrative of the uses of judicial battle implements, we do not intend to suggest that these opinions exhibit *more* or *different* uses of the implements than could be found in the opinions of Justices who are doing battle on the other side. To the contrary, we believe that the implements are used by justices and judges of all ideological orientations and that similar implements are used by lawyers on both sides of every controversy, and by all sorts of critics and students of the law, ourselves included. By increasing their visibility, we hope to encourage increased attention to them wherever they are found; and we would be astounded if sensitive students and critics could not find them in abundance in our own book.

So, yes, we have a definite ideological point of view; and, yes, that point of view has had a lot to do with our selection of the legal texts that we examine in the following chapters. But our object is not to sell our ideological point of view or even to offer a dissent from the ideologies reflected in the texts. It is to increase vigilance and to sharpen scrutiny. If we succeed in that object, the reader will, we are sure, be astute to catch us out wherever our ideological leanings have influenced our interpretations or uses of categorization, narrative, rhetorics, and culture.

Here is a rough sketch of the following chapters: Where there be law, so too must there be categories. For law defines categorically the limits of the permissible or, more often, of the impermissible. Since human imagination cannot conceive of the full variety of possible transgressions, law requires a system of categories to reduce that variety. So an innumerable array of natural and unnatural, potentially harm-wreaking temptations is dealt with under the rubric of "attractive nuisance," for example; and the courts must decide, case by case, whether the harm-wreaker at bar is indeed an *attractive nuisance* or nay. With regard to some categories—such as the "liberty" protected by the Constitution's Due Process Clauses—one would be hard-pressed to capture their "defining" attributes in any compendious tag and would be tempted to allow as how they can only be defined by reference to a line of precedent. But how is a line of precedent to be understood—as a progressive refinement of the terms used to mark the boundaries of a legal rule, as some abstract idea evolving logically along lines dictated by the doctrine of *stare decisis,* as a continuing story to be spun by a succession of tale-tellers? The typical law dictionary is a *vade mecum* of category specifications, few of them safe to bank on. All the more astonishing that, in the main, the nature of legal categories has not been much studied.

In the following chapter we take a look at theories of categorization as they have emerged over recent years in fields like cognitive psychology, anthropology, and linguistics. It was, after all, "the category problem" that precipitated the Cognitive Revolution in modern psychology.[5] It was also a categorial question—whose categories matter, the anthropologist's or the native's?—that brought anthropology into modern times.[6] And it was Roman Jakobson's paramount contribution to show that at every level of language, category rules were crucial to well-formedness, whether of phonemes, words, or sentences.[7]

The burden of this new work in the human sciences, to oversimplify a bit, is that categories are *made in the mind* and not found in the world. They are made in response to certain demands that derive both from the nature of human cognition (that is, the human capacity to discriminate far more things than we can possibly respond to—such as the millions of colors we can differentiate but which we reduce for use to a few dozen color categories), and from the constraints on communal living in a human culture (as in the case of the distinction between kin and non-kin, or private and public property). The appropriate questions then become functional ones: What functions do categories serve in general, and what function is served by any particular category system? Why do we *create* our categories as we do, *justify* them in what are often very odd ways, and *put things into them or not* by what are often dubious procedures? How can categorizing lead us into trouble and error? After considering these questions, we conclude Chapter 2 with a look at one domain of legal categorizing—the category of incest—to see whether there is anything special about legal categories, even so highly charged a one as incest.

In Chapter 3, partner of the preceding one, we proceed not by undertaking a conspectus of legal categorizing, but by a close reading of two United States Supreme Court opinions in which issues of categorization are decisive. We look first at Chief Justice Rehnquist's opinion for the Court in *Missouri v. Jenkins,* holding that a lower federal court had gone too far in its efforts to desegregate the public schools of Kansas City. The case ultimately turns on his categorization of the lower court's orders as a forbidden "interdistrict remedy," but, as we shall see, the Chief Justice marches through an intriguing parade of other categorizing moves in setting this move up and bringing it off.

Our reading of the *Jenkins* opinion does not refrain from voicing some strong criticisms of the Chief Justice's categorizing methods. Indeed, it should be abundantly clear that, in our view, Chief Justice Rehnquist's opinion does not face up to the key issue of racial desegregation remedies presented by the case but skirts that issue by a specious categorization of the remedy ordered by the lower federal courts to desegregate the Kansas City, Missouri School District as "interdistrict" as opposed to "intradistrict." And when we get to Chapter 9, the reader will perceive that, again in our view, *Jenkins* represents a major step in the Supreme Court's retreat from the landmark desegregation decision in *Brown v. Board of Education.*

This brings us back to an issue we raised earlier: our inability to achieve—or even to aspire to—a stance of neutrality, *au dela de la bataille.* It is impossible to explore a Court's opinion with complete neutrality. To attempt to do so would entail considering all the alternative ways in which the Court *might have* categorized the issues in the case, *might have* told the story behind the litigation, *might have* deployed its arguments, and *might have* responded to contending strains in American culture. But to carry out such an analysis in full, one would also need to consider all those *might haves* from all possible legal and political perspectives. That kind of algorithm is beyond ordinary human capacity.

So our biases will show, sometimes clearly enough, as in our reading of Chief Justice Rehnquist's *Jenkins* opinion in Chapters 3 and 9, sometimes not. Even when our criticisms are addressed solely to particulars of narrative construction in an opinion, or to fine points of wording, or to the means through which claims to factuality are advanced, it is our own point of view that will steer us to the topics we take up. For writing, whether of love or law, in fiction or essay, is never alien to drama, designed to enliven, not simply to inform neutrally. And while some authors may aspire to recede further from the stage than others, the greatest distance we can hope to achieve from ours is rather like the posture of a Greek chorus, commenting on the passing scene yet remaining part of the play.

Now to the second half of Chapter 3. Here we inspect the pivotal categorizing move in an opinion by Justice Scalia, *Michael H. v. Gerald D.*, which concludes that the relationship between a natural father and the child born of his extramarital union with another man's wife is not such an interest in "liberty" as the Due Process Clause of the Fourteenth Amendment protects against destruction by state law. *Michael H.* will give us an early occasion to observe the powerful interdependence of legal categorization and narrative. Justice Scalia, intentionally or not, draws his categories not just from the law but from an ancient, almost mythic story of adultery, a precursor of the classic tale of Lancelot, Guinevere, and King Arthur. We examine the story in some detail and try to place Justice Scalia's opinion in that narrative line, to understand his categories in relation to the narrative choices available within it. For adultery is not defined merely by legal statute; its canonical variants take their life from archaic but changing habits of thought—and of storytelling. It is by examining that immemorial but still emerging narrative tradition that we can fully appreciate the power of the Guinevere legend in shaping Justice Scalia's portrayal of adultery—and, perhaps as well, the very lives of the case's troubled protagonists. It is not just a Fourteenth Amendment "liberty interest" and a State's prerogatives that are at issue in *Michael H.*, but the narrative form by which we make sense of marriage, fidelity, and human bonds.

In the next pair of chapters, the central focus is on narrative. Why narrative, following categorization? Because we believe that the connection between the two processes exposed by our examination of *Michael H.* is not adventitious. When you inquire where categories come from, you quickly recognize that they are almost never constructed arbitrarily. Typically, they are extracted from some larger-scale, more encompassing way of looking at things—either from some *theory* about the world or from a *narrative* about the human condition and its vicissitudes. Theories are accounts of things framed in terms of causes and effects: lightning struck a barn and caused it to catch fire; a particular poison entered the bloodstream and caused a failure in the immune system. From theories of this sort we get such useful categories as "natural hazards" and "toxic agents."

Narratives cohere differently, not through the mechanics and chemistries of cause and effect but through the play of human intentions and purposeful acts in the worlds of striving, accomplishment and failure, victory and defeat. Narratives do not contradict theories but cut across them; the two are incommensurate. (Nonetheless, as we will discover later in the book, narrative may masquerade as theory— or vice versa—for the purpose of persuasion in particular situations where one or the other is supposedly more authoritative; and the implementation of this masquerade is one of the chief offices of rhetorics.) "Good faith effort" is a category extracted from narrative; so is "golden opportunity" and "gutsy kid." And so are "willful ignorance" and "informed consent" and "malice aforethought."

Because so many legal categories derive from narratives, we examine the nature of narrative in general in Chapter 4 and then focus on narrative at work in judicial decisionmaking in Chapter 5. Still another reason for our concentration on narrative—or perhaps simply a different expression of the same reason—is that litigation, a crucial law-making procedure in the Anglo-American common-law tradition, is centrally concerned with the *fit* of competing stories to presumably controlling points of law. This is what is usually afoot in the process that lawyers call (with a confident simplicity that is truly astounding when one considers the mysteriousness of the process) "applying the law to the facts."

Chapter 4 sets the stage, summarizing what we know about narrative from literary theory, linguistics, classics, psychology, historiography, even biblical exegesis. What makes a narrative, what does it do to the "facts" that it comprises, how does it manage to impose its values and its reality, even when it is admittedly fiction? In Chapter 5, again we look at two illustrative Supreme Court opinions: Justice Story's classic opinion in the 1842 case of *Prigg v. Pennsylvania* and Justice Kennedy's majority opinion in the 1992 case of *Freeman v. Pitts*. These cases deal with issues of race and federalism; and although they have no ostensible point of contact in traditional legal analysis, we suggest that they bear instructive comparison when their narrative structures are exposed.

In both cases a conventional but implicit narrative structure spills over into explicit judicial rule-formulation. But the choice of narratives is strikingly different. *Prigg* is concerned with a State's right to protect free Negroes under its jurisdiction against kidnapping and transportation into bondage by slave snatchers. Pennsylvania, in effect, was denied that right because its interference with the rights of southern slaveholders to retake their runaways was thought intolerable. Justice Story's opinion announcing the Court's decision invokes a historical narrative featuring the Sacred Peace-Keeping Compact sworn between slave and free States at the Constitutional Convention of the Founders—a narrative which, as we discover, was in use even before Homer to enact the danger of impending chaos and the need for strong, centralized power to avert that danger. *Freeman* deals with the duties of a Georgia county school board to continue carrying out court-ordered desegregation remedies. Here a stock narrative about the danger of *too much* strong, centralized power, combined with the theme that human efforts cannot stay the forces of nature, is used to justify the beginning of the end of the school-desegregation effort launched by *Brown v. Board of Education*. Later in the book (Chapter 9) we return to both of these cases and explore what might underlie their dialectical play in the adjudication of constitutional issues involving race—observing, in particular, how competing narrative frames or "creeds" are evoked in the rise and fall of constitutional doctrine.

Following the pair of chapters on narrative comes a pair on rhetorics (Chapters 6 and 7). These require some preliminary explanation. Not that rhetorics are out of place in a book such as this one: far from it. But categorizing and narrative are often treated nowadays as if they both were concerned with "representing the world" validly or invalidly—and one might well ask what rhetorics have to do with this, or, for that matter, with judicial opinions, which have been our primary legal focus in Chapters 2 through 5.

We believe that there is much more to legal categorization and narrative, and to judicial opinions, than a striving for validity in representing something "out there" in the world, or even in expressing one's logically reasoned notions of how things "out there" ought to work. And the "much more" is principally about rhetorics: ways of winning others over to our views, and of justifying those views to ourselves as well as others, when the question of how things in the world ought to work is *contested* or *contestable*. For much of the province of the law is contested territory, which, of course, is why we see no inconsistency between the canons that enjoin lawyers simultaneously to avoid dishonesty and to advocate their client's cause with partisan fidelity. And an even larger tract of law's territory would be contestable—frighteningly so, because of the fragility of institutions that are ceaselessly contested—if it were not for the constant efforts of lawyers and judges to conceal its susceptibility to contest. Both the contests actually waged and the feints and counterfeints that avert broader contests are the fields of action of rhetorics.

Rhetorics enable lawyers in the service of their clients (and also judges in the service of whatever loyalties constrain *them*) to justify their categorizations and to tell their stories in a language that navigates adroitly between certifiable misrepresentation and acknowledgment of the weakness of their client's positions (or the strength of their doubts). It is a subtle discourse, full of implications that it insulates from the risk of refutation by stopping millimeters short of assertion, and from the risk of backfire by embroidering with equivocations at the margins of commitment.

We examine the makings of these subtle rhetorics in Chapter 6. There we consider such matters in the domains of linguistics and pragmatics as speech act theory, the Gricean cooperative maxims, felicity conditions, and presuppositions, all with a view to discerning how "reality" can be represented in discourse so as to make it more convincing, more believable, more compelling. Inevitably, we revisit the age-old topic of the rhetor's tools (or, if you would vie with the rhetor, "tricks"). Chapter 7 then considers how these tools are used to decide issues of life or death: we analyze Justice Powell's majority opinion in *McCleskey v. Kemp,* where the Supreme Court held by a vote of five to four that a demonstrated pattern of racial bias in the capital sentences imposed by the Georgia state courts for the crime of murder was a matter of no federal constitutional concern.

We see the *McCleskey* opinion as a study of the power of rhetorics to obscure both the difficulty of issues and the range of choices available to deal with them. The Court linguistically erodes any cause for worry that racial discrimination may be affecting the selection of convicted murderers to be sentenced to death in the United States; it linguistically reinforces the *necessary* power of the state to use capital punishment as an instrument of public safety; and it linguistically posits an either/or choice between permitting judicial scrutiny of racial discrepancies in capital sentencing outcomes and permitting state governments to use the death penalty at all. It is interesting that the *McCleskey* opinion frames the issues in this way and finds the resulting tradeoff easy to resolve, at a time when public sentiment in the United States in favor of the death penalty was at a 50-year high,[8] although in most of the rest of the world the use of the penalty was either declining or becoming increasingly controversial.[9] Could it be the case, then, that the way people categorize, tell stories, and use rhetorics to make sense of their world and decisions affecting it is influenced by *culture*—and that judges, too, reflect this influence when they make law and legal decisions? Can activities of these sorts be understood without taking into account the culture in which they are going on?

Such questions lead us, in Chapter 8, to explore the nature and workings of culture. The chapter opens with a review of the unquiet status of the concept of culture in modern anthropology. Anthropologists are divided on the issue of whether a culture should be regarded as a set of institutional arrangements that provide the consensual pattern for the commonplace exchanges constituting communal life in a society, or rather as an ensemble of ways of thinking, feeling, and believing shared by the members of the society. But even a cursory look at accounts of different cultures makes it plain that both forms of description—outside-in institutional and inside-out subjective—are indispensable. Neither institutional arrangements alone nor shared subjectivity can capture the curious complexity of human cultures.

We therefore propose to conceive of culture as an interplay of the two—a dialectic between the canonical ways laid down by a society's institutional forms and the possible worlds generated by the rich imaginations of its members, who nonetheless must remain dependent to a large extent upon the society's institutional arrangements. In some deep sense, a culture's canonical ways are brought into question by the products of its collective imagination of the possible—its *noetic space,* as we call it. Yet the culture tolerates those possible worlds in noetic space; they are even nurtured by such "marginal" institutions as theater, novels, dissenting political movements, styles of gossip and fantasy; some of them come in time to gain more solid support; and a few may eventually co-opt or replace institutions at the core of the society's canon. The "dialectic" of culture, as we see it, is a kind of yin-and-yang tension that produces continual small shiftings and occasional large readjustments in the balances among a society's institutions and imaginings, its actualities and its possibilities.

Chapter 9 examines this tension as it plays out in a century of Supreme Court case law. Against the backdrop of our conception of culture and the ideas explored in earlier chapters, we trace the Court's progress through a series of cases dealing with race discrimination and the Equal Protection Clause of the Fourteenth Amendment. The route runs from *Plessy v. Ferguson,* in the closing years of the nineteenth century, through the mid-twentieth-century landmark decision in *Brown v. Board of Education,* to the present, where we revisit cases discussed in earlier chapters, most notably *Freeman v. Pitts* and *Missouri v. Jenkins.* This trail can be seen as marking the fall, the rise, and the fall again of a brightly egalitarian and progressive American Creed—or as marking the rise, the fall, and the rise again of an equally potent, darkly suspicious American Caution.

But we find one other characteristic dynamism in American culture besides this primary and substantive dialectic, one that makes the Creed and the Caution difficult to bring together manageably. It is a collective way of thought disposed to all-or-none judgments, to sharp polarization, to defining the Other as simply non-Us, to defining Us as non-Them. It renders us insensitive to middle grounds and the subtle qualities of Others. We Americans find it peculiarly hard to appreciate mitigating circumstances, peculiarly tempting to cast blame rather than find explanation. Put them in jail, one-two-three out, for-us or against-us! This turn of collective thought reflects itself, we suspect, in resistance to affirmative action, in our reluctance to carry the American Creed "too far," in unwillingness to abolish the death penalty, and above all, in our stumbling efforts to come to terms with our racism—Them and Us.

This is the order of business that concerns us in Chapter 9 as we pass in review a century of wild swings not only in American public opinion but in the actions of our courts. This dizzying dialectic appears not simply in the policies we practice as a nation, but in the small coin of categories that we use for sorting our realities, in the stories we prefer to tell, in the rhetorics we use for convincing ourselves as well as others.

Chapter 10 sums up our explorations. We have no nostrums to peddle—no patent medicines guaranteed to cure the courts of everything that ails them in the vital functions of categorization, narrative, and rhetorics. Nor do we have a program for reshaping American culture or establishing a fairer, more decent ordering of values in American civic life. This book announces no new theory of jurisprudence, provides no ready formulas for teasing truth from legal texts or detecting error in them. All it offers is a way of thinking about the law that is intended to enliven consciousness as a ward against the numb acceptance of injustices and inhumanities so rooted in routine that they seem natural, inevitable, or not really to be going on at all.[10]

Finally, a word about the audience for whom this book is intended. As lawyers in particular know—though perhaps they know it no better than any others who concern themselves professionally with human troubles—intentions are never to be taken at face value. We can easily tell about our own, though we do so with no illusions regarding their relevance to others. Plainly, as teachers in a law school, we had in mind law students as part of our audience. After all, many of the ideas explored in the following chapters were first developed in the long-continuing seminar for second- and third-year law students mentioned earlier. But that seminar, somewhat offbeat by conventional law-school standards, also turned our thoughts to how our colleagues would take our approach. So this book is also intended for law school teachers, in the hope that they may find ideas in it that make their teaching and their study of the law more exhilarating. (Law teaching is not exactly nonstop fun.) Which, of course, led us on to think about practicing lawyers, who so often complain that there are too few opportunities in their working lives to reflect upon what they are doing. May this book provide them such an opportunity—if only "after hours."

But we also have in mind readers who are interested in the workings of the law even though they have no technical training in it. To make this book accessible to them, we have tried to keep legal jargon to a minimum (no small task when one is analyzing, among other things, the language of judicial opinions); and, when we had to give in, we have offered translations of, say, "granting *certiorari*" as the Supreme Court's action in agreeing to hear a case. (The Supreme Court refuses to hear most of the cases which it is asked to review.) Yet we have not hesitated to plunge our lay readers into the intricacies of real cases and of judicial opinions as actually delivered. For the "real thing" is typically fraught with drama—Athenians, it is said, repaired to the law courts when plays by Euripides, Aeschylus, or Sophocles were not on the boards. Moreover, it is *in* the text of court opinions that law is often made, and where it may even happen that rights not specified in constitutions or codes are boldly deduced from those that are—like the "right to travel" from state to state, for example.[11]

Finally, we hope to find the ear of our colleagues in the human sciences and in literary and rhetorical studies—if only to express our gratitude for the insights they have provided about the ubiquitousness and power of categories, narratives, rhetorics, and culture, in law as in the rest of life. Perhaps they'll be pleased to learn that life does not stop at the courthouse steps!

CHAPTER TWO

On Categories

Categories are ubiquitous and inescapable in the use of mind. Nobody can do without them—not lawyers or judges, Hottentot farmers or school children, not even iconoclasts. Categories are the badges of our sociopolitical allegiances, the tools of our mental life, the organizers of our perception.

Though we all use categories, we do not, of course, use identical ones. Our categories resemble Woody Allen's mythical beast that had the head of a lion and the body of a lion, but not the *same* lion. Acquiring and negotiating our categories is part of the business of growing up, of becoming a member of a family or a group of friends or a culture, of learning a trade or a profession, of trying to understand the elusive and the counterintuitive. Whether the categories deal with nearly universal human experience—like "rectangles" and "triangles"—or are found only in specialists' reference books—like the legal digest headings "Arbitration," "Armed Services," "Arrest," "Arson," and so forth—we need to get them *right* both to make sense of the world and to communicate with one another about it.

That means we are always at risk that our categories may lead us astray. Indispensable instruments, they are also inevitable beguilers. To interrogate their uses and their dangers is a necessary part of legal studies, as it is of any preparation for considered thought and action. So we spend this chapter and the next asking a lot of questions about categories and trying to answer a few of them. We can hardly hope to plumb the subject. These are questions that have long bedeviled linguists, logicians, psychologists, anthropologists, philosophers—all who ponder what kind of sense underlies "common sense." For common sense, like common law, is a great concealer of the origins and artifices of its categories. In Chapter 3, we will explore some uses and abuses of categories in the law. The present chapter looks at categorization more generally.

Part I proposes a start-up definition of a "category." Part II summarizes the functions that categories serve in cognition. Part III describes a half-dozen elemental rules of play for thinking about categories. Part IV looks at where we get our categories from, and Part V looks at how we put things into them under various circumstances, including adversarial circumstances. Part VI identifies some hazards of categorization.

I. Categories: A Starting Definition

What do we mean by *categories* anyway? Categories and category systems vary from formal mathematical ones like prime and non-prime numbers, to legal ones like "attractive nuisance" or "custody" (which is apparently not the same lion in family law as in the law of *habeas corpus*), to practical ones like "things I can use to scrape the ice off the windshield," to ones that strike us as *natural kinds*—apples, or oranges, seemingly the products of an abounding nature rather than anything we put together. Or what about the paranoid's smudgy category of "people who are out to get me"?

Let's concoct one of those bare but useful definitions that are designed not to settle matters but to open them to closer inspection. Here is one such:

> A category is a set of things or creatures or events or actions (or whatever) treated as if they were, for the purposes at hand, similar or equivalent or somehow substitutable for each other.

We'll unpack some of these terms very soon. But before we do that—and to help us on the way—we need to have a quick look at the question of what our categories do for us, what functions they serve. That will help us understand the limits and pitfalls of trying to pin down our quarry simply by defining it.

II. The Functions of Categorizing

Mental economy. Probably the simplest function of categories in our personal, social, and institutional life is mental economy. Nobody has the time or mental energy to deal with everything encountered as if it were unique, *for the first time.* So we use the past to manage the present. We need to be able to say, as William James put it, "here comes a thingumabob again." Another way to put it is that categorization minimizes surprise, allows us to treat things *as if* they were the same as what we had encountered before. It ensures that the limited number of slots we have for processing what is going on around us are used to good purpose,[1] not wasted on lavish particularity.[2]

To deal with the millions of discriminately different colors around us, which would be a full-time occupation if we attended to them all, we batch tens of thousands into the category "blue," other tens of thousands into "green." We learn this labor-saving convention early in life, and we stick with it unless we have a reason not to—like fashion designers with their latest modes in taupe and tan and beige. Not that most of us can't see the difference between taupe and tan and beige if it is brought to our attention. But for most purposes it's quite enough to call them and even *see* them as simply "tan." At least in our culture. We're more particular about blue and green, though in some cultures people do not distinguish blue from green in their ordinary discourse, just as in other cultures they treat yellows and oranges as if they were the same.

But it isn't all a matter of cultural convention. There is something else, something that has to do with how the mind works, wherever it happens to find itself. There is a famous study by Berlin and Kay,[3] for example, that explores everyday color categories in the languages of the world—the commonly used single words we employ to group thousands of different colors as workaday equivalents. It shows that the black/white distinction is the first to emerge: if a language has *any* color terms, they will be "black" and "white." If it has another one beyond those two, it will be "red." Beyond that, "yellow" will be added, and so on. Nobody quite understands why this order prevails, though there has been much speculation over the centuries about whether some colors are "primary."

All of which does not mean, of course, that a people whose everyday single-word color lexicon includes only "black," "white," and "red" can't discriminate thousands of other colors if their attention is called to the differences—like us with "taupe" and "beige." In all languages one can use object-names like "banana color" or "leaf color." But generally speaking, the more condensed or shorter a term is, the more likely it will be used; or the more often used, the shorter it will become—as in the historical transition from "moving pictures" to "movies" to "flicks."[4] It is only when there is some special need that we violate the principle of economy and resort to a non-ordinary category with its strange or more cumbersome name.

Which brings us to the second function of categorizing:

Pragmatic utility. If you happen to be a physicist, you'll probably want to use spectral wavelengths to categorize colors rather than the crude lexicon of your language. You'll even get yourself a spectrometer so you can determine the millimicra of wavelength of your color source. It's necessary for your work, you'll say. And that is what we mean by pragmatic utility—to do some job or to pursue some interest.

The marketing departments at GM and Honda, for example, want categories that are useful for their sales pitch. So, in order to be sure that they are targeting their products correctly, they do market research and divide car colors into two categories: those preferred by "younger" and by "more mature" buyers. For the same reason, lawyers find it too amateurish (save under rhetorical pressure) to use so gross a category as "a crime" without specifying whether they are talking about a felony, a misdemeanor, or an infraction. Consequences that it is their job to worry over (the severity of the maximum sentence their client faces, the client's right to a jury trial, and so forth) call for drawing these finer distinctions. And such consequences may call for *redrawing* them from time to time—a possibility implicit in the utilitarian function of categorization. More usually, the mental-economy function lulls us into mindlessness until some alarm of necessity awakens us or catches us blindsided by awakening others. Then we eagerly redefine categories that we had supposed to be "just there" and inherently changeless.

Reference group relevance. It should be clear already that categories are neither arbitrary nor out-of-the-blue. They are derived, consciously or unconsciously, from some larger-scale theory or narrative about the canonical or desirable state of things in the world. Categories like "hero" and "villain" are inconceivable without reference to some sort of folk conception of a *story* and its ordinary ingredients. In science, the taxonomic categories of biology derive from a theory of evolution. Mendeleev's elegant table of the elements—an entire *system* of categories specified in terms of atomic weight—is based upon a theory of matter which in turn is based upon a theory of atoms. In law, the category of "felon" requires a whole body of legal rules and protocols, not simply to define it but to make the definition count for something. Censorship categories, like those in Hollywood's classification of films, are based upon an elaborate conception of morality, including theories about the responsibility of adults for children, as with films rated "PG" or as suitable only for *accompanied* children.

In short, our categories are grounded in conceptions of *what matters* to ourselves and those on whom we depend—our reference groups, as sociologists like to call the people with whom we feel interdependent in the conduct of life. This even holds for the categories of sounds we use in our native language, our phonemes—speech sounds grouped as equivalent according to whether they make a difference in the meaning of words in our daily speech. As an English speaker, you are mystified by the word "robster"; there ain't no such thing. Any native Japanese speaker will tell you without hesitation that it is the same as what you call *lobster*. For the /r/ and /l/ phonemes that you, as an English speaker, recognize as different are simply not distinguished by a Japanese speaker. For you, their difference is the basis for your ability to tell *rob* from *lob, rip* from *lip, rate* from *late.* There are no words in Japanese that are distinguished by this phoneme contrast, so the Japanese don't "hear" it. Similarly, we native English speakers can't distinguish the /p/ in *pit* from the /p/ in *spit,* though one of these allophones of the phoneme /p/ (the aspirated one in *pit*) will blow out a match held close to the mouth, while the other won't even make it flicker. Aspirating /p/ doesn't change the meanings of words in English, so a category bounded by the aspirated-/p/ sound doesn't exist for us—unless we create it "unnaturally" by, say, demonstrating its existence with a lighted match.

Our categories reflect who we are, with whom we feel related, with whom we have to get on. The category systems we use are instruments for getting on with others, for relating to our reference groups. But we have lots of reference groups—our family, our profession, our social class, and so on. This means that the category system we use will vary according to whom we have in mind. And *what* we have in mind.[5]

Which leads us to yet another function of categorizing:

Communal power. A society's shared categories—including but not limited to those of its common language—function to create and promote communal solidarity. For all that we speak disparagingly of consensual categories as "stereotypes," the familiarity of these stereotypes provides a basis for a people's sense of identity as a community, the grounding for their culture.[6] (We will return to the large subject of *culture* in Chapter 8.) So societies do what they can to assure that a consensus about category systems continues to exist as a means of assuring cultural cohesion. They obey the rules laid down by precedent in the law, by the institutionalization of customs, by tradition or entrenched protocol or immemorial convention—all rooted in some recognizable theory or narrative of government, guild, community, folk, or *who we are.* These are our emblems of communion, and we explicate and justify our categories in terms of them. The content of any particular category—"eligible voters" or "responsible parents" or "a decent respect" or "what's equitable"—may change over time, but the persistence of the category itself expresses a continuing adherence to a particular understanding of human affairs and the values by which they should be measured; and to participate in this understanding is, quite simply, to *belong.*

There is, of course, a negative side to this as well. For category systems are often used hegemonically, as instruments of power. Gender-based category systems usually imply a hierarchy in which women are at the bottom, men at the top—whether in strength, reliability, competence, or whatever trait is important—so that attributes possessed by both sexes but predominantly associated with women are devalued,[7] women are generically disempowered, and their disempowerment is insulated from reexamination. In much the same way, race-based category systems have been a powerful, traditional American means of racial discrimination,[8] a matter that will be of specific concern to us in Chapter 9.

Recognition of the hegemonic use of category systems is characteristic of our times, some say of our "postmodern condition."[9] Unfortunately, recognition is an insufficient (though a necessary) step toward correction. American constitutional jurisprudence, for example, responded to the risks of hegemonic category usage 50 years ago by developing a doctrine of "suspect classifications," which says that laws that allocate burdens or benefits on the basis of categories conspicuously aligned with historically documented patterns of invidious discrimination are subject to "strict scrutiny" under the Equal Protection Clause of the Fourteenth Amendment.[10] But lately the suspect-classification doctrine has taken turns that locate it somewhere between a bust and a backfire. First it proved too unsophisticated to deal with the problem that often the most important locus of discrimination is *implicit category systems* rather than their *explicit categories,* so that courts applying the doctrine were unable to identify as "suspect" even the most obvious proxies for historically discriminatory classifications.[11] Then the doctrine proved so rigid that it could not discern the difference, for example, between the use of racial classifications to *disempower* and to *empower* historically disadvantaged groups[12]— ending, like Anatole France's parody of the Law in Its Majestic Equality, by decreeing deadpan that neither the Rich nor the Poor could sleep under the bridges of Paris. This too is a subject we will revisit in Chapter 9.

Personal gratification. Our categories also serve our personal needs and quirks. We all have a category of "suspicious-looking people," although its use will be classified as paranoid if the category gets too rampantly subjective. (What counts as too rampantly subjective depends partly upon the medical community's conceptions of what is disabling, partly upon the legal system's conceptions of what is extenuating,[13] and partly upon the culture's conceptions of what is inherently impossible.[14]) Far short of that, we each recognize (perhaps more often in others than in ourselves) a certain personal idiosyncrasy in the category schemes that people bring to their everyday lives— whether it be Julien Sorel's sensitivity to status and power distinctions in Stendhal's *Le Rouge et le Noir* or a six-year-old's preoccupation with the difference between what's "fair" and "unfair" in grownups' demands.

Risk regulation. Finally, one's category uses serve to regulate risk. The most obvious example is in categorizing people as "friend" or "foe." Sentries in combat zones are the exemplary case for playing it safe: Shoot before you get shot; when in doubt, categorize the shadowy figure as "foe." That's why passwords are needed; and even at that, posted sentries are often as dangerous for returning patrols as the enemy troops they were sent out to reconnoiter. It hardly stops there. Racist suspicion often takes a similar form, as when a householder in Louisiana shot to death a young Japanese stranger who approached the house in the mistaken belief that it was the site of a

Halloween party to which he had been invited,[15] or when America interned loyal citizens of Japanese extraction during World War II.[16] Impatient custodial interventions in child-protection proceedings[17] and mandatory life sentences for "three-time offenders" are other examples of risk-regulating overkill.

But categorical risk regulation shouldn't get a black eye just because it is so often abused. For those interested in its more rational employment, there is an enormous literature on decision theory dealing with the means whereby human beings guard themselves against error, optimize utility, even minimize chagrin.[18] Indeed, much of modern investment theory and some civil law jurisprudence[19] is based upon conceptions of categorizing as a form of risk regulation, although these are matters too technical to concern us here. So too is the domain of Rational Choice Theory, the branch of sociology concerned with ways in which considerations of probability and value of outcome affect the classification of situations for purposes of deciding how people should behave.[20]

III. Rules of the Game

Using categories, it should now be plain, is one of those complicated games people play, like Wittgenstein's celebrated language games and the very ways of life that language games express. The game is far too intricate and subtle to be captured by a set of rules. How the category game is played is among the founding quandaries of the philosophy of mind, of theories of knowledge, even of metaphysics—a quandary renowned for slipperiness, both logically and psychologically.

Its ill-renown is all too well deserved. For "the category problem" is a triple-threat quandary. First, the human capacity to categorize seems inexhaustible, irreducible, and often unpredictable: human beings armed with categories can cut the universe into so many and such myriad shapes that it is difficult to figure out a common *modus operandi* in what they're doing. Second, we human beings seem strangely unconscious—sometimes almost totally unaware—of many of the common categories that figure in our cognitive activities, rather like fish, aphoristically slow to discover water. We *experience the world as categorized* and simply take this experience for granted, as given. Perhaps this is because categorizing in the process of the super-swift act of perceiving is too automatic to be caught by consciousness. So, like the early pre-Socratic philosophers, we fall into believing that things come into our minds from the outside already categorized as cabbages, kings, equilateral triangles.

The third aspect of the category quandary is that our categories are derived from more encompassing notions about how the world *really* is—notions that, again, we take so much for granted as to lose sight of them. (This is why we need jarring and disorienting reminders like Magritte's famous tease of labeling his pipe painting, "This is not a pipe.") We want to take the world as processed through our comprehension of it as though it were simply *there*, unaltered and unalterable by our own conceptions about its nature.

With all of these complexities, categorization does not submit to definitive explanation, let alone instructive summary. Yet there are a few basic principles that can help us keep our thinking about categories in order, and they are worth spelling out preliminarily even if they oversimplify the subject. We will have occasions to recapture its complexities soon enough, when we turn to questions like where our categories come from and in what ways they stand for the world outside our minds. To guide our approach to those questions, let us start by setting out a half-dozen rules for the wary in exploring the category game as usually played.

(1) Categories Are Made, Not Found

For the most part, our categories do not derive from the shape of the world but create it. We inherit an important few from our phylogenetic past: survival categories that predispose even newborn infants to divide up the world in characteristically human ways. (Thus, human infants sort out "faces" and differentiate them from all other shapes: they will smile at schematized circles containing two dark spots *as if* they were "faces.")[21] But most of our category systems are inherited not from our genetic makeup but from our culture, like the phoneme contrasts mentioned earlier that different language speakers notice— or fail to notice—in speech sounds. These categories direct attention to what a culture deems important for one reason or another, often quite local. (The quintessential trite example is the linguists' observation that Eskimos have approximately twenty words for "snow.")

This is not to say that we are stuck once for all with our culture's categorical practices. People have a great capacity for modifying received categories or constructing new ones under appropriate conditions—usually as a means of solving particular problems. Sometimes we deliberately stretch existing categories, as when a lawyer argues that some novel arrangement is a "constructive trust" or that some previously never-sued-for injurious act is a "tort" or that some high-tech depredation is a "theft" of intellectual property. Lawyers are notoriously ingenious in such stretching (or shrinking) exercises, the notion of "intellectual property" itself being a striking illustration of the former. But they are not alone. We all stretch categories to deal with special circumstances—often inexplicitly and without conceiving of what we are doing as the category work it is—as when, say, we see a loose fence board and, being too lazy to return to the house for a hammer, we include a nearby rusty horseshoe in our "hammer" category.

Still, category *systems* do not change easily. This is an important point to which we will return. Our category systems derive from canonical general theories of the world and template narratives about life; and when these theories or narratives are contorted too much or too obviously, when they come to be seen as endangered, we have culture wars and fierce debates about paradigm shifts—as when the category of *art* exceeded the bounds of "representation," or when *physical laws* began incorporating such violations of causality as an "uncertainty" principle. And this brings us to our second rule of the category game:

(2) Categorizing Is an Act of Meaning Making

To put something in a category is to assign it a meaning, to place it in a particular context of ideas. Though we each may have some private categories or private adaptations of shared categories, for the most part our categories are public, *held in common with other people,* and they express that community's understanding of what is happening and what is important in the world. To categorize somebody out of work as a "victim of capitalism" on the one hand or as a statistic of the current rate of "frictional unemployment" on the other is to assign very different meanings, with very different social consequences, to the same person on the basis of the same characteristic. In the philosopher's perspective, categorization is not only an act of *reference,* specifying what the thing in question *is,* but also an act of *sense making,* specifying how the category that includes this thing fits into our larger picture of the Shape of Things. Meaning making, as Frege[22] long ago pointed out, includes both.

This by now self-evident truism leads us to yet another of those philosophical quandaries. What kinds of systems of sense making do categories usually rest on? What kinds of worlds do these systems imply? For another rule of the game is:

(3) Categories Imply a World That Contains Them

We remarked earlier that categories are usually derived or abstracted from either theories or stories—*atoms* being an example of the first, *heroes* and *villains* of the second. This, of course, is an oversimplification, though a useful one. Theories and stories are themselves a multiplicity of things, various and compound. It would be pointless to go into the particularities of how human thought or knowledge is organized under these two large headings. Our object is simply to note that whenever we categorize something, our choice of category implies (often unintentionally) some conception about where and how that something fits into a broader vision of the world. It is worth pausing for a moment over this point.

There are theories and theories. They vary in scope, ranging from how to keep your fireplace from smoking to the laws of thermodynamics. They vary in their derivational depth—whether they are derived from first principles (as with "thermo") or are developed *ad hoc* (as with fireplaces). They vary in what they are "about"—whether about physical nature, about the living world, about human beings, about literature or language or thought. And we have always had theories of history, intertwined with other theories. Sometimes our historical theories are grounded in cosmological ones (as with Hesiod's theory of the Ages of Humankind, which had humans going downhill from an Age of Gold through intermediate ages to an Age of Iron); sometimes they are derived from philosophical arguments (such as German idealism's argument for the eventual triumph of the human spirit); sometimes they are based on social-philosophical speculations (as with Karl Marx and Arnold Toynbee); there are even "scientific" theories of history. After all, Darwin's theory was taken by Herbert Spencer to be a theory of history, and is still often taken that way by neo-Darwinists in our own day.[23]

Theories in the sense in which we are using the term are intended to be verifiable, or at least falsifiable—subject to test. They are supposed to tell "how things happen," which usually implies explicating "what causes what" (although this is not always the case, as when a theory is principally taxonomic). Theories, accordingly, carry a certain authority, and so do the categories derived from them. This leads to a predictable abuse.

Categories are often employed as if they were derived from some tested theory which not only *places* a phenomenon but *explains it scientifically.* In the following chapter, for example, we will encounter Justice Scalia treating the category "unitary family" as if it were derived from a theory about nature—specifically, about a basic state of human social organization—and then using the category to construct the rationale for a Supreme Court opinion dealing with the visitation rights of an unmarried parent. The theory is never made explicit, but its presumed verifiability is nonetheless used as the foundation for Justice Scalia's reasoning. So, too, categories are typically attributed to a general theory of human development when judges write opinions justifying their decisions in child custody cases—although no verifiable theory exists. Quite a number of legal categories, indeed, implicitly and spuriously claim to have a basis in biological or psychological theory, like the category of "recidivist" or "habitual offender" implying a "criminal propensity" that is used to justify "three-strikes-and-you're-out" sentencing schemes and similar measures.

A second major source of categories, as noted, is story: folklore, myth, best-seller, all of the many genres of narrative. Story is quintessentially about people striving to attain some goal. When people in stories fail to get easily to the goals they're trying to reach, it is usually because something out of the ordinary, some obstacle (or what we will call "Trouble" when we return to the subject of narrative in later pages) has blocked them from doing so. The story provides an account of how its protagonists cope or fail to cope with the Trouble. Story, then, specializes in human agency, purposiveness, Trouble, and coping. It is also (usually covertly) normative, enlisting us to root for some agents to achieve some goals and overcome some Troubles, while (as in the Gothic genres) we root against others. Stories derive their convincing power not from verifiability but from verisimilitude: they will be true enough if they *ring true.*

So predisposed is the human mind to narrative that we even experience the events of everyday life in narrative form and assign them to categories derived from some particular kind of story. It simply will not do that events roll by us purposelessly, One Damn Thing After Another. We shape them into strivings and adversities, contests and rewards, vanquishings and setbacks. We do this, however sophisticated we may be. Indeed, sophistication may be nothing else than overlaying more and more elaborate stories on the simpler ones that continue to enthrall our imagination. Consider your own imaginative progress, for example, if you have read Northrop Frye's exquisite *Anatomy of Criticism*.[24] The book provides, among other things, an elaborate, explicitly theory-based taxonomy of categories for Western literary criticism. Doubtless, no one who has read its analyses of the tragic and the comic hero thinks about the category "hero" in the same way afterwards. Yet, for all of us, the figure of a hero continues to have features and implications that do not come from Frye's book, but from our readings of the stories of Antigone, of Robin Hood, and of the Argonauts, our television viewings of the Astronauts, the Star Trekkers, and so forth.[25]

Or consider the typical lawyer's category of a "murderer." At some times, for some purposes (and, one hopes, for the purpose of taking one's final examination in Criminal Law), it will reflect the technical definitions and distinctions of the law of homicide. But even for the most studious law student or the most experienced criminal practitioner, "murderer" will almost surely also call to mind, most of the time and for most purposes, images that have nothing to do with the Penal Code and everything to do with Jack the Ripper or Jimmy Cagney or Horror Comics. Thus are our narrative categories rooted in tales so implicit, so tacit, as to be beyond our ordinary awareness, unless we pull ourselves (or others) up short and insist on stopping to examine them afresh. As when Judge Constance Baker Motley, ruling on a motion to recuse her from presiding in a gender-discrimination case because she was a woman and therefore presumptively biased, observed with a becoming understatement that all the judges of her court were of *some* gender.[26]

Theories and narratives are hardly the only resources on which categories may be based. There is one other that needs to be looked at briefly before we move on, an obvious one. It is the regulative or overtly normative sphere, perhaps best illustrated by religion, although the law itself is another example. Normative knowledge is rarely organized *just* in terms of regulatory statutes: drive on the right, show your passport, file your tax returns by April 15. It is a system not only of rules or commands, but of justifications for them informed by some conception of what is right and wrong in the conduct of human affairs. And this conception needs grounding in a still broader conception about the origins of the world and of humankind, which, in every known culture, includes an account of a supreme and supernatural being or substance or principle.

If theories are about causes and connections in the natural world, and if narratives are about human agency and its vicissitudes in the enterprises of life, then normative-religious accounts are about human origins, human destiny, human responsibilities, and human plights. Their medium of expression is sometimes narrative (often mythic) in nature, sometimes theoretical (or metaphysical), but always ethically axiomatic. Their authority is based neither on verification nor on verisimilitude, but on their capacity to enlist belief as an act of faith. Their poles are Good and Evil, and their normative standards are oriented toward these. The great French sociologist Emile Durkheim[27] characterized the sphere of religious doctrine as having "exteriority and constraint," the former relating to the supernatural reality of religious creeds, the latter to their normative effect on believers.

Legal systems are shot through with religious doctrine, our Constitution being no exception.[28] Indeed, the very idea of a legal system is modeled structurally on religious doctrine, notably its mode of pronouncing and classifying edicts and decreeing the consequences of their violation. However much a legal system becomes secularized, its system of categories goes on reflecting its religious origins.

These, then, are the main sources from which category systems are drawn: the natural theoretical, the human narrative, and the supernatural religious. We shall have occasions to consider these further as we go along. Now we turn to yet another rule of the category game:

(4) Categories Serve Particular Functions

Any category system serves both individual and cultural functions.[29] We need not spend long on the individual, idiosyncratic functions of particular ways of categorizing. These are principally of concern to the student of personality and personal style. Yet not altogether so. French social scientists, for example, have long been interested in what they call *déformation professionelle*—the ways in which one's occupation or professional position leads one to cut up the world into particular kinds of categories. The teacher of contemporary litera- ture and the would-be movie producer doubtless sort the latest list of best-selling novels rather differently. The constitutional scholar and the high-school principal make different things of *United States v. Lopez*,[30] a Supreme Court decision resurrecting pre-New-Deal juris- prudence to limit Congress's power over interstate commerce and in- validate a federal ban on firearms in school zones. The bureaucrat prefers categories that are clear, definite, and free of ambiguity. The poet wants a world sorted into categories that have metaphorical ex- tension. At least that's how it probably goes on working weekdays— or is supposed to go. At least one major study has shown rather con- clusively that people who have authoritarian attitudes generally tend toward categories that are neat, tidy, and free of ambiguity, even when the objects being categorized are of no personal account to them.[31]

But let us turn to the functions that particular category systems serve for a culture or community or society—a subject we must talk about a bit now although we will discuss it more fully in Chapter 8. To begin with, take that most crucial distinction—which people are eligible mates for marriage, and which ones are not. Lévi-Strauss ar- gues that the line is drawn (and enforced by the taboo against marry- ing "close" relatives) in order to guarantee that clans exchange their eligible young women for reliable outside-the-clan allies.[32] There is no secret genetic wisdom in this taboo arrangement: it is obligatory even if clan kin are only distant cousins. Yet the taboo, with its quasi-reli- gious overtones, comes to condition the very way in which individual members of a society see one another: it even affects whether mem- bers of the opposite sex look "sexy."

Over time, category systems that originally reflected one set of pre- occupations or priorities of a culture may become the repository of others. A category system that embodies the tenets of a culture's dom- inant sectarian religion may, for example, come to serve the culture also as a framework for expressing or understanding human quests and plights and situations that are not sectarian or even essentially re- ligious.[33] A striking legal example of the evolution of a category sys- tem to serve multiple cultural functions is the history of the writ of *habeas corpus* in the courts of the United States from the days of Calhoun right through the 1996 Session of Congress. Through that long period, the debates and decisions that have determined which individuals "in custody" are entitled to seek redress by *habeas corpus* proceedings in a federal court have used the contours of the writ sometimes as an emblem of the worth that our society attributes to personal liberty in contrast to other values,[34] sometimes as a measure of the power balance between the states and the federal government,[35] sometimes as a means of mobilizing political rhetoric for the War on Crime,[36] and sometimes all these things at once.

In general, we can say that category systems serve two major cultural functions, often simultaneously. One is to promote cohesiveness within cultural groups: to enable in-group members to sort out the world in the same or in complementary ways. This is, of course, how the initiates of religious and political and artistic communities (and many others) form or maintain their cognitive solidarity: by seeing the world in a similar manner. It gives them a powerful bond and gives their group a unique identity.

But almost by virtue of that function, category systems can also serve to dominate other groups: to impose *your* system on *them*. As we have noted, this hegemonic function of category systems is generally acknowledged as a theoretical matter by virtually all students of culture in our time; and those who struggle to break the grip of long-established hegemonies have come increasingly to include among their strategies some form of radical criticism of long-established categories. A classic case is the feminist movement's early insistence on "consciousness raising," a strategy directed in large part at making women aware of the imposition of a male-centered category system on those it would control. In a similar vein, Roland Barthes suggested that public education had as one of its functions to impose the bourgeois mode of sorting out the world on those who were to serve the ends of bourgeois society[37]—a point also associated with Antonio Gramsci.[38] Analyses of discourse in the mode of Michel Foucault, with attention to the ways in which its categories represent power relationships (in a double sense), illustrate the same strategy.

All of this has made contests for control of at least some category systems more visible. At the same time, it has counseled the tacticians of many political movements covertly to fashion and popularize forms of discourse calculated to categorize the world's woes according to the prescriptions they are motivated or positioned to sell. Punitive prescriptions are hawked in the language of the War on Crime, which includes characterizing any proposal to retract the reach of the criminal law as "soft on crime" or as "coddling criminals." Proponents of the proposals prefer to talk about them as "decriminalization" and to hawk them in language that attributes the "crime problem" to "economic conditions" rather than to the acts of moral agents. Explicit debate about which of several available category systems is the conventionally "proper" one, the politically "legitimate" one, or the legally "authoritative" one for discussing this or that problem sometimes surfaces, but for the most part the never-ending struggle to dictate the categories that carve problems into *issues* remains tacit.

We will witness the struggle again and again in later chapters. Is a federal court's desegregation order a "remedy for a constitutional violation" or is it "running the public schools" (Chapter 3)? Is the shift of population in the Atlanta suburbs sprawling across DeKalb County a "natural demographic shift" or is it "white flight" (Chapter 5)? As we have already hinted, these are questions that bedevil not only Supreme Court Justices, Presidents, and "spin doctors"—each from a vastly different perspective. They also bedevil those foolhardy enough to write books about such dilemma-bound subjects as the relation of law, mind, and culture! For we too need to take stances. Stance, after all, is perspective in action—the condition for knowing.

So some of the categories we will use as we go along, like the categories used by the Justices whose opinions we will examine, bespeak our predispositions and preferences—which some will no doubt categorize (using no less plausible ones) as those of "lefty liberals." But we do not deploy them on the assumption that they represent the "right" way of framing things, or to argue that alternative category systems are "wrong." They simply give us a place to stand, from which to look at the motivated quality of *all* category systems.

The basic point of our Fourth Rule of Categorization is that category systems are, in the main, under human control. They are *for something*, and it matters greatly what they are for. Their consequences are serious, whether in holding a community together or establishing its hegemony over another. Category systems are rarely innocent. They impose larger-scale ideological structures not only on the workings of courts and legislatures—and the interpretations of them by their observers—but on the conduct of everyday life. That is why we are so deeply concerned with them, and why we will return again and again to the problem of categorization in later chapters.

(5) Categories Become Entrenched in Practice

Ways of categorizing get entrenched in institutions, in habits of life, in the very language we speak. Cultural historians take this process for granted.[39] Even physics is subject to the process, as we know from Kuhn's classic work on the resistance of scientific paradigms to disproof.[40] And it is explicit in the law. The familiar legal canon that courts are "never to anticipate a question of constitutional law in advance of the necessity of deciding it"[41] expresses the notion that entrenched categories are privileged not only against precipitous amendment but against presumptuous inquiry.

Entrenchment is not only institutional: it expresses itself in habits of mind—even in something as private as the process of perceptual recognition. An odd experiment that one of us did some years ago can serve to illustrate. Subjects in the experiment were shown playing cards one at a time in a tachistoscope (an apparatus for displaying a visual stimulus as briefly as one wishes) and were asked to say when they recognized the card displayed. Some of the cards were normal in the sense of having normally matched colors and suits—red hearts and diamonds, black spades and clubs. Some were trick cards like, say, a red six of clubs or a black four of diamonds. Subjects needed four times as much time exposure to recognize these trick cards, and they clung to the entrenched version of "reality" by reporting, for example, at well above normal recognition exposure, that the red six of clubs was "just a six of clubs, but the light that comes in is reddish," or that the black four of diamonds was "OK, a four of diamonds, except it's in heavy shadow." Indeed, even when subjects had already been exposed to one of those contrary-to-nature playing cards, they still couldn't quite believe another one when they "saw" it.[42] The visual system seems to be as entrenched in precedent as the Supreme Court. And, of course, language puts an institutional cement into this process even at the perceptual level: in general, the more often a word appears in print, the less time necessary to recognize it. But note also—a matter that will concern us later—that speed of recognition is greater when the word in question happens to conform to something you value.[43]

Then, of course, there is that entrenchment phenomenon in language known as the Whorfian hypothesis: the doctrine (probably exaggerated in popular accounts) that one makes distinctions in experience more easily if the distinction is present in the lexicon of your language—the corollary of this being that we entrench in the lexicon only those categorical distinctions that are *useful* in a linguistic community. So entrenchment of one kind or another seems always to have us in its grip—at least when we are operating on automatic pilot rather than practicing "strict scrutiny." Nevertheless:

(6) Categories Are Never Final

Our last maxim is a reminder that both minds and cultures change under conducive conditions. When those conditions come about, categories crumble; Supreme Courts render landmark decisions; paradigm shifts (in the fashionable terminology) happen; all of us manage suddenly to see things differently—even when it hurts. And categories, together with the other canons and conventions of any culture, are perpetually under threat of excavation or sapping by those at its fringes, by those less privileged, by the culture's parodists, its playwrights, its comics. Our First Rule of the category game was that categories are made, not found. Our Last Rule is intended to restate that first one. Neither habit nor culture has the final word on how we categorize things in our worlds.

IV. Where Do Our Categories Come From?

We have already begun to address this question by noting that categories are derived or abstracted from larger-scale theories, stories, or normative redes about "reality." We must now look more closely at the matter.

A first point is as important as it is banal. We take or make our categories out of ordinary "logic," by dint of commonplace rationality that tells us, say, that something can't be both A and not-A. This is what is called *necessary knowledge.* The mind seems to have certain irresistible ways of creating categories, to paraphrase Kant. But what can we say about the range or scope of such necessary knowledge? Are there only certain prescribed ways in which the mind can compute?

In Kant's original account, space and time and causality were singled out as the irresistible sources of our categories: humankind could not experience a world without them.[44] Later he added a moral dimension: we cannot experience the world non-evaluatively. In more recent times, philosophers and human scientists have been exploring other domains of necessary knowledge, irresistible ways of making sense of the world, of cutting it up into categories.

This inquiry usually posits some form of "innate knowledge." So, for example, the claim has been made that our knowledge of language, specifically our knowledge of syntax and phonology, is innate and so abstract that it fits all the languages of the world. All we need, according to this view, is a minimum instantiation of how some abstract syntactic rule is "realized" in our mother language, and we "recognize" it and adopt it forthwith. Specific languages, on this view, do not have to be taught, only "modeled" by some competent speaker in the infant's earshot. The infant already has the deep-structure knowledge necessary to recognize the model as a "right" rule.[45]

While this nativist view has been widely criticized for being overgeneralized, it has stimulated a great deal of inquiry about the nature and function of innate knowledge. Briefly, innate knowledge is evidenced by irresistible inference: given a certain input from the world, we cannot experience or understand it as anything *other* than as of a certain kind. Some examples might help. Even infants of a few months see the behavior of those around them as *intended*. We know this from an ingenious experiment in which infants watch an adult trying to perform a task (put a ball into a container) at which the adult is thwarted by various obstacles. The infant's subsequent behavior is observed when the infant has the same materials available. Infants typically proceed to imitate what the adult was *trying* to do, and they carry out the task *to its intended end*.[46] From this we judge that very young infants perceive the intent in human action: the category "intention" is an innate one. In a similar vein, we now know that human infants also have a "theory of mind"—that they *know* from very early on that their conspecifics have subjective states like beliefs, intentions, fears.[47]

We mention these studies not to argue that human category systems are themselves innate or "necessary," but only to note that initially they take certain characteristic shapes or forms rather than others. Humans seem to find it easy and natural to categorize people's actions as intentional; they have much more difficulty seeing people's behavior as, say, circumstantially or structurally determined. It seems less effortful to see unemployed persons as suffering their misfortune because of not "trying" hard enough than because of structural shortcomings, say, in a capitalist system or of socialist planning.

So an initial answer to the question "Where do categories come from?" is that they are products of the human imagination. They often get born as *empty categories,* constructed to explore hypothetical possibilities—like female Popes, visiting presidents of universities, or any category that takes us beyond the given of the here and now. Science and mathematics have even formalized ways of making such leaps into the possible; quarks and neutrinos often come out of mathematical deduction before ever they show up on a telescope or in a cloud chamber. Novelists and playwrights have their more mysterious forms of intuition. They too get there before the real thing; else there would be no boast that "Life imitates Art."

All of this makes plain that the only voucher for the truth of human categories is the human imagination itself. But it is the human imagination operating within the confines of human mental life, with some imaginative products coming more easily than others. Supernatural, all-powerful creatures come more easily to young children's imagination, and we grow into adults who can imagine less fantastic forms of powerful beings. We seem so predisposed to think of the category "human beings" as possessed of "will" or "intention" that we can scarcely imagine them without—until we generate the possibility of "zombies" who have no will at all. And this reflects another property of human imagination—the generating of contrast categories: God generates Devil; government, anarchy; freedom, slavery; good fairies, bad ones.

We have made it seem as if imagination works in a vacuum, "mind in a vat." But of course it does not. As Clifford Geertz has made a point of reminding us through his long and distinguished career (with many other anthropologists assenting), there is no mind without culture.[48] If culture is anything, it is a network of models of the world, of ways of getting on in it, of tools for thinking and imagining that range from systems of mathematics to genres of storytelling.

Not a lot is known about how cultures generate and traditionalize their ways of looking at the world. We will consider this subject—what we call "the dialectic of culture"—in Chapter 8. For now it suffices to say that cultures seem to have been and continue to be enormously tenacious in holding onto and passing on their traditional theories, narrative forms, and normative system. And when we refine the question "Where do category systems come from?" the answer has got to be that they come not just *de novo* from human imagination, but from the storehouse of any culture's ways of construing the world.

Yet to this we must add the proviso that, for all their diversity, human cultures are by no means a free-for-all. Human beings, as the anthropologist Dan Sperber likes to put it, have varying hospitality for different ways of thinking and organizing experience. In consequence there is something like an *epidemiology* with respect to different cultural notions and cultural ways. We fall victim to some narrative forms more readily than others, certain power relations more than others, causal accounts more than probabilistic ones.[49] Thus, while cultures and particular circumstances offer many possible sources for category systems, not all shapes and varieties of them take hold and become part of a people's canonical ways. There are (as some call them) *human universals,* constraints on what human beings living in cultures will accept, will "come down with," to use Sperber's epidemiological metaphor.

It is worth noting one interesting matter of detail that has recently grown out of a half-century of research lavished by psychologists on the subject of categorizing or "concept formation" (as it is usually labeled). We call attention to it principally because it can serve to distinguish an older, more rationalistic way of looking at categorization from a newer, more experiential way that has challenged the old rationalism. It concerns how categories are formed and, indirectly, where they come from.

The rationalist assumption was that categories and category systems resulted from rather straightforward combinatorial mental operations—contrast (as with the category "citizen" presuming the category "non-citizens"), overlapping (as in Venn diagrams when two categories, say "women" and "U.S. Presidents," are combined to yield "female U.S. Presidents"), and the like. The shortcoming of this approach is that it failed to distinguish more *natural-seeming* experiential categories like "apples" or "birds" from artificial or made-up ones like "attractive nuisances" or "intellectual property." In recent years, thanks principally to the pioneering work of Eleanor Rosch and George Lakoff, this problem has been pursued with a passion.[50] Rosch was among the first to argue that natural-kind categories do not come from logic-like combining but, rather, grow up around a *prototype* experience of some sort of salient thing or event that then serves as an emblematic instance of a category, with other instances gaining entry into the category by their resemblance to the proto- type. A sparrow, for example, may be the prototype of the category "BIRD"; penguins are, as it were, outliers in this category. The *closer* something is to the prototype, the more confident we are that it is *in* the category.

There are two rich questions that this approach leaves open, both of interest in trying to understand how legal categories come into be- ing and are used. The first, of course, is *what kind of salience* makes something into a prototype. Sparrow may be the prototype "bird," but we have a tendency to create additional prototypes for all sorts of subcategories of birds. Probably, most people would see the eagle or the hawk as the prototype bird-of-prey, the seagull as the prototype seabird. It would seem that practically any category we create either originates with or generates a prototype to go with it, or to serve somehow as a trope for it; and the "somehow" may have to do with typicality or *commonness* (for the sparrow as prototype bird), or with *vividness* or *iconicity* (for the eagle prototype), or whatever.

But surely John Wayne was neither the most typical nor the most vivid Western Hero, though he was for a long time the prototype of the class. What creates prototypicality is a puzzle. We tend toward the view that prototypes are somewhat like tropes: they function *tropo- logically* to capture the nature of the *system* from which a set of cate- gories emerges or is derived. So, for example, Theseus was the proto- type Greek mythic hero, by dint of his wily killing of the terrorizing Minotaur. He fit the role of hero in Greek mythic narrative to a T. Not only filled it, but somehow condensed it into a negotiable image. And so with the lion as "king of beasts," filling the bill for the legend of fe- rocity, or the hyena that of the legendary cowardly beast, or caviar the legendary luxury food. Science, too, generates trope prototypes: the frictionless plane, the visible rainbow, the red-yellow-white molecular turning points in heated metals. And music as well: the C major chord in the Western musical canon.

This leaves open the question whether natural-kind categories always *originate in response to* some particular object, event, or whatever that, as it were, serves as a prototype and *then* gives birth to the category. This is probably not a question that anybody can answer in our present state of knowledge. But somehow it seems unlikely, given the presence of fantasy categories like "goblins" with their upsetting prototypes.

We've not yet asked the second puzzling question alluded to above—the so-called *similarity question:* how similar to the prototype must a newly encountered event be to qualify for inclusion in a category? And similar in what respect? Similarity depends on what *dimension* or *axis* of comparison one uses. *Tristram Shandy* and *Brown v. Board of Education* are alike in their emphasis on "inwardness"—if that is the dimension along which you are judging their likeness. On the other hand, *Brown* is like *Plessy v. Ferguson* in their both being U.S. Supreme Court decisions about Equal Protection. So, the question of what composes a category of similar things seems to be a matter of one's choice of criteria. If you're thinking in terms of epistemology, *Brown* and *Tristram* go together; if jurisprudence, then *Brown* and *Plessy*. Or as Keil[51] and Carey[52] tried to show, once categories are framed in a particular way, in light of a more general theory or story, much more follows. If you categorize a paramecium as an *animal,* you get committed to lots of other things. Having placed it in the "animal kingdom," you will see one structural feature of it as a mouth, another as its cloacum, and so forth. Put it in the plant kingdom, and quite different commitments come into play.

All of which argues that neither categories nor their prototypes are fixed and once-for-all. Categories form in response to what you are up to, talking about, thinking about. Your category of a "great teacher" is not the same in the morning, when you are choosing your law school courses for next semester, and in the evening, when you are chatting with the parents of your child's third-grade classmates at a PTA meeting.

V. How We Put Things into Categories

We come now to the conditions under which people put things into one category or another. Category placements suppose some process for arriving at a judgment that the pertinent characteristics of the instance you are seeking to place *fit* the criteria you take to be indicative of category membership. Because this seems intuitively obvious, the most common model of the process—both in popular science (with its images of all knowlege laid out in Linnaean grids) and in legal thinking (with its writ systems and subchapters laid out in similar fashion)—is simply to *match the observed attributes of the instance in question with the defining properties of each category into which it might fit.* A process of this sort is consistent with what we have called the older, more rationalistic notion of category formation: a category is first staked out by enumerating the necessary and sufficient conditions for membership in it; then those conditions are used as a checklist to test the qualifications of any putative candidate for admission.

Such a model hardly fits every kind of category placement. We have already noted psychological research suggesting that category placements are often made by assimilating the thing-to-be-categorized to a *prototype* rather than by comparing its observed attributes with a checklist of definitional components. So, jurors deciding whether a defendant is guilty or innocent of murder might well respond not only to the legal elements of the crime of murder as defined in the judge's instructions, but also to their prototype of what a "murderer" looks like. And even judges might not avoid prototype-based categorizations in deciding what conduct constitutes an actionable "nuisance" or "invasion of privacy." But this is only the beginning of the difficulty in supposing that category placements are usually made by the systematic application of taxonomic definitions to perceptual observations. Neither life nor law is a well-run laboratory; both are worlds where, as Richard Rorty puts it laconically, "*no* interesting descriptive term has any interesting necessary and sufficient conditions."[53] Nor does life or law often offer any single, correct viewing position that assures a correspondence between appearance and reality. So all cannot be settled simply by invoking Bertrand Russell's "close look" theory. Indeed, the very question of how closely one will look depends, commonly, on what's at stake.[54]

Of course, all societies and legal systems have procedures for rendering certain kinds of categorizing relatively non-problematic, even foolproof, whether for reasons of state or on some more pragmatic basis. We have passports to attest to our nationality, driver's licenses to bear witness to our navigating skills, intricate watermarks to "prove" the genuineness of our legal tender. These procedures are designed to take the uncertainty out of category placement through the use of *formal category structures* that have specifications sufficiently well-formed as to be virtually independent of the context in which any particular categorizing judgment is made. Placing people in or outside the category of "eligible voters" is a job we try to make so uncontroversial that a handful of registration officials can quick-classify millions of individuals by election day: a voter must be over 18 years old, must have resided in a certain district for a certain length of time, must not be a convicted felon, and so forth.

The (small) trouble with such formal category systems is that the very artificiality that makes them serviceable sorting instruments also tends—or should tend—to remind us how provisionally, transiently, and superficially they are entitled to command our acceptance. They can hold our operating programs but not our dreams or values or anything we care enough about to contest. They work, for the most part, only if the work to be done is doable by scanners, computers, and like-minded creatures. Suppose an election forecast to be so precarious that some candidate is moved to question whether persons who are "eligible voters" under the Election Code are really "eligible voters" under the Constitution. We would be foolish to expect that in the ensuing litigation any formal category system could supply the answers.

Unless it masqueraded as something else. And that is the *big* trouble with formal category systems. They too often conceal their limited potential usefulness and their contestable pedigree by posing as *real*, as in the world, *eo ipso,* "natural." In consequence, when a proposal is made to change the criteria of some formally defined category— when the franchise is extended to women, or when the Fifteenth Amendment right to vote is extended to primary elections—there is a cry in the land as if Nature had been betrayed. We will see an instance of this in the following chapter when we examine Justice Scalia's invocation of Nature to categorize the "family"—and thereby the "liberty" protected by the Fourteenth Amendment—in the case of *Michael H. v. Gerald D.*[55]

In any event, formal category systems fail (and do not even try) to map more than a minute and superficial sector of the human scene in which we live our lives and do our thing. We ordinarily look at the people around us, their strivings and conditions, not in terms of some Linnaean chart or Field Guide to Flowering Plants, but in terms of implicit praxic knowledge, *folk psychology.*[56] This is the kind of understanding about how the world operates that typically takes the form, "the right way to do that is so-and-so"—some prescriptive account of *what you do* to avoid snakes, to counteract spells of witchcraft, to show guests a good time, to survive New York City street life, to win lawsuits, or whatever. Virtually everything we do in daily life is kept on course by such praxic understandings; and if you ask people to explain why they are following a particular line of action, they will typically tell you what-you-are-supposed-to-do and then recite some beliefs about how the business at hand "works."

There is always something obligatory about these accounts of actions-to-be-taken and the beliefs underlying them. It is often expressed by reciting in tandem how things *actually* happen and how things *should* happen. What characterizes such recountings is that they are about particular *paths* to follow. These are rarely mapped on aerial diagrams of the whole terrain of possibilities: they are not, as we would say nowadays, layouts of possible worlds. They represent the route instructions ("two blocks south to the first light, then turn left") by which, if only to save effort, we "think in the small."

We test a line of practice against these "think small" expectancies, and if the TEST[57] seems to produce the expected outcome, we go through with the line of practice and EXIT. Every language has a primitive form for indicating that we're done—*ecco fatto, c'est ça, that's it*—and usually the first action-marking demonstrative encountered in infant speech (related to eating or drinking) is *all gone*. You'll sense immediately that these praxic understandings come very close to being little stories—scripts and narratives.

We'll have more to say about scripts and narratives (and about the difference and relationships between them) in Chapter 4. For now, it is enough to introduce these two kinds of stories and to note the importance of their role in category placements. We use the term *scripts* to refer to stories that provide walk-through models of a culture's canonical expectations, and *narratives* to refer to stories that illustrate what happens when a script is thrown off track or threatened with derailment.

Scripts contain familiar characters taking appropriate actions in typical settings. They play out *recurrent* situations in our lives, and we don't so much create them as assimilate them from the people with whom we live. Probably, our first categories are homely little abstractions from these useful everyday scripts. They continue to reek of their scriptish origins even after they have been abstracted, so that kids say things like "a hole is to dig" or "a waiter is somebody who waits on you in a restaurant." Notice that the script for "waiter" is a customer's-eye view of how a waiter behaves, not a waiter's-eye view; we would have a different script for "waiter" if we worked for a while in a restaurant. Each script centers on what *we* expect from the activity related in the script.

Narratives are more complex, precisely because they involve some violation of a script and so must also embed or imply the violated script. Narratives do not simply reflect expectations; they confront expectations with dangers and obstacles. They are about the Troubles people encounter while following scripts. So they introduce categories of unexpected outcomes (like comedies and tragedies) and categories of what precipitates trouble and of what redresses trouble. (The latter two categories are of particular interest to the law, of course.) Narratives are about "treachery" and "revenge" and "honor" and "reward" and "defeat" and "overcoming." It is through narratives that we come to see people as heroes, villains, tricksters, stooges (and so forth), and that we come to see situations as victories, humiliations, career opportunities, tests of character, menaces to dignity (and so forth).

The essential elements of narrative are Agents who Act to achieve Goals in a recognizable Setting by the use of certain Means and who run into Trouble. The Agents are human-like characters capable of willing their Goals and of choosing their Acts—although they need not be people; they can be foxes and cranes, as in Aesop; or they can be the Church, or the Nation, or the States, as in "States' Rights."[58] Their story typically moves from *an anterior steady state* (the prevalence or promise of a usual, expected, legitimate state of affairs) through some setback, reversal, or disruption (the Trouble) through strivings to correct or cope with the Trouble (which may succeed or fail) to either *a restoration of the old steady state* or *the establishment of a new one.*

Although narratives are far more varied than scripts, they are not infinitely varied. Not only do most of them adhere to the basic structure we have just described, but there is an astonishingly small number of subspecies ("genres") of narratives. Northrop Frye argued for four: tragedy, comedy, romance, and irony.[59] Alistair Fowler maintains that genres are more like pigeons than pigeonholes, constantly being reinvented and transformed to fit the contemporary condition.[60] However they may change, at any time in any culture we find precious few of them. They express that culture's current way of conceiving of the human condition, the plights that plague it, and how they will play out.

Either that, or the culture reflects its narratives. Doubtless both are true, art imitating life just as tenaciously as life imitates art. So both in Tonight's News and in the newest fiction, "True Romance" will either Win Through or leave its Poignant Pain; "Betrayal" will bereave both Betrayer and Betrayed; there will Come a Moment and God Help Those Who Fail to Seize It, etc. These narratives, their characters, plots, and predicaments, constantly furnish us a standard library of categories by which to classify and interpret the human scene.

Placing things, events, and people in these categories is very much a matter of *what stock script one recognizes* as being in play[61] or *what story one chooses to tell*.[62] In a well-known experiment by Thomas Gilovich, for example, political science students given a hypothetical "foreign policy crisis" involving the threatened invasion of a "democratic" country by its "totalitarian" neighbor tended to categorize the situation as appropriate for U.S. intervention when they had been cued to tell themselves a story about the consequences of appeasing Hitler on the eve of World War II as contrasted with a story about the consequences of U.S. engagement in Vietnam.[63] And, as another example, we shall see in the following chapter that Chief Justice Rehnquist's majority opinion for the Supreme Court in *Missouri v. Jenkins* categorizes white flight as a result-of-desegregation, *not* a result-of-*de-jure*-segregation, by telling a story in which (1) the anterior steady state is a school district running its own schools, and (2) the disruptive Trouble is a federal court's desegregation order issued under *Brown v. Board of Education*—in contrast to a story in which (1) the Trouble is segregation, and (2) *Brown* is part of the rectification of that Trouble.[64]

Stock scripts and familiar stories will powerfully influence the categories that come readily to mind and the ones we choose to contain— and therefore to shape—our observations and experiences. We are quicker to see the expected than the unexpected, as the tachistoscope experiment with red and black fours of diamonds reminds us. And the deck is often stacked in ways that can deceive the unselfconscious. For example, white subjects viewing a videotape of an altercation in which an African-American actor gives a white actor an ambiguous shove will categorize this behavior as "violent" (not as "playing around" or "dramatizing") far more often than when the white actor gives the African-American actor the same shove.[65]

Which is not to suggest that self-consciousness is a sufficient guarantor against biased category placements. Consider an example from the law. When a client hands a document to a lawyer and says "I want your opinion as to whether this is a legally binding contract," any self-conscious, sensible attorney will reply with counter-questions: "Do you want to break it or enforce it?"; "Does your question relate to something you have already done or something you are thinking about doing?"; and so forth. This is very different from the sentry deciding whether the approaching figure in the dusk is friend or foe. For the figure approaching the lawyer might conceivably turn out to be either friend or foe, depending on which the lawyer chooses to make it.

So, what does our lawyer do? In effect, the lawyer designs a *rhetorical strategy*. To be sure, the lawyer's (and the client's) categorization problem will eventually require a decision, but it will not be solely the lawyer's decision. It will involve an arbiter (real or imagined) who must decide which of two (or more) *contending categorizations* is the fitter one. The lawyer is called upon to present (or imagine) the best possible case for the contract being either valid or invalid, and must do so in full knowledge that a lawyer for the other party may, presumably with equal assiduity, present a contrary brief. Immediately or potentially, categorizing under law is an adversary process (though, to be sure, much of legal practice consists of advising clients how to avoid entanglement in formal adversarial procedures). In the end it is guilty as charged or not, liable or not, contract performed or not.

Obviously, there are also other walks of life where one must make one's case before an arbiter—a tribunal charged with saying yea or nay to one's categorial claims—sometimes in a more formal sense, sometimes less so. As a Diaspora Jew, do you have the "right of return"? As an art auctioneer, can you classify this painting as a "genuine" Van Gogh? As a literary scholar, do you take *Tristram Shandy* to be the *first* (or the prototype) of the "inward turning" novels? These are all categorizations to be made in the contemplation of controversy. And so they will enlist *rhetorics,* a subject of sufficient importance and complexity to deserve a later chapter of its own.[66]

VI. *The Hazards of Categorization*

What has been said already should suffice to warn us of at least the most apparent pitfalls of categorization. Once we put a creature, thing, or situation in a category, we will attribute to it the features of that category and fail to see the features of it that don't fit. We will miss the opportunities that might have existed in all the alternative categories we did *not* use. We will see distinctions where there may be no differences and ignore differences because we fail to see distinctions.

All of this is well known. We want to close by mentioning a few less obvious shoals on which legal categorization, in particular, may run aground.

The appeal to similarity. When one raises a question whether any particular legal category, category system, or category placement is defensible by anything but *fiat,* one is more often than not met with the claim that there must be some substance to the challenged categorization because things within the category are more *similar* to one another than to things outside the category. And often the similarity adverted to is undeniable, even glaring. But beware the *other* similarities that were ignored when the adverted-to similarity was selected for attention.

For the fact is that human beings have an exquisite, ubiquitous capacity to register endless sources of similarity. And any judgment of similarity depends upon the criteria chosen to measure likeness or unlikeness. Similarity for what? is the question. Two dachshunds are more like each other than like a Doberman, *unless* one of the dachshunds belongs to me; then the other dachshund and the Doberman are more alike because they are "not mine." Save in highly specialized instances (as with faces), similarity is the result of categorization rather than the cause of it. The Serbs in Sarajevo see the Serbs in, say, Belgrade as more akin to them than their Muslim neighbors in Sarajevo. But that is due to category criteria, not to "natural" similarities between Serbs, Muslims, and Sarajevans. The eminent logician-philosopher W. V. Quine put it well:

"The brute irrationality of our sense of similarity, its irrelevance to anything in logic or mathematics, offers little reason to expect that this sense is somehow in tune with the world."[67]

The observation that things are similar—like the observation that a legal precedent has features in common with the case at bar—says only that there is an available ground on which to treat the two alike *if we choose to deem that commonality relevant. Which* commonalities we deem relevant almost always depends on something else: history, commitments, values, principles, sometimes simply the failure to take a second look after we think we have seen some similarity in the first.[68]

The appeal to natural kinds. We mentioned "natural-kind" categories earlier. The concept is appealing: "dogs," say, seems indeed to be a more natural category than "postmodern poetry." This appearance of naturalness may increase the likelihood that your "dog" category is organized prototypically rather than definitionally; it will almost certainly decrease the likelihood that you will reconsider its boundaries critically whenever you put things into it. For these reasons, it is particularly important to keep in mind what people often do not: that "naturalness" itself is a creature of our conceptions and our circumstances, of our theories and our praxic understandings about how things work. A "cripple" becomes a less natural category to the extent that prosthetic technologies become available; it is a particularly natural category when a culture not only lacks technological resources but regards physical afflictions as punishments for one's misbehavior in a prior life.

The claim of naturalness for particular categories often rests cryptically upon some notion of coherence: either that the category was *caused* by natural forces or that it has a special ontological status (like the claim that races were *created* different). The last example points up how easy it is to abuse the natural-kinds argument in defending entrenched categories. Another example is the persistent effort to convert "criminal" from a legal category into a natural kind. Criminality is observed to run in families, to be statistically associated with a particular race, even to be related to a particular gene; it is but a step, then, to the need for a natural remedy (like the three-strikes-and-you're-out rule of recidivist sentencing), and another small step to "root and branch" remedies like sterilization. Or: the explicit or implicit suggestion is made that poverty is "caused" by low IQs; the poor then become a natural category; and society is absolved.

The rhetoric of categorization. Given its complexities and centrality, categorization inspires a nearly suffocating rhetoric. Little wonder that the advice of the *Rhetorica ad Herennium* is so widely followed:

> "[I]f it is at all possible, we shall show that what our opponent calls justice is cowardice . . . and perverse generosity; what he has called wisdom we shall term impertinent, babbling, and offensive cleverness; what he declares to be temperance we shall declare to be inaction and lax indifference; what he has named courage we shall term the reckless temerity of a gladiator."[69]

The protection against rhetoric is, of course, to unpack it by debate—to bring its baggage under conscious scrutiny. But, as we noted at the outset of this chapter, awareness of our habitual categories does not come easy. Even after the women's movement of the 1960s kicked off a quarter-century of close scrutiny of our culture's genderizing categories, we remain no more than partly conscious of the gender distinctions we are using in our daily vocabularies and lives. It is especially difficult to make people aware of the broader, value-loaded narrative and conceptual frameworks from which particular categories are being derived for a purpose at hand—for example, when welfare is classified as a "handout" rather than a "safety net" in order to justify killing it off. "Strict scrutiny" all too often comes into play, alas, only after such rhetorical tricks have had their effect.

In a word, then, categorization is always serving some function.[70] It is always subject to change, always somewhat elusive. Pigeonholes should never be taken for granted. And this is as true in the law as elsewhere.

The legal category of acts that we loosely call *incest* is a good illustration. To begin with, it is defined differently in different indigenous cultures and in different legal systems within more technologically advanced societies. In many indigenous cultures, for example, marriage between males and females of the same totemic clan or moiety is taken to be incest and is tabooed. In other cultures, the incest taboo applies to unions between partners who bear some specified kinship relation to each other; the offspring of one's father's brothers are maritally off-limits, for example. As we have mentioned, Lévi-Strauss sought to explain such taboos and prohibitions in terms of a "theory of exchange," according to which women were married out into families with whom a broader alliance was sought rather than into families with whom such an alliance was already specified by custom.[71] Interestingly, Leigh Bienen's recent study of incest laws in the United States suggests that some late colonial and early state exogamy statutes included a similar economic or *alliance* function. Thus, "[m]arrying your wife's cousin by marriage . . . [was] prohibited not because it would be inbreeding, but because it would confuse an existing, rigidly structured, kinship relationship with your wife's family," and this was a consummation devoutly to be avoided in a "patriarchal, property-based clan system"[72] such as prevailed in the colonies and continued long after the Revolution.

Bienen traces the evolution of American incest laws during the nineteenth and twentieth centuries and shows that they underwent a marked change in function. At the end of the eighteenth century, the statutes took the form of prohibitions of marriage or carnal copulation between persons having a defined familial relationship. The harm to be prevented was that "the parties have sinned against God's order and against the social structure upheld by marriage and kinship relationships governing the ownership of property."[73] But over time, the incest statutes increasingly became instruments for providing legal protection to young girls who had been sexually assaulted by older male members of their family, most often by a father or stepfather.[74] There was considerable variation in the extent to which the laws were enforced by prosecution, but successful prosecutions were rare.[75] Then in the 1970s and 1980s, when the national women's movement focused public attention upon sex crimes against women and undertook a campaign to reform the laws defining sexual offenses, the idea of "recharacterizing sex offenses involving children became a powerful and persuasive component of both the practical and the political arguments for . . . changing the criminal justice system's response to sex crimes generally."[76] As a consequence, reform "statutes introduced an entirely new concept of Incest in their description of the behavior to be prohibited, the proof requirements, the penalties, and the perceived harm."[77]

> "Offenses involving adults and minors when the adult was in a position of familial authority became a special case of the redefined and retitled sex offenses. The transformation of family, with its emphasis on blood

relations, into a concept of 'position of authority' was one of the most profound philosophical changes."[78]

As Bienen concludes, "changes in the statutory definitions of Incest and their myriad interpretations . . . allow us to glimpse . . . [how] the law . . . stretches and tears, across time and place, and then connects itself again to the living body of the society."[79]

Now we are ready to look closely at some other cases of categorizing in the law.

CHAPTER THREE

Categorizing at the Supreme Court

Missouri v. Jenkins and *Michael H. v. Gerald D.*

Two case studies will introduce us to the complex ways of categorization in the law. The first, a sort of aerial survey aimed at getting a general sense of the terrain, maps the sheer range of categorizing devices used in one opinion of the Supreme Court of the United States. The second focuses upon a different Supreme Court opinion and explores its central categorizing move in depth.

It is unremarkable that judicial opinions involve a lot of categorization. Deciding that a particular set of facts does or does not constitute a "libel" or a "nuisance" or a "cruel and unusual punishment" or an "unreasonable search" forbidden by the Fourth Amendment or a "liberty" protected by the Fourteenth Amendment is, after all, what courts take to be their primary task. But we seldom pause to consider the wide variety of ways in which judicial opinions create categories and put things into them, or the wide variety of effects that they produce by these operations. To attend to this is the object of our first study, which surveys Chief Justice Rehnquist's majority opinion in the 1995 school-desegregation case of *Missouri v. Jenkins*.[1]

Our aim at this preliminary stage is not to criticize the *Jenkins* opinion or even the particular categorizing moves that we will isolate for observation. Criticism would require perspectives that we have not yet developed. We will revisit *Jenkins* with those perspectives in Chapter 9; for now, our aim is simply to take notice of a broad sample of the categorizing moves that are made in the *Jenkins* opinion, to get a sense of the extent to which its reasoning depends on categorization.[2]

MISSOURI V. JENKINS

I. The Background

To prepare for our examination of the *Jenkins* opinion, we need to say something about the Supreme Court's school-desegregation jurisprudence before 1995 and about the facts and issues in the *Jenkins* case itself. In 1954, in *Brown v. Board of Education*[3] (commonly called "*Brown I*"), the Supreme Court of the United States decided that governmentally enforced racial segregation in the public schools violated the Equal Protection Clause of the Fourteenth Amendment. Recognizing that this ruling would require major changes in the way that schools were administered in many regions, the Court postponed decision of the question of "appropriate relief"[4]—that is, how its *Brown I* decision should be implemented by the formulation of court orders disestablishing the dual school systems in the segregated states. After deliberating further, the Court decided in 1955 (in "*Brown II*") that the lower federal courts should be given discretion to craft desegregation orders in the light of local conditions and to "consider the adequacy of any plans . . . [that school authorities] may propose to meet . . . [local administrative] problems and to effectuate a transition to a racially nondiscriminatory school system."[5] During the "period of transition," the lower courts were to "retain jurisdiction" with a view to conducting whatever proceedings were "necessary and proper to admit . . . [the class of African-American children] to public schools on a racially nondiscriminatory basis with all deliberate speed."[6]

For more than a generation after *Brown II*, the "failure of local authorities to meet their constitutional obligations aggravated the massive problem of converting from the state-enforced discrimination of racially separate school systems."[7] The Supreme Court increasingly expressed impatience with the long delays in achieving desegregation, saying in 1964 that "[t]he time for mere 'deliberate speed' has run out,"[8] in 1968 that "[t]he burden on a school board today is to come forward with a plan that promises realistically to work,

and promises realistically to work *now*,"[9] and in 1971 that school desegregation remedies "must be implemented *forthwith*."[10] The last of
these pronouncements was made in the case of *Swann v. Charlotte-
Mecklenburg Board of Education,* where the Court took pains to
spell out an updated canon of school-desegregation principles.[11]

Swann authorized the federal courts to use a broad range of devices, including court-ordered busing and "a frank—and sometimes
drastic—gerrymandering of school attendance zones,"[12] to "eliminate
from the public schools all vestiges of state-imposed segregation."[13] It
said that "'[r]acially neutral' [pupil] assignment plans . . . may be inadequate [because they] . . . may fail to counteract the continuing effects of past school segregation resulting from discriminatory location
of school sites or distortion of school size in order to achieve or maintain an artificial racial separation."[14] On the other hand, *Swann* emphasized that "judicial powers may be exercised only on the basis of a
constitutional violation"[15]—that is, "racially separate public schools
established and maintained by state action"[16]—and that "once the
affirmative duty to desegregate has been accomplished and racial discrimination through official action is eliminated from the system,"
neither "school authorities nor district courts are constitutionally required to make year-by-year adjustments of the racial composition of
student bodies."[17] Desegregation does not require "that every school
in every community must always reflect the racial composition of the
school system as a whole."[18] In metropolitan areas where "minority
groups are . . . concentrated [residentially] in one part of the city," the
"existence of some small number of one-race, or virtually one-race,
schools . . . is not in and of itself the mark of a system that still practices segregation by law."[19] But "in a system with a history of segregation," there is a "presumption against schools that are substantially disproportionate in their racial composition," and "[t]he district
judge or school authorities should make every effort to achieve the
greatest possible degree of actual desegregation and will thus necessarily be concerned with the elimination of one-race schools."[20]

In 1974, in *Milliken v. Bradley*[21] (commonly called "*Milliken I*"),
the Supreme Court was confronted with a question of the extent to
which local school district boundaries had to be respected by federal
judges framing desegregation decrees. A federal district judge had
found that Michigan state officials and the Detroit Board of Edu-

cation together contrived to create a system of racially segregated schools within the Detroit school district. The judge first ordered "the state defendants . . . to submit desegregation plans encompassing the three-county metropolitan area despite the fact that the 85 outlying school districts of these three counties were not parties to the action and despite the fact that there had been no claim that these outlying districts had committed constitutional violations";[22] after consideration of the proposed plans, the judge "designated 53 of the 85 suburban school districts plus Detroit as the 'desegregation area' and appointed a panel to prepare and submit 'an effective desegregation plan' for the Detroit schools that would encompass the entire desegregation area."[23] The Supreme Court observed that the district judge's "metropolitan remedy would require, in effect, consolidation of 54 independent school districts historically administered as separate units into a vast new super school district" and "give rise to an array of . . . problems" such as: "Would the children of Detroit be within the jurisdiction and operating control of a school board elected by the parents and residents of other districts? What board or boards would levy taxes for school operations in these 54 districts constituting the consolidated metropolitan area?"[24] It concluded that "a remedy mandating cross-district or interdistrict consolidation [was improper] to remedy a condition of segregation found to exist in only one district."[25] "Before the boundaries of separate and autonomous school districts may be set aside by consolidating the separate units for remedial purposes or by imposing a cross-district remedy, it must first be shown that there has been a constitutional violation within one district that produces a significant segregative effect in another district."[26] "[W]ithout an interdistrict violation and interdistrict effect, there is no constitutional wrong calling for an interdistrict remedy."[27]

In 1976 the Supreme Court identified another instance in which a federal district court had exceeded its discretion in fashioning a desegregation remedy. In *Pasadena City Board of Education v. Spangler*,[28] the district court had found that various school board policies and procedures had segregated Pasadena's city schools, and it included in its desegregation order a requirement that by the following school year no school was to be assigned a majority of nonwhite students. The school board complied with the court's order; there were no majority-nonwhite schools in the Pasadena system the next year; but by the following year "some of the Pasadena schools had 'slipped out of compliance' with the literal terms of the [no majority-nonwhite schools] order";[29] and four years later the school board requested that the court modify this provision of the order. The district judge refused to modify it, saying that his original order had "'meant to me that at least during my lifetime there would be no majority of any minority in any school in Pasadena.'"[30] The Supreme Court held that such a ruling was impermissible insofar as it "appears to contemplate the 'substantive constitutional right [to a] particular degree of racial balance or mixing' which the Court in *Swann* expressly disapproved" and to impose "an 'inflexible requirement,' . . . to be applied anew each year . . . [e]ven though subsequent changes to the racial mix in the Pasadena schools might be caused by factors for which the . . . [school authorities] could not be considered responsible."[31] The Court noted that in fact there was "no showing . . . that those . . . changes in the racial mix of some Pasadena schools . . . were in any manner caused by segregative actions chargeable to" school officials, and that the "District Court rejected . . . [an] assertion that the movement was caused by so-called 'white flight' traceable to the decree itself."[32] Under these circumstances, the Court thought the case was governed by the principle of *Swann* that "'[n]either school authorities nor district courts are constitutionally required to make year-by-year adjustments of the racial composition of student bodies once the affirmative duty to desegregate has been accomplished and racial discrimination through official action is eliminated from the system.'"[33]

As time went on, the Supreme Court's attitude toward school cases shifted. No longer impatient about how long it was taking state authorities to comply with judicial desegregation orders, the Court now began to express impatience with the duration of the desegregation orders themselves.[34] We will see one instance of this in Chapter 5 when we discuss the case of *Freeman v. Pitts*,[35] which holds that federal district courts may relinquish jurisdiction over aspects of a school system (such as pupil assignment) in which the school authorities have achieved compliance with desegregation orders even though in other aspects of the system (such as faculty and administrative assignments) there remain vestiges of segregation. The *Pitts* opinion, written by Justice Kennedy, is notable for introducing the idea that in a school desegregation case, "the court's end purpose must be to remedy the violation and *in addition to restore state and local authorities to the control of a school system that is operating in compliance with the Constitution.*"[36] From *Brown II* on, of course, it had been understood that federal-court supervision of school districts was a temporary measure; but now the termination of such supervision was being called the *purpose* of desegregation litigation. In any event, when the case of *Missouri v. Jenkins* came before the Supreme Court in 1990 for the second time,[37] raising the question whether a federal court has power to order a school district to levy taxes in excess of state statutory limits in order to pay the costs of court-ordered desegregation provisions,[38] Justice Kennedy wrote a lengthy separate opinion (speaking for himself and three other Justices, including Chief Justice Rehnquist) that features a caustic criticism of the extent and costliness of the desegregation plan approved by the lower federal courts for the Kansas City, Missouri, public schools.[39] All of this is prelude to the 1995 phase of the *Jenkins* case, to which we now turn.

II. The Jenkins Decision and Opinion

This phase of *Jenkins* involved orders entered by the federal district court during the seventh and eighth years of its efforts to remedy unconstitutional racial segregation in the public schools of the Kansas City, Missouri, School District (KCMSD). The orders included provisions requiring the State of Missouri to (1) pay for salary increases for the KCMSD staff and (2) continue to fund certain programs previously instituted to improve the quality of education offered to KCMSD students. The Court of Appeals for the Eighth Circuit affirmed the orders, but the Supreme Court reversed the court of appeals in the opinion that is our text for analysis.

Chief Justice Rehnquist begins this opinion by addressing a point of procedure. As a matter of Supreme Court practice, a party who undertakes to bring a case before the Court by a petition for a writ of *certiorari*—the technical name for a request to the Supreme Court of the United States to review the decision of a lower court—is required to specify in the petition the "Questions Presented" for the Supreme Court's review. If *certiorari* is granted—which means that the Supreme Court agrees to review the lower court's decision[40]—the Court hears argument from both sides on the merits. At this stage, the petitioner is not permitted to challenge any ruling of the lower court that is not fairly encompassed within one of the Questions Presented in the *certiorari* petition. In the 1995 phase of *Jenkins*, Missouri's *certiorari* petition had questioned whether the district court's order "granting salary increases to virtually every employee of a school district" violated the principle that "remedial components must directly address and relate to the constitutional violation and be tailored to cure the condition that offends the Constitution." Chief Justice Rehnquist launches the *Jenkins* opinion by holding that this Question Presented allows the State to argue on the merits that the salary-increase order was improper because it was designed to achieve an *objective* that exceeded the district court's remedial authority.

Regarding the objective of the order, Chief Justice Rehnquist finds that it was aimed at "'improving the desegregative attractiveness of the KCMSD'"[41] so that white students would be motivated to attend KCMSD public schools instead of fleeing to suburban or private schools. He declares that an order having such an aim is an *interdistrict* remedy; that an *interdistrict* remedy cannot properly be ordered in the absence of an *interdistrict* violation; that the only constitutional violation established by the segregation of African-American from white children in the KCMSD was an *intradistrict* violation; and therefore that the salary-increase order was impermissible.

He then goes on to disapprove the district court's order requiring continued funding of quality-education programs. He reads this order as responsive to the concern that "student achievement levels were still 'at or below national norms at many grade levels,'"[42] and he holds that the performance of minority students on nationally-normed achievement tests is an inappropriate criterion of desegregation.

In the course of these rulings, the Chief Justice expresses displeasure with protracted federal-court involvement in the affairs of local school districts. He itemizes and returns frequently to the large sums of money that the federal courts have required Missouri to expend on the KCMSD, and he ends by sending the case back to the lower courts with the observation that the district court "should consider that many goals of its quality education plan already have been attained"[43] and that

"its end purpose is not only 'to remedy the violation' to the extent practicable, but also 'to restore state and local authorities to the control of a
school system that is operating in compliance with the Constitution.'"[44]

III. A Tour of the Chief Justice's Categorizing Moves

The preceding synopses, although sparse, should provide enough
background for us to survey the variety of kinds and uses of categorization in Chief Justice Rehnquist's *Jenkins* opinion. We will pause at
each example no longer than is necessary to see *that* a categorizing
move is being made, *how* the move is accomplished, and *what function* it serves in the larger movement of the opinion. Think of these
varied sights, if you will, as scenes encountered on a Cook's Tour.[45]

Scene 1

The opinion's first substantive holding is that the district court erred
in ordering salary increases for KCMSD employees. This holding is
made to appear as if it rested on a commonplace form of category-
placement: deciding whether the facts before the court *fit inside or
outside* the classificatory formula supplied by an applicable general
rule. Straightforward *definition-matching*? It seems so. All that is involved is to specify the circumstances of the case at hand, match them
with the terms set out in a doctrinal rule ordaining the result when
that category of circumstances is found, and give judgment accordingly.

Chief Justice Rehnquist's version of this ordinary-seeming procedure starts with a review of prior Supreme Court decisions (principally *Milliken I*) in pursuit of the doctrinal rule that is to govern his
category placement. He emerges with a doctrinal rule containing two
category labels: Without an *interdistrict violation and interdistrict effect* there can be no *interdistrict remedy*. He categorizes the circumstances of the present case as falling outside the boundaries of the first
label and inside the boundaries of the second: *The courts below found
no interdistrict violation and interdistrict effect; they did order an
interdistrict remedy*. He then announces the syllogistically determined
result: *The courts below erred*.

One of the two noun phrases that constitute the category labels (interdistrict violation and interdistrict effect) is explicitly defined in the *Jenkins* opinion.[46] But this definition is not used to classify the circumstances of the case. The classification is achieved solely by quoting and paraphrasing statements of the lower courts that use the label itself—i.e., by saying that the lower courts *expressly* disavowed finding "'interdistrict effects.'"[47] Thus, while the display of a definition serves to confirm an appearance that definition-matching logic is in use, it does not advance that logic or play any functional part in the reasoning that leads to the Court's decision.

The other doctrinal label (interdistrict remedy) is never defined. It is treated, without explanation, as meaning a remedy having "an interdistrict purpose" (or an "interdistrict goal"); and the latter term is implicitly equated with a *purpose to motivate parents and children to choose one school district over another when they have an option.* Thus elaborated, the label comes to subsume the district court's salary-increase order because the district court itself explained that order as aimed at "'improving the desegregative attractiveness of the KCMSD.'"

Notably, the *second* step in this two-step elaboration of the category label "interdistrict remedy" is wholly covert. It is neither acknowledged nor defended. It represents categorization—and thereby constitutional lawmaking—entirely by *fiat,* pun, or question-begging. There are many meanings of "interdistrict goal"—for example, a purpose to *compel* or *require* children living in one school district to go to school in another—which would not subsume the *Jenkins* district court's purpose to *offer educational incentives* to parents to *choose to reside* in the KCMSD. Chief Justice Rehnquist simply removes these meanings from the realm of possible analysis by declining to notice their existence.

His *first* step in elaborating the "interdistrict remedy" label is, by contrast, overt. It is acknowledged and defended—but not as a legal ruling that the Court is making on its own responsibility in *Jenkins.* It is depicted as a rule laid down by precedent. Toward the beginning of his legal analysis, Chief Justice Rehnquist cites and quotes *Milliken I* as establishing the legal rule that "'[W]ithout an interdistrict violation . . . there [can be no] . . . interdistrict remedy.'"[48] At this point in his opinion, he omits any mention of the nature of the desegregation order which *Milliken I* used the label "interdistrict remedy" to describe: namely, an order *mandating the consolidation of city with suburban school districts* in order to correct unconstitutional racial segregation found only within the city. *That* sort of remedy can obviously be categorized as "interdistrict" without reference to its *goal*. So how does Chief Justice Rehnquist get from *Milliken I* to an equation of "interdistrict remedy" with "interdistrict goal"? Three pages later in *Jenkins* (after he has already made the equation implicitly, simply by using the terms interchangeably),[49] he returns to *Milliken I*, recites that *Milliken I* coined the term *interdistrict remedy* in the course of holding that "a desegregation remedy *that would require mandatory interdistrict reassignment of students* throughout the Detroit metropolitan area was an impermissible interdistrict response to [an] . . . intradistrict violation,"[50] and then goes on to say:

> "Nothing in *Milliken I* suggests that the District Court in that case could have circumvented the limits on its remedial authority by requiring the State of Michigan, a constitutional violator, to implement a magnet program designed to achieve the same interdistrict transfer of students that we held was beyond its remedial authority. Here, the District Court has done just that: created a magnet district of the KCMSD in order to serve the *inter*district goal of attracting nonminority students from the surrounding SSD's and redistributing them within the KCMSD."[51]

This passage cannot be taken at face value. For, plainly, the fact that "[n]othing in *Milliken I*" was said about the propriety of the district court in that case doing something which it didn't do—and which no court or party in *Milliken I* ever remotely contemplated or had any occasion to contemplate—is not a persuasive reason to read *Milliken I* as a precedent for the equation of "interdistrict remedy" with "interdistrict goal." So if the passage has any persuasiveness as an interpretation of *Milliken I*, that persuasiveness derives from some other source than its ostensible logic. It derives, we think, from another kind and function of categorization:

Scene 2

The quoted passage categorizes what the *Milliken I* district court did not do—and thereby what the *Jenkins* district court "has done"—as "circumvent[ing] the limits on its remedial authority." The same categorization appears a page earlier in the *Jenkins* opinion: "In effect, the District Court has devised a remedy to accomplish indirectly what it admittedly lacks the remedial authority to mandate directly: the interdistrict transfer of students."[52] This categorization implicitly triggers a hoary legal maxim: *It is impermissible to do indirectly what you are forbidden to do directly.*

By linking such a maxim to *Milliken I* on the one hand and to the *Jenkins* district court's salary-increase order on the other, the opinion increases the apparent plausibility of its reading of *Milliken I* in two ways: (1) The *Milliken I* opinion might conceivably have discussed a potential *evasion,* as distinguished from an utter irrelevancy. (2) If the district court in *Jenkins* was being *evasive,* there must have been some rule—presumably established by *Milliken I*—for it to seek to evade. And implying that the *Jenkins* district court's behavior falls within the maxim against evasiveness produces two additional rhetorical effects: (3) It casts the district judge as a tricksy villain who should not be permitted to get away with such villainy; and (4) it locates that villainy in the district judge's *intentions,* thereby making the district court's pursuit of an "interdistrict goal" particularly vulnerable to condemnation.

But how is this categorization achieved in the first place? The process is similar to, although a bit more subtle than, the process by which we saw Chief Justice Rehnquist equate the term "interdistrict goal" with a *purpose to motivate parents and children in their choice of school districts.* The process consists of (a) describing what the *Jenkins* district court did (and what the *Milliken I* district court didn't do) in words traditionally associated with the maxim against evasiveness and (b) *not* reasoning expressly from or about the maxim, so as to escape any necessity for analyzing it.

The avoidance of analysis is indispensable to this particular categorizing move. For even the most rudimentary thinking about the maxim "It is impermissible to do indirectly what you are forbidden to do directly" would expose that it is concerned exclusively with cases of illicit ends, and not with cases of illicit means. When an *end* is prohibited, its accomplishment by roundabout means is no more permissible than its accomplishment by straightforward means; and this is what the maxim expresses—together with a characteristic Anglo-American distaste for underhandedness. But when it is only some particular *means* to an end that is prohibited, of course that does not imply the impermissibility of achieving the same end by a different means; quite the contrary. So the applicability of the maxim to the situations of the district courts in *Milliken I* and *Jenkins* turns on whether what was prohibited in *Milliken I* was the end sought by the district court in that case (decreasing the racial isolation of African-American students in the Detroit city schools by drawing white students from the suburbs to attend those schools) or the *means* used by the district court to achieve that end (court-ordered consolidation of city and suburban school districts). But this question of the proper interpretation of *Milliken I*—which needs to be resolved before the maxim can be brought into play at all—is exactly the same question of interpretation of *Milliken I* that Chief Justice Rehnquist is invoking the maxim allusively to address: whether a district court order designed to motivate white students to come in from the suburbs and attend center-city schools *voluntarily* constitutes an "interdistrict remedy" in the same category as *Milliken I*'s order *mandating* the interdistrict reassignment of students. So once again the Chief Justice performs his categorizing by assuming his conclusion and selecting the implicit category definitions necessary to produce it. Here, however, the entire process is more subtle and opaque than in Scene 1. To be aware that any categorization is going on at all, a reader needs to keep in mind the easily forgotten point that even tacit invocation of a maxim or a commonplace supposes that the present subject of discussion comes within the category of situations to which the maxim or the commonplace applies.

The salary-increase order is faulted on two additional grounds that demonstrate two additional kinds and functions of categorization:[53]

Scene 3

The opinion says that "the District Court's reliance upon desegregative attractiveness . . . [cannot be] justified . . . [by] the District Court's statement that segregation has 'led to white flight from the KCMSD to suburban districts'" because "[t]he lower courts' 'findings' as to 'white flight' are both inconsistent internally, and inconsistent with the typical supposition, bolstered here by the record evidence, that 'white flight' may result from desgregation, not *de jure* segregation."[54] Both of the asserted inconsistencies are produced by the opinion's own binary, antipodal categorization of the possible causes of white flight as *either* segregation *or* desegregation. This kind of oppositional pairing of mutually exclusive categories is calculated to trigger a basic rule of Aristotelian logic: *A cannot be not-A*. By this logic, "desegregation" is to "*de jure* segregation" as "cure" is to "disease."

But why select the binary category structure and its logic in the first place? Chief Justice Rehnquist's reference to a "typical supposition" suggests the source from which the structure draws its superficial plausibility. *In relation to each other*, "desegregation" is typically thought of as the *cure* for the *disease* of "segregation": that much is instinct in the talk about "remedies" in *Brown II* and its progeny. *In relation to other consequences*, however, there needs be no such fixed opposition between *cure* and *disease*. (Suppose I break my leg in an accident. I am taken to the emergency room of the nearest hospital for treatment of the broken leg. While in the emergency room, I contract a staph infection. Is my staph infection the result of my broken leg *or* of its cure?)

Analytically, Scene 3 in the *Jenkins* opinion is akin to the logical fallacy of the excluded middle term. For purposes of our tour of categorization techniques, we can classify it as the use of category structure to foreclose potential lines of reasoning (for example, that white flight is the result of *both* segregation and desegregation) as apparent logical impossibilities.

Scene 4

The opinion says that the lower courts "felt that because the KCMSD's enrollment remained 68.3% black, a purely *intra*district remedy would be insufficient."[55] Such a concern is held to be inconsistent with the doctrinal rule established by *Swann* and *Milliken I* and *Spangler* that "'racial imbalance in the schools'" does not violate the Constitution when it merely mirrors "'the racial makeup of the school district's population.'"[56] This inconsistency is produced by categorizing the lower courts' concerns in terms of their *subject* rather than their *reason*. Chief Justice Rehnquist's *Jenkins* opinion meticulously states that the lower courts were concerned about the 68.3% black-student-enrollment figure;[57] it entirely neglects to state that they were concerned about it because they had found that it was a result of state-maintained *de jure* segregation.[58]

Here, as in Scene 1, categorization overtly serves a form of definition-matching logic. It appears to be based upon a rule defining the permissible subjects of judicial concern in resolving a problem, and it appears to determine whether rulings of a lower court are permissible or impermissible simply by categorizing the lower court's articulated concerns as either *inside* or *outside* the defining terms set forth in the rule. But because the rule and its categories are ambiguous about whether they are specifying the proper subjects of judicial attention from the perspective of what may be looked *at* or from the perspective of what may be looked *for,* those defining terms can be covertly manipulated—and a lower court decision can be approved or disapproved—by focusing alternatively on one perspective or the other.

A few further examples of the uses of categorization in definition-matching logics will suggest their variety and frequency. Two are central to the portion of Chief Justice Rehnquist's opinion holding that the merits of the salary-increase order are properly before the Supreme Court for review:[59]

Scene 5

There is one aspect of Supreme Court procedure that intrinsically calls for a definition-matching approach. This is the rule requiring a party who files a petition for *certiorari* to set forth in it "the questions presented for review" and forbidding such a party to contest any ruling by the lower courts that is not "fairly included" within these questions.[60] In deciding whether an argument is out of bounds under this rule, the Supreme Court treats a *certiorari* petitioner's Questions Presented as defining a category of potential contentions and asks whether or not each argument advanced by the petitioner falls within the category.

In *Jenkins,* Chief Justice Rehnquist concludes that Missouri's challenge to the "interdistrict" character of the lower courts' attempted desegregation efforts is included within one of the Questions Presented by the State's petition for *certiorari.* His reasoning is as follows: He first takes Missouri's Question Presented concerning the district court's salary-increase order, namely:

(1) "'Whether a federal court order granting salary increases to virtually every employee of a school district—including non-instructional

personnel—as part of a school desegregation remedy conflicts with applicable decisions of this court which require that remedial components
must directly address and relate to the constitutional violation and be
tailored to cure the condition that offends the Constitution?'"[61]

and characterizes it as a claim that

(2) "the order of salary increases is beyond the District Court's remedial
authority."[62]

He then takes Missouri's argument that

(3) "the order approving salary increases is beyond the District Court's
authority because it was crafted to serve an 'interdistrict goal' [i.e.,
to make KCMSD schools attractive for voluntary enrollment by
whites], in spite of the fact that the constitutional violation in this
case is 'intradistrict' in nature"[63]

and abstracts it as

(4) "the State's challenge to [the salary increase] order,"[64]

which he categorizes in turn as

(5) "a challenge to the scope of the District Court's remedy."[65]

So the rubber issue (in every sense) becomes whether formula (5) fits
inside formula (2); and Chief Justice Rehnquist unsurprisingly finds
that it does: "An analysis of the permissible scope of the District
Court's remedial authority is necessary for a proper determination of
whether the order of salary increases is beyond the District Court's remedial authority."[66] Never mind that item (3), Missouri's actual argument, conspicuously fails to fit inside item (1), Missouri's actual Question Presented.[67]

Scene 6

In a dissenting opinion, Justice Souter contends *(inter alia)* that the
Court should not read Missouri's Question Presented so broadly
because the narrow framing of the question misled the lawyers for
the school-desegregation plaintiffs to argue their case before the Supreme Court without fair warning that the "interdistrict goal" issue would turn out to be crucially important. Chief Justice Rehnquist
responds to this contention by (1) paraphrasing it as a contention

that "factors such as our failure to grant certiorari on the State's challenge to the District Court's remedial authority [when the *Jenkins* case was previously brought before the Court in 1989] . . . 'lulled . . . [the plaintiffs' lawyers] into addressing the [present phase of the] case without sufficient attention to the . . . ["interdistrict goal"] issue,'" and (2) declaring such a contention untenable because it ignores the oft-repeated doctrinal precept that "'[t]he denial of a writ of certiorari imports no expression of opinion upon the merits of the case.'"[68] Here the Chief Justice's category work consists primarily of decontextualizing both the oft-repeated doctrinal precept and Justice Souter's argument so as to produce an apparent conflict between them.

What the oft-repeated precept means is simply this: Because the United States Supreme Court's choice of whether or not to review the decision of a lower court by granting a writ of *certiorari* is wholly discretionary and depends on many factors other than whether the lower court's judgment is right or wrong, the Court's denial of *certiorari* cannot be viewed as a determination that the lower court correctly decided the case or any particular point of law involved in it. Therefore, a denial of *certiorari* cannot be cited as a precedent establishing a rule of law with implications for any other case;[69] nor can it be taken as settling the substantive rules to be applied in subsequent stages of the same case.[70] Justice Souter's argument in *Jenkins* makes no such uses of the Court's 1989 refusal to review the "interdistrict-goal" issue presented by Missouri's earlier petition for *certiorari*. He argues, rather, that in the wake of such a refusal, the plaintiffs' lawyers were entitled to assume that the Court would not (at least without fair notice) turn around and elect to review the selfsame issue that the Court had earlier specifically declined to review.[71] There is no inconsistency between this argument and the doctrinal precept with which Chief Justice Rehnquist purports to confound it—only between the Chief Justice's stripped-down versions of each.

Both of the last two examples involved effects of categorization as *generalization.* By stating propositions at higher levels of abstraction, Chief Justice Rehnquist pruned them of elements that would have brought them into conflict (in Scene 5) or kept them out of conflict (in Scene 6). A similar effect can be produced by stating a case that is cited as a precedent more or less abstractly:

Scene 7

Consider, for example, Chief Justice Rehnquist's treatment of the landmark precedent of *Swann*. He begins his substantive analysis in Jenkins by emphasizing *Swann*'s authoritative status, giving *Swann* the pride of place that earlier desegregation opinions tended to give *Brown* itself: "Almost 25 years ago, in *Swann v. Charlotte-Mecklenburg Bd. of Ed. . . .*, we dealt with the authority of a district court to fashion remedies for a school district that had been segregated in law in violation of the Equal Protection Clause . . ."[72] Chief Justice Rehnquist does not describe the issues or the arguments in *Swann*;[73] he simply says that *Swann* "recognized the limits on . . . [the discretionary] power" of a federal district court to fashion desegregation remedies and then quotes *Swann* as follows:

> "'[E]limination of racial discrimination in public schools is a large task and one that should not be retarded by efforts to achieve broader purposes lying beyond the jurisdiction of the school authorities. One vehicle can carry only a limited amount of baggage. It would not serve the important objective of *Brown I* to seek to use school desegregation cases for purposes beyond their scope, although desegregation of schools will ultimately have impact on other forms of discrimination.'"[74]

Thus, the admonition of *Swann* not to load too much "baggage" into a school-desegregation order is presented as a precept addressed to school-desegregation issues generally, without distinction or particularization.

That was not, however, the tenor of the admonition in *Swann*. The *Swann* opinion noted that "the cases before us are primarily concerned with problems of student assignment" and that it would address those problems after "a brief discussion of other aspects of the [desegregation] process."[75] One of the prefatory aspects was the construction of new schools and the closing of old ones, a matter that the Court described as important and complex because school location can affect patterns of residential development.[76] School-location decisions aimed at furthering segregation would do "more than simply influence the short-run composition of the student body of a new school"; they might also "promote segregated residential patterns which, when combined with 'neighborhood zoning,' further lock the school system into the mold of separation of the races."[77] The *Swann* opinion concluded that federal courts "may consider this [phenomenon] in fashioning a remedy."[78] It then turned to the issue of student assignment[79] and, at the outset, put aside consideration of *racially discriminatory decisions made by public agencies other than school authorities*—public-housing location decisions, zoning decisions, and so forth. The passage quoted by Chief Justice Rehnquist in *Jenkins* was preceded and followed by sentences making clear that its point was that *school desegregation orders should not undertake to remedy racial discrimination in sectors other than public education.*[80] It is only by treating the quotation as addressed to the whole category of school-desegregation issues that Chief Justice Rehnquist has gotten *Swann* to sing in a different and distinctly funerary key.

Scene 8

Another kind of category work serves to put a new emphasis on the precedential teaching of *Freeman v. Pitts*. As we have seen, *Freeman* inaugurated the notion that a court in a school-desegregation lawsuit has *two* objectives: to terminate segregation and to terminate the lawsuit.[81] *Freeman* did this by aggregating the two objectives into a single category: "*the* end purpose" of a school-desegregation case—an aggregation necessary to avoid attributing to *Brown* the absurdity of having put the federal courts *in* the school-desegregation business for the distinct "end purpose" of getting them *out*. But now in *Jenkins*, Chief Justice Rehnquist *dis*aggregates the category, restating *Freeman*'s pronouncement that

> "the court's end purpose must be to remedy the violation and in addition to restore state and local authorities to the control of a school system that is operating in compliance with the Constitution"

in the form:

> "On remand, the District Court must bear in mind that its end purpose is not only 'to remedy the violation' to the extent practicable, but also 'to restore state and local authorities to the control of a school system that is operating in compliance with the Constitution.'"[82]

This disaggregation permits the two purposes to be represented as in tension, with *Brown*'s goal of terminating segregation subordinated—both grammatically, in a "not only" phrase, and by the casual insertion of the seemingly innocuous qualifier "to the extent practicable"—to the now-competing goal of getting the court out of the school-desegregation business as fast as possible.

So far we have seen categorization at work primarily as an adjunct to the legal or logical reasoning in the Chief Justice's *Jenkins* opinion. But categorization also serves to construct or deconstruct what counts as the "facts" of the *Jenkins* case:

Scene 9

From its first sentence to its last, Chief Justice Rehnquist's opinion breathes an unmistakable impatience with the sheer duration of federal-court involvement in the Kansas City schools. This impatience animates the Court's resolution of the two issues before it[83] and leads it to go beyond those issues in closing its opinion with the pointed instructions that "[t]he District Court also should consider that many goals of its quality education plan already have been attained" and "must bear in mind" that returning school systems to local control is a matter of the highest priority.[84]

But how long *have* the federal courts been involved in desegregating the KCMSD? Chief Justice Rehnquist answers that question by locutions like these:

"*As this school desegregation litigation enters its 18th year,* we are called upon again to review the decisions of the lower courts."[85]

"*Sixteen years after this litigation began,* the District Court recognized that the KCMSD has yet to offer a viable method of financing the 'wonderful school system being built. . . .'"[86]

So the category of relevant doings apparently begins with the filing of the *Jenkins* litigation in 1977 rather than with the entry of the district court's first remedial order in 1984. That is a particularly interesting choice of category boundary inasmuch as the sole subject of the case before the Court and of Chief Justice Rehnquist's substantive analysis is the propriety of two specific orders of the district court implementing and extending its first remedial order. Chief Justice Rehnquist says nothing at all about the existence, nature, or extent of the constitutional violation found by the district court as the basis for its first remedial order—except that this was "an intradistrict violation"—and he says nothing above the footnote line about events or conditions in Kansas City, in Missouri, or anywhere before 1971 (when *Swann,* a case about *desegregation remedies,* was decided).[87] Segregation and *Brown v. Board of Education* appear in the Chief Justice's opinion only in a footnote[88] setting out the percentages of African-American students in the KCMSD's student population in various eras. Thus, this is a case entering its eighteenth year for purposes of impatience but not for purposes of identifying the issues or the scope of relevant facts and concerns. What the relevant facts and concerns should be, and how impatient one should be with whom, might look very different if the *Jenkins* opinion had catalogued events as follows:

1954:   *Brown v. Board* was decided.

1977:   The *Jenkins* suit was filed.

1984:   The district court held that the KCMSD and the State of Missouri had done nothing to correct the concentration of African-American students in the separate and unequal racially identifiable schools established pursuant to state law before *Brown.*

1985:   The district court entered its first remedial order.

1992–1993:   The district court entered the orders presently before the Supreme Court for review.

Scene 10

In addition to reversing the district court's salary-increase order, the *Jenkins* majority reverses the district court's order "requiring the State to continue to fund the quality education programs because student achievement levels were still 'at or below national norms at many grade levels' . . ."[89] Central to this holding is the factual assumption that the district court failed to distinguish between two categories of shortfall in KCMSD student achievement: a *portion* of the shortfall that was "attributable to segregation" (hence, properly remediable) and a *portion* that was attributable to "numerous external factors beyond the control of the KCMSD and the State" (hence, not properly remediable):[90]

"The District Court determined that '[s]egregation ha[d] caused a system wide *reduction* in student achievement in the schools of the

KCMSD.' . . . The District Court made no particularized findings regarding the extent that student achievement had been reduced or *what portion of that reduction was attributable to segregation.*"[91]

"Although the District Court has determined that '[s]egregation has caused a system wide *reduction* in achievement [*sic*] in the schools of the KCMSD' . . ., it never has identified *the incremental effect that segregation has had* on minority student achievement. . . ."[92]

In these passages, the division of a category structure employed by the district court in its findings ("reduction in student achievement") into subcategories (some **"portion of that reduction . . . attributable to segregation"** and some *other* portion; the **"incremental effect"** and some *non-incremental* effect) implies the existence of contents in the italicized subcategories which must be excluded from the contents of the boldface subcategories before the latter can count for anything. But the majority opinion points to no evidence—and the record contains no evidence—that there are any contents in the italicized subcategories. In fact, they are evidentially empty categories, created by the *Jenkins* majority opinion itself solely by the verbal act of categorizing.[93]

Scene 11

Although the majority opinion disparages the district court's consideration of nationally-normed achievement-test scores as a measure of the need for State-funded quality education programs in the KCMSD,[94] the opinion devotes considerable attention to *comparing* the KCMSD with other school districts in the dimensions of *cost* and what might be called *ambitiousness* of programs. The comparisons are made both explicitly and implicitly. For example:

Explicit cost comparisons: "The expenditures per pupil in the KCMSD currently far exceed those in the neighboring SSD's."[95] "The annual cost per pupil at the KCMSD far exceeds that of the neighboring SSD's or of any school district in Missouri."[96]

Implicit cost comparisons: "Since . . . [1990], the total cost of capital improvements ordered has *soared* to over $540 million."[97] KCMSD "has continued to propose *ever more expensive programs* . . . [and a]s a result, the desegregation costs have *escalated* and now are approaching an annual cost of $200 million. These *massive expenditures* have financed [a list of amenities including air-conditioned classrooms, a 25-acre farm with an air-conditioned meeting room for 104 people, broadcast-capable radio and TV studios, swimming pools, etc.]."[98]

Explicit "ambitiousness" comparisons: "[T]he KCMSD now is equipped with 'facilities and opportunities not available anywhere else in the country.'"[99] "The District Court's desegregation plan has been described as the most ambitious and expensive remedial program in the history of school desegregation."[100] "'KCMSD students have in place a system that offers more educational opportunity than anywhere in America.'"[101]

Implicit "ambitiousness" comparisons: "The District Court candidly has acknowledged that it has 'allowed the District planners to dream' and 'provided the mechanism for th[ose] dreams to be realized.'"[102]

The opinion nowhere explains why these comparisons are relevant—let alone why, if they are relevant, the comparative position of KCMSD children on nationwide achievement tests is not. As the opinion is structured, there appears to be no place or need for such explanations, because the quoted passages purport to be simply descriptive, not analytic. The technique here is to describe the "facts" of the case through a category structure that makes selective, rhetorically cogent comparisons with no need to justify them.[103]

Scene 12

The *Jenkins* opinion also engages in a more pervasive categorization of the data that it describes as constituting the relevant facts: a categorization of information according to its epistemological status as *known* or *unknown, sure* or *unsure.* For example:

"The District Court *made no particularized findings regarding the extent* that student achievement had been reduced" as a result of segregation.[104]

"[W]e granted certiorari to consider . . . whether the District Court properly relied upon the fact that student achievement test scores had failed to rise *to some unspecified level* when it declined to find that the State had achieved partial unitary status as to the quality education programs."[105]

"It is certainly *theoretically possible* that the greater the expenditure per pupil within the KCMSD, the more likely it is that *some unknowable*

number of nonminority students not presently attending schools in the
KCSMD will choose to enroll. . . . Under this reasoning, however, every
increased expenditure . . . will make the KCMSD *in some way* more attractive, and thereby *perhaps* induce nonminority students to enroll. . . .
But this rationale is not susceptible to any objective limitation."[106]

"The District Court's pursuit of the goal of 'desegregative attractiveness'
results in *so many imponderables. . . .*"[107]

The State "challenges the requirement of *indefinite funding* of a quality
education program" and its "*indefinite extension.*"[108]

"*Apparently,* the Court of Appeals *extrapolated from the findings* regarding the magnet school program and later orders and *imported those
findings wholesale* to reject the State's request for a determination of
partial unitary status" under *Freeman v. Pitts.*[109]

Again the categorization is performed in such a way as to produce its
rhetorical effects without explaining or justifying the categories involved or the criteria for placing items in them. This avoids the need
for facing up to issues that would have to be addressed if the category
work were more explicit—such as what level of confidence is necessary in making the predictive judgments that underlie the formulation
of a school desegregation order (or any other form of injunctive relief,
for that matter); which party bears the burden of producing evidence
to inform those judgments; and what standard of review should govern the Supreme Court's reexamination of the evidentiary basis for
such judgments by the lower courts.

Scene 13

Scene 13 is a non-scene, an example of a noteworthy non-happen-
ing:[110] The *Jenkins* majority opinion quotes *Milliken I* to the effect
that "a desegregation remedy 'is necessarily designed, as all remedies
are, to restore the victims of discriminatory conduct to the position
they would have occupied in the absence of such conduct.'"[111] This
pronouncement is thrice repeated in terms that make it mean that the
lower courts are not permitted to *go beyond* restoring the victims of
discriminatory conduct to "the position they would have occupied in
the absence of such conduct."[112] And nothing more is said about the
subject.

Ah, but what possible categories might be designated by the phrase "position they would have occupied" if that phrase were taken to be a command as well as a limitation and examined as well as reiterated? Position in regard to *what?* In regard to the distribution of African-American students among the various schools in the KCMSD that would exist today if Missouri had not forbidden African-Americans to be educated with whites for more than 100 years before *Brown v. Board of Education* and then disregarded *Brown* for 30 years more? In regard to equal educational opportunities?[113] In regard to freedom from "a feeling of inferiority as to their status in the community that may affect their hearts and minds in a way unlikely ever to be undone"?[114] Questions unasked are categories uncreated; and categories uncreated are universes of possibility left unexplored.

We have toured Chief Justice Rehnquist's *Jenkins* opinion only to observe its performances of categorization, not to excavate its ideological agenda or even its jurisprudential basis. A fuller examination of *Jenkins* had best be postponed until almost the end of this volume, after we discuss how narrative and rhetorics interact with categorization in judicial opinions, and also how cultural predilections find their way into the adjudicative process. We shall not even pause for summary here. Rather, we want to turn immediately to our second case study, which will explore a single categorizing move in detail. In particular, it will enable us to see how the system of categories applied in making one such move is rooted in a complex mythic, folk-psychological matrix, and how that matrix affects the process of categorizing under its influence.

THE CASE OF *MICHAEL H.*

The focus of this study is Justice Scalia's 1989 opinion in *Michael H. v. Gerald D.*[1] The case involved four parties: a child named Victoria; Victoria's mother, Carole; Carole's husband, Gerald; and Carole's lover, Michael, who offered to prove he was Victoria's biological father so that he could get a court's permission to visit with Victoria from time to time.

Victoria wanted to maintain her bonds with both Michael and Gerald, but Gerald (subsequently joined by Carole) opposed the judicial recognition of a paternal relationship or any visitation between Michael and Victoria. Gerald and Carole invoked a California statute providing essentially that every child born to a married woman living with her husband is conclusively presumed to be the husband's child, and that no court is permitted to receive any factual evidence to the contrary. Michael and Victoria responded that this statute was unconstitutional insofar as it purported to deny them the opportunity to prove their actual blood relationship as the basis for visitation rights. They relied primarily on the Due Process Clause of the Fourteenth Amendment to the Constitution of the United States, which forbids any State to "deprive any person of life, liberty, or property, without due process of law."

Under the United States Supreme Court's standard methodology for analyzing controversies of this sort, a crucial threshold question was whether the relationship for which Michael and Victoria claimed constitutional protection—the tie between a natural father and his child born to another man's wedded wife—was within the category of interests defined by the term "liberty" in the Due Process Clause. If it was not, their case was lost from the start, because a State is only required to comply with the commands of "due process" (whatever those commands may be) when it acts to "deprive any person of . . . *liberty*" (or of "life" or "property," neither of which was in issue in *Michael H.*). This definitional question is the entire subject of Justice Scalia's *Michael H.* opinion as a technical matter; and we have chosen the opinion for examination here because it centers on the kind of categorizing process most familiar in judicial decisionmaking: *deciding that the facts before the court do or do not come within a defining term in some doctrinal rule.*

By examining an instance of that familiar process, we hope to expose some of the complications that its familiarity conceals. But to do this we will need to navigate back and forth between the opinion and several strata of ideas, images, and stories in which the opinion is grounded. For, as we said in the preceding chapter, categories are formed and categorization is performed against a ground of notions and narratives about the nature of the world; and often these are less discernible the more elemental they are. In Justice Scalia's *Michael H.* opinion, they turn out to be among Western culture's most elemental and enduring myths.

So we ask the reader's indulgence for a style of exposition that will sometimes deviate from the ordinary figure/ground balance. We will begin with the facts of the *Michael H.* case (in Part I) and with the text of Justice Scalia's opinion (in Part II), but we will almost immediately jump off from that text (in Part III) to explore the basic scripts for literary stories of adultery. The exploration will lead us to a parallel set of scripts for apocalyptic tales, thence to *Star Wars*, the rhetoric of Ronald Reagan and other combat myths of the 1980s, a structural comparison of combat myths and a subspecies of adultery story, and then back to Justice Scalia's text for a look at its structural properties anatomized in the manner of Vladimir Propp.[2] That excursus will equip us to refine our analysis of both the story that Justice Scalia chooses to tell (in Part IV) and his methods of telling it (in Parts V and VI). The analysis concludes (in Part VII) with preliminary reflections on Justice Scalia's categorizing procedure in *Michael H.* that relate it to the subjects of the following chapters: narrative, rhetorics, and culture.

I. The Facts and Proceedings in the Case

Carole and Gerald were ceremonially married in 1976 and lived together in California when neither was away on business. In 1978 Carole and Michael entered into a romantic relationship that lasted, on and off, until 1984. Victoria was born to Carole in 1981. Five months after Victoria's birth, Gerald moved to New York. During the next three and a half years, Carole and Victoria lived briefly in St. Thomas (in the Virgin Islands) with Michael, briefly in New York with Gerald, but most often in California by themselves or with Michael or with a man named Scott.

Shortly after Victoria's birth, Carole told Michael that she believed he was Victoria's father. They underwent blood testing which showed a 98.07% probability of Michael's paternity. Thereafter, during the periods when Carole and Michael were living together—a total of seven or eight months over three and a half years—Michael publicly treated Victoria as his daughter. Gerald also publicly treated Victoria as his daughter, and Gerald was listed as the father on Victoria's birth certificate.

For a time in 1982, Carole refused to let Michael see Victoria. This led Michael to file a legal action for a declaration of paternity and visitation rights. Through a court-appointed guardian *ad litem*,[3] Victoria asked the court to permit her to maintain a filial relationship with both Michael and Gerald. At the recommendation of a psychologist who had evaluated all the parties, the court gave Michael restricted visitation rights while leaving Victoria in Carole's sole custody during the pendency of the litigation.

In the summer of 1984, Carole and Victoria moved to New York and resumed living with Gerald. Gerald intervened in Michael's paternity action and moved for summary judgment on the ground that there were no triable issues of fact[4] regarding Victoria's paternity because the applicable California statute provided that "the issue of a wife cohabiting with her husband, who is not impotent or sterile, is conclusively presumed to be a child of the marriage."[5] Michael and Victoria responded by asserting (among other arguments) that the statute would violate their rights to due process of law if it were applied to forbid them to prove factually that Michael was Victoria's father.

The California trial court rejected their constitutional arguments, refused to receive any evidence of Michael's paternity, and granted Gerald's motion for summary judgment. It also denied Michael's and Victoria's motions for continued visitation pending appeal because it found that any further recognition of a relationship between them would be inconsistent with the statutory presumption of Gerald's exclusive parentage. The California Court of Appeal affirmed each of these rulings, and the California Supreme Court declined discretionary review.

Michael and Victoria then appealed to the Supreme Court of the United States. That Court rejected their constitutional claims by a vote of five to four. In the opinion we shall examine, Justice Scalia—joined by Chief Justice Rehnquist and, except for one footnote, by Justices O'Connor and Kennedy—rendered judgment against Michael and Victoria on the ground that the relationship between them did not qualify as the sort of "liberty" protected by the Due Process Clause of the Fourteenth Amendment and could therefore be extinguished through whatever process California law decreed, without federal constitutional limitation. Justice Stevens disagreed with this conclusion but concurred in rejecting Michael's and Victoria's constitutional arguments on a narrow, fact-specific ground.[6] Two dissenting opinions—one by Justice Brennan (joined by Justices Marshall and Blackmun) and one by Justice White (joined by Justice Brennan)—argued that the relationship claimed by Michael and Victoria deserved constitutional recognition as a form of Fourteenth Amendment "liberty" and could not be terminated consistently with the Due Process Clause on the sole ground that a statutory presumption deemed Gerald's paternity conclusive and exclusive.

II. Starting to Read Justice Scalia's Opinion

Justice Scalia's opinion opens by saying that "[u]nder California law, a child born to a married woman living with her husband is presumed to be a child of the marriage" and that the case before the Court "presents the claim that this presumption infringes upon the due process rights" of Michael and Victoria.[7] It then proceeds to set out "[t]he facts of this case"[8] (in a rather special way, as we shall soon see), and (after reciting that "[t]he California statute that is the subject of this litigation is . . . more than a century old")[9] it quotes the statutory text *verbatim* for more than a page. Next comes Justice Scalia's analysis of the issues, which begins as follows:

> "We address first the claims of Michael. At the outset, it is necessary to clarify what he sought and what he was denied. California law, like nature itself, makes no provision for dual fatherhood. Michael was seeking to be declared *the* father of Victoria."[10]

"Like nature itself"? And there, in three words, within three lines of the ostensible beginning of his legal analysis, Justice Scalia has installed the conceptual and narrative engine that will power everything to come—the necessary and sufficient machinery to demolish all of Michael's and Victoria's constitutional claims. We pause to see why this is so.

III. The Opinion's Core Construct: Adultery as Combat Myth

Not only does Justice Scalia's definition of the issues to be decided in the case depend explicitly upon the declaration that "California law, like nature itself, makes no provision for dual fatherhood," but this axiomatic pronouncement is central to his opinion in several ways.

First, the "natural" impossibility of dual fatherhood is ultimately what renders inconceivable the federal constitutional protection of an interest in that sort of fatherhood. The circumstance (recounted in the same sentence) that California law "makes no provision" for such an interest is not dispositive of the question whether the interest should be recognized as encompassed in the "liberty" protected by the Fourteenth Amendment. The Amendment protects many "liberty" interests that are not acknowledged by state law,[11] including a number of interests associated with family life.[12] But an interest that is unnatural is quite simply unimaginable.

Second, the rule against dual fatherhood allows Justice Scalia to cast Gerald and Michael as *rivals* for Victoria: "Here, to *provide* protection to an adulterous natural father is to *deny* protection to a marital father, and vice versa."[13] Thus Michael's claim is freighted from the outset with the burden of justifying a despoiler.

Third, the rule against dual fatherhood leads Justice Scalia to conclude that the only constitutionally protected family relationships are those that arise within what he calls "the unitary family."[14] His unstated but uncompromising definition of the unitary family is a family in which there is no more than one "father" because there is no more than one mating pair.

This last point provides a clue to the real source of Justice Scalia's one-father axiom. There is in fact no natural rule—or even any Anglo-American cultural rule—against dual fatherhood. Many good little girls and boys in impeccably traditional mainline families have two fathers, although one of them is called "dad" and one is called teacher, scout leader, counselor, mentor, or Uncle Joe. Indeed, without dual fatherhood, Western culture would lose rather more than its scout leaders. For, as students of its central myths have long pointed out, having two fathers is a quintessential hallmark of the Hero Figure from Heracles, Perseus, Theseus, and Oedipus to Moses and Jesus Christ:[15] "[T]he hero almost always has a double parentage."[16] So what is "unnatural" and inconceivable about the relationships that Justice Scalia cannot countenance in *Michael H.*[17] is *not* that Victoria should have two acknowledged fathers, but rather that Victoria's mother should have two acknowledged lovers. It is this licentious model which cannot be squared with Justice Scalia's cuckold-phobic vision of the "unitary family."

A lot is invested in that vision. There are strong reasons for Justice Scalia to extol "the family" (in the manner of the Contract with America)[18] while keeping *family* narrowly defined.[19] This approach perpetuates a basic symbol of established hegemonies—political and religious, as well as social and sexual—by consecrating a patriarchal notion of the family that simultaneously excludes outsiders and rank-orders insiders in proper top-down fashion.[20]

Punishing the adulterous lover serves the same ends[21] and more. It binds *domus* to *Dominus* by reenacting one of Christian culture's most dramatic plots, the apocalyptic story of Satan who, through sin, seduces humankind to disobey its rightful God, and then must be cast out in order to restore divine dominion. The mirroring of this plot in narratives of adultery is no accident, historically[22] or structurally.

Consider that there are two traditional ways to tell a tragic or a moralistic story about a human situation in which a wife has an adulterous lover—one centering on "lack," the other on "villainy." These precipitating incidents match Vladimir Propp's classic definitions of the alternative ways in which "the actual movement of . . . [any] tale is created."[23] "Lack" can be a physical or moral incapacity of the husband—as in the cases of D. H. Lawrence's Lady Chatterley or Tennyson's (and Malory's) Isolt, "misyoked with such a want of man [as Mark],"[24]—or it can be something more basic or more subtle that is missing in the marriage or the world.[25] If the tale is told as a case of "lack," we get a Tristan and Iseult story, a Little-Musgrave/Matty-Grove story,[26] or some other story that, while ending badly, treats the lover-wife relationship with a degree of understanding and compassion ("as knowing that some deep life-matter—which, if full of sin, was full of anguish and repentance likewise—[is] . . . laid open").[27] If the tale is told as a case of "villainy," we get an Aegisthus story[28] or some other form of Demon Lover story[29] and a simpler ending: the lover is condemned and cut down, with or without his sexual partner.

These two forms of adultery stories parallel the two principal renditions of the Christian eschatological account of Universal History:[30] one, a combat myth in which Satan or Evil is an Invading Principle, a living presence assaulting God's Creation, and one in which Evil is nothing but a deficiency of goodness, to be understood as a kind of degenerative disease[31] or falling away[32] from the Light.[33] Elaine Pagels has pointed out the connection between a preference for the first rendition—the dualistic, invasive, combat mythology culminating in a shootout Apocalypse—and the findings of "[m]any anthropologists . . . that the worldview of most peoples consists essentially of two pairs of binary oppositions: human/not human and we/they."[34] The combat mythology is particularly useful, Pagels suggests, when a subgroup within a fractious culture feels the need to draw a hard and hostile line between its adherents and people who interpret their common cultural legacy differently. By posing the question "'which of us . . . really are on God's side'" and by projecting a cosmic combat myth that features "God's antagonist, his enemy, even his rival"[35] as the Seducer of the Faithful and Source of All Apostasy, such a subgroup can simultaneously explain and cast out their "intimate enemies"[36]—can turn them into "former insiders [who] have now become outsiders"[37]— through any culturally available narrative (demonic possession, the Communist conspiracy, the perverting influence of rock music, and so on) that "draws the battle lines between the 'sons of light' and the 'sons of darkness.'"[38]

The cosmic combat myth was a major feature of American culture and iconography from the late 1970s through the 1990s.[39] In particular, the *Star Wars* movies, released between 1977 and 1983, dominated public consciousness and provided metaphors for every aspect of the contemporary human condition. President Reagan tapped this source when he described the Soviet leadership as the declared enemies of religion and called upon the American people to side with God against "the aggressive impulses of an evil empire" in the latest chapter of "the struggle between right and wrong and good and evil."[40]

The political rhetoric of the Reagan presidency was designed to encode this struggle in a set of slogans stretching from the hearth to the heavens. "For us, faith, work, family, neighborhood, freedom, and peace are not just words: they're expressions of what America means, definitions of what makes us a good and loving people."[41] The slogans idolized "those vital communities like the family, [and] the neighborhood . . . which are found at the center of our society between government and the individual."[42] In this rhetoric, "family" emerged as a bastion to be shored up against the assaults of dissipation and disorder on the one hand and the risks of overdependence upon soulless, godless Government on the other.[43] Defending the traditional family was portrayed as a vital theater of the cosmic war.

Now let us look at the narrative *structures* of the apocalyptic combat myth, on the one hand, and the villainous form of the adultery story, on the other. Neil Forsyth has done half of this work for us,[44] applying Propp's "morphological" approach to a wide range of Near Eastern and Western stories of battles between the High Hero and the Abysmal Adversary. Forsyth finds that all of these tales—everything from the Sumerian Gilgamesh/Huwawa struggle to the Christian battle between Christ and Satan—exhibit the same basic sequence. They proceed in twelve movements (or "functions," to use the usual Proppian term):[45] LACK/VILLAINY; HERO EMERGES/PREPARES TO ACT; DONOR/CONSULTATION; JOURNEY; BATTLE; DEFEAT; ENEMY ASCENDANT; HERO RECOVERS/NEW HERO; BATTLE REJOINED; VICTORY; ENEMY PUNISHED; TRIUMPH.[46]

It is instructive to compare Forsyth's sequence with that found in tales of cuckoldry precipitated by "villainy." A few Arthurian exemplars will serve this purpose well, because of the central preoccupation of much Arthurian material with the problem of King Arthur and Queen Guinevere. The Arthur-Guinevere-Lancelot legend—like the Mark-Iseult-Tristan legend with which it was frequently conjoined—is most often told as a "lack" story, with some understanding of the plight of the adulterous lovers, however harshly their sins may be arraigned.[47] But the earliest tales of Arthur and Guinevere were "villainy" stories and drew other "villainy" stories into orbit around them.

The early stories apparently grew out of a traditional form of Celtic abduction or elopement narrative in which a married woman was carried off by a ravisher from Otherworld; her husband pursued and rescued her.[48] Guinevere's first adulterous lovers were of this Otherworld-Ravisher type, less sympathetic than the later peerless-Lancelot-torn-by-love-of-Queen-and-loyalty-to-King.[49] Even after peerless Lancelot was brought into the story, vestiges of the ravisher often remained, sublimated in subplots. For example, in Chrétien de Troyes's late twelfth century *Knight of the Cart*, Guenever is abducted by Meleagant and is rescued by Lancelot himself, whereas in earlier incarnations the figure cast by Chrétien as "Meleagant" was Melwas, Lord of the Summer Country (or of the Isle of Glass), who abducted and ravished Guenever and was pursued and forced to yield the queen by her husband, Arthur.[50] In Malory's *Le Morte D'Arthur* (circa 1470), a more craven variant of Chrétien's Meleagant figure ("Meliagaunt") kidnaps Guenever and is pursued and punished by Launcelot as one episode in the larger story dominated by the classic triangle of Arthur/Husband/King—Guenever/Wife/Queen—Launcelot/Lover/Knight.[51]

Three Arthurian examplars are charted below: (1) Malory's Meliagaunt episode; (2) another subplot in Malory—the story of a giant ogre who lairs on Mont St. Michel and is slain by Arthur during Arthur's continental campaigns;[52] and (3) the climax of *Morte Arthure,* a poem predating Malory by three-quarters of a century, in which Lancelot and Guinevere are not linked but Guinevere is carried off and wedded by Arthur's recusant regent, Mordred.[53] As you'll see, the Forsyth sequence maps each of these stories quite well, although the stories otherwise differ considerably from one another.

LACK/VILLAINY

Giant Ogre of Mont St. Michel: The ogre abducts the Duchess of Brittany, Lady Howell, and takes her to his mountain lair to ravish her and lie with her until her life's end.

Meliagaunt: Meliagaunt abducts Queen Guenever.

Mordred: Mordred, whom Arthur has appointed regent while Arthur is campaigning abroad, oppresses the people, takes Guinevere for his own wife, and gets her with child.

HERO EMERGES/PREPARES TO ACT

Giant Ogre of Mont St. Michel: King Arthur declares the abduction a great mischief and orders Sir Kay and Sir Bedivere to ready horse and harness.

Meliagaunt: Launcelot vows to rescue the Queen from dishonor. Launcelot arms and takes to horse.

Mordred: Arthur, told of Mordred's doings, vows revenge and musters his troops.

DONOR/CONSULTATION

[In all three narratives, this function and the following one are transposed. See the item after next.]

JOURNEY

Giant Ogre of Mont St. Michel: Arthur, Kay, and Bedivere ride to the ogre's mountain and Arthur climbs the mountain. He finds a dolorous widow, who tells him that the ogre has murdered Lady Howell.

Meliagaunt: Launcelot rides out in pursuit of Meliagaunt and Guenever. He is ambushed by Meliagaunt's archers and his horse is killed.

Mordred: Arthur returns by forced marches and fast ships to Britain.

DONOR/CONSULTATION

Giant Ogre of Mont St. Michel: Arthur tells the widow that he has come to treat with the ogre. The widow warns Arthur that the ogre will not treat with anyone, cautions him not to approach the ogre too closely, and directs him to where the ogre is.

Meliagaunt: Launcelot encounters a cart and compels the carter to carry him to Meliagaunt's castle. The carter does.

Mordred: [The essence of this function—the confirmation that the hero is fitted for the hero's task—is supplied by a description of Arthur's banners and shield.]

BATTLE

Giant Ogre of Mont St. Michel: Arthur accosts, accuses, and challenges the ogre, who smites Arthur and knocks his coronal to earth. Arthur disembowels and castrates the ogre.

Meliagaunt: Launcelot calls out, accuses, and challenges Meliagaunt.

Mordred: Arthur's and Mordred's ships clash in battle.

DEFEAT

Giant Ogre of Mont St. Michel: The ogre catches Arthur in his arms and crushes Arthur's ribs.

Meliagaunt: Meliagaunt at first refuses to fight. Launcelot and Guenever make love in her chamber. Meliagaunt finds Guenever's bed stained with blood from Launcelot's cut hand and accuses her of taking a lover. Meliagaunt and Launcelot set a date to try the accusation by battle, but Meliagaunt decoys Launcelot into a drop-trap and imprisons him.

Mordred: Mordred overwhelms and kills Arthur's advance troops and their leader, Sir Gawain. Arthur swoons with grief for Gawain, his chief warrior and counselor.

ENEMY ASCENDANT

Giant Ogre of Mont St. Michel: Three maidens who are witnessing the battle call upon Christ to help Arthur.

Meliagaunt: With Launcelot detained in a cell, Meliagaunt goes to the appointed place of battle and demands that Guenever be brought to the fire to be burned. The hour for battle arrives, but there is no sign of Launcelot.

Mordred: Arthur's heart near bursts in woe. He is chastised by Sir Ewain and his other high lords for excessive and unseemly weeping and hand-wringing.

HERO RECOVERS/NEW HERO

Giant Ogre of Mont St. Michel: Arthur welters and wrings so that he is sometimes beneath and sometimes above the ogre.

Meliagaunt: Launcelot, who has escaped, rides up just in time and tells of Meliagaunt's trick.

Mordred: Arthur swears vengeance for Gawain's death.

BATTLE REJOINED

Giant Ogre of Mont St. Michel: Weltering and wallowing, Arthur and the ogre roll down the mountain with Arthur locked in the ogre's arms.

Meliagaunt: Launcelot and Meliagaunt do battle.

Mordred: Arthur pursues Mordred into Cornwall. Arthur's and Mordred's armies meet in battle. Mordred attempts to evade Arthur by changing his colors, but Arthur recognizes him and engages him in personal combat.

VICTORY

Giant Ogre of Mont St. Michel: Arthur smites the ogre with his dagger and kills him. Kay and Bedivere release Arthur from the ogre's grip.

Meliagaunt: Launcelot beats Meliagaunt to the ground. Meliagaunt yields and begs for his life.

Mordred: Arthur and Mordred give each other death blows. Mordred, his sword hand cut off, squirms on Arthur's sword point and expires. Arthur only laments that so false a felon should die in so fair a fashion. Mordred's troops are killed to the last soldier.

ENEMY PUNISHED

Giant Ogre of Mont St. Michel: Arthur orders Kay to cut off the ogre's head, set it on a spear, carry it to Lord Howell, and then bind it to a barbican for public display.

Meliagaunt: Guenever signals Launcelot not to let Meliagaunt live. Launcelot offers to resume the fight with his left side unarmed. Meliagaunt accepts these shameful terms. Launcelot cleaves his head into two pieces.

Mordred: Arthur orders his followers to be stern and see that Mordred's offspring are slain and slung in the sea.

TRIUMPH

Giant Ogre of Mont St. Michel: The people come and give thanks to Arthur. He responds that they should give thanks to God. He distributes the ogre's treasure to the people and orders Lord Howell to build a church to St. Michael on the former ogre's hill.

Meliagaunt: Launcelot is cherished and honored by Arthur and Guenever.

Mordred: Arthur takes the sacrament, forgives all offenses and Guinevere, and dies. He is interred with the highest honor and ceremony.

Essentially the same structure is found in Chrétien's version of the Meleagant tale[54] and in the giant ogre episode in *Morte Arthure.*[55] Its basic features are recognizable in a wide range of ravisher-and-revenge stories from Theassi's abduction of Idunn[56] and Tarquin's rape of Lucretia[57] through folktales[58] and fantasy[59] to science fiction[60] and suburban saga.[61] And it is unmistakably the prototype for Justice Scalia's statement of the case in *Michael H.*, which we are now ready to review:[62]

LACK/VILLAINY

Two years after Carole and Gerald were married and "established a home" in California (113, para. 2, lines 2–5), Carole "became involved in an adulterous affair with a neighbor, Michael . . ." (113, para. 2, lines 7–8)

HERO EMERGES/PREPARES TO ACT

Victoria being born, "Gerald was listed as the father on the birth certificate and . . . always held Victoria out to the world as his daughter." (113, para. 2, line 9 – 114, para. 1, line 1)

DONOR/CONSULTATION

[This function and the following one are transposed. See the item after next.]

JOURNEY

Gerald "moved to New York City to pursue his business interests." (114, para. 2, lines 3–4) Carole chose to remain in California, but soon she and Victoria visited Michael in St. Thomas, where his primary business interests were based. (114, para. 2, lines 4–5) Carole [with Victoria] left Michael, returned to California, took up residence with "yet another man," Scott (114, para. 2, lines 10–12), spent time with Gerald in New York, vacationed, and returned to Scott in California. (114, para. 2, lines 12–16)

DONOR/CONSULTATION

Michael was "rebuffed in his attempts to visit Victoria." (114, para. 3, lines 1–2) This recitation, following a statement that Carole and Victoria were living with Scott, casts Scott— otherwise a transient in the tale—in the donor/helper's role.

BATTLE

"Michael filed a filiation action." (114, para. 3, lines 1–2) Carole, who was now "again living with Gerald in New York," responded by "fil[ing] a motion for summary judgment." (114, para. 3, lines 9–12)

DEFEAT

Carole "returned to California, [and] became involved once again with Michael. . . ." (114, para. 3, lines 12–13)

ENEMY ASCENDANT

Carole "instructed her attorneys to remove the summary judgment motion from the calendar." (114, para. 3, lines 13–15) For the next eight months, Michael mostly lived with Carole and Victoria in Carole's apartment and held Victoria out as his daughter. (114, para. 4, lines 1–3) Carole and Michael signed a stipulation that Michael was Victoria's natural father. (114, para. 4, line 4 – 115, para. 1, line 1)

HERO RECOVERS/NEW HERO

Carole "left Michael the next month . . . and instructed her attorneys not to file the stipulation." (115, para. 1, lines 1–3)

BATTLE REJOINED

Carole "reconciled with Gerald and joined him in New York, where they now live with Victoria and two other children since born into the marriage." (115, para. 1, lines 3–6) Michael and Victoria sought visitation rights for Michael *pendente lite.* (115, para. 2, lines 1–2) Gerald, "who had intervened in the action, moved for summary judgment." (115, para. 3, lines 1–4)

VICTORY

The trial court granted Gerald's motion for summary judgment, "reject[ed] Michael's and Gerald's constitutional challenges," and denied continued visitation pending appeal. (115, para. 4, lines 1–8)

ENEMY PUNISHED

The court "found that allowing such visitation would 'violat[e] the intention of the Legislature by impugning the integrity of the family unit.'" (116, para. 1, lines 3–5)

TRIUMPH

The California Court of Appeal affirmed and the California Supreme Court denied discretionary review. (116, para. 2, line 10 – para. 3, line 3)

So much for the facts of the case. Here, as Forsyth says in a similar context, "the telling of a story is also the interpretation of a story: narrative is also theology."[63]

IV. How the Opinion Enacts the Myth in Words

It is not just the opening statement of the facts but the linguistic microstructure of Justice Scalia's entire opinion that molds the universe of *Michael H.* around a core of combat mythology.[64] Consider the verbs that Justice Scalia uses to portray Michael and Gerald each as doing things in the world. The following chart sets out every active

ACTIVE VERBS ASSIGNED TO MICHAEL AND GERALD RESPECTIVELY

Michael *seeks*
Michael *seeks* to be declared the father
Michael *seeks*
    to *obtain* a benefit
Michael *asserts* a claim
Michael *asserts* a claim
Michael *asserts* [a legal contention]
Michael *asserts* an alleged substantive right
Michael *asserts* that his rights are violated
Michael *asserts* a right
    to *have himself declared* the natural
      father
    and thereby to *obtain* parental
      prerogatives
Michael [according to the dissent] *does not
claim*
    and in order *to prevail*
    need not claim a substantive right
    to *maintain* a parental relationship
Michael *contends*
Michael *reads* the cases as establishing [a
legal contention]
Michael *raises* two challenges
Michael *must establish*
Michael [is obliged] to *establish*
Michael [is not afforded an opportunity]
    to *demonstrate* his paternity
Michael *establishes* a parental relationship
Michael *files* a filiation action   Gerald *intervenes* in the action
    to *establish* his paternity   Gerald *moves* for summary judgment
    and right to visitation
Michael [assertedly] *has* a constitutionally
    protected liberty interest
Michael [according to the dissent] *has* a   Gerald *must have* a "freedom
    "freedom *not to conform*" (whatever   *to conform*"
      that means)
Michael [according to Victoria] *should stand*
    as her legal father, not Gerald
Michael *lives* with Carole and Victoria in
    Carole's apartment
Michael *stays* with her [Carole] and the
    child
Michael *holds* Victoria *out* as his child   Gerald *holds* Victoria *out* to the world
Michael *holds* Victoria *out* as his daughter   as his daughter

Michael [is rebuffed in his attempts] to *visit* Victoria

Michael [is unable] to *act* as the father of the child
    he adulterously *begets*

Gerald [is unable] to *preserve* the integrity of the traditional family unit

Michael [hypothetically] *begets* Victoria by rape

Gerald *moves* to New York
    to *pursue* his business interests

Michael & Carole *have* blood tests

Gerald & Carole *establish* a home

Gerald & Carole *reside* as husband and wife

Gerald & Carole *cohabit*

Gerald & Carole *live* with Victoria and two other children born into the marriage

Michael & Carole *sign* a stipulation that Michael is Victoria's natural father

Gerald & Carole *acknowledge* the child to be theirs

Gerald & Carole *wish*
    to *raise* the child as their own

Gerald & Carole *wish*
    to *raise* the child as the offspring of their union

Gerald & Carole *wish*
    to *raise* her child jointly

---

verb in his opinion that has as its subject (1) Michael alone [left column, top], (2) Gerald alone [right column, top], (3) Michael and Carole jointly [left column, bottom], and (4) Gerald and Carole jointly [right column, bottom].[65]

Although Michael is portrayed as substantially more active than Gerald throughout the opinion (there are 37 active verbs predicating action by Michael alone, 8 predicating action by Gerald alone),[66] not a single verb depicts Michael going about the ordinary, productive, workaday business of life: his entire activity consists of *distraining, disputing, and despoiling.* This is the recognizable figure of the traditional Satan as a "being without a center, . . . [one who] has no essence,"[67] one who is simply the Adversary, the Opponent, the *diabolos,* and "as the adversary, . . . must always be a function of another, not an independent entity."[68] The Adversary's Other is Gerald, whose activities are *providing* and *preserving*—and whose preserve must *naturally* be protected against poaching.

Of course this kind of summary chart can convey only a gross sense of Justice Scalia's word portraiture. To see how it plays out in the particular, look at how he describes identical behavior by Gerald and Michael: "In October 1981, Gerald *moved* to New York City *to pursue* his business interests."[69] "In January 1982, Carole visited Michael in St. Thomas, where his primary business interests were based."[70] Both men would seem to have been engaged in economically productive activity, but Gerald's is made explicit in two active—very active—verbs, while Michael's is tucked under the verbal rug. Or compare these two predications: "The couple [Gerald and Carole] *established* a home in Playa del Rey, California, in which they *resided* as husband and wife when one or the other was not out of the country *on business.*"[71] "For the ensuing eight months, when Michael was not *in St. Thomas* he lived with Carole and Victoria in Carole's apartment in Los Angeles. . . ."[72] The sentence about Gerald has a compound subject literally conjoining Gerald and Carole and packing into three lines the complete tale of a Happy Marriage of Two Productive Partners. The sentence about Michael describes *his* business travel as being "in St. Thomas";[73] it denies Carole any activity whatsoever; Michael is the solo subject of the verb; and the verb's activity is parasitic. Later, Justice Scalia will repeat the sentence about Michael and Carole in slightly stronger language, talking about an "8 month period when, if he *happened to be* in Los Angeles, he *stayed with her* and the child."[74] The image of Satan "going to and fro in the earth, and . . . walking up and down in it"[75] making trouble for humankind until confounded is unmistakable. Thus does Justice Scalia set the scene for the inevitable shootout on the threshold of Eternity, in which either Michael or Gerald "will pay a price . . . —Michael by being unable to act as father of the child he has adulterously begotten, or Gerald by being unable to preserve the integrity of the traditional family unit he and Victoria have established."[76] We are surely not left without verbal and narrative clues about who will win the shootout or whom to root for.

V. *How the Opinion Embodies the Myth*

Having set forth the case of *Michael H.* as a combat myth even in his choice of words, Justice Scalia keeps the case locked into that frame by an assortment of techniques.[77] We will take up separately techniques that center in *plot elaboration, legal analysis,* and *judicial philosophy,* although these are simply categories of convenience and their contents are connected. A fourth category that we can call *ontological construction* overlaps the others and is best discussed alongside each of them.

Plot Elaboration

For Justice Scalia, as for any successful storyteller, it is crucial that his ending seem inevitable. The circumstances, motivations, and behaviors of the characters must all be developed so as to drive the combat myth to its ordained conclusion.[78]

Justice Scalia begins this process in the first half-dozen lines of his legal analysis. Immediately after the pronouncement that "California law, like nature itself, makes no provision for dual fatherhood,"[79] he goes on to describe the Trouble posed by Michael in the light of this Rule of Nature:

> "Michael was seeking to be declared *the* father of Victoria. The immediate benefit he evidently sought to obtain from that status was visitation rights. . . . But if Michael succeeded in being declared the father, other rights would follow—most importantly, the right to be considered as the parent who should have custody, . . . a status which 'embrace[s] the sum of parental rights with respect to the rearing of a child, including . . . [rights enumerated in five divisions and numerous subdivisions quoted *verbatim* from a California family law hornbook].'"[80]

The case is thus presented as a winner-take-all struggle between Michael and Gerald, with "'the sum of parental rights'" set at stake and embellished like a Champion's Portion displayed to goad potential rivals into battle fury.[81] So elaborated, the combat plot has four self-evident entailments: since Michael seeks an elevated prize, he must make an elevated showing to obtain it;[82] his showing must *trump* Gerald's showing;[83] no accommodation is possible between the combatants;[84] and this war-to-the-death is not only of Michael's making[85] but of Michael's choosing.[86] Any reader who accepts this story line must anticipate and relish Michael's come-down at the destined conclusion.

How does Justice Scalia promote this story line? One of his major devices is to give a seemingly ontological status to the major elements of his plot. Look again at the first substantive paragraph of his opinion. But first, here is an opening paragraph that he *might* have written:

> "We take Michael's claims first. California law makes parental rights indivisible, requiring that either Michael get them all or Gerald get them all. Nature requires the same all-and-nothing distribution. Because of these requirements, we must deem Michael's claims to be that he is entitled to enjoy all parental rights with respect to Victoria and that Gerald is entitled to enjoy none. Michael's filiation action requested a declaration of paternity for (so far as we can tell) the purpose of obtaining visitation rights. But California law and nature deny him the option of making so modest a claim, and we are bound to treat him as seeking everything that California law and nature make inseparable from what he sued for."

Now, here is what he wrote:

> "We address first the claims of Michael. At the outset, it is necessary to clarify what he sought and what he was denied. California law, like nature itself, makes no provision for dual fatherhood. Michael was seeking to be declared *the* father of Victoria. The immediate benefit he evidently sought to obtain from that status was visitation rights. . . . But if Michael were successful in being declared the father, other rights would follow—most importantly, the right to be considered as the parent who should have custody, . . . a status which 'embrace[s] the sum of parental rights with respect to the rearing of a child, including the child's care; the right to the child's services and earnings; . . .'" etc.[87]

Confronted by the first passage, the reader would be moved to ask some troubling questions. California law makes parental rights indivisible. But *can* California law do that? The very California law that Michael says is federally unconstitutional? If the U.S. Supreme Court can declare California law federally unconstitutional, why is it *bound* to accept California law's requirement that Michael stand or fall on an all-or-nothing claim? Indeed, isn't this case about precisely that question: whether California can constitutionally package parental rights in all-or-nothing bundles?

Nature requires the all-or-nothing packaging of parental rights? Does it?[88] Does nature say anything at all about parental rights, or are parental rights a legal construct rather than a natural trait?[89] And if nature's brand of indivisible fatherhood is binding, Michael wins the case hands down, right?

But even assuming that California law and nature constrain Michael and the federal Constitution to an all-or-nothing move, why is *Michael* to be treated as the maker and the seeker of the consequent all-or-nothing combat? He had no opportunity to limit the scope of conflict.

Justice Scalia's actual passage avoids all of these questions by portraying his plot elements as features of reality instead of cognitive constructions. His first sentence casts the Court as responsive to ("*address[ing]*") "the claims of Michael." His second sentence literally reifies those claims after taking on the posture of objective and omniscient narrator: "it is necessary to clarify *what* he [Michael] sought and *what* he was denied." It is not that the shape of California law compels the U.S. Supreme Court to treat Michael's claim as being X because it legally entails X and the Court accepts that entailment. Rather, "Michael *was seeking* to be declared *the* father of Victoria," and "if Michael were *successful* in being declared the father, other rights *would follow*. . . ." The same linguistic strategies are used whenever the *real* nature of Michael's (or Victoria's) claims are described by Justice Scalia: for example,

> "As noted earlier, *what* is at issue here is not entitlement to a state pronouncement that Victoria was begotten by Michael. . . . *What* Michael *asserts* here is a right to have himself declared the father *and thereby to obtain parental prerogatives.*"[90]

This reality is deepened by the superb sentence elaborating Michael's motivation: "The *immediate* benefit he *evidently* sought to obtain . . . was visitation rights." The adjective and adverb set up the binary ontological pairings[91] *immediate/long-range* and *evidently/really* so as to imply that Michael's *real* aims were more extensive than his pleadings stated. An indefensible implication created through such techniques will never have to be defended because, if the techniques go unnoticed, the implication works on the reader; but if the reader notices and questions the techniques, Justice Scalia can deny that any implication was intended. The same procedure of ontological construction with an escape hatch is followed in the foundational sentence: "California law, like nature itself, makes no provision for dual fatherhood." If the *nature* phrase goes unquestioned, it sets up the quintessential *normal* : *normative* transition;[92] if it is questioned, Justice Scalia can disavow it as nothing more than a cute metaphor.

Similar techniques are used to reify Victoria's claims in forms that offend the natural order[93] and give rise to an irreconcilable conflict plot. Victoria's due process claim, we are told, "*is not*" that California has denied her an opportunity to choose between contending father figures: "Rather, *she claims* a . . . right to maintain filial relationships with both Michael and Gerald;"[94] and this unnatural and greedy desire[95] "merits little discussion."[96] Victoria's equal protection claim—that "unlike her mother and presumed father, she had no opportunity to rebut the presumption of her legitimacy"[97]—is then set at war with a generic mother's and father's interests in marital privacy and harmony and is resoundingly trounced:

> "The primary rationale underlying [California's] . . . limitation on those who may rebut the presumption of legitimacy is a concern that allowing persons other than the husband or wife to do so may undermine the integrity of the marital union. When the husband or wife contests the legitimacy of their child, the stability of the marriage has already been shaken. In contrast, allowing a claim of illegitimacy to be pressed by the child—or, more accurately, by a court-appointed guardian ad litem— may well disrupt an otherwise peaceful union. Since it pursues a legitimate end by rational means, California's decision to treat Victoria differently from her parents is not a denial of equal protection."[98]

It is noteworthy how this passage tacks from radical idealism to radical (if cynical) pragmatism in order to maintain its plot line. Juxtaposing the second and third sentences has the effect of implying that *unless* a husband or wife contests a child's legitimacy, the "stability of the marriage" has *not* "already been shaken." Whatever truth that proposition might have in some prototypical case, the proposition stands in the starkest possible contrast to the history of Gerald's and Carole's marriage which Justice Scalia has described in his statement of the facts.[99] It is an idealized if not an utterly unworldly abstraction.[100] The idealism vanishes a half-sentence later, when "a court-appointed guardian ad litem" is disaggregated from his or her ward— without regard to the role that such a guardian is supposed or required to play under California law—and personified as an indiscreet, Tom-peeping mischief-maker in order to provide a villain for a plot to "disrupt an otherwise peaceful union" who is somewhat more credible in the role than Victoria or any other toddler could be.[101]

The converse technique, aggregation-and-personification, is used to create the heroic couple of the plot. Michael's and Victoria's claims must fail, says Justice Scalia, because "our traditions have protected the marital family (Gerald, Carole, and the child they acknowledge to be theirs) against [this] . . . sort of claim. . . ."[102] The parenthetical phrase or its equivalent is repeated throughout the opinion[103] and has enough importance in Justice Scalia's view to warrant a footnote defending it against a challenge by Justice Brennan's dissent to an aspect of its reasoning.[104] The more basic question of its construction is never explained, but the explanation must be that it is constructed either by (1) treating Carole as a static, changeless character[105] and treating her present litigation posture as her attitude at all relevant times, or (2) treating Gerald and Carole aggregatively, by conjoining them with plural verbs such as "acknowledge" and "wish" and with pronouns such as "theirs."

This way of treating Carole simply as Gerald's *ux*, who lacks any independent agentive stance, is, of course, a major feature of the Demon Lover adultery tale, the tale that Justice Scalia chooses to tell. He decries Carole's wanton behavior but portrays it as a sort of unmotivated libidinousness at the beck of male marauders such as Michael.[106] It is *beneath* censure. Justice Scalia thereby escapes the need to condemn and punish Carole that would arise if, say, she were portrayed as the Villain Wife in the typical tale of that genre.[107] With Michael as the sole villain, the story allows the "unitary family" to be reconstituted and to emerge Triumphant.

Legal Analysis

The combat myth also marks Justice Scalia's legal analyses.

First, he frames the issues as unavoidably conflictual. This is done, once again, by linguistic techniques that embed antithesis in the very structure of reality. Consider how he might have begun his discussion of Michael's substantive due process claim:

> "Michael contends as a matter of substantive due process that California has impermissibly abridged his liberty interest in the parental relationship which he has established with Victoria. This argument is, of course, predicated on the assertion that a relationship of this kind comes within the 'liberty' protected by the Due Process Clause."

And then consider how he did begin it:

> "Michael contends as a matter of substantive due process that, because he has established a parental relationship with Victoria, protection of Gerald's and Carole's marital union is an insufficient state interest to support termination of that relationship. This argument is, of course, predicated on the assertion that Michael has a constitutionally protected liberty interest in his relationship with Victoria."[108]

Justice Scalia is plainly getting ahead of his story and weaving a pattern of polar opposition into its ontological fabric.[109] *Protection of the Michael/Victoria relationship* is presented as *inherently* opposed to *protection of the Gerald/Carole relationship*. This pattern is repeated throughout the opinion. For example, in discussing the precedents on which Michael relies, Justice Scalia notes that one of them acknowledged that biological fatherhood has a particular significance—specifically, it "'offers the natural father an opportunity that no other male possesses to develop a relationship with his offspring'"[110]—and (Justice Scalia continues in his own words) "we assumed that the Constitution might require some protection of that opportunity."[111] Having formed a composite body out of the notions *opportunity* and *legally protected* and *no other male,* Justice Scalia can then pit this body against an antagonistic Double:

> "Where, however, the child is born into an extant marital family, the natural father's *unique opportunity* conflicts with the similarly *unique opportunity* of the husband of the marriage; and it is not unconstitutional for the State to give categorical preference to the latter."[112]

Or:

> "Here, to *provide* protection to an adulterous natural father is to *deny* protection to a marital father, and vice versa."[113]

Second, an agonistic temper is reflected in the way in which Justice Scalia rejects Michael's procedural due process claim:[114] by reading the precedents on which it is based as "not . . . rest[ing] upon *procedural* due process" but upon a substantive due process (or equal protection) principle requiring the States to justify "the adequacy of the 'fit' between [a] classification and the policy that the classification serves."[115] This is a plausible explanation of the precedents,[116] although it is not the only plausible explanation of them,[117] nor the only one that could support rejecting Michael's claim.[118] The interesting thing about Justice Scalia's choice of rationale is that it converts precedents which talk as though they were based upon procedural due process[119] into precedents which restrict the state legislatures' power to enact substantive classifications, and it does this without discussing the doctrinal effects of the conversion.[120] The principal effect is to intensify the potential for friction between the Fourteenth Amendment and state policies in a range of substantive fields. (The doctrine subjecting state-enacted substantive classifications to federal constitutional review for fitness[121] was a frequent instrument of pre–New Deal judicial invalidation of divers state statutes.[122] Conversely, procedural due process doctrines have served largely to avoid occasions for broad-scale conflict between state law and federal constitutional constraint.)[123] Conflict-avoidance, ordinarily a strong consideration in a jurisprudence concerned with federalism[124]—as the *Michael H.* plurality opinion purports to be[125]—is simply disregarded in Justice Scalia's zeal to put all of Michael's contentions decisively to the sword.[126]

Still another reflection of combat mentality in Justice Scalia's legal reasoning is his construction of two bodies of warring precedent. One body is composed of cases in which "we have *insisted* not merely that [an] . . . interest [seeking Due Process protection] . . . as a 'liberty' be 'fundamental' (a concept that, in isolation, is hard to objectify), but also that it be an interest traditionally protected by our society."[127] This body of case law is depicted as having been decided "[i]n an attempt to limit and guide interpretation of the [Due Process] Clause" because of "the need for restraint" presented by another body of case law that is described in equally forceful terms: "It is *an established part of our constitutional jurisprudence* that the term 'liberty' in the Due Process Clause extends beyond freedom from physical restraint."[128] But the "established" feature of the liberty-extending body of case law is not emphasized as a reason for respecting it. Rather, its rootedness is a measure of its *treachery*[129] and the difficulty of dominating it.[130] Constitutional law, in this conception, is neither a harmonious pattern nor a set of carefully calibrated accommodations but a deadly war. Choosing sides and gathering up the biggest available bombs becomes the order of the day for an ancient and unquestionable cause: an Evil Principle is loose among the stars.[131]

Judicial Philosophy

Where Satan emerges, so, too, will heretics.[132] Justice Scalia moves immediately from the treacherousness that lurks in the Due Process precedents to "'concern lest the only limits to . . . judicial intervention become the predilections of those who happen at the time to be Members of this Court.'"[133]

Both constitutional doctrine and the judicial function need to be defined in terms of the extreme danger posed by these would-be Traitor Members. Their allegiance is unknown but they are always to be feared, lying in wait for the slightest opportunity to "dictate rather than discern the society's views."[134] Their motivation may be obscure, even unimaginable, but their willfulness is manifest.[135] Justice Scalia does not undertake to tell their tale directly; he assumes his readers know it and he uses it figurally[136] to interpret Justice Brennan's dissent[137] and draw appropriate morals for judging.

Unmistakably, "[t]his is history as rebellion myth."[138] Adjudication becomes less a matter of deciding the case before the Court than of scorching all surrounding constitutional thickets to interdict the approaches of the Enemy. Michael cannot merely be adjudged to have lost a close and arguable controversy; he and his supporters must be annihilated.

VI. How the Opinion Lays Down the Law and, with It, Michael

This, then is the mission to which Justice Scalia is inexorably called: to punish Michael's villainy, prosecute the larger war against encroaching Evil, and restore security to territory threatened by seductive, wanton, and rebellious powers. It is the formulaic situation for exerting stern authority, in narrative[139] and history[140] alike. Sexual promiscuity vaguely linked with menacing malignity will always call for laying down the law. These are circumstances under which an empathy for malefactors risks confusion or perversion of the righteous;[141] safer 'tis to rally 'round time-honored values and to tighten ranks against their violators.

The law laid down by Justice Scalia fully meets these rigorous necessities. As a matter of constitutional doctrine, the law is that only "an interest traditionally protected by our society" qualifies for Due

Process protection;[142] that the tradition to be consulted is "the most specific tradition available";[143] that "[s]ince it is Michael's burden to establish that . . . [the interest for which he seeks Due Process protection] is so deeply embedded within our traditions as to be a fundamental right, the lack of evidence alone might defeat his case";[144] and that, in any event, "the existence" of a "long-standing and still extant societal tradition withholding the very right" for which Michael seeks recognition "refutes any possible contention that the alleged right is 'so rooted. . . .'"[145] The next task is to make these decrees plausibly defeat Michael's claims; and the ways in which Justice Scalia undertakes the task are interesting.

To begin with, Justice Scalia adopts the stance of the defender of traditional values through the rhetorical device of repetition:[146] he swears allegiance to tradition so incessantly that it becomes difficult to imagine that he could have any other loyalties.[147] To this he adds the device of hyperbole:[148] he says that the Court's earlier parental-rights cases rest upon "the historic respect—indeed, sanctity would not be too strong a term—traditionally accorded to the relationships that develop within the unitary family,"[149] and he quotes a passage in one of those cases saying that "'[o]ur decisions establish that the Constitution protects the *sanctity* of the family precisely because the institution of the family is deeply rooted in this Nation's history and tradition.'"[150] What goes unsaid is that Justice Scalia must distinguish literally all of those prior cases in order to reach his result in *Michael H.*; he makes this feat invisible by doing it in three swift moves within successive sentences—first, ushering in the cases as those which "Michael reads . . . as establishing [Michael's position]";[151] second, saying: "We think that distorts the rationale of those cases";[152] and third, announcing that the cases "rest not upon such isolated factors"[153] as they have in common with Michael's case[154] but upon the *sanctity* attached to *the unitary family*[155]—and he thereafter implies that all of the cases support his position by quoting from them such isolated phrases as do,[156] without bothering to discuss any aspects of them which are coherent with Michael's position and incoherent with his own. The cases are not treated as part of the legal tradition to be consulted or as illuminating it; *that* tradition is reified independently of anything that the Supreme Court has said about parental rights. And there can be no question about which tradition is *the* tradition to be consulted: the disagreement between Justice Scalia's opinion and Justice Brennan's dissent concerns not how to read our traditions but simply whether to honor them or to abandon all tradition.

This last point is crucial: if it is questioned, Justice Scalia's whole opinion comes unstuck. A reader of the opinion might then ask Justice Scalia: But isn't the judge's job in this case to figure out the most appropriate methodology to use in constructing the concept and the content of the *tradition* with which s/he will work? Isn't *tradition* composed of multiple strands—the common law (and its progression through centuries), state statutes (and their evolution), the High Court's constitutional case law (and its line of development), the ideas and values reflected and growing in all of these sources? Isn't the disagreement between you and Justice Brennan—who is just as much a laborer within these traditions as you are (and can no more get outside them)—mostly a matter of reading your common traditions differently?[157] And if that's right, shouldn't your opinion address the reasons for preferring some ideas and values to others, or for accommodating them in one fashion rather than another, instead of denigrating this difficult work as "'balancing'"[158] and saying, as you do, that:

> "we rest our decision not upon our independent 'balancing' of . . . interests, but upon the absence of any constitutionally protected right . . . in Michael's situation, as evidenced by long tradition. That tradition reflects a 'balancing' that has already been made by society itself"[159]?

A reader in the grip of Justice Scalia's prose will not be prone to ask these questions, for several reasons:

First, the basic structural features of the opinion that we have already noted—the combat-myth plot line, Justice Scalia's self-presentation as the Defender of Tradition, his depiction of Justice Brennan as the Rebel against Tradition—crystallize the notion that the two Justices are engaged in wholly different tasks, with different and opposing motivations.

Second, throughout the text of Justice Scalia's opinion, everywhere above the footnote line, the image of *our tradition* or *our traditions* is projected as a monolith: single-stoned, definitively bounded, either present or absent but unmistakable when present, undivided and indivisible. Conceptually, what is involved here is very like the Idea of Universal History;[160] rhetorically, it is reification: "tradition" is *thingified* into inseparability.[161] In one footnote, Justice Scalia admits that "tradition" might not have this monolithic quality at all; elsewhere, both before and after the footnote, tradition's monolithic quality is simply taken as a given. The footnote (footnote 6) taxes Justice Brennan for preferring a more "general" to a more "specific" formulation of what counts as "tradition."[162] "One would think that JUSTICE BRENNAN would appreciate the value of consulting the most specific tradition available" because he admits the imprecision of "general traditions."[163] There is

> "a need, if arbitrary decisionmaking is to be avoided, to adopt the most specific tradition as the point of reference—or at least to announce, as JUSTICE BRENNAN declines to do, some other criterion for selecting among *the innumerable relevant traditions that could be consulted . . .* [because] a rule of law that binds neither by text nor by any particular, identifiable tradition is no rule of law at all."[164]

The strategy here is precisely like the one that we observed Justice Scalia using when he allowed that the liberty protected by Due Process "extends beyond" freedom from physical restraint but then treated this extensibility as a menace.[165] The possibility of a rule-relaxing conception is admitted only to exaggerate it into a threat of rule-destroying disorder and justify reverting to another form of rigid rule.

Third, the ultimate rule that promises salvation is presented as impervious to change or to interpretation. Justice Scalia simultaneously creates the category of "the unitary family" and *sanctifies* it.[166] Thus elevated into the realm of the numinous, the concept is insulated against fraying at the fringes. There can be no indeterminacy or triviality about the line that separates sacred space from profane space.[167] By its very nature, the location of such a line cannot turn on whatever "isolated factors" Michael may cite as common to his case and to the precedents[168] that give Due Process protection to "*certain* parental rights";[169] nor can the boundaries of sacred space be "stretched so far" as to include Michael's case in all its tawdry particularities.[170]

Fourth, the world of Justice Scalia's opinion is elementally designed so as to preserve his orderly and hard-edged rules against the messy little facts that might disorder them. From start to finish,[171] he uses three well-known rhetorical techniques for doing this.

He devalues the concrete. Throughout the opinion, abstract categories are made to seem realer than the concrete specifics that they encompass. In stating "[t]he facts of this case,"[172] concrete circumstances are reduced to classificatory labels: for example, "[i]n the first three years of her life, Victoria . . . found herself within a variety of quasi-family units."[173] This is hardly a description that conveys the circumstances or the life of a newborn-through-three-year-old child. Yet it sets up very nicely Justice Scalia's recitation of the California trial court's legal ruling that to grant Michael visitation rights after his failed attempt to prove paternity "would 'violat[e] the intention of the Legislature by impugning the integrity of the family unit.'"[174] And it implicitly warrants Justice Scalia's ultimate framing of the constitutional issue presented by this ruling as an either/or choice between allowing Michael "to act as father of the child he has adulterously begotten" and enabling Gerald "to preserve the integrity of the traditional family unit he and Victoria have established."[175] On the one hand, Justice Scalia consistently treats the details of daily life in which Michael and Victoria claim to have an interest (like visitation) as fleeting, superficial incidents of more enduring and important essences ("the right to be considered as the parent who should have custody"; *legal* "status"; "'the sum of parental rights'"; and so forth).[176] On the other hand, he treats legally-prescribed connections as features of the God-given Universe[177] and describes their premises in terms of sweeping generalizations that he declares to be universal truths about human nature.[178] The cumulative effect of these devices is to create a powerful set in favor of tailoring facts to rules instead of vice versa in the processes of categorization.

He devalues the individual. Throughout the opinion, quantitative values trump qualitative values: the general is privileged over the unique.[179] At first blush, this may seem to be nothing more than an employment of the standard methodologies of Due Process adjudication—evaluating claims in terms of the antiquity[180] and extensiveness[181] of their acceptance—and the subspecialties of those methodologies, such as historical surveys[182] and jurisdictional nose counts.[183] But Justice Scalia is *driving* those methodologies while appearing merely to ride them. Consider, for example, his formulation of the teaching of the Supreme Court's parental-rights precedents: "they rest . . . upon the historic respect—indeed, sanctity . . . —traditionally accorded to relationships that develop within the unitary family."[184] One might go in either of two directions from this premise. One might say: *There must be something very special about the kinds of relation-*

ships that develop within a unitary family to command respect so widespread, enduring, and intense; let us see whether we can identify that special quality, search the circumstances now before us for indicators of its presence or absence, and honor it to the extent we find it present. Or one might say: *Whatever is special about those relationships must derive exclusively from the pervasiveness, duration, and intensity of the respect they have commanded; so let us ask what forms of relationship have received the requisitely widespread, enduring, and intense respect, and let us honor only those forms.* The first direction is entirely consistent with Due Process precedents,[185] including the leading precedent on which Michael based his claim.[186] But Justice Scalia takes the second direction as though it were the sole road out of the starting gate, and thus he portrays the case as *reducing itself* to purely quantitative inquiries.[187] Approaches that place a higher value on unique circumstances are ruled out, indeed, by the very first sentence of Justice Scalia's statement of the facts: "The facts of this case are, we must hope, extraordinary."[188] In this opening, Justice Scalia is not simply expressing disapproval of Michael's and Carole's promiscuous behavior; he is implicitly asserting that only *the ordinary* counts and that the *extraordinary* can be written off as unimportant.[189]

He devalues the uncertain. Similarly, Justice Scalia implies that nothing is important that cannot be known with certainty. He begins his legal analysis by saying that it is "necessary to clarify" what Michael is seeking.[190] He says that Michael's procedural Due Process claim "derives from a fundamental misconception of the nature" of the California statute[191] and that the precedents on which Michael relies "must ultimately be analyzed" in terms other than procedural Due Process.[192] These Foundational Imperatives accompany a legal analysis that reads the precedents as concerned with "the adequacy of the 'fit' between . . . [a legislative] classification and the policy that the classification serves" rather than with the adequacy of fact-finding procedures—an analysis implying that facts and their finding are of scant constitutional moment.[193] Justice Scalia's standard locution for describing the teaching of a line of precedent is: "we have *insisted*."[194] The precedents "establish" a particular rule or do not.[195] Justice Scalia's standard locution for conceding a point is "of course."[196] His standard locutions for rejecting a point are to say that it has "no" claim to credibility[197] or that it is "impossible to find" the point.[198] His standard response to arguments made in Justice Brennan's dissent is that they are unintelligible.[199] In his twenty-page opinion, he does not once allow that any view which he rejects is *possible;* he recognizes only twice that any logic may be *possible* which is not *necessary;*[200] and he makes only one nuanced assertion.[201] A world configured in these ways does not provide much room for adjusting categorical rules to the circumstances of animate existence: life's little gleam of Time between Two Eternities appears too insignificant and sloppy to be worth that effort.

VII. *The Last Stop, This Trip*

So where has this extended, sometimes fussy dissection of the prevailing *Michael H.* opinion brought us? We close with one irony, one metacritical comment, and one intriguing speculation.

First, it is an extraordinary irony that the stated justification for Justice Scalia's tradition-focused approach to Due Process analysis[202] is the danger of constitutional law-making whose "'only limits . . . [are] the predilections of . . . [the] Members of this Court,'"[203] and that his proclaimed "methodology in using historical traditions"—to "refer to the most specific level at which a relevant tradition . . . can be identified"—is supposed to deny judges the power "to dictate rather than discern the society's views."[204] His entire opinion is a demonstration of the limitless license that judges acquire to reify or deify their predilections when they pretend to themselves or others that their job involves no interpretive work but consists simply of sorting the *objective* facts of cases into the *objective* categories of *objective* rules.

Second, once Justice Scalia's methodology is probed to any depth, it is seen as relying upon narrative and rhetoric to construct categories, classify facts by categories, and conceal these operations in a made-to-order universe where they look natural, logical, unproblematic. In unpacking opinions like *Michael H.*, the perspectives and techniques of literary and linguistic study and rhetorical criticism can therefore be useful supplements to more traditional modes of legal analysis. We will offer more of them in later chapters.

Third—and here we enter upon the speculative—it may be that judges (and other legal categorizers) will decide cases rather differently depending upon whether the judge (or other legal categorizer) is relatively category-centered or relatively situation-centered.[205]

At root, every act of categorization involves matching *some awareness of the situation one is in* with *some standard for what a situation of this sort should be like.* In this regard, the question "Is Michael's relationship with Victoria a 'liberty' protected by Due Process?" is not unlike the question "Is that a dog?" or "Is that art?" One has a *concept,* a general model that is a subpart of the ordering structure of one's intellectual universe (which may take the form of a definition, a prototype, an ideal, a rule, or whatever); one has a sensitivity to the *immediate context;* and one has to put these two together in some manner.

Something almost always has to give way in the process. No system of concepts that serves as an ordering structure can have definitions, prototypes, or whatever, that are as numerous, variegated, and nuanced as the circumstances which bring the system to mind. The functional efficiency and the aesthetic elegance of the system both depend on Procrustean prunings. The word "dog" is conceptually enriched and contextually impoverished as soon as we apply it to two different four-legged beasts.

So the question is what will give way, and how much, when something has to give way? Will the situation get carved down, in the manner of Procrustes, to fit the system of concepts? Or will a patch get sewn onto the system of concepts, to fit the situation? Or a bit of both? The answer is likely to turn in part on the value one attaches to preserving the coherence of the system, on the one hand, and the richness of the situation, on the other.

CHAPTER FOUR

On Narrative

Law lives on narrative, for reasons both banal and deep.[1] For one, the law is awash in storytelling. Clients tell stories to lawyers, who must figure out what to make of what they hear. As clients and lawyers talk, the client's story gets recast into plights and prospects, plots and pilgrimages into possible worlds. (What lawyers call "thinking through a course of action" is a narrative projection of the perils of embarking on one pilgrimage or another.) If circumstances warrant, the lawyers retell their clients' stories in the form of pleas and arguments to judges and testimony to juries. (As Janet Malcolm has recently reminded us, "[t]he law's demand that witnesses speak 'nothing but the truth' is a demand no witness can fulfill, . . . even with God's help. It runs counter to the law of language, which proscribes unregulated truth-telling and requires that our utterances tell coherent, and thus never merely true, stories."[2] Next, judges and jurors retell the stories to themselves or to each other in the form of instructions, deliberations, a verdict, a set of findings, or an opinion. And then it is the turn of journalists, commentators, and critics. This endless telling and retelling, casting and recasting is essential to the conduct of the law. It is how law's actors comprehend whatever series of events they make the subject of their legal actions. It is how they try to make their actions comprehensible again within some larger series of events they take to constitute the legal system and the culture that sustains it.[3]

As a practical matter, the administration of the law and even much of its conceptualization rest upon "getting the facts." Every recognized legal situation (whether problem or solution) is taken to involve a distinctive state of facts (actual or potential).[4] In each such situation, some arbiter or agency or adviser is presumed to be able to decide what the facts *are*, at least for the purposes at hand. *Relevant facts,* "found" or hypothetically imagined, are presumed to frame the issue in debate, delimit the choices of action that can be pursued, determine the visitation or the vindication to be authoritatively pronounced. Did Joseph Jones suffocate his infant child, did he do it deliberately, was he mentally disordered at the time? Did Linda Lee lose her hand as a result of a design defect in the Truecut Power Saw, through some negligence in how she used the tool, or both? Is the Surefire Barbecue Company's latest self-igniting model safe to market? Do New Jersey State Highway Patrol Officers ticket a disproportionate number of African-American drivers for traffic violations, and is this a tactic designed for making drug-check stops based on a race-specific courier profile?

The traditional supposition of the law has been that questions like these can be answered by examining free-standing factual data selected on grounds of their logical pertinency. But increasingly we are coming to recognize that both the questions and the answers in such matters of "fact" depend largely upon one's choice (considered or unconsidered) of some overall narrative as best describing *what happened* or *how the world works*. We now understand that stories are not just recipes for stringing together a set of "hard facts"; that, in some profound, often puzzling way, stories *construct* the facts that comprise them. For this reason, much of human reality and its "facts" are not merely recounted by narrative but *constituted* by it.[5] To the extent that law is fact-contingent, it is inescapably rooted in narrative.

Reasoning within the law, finally, depends not only upon conceptions about *specific* states of facts but also upon notions about the nature of things generally, what they are and how they are related—the classic *de rerum natura*. These "things" are often not all that thing-like. They may take the shape of rules and principles, institutions and sources of authority, rights and obligations, freedoms and commitments, values and goals. However we conceive of them, they are grounded in what our culture designates as *mattering*. And what does or doesn't matter to a culture can be traced back through the culture's stories, its genres, to its enduring myths.

Narrative is the carrier of those myths and, at the same time, our means for recognizing that a present situation needs telling in a way linked to this myth or that one. How and what we tell ourselves about legal situations is no exception. Indeed, the very writs that defined causes of action at common law (*quare clausum fregit* and so forth) were rather like plot summaries of the founding narratives of various myth-like narrative genres.[6]

So, it is unsurprising that the connections between narrative and law are ancient—and tangled.[7] To begin to explore them, we need to consider narrative in its own right. What is it? How does it work?

Narrative is puzzling in the way familiar things sometimes are: it is simple, *but*. Telling and hearing stories come as second nature to us, but that doesn't quite lead us to understand what makes them hang together (sometimes memorably). We deploy them with great skill, practically all of us, and for purposes as varied as offering excuses for being late, amusing our children, and telling the story of our last trip—or of our life. If pressed about the factuality of their "true" stories, most people simply reply "but that's how it happened." Even fiction needs that touch of *lifelikeness* to seem right.

This chapter takes an introductory look at the why's and ways of narrative in its different guises.[8] Although we may not reach its heartland, we can at least enjoy the company we'll be keeping on our voyage. For some of the finest minds in the history of thought, beginning perhaps with Aristotle,[9] have addressed the puzzles of narrative, although never, alas, with the resounding triumph of a Galileo unlocking the secrets of the firmament.

We begin with an austere definition of narrative, compressing what we said about the subject in Chapter 2 into something like an Identikit of the basics that scholars over the centuries have taken to be narrative's elemental features. We then turn briefly to *theories of narrative*, efforts to explain its origins, functions, or course of development. All of these turn out to be so broad, so narrow, so incoherent, or so untestable as to shed little light on the question why narrative is as it is. So, what our theoretical excursion yields is the truism that narrative forms are affected by the nature of mind, language, and/or culture, and that they in turn shape how we look at people, the world, and the human condition.

Thus frustrated, we return once more to the austere particulars of narrative, to those essential features that give it its form and that serve to convert "things in the world" into *story,* real or fictional. In particular, we examine how stories are framed in order to speak to the questions:

- what is ordinary and legitimate,
- what constitutes time,
- what human beings strive for,
- what comprises *Trouble,*
- what makes character, and
- what shape human plights can take.

Well-wrought narratives are so successful in making their answers to these questions seem like "the real thing" that they virtually blind us to the subtle architecture of their construction. But we'll try to dig up clues about this architecture as we go along.

Finally, we'll turn to some particular problems of narrative in the law—how story is subordinated to the requirements of persuasion in courts as in lawyers' offices, how our very success in making things narratively believable often seduces us into unintended conventional stances toward the world. In the end we will suggest that narrative—with all its pretensions to stand for "reality"—is the *necessary* discourse of the law, and that recognizing this necessity is an important step toward enriching the possibilities of storytelling in the legal process *and* guarding against its perils.

I. An Austere Definition

Our bare-bones definition of narrative reminds us what is necessary to make a story. It is like a protocol for a story pilot's instrument check before flying narratively—both a guide and a set of cautions:

A narrative can purport to be either a fiction or a real account of events; it does not have to specify which. It needs a *cast of human-like characters,* beings capable of *willing their own actions, forming intentions, holding beliefs, having feelings.* It also needs a *plot* with a beginning, a middle, and an end, in which particular characters are involved in particular events. The unfolding of the plot requires (implicitly or explicitly):

(1) an initial *steady state* grounded in the legitimate ordinariness of things

(2) that gets disrupted by a *Trouble* consisting of circumstances attributable to human agency or susceptible to change by human intervention,

(3) in turn evoking *efforts* at redress or transformation, which succeed or fail,

(4) so that the old steady state is *restored* or a new (*transformed*) steady state is created,

(5) and the story concludes by drawing the then-and-there of the tale that has been told into the here-and-now of the telling through some *coda*—say, for example, Aesop's characteristic *moral of the story.*

That is the bare bones of it. One could add more, though not without getting into quarrels with some narratologist or other. For example, does a narrative imply a narrator with a *point of view?* Well, perhaps, though novelists until recently tried to create the illusion that their narrator was omniscient and therefore needed no point of view. Or, does narrative imply "commitment" or caring in its characters (*Sorge,* as Ricoeur calls it)?[10] To those who say yes, postmodernists say no.[11] We think our present list of features is long enough to provide ample room for thought about such matters later.

II. Theories about Narrative

So why narrative? What functions does it serve? How did it come into being? These are the kinds of daunting questions that face a theorist bold (or foolish) enough to try *explaining* narrative. Alas, they get no less daunting when reduced to more manageable specifics. Why, for example, are narratives so ubiquitous in human discourse? Among blue-collar white families in Baltimore, to take a case in point, mothers' conversations with their preschool children or within earshot of the children average one narrative every seven minutes.[12] It is said that no culture, no language group is without stories.[13] Why do peoples everywhere revere the skilled storyteller so highly, especially for telling stories that they know are not factual? And why, in all cultures, do stories fall into locally recognizable kinds or genres—be they creation stories, excuses for aberrant behavior, comic tales to amuse, or whatever?

It seems almost as if humankind is unable to get on without stories. Knowing how to tell them and to comprehend them may be part of the human survival kit. And there appears to be something surreptitiously value-laden or value-promoting about storytelling. It isn't just for their literary technique that we give good storytellers laurel wreaths (or hemlock!), but because we understand that their stories *do* something beyond spinning a tale. Their stories give comfort, inspire, provide insight; they forewarn, betray, reveal, legitimize, convince. You can declare your love by telling just the right story at the right time; you can be Iago and create mad suspicion; you can spur Billy Budd to strike Claggart dead. There is obviously something more to story than the sheer transfer of information.

We should be forewarned, then, that narrative and its forms do not sit quietly for the theorist bent on portraying them in the abstract. They are too value-laden, too multipurpose, too mutable and sensitive to context. For all that, such crude theoretical efforts as have been made to explain narrative do pose interesting questions even if they are unable to yield answers. So let us have a brief look at these explanatory theories—not so much at particular theories, but at the basic kinds of theories that are on offer.

First, there are what might be called *endogenous* theories of narrative. Their central claim, typically, is that narrative is inherent either in the nature of the human mind, in the nature of language, or in those supposed programs alleged to run our nervous systems. Simply to claim that storytelling is doing-what-comes-naturally is hardly to explain it; but even so, endogenous theories entail certain presuppositions that are not altogether trivial—like the implicit claim that narrative is a human *universal,* within reach of everybody regardless of culture, language, intelligence, or condition of life. For not all anthropologists buy into claims about human universals.[14]

Consider an example of *linguistic* endogenous theories. Perhaps the most famous is Charles Fillmore's.[15] He argues that all known languages have some version of "case grammar," a system for syntactically marking forms like *agent, action, recipient, instrument* (or means), *progress to goal,* etc., in discourse. These are the so-called *arguments of action* that logicians distinguish; and Fillmore views them as innate in human thinking. They comprise the bare bones of story. A somewhat weaker claim is that this presumed innateness is what *causes* languages to make the case-grammatical distinctions they do. The implied theory (Fillmore never quite states it explicitly) is that a case-grammatical language has just the sorts of categories needed for telling stories like those described in our Austere Definition. Fillmore's implicit claim was made somewhat more explicit in a study of the spontaneous bedtime, pre-sleep soliloquies of a young child, Emmy, in the early stages of mastering English.[16] In this study, new case-grammatical forms were learned when needed to fit the requirements of the stories that Emmy was trying to tell—as if English were being mastered to help her tell her tales.

Endogenous theories might be propped up on evolutionary arguments—for example, that evolutionary selection favored hominids whose language had a grammar that made it easy for them to encode, say, deviations from the ordinary (as in our Austere Definition).[17] Good for intra-species warning, and all that. More interesting and less like a "Just So"-story is Merlin Donald's[18] suggestion that narrative grew from the mimetic system of representation that preceded the explosion of language and of brain size roughly a million years ago. New systems typically use and build on old systems, so the notion here is that narrative forms replicated and extended purely mimetic imitation. This sounds reasonable, but while we have skull endocasts to confirm what happened to the hominid brain a million years ago, early hominid storytelling has long since dissolved, literally into thin air.

Perhaps the most suggestive implication of endogenous theories of narrative comes from their implicitly Kantian stance: that narrative *constructs* a world not just according to how the world *is,* but according to its own categories. In that aspect, endogenous theories have usually been seen as an expression of constructivism (the view that the world is constructed by mental activity rather than "found" out there by the senses), a subject we discussed in Chapter 2.

In the end, what is inherently weak about endogenous theories is not what they claim, but what they leave unspecified. To say that narrative is innate is to say considerably less than it might appear—somewhat like saying that language is innate. Who doubts it? The real issue is *what* is innate about it, and how it works to constrain the ways we speak, what we say when, what is possible to talk about, and so on. These are not obvious matters. All languages, for example, use linguistic means for marking polite or respectful discourse.[19] Is politeness, then, innate in language, or is it a feature of social organization that language usage accommodates?

There is a second kind of narrative theory that involves culture and human interaction much more directly. It needs a word of background. About two decades ago the literary critic and linguist Roland Barthes proposed that narrative form provides the solution to the problem of translating *knowing* into *telling*.[20] He suggested that the two somehow grow alike or grow together, whether by experience coming to fit the confines of language or language coming to fit the forms of experience, or both. For Barthes, the confluence of the two was like Henry James's remark that "adventures happen only to people who can tell adventure stories."[21] Way-of-knowing and way-of-telling somehow fuse.

This second sort of theory seems to argue that narratives and genres of narrative serve to *model* characteristic plights of culture-sharing human groups.[22] On this view, cultures convert their plights and aspirations into narrative forms that represent both the culture's ordinary legitimacies and possible threats to them. Narratives function not simply to make experience communicable and thereby increase cultural solidarity, but also to give a certain practical predictability to the plights of communal life and a certain direction to the efforts needed to resolve them. Extended a bit further, the "social plight" view can even be given a legal turn, as Robert Cover[23] and James Boyd White[24] have given it. In their account, narratives that engender potentially disturbing conflicts of construal get incorporated in an idealized form into a *corpus juris,* with the objective of minimizing disruption. Notions like legitimacy, violation, good-faith effort, redress, and so on are prescribed in a form fitted for determination by legal rules and procedures rather than being left to spontaneous, face-to-face working out.

Legal narrative does, by and large, tend to conform to this second view of narrative. Indeed, some would say that by conforming *too* well, it creates its own kinds of discontents. In litigation, the plaintiff's lawyer is required to tell a story in which there has been trouble in the world that has affected the plaintiff adversely and is attributable to the acts of the defendant. The defendant must counter with a story in which it is claimed that nothing wrong happened to the plaintiff (or that the plaintiff's conception of wrong does not fit the law's definition), or, if there has been a legally cognizable wrong, then it is not the defendant's fault. Those are the obligatory plots of the law's adversarial process. At common law, moreover, the plaintiff's story-argument is classically shaped to fit a particular *writ,* which, as we have said, is a kind of plot précis of what is at issue—trespass, *indebitatus assumpsit,* or whatever. And the defendant typically counters the plaintiff's writ-informed narrative with one known or believed to have been used successfully to that end.

A lawyer's work is full of narrative labor designed to cook up "winning" stories according to hornbook recipes—how to unmask the false hero and disclose the true villain of the tale told by one's opponent, how to discomfit the opponent's witnesses, how to delve a yard below the opponent's precedents and blow them at the moon. The prosecution's case of cold-blooded murder, for example, has failed to take into account that the defendant was lashed into uncontrollable rage by some [standard] unsufferable provocation, reduced to blind instinct by some [recognized] source of mind-blowing fear, and so forth.

An inevitable consequence of such adversarial storytelling is that it tends to focus the attention of storytellers and hearers alike upon certain considerations rather than others, and to put a premium on type-casting the elements of every tale to fit the stock model of the "relevant" considerations. In addition, as a friend of ours once put it, the court may be compelled to make decisions that are essentially "comic" in contrast to the "tragic" circumstances that brought the case to law in the first place. The judge and jury often have no choices but to grant *or* deny "redress," say, by compensating the plaintiff or penalizing the defendant. The outcomes of adjudication, given the specialized nature of adversarial storytelling and the limited choices that emerge from it, are a bit too pat.

Supreme Court Justice Hugo Black frequently recounted a tale that makes the point. A jury in rural Alabama was called to try a poor farmer charged with stealing a mule from a rich one. The jury's first verdict was: "Not guilty, provided he returns the mule." The judge refused to accept the verdict, telling the jury that it was impermissibly conditional. The jury resumed deliberations and rendered a second verdict: "Not guilty, but he has to return the mule." When the judge again rejected the verdict, telling the jury that it was impermissibly contradictory, the jury came back with a third verdict, which the judge finally accepted: "Not guilty, let him keep the damn mule." One might perhaps view the outcome of the *Michael H.* case, discussed in the preceding chapter, as a sort of converse verdict—"Guilty, don't let him keep the mule"—rendered under similar, self-enforced constraints. At the end of the present chapter we will revert to this matter of the nature of adversarial storytelling and some of its implications.

The *endogenous* and the *plight-modeling* approaches are the two major ways of explaining narrative theoretically, insofar as theory attempts to account for narrativity in general rather than particular kinds or uses of narrative. One approach is principally *inside → out,* the other *outside → in.* Despite their seeming to be the classic "A and not-A," they might both be right.

Particular kinds and uses of narrative—theater, novels, or films; different genres like tragedy or comedy; storytelling on the psychoanalytic couch—have generated more theories than has narrative in general. Witness Aristotle's claim that the function of tragedy is to provide catharsis (a matter we'll visit again in Chapter 8), or Bergson's claim that the function of comedy is to reprove vanity and other separatist tendencies that threaten a society's adaptability, or Freud's claim that the function of storytelling for the neurotic is vicarious wish-fulfillment · and defense against the anxiety of self-discovery, or Eliade's claim that the function of myth is to validate the meaning of human existence by reiterating the primordial events that made humankind what it is today—"mortal, sexed, organized in a society, obliged to work in order to live, and working in accordance with certain rules."[25] Or consider the well-argued view that narrative fiction is *dramaturgic,* that its function is to create excitement, to explore the endlessness of desire, to mitigate boredom and dead certainty—particularly the ultimate dead certainty, death itself.[26] The very richness and variety of these mini-theories suggest that we are not likely soon to have a satisfactory "maxi-theory," capable of ordering the whole cosmos of narrative according to a single, harmonious plan. Certainly, the smaller theories of genres and their functions are the best that theorizing has been able to do so far, despite (or, a pessimist might say, because of) their localism, diversity, and incommensurability. For the extant general theories of narrative, its origins and functions, fall conspicuously short.

Their shortfalls are too numerous to canvass, but three of them are worth noting here because they play an important part in our own agenda.

The first is a shortfall regarding the whole crucial sphere of the *rhetorical.* As every classical rhetorician from Isocrates through Quintilian and from Seneca to Tertullian would have told you, a central problem of persuasion (and we'll propose for the moment that any good story must persuade, whatever else it does) is to find a way between being *convincing* or *believable* and being *true* or *truthlike.* But a storyteller must also find the way between *truth* and *excitement*, between *believability* and *epiphany*, between *truth* (or *believability*) and *desire*.[27] There is not a clue in any general theory of narrative about how to solve these navigation problems—or even about how to identify the rocks and whirlpools.

Second, there is a shortfall regarding *time*. Why are stories always about events extended over time, and why does the artfulness of their telling depend upon the management of timing within the telling itself—upon pace, plotting, interruption, suspense, foreshadowing, flashback, and all of the other manipulations of temporality that enter into a story's elaboration?[28] To say that storytelling comes naturally or models social plights does not begin to help us understand why it depends so fundamentally upon the manipulation of time as "the primary category of experience, the most important and fundamental aspect of life."[29]

And third, there is a shortfall with respect to *resolution*. This one is particularly important to legal storytellers. Our Austere Definition included the generalization that narratives arrive at a resolution which either restores the old steady state or legitimates a new one. But which of these will it be? The difference between a restorative resolution and a transformative one will often be the difference between a winning plaintiff's story and a winning defendant's story—between a legal ruling that entrenches old ways and a legal ruling that enables new ones. Our theoretical journey yields no clue on this matter—nothing about why some stories seem to do best by reaching for the new while others are made to glow by espousing the return to the immemorial.

So we must take the next step, perhaps a step back, and examine more minutely how narratives are made, particularly how they are purpose-built for different tasks, and with different kinds of bricks and scaffolds. This will bring us closer to the work of narratologists who strive to make sense of particular genres, variations, and situations of storytelling. And closer, too, to efforts to understand the various specializations of narrative—as in history, the law, and folklore.

III. The Narrative Forge

We need to look at the forge where narrative is hammered out. Why does it require those basic, essential features that we itemized so matter-of-factly in our Austere Definition? We want to explore how these features make a story and affect the overall structure of the story that gets told. This may help us to glimpse what narrative does to our fix on "reality," and through what means.

Ordinariness and Legitimacy

Narratives, we know, are deeply concerned with legitimacy: they are about threats to normatively valued states of affairs and what it takes to overcome those threats. In examining the subtle relation between the ordinary and the aberrant, it will be useful to keep in mind the distinction between *scripts*[30] and *narratives*.

Scripts embody normal expectations and normal practice in a culture; they capture the normal ways in which people go about and are expected to go about their ordinary daily lives: how to get a meal at a restaurant, how to plead before a court of law. Much of our background knowledge of the culture is organized in terms of such scripts. Even young children organize their expectancies by them.[31]

Some situations are ambiguous as to scripting—for instance, what you're supposed to say to an ex-spouse when you meet at the funeral of a mutual friend. Scripts eventually get established to cope with yesterday's social anomalies. Until they are established, the uncertainty itself provides fertile ground for storytelling: those stories about "whatever should one have done when . . ." that are the rootstock of the novel of manners. In Chapter 8, we'll explore the importance of such *script uncertainties* in the dynamics of cultural communities, how stories built around them reconnoiter possible worlds that are competing for a place in a culture's canon.

Established scripts (sometimes called *stock scripts*) are the hidden cargo in narratives, often tacit rather than explicit, but always there. Their presence is a precondition for narratives, which earn their right to be told only because some script has been breached or threatened with violation. You do not *tell* about a visit to the restaurant unless something not in the script occurs.[32] King Alfred hiding in that cottage is not worth telling about without his distractedly letting the muffins burn. His ruining the muffins, after the good lady has warned him to watch out for them, releases a range of possible narrative resolutions. Scripts, in short, embody the norms with whose violation narrative is preoccupied; and the first rule for anyone who wants to dig below the surface of a narrative is to get a good measure of the hidden cargo that is its underlying script—what norms the script embodies, what vicissitudes derail the script, and what consequences follow its derailment.

So, narrative takes its impetus from the breach (or from the possibility of the breach) of some script, and it holds its interest for us by confronting us with the question, "What may happen when the script goes awry?" *Narratives* serve to warn us of the ever-present dangers that beset our scripts, of the fragility of the ordinary. Yet, in two important ways, narratives also work to reinforce the scripts. First, narrative's very reminder of the inevitability that scripts will sometimes be broken is what enables the scripts to retain their coherence despite those breakings. Second, narrative has a way of domesticating the breakings themselves. Told often enough, any particular narrative version of norm-violation founds a tradition, becomes the kernel of a genre, of an accounting of "how the world is." Thus, the fateful ardor of the young leads Iseult to an illicit love affair with Tristan; and how then shall the lovers and the aging King Mark play out their tangled roles? In time, the Tristan-Iseult dilemma comes to be the formula for a recognizable type of narrative: it achieves its own sort of ordinariness as a *plight*. Unlike a script, it has no single, pat progression, no one-right-way of ending. It *explores* the store of possibilities inherent in this now-familiar plight. And in the process, links are forged between the unexceptional and the exceptional—scripts are breached, but nonetheless survive.[33]

The narrative form seems almost designed for such use. William Labov,[34] one of the outstanding students of the language of narrative, describes first-person oral narratives as beginning with a preamble setting forth or subtly implying the state of affairs legitimately to be expected by the protagonists in a story—and by the listener or reader as well. The preamble is followed by a reversal or threatened reversal of expectation (like Aristotle's peripeteia);[35] and this is followed in turn by the action of the story proper, leading either to the restoration of the initial state of things or to its replacement by another stable, steady state. Often this finale is followed by a coda, serving to bring the hearer back into the world of the present, and perhaps explicating the "moral" of the story.

As Labov notes, narrative forms develop distinctive, conventionalized linguistic styles. Thus, a story's preamble, reversal, action, and coda are typically differentiated linguistically in the telling—often quite subtly—to create an illusion of separateness. For example: "I was walking down this street in midtown, and this guy comes up to me and asks if I'm interested in buying some theories. So I said, 'Hey, what kind of proposition's that?'" Notice the shift in tense from past progressive to present as we go from the preamble, recounting an ordinary day's activity, to its reversal by a most extraordinary request; and then another shift to simple past tense for the start of the action. The deaf even place their signing hands in different positions to distinguish the preamble from the reversal, often returning to the start position for the coda. The reality of the ordinary "street in midtown," with its normative expectations, needs to be differentiated from the oddball offer of theories for sale. In time, genres develop not only conventionalized situations, but conventionalized ways of telling about them—which in turn can be violated to create the subtle shadings of meaning that Grice calls "implicatures."[36]

Affixing the stamp of the ordinary and the legitimate is a crucial part of historical narrative. Hayden White gives a striking précis of it, how historical accounts evolve from *annales* to *chronique* to *histoire*.[37] As one progresses from the bare chronological listing of events in the *annales* to the "rightful" doings of a ruler in the *chronique* to the legitimacies of a dynasty in the *histoire* or "history proper," the recounting becomes an increasingly realized story, making the historical normativity more explicit at each step.

Small wonder that narrative history withstands the claims of modern social science to reduce the past to a timeless theory. Timeless theory has no way of spelling out ordinariness and its breaches—except by indicating mean frequencies and variances. Statistics can tell us that we are in, say, the lowest quartile of income in the city; but only through narrative do we come to understand whether that is bad luck, a sign of personal fecklessness, or an injustice. Samuel Stouffer's atemporal "covering law"[38] about migration correlating with intervening opportunities will never replace the tales of pioneers on the Oregon Trail or Willa Cather's women on the Nebraska plains. "All the steam in the world could not, like the Virgin, build Chartres."[39] Narrative defines its cast of characters as agents or victims, gives their aspirations legitimacy (or not), looks at them in the light of a culture's time-tested scripts—scripts that set forth and exemplify the expectable order of things—and thus connects the happening of events over time into patterns that enact the culture's normative understanding of its people's straits and destinies.

Narrative Time

This is a vast subject;[40] we will only scratch the surface. Narrative time is not measured by clocks and calendars. Those can merely date the doings that a narrative takes as its beginning, middle, or end. What constitutes the beginning and the end and the plenum between them is defined by the story itself. Stories are about events, not minutes or hours. And the events are not found in nature but created by our telling; they are of our own making, fitted to the requirements of our narrative account. If an event *matters,* we dwell on it; we take longer to tell it than it could ever take to happen—as with Proust, for example, elaborating on that glance at the *madeleine.*

Thus, the temporal fabric of narrative reflects the shape of our concerns, not the metrical ticking away of seconds or days or centuries as a chronometer would count them. Consider Justice Kennedy's choice of time frame for his recounting of the history of school desegregation in *Freeman v. Pitts,*[41] or Chief Justice Rehnquist's account of the duration of the litigation in *Missouri v. Jenkins.*[42] In both cases, the opinions limited the powers of the lower federal courts to continue school-desegregation efforts; both opinions focused with impatience on *how long* the federal courts had taken to return the supervision of the public schools to local school boards; and Justice Rehnquist, for example, talked about *Jenkins* as a "school desegregation case enter[ing] its 18th year." But what, we may ask, could and should count as the beginning of the story in *Jenkins?* Are we to date it from the finding of Missouri's non-compliance with the Constitution, from the filing of the complaint, from the decision of *Brown v. Board of Education,* from the Emancipation Proclamation, or from the first days of importation of African slaves into the southern United States? Where one chooses to begin one's story is a part of the hidden-cargo script that defines what's to be taken as ordinary or as mattering in the narrative.[43]

So, in trying to decipher narrative time, we must bear in mind not only *what* is said about things in the world, but *how* it is said. In this, narrative again has natural language as its willing steward. Narrative's needs are miraculously met by language—so much so that some have even wondered whether grammar itself grew in response to our need to narrate. For one thing, language permits us to *mark* or structure time by devices that, for all their familiarity, are quite astonishing. Indeed, grammatical time marking literally invents human time.

Take *tense*. It uses "the present" as its anchor. *Within* that "present" is *the present tense*. And you are thereby obliged (though hardly aware of it) to invent a specious present. Suppose you have been involved in, say, a patent infringement litigation for eighteen months. You say in the present tense, "This is the damnedest case I've ever worked on." A little while later, you lean over to a colleague and say of some testimony given several seconds ago, "He was lying through his teeth"—in *the past tense*. The specious present is devised to frame time to the matter at hand—or more properly, to the matter in mind. Tense is our ally in the narrative humanization of time.

But it is only one ally. Take the sentence, "Yesterday as I was strolling down O'Connell Street, suddenly there is Buck Mulligan bearing down on me." There, in seventeen words, we've set forth a dense little temporal microcosm. Six of the words, a third of them, are time-marked. They are marked to tell about space-time relations (like *strolling*), about when things happened—but not quite that, for the *yesterday* and *was* are at the same time as the *is* in Buck Mulligan's appearing. *Is* is not so much tense as *aspect*, a subtle grammatical device that relates time to the progress of reference events.

And since narratives require beginnings, middles, and ends, *aspect* rather than *tense* may be what you want to attend to. Consider "He started for the village early, walking quietly from one familiar shop to another, until he found just the size carton he was looking for." Tense remains constant throughout; aspect relates events to the progress of the task at hand. The telltale phrase "until he found" brings time to its climax by binding everything to a quest. But remember too that there are ways to undo your aspect-created time, by introducing another aspect horizon. For example, when we look more closely at *Freeman v. Pitts* in the following chapter, we will notice the way in which the aspect-based *quest line* embodied in court-ordered desegregation is undermined by a counter-narrative about "inevitable" demographic "shifts" that have altered DeKalb County, Georgia, and annulled the desegregation quest along with human power to achieve it.

Language marking even provides a resource for hitching a time line to the relation between the teller of a tale, the hearer, and the people that the tale is about. This resource goes by the fancy name of *time deixis*. We use it all the time, as Moliere's bourgeois gentilhomme used prose. (There's also *space deixis:* I say *here* and *there* in conversation with somebody as relating to the space around me, not them. With the comparable *now* and *then* I have to be a little more careful to specify whose time frame I have in mind.)

Time deixis lets us do all sorts of canny things about time. Think about the difference in time between when I put something into words and when you finally receive and make sense of the message. When we're in face-to-face conversation, there is no difference, or very little. But consider the epistolary mode, telling stories by letter. You're on vacation in the Southwest, say, and write your friend, "I'm writing this while chewing peyote with an old acquaintance." And you continue, "You're doubtless thinking how reckless of me to be chewing peyote and hope I've stopped by now." Now add a story protagonist and consider this epistolary passage: "Jane will be furious when she hears that I've discussed this matter with you before consulting her."

No wonder clocks aren't much help to the narrator, except in providing background reference knowledge. And even then, the listener had better know when time is no more—as in those timeless utterances by which we proclaim that some initial state of affairs was presumed to be forever. The two-year-old whose bedtime monologues we studied—the famous "Emmy"[44]—was fond of telling rather swift-paced stories about her day's doings or imaginings. But then she might, in the midst of these, shift to the enduring regularities, usually marked in the *timeless present* of English: "Saturdays we have corn-bread." This might then be followed by the misadventures of, say, the preceding Saturday, carefully nuanced into what came first, next, and so on.[45]

Still, one must not be literal in parsing the order of time within narrative. Both Labov[46] and Propp[47] went too far in claiming that a story's "proposition" has to follow a fixed, sequential time order. A minimum set of ordered propositions might be:

The King died.
The Queen cried.

—with the narrative work being in the connection between the two. But what about prolepsis and analepsis (flashforward and flashback):

The Queen cried.
She couldn't get the King's death off her mind.
They were so happy together all those years.

Narrative is embedded in time, but it is time "in the head," not necessarily on the page or the screen.

Time-based narrative contrasts sharply with time-independent propositional thinking. "If p then q; and p" leads to q as a conclusion in a way that is timelessly and logically necessary. That is very different from the time-bound business of *narrative* necessity—there was nothing left for Oedipus to do in the end save tear out his eyes. Powerful narrative has the quality of leaving the hearer or reader uncertain about whether a story reaches, as it were, a timeless *logical* conclusion, or a time-bound *narrative* one. Neither is quite the whole of it because narrative necessity—the sense of the appropriateness or compellingness of a story as it reaches its resolution—is more than a function of an arrow of time moving toward its terminus. Narrative also has a logic-like internal consistency that is instinct in how its parts or constituents fit together. To deal with the nature of this fitness, we need to consider one more element in our account:

The Narrative Teleology of Human Striving

Stories go somewhere. They have an end, a *telos*. If someone drifts in telling a story, we urge him or her to "get to the point." What gives stories this "point" is that, just as they have a *telos*, they also have to do with some *obstacle* blocking progress toward it. If there is no obstacle, no Trouble, there is no story—only a recital of some happening that unfolded banally with nothing untoward to tell about.

A good story is one in which there is some appropriate *match* between a story's *telos* and the obstacle to its attainment. We cherish stories, for example, where the chief protagonist is "hoist with his own petard"—the special form of match that Aristotle identified with tragedy, one in which the very virtues of the hero end up causing his downfall.[48] Nobody, so far as we know, has ever come up with a convincing theory (or even a good rule of thumb) about what it is that makes a good match between *telos* and obstacle.

But it is sometimes claimed that one of the functions of a culture's mythology—its storehouse of *charter narratives*—is to create and conventionalize appropriate links between *telos* and obstacle. Heroes, for example, can be thwarted in their noble quest only by something or somebody equally extraordinary, bearing (to use a mathematical term) an opposite sign. It isn't exactly that mythic conventions need to be followed in matching *telos* and obstacle, but, rather, that these conventions will be in the minds of both storytellers and their hearers. They prefigure the kind of match-up that we expect.

Indeed, so goes the claim, we use these charter *telos*-obstacle match-ups even in "reading" our own experience, turning the quotidian into the stories we tell ourselves. Perhaps this is the route by which, in that hackneyed phrase, "life comes to imitate art." What makes this claim compelling is not only that intuitively it sounds right (or at least plausible), but that it draws a certain amount of support from some interesting research findings.

For example, even at eighteen months of age, children are sensitive to both *telos* and obstacle in the events around them. When they imitate an adult, they imitate what the adult was *trying to do,* not what the adult *did,* what actually *happened.* If an adult is trying to get a ball off a stick on which it's impaled but can't succeed, the kids imitate the action not as the adult being thwarted (which is what they saw), but as pulling the ball right off. They do not, for example, imitate the adult's frustrated yanking.[49] In another study, comparing how ten-year-olds, adolescents, and adults repeat a story told to them, we can observe conventionalization at work. The youngest ones concentrate almost exclusively on plot—i.e., the *telos* and its obstacle; and that's it. The adolescents embroider the plot with an inner landscape of subjectivity—how protagonists saw things and felt about them, moral stances, and the like. The adults take the next step: they retell the story as an example of a conventional genre, noting violations of genre as particular "unusual" features.[50] We most certainly come to recognize narrative necessities by the time we're grown—no surprise—but what is so intriguing is how early the process begins and how steadily it seems to progress.

Somewhere along the way we become quite sensitive, in particular, to imbalances and incongruities between *telos* and obstacle in the stories we hear. We know all too well when a story "has something missing," has "a weak ending," or "doesn't quite ring true." Stories that reach their resolution by the sudden intervention of a munificent, hitherto unmentioned rich uncle from Australia or Aristotle's god-in-a-car[51] are immediately dismissed as shallow or contrived. Stories in which Virtue Triumphs by the simple expedient of taking itself and nothing else seriously are rejected as melodrama—what Northrop Frye has called "comedy without humor"[52]—or mere moralizing. Stories in which the Trouble is wished away without being worked through leave us with the cloying discontent of premature closure.[53] In these and similar cases, our sense of fitness is offended by a manifest misalignment between *telos* and obstacle, between getting to the goal and what stands in the way. And it may well be that this sense of fitness is narrative in its origins as well as in its logic—that we learn it as much from stories as from life itself.

The Nature of Trouble

Trouble in narrative is not as simple as it sounds. In order to make a good story, Trouble needs not only the collision of *telos* and obstacle but some discernible coherence—what is sometimes called *systematicity* or orderedness. Random or fortuitous setbacks may not be uninteresting; but the only reaction they produce is likely to be "Tough luck, Jack." For narrativity, we seem to need an orderedness in Trouble.

Now, orderedness is easily defined in logic or grammar. In logic, when $A > B$ and $B > C$, it "follows" that $A > C$. Or in grammar, an anaphoric pronoun requires the same number marking as the noun for which it stands: "Confident that his *daughters* could be trusted to get on together, Smith made *them* joint trustees." But what about the orderedness of Trouble in narrative?

The great Vladimir Propp,[54] who virtually founded modern narrative studies, noted that events and protagonists in a folktale serve as "functions" of the tale as a whole. In other words, we understand that a hero is such by virtue of the role that he or she performs in the tale. But how does it come about that the tale-as-a-whole imposes its pattern or orderedness on everything within it? Including its Trouble?

Consider, for example, the stories one uses as *excuses*.[55] It would somehow be *wrong* to offer as an excuse for being late to dinner at a friend's that you were timing the red and green lights on the corner of Broadway and Bleecker—unless you mumble something to the effect that you happen to be working on a doctoral dissertation on traffic lights. Right narrative excuses give ordered justification to what might otherwise seem incomprehensible, "crazy," capricious, or random troubles. They supply "reasonable accountability," a notion that things are as they *ought* to be.

What about orderedness in other kinds of narrative? We can take instruction on that subject from Kenneth Burke,[56] another of the great figures in this century's study of narrative. He richly (but vaguely) characterized *dramatism* as deriving from an imbalance or misalignment among his five minimally required constituents of narrative—his famous "Pentad:" Agent, Act, Purpose (or Goal), Agency (or Means), and Scene. A disjunction between any of these produces Trouble, the engine of drama.[57] Trouble, then, may emerge when an Act toward a Goal is inappropriate in a particular Scene, as with Don Quixote's antic maneuvers in search of chivalric ends; when an Agent does not fit the Scene, as with K in Kafka's *The Trial* or with Nora at home in Ibsen's *A Doll's House;* or when an Agent's Goal seems hopelessly unattainable given the Means available, as in Jamaica Kincaid's touching *Annie John.*

These imbalances become even more "Troublesome," sometimes grotesquely so, in the high form of myth: Psyche is to take prototypically handsome Cupid as her lover, yes, but she must never look upon him in the light; Cassandra receives the gift of prophecy from Apollo, yes, but she is destined never to be believed. Trouble in both tales is further exaggerated by being nested in other Troubles. Cupid has been ordered by his mother, Venus, to infatuate Psyche with a monster because the girl's beauty has won her admiration as a "second Venus"; so Psyche must not discover who Cupid is lest Venus find out that instead of degrading Psyche, he has taken her as his beloved. Or Apollo, who has given Cassandra her gift of prophecy in an effort to seduce her, cannot take it back, and so must curse her with unbelievability. And violence must go on and on in the House of Atreus—Iphigenia at the hands of Agamemnon, Agamemnon at the hands of Clytemnestra, Clytemnestra done in by Orestes, and he by the Furies—until Athena cries "Enough" and creates a court of Athenians empowered to judge matters of blood-guilt for all time, under standards of Justice.

Excuse stories, then, domesticate Trouble—or try to; secular drama explores the forms and fates of Trouble and how mortals cope with them—or try to; mythic drama specializes in the inevitability of Trouble and its inescapability even among the gods. In each of these domains (and perhaps there is an endless number of them, each with its own genre conventions), Trouble takes off from what is canonical or moral or to be taken as the accepted and orderly set of things. And it is precisely that canonicity—which, as it were, locates Trouble in the world—that gives Trouble its orderedness and systematicity. So we can develop a shorthand, like lifers in prison who end up telling a fully elaborated story by just reciting its assigned number: we identify a form of Trouble, and a whole clutch of circumstances comes with it—Boyfriend Trouble; Trouble with the Bank; Trouble with the Boss; Marriage Trouble; Teenage Trouble.

Small wonder, then, that story is the favored form for teaching what Ought-to-Be, what is the Right Order, what is the likely agenda of Troubles. It serves that function still and has served it from the start, whether in technologically simpler cultures, or in the moral teaching of the classic Greek and Hebrew traditions.[58]

So, too, in the case of Trouble with the Law. Earlier in this chapter we mentioned the robust adversarial stories of prosecution and defense, and commented on how they grew out of traditional narrative stances. But the law is not *just* a contest of legal stories, the best-formed one the winner. Although well-formed stories go part of the way in court, Athena had her wish, too. There *is* a system that aims to do enduring justice; and if it isn't quite the Goddess's hoped-for Athens, it makes its own demands.

But we move too fast. We'll return to this matter further along. All we need to say now is that in discussing narrative, we seem to be grappling with something like a culture's canonical necessities.

The Fate of Protagonists

Narrative deals out fates to protagonists. Recall Amelie Rorty's[59] typology of narrative protagonists, Agents, as reflecting *idealized lives* in a culture. She distinguishes between *characters, figures, persons,* and *individuals*. On her view, they are "forms of life" inherent in a culture's world view, embodied and instantiated in its lore and myths.

A *character* is based on the Greek conception of a hero—known by his deeds and bound by a code. He needs no subjective unity, for he does not brood over alternative ways. He is, as it were, his necessary deeds. He suffers no identity crises: he is ineluctably what he is. A character embodies a particular set of circumstances in life; when these change, his plight is to lose his function. Achilles and Ajax are both characters.

Figures are characters writ large as figureheads to take their place in an unfolding drama. They exist to occupy a particular role—a Mary or Martha, a Che Guevara. They are neither formed by nor own their experience: they simply fill a place in a plot. Great figures, as Jaroslav Pelikan[60] has vividly illustrated in his study of what different eras have made of the Virgin Mary, are characteristically transmuted to fit the changing plot: they become figures for all future seasons.

Persons take their origin in the concept (common to law and drama) that there is a unified center of action and choice which is the locus of legal and moral responsibility. Persons are actors whose being is coextensive with their power to affect others. When they become conscious of their own acts, they develop selfhood. Trollope's novels are full of persons, many of whom have a degree of selfhood. They fill roles in a society—sometimes wittingly, sometimes unwittingly.

Individuals organize their actions around a sense of selfhood and often see themselves *versus* society, which is seen as binding or fettering their self-development.

We have scarcely done justice to Rorty, but this brief summary captures her point well enough for our purposes. Narrative, in a word, models a culture's conception of human character and its plights. Given any degree of imagination, it also explores the culture's counter-conceptions: its rogues and mountebanks and monks, its idiots and innocents, its renegades and regicides.[61] And it puts them on the same stage together—Quixote and Sancho Panza, Lear and his daughters, Jacques et Le Maître, Jakobowsky and the Colonel, even Laurel and Hardy—*characters, figures, persons,* or *individuals.* Perhaps that is why narrative is so penetrating a preview of moral possibility as well as of evil. Must Oedipus act out his characterhood and tear out his eyes? Or might he conclude (on learning who Jocasta really was) to shrug the whole thing off with "What the hell. Accidents happen. What can you do?"

This brings us to still another feature of a narrative's work:

Delineating Plights

We rarely hear a story but that we're reminded of one like it. We speak of "like" stories as genres. *Genre* is an elaborate topic. While no two stories are the same, some of them are more alike than others. We want to suggest, with the promise of elaborating on the matter in Chapter 8, that narrative genres are *mental models representing possible ways in which events in the human world can go.* They give body to—they virtually institutionalize—the possible worlds we believe to be open to us. They weave into a pattern the kinds of projections we've been discussing in the preceding sections—our culture's constructions of what is ordinary or legitimate, what is the structure of time, what are the ends of human striving, what are the shapes of human trouble, what are the forms that human character can take, and more. All together, these amount to a kind of inventory of the humanly possible, the range of a culture's plights. Perhaps it is because they have the power to expand the boundaries of possibility that the invention of new literary or political or legal genres is so important— again, a matter that we will take up in Chapter 8. For just as a paradigm-breaking scientific theory opens a new way of conceiving the world of nature, a new genre provides a new way of conceiving human plights.

Greek tragedy, as we saw earlier, provided a way of conceiving of a protagonist's virtue precipitating his downfall. Its roots were deep in classical Greek culture. The Chancery clerks in England captured their times by formulating writs that defined what (as we would now say) were justiciable matters—genres of actionable disputes. Laurence Sterne, it is said, created a new human possibility by starting a genre of consciousness with *Tristram Shandy.* Perhaps Ionesco and Genet launched new possibilities with their creation of the theater of the absurd. Breaking established genres and creating new ones is a major force in changing cultures, in changing legal systems, in opening new worlds.

So, in effect, we have come to think of genres as tools of narrative problem-solving applicable not only to the making of fiction (as the familiar literary genres are usually supposed to be) but also to the shaping of human encounters in the small and institutional arrangements in the large. To return to an earlier question, this may give us some hint as to why certain narratives drive to certain endings and not others—why the right ending for some tales is restorative of an anterior steady state, while the right ending for other tales is transformative. Some long-established genres feature the inexorable unfolding of human destiny, while others, almost as ancient, celebrate the agentive exploitation of human possibility. The tragic hero has no choice but to succumb to what has been forever fated: he *is* his plight. The hero in Greek New Comedy, on the other hand, must win through and found a new order because the *cognitio*—the essential comic moment of discovery or reconstitution—ever beckons up ahead.

One of us has commented elsewhere[62] on the shift from an *ideology of fate* to an *ideology of the possible* that characterized the transformation of European thought from the Age of Faith to the Age of Reason. It amounted to a shift in "genre addiction," as one might call it, a new addiction related to a new conception of the world. We suspect that shifts of this kind are constantly in progress and that one of the ways of spotting them is by looking at how we deploy our narrative gifts not only in fiction, but in the conduct of the law. If we are to rescue consciousness from its slavish attraction to banality, "to make the familiar strange again," in Viktor Shklovsky's renowned motto for the poet,[63] then perhaps we can do the same for the law by considering it in its narrative guise.

IV. The Rhetoric of Narrative

The law abounds in *rhetorical narratives*: pleadings, stories told to persuade somebody to believe something or to do something, partisan briefs and arguments. By way of a preliminary, note that rhetorical narratives have a few basic features in common, whatever their aim or audience—whether they are spun to convince a judge on the bench or a lawyer across the bargaining table, to reassure a hesitant client, or (in either a legal or a non-legal setting) to persuade a listener for any reason that a particular version of events is "the way it happened."

Rhetorical narratives use a story rather than a set of propositional assertions to *prove* something persuasively. "The proof is in the pudding," the rhetorical story implicitly proclaims, while it serves up fare far spicier than pudding. As a homey example, a lawyer might urge a client to buy life insurance like this:

> "You know, most of us in our early and middle years like to push aside possibilities that anything seriously damaging will ever happen to us. Well, my roommate in law school was one of those real Type A strivers—made the editorial board on the law review, went with one of the big, high-powered firms, married a very nice sculptor and they had a couple of lovely kids. And he just went on gung-ho working his eighty-

hour week, thinking all the while his pension and his savings would look after everything. We all do it. Then the inevitable: a heart attack at 42, and gone two years later. It was a real blow. Fortunately, her family had a little money, but it was pretty bad anyway. She had to give up her sculpturing; the kids had to change schools; and you can imagine the rest. Let me tell you most of us aren't that much smarter. It's easy to say that he would have been much wiser if he'd thought about it in advance and gotten a life policy when it was cheap. But most of us are like that. It's really worth thinking about, even if it's something we'd rather push out of consciousness."

Narrative persuasion is plainly not just a logical demonstration in the form: *All human beings die; you are a human being; therefore you are mortal; face it; buy life insurance.* We convert our telling into some sort of "higher common sense" by *personalizing* it, playing on the hearer's *identification,* giving it a vivid *time arrow,* and the rest. To paraphrase the adage about well-wrought fiction, good narrative leads to the suspension of disbelief—and thus serves the ends of rhetoric very well indeed.

We'll examine the complexities of rhetoric in Chapter 6, but some preliminary remarks about the rhetorical side of narrative should be made now. For there are a few matters, often either overlooked or trivialized in popular discussion, that need to be kept in mind in reading the two Supreme Court cases discussed in Chapter 5.

The first has to do with what might be called the value-laden nature of stories. We can take a hint on this score from William Labov, whose work on narrative we discussed earlier in the chapter. Recall that he distinguished between the preamble of a story, in which the ordinary or expected state of things is set out (or implied), and the part that goes on to tell about the precipitating incident that brings that ordinariness into question. He notes that it is the contrast between the two that lends a story its implicit *evaluation:* "I rightly expected this, but instead I got that." The implicit evaluation of things is a crucial element in the rhetoric of storytelling—like our lawyer laying out the cautionary insurance tale.

But this feature of narrative structure is far more powerful than just as a device for convincing people to *do* something. It is the means, par excellence, by which a story shapes reality. It can be found in all novels that have, as we say, some sort of "moral message." James Joyce, intent on awakening readers to the epiphanies of ordinariness, crafts the stories in his *Dubliners* with that rhetorical end always just below the surface. Even a streetcar ride becomes oddly mysterious in his hands. Herman Melville, possessed by the contradictions inherent in authority, casts Captain Vere in *Billy Budd* in the plight of having to try the angelic Billy for killing the satanic Claggart. Even postmodern novelists, with their proclaimed distaste for "plot," contrive to tell their story in a way that undermines the reader's faith in narrative itself.

So, too, in Justice Holmes's famous *Lochner* dissent,[64] where he leaves us not just with his view of *this* case, but of what he takes to be the judicial role under the Constitution. The right of a New York bakery worker to a less-than-ten-hour workday is the *vehicle,* not the *destination,* of his dissent. The vehicle is fitted to get to its destination. And this must be so because, as Holmes himself says, a judge's decision "will depend on a judgment or intuition more subtle than any articulate major premise."[65]

The second matter has to do with tailoring a story to suit an audience—as old an art as there is.[66] The only fresh thing to report on this subject is that it is now widely believed among linguists and students of discourse processes that the most critical aspect of fitting story to audience is not "buttering them up" or "talking down" to them à la Dale Carnegie, but *entering into dialogue* with them—a particularly difficult feat in, say, filing a brief or writing a book. But it is perhaps not all that impossible. For much has been learned about the language, the tropes, the "styles" of dialogic discourse. The gist of it is that without the feel and substance of *intersubjectivity* characteristic of back-and-forth discourse, rhetorical "tailoring" for an audience becomes empty and seems "false."[67] The rather wry conclusion of this work has to be that the best way to fit one's story and its message to an audience is to get some good sense of what your audience has in mind. Doubtless this is why research tools like "focus groups" have become so popular with political storytellers; they are a step beyond Aristotle's efforts to read an audience's mind on the basis of his character studies of old men and young ones (like the pity of the young rising from their humanity; the pity of the old, from their weakness).[68]

A third matter has to do with conventionality—what we have been referring to as *canonicity.* This is a concept that will concern us centrally in our discussion of the dialectic of culture in Chapter 8. Its bearing on the rhetoric of narrative is powerful but not simple. On the one hand, the advocate who can couch his or her argument in the form of a canonical tale is ordinarily a long way toward persuading the auditor that the outcome of the tale should be the familiar, expected ending.[69] On the other hand, canonicity has an interesting—indeed, amusing—vulnerability. A point we shall develop later is that while conventional ways of doing things (including administering the law) become firmly entrenched in the institutional routines of a culture, they also become "sitting ducks" for contrarians. The canon easily becomes a target not only for well-reasoned dissent—and how could it not, given the contending values that characterize human societies?—but also for all the doubt-generating tropes that dissenters can muster. Not so surprising then, that wit and humor often become the dissenter's sharpest arrows against the canon. After all, their main object is not so much to *create* belief but to *destroy* it. As in Arthur Koestler's witty anti-clerical tale about a certain French Marquis who, arriving home unexpectedly, finds his wife in bed with the local Bishop. The Marquis walks to the doors leading out onto the balcony, steps out, and proceeds to make the sign of the cross over the people passing below. "What are you doing?" his wife cries out. "Ah," he replies, "the Monseigneur is performing my function . . . so I am performing his."[70] This sort of lampooning role reversal is not unknown even in such august tribunals as the Supreme Court of the United States. Consider, for example, Justice Frankfurter's put-down of the urbane John W. Davis, during the 1952 oral argument of the school desegregation cases that produced the Court's decision in *Brown v. Board of Education*. Davis, arguing in defense of the southern states' right to maintain separate schools for white and African-American children, contends that the Equal Protection Clause of the Fourteenth Amendment must be construed according to its original 1868 understanding, which did not contemplate racially mixed schools. He concedes that "changed conditions may bring things within the scope of the Constitution which were not originally contemplated," and he says that "perhaps the aptest illustration is the interstate commerce clause," which was read as including forms of commerce unknown to the Constitution's framers; but, so far as Equal Protection goes, he insists that changed circumstances "do not alter, expand, or change the language that the framers . . . have employed." This exchange follows:

Justice Frankfurter: "Mr. Davis, do you think that 'equal' is a less fluid term than 'commerce between the states'?"
Mr. Davis: "Less fluid?"

Justice Frankfurter: "Yes."
Mr. Davis: "I have not compared the two on the point of fluidity."
Justice Frankfurter: "Suppose you do it now."[71]

Or consider, once again, Justice Holmes's biting dissent in *Lochner*.

A last preliminary matter touching rhetorical narrative has to do with the *believability* of stories—the persistent and ancient problem of verisimilitude. It is a problem that can, and has, filled volumes. What, indeed, makes a story "truthlike" even when we know it to be fiction?[72] Surely, as William James so eloquently argued a century ago, there is some deep-seated human "will to believe," or, as we would put it today, some human "effort after meaning."[73] What we know, and what we have known forever, is that there are many routes to belief, some of them quite specific to believing stories. The paths of logic and familiarity are, of course, two of the super-highways; but human beings also have a remarkable capacity to believe many things that do not conform either to their rules of logical reasoning or to their experience of the world.[74]

What is most striking, and most puzzling, is that the believability of stories seems to have a twofold specification, a kind of double-entry accounting system—one relating to the *teller* and the other to the *tale* told, the source and the text. Hence the infamous "usually reliable sources" in the press's attribution. Such "reliability" is classically related to two oddly disjoint characteristics of tellers: sincerity and competence.[75]

Sincerity, in contemporary common sense, is contrasted with self-interest, and is considered a gift requiring objectivity or dispassion. One's impression of another's sincerity is undermined by signs of a hard sell or over-heated rhetoric, by any conspicuous show of tailoring story to audience, or even of hedging one's bets by ambiguity. The teller, of course, can fall back on the second-order strategy of keeping these efforts as undetectable as possible—argue your story convincingly, but not *so* convincingly as to drown it out with the sound of a grinding axe. Thus did Aristotle, Cicero, and Quintilian, among many other instructors on classical rhetoric, emphasize the indispensability of art's concealing art.[76] We will come back to this maxim, as it plays itself out in legal discourse, in Chapter 6.

But there is a deeper issue lurking underneath those classical rhetors' canny advice. As Lionel Trilling reminded us some years ago, "sincerity" itself is a construct grounded in the values of a particular culture at a particular time.[77] He observed, for example, that the French believed that sincerity implied facing up to one's concealed moral delinquencies and confessing them, while the English required only that a person "communicate without deceiving or misleading," maintain "a single-minded commitment to whatever dutiful enterprise he may have in hand," and "be oneself . . . in deeds." Americans, Trilling suggested, were less class-conscious, more other-oriented, so they "shaped their speech not by the standards of a particular class or circle but by their sense of the opinion of the public."[78] But if *being sincere* is culture-specific, it is also occasion-specific within a given culture—forbidding, say, any deliberate factual misrepresentation in declarations between traders, any ulterior motive in declarations between partners, any inexplicit shifting of premises in declarations between philosophers, or any lapse from total devotion in declarations between lovers.

As for competence—the second warrant of a teller's credibility—it looms particularly large in a knowledge-driven, technological society like ours. "A physicist I know told me that some version of Three Mile Island or Chernobyl can happen anywhere in America." Compare that with "A conservationist friend of mine told me . . ." To be sure, sincerity and competence are confounded in this example: conservationists are usually seen as lacking objectivity, in contrast to physicists. Yet it is certainly the physicist's presumed competence that invests his or her scare story with its peculiar credibility,[79] its almost priestly infallibility.[80]

We began our observations on the believability of stories by noting that it is rooted in both the teller and the told. We shall put off our consideration of the latter—the text itself—until Chapter 6, where we deal with rhetorics more generally. For stories derive their convincing power from both narrative and rhetorical resources; and although the two are interdependent, it would be too complicated to discuss them both at once.

V. Narrative and Law

We want to return finally to the intimate link between narrative and law, a matter we have touched on several times. Why does narrative seem so essential to the practice of the law—to conducting litigation and negotiation, to imaginative legal counseling, to establishing the continuity of a line of precedent or simply justifying a judicial holding, and especially to breathing new meaning into time-worn doctrine or launching a new line of reasoning?

It is not enough to say that since law is about troubles and their management, it turns naturally to narrative, recognizing narrative's singularity in elucidating Trouble. That is part of the reason for law's resort to narrative, surely, but there is also something deeper going on.

Law is one of society's means for maintaining continuity in value judgments across time and changing conditions. It does not encompass *all* value judgments but is centrally concerned with those that are seen as affecting the stability of a community—including the criteria for determining which ones these are. Such value judgments must evolve through a process of repeated applications in which they are simultaneously reaffirmed and tested, made to fit anew through mutation and thereby preserved. So it is the nature of the *corpus juris* to prescribe general rules about what is permissible and impermissible in delineated spheres of human activity and to establish institutions and procedures for constantly instantiating those rules with reference to specific cases.

It does not matter what theory one holds about the origination of the rules—whether they are thought to derive from a body of "natural law" through the exercise of reason, or to represent the commands of a sovereign (or some other authority legitimated politically or historically), or to be formulated pragmatically in such a way as to keep cycles of vengeance from spinning out of control, or to harden a society's conventional values once its people have undergone diaspora and can no longer negotiate those values face-to-face. Thoughtful students of jurisprudence have taken each of these views, and more. But whatever law's *primum mobile* may be, law could not operate without a means of going from its generalities to the particularities of individual cases. For however grand and majestic is the law in general, *law must also be in the small.*

The grand and majestic may be embodied in the supposedly eternal truisms of the common law ("memory runneth not to the contrary") or in the ringing aphorisms penned by ancestral Founding Figures on some symbolic occasion in a distant past ("due process of law"; "equal protection of the laws"). But the individual cases to which these timeless, abstract principles must be applied are here and now, often painfully particular.

Narrative in its very nature makes it *humanly* possible to relate the Grand and Timeless Principles of a *corpus juris* to the current particularities of the cases we adjudicate or arbitrate or negotiate, or those in which we help our clients comprehend the circumstances of their lives within the framework of the law or vice versa. "Humanly" possible, because it is through narrative that we provide humanly, culturally comprehensible justifications for our principled decisions and opinions. It is through narrative, rather than through some impeccable, impersonal argument from first precepts, that we show how or why the plaintiff's or the defendant's case is to be judged as we judge it. Narrative's inherent structure fits it for this task.

For one thing, narrative is a mode of discourse that takes directly into account the normative element upon which law is based—the existence of a legitimate, canonical state of things that has been complicated by some human action in some particular context or setting. Narrative takes for granted—indeed, takes it as a necessary condition—that in human affairs, the actors are agents whose acts are in some significant way under their own responsible control. Narratives require and provide an accounting of the justifiability of those acts that are alleged to have violated the legitimate expectations of another party or of the community. And in its very nature, narrative requires resolution.

Narrative, moreover, differs from purely logical argument in that it takes for granted that the puzzling problems with which it deals do not have a single "right" solution—one and only one answer that is logically permissible. It takes for granted, too, that a set of contested events can be organized into alternate narratives and that a choice between them may depend upon perspective, circumstances, interpretive frameworks. In a word, it leaves room for the possibility that things have changed. It is this feature of narrative that makes it invaluable in relating the past to the present and the abstract to the particular.

As Ronald Dworkin[81] has remarked, a line of precedent is like a continuing story, with the links between its continuing episodes forged as much by metaphor and analogy as by any strictly logical derivation from first principles. The *separate but equal* doctrine of *Plessy v. Ferguson* is replaced by an *equality of opportunity* doctrine in *Brown v. Board of Education* on the ground that the former cannot keep the Fourteenth Amendment's promise of "equal protection" under twentieth-century conditions but the latter might. Narrative continuity is maintained, however much the once-subtle reasoning of *Plessy* is rejected.[82]

One more general observation before we, too, get down to cases in the next chapter: There is a well-known claim—perhaps as controversial as it is well-known—that a people's mode of thinking is powerfully influenced (if not determined) by the structure of the language they use for communicating their thoughts. It is variously known as the Humboldt Principle or the Whorf-Sapir hypothesis.[83] In its trivialized form, the hypothesis is taken to mean, say, that if an Eskimo tribe has twenty different words for kinds of snow, its members experience twenty different kinds of snow. The weakness of this argument, of course, is that it fails to take account of the many ways in which human languages can use circumlocutions and metaphors: "snow that falls like feathers," for instance. Nonetheless, Benjamin Lee Whorf, who was a high-ranking insurance executive as well as an after-work linguist, offered many examples of linguistically constituted circumstances producing real-life disasters—like the case of the factory workers who should have known better but threw their still-lit cigarettes into an "empty" barrel that had recently contained an explosively flammable chemical. The consequences were predictably dreadful, including the size of the insurance claim; Whorf argued that the word *empty* had produced the disaster.

The question that we want to raise before passing on is whether law's dependence upon narrative for the conduct of its discourse may not produce a kind of Whorfian effect. Is there a Whorfian tendency to overemphasize the role of agency rather than circumstances, fault rather than unindictable conditions, intent rather than cultural conscription? The question goes beyond the obvious potential of narrative conventions to produce distortion in the interpretive work of the law through their stereotyped plots, stock characters, and potted situations. More broadly, one must wonder whether the inherent *drama* of narrative tends also to over-dramatize legal thinking in a manner out of keeping with law's function as a cooler of conflict. While it may be true that "hard cases make bad law," they make very good theater. So, do the ways of thought promoted by a histrionic tendency warp the systems of law into which they find their way? We shall have occasion to revisit this troubling matter in Chapters 8 and 9 when we discuss the noetic space that a culture and its myths create.

CHAPTER FIVE

Narratives at Court

Prigg v. Pennsylvania and *Freeman v. Pitts*

The two Supreme Court decisions that we examine in this chapter—
Prigg v. Pennsylvania[1] and *Freeman v. Pitts*[2]—are separated by 150
years. In the manner of the annalists, we might set them in a chronological sequence like this:

1788   United States of America established by adoption of
Constitution. Art. IV, sect. 2, cl. 3 says persons held to service or
labour in one State escaping to another should not be freed but
returned when claimed.

1842   *Prigg v. Pennsylvania* decided. Justice Story's leading
opinion holds that the federal Congress has exclusive power to
regulate rendition of runaway slaves and that Pennsylvania's law
punishing the abduction of negroes into slavery is void.

1868   Article XIV of Amendments to the Constitution ratified.
Sect. 1 says no State shall deny any person the equal protection
of the laws.

1954   *Brown v. Board of Education* decided. Chief Justice
Warren's opinion for the Court holds that the Fourteenth
Amendment forbids the States to maintain racially segregated
public schools.

1992   *Freeman v. Pitts* decided. Justice Kennedy's opinion for the
Court holds that federal judges should give up supervising pupil
assignment in school systems where African-American children

remain isolated in separate schools if the isolation results from demographic shifts not attributable to official state policy.

These annals obviously omit much that is important. So will the following pages. They examine Story's *Prigg* opinion and Kennedy's *Pitts* opinion as narrative constructions. They do not examine the opinions' legal reasonings, psychological motivations, political and sociological settings, agendas, or results.[3]

Our object is to learn what we can discover by reading these judicial opinions as stories.[4] We do this in the spirit of our purpose—and of Shklovsky's challenge, mentioned toward the end of the preceding chapter—"to make the familiar strange again." We want particularly to invite law-trained readers to look at the opinions in *Prigg* and *Pitts* from a narrative perspective *because* it is an unfamiliar perspective, beyond the standard range of ways of reading judicial opinions in which lawyers have been incessantly drilled. As for the non-lawyers among our readers, perhaps they will be struck by the classical, almost timeless quality of legal opinions written to deal with particular cases in particular places at particular times.

Be forewarned that among the things we'll discover are parallels between the structures of our two judicial texts and those of some of the founding narratives of the Western literary canon. We trust that you will understand what we are *not* implying by observing these parallels. We are not suggesting that Justice Kennedy copied Aeschylus or that Justice Story copied Homer knowingly or unknowingly—that some Freudian vulture of a plot lurks beneath the Leonardo's surface of their prose—or that their opinions participate (whether in the transcendental manner of Jung or in the manner that contemporary literary criticism calls "intertextual") in the great myths of Agamemnon and Helen of Troy.[5] Nor are we suggesting a mode of narrative analysis that, as Barbara Herrnstein Smith once warned, ends by making "all stories [turn] . . . out to be versions of *Cinderella*" or by making *Cinderella* "turn out to be basically all stories."[6] We imply nothing more than that judicial opinions, like other texts, contain the world of which they speak and, by impressing their structure on it, create it in their image.[7] In Chapter 4 we saw that narrative offers a unique store of resources for this kind of world-making.[8] So now let us assume *arguendo*—simply to explore where the assumption may lead us— that judges writing opinions may be using these very resources, just as literary storytellers[9] and historians[10] do, and as lawyers arguing cases can.[11] On the assumption that a judicial opinion may employ narrative means to create its distinctive world, what worlds do the *Prigg* and *Pitts* opinions create? And how do they go about doing it?

I. The Plot Outlines

Tracked summarily and stripped of legal material, the opinions unfold this way:[12]

Justice Story's *Prigg* Opinion

Prigg was charged with violating a Pennsylvania statute by abducting a Negro woman from Pennsylvania to Maryland with the intention of causing her to be kept as a slave. At trial the jury found these facts by a special verdict: The Negro woman was a slave in Maryland. She escaped and fled to Pennsylvania. Prigg, as agent of the woman's master, had the woman apprehended as a fugitive and taken before a Pennsylvania magistrate, but the magistrate refused to act. Prigg then removed the woman to Maryland and delivered her to her master.[13]

Upon this special verdict, the trial court convicted Prigg. Pennsylvania's highest court affirmed. The States of Pennsylvania and Maryland cooperated cordially in conducting the case in the Pennsylvania courts and bringing it to the Supreme Court of the United States, so that the Supreme Court could resolve questions that had interrupted the harmony between them and that they had failed to solve despite their own well-intended efforts at accommodation.[14]

The question posed is whether the Pennsylvania statute is unconstitutional. Its unconstitutionality is asserted on three grounds: that Congress has the exclusive power to regulate the rendition of fugitive slaves; that if any concurrent power exists in the state legislatures, it was suspended by Congress's enactment of the Fugitive Slave Act in 1793; and that, in any event, the provisions of the 1793 Act conflict directly with and invalidate the Pennsylvania statute. These are extraordinarily delicate and important issues, in which the public may be presumed to feel a profound and pervading interest.[15]

The issues presented cannot be resolved by general principles because the Constitution has no uniform logic; it is a practical historical instrument whose provisions embodied various compromises.[16] The provision concerning fugitives from labor was designed to secure the property rights of citizens of the slaveholding States against intermeddling by the non-slaveholding States, and these rights were so vital to the preservation of the domestic concerns of the slaveholders that the Union could not have been formed without such a provision.[17] In its absence, the non-slaveholding States could have immunized runaway slaves from the claims of their masters, a course destructive to the slaveholding States and sure to generate bitter animosities and perpetual strife between States.[18]

To avert this outcome, the framers of the Constitution unanimously adopted the very Clause whose meaning is now contested between Maryland and Pennsylvania. And how is the Court to interpret this Clause? So as to effectuate its object.[19] After full examination, Story can only conclude that it confers exclusive power on the Legislature of the Union to regulate the rendition of fugitive slaves; that Congress has exercised this power; and that Pennsylvania may not interfere in any aspect of the subject.[20] Thus is the controversy between it and Maryland resolved in accordance with the foresight of the framers: Pennsylvania's statute and Prigg's conviction must fall. It is not for a non-slaveholding State to punish as an abduction "the very act of seizing and removing a slave by his master, which the Constitution of the United States was designed to justify and uphold."[21]

Justice Kennedy's *Pitts* Opinion

DeKalb County, Georgia, is a major suburban area of Atlanta. Its school system, serving 73,000 students, is one of the nation's largest. For more than 20 years, it has been subject to supervision by a federal district court. A generation after the initial court order designed to integrate the system's public schools, the court finally decided to relinquish control over some aspects of school business, while retaining authority over others. But an appellate court refused to allow this gradual phasing out of federal judicial control.[22]

Before *Brown v. Board of Education*,[23] the DeKalb County school system was segregated by law.[24] It did little to desegregate through 1968, when the Supreme Court in *Green v. New Kent County School Board*[25] informed segregated school districts that delay would no longer be tolerated.[26] Immediately after *Green*, African-American children and their parents filed the present lawsuit; the school district set to work to devise a comprehensive, final desegregation plan; and the court ordered the plan into effect in 1969 with consent of all the parties. During the next 17 years, the African-American plaintiffs sought little additional judicial action and no significant changes in the student-assignment features of the plan.[27] The court tinkered with the plan in minor regards.

In 1986, the School Board sought to have the litigation dismissed with a declaration that it had fulfilled its duty to desegregate. The district court agreed that the Board had achieved almost complete desegregation. The court therefore withdrew from overseeing certain aspects of the Board's affairs (including all student-assignment matters) but retained control over other aspects (including teacher and principal assignments) and ordered the Board to cure the problems remaining in the latter areas.[28]

The district court based its ruling on an assessment of the current situation in the DeKalb County schools. It made an extensive record. One fact stands out: by 1986 the School Board and the court were confronted with a very different student population from the one they had set out to integrate 17 years earlier in 1969.[29] The difference was produced by dramatic changes in demographic patterns[30]—changes complex in their nature and causes[31] and particularly difficult to work with[32] because of their complicated interrelationship with the myriad details involved in planning and administering a large school system.[33]

Despite these problems, the School Board had taken action after action to combat the adverse effects of demographic changes on the racial mix of the schools and thereby to preserve the desegregated status attained for at least a short period under the 1969 plan.[34] Although the African-American plaintiffs contended that desegregative techniques not deployed by the Board would have done a better job, the district court concluded otherwise, finding the Board's expert witnesses more reliable. The court specifically found that the Board had gone to great lengths to achieve maximum practical desegregation;[35] that any remaining shortcomings were not due to the Board's lack of efforts but were inevitable in the face of demographic changes;[36] and that, while there would always be something more that could be done to improve the education of African-American students, the Board had worked innovatively to enrich the academic potential of all students and had targeted many remedial programs in the predominantly African-American schools.[37] The district court accordingly discontinued its supervision over some—not all—aspects of the Board's affairs.[38]

But a federal court of appeals rejected this incremental approach and held that the lower court must continue to supervise all aspects of the DeKalb County system and must order administratively awkward, inconvenient, even bizarre remedies to correct racial imbalances produced by demographic shifts.[39]

After full examination, the Supreme Court could only conclude that the Court of Appeals had got it wrong[40] and that the district court should be permitted to go forward with its plan for using incremental means together with a phased withdrawal to achieve the twin objectives of *Brown v. Board of Education*—to eliminate racial discrimination in the public schools[41] and to return the system thus desegregated to the control of responsible local authorities.[42]

II. The Orientations: Setting the Scenes

In Chapter 4 we mentioned the importance of the preamble that often precedes the action of a narrative. In many narratives, the preamble contains an orientation or an abstract featuring a *display of tellability*.[43] The display of tellability enlists the listener's or reader's attention by connecting the tale being told to the occasion of the telling. If the narrative is designed to have implications for action, they will often be embedded in (and can sometimes be discerned from) this connection. So when a narrator is telling you a story and starts by saying, *Before I begin, let me just note . . .,* beware.

Justice Story's *Prigg* opinion does this *twice*. His first "[b]efore proceeding" passage notes prefatorily that the case at bar "has been brought here by the co-operation of the State of Maryland and the State of Pennsylvania, in the most friendly and courteous spirit, with a view to have [the] . . . questions [presented] finally disposed of by the adjudication of this court, so that the agitations on this subject in both States, which have had a tendency to interrupt the harmony between them may subside. . . ."[44] It adds that Pennsylvania had tried unilaterally to accommodate Maryland's wishes but only made the situation worse.[45]

The *Prigg* case is thus *about* a conflict between two governmental entities, both well-intended and cooperative, who can't get their act together without help from the organs of the Union established by the Constitution. People—individuals—are not on the game board. The game is harmonizing relations between the States.

That game must be played by interpreting the Constitution of the Union. And here comes Story's second "[b]efore . . . we proceed" passage. This says that in interpreting the pertinent part of the Constitution, the Court will eschew "rules of interpretation of a more general nature."[46] It will resolve the problem at hand without committing itself to principles that may impact any other part of the Constitution—a flexible approach particularly prudent in view of "the known historical fact that many of [the Constitution's] . . . provisions were matters of compromise of opposing interests and opinions."[47] (Later, Story will describe the Fugitive Slave clause as a "practical necessity"[48] designed to avoid "the most bitter animosities, and . . . perpetual strife between the different States,"[49] and "a fundamental article, without the adoption of which the Union could not have been formed.")[50]

The tale to be told then, is how the States came together to form a Union to guarantee harmonious relations between them; and this tale is being told on the occasion of a disharmony resulting from the inability of the States to work out a practical mutual accommodation despite their best cooperative efforts. "Before . . . proceeding" to the content of the tale, can you doubt the ending? Is any other ending possible than that the Congress of the United States—the organ of the Union which is best equipped to manage the political and practical task of averting "perpetual strife" arising from "opposing interests and opinions" among the States—has and suitably exercises an exclusive jurisdiction over the problem of fugitive slaves?

The orientation of Justice Kennedy's *Pitts* opinion is more straightforward. It consists of an ostentatiously conventional statement-of-the-facts and follows an ostentatiously business-like abstract. We say that the statement-of-the-facts is conventional because it follows the cookbook recipe for setting out the facts at the beginning of a judicial opinion. We say that it is ostentatious because it flaunts the fact that it is doing so—by supplying separately labeled subsections that recite the procedural history of the case and then summarize the evidence;[51] by introducing the evidence subsection with the emphatic commentary that "Proper resolution of any desegregation case turns on a careful assessment of its facts";[52] and by appearing to spell out the evidentiary facts in meticulous detail. Within this framework, the information conveyed—a dense array of statistics laced with tag labels saying that the statistics are about "radical demographic changes"[53] and "demographic shifts"[54]—does not seem out of place; and it seems altogether fitting that the prose reads exactly like an educational consultant's report to a school board about the difficulties of maintaining racially balanced schools in the face of shifting residential patterns. The management-promoting tone is highlighted by what we have called the opinion's ostentatiously business-like abstract, for this is nothing more or less than a standard-form executive summary.[55] When the opinion finally comes to an explicit discussion of the merits of the case, we will not be surprised to discover that the Court deems "facts" of this texture to be far more suitable for administrative decisionmaking than for judicial contemplation.

III. Casting: Putting the Players Onstage

To continue reading the opinions as stories, we must next consider whom they are about—who counts as a player in the events discussed. For both opinions, the plot outlines suggest that the principal players are not individuals or groups of human beings but governmental entities: the United States, the States, their organs, subdivisions, and agents. *People* do not figure prominently in these plots.

The full extent to which governmental players dominate the scene becomes apparent only through a detailed examination of the entire text of each opinion. The Appendix found on page 293 contains such an examination.[56] It analyzes the frequencies of nouns and verbs referring to human and governmental beings and their actions in the *Prigg* and *Pitts* opinions[57] and—for comparison—in Chief Justice Warren's 1954 opinion declaring public school segregation unconstitutional in *Brown v. Board of Education I*.[58] The results are striking. We summarize just a few of them here.

Taking all of the nouns that refer to people and to governmental entities in *Prigg, Pitts,* and *Brown,* we can divide them into four groups—nouns designating black persons, white persons, persons not identifiable in terms of race, and governments and governmental agencies. Here are the total number of nouns in each category in the three opinions:

| referents of all nouns | | | |
	blacks	people	whites	governmental entities
Prigg	60	45	53	222
Pitts	76	59	18	413
Brown	55	20	17	95

Thus, in *Prigg,* nouns referring to governmental entities occur almost one and a half times as frequently as nouns referring to all groups of persons combined, and more than three and a half times as frequently as nouns referring to black persons. In *Pitts,* nouns referring to governmental entities occur more than two and a half times as frequently as nouns referring to all groups of persons combined, and almost five and a half times as frequently as nouns referring to black persons. In *Brown,* there is an almost equal number of nouns referring to governmental entities and to people, and "government" nouns occur less than twice as frequently as nouns referring to black persons alone.

But this is only the beginning of the lexical composition of the stories told in these opinions. We must also look at how the nouns are *used* in the opinions, how they are put into sentences[59]—whether, for example, they are *portrayed as agentive by being made the subjects of active verbs* or are *portrayed as subordinate to other actors by being made the direct objects of verbs that take the other actors as subjects.* If we differentiate the uses of nouns in terms of the degrees of agentivity and dominance involved in each use, we find the following numbers of nouns associated with *the most agentivity and dominance* in each of our four categories:

| nouns showing the most agentivity/dominance | | | |
	blacks	people	whites	governmental entities
Prigg	3	12	36	109
Pitts	35	21	8	268
Brown	23	12	5	50

And we find the following numbers of nouns associated with *the least agentivity and dominance* in each category:

nouns showing the least agentivity/dominance

	blacks	people	whites	governmental entities
Prigg	31	16	8	12
Pitts	20	24	4	20
Brown	9	4	4	3

We include a more detailed analysis of the nouns—together with a parallel analysis of verbs—in the Appendix. (The analysis of verbs shows, for example, that governmental entities are depicted as the agents of active verbs more than twenty-two times as frequently as black people in *Prigg*, almost thirteen times as frequently as black people in *Pitts*, but only about four times as frequently as black people in *Brown*.) Taken together, the analyses come down to this:

In the world created by the language of Justice Story's *Prigg* opinion, governmental entities appear and act somewhat more frequently than human beings. Human beings of African descent appear as frequently as other human beings, but they act less frequently and much less powerfully. Governments and their functionaries are substantially more powerful than any humans, and incomparably more powerful than humans of African descent.

In the world of Justice Kennedy's *Pitts* opinion, governmental presence and activity vastly overloom anything human. African-Americans appear and act more frequently than other humans, but all are rendered inconspicuous by the sheer volume and controlling character of governmental goings-on.

The world of *Brown* is less dominated by government. Governmental actors take center stage but leave room for people.

IV. The Time Frames

Consider now the points in time at which the stories told in *Prigg* and *Pitts* begin and end. The starting points are particularly noteworthy because the time at which a narrative begins[60] will ordinarily serve both to delimit the action—excluding or backgrounding everything that might have gone before—and also to frame what follows so that occurrences become *events* that have a particular meaning and narrative necessity.[61] In the welter of human doings, there are no "natural" beginnings and no "natural" endings: the solution to Problem One generates (or becomes) Problem Two, and so on.[62] What is Trouble and what is Resolution are determined largely by where the teller of the tale chooses to begin it.

In *Prigg*, immediately after stating the case that is the occasion for the present narration,[63] Justice Story begins his saga with the difficulties of forming the Union through the "compromise of opposing interests and opinions"[64] which, if not reconciled, "would have created the most bitter animosities and engendered perpetual strife between the different States."[65] As Story tells it, this difficulty is the Great Original Trouble which precisely prefigures the current controversy between Pennsylvania and Maryland. By making the overcoming of this Trouble the quintessential Origin Myth, Story privileges it both as a means and as an end; he can then simultaneously interpret and reenact it in the Pennsylvania-Maryland confrontation.[66] He need not delve beneath it to consider, for example, whether the formation of the Union was itself only a part of some larger narrative.[67]

In *Pitts*, after briefly stating the case in an opening passage[68] that makes Georgia's government officials and the federal courts the only real players,[69] Justice Kennedy begins with the decisions in *Brown I* and *Brown II*.[70] The entire *Pitts* opinion is one long tale of unrelenting efforts to cope with the Trouble precipitated by the decisions in *Brown*. Or, rather, it is one short story made to seem long: an ancillary effect of Kennedy's starting point is precisely to stretch the temporal perspective so as to increase the apparent duration of the Trouble. (It is distinctly easier to view federal-court supervision of the Atlanta public schools for twenty-five years as a Vast Trouble—a Trouble beyond enduring—if history begins in 1954 and comprises forty years in total than if the preceding three centuries of white domination of blacks in North America are part of the story.)

V. The Plots

The plot of Kennedy's *Pitts* opinion is a stock item: it is the classic story of the Conquering Hero Turned Tyrant. Although the various versions of this tale involve very different motivations on the characters' parts[71] and diverse dramatic and ideological projects on the authors',[72] the basic structure is readily recognizable:[73]

1. The story starts with Conqueror's ascension to the peak of power: Caesar, for example, comes victorious to Rome, where Antony thrice makes to crown him. Agamemnon's sail is seen as he returns victorious to Argos with the spoils of gutted Troy. Creon, having just ascended to the throne of Thebes, forbids dead Polynices's burial. Othello, barely nine months from the field of glorious battle, chooses his lieutenant and weds the Senator Brabantio's daughter. Nero first emancipates himself from Agrippina and begins to act the part of emperor in earnest.[74] [In *Pitts,* Brown's reign is heralded in the first active sentence[75] and is re-trumpeted to spark each successive stage of the action.[76] *Brown* begins as Conqueror over past wrongs.]

2. Enter Detractor (Cassius; Aegisthus; Antigone; Iago; Agrippina), who denounces Conqueror as a tyrant.[77] [The DeKalb County School System ["DCSS"], first onstage and boldly etched in *Pitts,*[78] undertakes to respond to *Brown*'s onerous commands[79] and then declares its duty done.][80]

3. Often there is enmity between Detractor and Conqueror; they or their forebears have wronged one another. It is difficult to know whether this enmity gives Detractor a unique insight into Conqueror's tyrannical character or whether the enmity causes Detractor to make a false accusation of tyranny as the pretext for a spiteful attack on Conqueror's authority, or whether both Conqueror's tyrannical character and Detractor's spite are real.[81] [DCSS for a long time declined to comply with *Brown,* and then, when sued by African-American children, "voluntarily" began working with federal education officials to desegregate.][82] In any event, Conqueror's potentially tyrannical power was won by indisputable courage and worth.[83]

4. Enter Defender (Brutus; Electra; Haemon; Desdemona; Burrus), who gives praise or obedience to Conqueror.[84] ["Within two months of our ruling in *Green,* [the *Pitts* plaintiffs,] . . . black school children and their parents, instituted this class action."][85]

5. Often there is a close bond between Defender and Conqueror; Defender has loyalties to Conqueror; it is difficult to know whether these loyalties give Defender a unique insight into Conqueror's true merit or whether they blind Defender to Conqueror's tyrannical character, or whether Conqueror's character is both meritorious and ty-

rannical.[86] [The *Pitts* opinion consistently depicts the class plaintiffs as the natural objects of *Brown*'s bounty.][87] In any event, Conqueror's courage and worth have now put Conqueror in a position to exercise tyrannical power.[88]

6. Detractor and Defender debate; the enormity of the stakes becomes apparent; but unclarity remains as to whether Conqueror's character is tyrannical, or at least as to whether it is irredeemably so.[89] [Most of the *Pitts* opinion recounts struggles to come to terms with *Brown*, logistically,[90] testimonially,[91] and rhetorically[92]: e.g., "[a]lthough this temporary measure [judicial supervision of schools] has lasted for decades, the ultimate objective has not changed—to return school districts to the control of local authorities."][93]

7. Enter (or reenter) Conqueror, whose conduct is now ambiguous.[94] (In some cases, Conqueror's initial entry may occur as early as stage 2.) [In *Pitts*, *Green*'s declaration of the demise of deliberate speed brings *Brown*'s reign to DeKalb County with considerable clatter.][95]

8. Conqueror reveals some unmistakable sign of tyrannical character, and the tragic outcome is unleashed.[96] [This, as we will shortly see, is the very pit of *Pitts*. In its old age, *Brown* is revealed to have become most harsh and unreasonable.]

The Conquering-Hero-Turned-Tyrant story has two structural features that mark it as a distinct subspecies of the Tyrant Tale.[97] The first is its starting point—where it begins—summarized in paragraph number 1 above. The action must start at precisely the right moment, immediately after the noble deeds of the Conqueror-That-Was are finished and done with (so that the audience is not enlisted in those deeds) and just before the Tyrant-That-Will-Be takes the irreversible plunge into corruption (so that the audience experiences not only the full plunge but the moment of teetering preceding it).[98] Justice Kennedy does this in *Pitts* through the remarkable lines with which he begins Part I of his opinion: a couplet that literally catches *Brown* (by both legs) at the peak of its trajectory. (This is set out in endnote 70 on page 369.)

The second key feature is the dramatic heightening of the moment at which the Conqueror decisively commits himself to a tyrannical course (paragraph number 8 above). Kennedy does this in the last two lines of Part I:

"The Court of Appeals held that [DCSS] . . . bore the responsibility for the racial imbalance, and in order to correct that imbalance would have to take actions that 'may be administratively awkward, inconvenient, and even bizarre in some situations,' . . . We granted certiorari."[99]

He then repeats the refrain before thrusting home:

"The Court of Appeals' rejection of the District Court's order rests on [the premise that] . . . until there is full compliance, heroic measures must be taken to ensure racial balance in student assignments system-wide. . . . The Court of Appeals was mistaken in ruling that our opinion in *Swann* requires 'awkward,' 'inconvenient,' and 'even bizarre' measures to achieve racial balance in student assignments in the late phases of carrying out a decree, when the imbalance is attributable to . . . demographic forces."[100]

Thus does the Court of Appeals, speaking for *Brown,* o'erleap the limits of the responsible Conqueror and vault into the Tyrant's own doctrinaire single-mindedness, rejecting restraint counseled either by the views of others or by the necessities of practicality and reason. This is the tragic step of Sophocles' Creon;[101] and, like Sophocles' Creon, *Brown* is now assuredly condemned to suffer the ultimate degradation of living too long—unless the Supreme Court, per Justice Kennedy, steps in and rescues it from this awful fate.

Shift back to *Prigg* now. One can easily imagine a number of ways in which the story of the Fugitives-From-Service-Or-Labor Clause of the Constitution could be told in 1842 as a tale of the Conquering-Hero-Turned-Tyrant.[102] But that is not the tale that Justice Story tells in *Prigg.* His tale, rather, resembles another of ancient fame that long predates the common-law doctrines of recaption which he quotes ("'when any one hath deprived another of his property in goods or chattels personal, or wrongfully detains one's wife, child or servant . . .[,] the owner of the goods and the husband, parent or master may lawfully claim and retake them, wherever he happens to find them, so it be not in a riotous manner, or attended with a breach of the peace'").[103] The tale, in its conventional form, goes like this:

1. When Helen, who was foster daughter to Tyndareus, the King of Sparta, reached a marriageable age, every prince of Greece came (or sent representatives) to sue for her hand. But Tyndareus neither accepted nor rejected any suitor, for fear of sparking a general conflict. He worried that if he gave Helen to one, the others would resort to vi-

olence.[104] [Justice Story, in his version, begins by reciting the "known historical fact that many of [the Constitution's] . . . provisions were matters of compromise of opposing interests and opinions"[105] and says that if the Fugitives-From-Service-Or-Labor Clause had not been included in the Constitution, "every non-slaveholding State in the Union would have been at liberty to have declared free all runaway slaves coming within its limits . . .; a course which would have created the most bitter animosities, and engendered perpetual strife between the different States."][106]

2. Odysseus perceived the problem and proposed a solution. Tyndareus was to insist that each of Helen's suitors swear to defend her future husband against all despoilers.[107] Tyndareus agreed and made the suitors swear the oath.[108] [In *Prigg*, the Fugitives-From-Service-Or-Labor "clause was accordingly adopted into the Constitution by the unanimous consent of the framers of it; a proof at once of its intrinsic and practical necessity."][109]

3. The rich Menelaus (represented in Tyndareus' halls by Tyndareus' son-in-law and Menelaus' brother, Agamemnon) was chosen to be Helen's husband, and he ascended the throne of Sparta after Tyndareus' death. Paris, son of Priam of Troy, then came to Sparta, seduced Helen, and eloped with her to his father's city.[110] ["The [Fugitives-From-Service-or-Labor] clause manifestly contemplates the existence of a positive, unqualified right on the part of the owner of the slave, which no State law or regulation can in any way qualify, regulate, control, or restrain. The slave is not to be discharged from service or labor, in consequence of any State law or regulation. Now, . . . any State law or State regulation, which interrupts, limits, delays, or postpones the right of the owner to the immediate possession of the slave, and the immediate command of his service and labor, operates *pro tanto*, a discharge of the slave therefrom."[111] In other words, the Pennsylvania law forbidding kidnapping, insofar as it forces slave-catchers to employ legal process and abide the attendant delays, *takes away* from the slave's owner the right to use the slave's services during the period of those delays. Notice how neatly Pennsylvania's anti-kidnapping statute has been recast as a kidnapper.]

4. Menelaus rushed immediately to Agamemnon, whom he urged to raise the Greeks and lead them against Troy. Agamemnon agreed to do so if, indeed, the Trojans refused to return Helen with compensation. Agamemnon sent envoys to Troy, but Priam claimed to have

no knowledge of the abduction, and he fobbed the envoys off by reminding them that his own requests for reparation for the abduction of Hesione (Priam's sister) by the Greek Telamon had been spurned. Menelaus thereupon sent heralds to every Greek prince who had taken Tyndareus' oath, asserting that Paris' abduction of Helen affronted all of Greece, and warning each to look to the safety of his own wife if this affront were not rectified.[112] [In *Prigg*, as Justice Story tells it: "The question can never be, how much the slave is discharged from; but whether he is discharged from any, by the natural or necessary operation of State laws or State regulations. . . . Many cases must arise in which, if the remedy of the owner were confined to the mere right of seizure and recaption, he would be utterly without any adequate redress. He may not be able to lay his hands upon the slave. He may not be able to enforce his rights against persons who either secrete or conceal, or withhold the slave. He may be restricted by local legislation as to the mode of proofs of his ownership, as to the courts in which he shall sue and as to the actions which he may bring, or the process he may use to compel the delivery of the slave. Nay, the local legislation may be utterly inadequate to furnish the appropriate redress. . . ."][113]

5. The Greeks then sent an embassy of Menelaus and Odysseus to demand Helen's return. The Trojans spurned (and came near to murdering) the envoys.[114] ["If, therefore, the clause of the Constitution had stopped at the mere recognition of the right, without providing or contemplating any means, by which it might be established and enforced . . ., it . . . would have been, in a great variety of cases, a delusive and empty annunciation. If it did not contemplate any action either through State or national legislation, as auxiliaries to its more perfect enforcement in the form of remedy, or of protection, then, as there would be no duty on either to aid the right, it would be left to the mere comity of the States to act as they should please, and would depend for its security upon the changing course of public opinion. . . ."][115]

6. Whereupon, the Greek army, under Agamemnon, attacked Troy; and thus began the war that decimated both.[116] [Fortunately, however, in *Prigg* the cordial cooperation of Maryland and Pennsylvania gives the Supreme Court a chance to settle the war—a last opportunity to avert disaster[117]—akin to the last-hope opportunity offered by the

abortive personal combat between Menelaus and Paris reported in Book III of *The Iliad*.]

Both tales, indeed, end just short of their respective catastrophes. The judgments announced in *Prigg* and *Pitts* are designed precisely to avert those catastrophes. Only "construe the right of legislation as exclusive in Congress," says Justice Story, "and every evil and every danger vanishes."[118] Says Justice Kennedy: "When the school district and [the other] . . . state entities . . . operating the schools make decisions in the absence of judicial supervision, they can be held accountable to the citizenry, to the political process, and to the courts in the ordinary course"[119]—that is, to courts not swollen by tyrannical ambitions born of *Brown* to go "beyond the[ir] authority and beyond the[ir] practical ability" and attempt "ongoing and never-ending supervision . . . of school districts simply because they were once de jure segregated."[120] After the catastrophic outcomes of the tales have been foretold, timely judicial action to avoid them becomes imperative.

VI. The Dooms

Justice Story's choice of an action to avert catastrophe in *Prigg* is to *concentrate* power in the central government and to let that government take charge of the situation, predictably by employing the federal courts in the ongoing work of returning runaway slaves.[121] Justice Kennedy's choice of an action to avert catastrophe in *Pitts* is to *disperse* power, leaving local governments to do their thing and largely withdrawing the federal courts from the work of overseeing school systems. Story's plot line, with its Trouble in the form of discord among warring principates, demands an *integrative* fix; Kennedy's plot line, with its nascent tyrant Trouble, demands a *disintegrative* one.

But what drives the two opinions to these poles is not simply their respective choices between the tired bogies[122] and contrastive metaphors of anarchy and tyranny, chaos and constriction, rock and whirlpool, explosion and implosion. Both go further. Story's narrative justifies the strengthening of central dominion by exuding confidence that humankind can use *increased* federal power to control its fate, while Kennedy's narrative secures the acceptance of *decreased* federal power by inspiring pessimism that any good can ever come of human efforts to do more than muddle through.

This aspect of the opinions can be seen by comparing key passages that depict the root of the Trouble in each. First, a passage from *Prigg*:

"If, then, the States have a right, in the absence of legislation by Congress, to act upon the subject, each State is at liberty to prescribe just such regulations as suit its own policy, local convenience, and local feelings. The legislation of one State may not only be different from, but utterly repugnant to and incompatible with that of another. The time, and mode, and limitation of the remedy, the proofs of the title, and all other incidents applicable thereto, may be prescribed in one State which are rejected or disclaimed in another. One State may require the owner to sue in one mode, another in a different mode. One State may make a statute of limitations as to the remedy, in its own tribunals, short and summary; another may prolong the period and yet restrict the proofs. Nay, some States may utterly refuse to act upon the subject at all; and others may refuse to open its [*sic*] courts to any remedies *in rem*, because they would interfere with their own domestic policy, institutions, or habits. The right, therefore, would never, in a practical sense, be the same in all the States. It would have no unity of purpose, or uniformity of operation. The duty might be enforced in some States, retarded or limited in others, and denied as compulsory in many, if not in all. Consequences like these must have been foreseen as very likely to occur in the non-slaveholding States, where legislation, if not silent on the subject, and purely voluntary, could scarcely be presumed to be favorable to the exercise of the rights of the owner.

"It is scarcely conceivable that the slaveholding States would have been satisfied with leaving to the legislation of the non-slaveholding States a power of regulation, in the absence of that of Congress, which would or might practically amount to a power to destroy the rights of the owner. . . ."[123]

And next a passage from *Pitts:*

"The findings of the District Court that the population changes which occurred in DeKalb County were not caused by the policies of the school district, but rather by independent factors, are consistent with the mobility that is a distinct characteristic of our society. In one year (from 1987 to 1988) over 40 million Americans, or 17.6 percent of the total population, moved households. . . . [citation omitted] Over a third of those people moved to a different county, and over six million migrated between States. . . . [citation omitted] In such a society, it is inevitable that the demographic makeup of school districts, based as they are on political subdivisions . . ., may undergo rapid change.

"The effect of changing residential patterns on the racial composition of schools though not always fortunate is somewhat predictable. Studies show a high correlation between residential segregation and school segregation. . . . [citations omitted] The District Court in this case heard evidence tending to show that racially stable neighborhoods are not likely to emerge because whites prefer a racial mix of 80% white and 20% black, while blacks prefer a 50%-50% mix.

"Where resegregation is a product not of state action but of private choices, it does not have constitutional implications. It is beyond the authority and beyond the practical ability of the federal courts to try to counteract these kinds of continuous and massive demographic shifts. To attempt such results would require ongoing and never-ending supervision by the courts of school districts simply because they were once de jure segregated. Residential housing choices, and their attendant effects on the racial composition of schools, present an ever-changing pattern, one difficult to address through judicial remedies."[124]

Passage after passage in the *Pitts* opinion refers to "tremendous demographic shifts that were taking place"[125] or to "demographic changes that occurred,"[126] recites that "dramatic demographic changes altered residential patterns"[127] or that "demographic shifts have had 'an immense effect,'"[128] and says that these "'demographic shifts were inevitable.'"[129] Such phrases serve to reify brute happenings, which then become the subjects of active verbs or copulas (linking verbs). Formulations of this sort recur *forty-nine times* throughout Kennedy's *Pitts* opinion. It is all about trends in Nature rather than about what people do. Not so in *Prigg*, where the closest Story comes to talking about general tendencies is one reference to "the changing course of public opinion,"[130] one reference to "mutations of public policy,"[131] a reference to "the natural or necessary operation of State laws,"[132] and two other references to the "operation[s]" of law or government[133]—and *none* of these phrases are used as the subject of a verb. So, too, in Warren's *Brown* opinion there is very little use of verbal formulations that turn human affairs into Things That Just Occur.[134] Whereas in *Prigg* (and in *Brown*) the tale is driven almost solely by what governments and people actively *accomplish,* in *Pitts* the tale is driven largely by what *happens to* them.[135] And whereas the fine descriptive texture in Story's *Prigg* opinion is preoccupied with *deliber-*

ate legal procedures and their functioning, in Kennedy's *Pitts* opinion it is lavished on statistics and the workings of demographic *chance*.

But this fatalism is only half of a double movement in *Pitts*. Despairing of the best of human efforts, Justice Kennedy reserves his concern for the worst of them. Compare a pair of passages from *Brown* and *Pitts*. First, *Brown*:

> "In *Sweatt v. Painter* . . ., in finding that a segregated law school for Negroes could not provide them equal educational opportunities, this Court relied in large part on 'those qualities which are incapable of objective measurement but which make for greatness in a law school.' In *McLaurin v. Oklahoma State Regents* . . ., the Court, in requiring that a Negro admitted to a white graduate school be treated like all other students, again resorted to intangible considerations: '. . . his ability to study, to engage in discussions and exchange views with other students, and, in general, to learn his profession.' Such considerations apply with added force to children in grade and high schools. To separate them from others of similar age and qualifications solely because of their race generates a feeling of inferiority as to their status in the community that may affect their hearts and minds in a way unlikely ever to be undone. The effect of this separation on their educational opportunities was well stated by a finding in the Kansas case by a court which nevertheless felt compelled to rule against the Negro plaintiffs:
>
> "'Segregation of white and colored children in public schools has a detrimental effect upon the colored children. The impact is greater when it has the sanction of the law; for the policy of separating the races is usually interpreted as denoting the inferiority of the negro group. A sense of inferiority affects the motivation of a child to learn. Segregation with the sanction of law, therefore, has a tendency to [retard] the educational and mental development of negro children and to deprive them of some of the benefits they would receive in a racial[ly] integrated school system.'
>
> "Whatever may have been the extent of psychological knowledge at the time of *Plessy v. Ferguson,* this finding is amply supported by modern authority. Any language in *Plessy v. Ferguson* contrary to this finding is rejected.
>
> "We conclude that in the field of public education the doctrine of 'separate but equal' has no place. Separate educational facilities are inherently unequal. Therefore, we hold that the plaintiffs and others similarly situated for whom the actions have been brought are, by reason of the segregation complained of, deprived of the equal protection of the laws guaranteed by the Fourteenth Amendment."[136]

Now, *Pitts:*

"The duty and responsibility of a school district once segregated by law is to take all steps necessary to eliminate the vestiges of the unconstitutional de jure system. This is required in order to insure that the principal wrong of the de jure system, the injuries and stigma inflicted upon the race disfavored by the violation, is no longer present. This was the rationale and the objective of Brown I and Brown II. In Brown I we said: 'to separate [black students] from others of similar age and qualifications solely because of their race generates a feeling of inferiority as to their status in the community that may affect their hearts and minds in a way unlikely ever to be undone.' . . . [citation omitted] We quoted a finding of the three-judge District Court in the underlying Kansas case that bears repeating here:

"'Segregation of white and colored children in public schools has a detrimental effect upon the colored children. The impact is greater when it has the sanction of the law; for the policy of separating the races is usually interpreted as denoting the inferiority of the negro group. A sense of inferiority affects the motivation of a child to learn. Segregation with the sanction of law, therefore, has a tendency to [retard] the educational and mental development of negro children and to deprive them of some of the benefits they would receive in a racial[ly] integrated school system.'

"The objective of Brown I was made more specific by our holding in Green that the duty of a former de jure district is to 'take whatever steps might be necessary to convert to a unitary system in which racial discrimination would be eliminated root and branch.' . . . [citation omitted] We also identified various parts of the school system which, in addition to student attendance patterns, must be free from racial discrimination before the mandate of Brown is met: faculty, staff, transportation, extracurricular activities and facilities. . . . [citation omitted] The Green factors are a measure of the racial identifiability of schools in a system that is not in compliance with Brown, and we instructed the District Courts to fashion remedies that address all these components of elementary and secondary school systems."[137]

Two other but related features of these texts stand out. The first is the way in which the *harm* of segregation is transmogrified from *Brown* to *Pitts*. In *Brown,* African-American children are held to be deprived of equal "educational opportunities" after due regard is given to "intangible considerations" of a psychological nature. The stigma implied when segregation has the sanction of law only makes the "'impact [of the motivational impairment] greater.'" In *Pitts*, this stigma has become the "principal wrong of the de jure system." If additional wrongs are tacitly acknowledged by the adjective "principal," they are not considered worth identifying or discussing. Meanwhile, those tangible "parts of the school system" enumerated in *Green* have become a "measure of [the] racial identifiability of schools" that does the stigmatizing. The inward turn from *Plessy* to *Brown* has been recurved; *Pitts* concerns itself exclusively with externals—with those listed "*Green* factors" that, when added up to a proper total of six, mark schools as "desegregated."

A second thing happens in *Pitts*—an implicit but inflexible linkage between *harm* and a *deliberate intention* to commit it. It is as if, when there is no intention to commit harm, harm cannot be said to occur. This notion is in stark contrast to *Brown*, where Chief Justice Warren's opinion takes pains to downplay any villainy on the part of the segregating States. To the extent that there is any villain on Chief Justice Warren's stage, it is *Plessy*, not the southern lawmakers. *Brown* explicitly uncouples *blame* from *unconstitutionality*[138] by defining the constitutional wrong it discerns as "depriv[ing] the children of the minority group of equal educational opportunities."[139] Such a wrong does not require an evildoer to commit it. But in *Pitts*, when the wrong becomes recast as stigmatization, it also becomes inseparable from the *animus* that stigmatization implies. Harm and the purpose to wreak it are portrayed as inextricable: where no deliberate evildoer can be found, the evil itself is exorcised—"no longer present."[140]

Pitts's plot both derives from and sustains this depiction of a world in which the only wrongs that call for attention are external and malevolent aggressions. Domineering violence is the very root of the Conquering-Hero-Turned-Tyrant Tale, the wellspring of its action and the measure of its deepest forebodings. Here the contrast to the Trojan War Tale is particularly marked, for the latter centers on disorders that can neither be accounted for nor ended by personifying evil in some monstrous evildoer.[141]

CHAPTER SIX

On Rhetorics

Categorization and narrative account for much of the weave of discourse. But discourse takes on special features in the presence or the prospect of dispute. Those features are the subject of this chapter and the next.

We call the subject "rhetorics" because it has to do in part with strategies of persuasion (the focus of classical Western rhetoric)[1] and in part with the use of symbols to construct alternative meaning frames (a focus of modern and postmodern rhetoric).[2] The old rhetoric and the new converge upon the means by which language deals with controversy or potential controversy—how it delimits what is contestable and in what terms. Rhetoric in today's popular sense of spin control is simply one of those means. So we take "rhetorics," the plural, to denote the various linguistic processes by which a speaker can create, address, avoid, or shape issues that the speaker wishes or is called upon to contest, or that a speaker suspects (at some level of awareness) may become contested.[3]

There are obvious reasons why legal discourse offers a particularly fertile field for rhetorics in this sense. Legal discourse is specialized for waging and negotiating controversy, on the one hand, and manipulating symbols, on the other. Talk becomes law-talk only when the way to do (or think about) something is contestable, when people want to settle the contest or its boundaries by ruling some of the contenders out of bounds, and when the ruling needs legitimation by resort to ideology. That is the time when advocates stand up to persuade a judge that their claims trump their opponents'; it is the time when judges sit down to convince themselves that their reasons justify their actions; collectively, it is the many times when the many participants in a legal system conspire to convince themselves and one another that the narrow range of values which their system takes into account can be preserved only by disregarding all of the other values in the known universe.[4] Each of these acts of persuasion or self-persuasion requires a language fitted for *selling,* not just *telling.* Statements uttered in such a language will bear the stamp of their rhetorical function.

Much of that function is to frame the questions open for debate or for consideration. Setting the agenda of contention is a crucial move for all rhetoricians: for lawyers arguing cases, for judges announcing their grounds of decision, for writers of political party platforms and cereal advertisements, for you or me choosing our words as we get out of our car to begin a conversation with the driver whose rear bumper we have just dented, for you or me articulating in our own heads the reasons why we should or shouldn't get a new car, take a new job, try a new cereal or a new political party, make a legal argument in one form or another. Every one of these situations requires us to choose our words with attention to the possibility that alternative, contending views may be taken of what is happening or should happen: our choice of language can precipitate or quash debate, locate the fronts along which debate might be joined, and establish what positions we will take, what arguments and commitments we will make or avoid in the course of debating. It will matter greatly, for example, whether our opening sentence to the owner of the dented bumper is accusatory or apologetic.

This conception of rhetorics as centered on debate-framing leads us to examine simultaneously the strategies that people use to convince other people and the strategies they use to convince themselves.[5] Because these strategies shape the arguments that individuals carry on internally as well as the arguments they make to other people, we are all at risk of becoming captives of our own strategies (in both settings), to the extent that they are unreflective.[6] So we will need to examine how they work—in both settings—to control the scope and terms of what is contested or even contestable. We will need to consider simultaneously the ways in which language poses, defines, structures, and connects (or isolates) issues and the ways in which language averts, blurs, preempts, and conceals issues.

We begin this exploration in Part I by examining the processes through which a speaker's words are almost always taken to mean more than they say, even when interpretation is not complicated by controversy, nor *telling* by *selling*. In Part II we add these complications, describing how communications in most legal settings are bedeviled by contestability and efforts to control it. In Part III we analyze various sorts of rhetorical control devices, their uses, and their dangers.

I. Saying Something and Meaning More

Human utterances are heard, understood, and processed *in a situational context*. Most of the things people say to one another are incomprehensible when parsed solely in accordance with the rules of grammar, dictionary definitions, and codes of formal logic. Their uptake is a product of interpretive activity conditioned by the nature and specific circumstances of the communicative setting. Briefly, *what is taken to be meant by what is said depends on what is perceived to be going on.*

This was John Austin's basic insight when he opposed a theory of *speech acts* to the claims of logical positivism.[7] The positivists' project was to specify a set of truth conditions such that every human pronouncement could be judged *true, false,* or *nonsense.* Austin's reply was that by such criteria a very large part of human discourse is palpably nonsense. Yet people understand it well enough to act on, for the most part; and how come?

Austin posed this question in a vocabulary that will be useful for our purposes. He and the speech-act theorists who followed him (most notably, John Searle)[8] distinguished three dimensions of any linguistic utterance: the *locutionary* dimension, the *illocutionary* dimension, and the *perlocutionary* dimension.

Suppose I tell you: "Sam drank some gin today." The locutionary dimension is the propositional content of my utterance, consisting basically of a *reference* to some subject ("Sam") and a *predication* about that subject ("drank some gin today"). The illocutionary dimension is what the speaker is doing with the proposition uttered: here, at first blush, *stating* or *asserting* it. (I *state* or *assert* that Sam drank some gin today.) Illocutionary activities include stating, declaring, commenting, suggesting, inviting, warning, questioning, requesting, demanding, arguing, criticizing, objecting, and so forth.

Different illocutionary acts can be performed with the same locutionary act. "Did Sam drink some gin today?" is (at first blush) the illocutionary act of *questioning*, using the same propositional elements (a reference to Sam as subject; a predication of Sam's drinking some gin) as in my previous act of stating or asserting. "Sam, drink some gin today!" is (at first blush) the illocutionary act of *commanding*, with the same locutionary elements.

The perlocutionary dimension has to do with the effects of the utterance on the hearer. For example, if you are Sam's spouse and Sam is an alcoholic who is supposed to be on the wagon, the perlocutionary consequence of my asserting that Sam drank some gin today may (at first blush) be to *alarm* you or to *upset* you. If you and I and Sam are on a desert island with a single gin bottle and strict sharing rules, the perlocutionary effect of my assertion may (at first blush) be to *anger* you or even to *incite you to mayhem*.

The reason for all these blushing qualifiers should be obvious. That first-blush illocutionary act of *asserting* that Sam drank some gin today would also constitute the illocutionary act of *apologizing* if, in the desert-island scenario, you were asleep and I was supposed to be guarding the gin bottle when Sam got at it. Or, if *you* were supposed to be guarding the gin bottle while *I* was sleeping, the same assertion on my part would constitute *accusing*. (Notice that the first-blush question form "Did Sam drink some gin today?" would also constitute *accusing* in the latter situation.) Or consider a different scenario, in which Sam is our revered mentor and the dialogue goes:

You: Nobody with brains drinks gin.
Me: Sam drank some gin today.

Here the illocutionary act is *denying* or *impeaching*. And the perlocutionary effects could range from *inspiring you to try gin* to *causing you to doubt my veracity* (or Sam's intelligence) to *persuading you to get a different mentor*.

It is perhaps less obvious but equally the case that even the locutionary or propositional dimension of my utterance is context-dependent. Suppose that we both know that Sam never drinks gin when he can lay his hands on scotch, and the dialogue is:

You: I had a bad day. Where's the scotch?
Me: Sam drank some gin today.

What I am telling you is that we are out of scotch. Or suppose that we both know that Sam drinks only when he is under heavy stress and the dialogue is:

You: Were things any better at the office today?
Me: Sam drank some gin today.

What I am telling you is that things were even worse than usual at the office today.

In both of these examples, the explicit propositional utterance is relatively inconsequential. What matters is its *implicature*. The locution counts only insofar as it implies something beyond what it says. And the truth of what it says doesn't count at all. In both cases, my assertion that Sam drank some gin today may be a pure fiction. Suppose that it is. It will nevertheless have conveyed to you exactly what it was intended to convey; you will have understood it; and the fact that what I *said* was false—perhaps demonstrably so—will not cause you to consider me a liar or even "wrong," provided that we *are* out of scotch or that I can document that today was a dreadful day at the office. (On the other hand, if I had begun by stating that things were worse at the office today; if you then *challenged* me to prove it; and if I *backed up* my assertion (or *offered proof* of it) by saying that Sam drank some gin today, the truth of the latter assertion would be crucial.)[9]

The point we are driving at (at first blush) is that human pronouncements ordinarily *mean* more than they *say*. If you got the point before we made it explicit, that's a demonstration of another way it can work. Call this one *inference*. You inferred the point we were driving at. We hinted at the point by multiplying examples. But notice that: (1) Until we stated explicitly what our point was, we were not committed to it. (The first sentence of this paragraph might have been "Our point is not that human pronouncements ordinarily mean more than they say, but only that they sometimes do." You could not have taxed us with inconsistency for disavowing an inference *you* drew from our earlier pronouncements.) (2) If we neither made the point explicitly nor disavowed it—but if you inferred it from our earlier pronouncements—you might have found it more persuasive than you do now that we have stated it explicitly. (The overtly quantitative adverb *ordinarily* invites critical scrutiny. How frequently is "ordinarily," and what's our proof that our handful of examples demonstrate a phenomenon of the requisite frequency?) (3) The actual first sentence of this paragraph actually had three more points than it said it did. (We've just numbered them.)

But let's leave off these language games.[10] The question recurs how one person goes about figuring out the meaning of another person's utterances insofar as meaning outstrips saying. Austin implied and Searle insisted that meaning and its interpretation are governed by conventional rules, so that, for example, the illocutionary force of an utterance is established by certain *felicity conditions*. My uttering X will amount to *promising* you that I will do A if, in uttering X, (1) I predicate of myself a future act, A; (2) you would prefer my doing A to not doing A, and I believe you would; (3) it is not obvious to both of us that I will do A in the normal course of future events; (4) I intend that the utterance of X will place me under an obligation to do A; and so forth. However, the felicity conditions for various illocutionary acts have turned out to be strongly resistant to any kind of comprehensive or unambiguous codification, except for a few highly ritualized speech acts like christening a ship, executing a testamentary instrument, and (sometimes) cursing somebody out. And even for those ritualized acts, the specification of necessary and sufficient conditions will hold good only within a narrow range of relatively commonplace circumstances.

Paul Grice made a famous contribution to the study of implicature by suggesting that *both* the observance *and* the manifest flouting of conventional rules can serve as the means of signaling that something more is meant than what is said, and of pointing (albeit not definitively) to what the "something more" might be.[11] There are, Grice suggested, *conversational implicatures* as well as *conventional implicatures*. The former sort of implicatures derive from a general principle of conversation, the "Cooperative Principle," which yields various maxims that people ordinarily observe when conversing. The Gricean Maxim of Quantity, for example, is *make your contribution no more or less informative than is required for the current purposes of the exchange*. The Gricean Maxim of Quality is *try to make your contribution one that is true*, and the Gricean Maxim of Relation is *be relevant*. The Gricean Maxim of Manner is *be perspicuous*; and it has corollaries like *avoid ambiguity; be brief; be orderly.* So, for example, if Sam says to you, "I could sure use a shot of gin," and you reply, "there is a bottle under the palm tree," you thereby imply that the bottle has gin in it—at least in the absence of any indication that you are violating a Gricean maxim or opting out of the Cooperative Principle. Similarly, if I say to you, "there seems to be a bit less gin in this bottle than there was before I took a nap," and you reply, "and Sam seems to be a bit more wobbly," you imply (and must imply, consistently with the maxim to *be relevant*) that Sam nipped while I napped. The notion is not that people never violate the maxims; on the contrary. But suppose that when Sam said to you "I could sure use a shot of gin," your reply had been, "Isn't the sunset magnificent this evening?" Here your flagrant disregard of the maxim of relevancy tells Sam that Sam shouldn't be thinking about the gin bottle, and that you don't want to think about it either.

Theorists since Grice have suggested a number of ways in which his approach to implicature can be refined and supplemented. Whereas Grice tended to treat the context of any particular utterance as a given and to use maxims like relevance as the starting point for calculating the implicature of the utterance *within* this given context, Dan Sperber and Deirdre Wilson emphasize that *the context itself is selected by the hearer in an active quest to make the new utterance relevant.* (A hearer can, in effect, expand the context by calling up memory stores; and s/he will do so in accordance with a general strategy of maximizing relevance.)[12] Stephen Levinson proposes that a key element of context is *activity type:* the species or *genre* of culturally recognized interactive behavior (like teaching a grade-school class or speaking at a PTA meeting, or participating in a job interview or a courtroom cross-examination) that is in progress when any particular utterance is made. (The structure characteristic of that activity type constrains what counts as an allowable verbal contribution to the activity; conversely, it influences how any verbal utterance will be interpreted.)[13] Language and its uptake within complex activity types become aspects of *genre knowledge,* learned "on the job" and "inherently dynamic, constantly (if gradually) changing over time in response to the sociocognitive needs of individual users."[14] Deborah Tannen sees context as a set of expectation structures or *frames* that overlap and interact. The frames include the general institutional and interpersonal situation (akin to Levinson's "activity type"); prior experience in analogous situations that may prompt notions of the proper perspective and role to take in this one; conceptions of how to tell and hear stories; stock scripts, generic characters, typical objects, model cause-effect relationships; and so forth. All of this is organized for recall (in an active searching process akin to that supposed by Sperber and Wilson) so that people act "as experienced and sophisticated veterans of perception" whose "structures of expectation make interpretation possible, but in the process they also reflect back on perception of the world to justify that interpretation."[15]

The roster of ways in which speakers convey and hearers apprehend implicatures remains wide open.[16] There is no reason to elaborate it further for our present purposes. Suffice it to say that people interpret any communication by assigning meaning to it in relation to the task at hand when it is uttered, goaded by some sort of presumption of relevancy (i.e., that what is being communicated makes sense in connection with that task) and guided by a bunch of fuzzy, convention-based, provisional/adaptable assumptions about what it is appropriate for a speaker to say in this connection. To bring the assumptions into play, additional assumptions or interpretations have to be made about what the task *is,* what objectives a speaker might plausibly be pursuing in regard to the task, and what sorts of communications might plausibly promote those objectives. We can call all of these assumptions, collectively, the *interpretive frame,* so long as we understand that "frame" does not imply something set in concrete beforehand but rather something constructed partly on the spot in an effort to make sense of the very communication that is in the process of being interpreted.[17]

Paul Grice himself hedged his entire system with an important *caveat:*

> "I have stated my maxims as if [the] . . . purpose [of human talk] were a maximally effective exchange of information; this specification is, of course, too narrow, and the scheme needs to be generalized to allow for such general purposes as influencing or directing the actions of others."[18]

And through this hedge—together hand in hand as to a tryst, and casually strolling (apparently)—now enter who? Why, law (of course) and rhetorics.

II. The Contestability at the Core of Law's Discourse

In ordinary communication outside of legal settings, what you mean by what you say is frequently equivocal but it is seldom contested or seriously likely to be contested. In law, controversy is the order of the day, and meanings are almost always vulnerable to being contested. People with differing interests in how to interpret communications are pitted against each other and primed by profession to question what constitutes the proper interpretive frame, to pick apart each other's proposed frames, and to advocate alternative plausible frames. Even if no interpretive challenger has yet appeared upon the scene, the legal setting warns you that one may. And the deeper you get into territory you associate with "law," the more nervous you become that somebody will pull the rhetorical rug of incontrovertible assumptions out from under your feet.[19]

In some legal settings, such as litigation, the very name of the game is to contest the meanings of communications and to take apart the components of an adversary's interpretive frame. Here, the contesting of interpretation is *expected*: the conventions of the genre call for oppositional debate. After rebuttal and traverse, a judge or arbiter accepts one competing interpretation and rejects another. So much for Grice's Cooperative Principle.

But while Grice's Principle finds no firm anchorage at the bottom of legal waters, it does retain a kind of sea-anchor traction on the surface. For legal discourse, even the language of adversary litigation, is dressed in the garb of ordinary discourse. It is typically in standard English (or some other mother tongue) and appears to make grammatically correct, logically reasonable, and narratively compelling assertions. It asks answerable, relevant questions and utters intelligible commands. Superficially at least, the rules of ordinary discourse are assumed to govern legal discourse: lawyers arguing cases and judges deciding them are expected to obey the Gricean maxims, respect the conventions for implicatures, conform to felicity conditions. They must give the impression of adhering to these canons, must *act as if* the Cooperative Principle remained in force.

It is the constant tension between these expectations—ordinariness and accommodation at the surface level, interpretive contestability just below the surface—that makes legal discourse treacherously fragile. Law-talk, particularly the law-talk used in litigation, is always subject to shattering without warning, as one or another of its users suddenly questions assumptions that had been accepted a moment before or turns some previously inconspicuous component of the interpretive frame into a subject of concern or controversy.

Contest is always to be expected, but its occasions and dimensions can rarely be foreseen exactly because adversaries choose their time, place, and terms of battle strategically. They do not rush to call attention to contestable points that their opponent or the judge may overlook. Each party to a litigation may have more than one line of attack or defense available, depending on what the other side (or the judge) does. Until another party violates or challenges the ordinary rules of discourse, the litigator may see an advantage in tacitly adhering to them. But the moment this advantage is threatened, a good litigator will be prepared to wage war over the rules themselves. And everybody knows this. So the ordinary rules are accepted only provisionally, with other modes of discourse readied to displace them or to debate their acceptability when expediency dictates.[20]

The vigilant awareness of contestability that underlies law-talk and gives it its fragility has several implications:

1. In legal discourse, and especially in litigation, all interpretations are inherently suspect. An interpretation offered by a litigator is not only vulnerable to attack by the adversary but is often viewed with suspicion by the arbiter. It is presumably self-interested, and its proponent is presumably capable of crafting it to look persuasive. So the arbiter may tend to discount it despite—or even because of—its seeming plausibility. (The more a story told by a visibly good advocate hangs together, for example, the more susceptible it is to being taken as a clever concoction.) In speech-act terminology, the illocutionary thrust of *every* truth claim made by an advocate is to *plead one's cause*. The principal felicity conditions of pleading one's cause are a need on the pleader's part to get the arbiter's vote and a belief by the pleader that this particular truth claim will hold up well enough to get it. There is no presumption that the pleader believes anything else about the claim, least of all that it is true. With no great cynicism, an arbiter may adopt *caveat emptor* as the only prudent principle of interpretation.

A pleader's assertions are always suspect of being custom-designed. Because they are presumably constructed to persuade the arbiter, the arbiter may read them as revealing what the pleader thinks the arbiter will regard as persuasive. It is this risk, more than any expectation of appearing disinterested or non-partisan, that leads pleaders to avoid obvious sales pitches and artfully contrived arguments,[21] as well as arguments that can be seen as calculated to appeal to stupidity, prejudice, fear, favor, or doctrinaire prejudgments (such as knee-jerk "liberalism" or knee-jerk "conservatism"). To reduce the risk, pleaders characteristically load the language of argumentation with exquisitely ambiguous double meanings.[22]

2. Because the arbiter is primed to suspect and question all interpretations, the opponent of any interpretation has more than ordinary leeway to cast doubt upon the obvious, the ordinary, the self-evident. In this setting, it becomes possible for pleaders to construct and sell uncommonly imaginative suggestions of alternative interpretive frames.

But their selling must be accomplished consistently with the preceding point: the sales pitch cannot be hawked too blatantly or couched in a form that allows the comeback that it is designed to appeal to gullibility or bias. The advocates on both sides must always fear that their arguments may be *discredited* (rather than simply countered) by the adversary.[23] To minimize this danger, they may choose formulations that contain some illocutionary ambiguity or even some locutionary fuzziness, trading off the cogency of precision for the security of deniability ("That's not at all what I was saying!").

3. For all of these reasons, legal pleaders cultivate a wealth of techniques for conveying meanings that they do not appear to be pleading, or even intending to convey.[24] In litigation particularly, the *illocutionary* dimension of speech-act analysis so central to philosophers and linguists is demoted to the status of a means for advancing one's *perlocutionary* aim of winning the contest. What matters most is not what you say or do or mean but what you can sell. Here Searle's axioms that "whatever can be meant can be said"[25] and that "unless . . . [a hearer] recognizes that I am trying to tell him something and what I am trying to tell him, I do not fully succeed in telling it to him"[26] are only partly correct. We can substitute "selling" for "telling" in the last axiom, but not if we also substitute "sell" for the repeated "tell."[27]

In short, what a speaker says in legal discourse needs to be made only reasonably and revocably clear to the hearer; and what the speaker *means* by what is said needs to be made only reasonably, revocably, and partly clear. Some part of what is meant will almost always be concealed or ambiguous, despite the fact that the hearer will often suspect that something more is there and even suspect what it is. This partial masking of the litigator's intended meanings is necessary in order to *keep up the appearance of using language in an ordinary way*—either in the present discourse or in general. For there will sometimes be occasions (whether or not the present occasion is one of them) on which the pleader will need to keep an arbiter uninformed about the various ways in which the pleader is trying to effect persuasion or preserve the deniability of things the pleader says; and the pleader's *general* mode of discourse must be such that it can be used indistinguishably on those occasions and others. A pleader would be dead in the water if s/he were ever reduced to saying *either* "This time I don't really mean it, judge," *or* "This time I really do." For everybody's sake, the language game in the law has got to be played in a way that substitutes lots of imprecise and deniable implicatures for precise propositional assertions while seeming not to.

4. This discourse shapes the language in which lawyers argue cases and in which judges decide them. It puts a premium on detecting and unmasking covert rhetorical tricks on the part of the other guy. But it also puts a premium on detecting and unmasking covert rhetorics in your own language. For both lawyers seeking to persuade judges what is right and judges seeking to persuade themselves that they have got it right are at grave risk of falling prey to rhetorical self-delusion.

Self-delusion becomes especially likely when contestability threatens to destabilize important premises of our accustomed reasoning. For when we get nervous that somebody might pull the rug of familiar assumptions out from under our feet, we are likely to experience the still more frightening suspicion that maybe we dreamed up the rug in the first place. We are at least as likely to use rhetorics to stifle such suspicions in ourselves as to wrestle with others for control of the rug. So we start to play the rhetorical game of making our assumptions more invulnerable to our own doubts. And we end up buying our own rhetorics as avidly as we sell them to others.[28] Perhaps this is why, as we shall shortly see, judges deciding cases often write exactly like advocates arguing them—even when, as is invariably true in the case of United States Supreme Court Justices, they sit on a court of last resort and need fear no subcelestial reversal.

III. Rhetorical Devices for Managing Contestability

Here is a short list of rhetorical techniques that are especially effective in concealing contestability and its discontents. They will doubtless suggest the workings of many similar techniques. We will not attempt a long list, let alone a complete one. The craving for completeness is what killed rhetoric (for the eighth certifiable time at least in recorded Western history) during the seventeenth century.

We have organized the list into three basic categories plus a fourth, fuzzy domain. First there are rhetorical devices for altering the solidity, inevitability, or nature of reality: *ontological* construction techniques. Second are devices for altering the certainty or scope of our knowledge of reality: *epistemological* construction techniques. Third are *storytelling* techniques—reminders of our earlier chapters on narrative. Our fourth domain includes some ways in which symbols are created, evoked, and used across (or beneath) the other three categories. All the techniques we will discuss have one thing in common: they are easy to use, perhaps too easy. And, given favoring circumstances, they are not easy to discern or unmask. That's what makes them such staples of persuasion and self-deception.

Ontological Construction Techniques

CONCRETIZING AND DECONCRETIZING
With rug-pullers about, better stand on a rock! To build upon one—or to kick one, as in Dr. Johnson's celebrated refutation of Bishop Berkeley—can be very reassuring to oneself and convincing to others. The trick is to make rocks look like they were there before you came.[29]

All languages let you range in your descriptions of things from the quite concrete to the quite abstract. We get more concreteness by using words that are more fine-grained, more vivid, more graphic.[30] Multiplying details (by, for example, the classical rhetorical devices of amplification)[31] also adds solidity.

Consider, for example, the opening paragraphs of two Supreme Court opinions announced on the same day and authored by the same Justice. The opinions decided two admiralty cases presenting common issues that had been argued together. In the first case, the Court is going to rule for the defendant. In the second case, the Court is going to rule for the plaintiff. The Justices will have to make their peace with these results. Will the statement of the facts at the outset of each opinion help? Perhaps.

The opening paragraph in the first case reads:

> "The administratrix of the estate of Walter J. Halecki brought this action against the owners of the pilot boat *New Jersey* to recover damages for Halecki's death, allegedly caused by inhalation of carbon tetrachloride fumes while working aboard that vessel. . . . Under instructions that either unseaworthiness of the vessel or negligence would render the defendants liable and that contributory negligence on the part of the decedent would serve only to mitigate damages, a jury returned a verdict for the administratrix, upon which judgment was entered. The Court of Appeals affirmed. . . ."[32]

The opening paragraph in the second case reads:

> "On the evening of December 5, 1952, the motor vessel *Tungus* docked at Bayonne, New Jersey, with a cargo of coconut oil in its deep tanks. . . . Shortly after midnight [a] . . . pump became defective, resulting in the spillage of a large quantity of oil over the adjacent deck area. . . . Carl Skovgaard, an El Dorado maintenance foreman, was . . . summoned from his home to assist in the repair work. After arriving on board he walked through an area from which the oil had not been removed, and in attempting to step from the hatch beams to the top of the partly uncovered port deep tank, he slipped and fell to his death in eight feet of hot coconut oil."[33]

In addition to the carping qualifier ("allegedly")[34] and the distancing tech-talk ("administratrix") in the first quotation, some less obvious devices are noteworthy. The whole story is being told in *procedural* terms: it is about the lawsuit, not Halecki's demise. Halecki's demise is blurred by *nominalization:* he doesn't *die;* rather, his "death" is caused by "inhalation."[35] In the case of Carl Skovgaard, by contrast, the story is very much about his demise, which is concretized as to time and place and recounted literally step by step after poor, faithful Carl has been fetched from home (an affecting detail of no conceivable legal relevance) to his rendezvous with destiny. The detailing is meticulous, down to the modification of adjectives by adverbs of degree ("*partly* uncovered port deep tank"). And observe how the powerful adjective "deep"—initially introduced with a tantalizing ambiguity as to whether it is deictic or descriptive—gains descriptive force by repetition until it opens onto the bottomless abyss where faithful, hastening Carl plunges to his gruesome, oozy death. Now turn back to the *Halecki* fact statement and you will find that the only word with the slightest evocative power or teleological thrust is "pilot"—used to classify the defendants' boat.

It is not always the case that the concretizing of facts enhances persuasive force; but when it does not, that is usually the result of some rhetorical counter-move. A legal advocate or a result-bent judge confronted with indissolubly sticky facts can sometimes escape them by taking to high ground through the use of an *essence : manifestation* schema, which comports the notion that *the idea is what's important,* and that details are mere distractions.[36] We have seen Justice Scalia employ a version of this tactic in the *Michael H.* case.[37] Or concreteness can be used to create a clutter that then calls for sweeping away. For example, as we shall see in Chapter 9, the devolution of *Brown v. Board of Education*[38] occurred through a process in which *Brown*'s command to desegregate the public schools was reduced to a formula requiring examination of a set of detailed "factors"; then the factors were disaggregated, so as to bury *Brown* in rubble.[39]

Ascending or descending the ladder of concreteness without announcement can also serve to make categorizations look foreordained.[40] We have seen examples in *Missouri v. Jenkins,* where Chief Justice Rehnquist squeezes things into categories or excludes them from categories by adjusting the degree of specificity with which he describes the thing, the category, or both.[41] Adjustments of this kind take potential issues out of play by shunting attention into channels where the issues don't arise.

PRESUPPOSING AND REIFYING

It is only philosophers who have trouble with the concept of creation *ex nihilo.* Lawyers, like most ordinary-language speakers, do it all the time.

The array of linguistic resources available for establishing the existence of something covertly—without stating it[42]—includes numerous presupposition-triggers,[43] like the so-called factive verbs. When I say: "I am confident that Your Honor will *see through* opposing counsel's effort to conflate the doctrines of waiver and estoppel," I have not asserted propositionally that opposing counsel is deliberately seeking to mislead the court; I have conveyed it by a factive *presupposition.*[44] I can also do it by the so-called cleft construction: "It is not I who am trying to mislead Your Honor."

Another device is the commonplace topic-and-comment structure of the first sentence in the preceding paragraph. "The array of linguistic resources" is the *topic* of the sentence; our statement of what is included in the array is a *comment* on that topic.[45] Notice that the proposition smuggled into the topic—that there *is* an array of resources—has an insinuating force that the comment does not. The mechanism at work here is often described by linguists in terms of a distinction between the *given* and the *new* within any sentence (or information unit).[46] In the preceding sentence, for example, you are attending to what is new—the nifty new vocabulary about "the *given* and the *new*"—so your attention is distracted from the given—that what the vocabulary is talking about *is* a "mechanism." (We have absolutely no basis for this mechanistic metaphor.)

Parallel to the *given : new* dichotomy is the dichotomy of the *marked* and the *unmarked.*[47] For example, "crime" is the unmarked case; "white-collar crime" and "economic crime" and "political crime" and "crime of passion" are marked cases. When a word is used with no marking, it will be understood in its ordinary or conventional sense—with its conventional associations—and its use will reinforce our notion of what that conventional sense is. This is why talk about "crime" *simpliciter* calls to mind violent, ruthless, predatory behavior, and why arguments that this or that rule of criminal procedure will "hamper the state's ability to prosecute crime" are so powerful rhetorically, even though statistically most crimes that are committed and most crimes that are prosecuted are not violent, ruthless, or predatory.

The *given : new* and the *marked : unmarked* distinctions impose an enormous presuppositional load on what is being said. So, for example, if we put an unmarked form into topic position—like "the criminal is never simply to be forgiven"—we have in one fell swoop presupposed that the criminal in question is violent and that the only new issue is whether we should ever forgive him. And that takes us to another matter.

For there are also script-cues at work. Suppose I tell you: "I just got back from the dentist's. The hygienist worked me over for an hour." Grammatically, it should be impermissible for me to use the definite article "The" at the beginning of the second sentence because its subject, "hygienist," has not been previously introduced. My usage violates the rules of what linguists call *anaphora*.[48] (Properly, I should have specified "*A* hygienist . . .," after which it would have become permissible to refer to that hygienist as "*the* hygienist.") So, if you didn't find the word "The" ungrammatical, that must be because your *script* for dentists' offices contains a hygienist. Each of these and many other creations *ex nihilo* can activate the common human tendency to accept the existence of X or to expect X to happen once we have done some connective reasoning on the assumption that X exists or will happen—even after we become aware that the assumption was hypothesized arbitrarily, with no factual foundation.[49]

Reification works similarly. Our predilection for nouns may predispose us to reification. By treating any construct as a Thing, we putatively endow it with the attributes of a Thing. It existed before we came to talk of it; we are not responsible for it; we cannot change it. As we saw in Chapter 3, Justice Scalia's *Michael H.* opinion relies heavily on these consequences of reification. Justice Scalia reifies the claims that he attributes to the parties invoking constitutional protection;[50] he reifies a "tradition" of denying such protection;[51] then he stands back and watches these two Things collide. It is none of his doing.[52] There's *really* no issue. But examined carefully, his opinion is full of nouns clashing under the protection of common language use.

STRUCTURING WHAT'S POSSIBLE AND IMAGINABLE

Issues arise when choices are possible and when the need to make them is perceived. Language can foreclose the logical possibility of certain choices or conceal the need to make them.

A striking example is the practice of many prosecutors in capital cases tried under a type of death-penalty statute that has become widespread in the United States since the mid-1970s. Where this kind of statute is in force, the jury is instructed that it may sentence a defendant convicted of first-degree murder to either death or life imprisonment, and that it should make its penalty decision by weighing "aggravating circumstances" against "mitigating circumstances." *Aggravating circumstances* are said to include certain statutorily defined circumstances (for example, that the murder was committed in the course of a robbery) and any other circumstances that militate in favor of a death sentence. *Mitigating circumstances* are said to include certain statutorily defined circumstances (for example, that the defendant has no significant history of prior criminal activity) and any other circumstances that militate against a death sentence. Prosecutors arguing to juries who will consider a case under these instructions frequently take up, one by one, all of the salient facts of the crime and the defendant's background (for example, that the defendant had taken drugs shortly before the murder and had a criminal record), asking about each fact: "Now, is that aggravating *or* mitigating?" Since the facts surrounding most murders are unattractive and the backgrounds of most people who commit murders are also relatively unattractive, this *either/or* logic produces a strong preponderance of aggravation over mitigation. It does this by eliding the preliminary issue of whether each fact taken up should count at all as either-aggravating-or-mitigating, or whether it is simply neutral. If defense counsel sees the gambit and is able to convince the jury that the answer to virtually all of the prosecutor's is-it-aggravating-or-mitigating questions is "neither" (it ain't pretty, but it doesn't single this murder out as either prettier or uglier than most), a whole different aggravation/mitigation balance becomes possible.

We saw binary logic structures used to foreclose possible alternative choices in both of the Supreme Court opinions examined in Chapter 3. In *Jenkins,* Chief Justice Rehnquist found that white flight could not be a result of *de jure* segregation because it was a result of desegregation; the possibility of conjunctive causation was eliminated by ignoring it.[53] In *Michael H.,* Justice Scalia's acceptance of a one-father-per-family rule as *definitional* of "family" set up an *either/or* battle between Michael and Gerald that drove the whole opinion.[54]

These are instances of invoking an axiom of logic[55] which seems so naturally fitted to the situation that its application is likely to go unquestioned. Another instance is Chief Justice Taney's invocation of the axiom *A cannot be not-A* to demonstrate in *Dred Scott* that the Nation's Founders could not have intended the egalitarian language of the Declaration of Independence to apply to "the enslaved African race":

> "[I]f the language, as understood in that day, would embrace them, the conduct of the distinguished men who framed the Declaration . . . would have been utterly and flagrantly inconsistent with the principles they as-

serted; and instead of the sympathy of mankind, to which they so confidently appealed, they would have deserved and received universal rebuke and reprobation.

"Yet the men who framed this Declaration were great men—high in literary acquirements—high in their sense of honor, and incapable of asserting principles inconsistent with those on which they were acting."[56]

In the face of this inspiring prose, a reader is not prone to ask such questions as (1) whether and why there need be any inconsistency involved in proclaiming a political ideal that one is not currently realizing; (2) whether, if there is some inconsistency, honorable people are necessarily immune to it; and (3) if not, whether they are most fitly honored by perpetuating their professed ideals or their inconsistent practices. The sanctity of the Founders for Chief Justice Taney—like the sanctity of the family for Justice Scalia[57]—imports an INTEGRITY IS INDIVISIBILITY metaphor, thereby triggering the *A/not-A* axiom.

Often, rhetoric not only triggers the apt logical axioms, but sets up the situation that makes them apt. It does this by embedding in the fabric of a discourse some Theory of the Way the World Works—the kind of theory that is sometimes called a "cultural model"[58] or an "idealized cognitive model,"[59] but that we have spoken of in Chapter 5 under the more numinous title of "doom." As we saw there, *Prigg v. Pennsylvania* and *Freeman v. Pitts* embed very different conceptions of whether, in Emerson's phrase, "Things are in the saddle, [a]nd ride mankind." And these conceptions entail, in turn, very different strategies of striving or resignation, power-aggregation or power-abdication, taking action or treading water. Judges, for example, who are predisposed or persuaded to regard sectors of the human condition as intractable to human agency are unlikely to hold events in those sectors *actionable*.[60]

A speaker's Theory of the Way the World Works may be implicitly conveyed by many linguistic techniques.[61] It may be announced explicitly on the authority of Nature,[62] or it may be made to seem "natural" by imagery that bespeaks the primal, the unspoiled, that-which-needs-no-artifice-to-create-nor-effort-to-maintain.[63] Or, if Nature offers no plausible harbor for one's theory, Civilization may.[64] Legal culture shares the ambivalence of our society generally as to whether that-which-needs-artifice-to-create-and-effort-to-maintain is therefore to be valued or devalued.[65] Rhetoric may appeal, alternatively, to What is Natural or to What Our Forbears Struggled to

Carve Out of the Wilderness.[66] Or to whatever categories are assumed to Exist in the Real World.[67]

Epistemological Construction Techniques

Epistemological indicators can also be used to make facts appear more or less certain and to open or close the range of admissible interpretive possibilities. In legal jargon, the option of describing things without or with procedural modifiers (like "alleged" or "asserted" or "presumed" or "conceded") adds a dimension to the ordinary narrative device of stabilizing or destabilizing facts by recounting them through an omniscient focalizor (or narrator), on the one hand, or a restricted focalizor (or narrator), on the other.[68] Various subjunctivizing forms (such as modal auxiliary verbs—"could," "might," "should"—and complex verb phrases that interweave cognition with its objects),[69] mental verbs ("I think," "I imagine," "it seems that") and hedges ("generally," "essentially," "basically"),[70] as well as qualifying adverbs ("probably," "apparently," "approximately"), serve "to qualify the force of our assertions and conclusions."[71]

Each and every one of these devices is available to serve as a tool for selective skepticism. Consider, for example, the opinion of the Supreme Court in *Branzburg v. Hayes*,[72] rejecting claims by news reporters of any First Amendment right to keep their confidential sources secret when subpoenaed by government investigating agencies. To support their arguments that such a right was necessary for protection of the freedom of the press, the two subpoenaed reporters presented affidavits from numerous nationally-known newspaper and broadcast journalists documenting (1) that investigative journalists commonly rely upon assurances of confidentiality to obtain information for major news stories; (2) that subpoena-compelled disclosure of informants' identities had caused previously willing sources to stop providing information to journalists; and (3) that the prospect of journalists being legally compelled to reveal their sources to government investigators would result in a wholesale drying up of vital news sources. In one of the two reporters' cases, the trial judge made explicit findings of these facts; in the other reporter's case, no contrary findings—and no explicit factual findings of any sort—were made.

Now, this was an era when the Supreme Court was in the process of creating a wide range of privileges against compulsory disclosure of confidential information—an attorney/client privilege, a police/informer privilege, an executive-official privilege, and a prison-snitch privilege (under another name)—all based upon the common-sense assumption that the prospect of disclosure of sensitive communications will cause people not to make them.[73] But when the news reporters presented the selfsame factual proposition to the Court in *Branzburg,* on a far more solid evidentiary record, the Court suddenly turned dubious. Justice White's majority opinion says, *inter alia:*

> "The argument that the flow of news will be diminished by compelling reporters to aid the grand jury in a criminal investigation is not irrational, nor are the records before us silent on the matter. *But we remain unclear how often and to what extent* informers are *actually* deterred from furnishing information when newsmen are forced to testify before a grand jury. The available data indicate that *some* newsmen rely a great deal on confidential sources and that *some* informants are *particularly* sensitive to the threat of exposure and *may* be silenced if it is held by this Court that, ordinarily, newsmen must testify pursuant to subpoenas, *but the evidence fails to demonstrate* that there would be a *significant* constriction of the flow of news to the public. . . . *Estimates* of the inhibiting effect of such subpoenas on the willingness of informants to make disclosures to newsmen are *widely divergent* and *to a great extent speculative.* It would be *difficult* to canvass the views of the informants themselves; surveys of reporters on this topic are *chiefly opinions* of *predicted informant behavior* and *must be viewed in the light of the professional self-interest of the interviewees.* Reliance by the press on confidential informants does not mean that *all* such sources will *in fact* dry up because of the later *possible* appearance of the newsman before a grand jury."[74]

After similar expressions of epistemological *angst* (e.g., "*[n]othing before us indicates* that *a large number or percentage* of *all* confidential news sources *fall into [a] . . . category* [that] . . . would *in any way* be deterred . . .*"),[75] the Court goes on to say that even if it assumed that "*an undetermined number* of informants . . . will *nevertheless, for whatever reason,* refuse to talk to newsmen if they fear identification,"[76] it would not adopt a constitutional rule that protected press sources at the expense of criminal prosecution. Why? Several reasons are given, but the one that stands out is that

> "[f]rom the beginning of our country the press has operated without constitutional protection for press informants, and the press has flourished. The existing constitutional rules have not been a serious obstacle

to either the development or retention of confidential news sources by the press."[77]

In *this* bold pronouncement, compacting more than 200 years of continental history into two sentences, there is not a trace of doubt. Nor does the Court hesitate to make sweeping generalizations like:

> "the relationship of many informants to the press is a symbiotic one which is unlikely to be greatly inhibited by the threat of subpoena: quite often, such informants are members of a minority political or cultural group that relies heavily on the media to propagate its views."[78]

There is no evidence of this supposed symbiosis anywhere in the record, so the Court's confident use of quantitative terms in describing it—"*many* informants," "*quite* often," "relies *heavily*"—stands in particularly stark contrast to the Court's hedges ("*unclear* . . . extent," "*undetermined* number," and so forth) when describing the journalists' uncontradicted evidence of sources scared off by subpoenas. And thus the native hue of resolution is (sometimes) sicklied o'er with the pale cast of thought.

Storytelling Techniques

We talked about the rhetorical potential of narrative in Chapter 4, and we have seen in each of our case studies of Supreme Court opinions how the elements of *story* can be used to invest some vision of the world with believability or to keep questions about its believability from arising. Here we need only emphasize that story elements can be more or less covertly embedded in a discourse,[79] so as to generate implicit ontological and epistemological claims and presuppositions.

Casting—what players are admitted onto the stage, and in what roles—is particularly important in the discourse of litigation, because the agonistic nature of the genre means that any potential interest or consideration that is not represented by a Champion tends to go unrecognized. (Personification of the States of the United States is both the necessary and the sufficient condition for talk about "States' rights.")[80] *Stock scripts*—like the script of the combat myth embedded in Justice Scalia's *Michael H.* opinion[81]—instruct us both about what we should expect and about what we must value.[82] More elaborate *narrative* plots[83]—like the Conquering-Hero-Turned-Tyrant plot of Justice Kennedy's *Pitts* opinion and the Helen-of-Troy plot of Justice Story's *Prigg* opinion[84]—drive toward endings that will need to be the *right* ending in order to confer significance on all that came before.[85] Any convincing story suspends, at least temporarily, the claims of competing interpretations to define contestable issues within the movement of events that the story recounts.

Techniques for Making Meaning through Symbols

EVOKING PROTOTYPES OR BREAKING TYPE SETS

Most of us harbor images of the *typical* "murderer," "welfare mother," "mailman," "post office," "school bus," and so forth, attributing personality traits and dispositions to these type-labels for people and attributing usages and physical features to these type-labels for things.[86] Use of the type-labels in discourse that we hear or address to ourselves or others ordinarily causes us to picture the bundle of associated attributes and to interpret the discourse through that focus. Our image of the characters who seem to us to be central to any set of events will affect the story that we discern in those events and the issues posed by the events for judgment or decision.[87] So, for example, our attitude toward general issues of welfare policy may depend upon our picture of the typical welfare recipient; and our willingness to terminate support payments in a case in which there is substantial (but not conclusive) evidence that a welfare recipient is concealing assets may depend on whether our attention is called to facts that *break the type set* by making this particular recipient look different (although not otherwise more or less attractive) from our prototype.[88]

Or consider the movement of American courts from initial rejection to eventual acceptance of a rule of contract law permitting an employer to enforce an agreement-for-services by getting an injunction to restrain a recreant employee from serving the employer's competitors. This movement came in a series of cases in which the employee was female: the American free-labor ideology that depicted each employee as the master of his fate failed to hold up when a woman stage performer was seen as having "bound herself" to a male theater owner and then proved unfaithful.[89]

ENGAGING OR DISENGAGING CODED MEANINGS

How much and which prototypes, stock scripts, and other meaning-templates affect our cognition at a particular moment depends partly on *prompting*. We are more likely to attend to templates insofar as we are prompted to do so;[90] and one of the resources of rhetoric has always been to provide cogent prompts.[91]

Prompting by means of slogans and similar formulas coded with powerful emotional content is a commonplace of propaganda[92] and political rhetoric.[93] Pollution imagery, for example, was a central feature of talk about the Jewish problem in Nazi Germany[94] and has long been a central feature of Anglo-American talk about the crime problem.[95] To connect any problem with a powerful slogan is to shape the very conception of what the problem *is* by locating it in a field of values dominated by the slogan. Thus, the proponents of the 1996 California constitutional amendment initiative outlawing publicly-supported affirmative action programs (Proposition 209) labeled it the "California Civil Rights Initiative" and worded its text this way: "The state *shall not discriminate against,* or grant preferential treatment to, any individual or group on the basis of race, sex, color, ethnicity, or national origin in the operation of public employment, public education, or public contracting." By the time a reader gets to the nub of the matter, it has been coded as an anti-discrimination provision.[96]

Or consider the wording of the United States Supreme Court's decision in *McCleskey v. Kemp,*[97] holding that a death-sentenced defendant could not establish a violation of the Equal Protection Clause of the Fourteenth Amendment by statistical evidence showing that black-defendant/white-victim homicides were significantly more likely to result in death sentences than any other homicides prosecuted in the State of Georgia when non-racial variables were held constant:

> "... McCleskey's statistical proffer must be viewed in the context of his challenge. McCleskey challenges decisions *at the heart of the State's criminal justice system.* '[O]ne of society's most basic tasks is that of protecting the lives of its citizens and one of the most basic ways in which it achieves the task is through criminal laws against murder.' ... Implementation of these laws necessarily requires discretionary judgments. Because discretion is *essential to the criminal justice process,* we would demand exceptionally clear proof before we would infer that the discretion has been abused."[98]

This invocation of the lion-hearted "criminal justice system" at risk—which recurs like a mantra throughout the *McCleskey* opinion[99] and other Supreme Court opinions of like vintage[100]—sounds entirely plausible at first blush. But suppose we launched the problem into orbit around a different luminary slogan, as follows:

> . . . McCleskey's statistical proffer must be viewed in the context of his challenge. McCleskey's challenge implicates the equal protection of the laws which goes *to the heart of the Nation's constitutional commitment to equality and justice.* One of society's most basic functions is to protect the life of every citizen and assure that it not be taken away except in accordance with the 'law of the land,' whose 'known certainty is the safety of all.' . . . Implementation of this protection necessarily requires some restraints upon a regime of totally discretionary decisionmaking in capital prosecutions. Because evenhandedness is *essential to the constitutional rule of law,* we must demand some explanation for racially disproportionate death-sentencing patterns which, if unexplained, would suggest an invidious abuse of discretion somewhere in the criminal justice machinery.

This alternative framing of the issue, which might compete with the Court's if attended to, is denied attention once "the context of [McCleskey's] . . . challenge" is declared to be "the State's criminal justice system" rather than America's longtime struggle to make its constitutional vision of equality real for African-Americans.

ENCODING MEANING INTO WORDS

Often rhetorics involve not only using words that come pre-coded but implanting words with new code meanings. One of the most effective ways to code a word is to use it repeatedly within the fabric of a narrative until it has taken on a meaning in that context,[101] and then to lift it out and use it elsewhere without examining or explaining it, simply treating its meaning as a given. We have seen Chief Justice Rehnquist do this with the key word "interdistrict" in *Missouri v. Jenkins.*[102] A more elaborate version of the technique appears in a body of Supreme Court cases upsetting lower courts' stays of execution of death sentences between 1982 and 1996, in which the Court coded words like "delay" and phrases like "abuse of the writ of habeas corpus" within the narrative frame of a conspiracy myth: Death-sentenced inmates and their scheming lawyers were manipulating postconviction procedures in an attempt to frustrate the will of the people and the authority of the Nation's highest court in an ideological war of attrition over capital punishment. Not surprisingly, the

Court and then Congress rose to the occasion by curbing the procedures, defunding the lawyers, and killing the inmates.[103]

The coding was particularly cogent in this instance because it tapped the metaphoric potential of "abuse" and similar code words.[104] "[M]etaphor is the rhetorical process by which discourse unleashes the power that certain fictions have to redescribe reality."[105] It locks the multiple denotations of a word in a bond that resists analytic detachment[106] and causes the use of the word in any one of its senses to trigger the thoughts and feelings that attend the others. Thus, by characterizing a particular habeas corpus petition as "abusive"—an adjective denoting, doctrinally, any second or successive petition raising new grounds that fails to explain on its face why the new grounds were not raised earlier—the Court could reap the benefits of all of the adjective's connotations: *excessive* ("drug abuse"; "alcohol abuse"), *exploitative* ("abuse of friendship"; "excuse abuse"), *perfidious* ("abuse of trust"; "abuse of confidence"), *vicious* or *perverted* ("child abuse"; "sexual abuse"), and so on.

Metaphoric rhetoric, indeed, has played a conspicuous role in the Supreme Court's periodic reconceptualizations of the proper scope of federal habeas corpus remedies for state prisoners who claim that their convictions or sentences are unconstitutional.[107] When the Warren Court expanded the reach of the writ in the controversial *Fay v. Noia* case,[108] its opinion discussed the interplay between habeas corpus procedure and legal change in language full of tropes about organic growth and the World Tree. The history of habeas corpus was described as "inextricably *intertwined with the growth of fundamental rights* of personal liberty."[109] Habeas was seen as a writ "'*throwing its root deep* into the genius of our common law.'"[110] Its "*root principle*" was said to be "that in a civilized society, government must always be accountable."[111] The "breadth of the federal courts' power . . . on habeas corpus," the Court wrote, "*stems* from the very nature of the writ,"[112] serving "to test any restraint contrary to fundamental law, which in England *stemmed* ultimately from Magna Charta."[113] And, although the English Habeas Corpus Act of 1679 concededly excepted "judicial detentions that have *ripened* into criminal convictions,"[114] the Court noted that "standards of due process have *evolved* over the centuries."[115]

On the other hand, when the Rehnquist Court later radically restricted the availability of federal habeas corpus relief for state prisoners in the controversial cases of *Teague v. Lane*[116] and *McCleskey v. Zant*,[117] its opinions discussed the interplay between habeas corpus procedure and legal change in language full of tropes about riven and eroded rock. In *Teague* the Court observed that a judicial decision "announces a new rule when it *breaks new ground*."[118] New rules should not be applied retroactively, the Court believed, when they "*constituted clear breaks* with the past."[119] This was because the "[a]pplication of constitutional rules not in existence at the time a criminal conviction became final seriously *undermines* the principle of finality."[120] The Court allowed an exception "for *watershed rules* of criminal procedure,"[121] but said that, even though "'it might be that time and growth in social capacity . . . will properly alter our understanding of the *bedrock procedural elements* that must be found to vitiate the fairness of a particular conviction,'"[122] the Justices "believe[d] it unlikely that many such components of *basic* due process have yet to *emerge*."[123] And similarly in *McCleskey,* the Court found it necessary to adopt rules to "curtail the abusive petitions that in recent years have threatened *to undermine* the integrity of the habeas corpus process"[124] because habeas corpus "litigation places a *heavy burden* on scarce federal judicial resources."[125] It said that "the writ *strikes at* finality,"[126] and causes even more "*severe . . . disruptions* when a claim is presented for the first time in a second or subsequent federal habeas petition";[127] accordingly, "[c]onsiderations of certainty and *stability* in our discharge of the judicial function *support* [the] adoption" of rules[128] to provide "'a *sound* and workable means of *channeling* the discretion of federal habeas courts,'"[129] and so forth.

Or consider the role of metaphor in Chief Justice Taney's *Dred Scott* opinion, where he declares and repeats three times that Americans of African descent are not entitled to admission to the "*political family*" of the United States.[130] He cannot read the Declaration of Independence as extending to "*embrace the whole human family*"[131] because the Declaration's language, when written, "would not, in any part of the civilized world, be supposed to *embrace* the negro race, which, by common consent, had been excluded from civilized governments and *the family of nations* and doomed to slavery."[132] The Chief Justice cites colonial legislation to prove this universal opinion, including Maryland's law "declaring 'that if any free negro or mulatto *intermarry* with any white woman, or if any white man shall *intermarry* with any negro or mulatto woman, such negro or mulatto shall become a slave during life'"[133] and Massachusetts' "'Act for the better *preventing of a spurious and mixed issue*'"[134]—statutes which, Taney concluded, show that "*intermarriages* between white persons and negroes or mulattoes were regarded as *unnatural and immoral.*"[135] The recurrent family trope simultaneously carries the messages of "we" and "they," all of the benevolently paternalistic intellectual baggage of slavery, a dramatic reminder of the dangers of interracial sex and miscegenation and of the Curse of Canaan crying that the Black children of Ham deserve eternal servitude because Ham saw his father Noah sleeping nude. Perhaps more than anything else in the Chief Justice's opinion, the family trope illuminates his conclusion that "the provisions of the Constitution, in relation to . . . personal rights and privileges [cannot be thought to have] . . . *embraced* the negro African race"[136] because they were "intended to *embrace* those only who were then members of the several state communities, or who should afterwards, by *birthright* or otherwise, become members. . . ."[137] The trope thus mediates between Taney's interpretation of the Naturalization Clause of Article I, section 8 as displaying "*caution* . . . in providing for the *admission of new members into this political family*"[138] and his conclusion that the Constitution intended "a perpetual and *impassable barrier* . . . to be erected between the white race and the one which they had reduced to slavery."[139]

IV. More Rhetorics

We think it evident that unexamined rhetorics can make trouble, in the law as elsewhere. But the moral of this story is a need for more examination, not less rhetoric. Less rhetoric, *pace* Plato, is impossible. Wayne Booth got it right when he wrote that an author "cannot choose to avoid rhetoric; he can choose only the kind of rhetoric he will employ."[140] And James Boyd White also got it right when he wrote:

> "Every time one speaks as a lawyer, one establishes for the moment a character—an ethical identity, or what the Greeks called an *ethos*—for oneself, for one's audience, and for those one talks about, and proposes a relationship among them. The lawyer's speech is thus always implicitly argumentative not only about the result—how should the case be decided?—and the language—in what terms should it be defined and talked about?—but about the rhetorical community of which one is at

that moment a part. One is always establishing in performance a response to the question 'What kind of community should we who are talking the language of the law establish with each other, with our clients, and with the rest of the world? What kind of conversation should the law constitute, should constitute the law?'"[141]

Well-considered rhetorics can moderate the tension between pleading and demanding in advocacy;[142] they can nurture polyphonic discourse in place of monologue;[143] they can open possibilities of interpretation instead of shutting them down;[144] they can facilitate, in various legal settings, "conversations in which both parties can remain tentative and exploratory as relevance is considered against a variety of norms."[145] Perhaps they can even serve to "create a new discursive space that allows for both diversity and community."[146] But these results cannot be achieved without working hard and thoughtfully to bring them about;[147] and a part of the work is to keep constantly aware of the ways in which many commonplace legal rhetorics function to *narrow* the range of discursive space and interpretive possibility. We examine a fatal instance of this in the following chapter.

CHAPTER SEVEN

The Rhetorics of Death

McCleskey v. Kemp

For our case study in rhetorics, we will examine Justice Lewis Powell's majority opinion in *McCleskey v. Kemp*.[1] Hindsight gives this 1987 opinion a special rhetorical interest. In *McCleskey,* the Supreme Court rejected a condemned murderer's claims that his death sentence violated the Cruel and Unusual Punishments Clause of the Eighth Amendment and the Equal Protection Clause of the Fourteenth Amendment because it had been imposed pursuant to a pattern of racially discriminatory capital sentencing in the State of Georgia. The decision was rendered by a vote of five to four, so Justice Powell's conclusion to uphold the death sentence was decisive and sealed McCleskey's fate.[2]

Yet barely four years later, when Justice Powell was interviewed by his biographer after his retirement from the Court and was asked "whether he would change his vote in any case," he replied: "'Yes, *McCleskey v. Kemp.*'" Powell explained that he had come to think that capital punishment should be abolished because it could not be regularly and fairly administered.[3] This change of heart did not mean that Powell was retrospectively persuaded by McCleskey's "'argument from statistics,'"[4] but it did mean that he was no longer able to accept his own grounds for rejecting McCleskey's argument.[5] Perhaps his *McCleskey* opinion will offer an instructive study of the means by which rhetorics achieve a self-justification that is strong enough to kill with, although not strong enough to endure much beyond the killing.

I. The Background, Facts, and Holding of the Case

The background of the *McCleskey* litigation is a long story briefly told. Since the time of the Scottsboro Boys case in the early 1930s, lawyers associated with national civil rights organizations had been called upon to represent African-American criminal defendants charged with capital crimes against white persons or already condemned to death for such crimes. Lawyers with experience in these cases at the NAACP Legal Defense Fund became convinced that their clients were often sentenced to die for offenses that would not ordinarily have resulted in a capital sentence—or even in conviction of a crime sufficiently serious to be potentially punishable by death—if the race of the defendant or the victim had been different. Their intuition that racial considerations were driving death sentencing was borne out in the mid-1960s by extensive empirical studies[6] and was in keeping with immemorial folk knowledge. The *Statement of the Law of Homicide in Tennessee,* proverbial among criminal trial lawyers, predicted exactly what the empirical studies later found: "If a black man kill a white man, that be first-degree murder; if a white man kill a white man, that be second-degree murder; if a black man kill a black man, that be mere manslaughter; whereas if a white man kill a black man that be excusable homicide (unless a woman be involved, in which case the black man died of natural causes)."

This trenchant précis of the legal rules was, of course, descriptive of the law in action, not of the statute books. Formally, the statutes in force in most of the States between the 1930s and the 1960s provided simply that, when a jury convicted a defendant of a crime punishable by death, the jury's verdict should specify either a sentence of imprisonment or a death sentence, at the jurors' discretion. In 1965, Legal Defense Fund attorneys, believing that racial discrimination was inevitable and ineradicable under discretionary death-penalty statutes of this kind, embarked on a systematic litigation campaign to get them declared unconstitutional. The campaign produced several results.

The jurisprudential result was a series of decisions by the Supreme Court of the United States imposing some, but not very stringent, constitutional restrictions upon the power of the States to inflict capital punishment. The first important decision of this sort was *Furman v. Georgia,*[7] handed down in 1972. In *Furman,* the Court held by a vote of five to four—in a confusing array of opinions by the several Justices—that the Cruel and Unusual Punishments Clause of the Eighth Amendment to the federal Constitution prohibits capital-sentencing procedures that create an undue risk of arbitrary and discriminatory distribution of death sentences. On this ground, the Justices struck down all of the then-ubiquitous statutes giving a jury unconstrained discretion to choose between the sentences of imprisonment and death when it convicted a defendant of a capital offense.

Thirty-odd States promptly enacted new statutes, of roughly two kinds. *Mandatory* death-penalty laws provided that every defendant convicted of a specified offense was automatically to be sentenced to death. *Guided-discretion* statutes provided that juries (or judges) could consider imposing a death sentence only if they made certain findings (such as a finding of one or more enumerated "aggravating circumstances"), usually in a separate sentencing hearing following a defendant's conviction of a capital offense. Most of the guided-discretion statutes also enumerated a list of "mitigating circumstances" that the jury was supposed to "weigh" against (or otherwise evaluate conjointly with) whatever aggravating circumstances it found in a particular case; and almost all such statutes directed a state appellate court to set aside the death sentence in any case in which the aggravating and mitigating circumstances appeared to be out of line with those in other cases in which death sentences were being imposed. In 1976, the Supreme Court upheld the constitutionality of the guided-discretion form of statute in *Gregg v. Georgia*[8] but invalidated the mandatory form of statute in *Woodson v. North Carolina*[9] on the ground that any infliction of the death penalty without consideration of the individual features of the particular case at bar was so inhumane as to constitute still another sort of cruel and unusual punishment.

In theory these rulings required that if a State wanted to use the death penalty, it had to design capital-sentencing procedures capable of steering between the Charybdis of *Furman* (too much discretion) and the Scylla of *Woodson* (too little discretion). However, during the next decade or so, the Supreme Court progressively broadened this constitutional strait. It continued to assert that the Eighth Amendment required capital-punishment statutes to "channel the sentencer's discretion by 'clear and objective standards' that provide 'specific and detailed guidance,' and that 'make rationally reviewable the process for imposing a sentence of death,'"[10] and it applied this principle to invalidate excessively vague definitions of aggravating circumstances, such as one permitting a death sentence to be imposed for murders that are "especially heinous, atrocious, or cruel."[11] Yet, once a single aggravating circumstance was found (or if a State narrowed its definition of capital murder),[12] little or no further guidance[13] or review[14] of the jurors' sentencing discretion was required.[15] On the lee side, the Court invalidated statutes that restricted the roster of *mitigating* circumstances so that the sentencer was "precluded from considering, as a mitigating factor, any aspect of a defendant's character or record and any of the circumstances of the offense that the defendant proffers as a basis for a sentence less than death."[16] But this principle, too, was applied with considerable flexibility.[17] All in all, the Court upheld most of the death-sentencing statutes that came before it, emphasizing that the Eighth Amendment tolerated a considerable range of differing state procedures.[18]

In the late 1970s and early 1980s, the Court handed down decisions that essentially restricted capital punishment to the offense of murder, on the theory that the Eighth Amendment requires a certain proportion between crime and punishment.[19] The result of this development was to eliminate the death penalty for rape, which had been the *locus classicus* of racial discrimination in the popular imagination[20] and the focus of the pioneering empirical studies documenting such discrimination.[21] During the same period, the Supreme Court also entertained constitutional challenges to a range of pretrial and trial procedures in capital cases, establishing some important safeguards for defendants[22] including the right of an African-American defendant charged with the murder of a white victim to question prospective jurors about race prejudice that might sway the sentencing decision.[23]

But by the mid-1980s, a second consequence of the Legal Defense Fund's capital litigation campaign had become apparent. This was the stoppage of practically all executions in the United States. Executions had ceased entirely between 1967 and 1977; they were slow to resume in the wake of the 1976 Supreme Court decisions sustaining some forms of capital sentencing statutes. The reasons for the holdup were complex. Novel issues of state law as well as federal constitutional issues were presented by the new death-penalty statutes enacted after *Furman* and after *Woodson*. The obscurity of those Supreme

Court decisions—rendered with no majority opinion to make their scope readily discernible—left the federal constitutional rules to be hammered out by the lower courts and by the Supreme Court bit by bit. Lower court judges faced with difficult legal issues and an imminent execution date usually granted the condemned inmate's request to stay the execution pending appeal and postconviction review proceedings. The Legal Defense Fund's visible position at the center of the capital litigation scene encouraged lawyers all over the country to seek its aid and enabled it to disseminate model stay-application papers and arguments addressing the still-unresolved legal issues.

For several Supreme Court Justices, including Justice Powell, the continuing stoppage of executions became increasingly galling. Their discontent was expressed in some very strident opinions beginning about 1980[24] and, in Justice Powell's case, in a widely reported speech to the Eleventh Circuit Conference in 1983.[25] These Justices believed that the Court's decisions upholding the constitutionality of the death penalty were not being taken seriously, and this *lèse majesté*—perceived as a threat that "undermines public confidence in our system of justice and the will and ability of the courts to administer it"—outraged them.[26] They were soon to lead the Court in its own campaign to escalate the flagging pace of executions.[27] Beginning in the mid-1980s, the Court's decisions on the merits of constitutional issues raised by death-sentenced inmates also began to run heavily against the inmates.[28]

A third consequence of the Legal Defense Fund's capital litigation campaign was probably that by the mid-1980s the Justices of the Supreme Court came to view the Fund's lawyers as abolitionist zealots, embarked on a crusade against the death penalty for its own sake. This may well have caused the Justices to believe that, on the part of these lawyers, even a claim of race discrimination that was obviously in the grain of the Fund's historic racial-justice mission was a mere tool or tease of abolitionist design. However that may be, by the time Warren McCleskey's claim of racial discrimination in the administration of the death penalty for murder in the State of Georgia reached the Supreme Court in 1986, some of the Justices at least must have been concerned that if they countenanced that claim, they would be opening the door to similar claims in other States; and that the extended postconviction evidentiary litigation necessary to resolve such empirically-based claims would further impede the States from getting on with the business of killing people under statutes that the Court had upheld fully ten years before.

Warren McCleskey was sentenced to death in Fulton County, Georgia, for the killing of a police officer who had responded to a silent alarm set off when four armed men including McCleskey attempted to rob a furniture store. McCleskey was black, the officer white. A jury consisting of eleven white jurors and one African-American juror convicted McCleskey of murder; it found that the murder involved two of the "aggravating circumstances" that authorize (but do not require) a death sentence under Georgia's homicide statute (the murder was committed during an armed robbery; and the victim was a peace officer); and it elected to sentence McCleskey to die.

McCleskey's death sentence in 1978 was the only one imposed in Fulton County for the killing of a police officer between 1973 (when Georgia's post-*Furman* statute was enacted) and 1980 (when attorneys for the Legal Defense Fund entered McCleskey's case on appeal). Sixteen other killers of police officers were sentenced to imprisonment in the county during these years. In only one police-killing case other than McCleskey's did Atlanta's predominantly white prosecuting authorities seek the death penalty, and in that case a black defendant convicted of killing a black officer was given a life sentence.

This local history led the Fund lawyers to ask the obvious question: *Why Warren McCleskey?* By the time they were ready to file federal habeas corpus proceedings on McCleskey's behalf two years later, they thought they had an answer that the federal courts might listen to. Their federal petition for McCleskey alleged that his death sentence was the product of a statewide pattern of racially biased death sentences in Georgia, and that it therefore violated both the Eighth Amendment rule of *Furman* prohibiting arbitrary and discriminatory capital sentencing and the Equal Protection Clause of the Fourteenth Amendment. In support of these claims, the Fund lawyers presented (among other evidence) two extensive studies of Georgia homicide cases between 1973 and 1979, conducted by Professor David C. Baldus of the University of Iowa and his colleagues.[29]

These studies examined data—mostly obtained from official state records kept by the Georgia Supreme Court and the Georgia Board of Pardons and Paroles—covering 2,484 cases of murder and non-negligent manslaughter. Using a highly refined protocol, the researchers collected information about more than 500 factors in each case. These included demographic and individual characteristics of the defendant and victim; the circumstances of the crime; the strength of the evidence of guilt; and the aggravating and mitigating factors in each case—both the factors specified by Georgia law for consideration in capital sentencing, and every other factor recognized in the legal and criminological literature as theoretically or actually likely to affect the choice of life or death. The Baldus research team subjected the data to a wide array of statistical procedures, including multiple-regression analyses based upon alternative models that controlled for as few as 10 or as many as 230 sentencing factors in each analysis. While presenting the results in court, Professor Baldus reanalyzed the data several more times to take account of every additional factor, combination of factors, or model for analysis of factors suggested by the State of Georgia's expert witnesses, its lawyers, and the federal trial judge.

Professor Baldus found, among other things, that:

1. Fewer than 40% of Georgia homicide cases involve white victims, but in 87% of the cases in which a death sentence is imposed the victim is white. White-victim cases are roughly eleven times more likely than black-victim cases to result in a sentence of death.

2. When the race of the defendant is added to the analysis, the following pattern appears: 22% of black defendants who kill white victims are sentenced to death; 8% of white defendants who kill white victims are sentenced to death; 1% of black defendants who kill black victims are sentenced to death; and 3% of white defendants who kill black victims are sentenced to death. (Only 64 of the approximately 2,500 homicide cases studied involved killings of blacks by whites, so the 3% figure in this category represents a total of two death sentences over a six-year period. Thus, the reason why a bias against black defendants is not even more apparent is that most black defendants have killed black victims; almost no cases are found of white defendants who have killed black victims; and virtually no defendant convicted of killing a black victim gets the death penalty.)

3. No factor other than race explains these racial patterns. The multiple-regression analysis with the greatest explanatory power shows that after controlling for non-racial factors, murderers of white victims receive a death sentence 4.3 times more frequently than murderers of black victims. The race of the victim proves to be as good a predictor of a capital sentence as the aggravating circumstances

spelled out in the Georgia statute, such as whether the defendant has a prior murder conviction or was the primary actor in the present murder.

4. Only 5% of Georgia killings result in a death sentence; yet, when more than 230 non-racial variables are controlled for, the death-sentencing rate is 6% higher in white-victim cases than in black-victim cases. A murderer therefore incurs less risk of death by committing the murder in the first place than by selecting a white victim instead of a black one.

5. The effects of race are not uniform across the spectrum of homicide cases. In the least aggravated cases, almost no defendants are sentenced to death; in the most aggravated cases, a high percentage of defendants are sentenced to death regardless of their race or their victim's; it is in the mid-range of cases—which, as it happens, includes cases like McCleskey's—that race has its greatest influence. In these mid-range cases, death sentences are imposed on 34% of the killers of white victims and 14% of the killers of black victims. In other words, twenty out of every thirty-four defendants sentenced to die for killing a white victim would *not* have received a death sentence if their victims had been black.

The federal district judge who heard this evidence concluded that it was not sufficient to show that racial factors were at work in Georgia's capital sentencing process, largely because the data collected by Baldus's researchers failed to capture all of the nuances of every possible aggravating and mitigating circumstance; because some data were missing for some of the 2,500 cases studied; and because there was no showing that all of the data regarding each case that was found in Georgia's official postconviction records had been known to the prosecutors and jurors before sentence was imposed. An intermediate appellate court, the United States Court of Appeals for the Eleventh Circuit, put aside these methodological criticisms, assumed that the Baldus study was methodologically valid, and assumed that it "showed that systematic and substantial disparities existed in the penalties imposed upon homicide defendants in Georgia based on race of the homicide victim, that the disparities existed at a less substantial rate in death sentencing based on race of defendants, and that the factors of race of the victim and defendant were at work in Fulton County."[30] The Court of Appeals nevertheless held that such a showing was legally inadequate to establish a violation of either the Eighth

Amendment or the Equal Protection Clause of the Fourteenth; and it was the correctness of those two legal rulings that the Supreme Court approved, five to four, in Justice Powell's majority opinion in the *McCleskey* case.

Justice Powell says to start with that the Supreme Court, like the Court of Appeals, will "assume the [Baldus] study is valid statistically."[31] He frames the question which the Supreme Court must decide as "whether a complex statistical study that indicates a risk that racial considerations enter into capital sentencing determinations proves that . . . McCleskey's capital sentence is unconstitutional under the Eighth or Fourteenth Amendment."[32] His answer to that question is no. With regard to the Fourteenth Amendment, he starts from the premise established by earlier Supreme Court precedents,[33] that the Equal Protection Clause prohibits only *purposeful* discrimination by some state-appointed actor, and that as a corollary a capital defendant asserting an Equal Protection violation "must prove that the decisionmakers in *his* case acted with discriminatory purpose."[34] Justice Powell finds that McCleskey has not proved this because statistical evidence of statewide (or even Fulton County) sentencing patterns cannot establish the requisite subjective racial *animus* of the prosecutor, jurors, judge, or other individual actors in McCleskey's case or of the legislators who enacted the post-*Furman* Georgia death-penalty statute.[35] With regard to the Eighth Amendment, Justice Powell concludes that the risk of racial bias demonstrated by the Baldus study is not sufficient to invalidate the Georgia statute as applied.[36] We will examine how he reaches these conclusions, paying special attention to his rhetorics.[37]

II. Justice Powell's Opinion for the Court

Virtually all of the rhetorical devices we described in Chapter 6 are put to use in Justice Powell's opinion to produce a single effect: the concealment of every debatable choice that the Court is making as it marches through a seemingly standard drill in legal reasoning. So many relevant matters remain unaddressed by the opinion that it is easy to fault Justice Powell's form simply as "slovenly judicial analysis."[38] But we think that more—and more interesting—things are involved. The question is how Justice Powell manages with such complete consistency to disregard whatever might obstruct his chosen line of march; and the answer, for the most part, is rhetorics.

Consider, for example, the obvious omissions at the center of his logic. Although purporting to assume the Baldus study shows "a risk" that death sentences are being meted out on grounds of race under the Georgia statute,[39] Justice Powell discounts the significance of this risk for both Equal Protection purposes and Eighth Amendment purposes. His Equal Protection analysis says that because "McCleskey challenges decisions at the heart of the State's criminal justice system," and because "discretion is essential to the criminal justice process, we would demand exceptionally clear proof before we would infer that the discretion has been abused."[40] His Eighth Amendment analysis says that "[w]here the discretion that is fundamental to our criminal process is involved, we decline to assume that what is unexplained is invidious."[41] The reasoning in the first passage has to do with how much risk of racially biased decisionmaking should be required "to support [a factual] . . . inference that any of the decisionmakers in McCleskey's case acted with discriminatory purpose."[42] The reasoning in the second passage has to do with how much risk of racially biased decisionmaking in the system as a whole is "'constitutionally unacceptable.'"[43] In both analyses the *importance of the criminal justice function that would be jeopardized if McCleskey's claims were recognized* is put forward as a powerful reason not to recognize those claims. The point is given added punch by passages throughout the opinion emphasizing that one of "'society's most basic tasks is that of protecting the lives of its citizens . . . through criminal laws against murder'"[44] and that "[i]mplementation of these laws necessarily requires discretionary judgments."[45]

Yet nowhere in the opinion is a single word said about the importance of the value of racial equality that would be jeopardized if McCleskey's claims are *not* recognized. This omission conspicuously leaves the opinion lacking half the makings of the cost/benefit analysis that Justice Powell is ostensibly conducting. The omission is the more conspicuous because it stands in stark contrast to the stirring professions of the importance of the value of racial equality that the Court in general and Justice Powell in particular are prone to pronounce—as much or more in criminal-justice contexts as in others[46]—whenever they elect to promote that value.[47] A similarly glaring omission is Justice Powell's failure to recognize the implications of his own declared value system insofar as they support McCleskey's claims. If, for example, one of "'society's most basic tasks is that of protecting the lives of its citizens . . . through criminal laws against murder,'" this consideration would seem to strengthen, not weaken, the argument for judicial vigilance lest Georgia use its murder laws to protect the lives of its black and white citizens unequally.[48]

It is not that Justice Powell's opinion totally neglects to mention the constitutional concern for racial equality, or explicitly disparages that concern. The first of these approaches would be difficult to bring off while saying anything at all about McCleskey's claims—a bit like trying to play Hamlet without the ghost. The second approach would require Justice Powell to face up squarely to the ordering of values that is driving his opinion. Nor does Justice Powell *overtly* assert as a factual matter that the constitutional concern for racial equality has been satisfied in the administration of Georgia's capital sentencing statute. That approach would compel him to come to grips with the embarrassing data revealed by the Baldus study; and even if he found a way to deny the persuasiveness of this particular study's conclusions, the approach would still leave Georgia's system and its counterparts in other states at risk of subsequent empirical challenge.

Rather, Justice Powell's rhetorical strategy is to portray the constitutional concern for racial equality as a Great and Honored Expectation—its honorific status attested by the fact that the Court *has* honored it ("we have engaged in 'unceasing efforts' to eradicate racial prejudice from our criminal justice system")[49]—and thus to put it on a wholly different ontological plane than the laws against murder, "the criminal justice system," "discretion," and all of the other constructs that he sees as threatened by McCleskey's claims. Racial equality is an *aspiration* that judges can salve their consciences by *striving* mightily (albeit ineffectually) to attain. Because it is disembodied, not quite real, society's failures to achieve it are also not quite real; and to carry the quest to the lengths advocated by McCleskey (and the four dissenting Justices) would be quixotic and unworldly.[50] By contrast, there is a hard reality and therefore an irresistible inevitability to such unquestionable facts as the states' efforts to protect the lives of their citizens by capital-punishment statutes, the criminal justice system, and discretion as an instrument of criminal justice. When aspiration and reality collide, the Supreme Court should certainly do as much as it practicably can to fulfill the aspiration but must ultimately bow to the reality.

Thus, the *McCleskey* opinion tells the edifying moral tale of that mature heroism which consists in making an honorable peace with the inescapable facts of the Universe.[51] As a subplot, it tells the equally familiar cautionary fable of the insatiate beneficiary with McCleskey cast in the leading role: instead of being grateful for all the constitutional gifts that the Court has already showered on him and his kind, the unappreciative wretch has the gall and greediness to ask for more.[52]

But how does the opinion create a world in which these stories can be told with plausibility?[53] Among the rhetorical devices made to do this work, perhaps the most interesting are (1) those that imbue selected features of the criminal justice system with unalterable factuality and conversely dematerialize the fact of racial discrimination; (2) those that depict capital sentencing procedures and other practices in the world as fathomable or unfathomable, predictable or unpredictable, according to the changing needs of Justice Powell's story line; and (3) those that make McCleskey's claims extravagant by ignoring the availability of category lines that could restrict their implications, while drawing category lines of a similar sort between McCleskey's claims and the precedents that support them. Consider each of these in turn:

Making Discretionary Justice Real and Discrimination Unreal

The structural framework for this rhetorical maneuver is one that we have seen before, most notably in Justice Scalia's *Michael H.* opinion.[54] The rectification of racial bias in capital sentencing sought by McCleskey and advocated by the dissenting Justices is locked into an *either/or* confrontation with capital punishment[55] *and* jury trial[56] *and* discretion in the administration of criminal justice (sometimes called "leniency"),[57] so that the Court cannot vindicate McCleskey's claims without immolating all these things. Then the Court has only to endow the things-to-be-sacrificed with unyielding materiality or necessity (or both) while attenuating the reasons-for-the-sacrifice into wraith-like immateriality, and there is *really* no difficult issue remaining to resolve.

Note the metaphors of centrality and the vocabulary of indispensability that Justice Powell uses to describe the things that
McCleskey's claim *challenges:*

> "... McCleskey's statistical proffer must be viewed in the context of his
> challenge. McCleskey challenges decisions *at the heart of the State's
> criminal justice system.* '[O]ne of society's most *basic* tasks is that of
> protecting the lives of its citizens and one of the most *basic* ways in
> which it achieves the task is through criminal laws against murder.' ...
> Implementation of these laws *necessarily* requires discretionary judg-
> ments.... [D]iscretion is *essential* to the criminal justice process...."[58]

This sort of heavy-gravity language is a standard feature[59] of the opinion's frequent assertions that the capital sentencing discretion which
McCleskey's claims would trammel "is fundamental to our criminal
process,"[60] "essential to a humane and fair system of criminal justice,"[61] and a matter of "necessity."[62] The density and repetition of
these pronouncements give them inescapable *presence:*[63] there is simply no getting away from them.

On the other hand, the racial bias of which McCleskey complains is
progressively rarefied until it becomes little more than an abstraction.
Justice Powell sets this process in motion in the very first sentence of
his opinion[64] by juxtaposing two things that a "complex statistical
study" might be said to do: *indicate a risk* or *prove a proposition.* He
willingly assumes that the Baldus study "indicates a risk that racial
considerations enter into capital sentencing determinations," and he
states the question flowing from this assumption as "whether [the] ...
study [thereby] ... proves that ... McCleskey's capital sentence is
unconstitutional." But then, as his opinion proceeds, Justice Powell
imbues the words "indicate" and "risk" with connotations of conjecture,[65] while he codes the word "prove" with connotations of actuality.[66] And he discovers in the end that his initial question has answered itself because the chasm between conjecture and actuality is
self-evidently unbridgeable.

This chasm is deepened by the order in which Justice Powell takes
up McCleskey's several constitutional claims. He first discusses—and
therefore first considers what the Court should make of the Baldus
study in the context of—McCleskey's Equal Protection claim. The Supreme Court's earlier cases construing the Equal Protection Clause of
the Fourteenth Amendment had laid down the rule that that Clause is

not violated when the enforcement of a state law or policy has an *unintended* disparate impact upon different racial groups; it is violated only when an agent of a State *intentionally* treats people differently on account of their race (or on some other invidious ground). This doctrinal rule permits Justice Powell to begin

"[o]ur analysis . . . with the basic principle that a defendant who alleges an equal protection violation has the burden of *proving* 'the *existence* of purposeful discrimination.' . . . Thus, to prevail under the Equal Protection Clause, McCleskey must *prove* that the decisionmakers *in his case* acted with discriminatory purpose. He offers *no evidence specific to his own case* that would support an *inference* that racial considerations played a part in his sentence. Instead, he relies solely on the Baldus study."[67]

Given that the occurrence of discrimination in the system as a whole (as distinguished from the individual case) is *legally* irrelevant under Equal-Protection doctrine, it is easy to demote that occurrence from the status of *fact* (of something having an "existence") to the status of *unspecific evidence*—abstract numbers from which an "inference" of discrimination may or may not be drawn.[68] Any systematic bias occurring in Georgia's capital-sentencing procedure is thus banished from the ontological onto the epistemological plane—dematerialized, made to appear a mere statistic, a possibility rather than an actuality. And so, when Justice Powell comes to McCleskey's Eighth Amendment claim—which does *not* require any showing of subjective discriminatory animus specific to McCleskey's own prosecution[69]—the occurrence of system-wide racial bias in Georgia's administration of the death penalty can again be treated as unreal:

"To evaluate McCleskey's challenge, we must examine *exactly* what the Baldus studies *may* show. Even Professor Baldus does not contend that his statistics *prove* that race enters into any capital sentencing decisions or that race was a factor in McCleskey's particular case. [footnote omitted] *Statistics at most may show only* a *likelihood* that a particular factor entered into *some* decisions. There is, of course, *some risk* of racial prejudice influencing a jury's decision in a criminal case. There are similar *risks* that other kinds of prejudice will influence other criminal trials. . . . The question 'is at what point that *risk* becomes constitutionally unacceptable,' . . . McCleskey asks us to accept the likelihood *allegedly* shown by the Baldus study as the constitutional measure of an unacceptable risk of racial prejudice influencing capital sentencing decisions. This we decline to do."[70]

Some of the rhetorics in this passage are obvious, like the ontologically subversive adverb "allegedly"[71] and the repeated use of the modal verb "may."[72] Others require a couple of readings to appreciate. Three are particularly interesting.

First, the passage opens with an ostentatiously no-nonsense declaration that "we must examine exactly what the Baldus studies may show." But it never gets around to saying ("exactly" or otherwise) what the Baldus studies may show. Rather, it is devoted exclusively to stating what the Baldus studies do *not* show. Nor does anything else in the section of Justice Powell's opinion that begins with this paragraph undertake to say what the Baldus studies do or may show. And the only sentence in the rest of the opinion that speaks to the subject contains two cumulative hedges: "*At most,* the Baldus study indicates a discrepancy that *appears to* correlate with race."[73] A reader would be led by Justice Powell's professed "assumption that the Baldus study is statistically valid"[74] to suppose that the study must show *something.* But Justice Powell resolutely avoids stating anything it shows in the form of a proposition of fact. Rhetorically, the Baldus study—the centerpiece of McCleskey's case—never enters the realm of factuality.[75]

Second, Justice Powell's statement of what the Baldus study does *not* show—or rather, what "*[e]ven* Professor Baldus does not *contend*"[76] that the Baldus study shows—is constructed on two mutually supporting, empty propositions. The second proposition (the study does not show "that race was a factor in McCleskey's particular case") is *factually* substantiated by a footnote appended to Justice Powell's text, quoting Baldus's testimony. But this proposition is irrelevant to the Eighth Amendment issue that Justice Powell is presently discussing.[77] The first proposition (the study does not show "that race enters into any capital sentencing decisions") is supported neither by the footnote nor by Professor Baldus's testimony: it is, indeed, contradicted by an earlier passage in Justice Powell's opinion and by the testimony quoted there:

> "Baldus argued in his testimony to the District Court that the effects of racial bias were most striking in the midrange cases. 'When the cases become tremendously aggravated . . ., the race effects go away. It's only in

the mid-range of cases where the decisionmakers have a real choice as to what to do. If there's room for the exercise of discretion, *then the [racial] factors begin to play a role.'* . . . According to Baldus, the facts of McCleskey's case placed it within the midrange."[78]

Neither of the two rhetorical devices that Justice Powell uses in tandem—cape work and selective forgetfulness—is particularly interesting in its own right, but their combination is instructive. It exemplifies how, by closely conjoining two points that are empty for different reasons, a speaker can create the appearance of saying something solid because each point deflects attention from the criticism that would come to mind immediately to defeat the other if the other were stated alone.

Finally, there is another notable sort of emptiness in the passage we are parsing. This one has to do with Justice Powell's analysis of "risk." He says that "some risk of racial prejudice" in Georgia's capital sentencing procedures is not enough to call for constitutional correction because there is always *some* risk; the decisive question must be "'at what point that risk becomes constitutionally unacceptable.'" This reasoning invokes the common-sense principle that risk is a matter of degree. To take the next common-sense step in such reasoning, one would expect Justice Powell to address the question: Just how big *is* the risk we're talking about? But neither here nor anywhere else in his opinion does he broach that question. Instead, he goes on: "Because of *the risk* that the factor of race *may* enter the criminal justice process, we have engaged in 'unceasing efforts' to eradicate racial prejudice from our criminal justice system."[79] There follows a three-page elaboration of the inevitability and benefits to criminal defendants of jury trial, merciful discretion, and other actualities—expressed with no ontological or epistemological uncertainty (for example: "a capital sentencing jury *assures* a 'diffused impartiality'").[80] Thereafter, Justice Powell returns to the issue of the acceptability of a risk but again avoids any assessment of the degree of risk in question:

"At most, the Baldus study indicates a discrepancy that *appears* to correlate with race. *Apparent* disparities in sentencing are an inevitable part of our criminal justice system. . . . As this Court has recognized, any mode for determining guilt or punishment 'has its weaknesses and the potential for misuse.' . . . Specifically, 'there can be "no perfect procedure for deciding in which cases . . . to impose death."' . . . Where the discretion that is fundamental to our criminal process is involved, we decline to assume that what is *unexplained* is invidious. In light of the safe-guards designed to minimize racial bias in the process, the fundamental value of jury trial in our criminal justice system, and the benefits that discretion provides to criminal defendants, we hold that the Baldus study does not demonstrate a constitutionally significant *risk* of racial bias affecting the Georgia capital sentencing process."[81]

The "risk," still unspecified but now verbally desolidified, is more than counterbalanced by such solid matters as "the *fundamental* value of jury trial" and "the benefits that discretion *provides*"—with no factual skepticism or demand for "proof" regarding the latter matters.[82]

These rhetorical strategies have the effect of allowing the Court to conceal from itself the reality of the choice that it is making when it concludes that the "risk of racial bias" shown by the Baldus study is not "constitutionally significant." On the Court's own stated assumptions,[83] what the Baldus study shows is that racial bias accounts for 20 out of every 34 death sentences imposed by Georgia juries in moderately aggravated murder cases like McCleskey's, *although no one can identify exactly which ones.* Should this kind of uncertainty be held fatal to McCleskey and his claims? Perhaps it should. But Justice Powell never faces that question because his rhetoric transmutes the genuine uncertainty about *which specific Georgia defendants will be put to death because of racial bias* into a factitious uncertainty *whether Georgia is putting people to death because of racial bias at all.*[84]

Making Capital Sentencing Too Disorderly to Study/Too Orderly to Fault

Sometimes Justice Powell portrays the capital sentencing process as so lacking in ascertainable standards that its outcomes defy prediction. Sometimes he portrays it as so principled and orderly that its outcomes can be confidently expected to be even-handed. Can the same process possess both of these qualities? Perhaps it can. But this, too, is a question that Justice Powell never faces, because he does not acknowledge any tension between his two portraits of the system. They appear and disappear as the needs of his arguments call for one portrait or the other.

Justice Powell first describes the capital sentencing process during his discussion of McCleskey's Equal Protection claim. In presenting that claim, McCleskey conceded that he had to show that Georgia's racially skewed distribution of death sentences was the result of conscious attention to race by some official decisionmaker or decisionmakers. He argued that the Baldus study showed this because it showed a pattern of outcomes that could be explained on a theory of race-conscious sentencing and could not be explained on any other theory. So, he said, he had proved his claim in the manner authorized by Supreme Court precedents holding that race-conscious decisionmaking can be proved circumstantially—and, in particular, by statistical evidence of exactly this sort—in cases involving claims of employment discrimination and of discrimination in the composition of jury panels.

Justice Powell rejects this argument, primarily on the ground that "the nature of the capital sentencing decision, and the relation of the statistics to that decision, are fundamentally different from the corresponding elements in the [employment-discrimination and jury-composition] . . . cases," so that "an inference drawn from the general statistics to a specific decision in a trial and sentencing simply is not comparable to . . . an inference drawn from general statistics to a specific [instance of decisionmaking in the latter settings]."[85] Employers' hiring, retention, and promotion decisions "may involve a number of relevant variables, [but] these variables are to a great extent uniform for all employees because . . . [i]dentifiable qualifications for a [particular] . . . job provide a common standard by which to assess each employee."[86] And when it comes to selecting citizens for jury service, "the factors that may be considered are limited, usually by statute" and "are uniform for all potential jurors." (Justice Powell quotes statutory qualifications that include "be[ing] 'of sound mind and good moral character,'" "'upright,'" and "'intelligent'"; and he observes that, "although some [of these] factors may be said to be subjective, they are limited and, to a great degree, objectively verifiable.")[87] By contrast, capital sentencing decisions "rest [and, as a consequence of the *Woodson* decision, are constitutionally required to rest] on consideration of innumerable factors that vary according to the characteristics of the individual defendant and the facts of the particular capital offense."[88] "[A] capital sentencing jury may consider *any* factor relevant to the defendant's background, character, and the offense. . . . There is no common standard by which to evaluate all defendants who have or have not received the death penalty."[89]

Leave aside the degree to which employment criteria are "uniform" or the degree to which jury-selection criteria that *"may be said* to be subjective" are "objectively verifiable." We will return in the following subsection to the techniques by which Justice Powell compares McCleskey's claims to other legal claims, including claims of discrimination in employment and jury selection. Here our focus is upon Justice Powell's portrayal of capital sentencing as so open-ended, case-specific, and idiosyncratic that it cannot be expected to exhibit the measure of regularity necessary for scientific study.[90] In this portrait, Georgia's capital sentencing procedure is *inherently* unpredictable, even by 230-variable multiple-regression methods such as those used by Professor Baldus.

But a distinctly different portrait emerges when Justice Powell comes to take up McCleskey's Eighth Amendment claims. Recall that the Eighth Amendment rule of *Furman* requires that a State's capital-sentencing procedures "channel the sentencer's discretion by 'clear and objective standards' that provide 'specific and detailed guidance,' and that 'make rationally reviewable the process for imposing a sentence of death.'"[91] To meet this requirement, the Eighth Amendment section of Justice Powell's opinion redescribes the Georgia capital sentencing process as impeccably regular and orderly:

> "McCleskey's sentence was imposed under Georgia sentencing procedures that focus discretion 'on the particularized nature of the crime and the particularized characteristics of the individual defendant. . . .'"[92] *Gregg* upheld this statute because "[n]umerous features [of it] . . . met the concerns articulated in *Furman*.[93] [Justice Powell here enumerates those features.[94]] . . . Thus, 'while some jury discretion still exists, "the discretion to be exercised is controlled by clear and objective standards so as to produce non-discriminatory application."'"[95] "*Gregg*-type statutes provid[e] for meticulous review of each sentence in both state and federal courts,"[96] and the state courts are forbidden to conduct their review in a way that may vitiate "the role of the aggravating circumstances in guiding the sentencing jury's discretion."[97] "[T]he State must establish rational criteria that narrow the decisionmaker's judgment as to whether the circumstances of a particular defendant's case" warrant consideration of a death sentence.[98] It is true that a State's constitutional power to restrict the jury's consideration of mitigating circumstances is limited,[99] but *Gregg* rejected the argument that "opportunities for discretionary leniency . . . rendered . . . capital sentences . . . arbitrary and capricious."[100] *Gregg* interpreted *Furman* as holding that "'the decision to impose [the death penalty] . . . had to be guided by standards so

that the sentencing authority would focus on the particularized circumstances of the crime and the defendant.'"[101] "The Constitution is not offended by inconsistency in results based on the objective circumstances of the crime."[102]

In a word, capital sentencing decisions are not susceptible to statistical examination because "[t]here is no common standard by which to evaluate all defendants who have or have not received the death penalty,"[103] but they are ""'controlled by clear and objective standards.'""[104] The latter standards—a credit to the Court's constitutional handiwork—assure Justice Powell that any "risk" of racial discrimination that "appears" to be "indicate[d]" by the Baldus study is constitutionally acceptable. And this assurance is reinforced by taking a second look at the Baldus study itself—a new look, which differs from Justice Powell's earlier treatment of the study as much as his two portraits of Georgia's capital sentencing process differ from each other. As we noted earlier, Justice Powell initially rejected the notion that the Baldus study "shows that racial considerations *actually* enter into any sentencing decisions in Georgia"[105] because "[s]tatistics *at most may* show *only a likelihood* that a particular factor entered into *some* decisions."[106] Yet all of this epistemological uncertainty vanishes as soon as Justice Powell can find some basis in the study to support his confidence in the regularity of the Georgia system:

> "The Baldus study *in fact confirms* that the Georgia system *results* in a reasonable level of proportionality among classes of murderers eligible for the death penalty. As Professor Baldus *confirmed*, the system sorts out cases where the sentence of death is highly likely and highly unlikely, leaving a midrange of cases where the imposition of the death penalty in any particular case is *less predictable*."[107]

Notice the powerfully concave conjunction of *"at most"* with *"may"* when doubt is wanted and the powerfully convex conjunction of *"in fact"* with *"confirms"* when doubt is unwanted.

Making Category Boundaries Shift At Will

By the end of Justice Powell's opinion, the price that would have to be paid if the Court upheld McCleskey's claims has increased dramatically. It is no longer merely the end of discretionary jury sentencing in capital cases under statutes having standards so lax that they produce a racially biased pattern of death sentences, but the end of *all* discretionary decisionmaking in any aspect of the criminal justice system whenever "some statistical study indicates" that "any arbitrary variable" may be at work to anybody's disadvantage. Justice Powell reaches this conclusion through a classic form of slippery-slope reasoning that denies the availability of any boundary lines which could restrict a ruling in McCleskey's favor short of cataclysmic leveling of the criminal law:

> "McCleskey's claim, *taken to its logical conclusion,* throws into serious question the principles that underlie our entire criminal justice system. The Eighth Amendment is not limited in application to capital punishment, but applies to all penalties. . . . Thus, if we accepted McCleskey's claim that racial bias has impermissibly tainted the capital sentencing decision, we could soon be faced with similar claims as to other types of penalty. Moreover, the claim that his sentence rests on the irrelevant factor of race easily could be extended to apply to claims based on unexplained discrepancies that correlate to membership in other minority groups, and even to gender. Similarly, since McCleskey's claim relates to the race of his victim, other claims could apply *with equally logical force* to statistical disparities that correlate with the race or sex of other actors in the criminal justice system, such as defense attorneys or judges. Also, there is *no logical reason* that such a claim need be limited to racial or sexual bias. If arbitrary and capricious punishment is the touchstone under the Eighth Amendment, such a claim could—*at least in theory*—be based upon any arbitrary variable, such as the defendant's facial characteristics, or the physical attractiveness of the defendant or the victim, that some statistical study indicates may be influential in jury decisionmaking. As these examples illustrate, *there is no limiting principle* to the type of challenge brought by McCleskey."[108]

This passage is rhetorically remarkable for more than one reason. It bears an uncanny resemblance to Thomas De Quincey's famous pastiche:

> "[I]f once a man indulges himself in murder, very soon he comes to think little of robbing, and from robbing he comes next to drinking and Sabbath-breaking, and from that to incivility and procrastination. Once begin upon this downward path, you never know where you are to stop."[109]

Significantly, Justice Powell's downward path hurdles several obvious retaining walls without acknowledging that he could stop at them.

Yes, the Eighth Amendment applies to all penalties. But the Supreme Court has held repeatedly, both before and after 1987, that the Eighth Amendment and other provisions of the Bill of Rights often impose more stringent controls upon procedures in capital cases than upon procedures in lesser criminal cases.[110] Yes, forms of arbitrariness other than racial discrimination may be matters of constitutional concern. But the Supreme Court has held repeatedly, both before and after 1987, that a special vigilance against racial discrimination is appropriate in the enforcement of a range of constitutional guarantees.[111] What Justice Powell says is literally accurate.[112] But what he does not say is that it need not lead him to decide the case the way he does. As so often in rhetorics, the unsaid conceals choices which, if faced up to, would render all of the justifications propounded for decision indecisive.

Moreover, Justice Powell's insistence on treating McCleskey's claims as subversive of "our entire criminal justice system" in the absence of some *theoretical* or *logical* "limiting principle" stands in stark contrast to his own use of *pragmatic, prudential, incremental, quantitative* reasoning to distinguish the proof requirements for claims of racial discrimination in capital sentencing from those for claims of racial discrimination in employment or jury composition. He drew those distinctions by saying that the latter claims involved "fewer entities" and "fewer variables"[113] and by talking about other matters of "degree" and "extent"—including differences that he discerned between the extent to which capital-sentencing standards and jury-selection standards (like "good moral character") are "objectively verifiable."[114] These are not distinctions grounded in "principle," "theory," or "logical force," but in supposedly practical considerations. To be sure, as we noted in Chapter 2, categories are created for different purposes and may legitimately have different kinds of boundaries. But to shift, without notice or explanation, between accepting category boundaries based on *differences of degree* and demanding category boundaries based on *differences of kind*[115] is to run considerable risk of falling into *ad hoc* reasoning or even self-deception.

A final matter to observe about this part of Justice Powell's opinion is that its language is suddenly quite abstract, full of generic nouns, conditional or subjunctive verbs, and particularly *coulds*. It doesn't say that anybody specific *does* or *will do* or *must do* anything. The only declarative sentence with an active verb—"McCleskey's claim, taken to its logical conclusion, throws into serious question the principles that underlie our entire criminal justice system"—features an incorporeal subject ("claim"), a philosophic hedge ("taken to its logical conclusion"), and a lofty but obscure object ("principles"). This is not a style in keeping with the stance of common-sensicality that Justice Powell has adopted as his principal posture in *McCleskey*. So we may perhaps learn something by restating this recondite passage of his argument in concrete, unhedged language:

> *If we rule for McCleskey, we will not be able to avoid invalidating every criminal statute on the books because none of them guarantees that jurors trying cases will not be influenced by the good looks of the defendant's lawyer.*

Had Justice Powell spelled out his reasoning in this straightforward form, he might have been better able to predict whether it would continue to convince him in the fullness of time, after some dust and blood had settled on it.[116]

III. Da Capo

No one can ever know what persuaded Justice Powell to vote the way he did in *McCleskey*. Doubtless it had much to do with the larger cultural stage on which issues of capital punishment and race played in the mid-1980s. We will talk about culture generally in the following chapter, and about some relevant aspects of contemporary American culture in Chapter 9.

But, almost certainly, whatever persuaded Justice Powell could not have been the reasoning in his *McCleskey* opinon. For that reasoning has the rhetorical features of a mask, concealing unstated convictions. Its rhetoric is not the less important on that account. To the contrary: providing ostensible reasons for acting that insulate one's other reasons from self-critical examination is all too often what rhetorics accomplish.

The opinion has its own drama. In it, Justice Powell argues with rhetorical skill, even passion, that the death penalty can be fairly enforced. That he ceased to believe this within four years is a striking symbol of rhetorics' magic—and of its limits.

CHAPTER EIGHT

On the Dialectic of Culture

We return once again to the nature and role of culture. We have used the term repeatedly in earlier chapters without specifying what we mean by it. For our purposes there, it sufficed to invoke "culture" in its commonplace sense, denoting the overall pattern in a people's collective way of life. Culture, so conceived, is some sort of "whole" that affects or shapes and grounds its "parts"—the general expressing itself in the particulars.

So we might say of Justice Story's opinion in *Prigg v. Pennsylvania*, for example, that it reflects basic aspects of antebellum American culture inasmuch as it (1) accepts as conceivable the notion that one human being can own another as a piece of property, (2) attempts to quell dangerous debates about the legality and rightness of that peculiar institution, and (3) avoids confronting the stark realities of slavery and sectional conflict by (4) retreating into realms of abstract theory in which States are personified and people are dehumanized, and by (5) waving the Flag. We can see aspect (1) more clearly as a cultural peculiarity now that it is defunct; we can see aspects (2) and (3) more clearly in the wake of a bloody civil war; and it has taken more than one twentieth-century war to highlight the question whether aspects (4) and (5) are characteristic Americana only in the antebellum period.

But what *is* "culture"? What kind of creature can be thought to assemble such a constellation of aspects as we have numbered (1) through (5)—fundamental views about the nature of humankind, goals, fears, debates, preoccupations, coping strategies, storytelling techniques, symbols, and Supreme Courts, for that matter? What does it mean to say that "culture" is "reflected" in a judicial opinion? If this means that "culture" shapes or affects the opinion (or its outcome, or its author), how does "culture" do these things?

How, indeed, can we detect some sort of Unmoved Mover called "culture" *behind* the effects that we invoke it to explain? Can we avoid the circularity—that dreaded hermeneutic circularity—of first making inferences about some culture-as-a-whole from observations of its particulars, and then seeking to explicate those particulars by reference to the culture as a whole? Does the idea of culture really provide a deeper, more coherent way of ordering the seemingly disparate particulars of a society? And what sort of conceptual ordering is this?

We turn naturally to anthropology for help with these questions. But anthropologists, alas, seem nowadays to be singularly doubtful about their own capacity to find answers. They are uncertain about how to define culture, how we "know" it, how it may be thought about as playing a role in the daily life of a people. All such questions, as contemporary anthropologists struggle over them, turn out to have an ideological as well as a philosophical side. They set anthropology's practitioners to wondering whether it can ever be a neutral, objective discipline and, if not, what special mandarin privilege it can claim in describing this culture or that. They wonder whether the reification of "American culture" or of any culture can ever be more than a hegemonic maneuver serving to impose somebody's self-interested point of view on whatever the "culture" is taken to encompass.

These misgivings—which we will examine further in a moment—should concern us. For epistemological issues, with or without an ideological dimension, almost always have consequences for how one goes about one's business. It is perhaps because anthropologists are preternaturally aware of this that they are presently in such a funk.

So, in Part I of this chapter we take a look at what is troubling anthropology. This appears, in the terms most relevant to our own enterprise, to involve a tension between two ways of understanding the central features of any society. One perspective emphasizes what is "outside" the minds of the society's members—what precedes and shapes the consciousness of any individual born into the society at a moment in time. The other perspective emphasizes what is "inside" the members' minds: it views the society as nothing more or less than the members' continuing, composite negotiation of the meaning of their communal life.

We describe this tension not in the hope of resolving it, but because its intensity testifies to the force of both of the contending perspectives. In Part II we suggest that each perspective focuses on a vital facet of existence of a people in a time and place and group: on the one hand, the group's web of received, more or less accepted arrangements for interacting and getting along and getting things done; on the other hand, the members' collective imaginative effort to interpret and direct what they are about—an effort that is constantly reshaping the web of arrangements, although only incrementally and arduously as a rule.

In Part III we note that anthropologists from both perspectives may be overly prone to see societies as unitary, as animated by a consistent, integrated set of practices and ideas. We posit a somewhat less tidy picture of how humans get on in culture—the picture of a continuing tug-of-war between the actual and the possible, between those arrangements-that-are and the arrangements-that-might-be.

Part IV summarizes and Part V speculates about the workings of this tug-of-war, this dialectic. We suppose that any society has its characteristic regime of ways for dealing with the here-and-now *and* its characteristic realm of byways for imagining and dreaming about other possible ways *and* its characteristic means for shuttling back and forth between the ways and byways. Part VI offers a few examples of this complex overlay.

I. Two Anthropological Conceptions of Culture

To start with, then, what is the debate going on within anthropology concerning culture? The principal contestants appear to divide up into two sides. At the risk of oversimplification, let us label them the "social-institutionalists" and the "interpretive-constructivists."

Social-institutionalists hold that a society or culture is a set of established arrangements for joint living, made up of such facts-of-life as kinship rules, systems of exchange, methods of conflict resolution, and the rest. In the now classic term introduced by Alfred Kroeber three-quarters of a century ago, a culture is "superorganic."[1] It is not "in" the minds of the individuals who compose a society but stands on a higher plane. The culture-at-large can only be inferred from the corpus of rules and traditional practices that exemplify each society's collective way of being.

The music of a culture, for example, inheres in practices from the past that have been absorbed into its instruments, harmonic forms, and compositional conventions—like keyboard instruments and counterpoint in Western music, or the drums and multiple-part rhythms perfected by some West African peoples—along with variations on these traditional practices. The institutionalized tradition is constituted in a canon that exemplifies ordinary musical appropriateness and the proper settings for its performance. Deviations from a musical canon can be tolerated, but only if explained or justified in the canon's terms. (Thus, the twelve-tone scale stands as a marked case in reference to the standard scale.) Common-law doctrines embody canons of much the same sort.

No single individual knows the entire culture, on this view. Yet, while the culture as a whole is beyond the ken of its individual members, all are expected to abide by its canons. There are many ways seemingly to circumvent the canons, but most of the ways are themselves highly conventional. When individuals fail to conform to a canon, they characteristically seek to legitimate their deviance in some canonically acceptable way, to which others may respond in an equally canonical way. As a whole, a culture offers a relatively restricted canon defining propriety, justifying or extenuating breaches in that propriety, and prescribing remedies and penalties for improprieties. Ignorance of the ways of one's culture may be mitigating, but never exculpating. In Durkheim's classic terms, a culture is "exterior" to the minds of its members, yet "constraining" on them.[2]

Epistemologically if not ontologically, this view implies that a culture exists in its own right, independent of the perspectives that individual participants may bring to it. Anthropologists are trained to discover the practices, rules, and values of the people they study. This is their expertise. Like good empiricists, they begin with detailed *ethnographic* observation and conclude with *ethnology*, theory. The former is objective, "factual"; the latter consists in a coherent ordering and interpreting of the facts to make such sense of them as one can. There may be different ethnologies of a people, but the choice between them is empirically principled by test against the ethnographic record. In Thomas Kuhn's sense,[3] this is "normal" science.

We have doubtless exaggerated institutionalism's focus upon externals, making it seem too much the acolyte of an objectivist positivism. In fact, even the most rigorous social-institutionalists were never so gripped by positivism as to deny multiple interpretations of the same society. Anthropologists in general have always been intrigued by how indigenous peoples interpret their worlds subjectively—perhaps because there is no getting away from the dramatic interpretive virtuosity of their informants.[4] And on occasion the clash of perspectives serves to remind every anthropologist that his or her own viewpoint is not wholly from on high. Even one so social-institutional as Evans-Pritchard[5] could not escape the reminder. Shortly before departing the Nuer in the Sudan, where he had been studying native religion, he invited his informants to ask him any questions they might have about *his* religious beliefs. They asked him, he reports, about the deity he wore around his wrist, the watch that he so often consulted before making decisions about what to do next.[6]

So the interpretive-constructivist critique of social-institutionalism, to which we turn now, was not primarily a rebellion against positivism. Both its target and its project were more sophisticated than that. What the interpretivists questioned was the institutionalists' *foundationalism*—the conviction that the trained anthropologist's account is *the benchmark account* of what is *really there*. For the interpretivist, as for Gertrude Stein, there is no "there."

Interpretive-constructivism fundamentally denies that there can be autonomous, free-standing, objective "facts," ethnographically observed or otherwise.[7] Facts are themselves born of interpretation. No theory about a culture can, then, be *verified* by mere reference to the facts; rather, the theory will drive what counts as fact. Facts inescapably derive from the interpretive stance of the knower, for it is the knower who bestows upon them the status of fact. The knower does so by interpreting, by narrating, by *making sense* of what the knower encounters. Each person's facts are simply that person's way of making sense under his or her conditions.

So any culture can be only the negotiated outcome of a people's effort to interpret their experience in living together. It is to the collective interpretive, meaning-making activities of the people themselves that the anthropologist must look for the crucial data.[8] Any theory of a culture is necessarily the anthropologist's interpretation of the interpretations of participants in the negotiation. Thus, the core concept of "culture" needs to be redescribed in terms of a society's systems for negotiating interpretation, for achieving communal meanings. And, as we shall later notice, an anthropologist can never be sure that he or she has gotten free enough of his or her own culture to acquire an insider's vision of another society's systems.

Obviously, history and tradition play a part, but not the usual one. For, as Foucault taught,[9] the past and its heritage are interpretive constructions as well, constantly subject to reconstruction in response to new requirements. Thus we are always engaged in the invention and reinvention of tradition, in Eric Hobsbawm's phraseology.[10] Although the past may be "fixed" in a society's institutions—in its caste system or its law courts or its musical scale—such institutional arrangements are subject to change, sometimes even rapid change, through continuing reinterpretation.[11] To maintain legitimacy, any particular arrangement or institution must *fit together* with a society's other interpretations and expectancies about the world—social, natural, and supernatural.

What, then, is the role of the outsider, the anthropologist, in the interpretive-constructivist account? For social-institutionalists, the anthropologist played the part of a wise (if not omniscient) expert, a trained eye. But under interpretivism, there are no antecedent naked truths to be discovered by the trained eye. Is the anthropologist, then, just another interpreter, and one slightly blinded by being *from away?* What status should this visitor's version of "the" culture enjoy, and among whom? Must Lévi-Strauss's sophisticated account of the Nambikwara,[12] for example, pass muster with those differently sophisticated nomads themselves? And what is "passing muster" anyway? Would Justice Story have to agree with our interpretation of his decision in *Prigg,* or Justice Scalia with our reading of his combat mythology in *Michael H.*? Or would they simply have to *understand* enough to disagree? Such dark questions, interpretive-constructivists insist, are even more complicated than they seem.

Perhaps. But are they any more complicated than the questions that historiographers pose for working historians combing the archives? Nobody believes any longer that there is a single objective record against which historians can check their accounts. But no records at all, only interpretations? Hardly. What of census reports, casualty lists, statutory texts, architectural remains, or sheer chronology for that matter?[13] As for a historian's account "passing muster" with those who "lived through it," that is a beguiling question but not a crucial one. It would be amusing and perhaps revealing to know how de Tocqueville's interpretation would have fared with Americans of the early nineteenth century, or Gibbon's with Romans of the fourth. But while we would be shaken if these indigenes, interrogated by some time traveler, testified that Gibbon had mistranslated the texts of particular documents or that de Tocqueville had got his information wrong about how communities provided for people who had come on hard times, we'd be unsurprised and rather unconcerned if these long-gone informants disagreed with our two authors' interpretations of what it was all about—or even failed to understand them.

Gibbon's interpretation of Rome's decline and fall, for example, was that of a man who believed profoundly in the ideal of civic self-discipline and public commitment. He was particularly discerning about those aspects of late Roman life that were salient from that perspective. So, he offers us a well-documented record of self-indulgence and moral decadence, all in recognizably eighteenth-century terms. A more "modern" historian, like Hugh Elton,[14] sees the same dissolution of Imperial Rome as reflecting internal struggles within the Roman bureaucracy and the army, and of course he is predisposed to analyzing documents appropriate to *that* perspective.[15] Both historians are exemplary institutional documentarists, both are rigorous questioners of the past, both are superb practitioners of the interpretive sensitivities of their own times. One does not render the other "wrong" or even any less suggestive. Perhaps some day a gifted historian will untangle—or invent—how moral self-indulgence and bureaucratic self-absorption go together. But that too will be an interpretation, not a "fact." Meanwhile we can only celebrate our good luck in having had both a Gibbon and an Elton among us. Never mind that the Romans might have found them both incomprehensible. *Their* difference sharpens *our* consciousness.

And so with anthropologists. One anthropologist's preoccupation with ritualization, for example, yields an enormously rich ethnography of dance forms, modes of polite address, techniques of self-decoration. Another, doing field work in the very same culture but interested principally in economics, will find, say, endless variants of primitive Keynesian wealth formation. Their ethnographies will almost certainly prime the theories they eventually end up writing. Again, what good fortune that both were around!

If, then, there is no absolute, right, or true interpretation of a culture, what makes one interpretation of Balinese cockfighting better than some other? Well, of course a good interpretation should be well-documented, thoroughgoing, attentive to detail, based on sources chosen for good reasons and cross-checked for bad information. But doing good ethnography itself requires more than following the Standard Guide to Field Work. It takes imagination. Consider Thomas Gladwin, during his study of Puluwat navigators, offering the skipper of an ocean-going outrigger canoe the use of a "real" Western compass (for which the skipper politely thanked Gladwin at the end of the long journey, with the comment that the compass might be useful under some conditions).[16] That kind of resourcefulness has the ingenuity of a Baker Street Irregular.

And even resourcefulness on the spot is not enough. In some profound sense, "telling a culture," like writing history, is also a literary act. It needs narrative coherence. This, in turn, demands an interweaving of theme and detail, a decent hermeneutic sensibility. It calls for both the creative and the critical skills required for making "true" stories *believable*—getting the parts and the whole in tune with each other, being aware of the pitfalls of perspective, interrogating one's own predispositions and penchants in framing issues and evaluating information.

And one thing more: having a decent respect for the people whose culture is being told. This appears to be the crux of the ideological issue that we mentioned earlier in describing the interpretivists' critique of the social-institutionalists. For many interpretivists, anthropology's longtime assumption that the outsider perspective of the professional anthropologist enjoyed some privileged status vis-à-vis the insider perspectives of a culture's participants was woefully lacking in the requisite respect. This criticism has served to raise consciousness—both within and beyond anthropology—of an ancient failing that remains an ever-present danger (again, both within and beyond anthropology).

That danger is the potential of any *legitimized* interpretation of a culture to become an instrument of hegemony. The technocrat's arrogant claim to own a preferred mode of understanding is not the only way of imposing hegemonic domination—of putting minorities, racial or religious groups, women, "savages," and "primitives" in their place. Western history is a running commentary on the efforts of the powerful to impose a conception of reality on those they would rule. The results are everywhere: in school curricula and academic agendas,[17] in forms of converse between the sexes,[18] in the language of legal representation,[19] in advertising and political discourse.

Contemporary anthropologists, understandably anti-ethnocentric and increasingly sensitive to the charge of Eurocentrism, have grown alert to the peril that their discipline will lend itself to hegemonic uses, whether colonialist in motive or not. Many of them have become convinced that peaceful human coexistence depends on people appreciating, respecting, and living with each others' often discordant constructions of social reality. It is this moral concern as much as any epistemological insight that has motivated the interpretive turn in anthropology. What the interpretivists are telling us is that if we are to live at peace with one another, we had better *all* become more interpretively anthropological toward "other" cultures—become more conscious, better informed multicultural readers.

II. Putting the Perspectives Together

What we take away from the clash of social-institutionalist and interpretive-constructivist positions in anthropology is a sense that each of these perspectives is onto something vital and unyielding. Whether they can be reconciled within the anthropological métier itself we have no competence to say. But for our purposes both perspectives are compelling, and they are no more contradictory in an epistemological sense than using both particle theory and wave theory in an effort to understand the physics of light, although the theories may be incommensurable. Nor are the institutional and interpretivist perspectives any more contradictory from a moral point of view than understanding the life of a community in the light of both human compassion and the principles of hard-knuckled economics, although the two may again be incommensurable. These paired searchlights cross, but the human condition remains more than half in darkness without both.

On the one hand, a respect for people and for what they sense to be their most immediate and meaningful experiences requires that we take seriously their understandings of their world and how it works.

This entails acceptance of the reality that "societies, like lives, contain their own interpretations."[20] And if they do, we think it follows, as Clifford Geertz has insisted, that "[t]he culture of a people is an ensemble of texts, themselves ensembles, which the anthropologist strains to read over the shoulders of those to whom they properly belong."[21]

On the other hand, this cannot be the *only* reality, for institutions are never *simply* interpretations of how the world should be understood. Undoubtedly all laws and practices are culturally constructed, the end products of a society's interpretive negotiations. But they have their own relentless being nonetheless. When Justice Story interpreted the Fugitives-From-Service-Or-Labor-Clause of the Constitution in *Prigg v. Pennsylvania* as though it had entirely to do with harmonizing polities and nothing to do with the whips and shackles of slavecatchers,[22] his interpretation did not alleviate the weight of those whips and shackles upon the black limbs he licensed them to fall on.[23] And when the Supreme Court of the United States today, setting aside a lower federal court's stay of execution of a death sentence, interprets the issue presented as whether the circumstances of the case make it appropriate "for a federal court to interfere with the orderly process of a state's criminal justice system,"[24] this interpretation does not prevent the decrease of the prisoner's body heat from 98.6 degrees to room temperature in the course of the "orderly process" thus conceptualized. These are realities *de rerum natura* that reside not merely in the mind of the interpretive beholder.

Any interpretive construction backed by the power of authority becomes a real social institution, implacably played out—in Robert Cover's celebrated phrase—upon "a field of pain and death."[25] It has consequences which are "biological fact[s] as well as . . . social event[s]."[26] These need always to be kept in view, alongside the discourses and conceptions and imaginings that people use to make some sense of them and sometimes to question them and change them.

III. The Disunity of Culture

Come back now to "culture as a whole," that SuperBeing manifested in all of the particularities of life. Is there Something Basic about Arabic and American culture, for example, that helps us to understand why a court of law governed by Arabic *haqq* jurisprudence emphasizes normative witnessing by people of high moral standing,[27] while a court governed by our own *Federal Rules of Evidence* puts such stress on "personal knowledge"—i.e., first-hand sensory observation—as the *sine qua non* of witness competency?[28] Something reflective of a reverence for rectitude in Arab society, and of a hard-bitten, skeptical empiricism in American? Perhaps. But is American or Islamic culture really so all-of-a-piece as that? What about our rules concerning expert testimony, which seem to stand all skeptical empiricism on its head?[29]

We suspect that anthropologists have had exaggerated expectations about the unity or coherence of the cultures they have studied, and that their expectations have often proved prophetic. "Finding" a goodly measure of coherence is, in the craft of anthropology, a mark of field work well done. To insist upon examining the messy texture of a culture in the fraying places where it doesn't hang together therefore seems a task most weary, flat and stale, to say nothing of unprofitable. The story of a culture, like the biography of an individual, makes better telling when it is a neat *unitas multiplex*. It follows a traditional literary-historical genre featuring National Character.

Take Salvador deMadariaga's unpretentious little classic of an earlier generation, *Englishmen, Frenchmen, Spaniards,* as a case in point.[30] For each culture, he contended, there is a central organizing metaphor (or small cluster of metaphors) that shapes a people's style of mind. *Le droit* for Frenchmen; *honor* for Spaniards; *fair play* for the English. DeMadariaga made no great claims, nor did he offer ethnographic protocols or statistical proofs. He deferentially admitted that his sole authority was that he was a seasoned diplomat of Spanish nationality, that his wife was French, and that they had spent many years living and working in England. The book is still delightful and useful reading. DeMadariaga provides us with something of a Greek chorus on the three cultures.

But what, for example, might the unemployed shipyard workers in the Clydeside make of the claim that *fair play* was the ruling metaphor of British culture? They might well ask what was fair about neglecting the laid-off toilers of an industry that had helped to make real the boast that the sun never sets on the British Empire. They might well choose as the key British metaphor or proverb *get it while you can.* And, indeed, reading George Dangerfield's historical masterpiece on the *Strange Death of Liberal England*,[31] one appreciates that both tropes were in play, even at war with each other. The dialectic between the two, some would say, is the tale of twentieth-century British culture.

Nearly a century after deMadariaga, a distinguished American social psychologist, Richard Nisbett, noted the comparatively high incidence of "non-acquisitive" violent crimes in the white American South and argued that their prevalence could be attributed to the pervasiveness of the ideal of "honor" in that culture[32]—a different conception of *honor* from the traditional Spanish one, to be sure, but nonetheless a real honor code. Nisbett saw this code as a source of unity in southern culture: southern whites fight and kill for "honor." But why, then, didn't the direct descendants of the culture's original white planters generalize their honor-orientation and oppose the shameful bully-terror of the Ku Klux Klan against helpless blacks? Well, in fact, some of them did: the Senator Bankheads and Hodding Carter IIIs. But more to the point, "honor" was itself part of a dialectic in the changing South. We know of this inner dialectical clash not from the canonical social- or political-history accounts, but from Lillian Hellman's *Little Foxes* and from William Faulkner, Tennessee Williams, Robert Penn Warren, and, more recently, Harper Lee and Michael Malone. It is of more than passing interest that African-American social scientists[33] and the perceptive Swedish student of American racism, Gunnar Myrdal,[34] have recognized the dilemma-like dialectic of southern culture. Perhaps it takes an outcast or an outsider—or a dramatist—to see it.

But what about abstract, formal, perhaps deep-structure analyses? Have they unearthed a core of cultural unity and coherence? Has anybody found an underlying grammar that renders a culture's surface messiness into a tidy set of rules? Did Saussure's renowned structuralist revolution in linguistics[35]—which excavated an orderly language system with formulable precepts *(la langue)* underneath the daily manifestations of speech *(la parole)*—pay off when applied to the equally semiotic domain of culture? To be sure, a certain gesture *stands for* respect, and a mode of dress *stands for* mourning in some language-like way. But does culture have an underlying *langue* in Saussure's sense, something that imposes a rule-bound regularity on the multiple performances of *la parole?*

"Structural" anthropology promised that it did, and many of its gifted adherents devoted their careers to making good on the promise, notably Claude Lévi-Strauss.[36] The sloppy surface of a culture, he argued, instantiates a body of underlying, structually coherent rules. We grasp *langue*-like rules about status, kinship, economic exchange, and symbolic communication, and are thereby enabled to recognize the local instantiations of these rules in everyday *parole*.[37] But the structuralist program never lived up to its elegant promise (though it was most successful when it dealt with language-like phenomena such as myth and folktale).[38] Structuralism had too little to say about why we are so often "of two minds" even about what we *should* intend or desire or believe, even in familiar situations. Why should there always be such contradictory cultural maxims as "love thy neighbor" and "stand up for your own"?[39] Why does it seem so inevitable in the business of living that "the values of my culture cannot be jointly implemented and kept intact," so that their daily accommodation requires constant, indeterminate compromises, "[a]nd this indeterminacy is the greater, the greater is the potential of my culture's flowering"?[40] It is not surprising that the structural anthropologist's search for underlying rules of cultural coherence fared poorly. Nor is it surprising that coherence-seeking anthropologists had their greatest difficulties when it came to getting down to the nitty-gritty of daily life. For the details are full of the messiness that results when institutionalized canonicity and imagined possibility are locked in a local dialectic.

One might expect that a culture's legal system would particularly reflect and reinforce a culture's underlying coherence, such as it is. Both the articulateness and the comprehensiveness of accommodations are at their highest premium in the law—if only because, as Lon Fuller observed long ago,[41] no legal system can last that yields arbitrary and unpredictable decisions. But there seems to be scant evidence that even formal legal systems express and preserve the coherence of some culture-as-a-whole.[42] Take, for example, Clifford Geertz's analysis of the jurisprudence of Islamic *haqq*, Indonesian *adat*, and Indic *dharma*, mentioned (in part) earlier.[43] In *dharma* jurisprudence, the evidentiary task is to determine "where in the local version of the grand taxonomy of dutiful behaviors a particular behavior fell."[44] So *dharma* is "obsessed with verdicts" and with the "'aptness of final judgments as to the total value of an individual's existence.'"[45] *Haqq* jurisprudence, on the other hand, is much more concerned with "establish[ing] fact by sorting out moral character and [is consequently] . . . obsessed with testimony."[46] This is a richly insightful interpretation that enhances our understanding of what the respective court systems are striving to accomplish, how this connects up with deep themes in their respective cultures, and how it drives their respective procedures. But does it reflect the "culture as a whole"? Not exhaustively,[47] and not necessarily for very long. In Thailand, as Geertz notes, when the King led a reform movement modifying *dharma* jurisprudence and appointed many new judges, not only did the rules change but even the court seal was duly changed from "a death-god king riding a lion" to the Roman scales of justice, now "enveloped in royal regalia."[48] Thai culture seems to have gone along with the change with no notable increase in grumbling about the ways of justice. As for *adat,* it had been forged from "a potpourri of vernacular rules,"[49] and after only a decade's absence Geertz found the system virtually turned on its head by an intervening, violent political revolution that the local judiciary had been unable to contain.[50]

Neither is our own legal system grounded in a monolithic cultural ethos that explains it all. We often hear the claim that American criminal procedure is extraordinarily protective of accused persons, and there are, of course, numerous opinions of the United States Supreme Court that not only express this aspiration and connect it to some value "at the core of our criminal justice system"[51] but actually enforce it[52] (to some extent).[53] However, all of these procedural protections are lodged in, or enforced through, the trial process; and the same Supreme Court has repeatedly refused to recognize any significant safeguards for accused persons in the plea-bargaining process by which upward of 90 percent of criminal cases are disposed of.[54] A cynic might say that our culture purchases the luxury of valorizing due process trials by ignoring the "undueness" of the only process that nine-tenths of its defendants can get. And even non-cynics must acknowledge that there are—in Herbert Packer's phrase—at least two models of criminal justice simultaneously in play here.[55] Similarly, although American legal culture is widely (and to some extent rightly) depicted as inveterately litigious, the rapid growth of alternative dispute resolution mechanisms—"ADRMs" of all sorts—in recent years attests to *some* countervailing values in the culture (if only the values of downsizing corporate litigation budgets).

In sum, then, presuppositions about the harmonious and integrated coherence of culture seem not to weather close scrutiny. Perhaps we could benefit from more monographs on indecisions and "fits and starts" among this tribe, or on interpretive disharmonies among that one. It may be, as Robert Cover argued, that once any small, intimacy-sharing group undergoes diaspora and spreads beyond the reach of common worship and mutual affection, its law-making process has to be increasingly specialized for adjudicating conflicting norms, for keeping the intrinsic dialectic of culture from turning into reverberating, increasingly irreconcilable conflicts.[56] In modern times, in any event, even the smallest, most harmonious of cultures splinter—and precisely because they are unable to be all of one mind for long.[57]

IV. A Sketch of a Cultural Dialectic

We seem to need a notion of culture that appreciates its integrity as a composite—as a system in tension unique to a people not in perpetuity but at a time and place. A culture does indeed require "exteriority and constraint," but it also needs an interpretive interiority that leaves room for the maneuverability of imagination.[58] Here is our brief and pragmatic formulation of the issue of culture:

1. All cultures are, inherently, negotiated compromises between the already established and the imaginatively possible.
2. Whatever internal coherence a culture achieves is attributable, not to some natural process (as with homeostasis in biology, say), but to the dialectical processes inherent in negotiation.
3. Given the centrality of such dialectical negotiation, we cannot dispense with either the social-institutional or the interpretive-constructivist conception of culture. The former serves to mark the importance of the forms of institutionalization and legitimation that all societies require for the establishment and maintenance of canonicity; the latter highlights the ubiquitous pressure exerted by both solitary and communal *possible-world* construction on institutionalized canonicity.

To put the matter more narratively, cultures in their very nature are marked by *contests for control over conceptions of reality*. In any culture, there are both canonical versions of *how things really are and should be* and countervailing visions about *what is alternatively pos-*

sible. What is alternatively possible comprises both what seems desirable or beguiling, and what seems disastrous and horrifying. The statutes and conventions and authorities and orthodoxies of a culture are always in a dialectical relationship with contrarian myths, dissenting fictions, and (most important of all) the restless powers of the human imagination. Canonicity and the ordinary are typically in conflict with imaginable "otherwises"—some inchoate and even private, some vocal or even clamorous, some quasi-institutionalized as cults or movements of dissent. The dialectic between the canonical and the imagined is not only inherent in human culture, but gives culture its dynamism and, in some unfathomable way, its unpredictability—its freedom.

We spell the matter out a bit more fully in the next section and then examine some pieces of it up close in section VI.

V. *The Dialectic Elaborated*

In any culture, there are right or canonical ways to think, feel, act, and affiliate with others. These make up a culture's overt normative structure. The norms vary in articulateness and in the degree to which people are aware of them. While some are highly explicit and accessible, even inscribed in legal statutes, others are so implicit as to require the efforts of gifted human scientists like Erving Goffman or Harold Garfinkel to explicate them,[59] or of novelists of manners like Trollope or Balzac to illuminate them in fiction.

Notwithstanding the obscurities and complications of leading one's life within the limits of a culture's canonicity, most of its members manage to do so much of the time, aided no doubt by some sort of principle of tolerance practiced by fellow members. (No culture expects its members to be paragons of the ordinary.) For all that, people everywhere spend a good deal of effort and time figuring out what they *ought* to do, with whom, when, and how, and then doing it—or, if they don't do it, then explaining or justifying why not. That much is common sense, but it is powerful common sense.

Heed for canonicity is not compelled principally by fear of punishment or reprisal. It is assured, rather, by that uniquely human adaptation that we so blithely call the "Self." We need not take up this topic in detail now,[60] except to note that the construction of Self typically entails internalizing maxims about how to interact with others, maxims we refine by a process of figuring out what we can expect from others and what they expect from us. We grow into the expectations people have of us. Adherence to expectation then becomes as much personal, individual, Self-related as it is cultural. Being mindful of our "place" and our roles is, in this sense, a matter of conscience as well as of social conformity. Different cultures create different patterns of selfhood—as with "shame" and "guilt" cultures.[61]

The Self, our experience of our own identity, obviously has deep biological roots in our postural orientation to gravity and in our distinctive sense of the seamless continuity of individual experience. But in its evolved, adult form, Self is profoundly dependent on two crucial, culturally patterned circumstances. These are worth a moment's pause, since they are critical to the discussion in the chapter that follows. The first is the obvious fact that Self is defined, in some critical way, with respect to or, often, in contrast to Other. That is to say, how we see Others is a condition for how we see ourselves. A proverb like "Blood is thicker than water" tells us that those Others we see as close kin are connected to our own Selfhood in ways that strangers are not. Self is defined by the social groupings with which we "identify"—the groups that give us a mark of our own identity. We are ourselves, of course, but we are also Ifaluk, or New Yorkers, or lawyers, or whatever. So we see Others not only as not-Us, but as belonging or not belonging to *our* clan, *our* family, *our* profession. And cultures vary widely in how those *not* belonging are perceived. In some cultures, the Stranger is virtually a nothing—not us, not of any group that gives us part of our identity, not anything. These cultures constitute the Stranger as a black hole—beyond ordinary empathy or fellow feeling, beyond any human likeness. Such radically strange Others easily come to be treated as objects, non-people, even property—excluded from the whole human race, as was done with the descendants of black Africans in *Dred Scott,*[62] or reduced to chattels, as was done with Margaret Morgan in *Prigg v. Pennsylvania.*[63] We will have much more to say about this baleful phenomenon in Chapter 9.

The second point to note is that the Self-Other relationship is unique to *Homo sapiens* and that its emergence—which dates back to the beginnings of the species only a half-million years ago—marks the watershed between Darwinian, biological evolution and modern cultural evolution.[64] Not that chimpanzees and other higher primates do not distinguish "self" from "other." They do,[65] but they do not con-

ceptualize the distinction in the same way. What is peculiar to enculturated human beings is precisely that their Self-Other distinction is
extraordinarily open to cultural influences—another matter that will
be at the center of our attention in the following chapter when we discuss the evolution of both public opinion and Supreme Court decisions in the century after Reconstruction.

Cultures, though they differ in their instrumentalities for enforcing
their members' self-imposed norms, have certain things in common.
No culture has ever been found that did not use ridicule as one way of
dealing with norm violations; and none in which humiliation was not
a mode of controlling violators or would-be violators of prevailing
norms.[66] Neither ridicule nor humiliation is conceivable without the
phenomenon of Selfhood with its attendant self-respect and *amour-
propre*. This is what provides the affective component of what we
have come to call in our times a *sense of identity*.

The sense of identity has a curious role in the picture we are setting out. It relates us to the groups on whose good opinions we rely
for self-esteem, and it fixes us to the roles and statuses that those
groups assign us as a condition for holding their good opinion. But no
individual's identity is ever preempted by a single group. Family, occupation, social class, gender, origins—all compete for the attention
and loyalty of the Self-presently-in-the-driver's-seat who must decide
which way to turn in the here-and-now. The tugs of various identities
have a way of fractioning the Self into a cast of characters, each seeking different, often contending forms of canonicity and/or possibility.
Perhaps that is why identity in the political sense of "identity politics"
is so very responsive to institutionalized support.

Institutionalized forms, to begin with, shape thought and action.
We behave and think "post-office" in the post-office, just as we behave and think "patient" at the doctor's. This is a basic feature of
enculturated human mental operations: in current jargon, mental activity is virtually always "situated." What this amounts to is that over
generations, people in any given culture *offload* as much mind as they
can on external devices in order to reduce mental load and mental effort. "We use intelligence to structure our environment so that we can
succeed with *less* intelligence. Our brains make the world smart so
that we can be dumb in peace!"[67] So we use measuring sticks, dictio-
naries, thermometers, story forms, various calculi, category systems,

law codes, rhetorical styles for proving our points—all "out there" in the public world. And of course, we pay for this in the same way that we pay for using any tool: tools and external devices generally make us their servants in return for their being ours. You don't *have to* frame your request to a salesperson in a New York store in the "New York" way, for example, or deal with municipal functionaries as a New Yorker would. But it's easier, and maybe even more effective. The world-made-easier by offloading our ways of dealing with things eventually eases us into canonical ways of thinking and feeling and acting. And soon we "become" New Yorkers, think New York thoughts, have New York suspicions, and expect the same of others who are situated as we are—rather like a computer with a default setting that runs along automatically when no other instructions have been given. Institutionalization locks these various culturally provided prosthetic devices into place, enabling us to navigate the everyday world largely on automatic pilot.

But cultures rarely let the matter rest there. They even institutionalize "sites" to aid us in possible-world construction, such as theater, fiction, and partisan politics. These sites often subvert the imagination and end by binding us more closely to the canonical. Yet sometimes they do not. They can harbor possible worlds—like *Uncle Tom's Cabin,* or the civil rights movement in America, or the early women's movement—that end up shaping tomorrow's canonicity.[68]

Cultures need such harbors. For there seems to be a distinctively human mental capacity that *compels* us to project our imaginations beyond the ordinary, the expectable, the legitimate—and to involve others in our imaginings. We are constantly outpacing our surroundings, envisioning alternatives to the here-and-now, generating the counterfactual, the absent, the *no*-thing ever experienced.[69] This proclivity is assisted by the creative power of language. For through language—stories, dramas, symbol systems, sacred revelations[70]—we get beyond the constraints of the present. And each human culture has its own rootstock of "starters" for prodding the sense of the possible in its members: myths of origin and purpose, fables, folktales, exemplary heroes and plights, Odysseys and Ragnaroks.

So, our species becomes unruly in ways strikingly different from—and, oddly, more communal than—anything resulting from mere biological variability.[71] The *communal* unruliness inheres in our ability to share our possible worlds with others, whether through language or in our species-specific ability to "read each other's minds" and to recruit others to our dreams.

Imagination flourishes in aggregation and exchange. Some, like Mikhail Bakhtin,[72] even argue that the origin of individual imagination is in dialogue. However that may be, an individual's possible worlds can readily become collective visions (utopian, apocalyptic, redemptive, demonic), later to be institutionalized in possible-world communities, political, religious, criminal. Perhaps the very unruliness of human imagination drives its possessors to seek the confirmation of company.

Every culture contains an *assembly* of possible-world constituencies, each animated to modify, bypass, or even destroy the existing canonical order—and sometimes one another. "Constituencies" is a better term than "communities" because the latter connotes too much duration and structure. Constituencies can be as episodic as a political rally, a freedom march, or a corporate retreat to a think tank. How these episodic rallyings become institutionalized and how, once institutionalized, constituencies achieve canonical status within a culture is, of course, the central topic of the study of social and political change. The means range from orderly but limits-testing protests, as when the civil rights movement of the 1960s undertook to register African-American voters against the resistance of white supremacists in the South, to the far more destabilizing acts of terrorist or paramilitary movements. Between these two extremes lie many alternatives: the "peace marches" in Great Britain in the 1970s, the Jacobin societies in North Italian cities in the years following the French Revolution, "ginger groups," "political theater," the political stand-up comic.

But protest itself must conform, somehow, to a culture's style of discourse. So there are conventions of protest, varying from culture to culture and from period to period. In the world of classical China, with its taboo against direct confrontation,[73] even logico-mathematical argumentation (as Geoffrey Lloyd reports) avoided the winner-take-all confrontations of Greek logic and philosophy. Contestation in Athens was not so inhibited. Still, it had its own code of regulations, as evidenced by those cautionary Greek choruses.

Imagination, like protest, gains intensity when it is channeled within a culture's recognized forms for challenging the canon. Pause a moment to reflect on how possible worlds are generated. Obviously, they involve imaginative projection. But that does not imply self-indulgent "primary process." To reduce the imaginative faculty to mere wish-fulfillment ignores both the *realism* of human imagination and the importance of social exchange in the life of the mind. Imagination is hardly just autistic; it is invested, *engaged,* in problem-solving. The problems are not always as well-formed as those that led Einstein to imagine relativity or Newton to understand that white light is a mix of the entire spectrum. Yet theater and political dissent have their own constraints, though they may be different from those that structure our understanding of the physical world.

One such constraint is implicit in the process of beginning afresh. To replace or reconstruct the familiar world, you must first defamiliarize what you would replace—make what was familiar or obvious seem strange again. Seeing the obvious as strange requires *metacognition,*[74] a clumsy word for making one's own thoughts the object of one's own thinking. The easiest way to make one's thoughts accessible to oneself is to discuss them with others—through dialogue.

Societies invariably provide rich opportunities for dialogue. They can (with varying degrees of toleration) harbor interlocutors who, whether by inclination or talent or profession, specialize in defamiliarizing the obvious. Artists and philosophers, novelists and playwrights, dissidents and agitators, the thoughtful and the discontented—all of them serve in that role, whether their discourse is from a soapbox or a university podium, from the stage or from behind bars. Almost every classroom has the kid who cocks a dubious eyebrow at what the others take for granted. And it was the classic function of carnival time to unchain a cast of characters tailored for turning the tables on the conventional.[75]

Disturbers of the canonical peace, these varied defamiliarizers may be disapproved by those in charge of the banal and obvious. But they are always left some elbow room to do their thing. Their activities lure us all into metacognition, into the imaginative space where mind can envision other possible worlds. Each culture maintains its distinctive imaginative space, teeming with alternatives to the actual. We want to call it the culture's *noetic space.*

The word "noetic" comes from the classical Greek *nous,* which includes not only the deliberations of the rational mind but its appetites and affections: what modern philosophers might call the mind's "intentional states"—beliefs, desires, feelings, hopes, intentions. Noetic space abounds in temptations to incite mind and imagination. No culture can exist long without it.[76]

Noetic space demands the free play of rhetorics, what in Chapter 6 we described as the interplay between *what is said* and *what might be meant*.[77] It is profoundly narrative in its ordering, nourished by stories however unfinished, incomplete, or sketchy.[78] But for all that, noetic space is a surprisingly *pragmatic* place. For both rhetorics and narrative require verisimilitude, and verisimilitude must be not only truthlike, but lifelike. Stories from life may be bizarre, their truths metaphoric, but they must honor the *limits* of lifelikeness—the limits beyond which they cannot go without losing the imaginative engagement of the audience. So noetic space, like imagination itself, is specialized for testing the limits of the possible.

Recall from Chapter 4 that story is organized around a human aim that is thrown off course by unforeseen circumstances, the rest of the tale having to do with the vicissitudes of repairing things to get them back to the old order or changing them to meet the new one. Aristotle poses the question in the *Poetics* why we enjoy tragedy, why we are intrigued by the grisly travails of an Oedipus or a Medea. His celebrated, though only briefly elaborated, answer is that tragedy provides *catharsis,* a discharge of emotions or release from pain.[79] Perhaps it does, although the evidence is thin. In our view, the pleasure in tragedy or any other narrative form is in getting a glimpse of the reach of possibility.

As Michael Silk recently put it, Aristotle "ignores . . . the dialectic between the suffering individuals [in the classical tragedy], and the anonymous human continuum that confronts us as the Chorus"—the voice of the culture.[80] It is the Chorus that echoes our queries: "What is this all about?" and "What else might have been?" We feel empathy, the more so because the protagonists in the drama are usually born to power or divinely sheltered, but they too can be brought to their knees by the unforeseen (as the Chorus typically and roundly assures us). Noetic space, in short, provides us with a well-annotated, yet elusive, map of the possible and its pitfalls.

Stocked with an Antigone, a King Lear, or a Hamlet, noetic space is no longer a *tabula rasa* or a penny arcade for working out wishful primary process. Its personae and plots serve as guides and cautions, as commentators and commentaries on human strength and frailty. They provide templates for tracing out first drafts of our own ventures into possibility. It is in that sense that life surely imitates art. And it is why art can appear so dangerous to those with an investment in seeming ordinariness.

VI. Two Instances of the Dialectic at Play

How does the dialectic of culture—the tug between a culture's canonical prescriptions for doing what conventionally wants doing and its imaginative stock of alternative possibilities—express itself in the lives of people and of peoples? Two examples will help us appreciate the nature and the range of the struggle.

We start with a familiar scene in which a culture's most timeless rituals come to the fore—a death and a funeral. At a funeral, everybody knows what's called for. The canon is deeply inscribed. Funerals are sacred, and on sacred occasions we expect to be guided by ritual.[81] The ritual has the function of composing and reintegrating the community's memory of the deceased while sending him or her forth into the Next World.

But even in such a sacred ritual, some imaginative improvisation is permitted. And, indeed, it is sometimes needed to come to terms with the peculiar, the aberrant, the offbeat, either in the life of the deceased or in the circumstances of his or her death. The aim of the improvisation is to reconcile the offbeat and the conventionally ordinary. When the improvisation is apt, it creates a new realm of possibility in which the offbeat is no longer odd—and in which the ordinary comes in for new scrutiny.

So it was once in a small Irish village where a well-loved pensioner—a former fisherman and handyman—died in the fullness of his years. He was to be buried with the customary mass and sermon at the local parish church. But this man was no model of orthodox piety, to be shunted into his grave with the usual ritual formulas. He was a heavy drinker even by local standards, where putting down a half dozen pints of Guinness in an evening at the pub was not all that uncommon. He'd done his share of running around in his day. He'd never married, never achieved a conventional respectability, probably never had a sixpence left after spending his monthly pension check.

Still, this man—let's call him Seamus—was special. Whatever he was up to, serious or playful, he remained his invariably jolly, good-

hearted self, the best-natured person in the village. In his days as a
lobsterman, the village boys would vie with each other to be asked
to come help tend pots with him. He was certainly no pillar of the
church; yet, for all that, he was a man of the community in every
sense: a beacon of good cheer and *craic*.[82] How to celebrate the last
rites of such a man in such a community? How to make the canonically sacred and the offbeat profane come together?

The local parish priest understood what was needed, and he did the
job with inspiration. Nobody in the village, he said, had failed to
benefit from the presence of this wonderful and boisterous man, never
mind his weaknesses. There was no question that his soul would go
to heaven, and a good thing too. Remember the Apostles, he said,
and think of them not as so many righteous stick figures, for they too
were human beings. They would welcome Seamus into heaven and be
blessed and comforted by his presence there as we had been here on
earth.

In the church vestry afterwards—the whole village was there, and
with scarcely a dry eye—there was an unusual buzz of subdued talk
among the parishioners. "How altogether Christian it had been."
Seamus had been "saved." A great-hearted boozer had been wel-
comed into heaven by the local priest. Sin had been domesticated that
day. And the Church's place in the community had been preserved in
the process.

Within a decade of that memorable day, the Irish Catholic Church
suffered a decline that would have been unimaginable at Seamus's funeral. Starting in the late 1980s, there was a seemingly endless series
of "priest scandals." Priests were not only denounced for violating
their vows of chastity, but accused and convicted of pederasty with
choir boys, sexual molestation of young girls in convent schools, and
other terrible acts. The papers were full of it, and talk of "pedophilia"
could be heard even in the pubs.

The initial response of the Church seemed evasive. Accused priests
were transferred, sent abroad, never mentioned. There was no facing up to the facts, no candid self-confrontation, by the Church itself. Even the faithful were stunned. It was not the priestly misconduct
that troubled people but the absence of dialogue, the silence of the
Church. There was surely a template in the Irish imagination for the
fallen priest,[83] but the Church never invoked it. There were not only

templates of transgression, but tradition-honored virtues of contrition and absolution that might have renewed the ties of understanding between the Church and its flock. Yet while secular courts convicted the accused pederasts, the Church appeared never to confess, not even to apologize. All that was left for the ordinary faithful was to insist that *their* parish priest was no Father Smyth—one of the most uncontrite and disaffecting of the convicted molesters.[84]

Before those years, the occasional remoteness of the Church from everyday Irish life had been only an ironic topic for "smart" young Irish playwrights at the Gate in Dublin or for on-the-make, brash young novelists. It now found its way into the correspondence columns of even the provincial newspapers. A new generation was beginning to emerge, skeptical and bitter—or so keened the commentators. And by mid-1997, the Church's repute had fallen so low that cooler heads were beginning to worry about the moral and political consequences for Ireland as a whole.

What had previously lived in the noetic space of novels and the theater came alive in the real world. Obviously, there had been stirrings of change even before the explosive scandals. The formerly banned expatriate novelist Edna O'Brien, for example, was being regularly invited to speak to packed audiences not just about her latest novel but about why her native Ireland was so off-putting to her as a place to work. The dialectic of Irish culture was simmering beneath the surface, heating up. Then, in the 1990s, it broke the surface. The widow of the former publican in Seamus's village declared, "These are terrible times; no telling what's next." Her daughter (age thirtyish) had a different take: "About time we woke up around here." The canonical—particularly if it could be dressed in the robes of the sacred—had become walled off from the imaginative, innovative side of Irish life. Like that rabbit-duck picture: see one *or* the other, but not the two together.

Compare this fractured scene with one in another setting, in a different culture, with a vastly different cultural history. The two have directly in common only the contested authority of the Church. But there is more to it than that. For just as our last scene showed Ireland struggling to go beyond an authoritative, Jansenist Catholicism, so our next scene shows another society, by quite other means, struggling out of an authoritative, aristocratic Catholic past—in this case, into a "Leftist" present. Both tales are about the tug-of-war between canonical ways and the new shape of the possible, first fashioned by imagination and then converted into institutional actuality.

So shift scene now to Reggio Emilia in the north of Italy. Reggio is an ancient city of some one hundred thousand inhabitants, a half-hour's drive down the *Autostrade* from Bologna. It is a proud little city, a place of great composure, even in its crowded twice-weekly open markets and its busy bicycle traffic with riders of every age and class going courteously about their affairs.[85] Its *provincia* (or catchment area, as we might say) is prosperous, perhaps as prosperous as any in Europe, and so is the surrounding region, Emilia Romagna, full of vibrant, bustling small cities: not just wealthy Bologna, but Modena (where Ferraris are built), and Parma (where Parmagiana cheese is only one of the products of its thriving agricultural industry). Even the old Roman Via Emilia, running down its middle, is now dotted with automated small factories turning out everything from specialized pumps to medical instruments. Its workers are skilled, independent, and well-educated.

Reggio, like most of its neighbors, has elected a Communist local government in every election since the Second World War, and at the time of writing still has a City Council dominated by the Partito Democratico della Sinistra (the "PDS"), successor to the former Communist Party of Italy (the old "PCI" in local alphabet talk). The Mayor, a much-admired, vigorous young woman, is also PDS. She is widely described as "very Reggiana," a term that does not translate easily but suggests that she is liked even by the opposition.

Reggio's out-of-power party is the Catholic-dominated rightist Christian Democrats. Wags in Bologna like to say that Reggiani are either devout communists or devout Catholics. The local Bishop is probably as powerful, though not as popular, as the town's young Mayor. Yet, while the two parties make no bones about their opposition to each other, they manage to get on amicably in the conduct of local affairs, particularly in matters of education and the provision of social services—the two spheres in which Reggio is famous throughout Italy.

There is abundant dialogue. The Left majority in Reggio is not the voice of an angry and dispossessed proletariat, nor is the Right an expression of single-minded Catholic militancy. Both sides are quite aware that they must occupy the same space, and have been long aware of it. So it is that even when the PDS was the PCI, its delegates marched in Reggio's Church-sponsored Saint's Day parades.

It has been rather like that since the end of the eighteenth century, when, inspired by the French Revolution, literate Reggiani organized themselves into local "Jacobin clubs" and rose against the reigning d'Este Dukes of Modena. Reggio officially established its own Republic in 1796, and a year later it enticed its neighbors, Bologna, Modena, and Ferrara, into joining a *Repubblica di Cispadania,* the Republic South of the Po.[86] In the Church, the Reggio Bishop at that time, Francesco d'Este—a cousin of the timidly self-exiled Duke of Modena—counseled his parish priests to moderation: "It will be easy for you to show that these same ideas of Equality and Liberty are not inconsistent in any way with the maxims of the Gospels, indeed, that they live together with them admirably. . . ."[87] Keep the dialogue going—and not just on Sundays.

After the d'Este Dukedom of Modena was restored to power in Reggio (the "cowardly" Duke returned), there were several further uprisings. By the middle of the nineteenth century, the city was savoring the promise of freedom under Italian unification in the Risorgimento. In 1899, Reggio elected what may have been the first Socialist city government in the world—certainly the first in Italy. Again, this was not a proletarian reaction to hard times, but a campaign led by a respected local bourgeois in whose honor the main Piazza of the city is now named. (Reggio's cathedral and its perpetually Left-dominated city hall stand together on the Piazza Prampolini today.) When a malaria epidemic struck the *provincia* a few years after the ascent of the first Socialist local government, the city council established a city-owned *farmacia* to assure that medication would be affordable to all. It was virtually unopposed at the time, and it is still there, still run by the *commune,* as the city still refers to itself.

There has been little open Catholic opposition to Reggio's professionally competent and expensive social services—services for families, for the elderly, even for new immigrants. One sometimes hears complaints that the children of well-off parents have a harder time being admitted into the Reggio preschools than immigrant children, for admission is partly governed by need. But social services are taken for granted locally, like clean streets and well-regulated open markets. The cultural wars heat up not over the pragmatics of running a proud town, but over what are marked as explicitly ideological issues. Even back in 1902, a bitter debate erupted over local financial support for the then obligatory religious instruction in public schools. On that issue, it was said that "the anti-clericalism of the Socialists was only equalled by the anti-socialism of the priests."[88] But the animosity did not go underground.

The rest of Reggio's history need not detain us. Not surprisingly, the city suffered badly under fascism, and its Leftist *partisani* payed a high price for their role in the Resistance.[89] Few were surprised when, in the first free election after the war, the city elected its first Communist government, the same party that has remained in power ever since. Yet the local Bishop continues to preside in Reggio, in a handsome *palazzo* off the square of San Prospero (who saved Reggio from the invading Visigoths by hiding it under a cloud in the fifth century); and the same little city which has become world-renowned for its free, communal preschools and social services also remains locally famous for its spacious Catholic seminary, often referred to ironically by locals as "the priest factory."

Partly through happenstance and partly through intention, Reggio is celebrating several important and ideologically disparate anniversaries in the last few years of the twentieth century. There have been many fetes and will be more: the centenary of the Italian flag (designed in Reggio); two hundred years since the Republican uprising; the millenarium of the Basilica of San Prospero; the centenary of local socialism. While there is a division of labor as to who presides over which celebration, all "sides" participate in all of them—and all with exquisite protocol. They know they are on opposite sides. But it is opposite sides of what seems to be a never-ending dialogue.

So what about that Bolognese quip regarding the devout Catholics and Communists in Reggio? Why has there not been more mayhem between them? Why haven't more Reggiani felt torn between their Catholic identity and their politics? Why do old PCI adherents who now vote PDS still baptize their children, get married in the Church, and depart the world blessed by its final rites? Catholic Christian Democrats are just as proud as others about Reggio's preschools and social services. When the old issue of religious instruction in the public schools raised its head again in the summer of 1997, there was sometimes bitter comment in the press and public discussion. But in that very same year, the nursery schools of the Catholic parish of Reggio made a deal with Reggio's communal preschools to have the parish's teachers trained along the lines of the Commune's preschools. The City Council immediately voted funds to pay for this. And there was even a full-day meeting at the local Catholic Seminary to discuss possible alternatives to religious instruction in the communal preschools, which is still required to be given to the children of parents who demand it although it is no longer compulsory for everybody. The meeting was altogether as courteous as it was inconclusive.

So Reggio goes on, despite two centuries of the struggle, without tearing itself to bits politically or culturally. How come? Perhaps the town's most famous literary son, Ariosto (who sped a sorceror to the moon in *Orlando Furioso* to recover Roland's common sense and thereby cure his raging madness), could give a better answer than we can. But surely managing the dialectic of culture commonsensibly depends in no small part on being awake to the dangers and possibilities of letting the dialectic die. Reggio, unlike Ireland, never had a hell-threatening Church,[90] never had foreign colonial masters intent on suppressing dissent and even the habit of dissent in dialogue.

The Bishop Francesco d'Este was shrewd enough to try to domesticate the spillover of the French Revolution into Reggio, much as the parish priest in our small Irish village domesticated the boisterous Seamus. And even though Reggio (at the heart of Italy's Red Belt) has now been politically Left for a century (with the infamous exception of two decades of fascism), its Left has taken the Catholic Right as a fact of life to be lived with; and its Catholic Right has reciprocated.[91] Even the famous Reggio preschools, born of the vision of a charismatic poet and writer of children's books, Loris Malaguzzi, boast of cultivating "the thousand voices of childhood." Dialogue is ever at the center of the local dialectic.

Lately, the Swedes and the Irish, the Americans and the Spaniards, have begun sending delegations to copy Reggio, the "Reggio approach." But can a cultural dialectic be "copied"?

CHAPTER NINE

Race, the Court, and America's Dialectic

From *Plessy* through *Brown* to *Pitts* and *Jenkins*

Let us see now whether the conception of culture developed in the preceding chapter opens any interesting vistas on the law. To that end, we will examine some major decisions of the Supreme Court of the United States dealing with issues of race under the Equal Protection Clause of the Fourteenth Amendment during the century from 1896 through 1995. In the process, we will also have a chance to reexamine our ideas about categories, narratives, and rhetorics in the light of the conception of culture set out in Chapter 8.

We have chosen this focus for several reasons. First, issues of race are among the central problems that have preoccupied American society since colonial times. The nation's efforts to grapple with those problems have crucially shaped its culture and been shaped by it, as Gunnar Myrdal, among other acute observers, saw.[1] Second, the race question becomes even more basic to an understanding of American culture under our own view that culture is constituted by the dialectic between and within a society's institutional systems and noetic space. For no other question involves a more acute tension between the possible worlds of which Americans dare to dream and the actual world that Americans inhabit; and on no other question is the disjuncture of these worlds so elaborately hidden by a screen of culture myths revealing in their deepest weave the strain of their intolerable justificatory burden.

Third, lawyers and judges are among the principal artificers of the screens.[2] As we saw in Chapter 7 in connection with *McCleskey v. Kemp*, the screens are often tissues of denial—denial that there is a problem, denial that the problem could be fixed if there were a problem, denial of judicial responsibility to fix the problem if it could be fixed. Because our aim in this book is to intensify awareness of the decisions and choices constantly being made by the people who make the law—and of the cognitive devices that those people are forever using to conceal their choices and avoid responsibility for their decisions—a study of the Supreme Court's constitutional jurisprudence of race may be particularly instructive.

Fourth, matters of race and racism depend heavily upon these very concealment devices. Race is not a fact found in the world but a *socially constructed* idea. Its construction is opportunistic, serving some end. Racism involves using the construct of race for hegemonic ends: to disempower the group constructed as "other" in order to empower *our group* by contrast to "them." This requires the creation and maintenance of an *essentialist,* "natural kinds" category scheme[3] that imbues the "others" with intrinsic, immutable qualities making them different from *us*. Particularly when the "others" coexist with us in close quarters so that their likenesses to us and the individual differences among "them" are difficult not to perceive, the essentialist category scheme at the core of racism needs to be continually shored up by *rituals of renewal* in which "they" are *re*racialized and their subordination to us is *re*justified—*re*instantiated in story or *re*inscribed in rhetorics time and again. As we noted in the last chapter, one of the aims of these rituals is to strip the "others" of all identity save their Otherness. Law provides a perpetual theater in which such rituals can be more or less consciously reenacted—and where, if they are at work, we can usefully investigate their workings.

Our method of investigation in this chapter will, as before, be to try to make the familiar strange. We will start by examining Supreme Court decisions at the beginning, in the middle, and at the end of our century of concern, not in their historical or doctrinal contexts but as single frames snipped from the hundred-year reel. We will compare these still-shots of the Court frozen in poses of action in 1896 (*Plessy v. Ferguson*), in 1954 (*Brown v. Board of Education*), and in the 1990s (*Freeman v. Pitts* and *Missouri v. Jenkins*), to see what the comparison reveals about the large similarities and differences in the Court's postures at these half-century intervals. Then, having immobilized Clio (in her role as the Muse of History) on our stage for the first act, we will unfetter her and see what songs and sagas she may inspire thereafter.

One last point before we plunge in. We make no claim to dispassion in our efforts to defamiliarize the history of Supreme Court adjudication of race issues. Like other Americans, we are tangled in the deeply disturbing American Dilemma about the social and legal rights of African-Americans and other racialized groups in this culture. Our biases were surely apparent in the previous chapters bearing on the subject. And again in what follows, our stance is no more objective than that of a Greek chorus commenting upon the action on a stage it shares with the principal players. Our perspective will be informed by our study of how protagonists on the living stage go about creating their categories, telling their stories, bending their arguments, and exemplifying the conflicts of their culture; but, at the same time, it will bear the unmistakable imprint of our own proclivities in each of these domains. So the reader will want to be critical about *our* predispositions and defects as we go about our work, just as we are critical of those we think we see in the work of Supreme Court Justices.

I. Three Snapshots of the Court in Action

Plessy v. Ferguson[4] involved a challenge to an 1890 Louisiana statute that required railroads to provide separate cars for whites and African-Americans, and forbade persons of each race to ride in the other's cars. Homer Plessy, who was one-eighth African-American although his skin was white, refused to obey a railroad conductor's order to leave a "white" car and was thereupon arrested and prosecuted. He sought to restrain the prosecution on the ground that the Louisiana statute violated the Equal Protection Clause of the Fourteenth Amendment and other provisions of the federal Constitution.

The Supreme Court rejected Plessy's claims and upheld the statute by a vote of seven to one.[5] As we read the majority opinion, its cardinal features are these:

1. *An unquestioning assumption that African-Americans and whites are inevitably different as a matter of the natural order of the Universe, and that judges could not change that fact if they wanted to.* "A statute which implies merely a legal distinction between the white and colored races—a distinction which is founded in the color of the

two races, and which must always exist so long as white men are distinguished from the other race by color—has no tendency to destroy the legal equality of the two races. . . ."[6] (The unquestioning nature of the assumption is all the more striking in that Plessy himself was not visibly "colored.") Thus, *"in the nature of things* [the Equal Protection Clause] . . . could not have been intended to abolish distinctions based upon color, or to enforce social, as distinguished from political equality. . . ."[7]

2. *A disavowal of judicial responsibility to attend to any problem that this state of affairs may present.* "If the two races are to meet on terms of social equality, it must be the result of natural affinities, a mutual appreciation of each other's merits and a voluntary consent of individuals. . . . '[T]his end can neither be accomplished nor promoted by laws which conflict with the general sentiment of the community upon whom they are designed to operate.'"[8]

3. *Conviction that whatever is, is right—that the measure of justice is its accommodation to existing public practices.* "[T]he case reduces itself to the question whether the statute of Louisiana is a reasonable regulation, and with respect to this . . . the legislature . . . is at liberty to act *with reference to the established usages, customs, and traditions of the people,* and with a view to the *promotion of their comfort,* and the preservation of the public peace and good order."[9]

4. *A disregard of inner life—of the reality of mind—and an exclusive attention to external forms.* "Laws permitting, and even requiring [the] . . . separation [of the races] . . . in places where they are liable to be brought into contact do not necessarily imply the inferiority of either race to the other. . . ."[10] This willful disregard of the psychological significance of institutional structures permits the Court to blame the victims for whatever offense they suffer. "We consider the underlying fallacy of the plaintiff's argument to consist in the assumption that the enforced separation of the two races stamps the colored race with a badge of inferiority. If this be so, it is not by reason of anything found in the act, but solely because the colored race chooses to put that construction upon it."[11]

In *Brown v. Board of Education,*[12] a half-century after *Plessy,* the Court took up the question whether state-enforced racial segregation in public schools was consistent with the Equal Protection Clause. African-American children challenged the systems of separate "white" and "colored" schools that had been established throughout the

South and in some border States since Reconstruction; the States defended their dual school systems under the "separate but equal" doctrine of *Plessy*. Passing over available narrower grounds of decision, a unanimous Supreme Court held that "in the field of public education the doctrine of 'separate but equal' has no place. Separate educational facilities are inherently unequal. Therefore, the [African-American children] . . . are, by reason of the segregation complained of, deprived of the equal protection of the laws guaranteed by the Fourteenth Amendment."[13]

As we read the *Brown* opinion, its cardinal features are these:

1. *Unwillingness to assume the inevitability of any particular institutional arrangement; a belief that if anything is inevitable, it is change; and a disinclination to view the prospect of change as frightening.* "In approaching this problem, we cannot turn the clock back to 1868 when the Amendment was adopted, or even to 1896 when *Plessy v. Ferguson* was written. We must consider public education in the light of its full development and its present place in American life throughout the Nation."[14]

2. *An acceptance of judicial responsibility for deciding when the time has come for a change: a refusal to invoke "the intent of the Framers" or any other ground for pretending that the Court is not making large value judgments in the exercise of its adjudicative function.* "[A]lthough [the historical] . . . sources cast some light, it is not enough to resolve the problem *with which we are faced*. At best, they are inconclusive."[15] "*Today*, education is perhaps the most important function of state and local governments. . . . *Today* it is a principal instrument [in preparing the child for life.] . . . *In these days*, it is [a necessary foundation for success in life]. . . ."[16] "*We come then to the question presented:* Does segregation of children in public schools solely on the basis of race, even though the physical facilities and other 'tangible' factors may be equal, deprive the children of the minority group of equal educational opportunities? *We believe that it does*."[17]

3. *A stance of idealism that takes the declarations of high-minded intention enshrined in the text of the Constitution as the measure of its commitments and of our society's obligations, rather than looking to the behavior of past generations as that measure; a willingness to imagine that our forebears may well have aspired more generously than they acted and to reconsider the compromises of expediency that*

they may have made between their professions and their conditions. "The most avid proponents of the post-War Amendments undoubtedly intended them to remove all legal distinctions among 'all persons born or naturalized in the United States.' Their opponents, just as certainly, were antagonistic to both the letter and the spirit of the Amendments and wished them to have the most limited effect. What others in Congress and the state legislatures had in mind cannot be determined with any degree of certainty,"[18] despite the historical fact that in the lifetimes of these people, segregated schools were established in more than two-thirds of the ratifying States. "We must look . . . to the effect of segregation itself on public education. . . . Only in this way can it be determined if segregation in public schools deprives these plaintiffs of the equal protection of the laws. . . . In these days, it is doubtful that any child may reasonably be expected to succeed in life if he is denied the opportunity of an education. Such an opportunity, where the state has undertaken to provide it, is a right which must be made available to all on equal terms."[19]

4. *An inward turn of vision that pays less attention to things-in-the-world than to things-in-the-mind, that defines "equality" in terms of equal opportunity to become something and equal opportunity for self-esteem, rather than as the sort of formal equality accepted as sufficient by* Plessy *or the equality of external resources accepted by the lower courts in applying* Plessy's *separate-but-equal doctrine to segregated schools.* Education "is a principal instrument in awakening the child to cultural values, in preparing him for later professional training, and in helping him to adjust normally to his environment."[20] "In *Sweatt v. Painter,* . . . in finding that a segregated law school for Negroes could not provide them equal educational opportunities, this Court relied in large part on 'those qualities which are incapable of objective measurement but which make for greatness in a law school.' In *McLaurin v. Oklahoma State Regents,* . . . the Court . . . again resorted to intangible considerations. . . . Such considerations apply with added force to children in grade and high schools. To separate them from others of similar age and qualifications solely because of their race generates a feeling of inferiority as to their status in the community that may affect their hearts and minds in a way unlikely ever to be undone."[21]

We have examined the 1992 case of *Freeman v. Pitts*[22] in Chapter 5, and the 1995 case of *Missouri v. Jenkins*[23] in Chapter 3. *Pitts* sends a message to the lower federal courts to start closing out the era of school-desegregation litigation promptly: it redefines the courts' "end purpose" in a desegregation case as being "to remedy the violation and in addition to restore state and local authorities to the control of a school system that is operating in compliance with the Constitution."[24] *Jenkins* intensifies the emphasis on the second member of this curious conjunction;[25] and both cases make it plain that, at least in metropolitan areas, "a school system . . . operating in compliance with the Constitution" means a ghetto district of predominantly African-American schools surrounded by a ring of largely white suburban school districts.

As we read the *Pitts* and *Jenkins* opinions, their cardinal features are these:

1. *An unquestioning assumption that African-Americans and whites will* inevitably *gravitate to different neighborhoods as a matter of the natural order of things, and that judges could not change that fact if they wanted to.* The overriding theme of the *Pitts* opinion is that judges must be resigned to the inexorable tides that make "'demographic shifts . . . inevitable as the result of suburbanization.'"[26] "The effect of changing residential patterns on the racial composition of schools though not always fortunate is somewhat predictable. . . . [R]acially stable neighborhoods are not likely to emerge because whites prefer a racial mix of 80% white and 20% black, while blacks prefer a 50%-50% mix."[27] "It is beyond the authority and *beyond the practical ability of the federal courts to try* to counteract these kinds of continuous and massive demographic shifts."[28] *Jenkins,* of course, goes on to turn this fatalism into a self-fulfilling prophecy by forbidding federal judges to fashion desegregation plans aimed in any part at motivating parents to choose to live in one school district rather than another.[29] And the same assumption of inevitability is reflected in the principal doctrinal apparatus of *Pitts* and *Jenkins,* the distinction between *de jure* school segregation (which is forbidden by the Equal Protection Clause according to *Brown*) and "*de facto*" school segregation (which is not).[30] The premise of the distinction thus drawn in metaphoric Latin seems to be that under some circumstances the uneven distribution of African-American and white children among public schools is simply a *fact,* something that happens without the intervention of human agency, *not* the result of decisions made by

human beings clothed with state authority to make them, like the decisions as to where school buildings will be located, how large they will be, what grades they will serve, how the neighborhoods around them will be zoned, where school district lines will be drawn, whether school districts will be separated or unified, and so forth.

2. *A disavowal of judicial responsibility to attend to any problem that this state of affairs may present.* As we have seen, *Pitts* and *Jenkins* are a pair of dissertations on the dangers and delusions of judicial over-ambitiousness about the work of school desegregation.[31] The emphasis in both opinions is upon the "duty [of the federal courts] to return the operations and control of schools to local authorities"[32] as soon as *de jure* segregation has been laid to rest. "In one sense of the term, vestiges of past segregation by state decree do remain in our society and in our schools. . . . But though we cannot escape our history, neither must we overstate its consequences in fixing legal responsibilities."[33] The courts need not be concerned with vestiges of discrimination unless they are "so real that they have a causal link to the de jure violation being remedied."[34] And to avoid finding such a reality in the case of white migration from center-city metropolitan schools to the suburbs, the Court in *Jenkins* uses an *either/or* rhetoric to establish that "white flight" must logically be seen as an irremediable vestige of desegregation rather than a remediable vestige of segregation.[35]

3. *Conviction that whatever is, is right—that the measure of justice is its accommodation to existing public practices.* The thrust of both *Pitts* and *Jenkins* is that it is past time for a return to normalcy after the unnatural exertions of the *Brown* era.[36] Normalcy is depicted as that state of good democratic government which will prevail when those who have always run our schools in accordance with the popular will are running them again. "Returning schools to the control of local authorities at the earliest practicable date is essential to restore their true accountability in our governmental system. When the school district and all state entities participating with it in operating the schools make decisions in the absence of judicial supervision, they can be held accountable to the citizenry, to the political process, and to the courts in the ordinary course."[37] This desideratum of democratic decisionmaking-as-usual exhausts the entire optative dimension of the *Pitts* and *Jenkins* opinions[38] and leaves the Court with no need

to examine possible complications of that dimension that might arise, for example, from the notion suggested in *Brown* that equality of opportunity is necessary to *fit* a people for democracy.

4. *A disregard of inner life—of the reality of mind—and an exclusive attention to external forms.* *Pitts* and *Jenkins* announce a standard to be used by the federal courts in determining when their work of desegregation is at an end. The standard is constructed by recasting a descriptive sentence found in a 1968 opinion, *Green v. County School Board of New Kent County,*[39] as a prescriptive checklist of the "various parts of the school system which, in addition to student attendance patterns, must be free from racial discrimination before the mandate of Brown is met: faculty, staff, transportation, extracurricular activities and facilities."[40] These "*Green* factors" are declared to be "a measure of the racial identifiability of schools in a system that is not in compliance with Brown,"[41] notwithstanding that any ordinary observer can plainly identify ghetto schools as *black schools* and suburban schools as *white schools* even when all six *Green* factors have been equalized *separately* within the center-city school districts on the one hand and the suburban districts on the other. The formal boundaries of school districts, initially drawn and always readjustable by the states for reasons of convenience or politics, are treated as uncrossable when a federal court comes to consider whether a State has done enough to meet its constitutional obligation to desegregate its schools.[42] Gone is *Brown*'s attention to those "intangible" features of the cultural landscape that any African-American child can see and that "may affect their hearts and minds in a way unlikely ever to be undone." What *Pitts* and *Jenkins* are concerned with, rather, is reducing *Brown* to a formula "susceptible to . . . objective limitation."[43]

II. Why Brown and Not Plessy Is the Law of the Land

On the face of this set of cases, it appears to us that the Supreme Court has marched the king's men up the hill and down again. This is not surprising in itself. Reversals of direction within a society over a period of a century are hardly uncommon. Nor is it surprising that the ascent of the hill was noisy and spectacular—Chief Justice Warren mustering a unanimous Court to declare *Plessy* defunct;[44] mobs in the streets; Governor Orval Faubus on television calling out the Arkansas National Guard to stand in the doorway of Little Rock's Central High

School to block the admission of black children under a federal court desegregation order;[45] the Supreme Court's responsive opinion in *Cooper v. Aaron*, unprecedentedly *superscribed* with the names of all nine Justices, requiring the enforcement of the desegregation order despite Faubus's armed resistance;[46] Birmingham, Alabama, with water cannons and police dogs savaging demonstrators; the March on Washington; the Civil Rights Act of 1964; Selma; Louisville—while the subsequent descent was quiet and almost inconspicuous. History offers plenty of examples of revolutions undone (indeed, co-opted) by a series of small, seemingly "technical" counterrevolutions.

What is interesting about this particular reversal—and what drives us to view it as a tricky puzzle—is that the Court's change of stance from *Plessy* to *Brown* has to be described quite differently than its change of stance from *Brown* to *Pitts* and *Jenkins* when the two changes are looked at today in their character as *law*. The easiest way to express the difference is to observe that if a would-be lawyer were asked on the bar examination whether *Plessy* is still an authoritative precedent in the wake of *Brown*, s/he would have to say "no" or flunk;[47] but if s/he answered "no" to the question whether *Brown* is still an authoritative precedent in the wake of *Pitts* and *Jenkins*, s/he would also flunk. And if a student on a Constitutional Law exam wrote: "*Brown* is still an authoritative precedent, except as applied to racial segregation in the public schools," s/he would flunk unless s/he added a footnote making clear that this was ironic commentary rather than an exposition of the doctrinal rules.

It is worth considering the reasons for these flunking grades. In many senses, *Brown* is still an authoritative precedent—"good law," as lawyers say—and *Plessy* is not. But some of those senses are no more than trivial, and others are less than obvious. Perhaps we can understand this better if we give a legal twist to the two aspects of culture discussed in Chapter 8: the canonical and the noetic. As a start, consider the following possible reasons why *Brown* must still be said to be "good law":

a. *Lower courts are still at work administering desegregation orders entered pursuant to* Brown. This is true but trivial today, both because it will not be true for many more years, and because there are more important senses in which *Brown* will remain good law even after it is no longer true. Most of the remaining decisions that the lower courts will make in these cases will be guided by the precedents of *Pitts* and *Jenkins*, which have glossed *Brown* so extensively as to render *Brown* irrelevant as a source of law.

b. *The lower courts would be obliged to "follow"* Brown, *and the Supreme Court itself would doubtless do so, in any new case presenting facts similar to* Brown's—*that is, cases of state laws explicitly requiring racial segregation.* This is true and not entirely trivial even though such cases will almost certainly never arise. It is not trivial because the notion that *Brown* is still good law is a part of the reason why the cases will not arise. In this regard, the rule of *Brown* is entrenched in our legal culture in much the same way that a people's musical canon is embodied in its musical instruments, as we noted in Chapter 8. It has acquired the exteriority necessary to function as a constraint without being the subject of conscious attention.

c. *The lower courts would be obliged to "follow"* Brown, *and the Supreme Court itself would doubtless do so, in new cases presenting facts that, while not similar to* Brown's, *are within the reach of its doctrinal or normative logic.* This is less true and more trivial than it would appear. It is more trivial because decisions like *Pitts* and *Jenkins* and *McCleskey* have confined the doctrinal and normative logic of *Brown* to such a small compass that there remain almost no circumstances in the real world under which a case invoking that logic can be proved.[48] It is less true because, as we have seen, these decisions themselves were not guided by any principles or values rooted in *Brown* but by a vision of the world that is considerably closer to *Plessy*'s. Although the Court's opinions continue to cite *Brown,* they are plainly not *following Brown* in the sense of reasoning under its influence, but are drawing from *Brown* whatever they can read into it that will support results driven by concerns that have nothing to do with *Brown*'s.[49] Witness the line of decisions from *Regents of the University of California v. Bakke*[50] to *Adarand Constructors, Inc. v. Pena,*[51] holding that white persons were denied the equal protection of the laws by governmental affirmative-action programs designed to increase the participation of racial minorities in sectors of American life from which they historically had been excluded. These cases commonly cite *Brown* for the proposition that laws treating people differently on the ground of race are per se invidious and presumptively offensive to the Equal Protection Clause. Yes, *Brown* can be read as standing for that proposition, but only through either or both of two procedures. One is to puff up *Brown*'s declaration of a right of racial equality to a ridiculous level of abstraction, in the manner of Anatole France declaiming that the Law in Its Majestic Equality forbids the rich and poor alike to sleep under the bridges of Paris. The other is to revert to the unseeing formalism of *Plessy* and profess to be unable to discern which of two segregated railway cars, the car reserved for whites or the car reserved for blacks, is the Jim Crow car.

d. Brown *is still respected as the icon of an ideal that the courts are free to disregard only after performing appropriate rituals of rationalization.* This seems quite true, and it is not trivial even though the Court's disregard of *Brown* has grown conventional and its rationalizations practically all-encompassing. For what the rituals declare is that *Brown* has been inscribed in the culture's noetic space and is a vital presence there in a way that *Plessy* is not. This is why in 1994 *Brown*'s fortieth anniversary evoked a tide of laudatory, largely self-congratulatory public prose, while two years later *Plessy*'s centennial went unremarked. It is also why, whenever a potentially reactionary nominee to any federal judicial office has been quizzed before the Senate Judiciary Committee during the past forty years, s/he has been put through the drill of swearing s/he believes that *Brown* was correctly decided, however moot the issue and patently insincere the oath may be.

How, then, account for the hold that *Brown* has obtained on America's political and legal imagination, and for its relative lack of traction on the nation's actual operating rules?

III. *The American Creed and Its Grim Counterpart*

A distinguished Johns Hopkins historian, John Higham, has offered an insightful explanatory thesis. We agree with it on the whole, with one major refinement and a few smaller ones.

Higham begins by observing that American history has been marked by three distinct waves of concern about the subordinated status of African-Americans, with each wave taking the same shape:[52] "A low swell, moving slowly, gains momentum. At a certain point it surges to a mighty crest that crashes with a roar. A wash of water flows onward, but the force is gone. The wave is receding."[53]

The first wave rises to its peak just after the American Revolution. Between 1780 and 1804, every northern State begins the process of emancipating slaves and ending slavery within its borders. During the same period, several southern State legislatures facilitate the voluntary manumission of slaves, and many slaveholders do let their slaves go free. The Northwest Ordinance of 1787 prohibits slavery in the Northwest Territory. The first Congress ratifies the Ordinance, assuring that new States formed north of the Ohio River will be free. By enactments in 1794, 1800, and 1807, Congress progressively outlaws the African slave trade.[54]

But then the antislavery fervor dies out rapidly. In the early years of the nineteenth century, southern legislatures tighten restrictions on manumission and on the rights of free blacks and enact harsher slave codes. In the North, the freed slaves are denied the right to serve on juries; they are excluded from some localities by ordinance and forbidden to immigrate to some States. Antimiscegenation laws are enacted or made more punitive everywhere. In 1820 the Missouri Compromise is struck. By 1836 the House of Representatives adopts a gag rule prohibiting discussion or consideration of any antislavery petition. Then comes *Prigg* in 1842, the Fugitive Slave Act of 1850, and *Dred Scott* in 1857.

The second wave rises to its peak during and after the Civil War. Antislavery becomes a religious and moral crusade throughout the North. President Lincoln issues the Emancipation Proclamation in 1863. The Thirteenth, Fourteenth, and Fifteenth Amendments are ratified between 1865 and 1870. Congress passes a series of civil rights and enforcement acts, protects the former slaves by temporarily installing the Freedman's Bureau and military authorities in the South, and undertakes to create permanent interracial governments in the southern States.

But again the fervor quickly dies away. The Supreme Court begins to read the postwar Amendments grudgingly, reducing the Privileges and Immunities Clause of the Fourteenth Amendment to a cipher as early as 1873 and thus returning most of the basic rights of individuals into the keeping of state law.[55] The Hayes-Tilden compromise of 1877 is cut; federal troops are withdrawn from the South; the Redeemer Governments begin to build the regime of White Supremacy and Jim Crow. In the North as well as the South, Social Darwinian "science" and other rationalizations for biological racism come into vogue and are widely accepted in a range of intellectualized and popular forms as the nineteenth century ends and the twentieth begins. *Plessy*, in 1896, speaks for its times.

The third wave rises to its peak after World War II. President Truman's Committee on Civil Rights recommends an end of all segregation in 1947. Assisted by the G.I. Bill, African-American veterans can attend colleges and graduate schools. Litigation challenging segregation in the graduate schools makes the first constitutional breach in Jim Crow laws. *Brown v. Board of Education* is decided by a unanimous Supreme Court in 1954. Southern resistance precipitates massive civil-rights protests that spark a powerful national reaction against Jim Crow. Congress enacts new civil-rights and voting-rights laws; not a few state legislatures and local governments do the same. Head Start and some affirmative-action programs open new avenues of educational opportunity to African-Americans.

And then again the wave crashes and recedes. Within a generation, the Supreme Court begins to back away from enforcing *Brown* and simultaneously starts to erode the new civil-rights statutes. *Bakke* and its offspring turn the Equal Protection Clause of the Fourteenth Amendment into a guarantee that white people will not be discriminatorily deprived of any of their traditional privileges. Affirmative action becomes a sinking ship, and the politicians all flee it.

Higham attributes this recurrent wave pattern to the waxing and waning of a "distinctive national ideology" which he follows Gunnar Myrdal in calling the American Creed and summarizes as follows:

> "One founding principle declared that the United States exists to secure the equal, unalienable rights that individuals receive from nature. Another enshrined a broadly Christian ethic of dedication to the common good. A third offered an embracing faith in human progress, with America in the lead."[56]

In each of the three historical waves, a major, victorious war gave rise to a "great upsurge of national idealism" centered upon this American Creed as expressive of "the principles that had given the nation its identity."[57] Before each war, there had been a "gradual . . . buildup of moral disquiet over the state of race relations"; then "the fervent nationalism of a great war energized [this] . . . long-standing moral concern, which had [previously] deeply troubled only a small minority of whites."[58] The wars served to "rais[e] aspirations and giv[e] demands for change a national hearing."[59] At the same time, they created economic conditions—a wartime need for military and civilian labor; a postwar period of full employment and prosperity—that enabled the United States to indulge "the altruistic inducement [that] each major war held out to Americans to locate themselves within and carry forward the Spirit of '76."[60]

But after each war, there was a "waning of idealistic nationalism and moral fervor."[61] New concentrations of African-American population, particularly in the nation's cities, aroused white fears. Then, when the postwar economic booms subsided, "self-interest crowded to the fore"[62] and people's attention turned from edifying moral themes to ruthless competition for jobs and other scarce resources. "Indifference at the top of the social scale and bare-knuckle antagonism down below again widened the racial chasm."[63]

Higham's perception of the crest-and-crash cycle of American egalitarian sentiment and its political realization seems to us quite right. But where he talks about a single American Creed and depicts the cycle in terms of the periodic falterings and resurgences of that one creed,[64] we see, rather, two contending visions of the world, both characteristically American,[65] constantly in tension, each a gradually mutating complex of ideas, assumptions, values, and arguments. And we view America's cycle of advances and retreats in egalitarianism partly as a function of the shifting battle lines as these two visions struggle for ascendance in the culture's noetic space and for controlling influence upon the country's legal, political, and economic institutions.

Our difference from Higham is not prompted by an urge to substitute some sort of metaphysical dualism for his monism. Rather, it is a matter of emphasizing that, in our view, the departing roar of the egalitarian tide, no less than its incoming crash, always involves an ideological and imaginative element. Both America's egalitarian advances and its egalitarian retreats have always been piped by appropriate, rousing tunes—familiar medleys of conceptualizations and justifications, categorizations, narratives, and rhetorics—that serve to give the advance or the retreat a cognitive coherence. Following Higham and Myrdal, we will call the medley usually heard as the tide rises the *American Creed,* hopeful, open-handed, companionable, and idealistic. But we will also speak of a second medley that is ordinarily heard as the tide falls: the *American Caution,* suspicious, grasping, clannish, and ruthless.

IV. The Dialectic of the Creed and the Caution

From the beginning, America has been caught in a dilemma born of its needs to incorporate both the American Creed and the American Caution into its identity. For the sake of economy, one might describe the competing needs as *the need to be inclusive* and *the need to be exclusive:* the need to recruit additional populations and the need to keep them subordinated so that the privileged status of their predecessors is preserved. This is, of course, an oversimplification: myths of national identity, as well as populations, evolve; peoples and the stories that they tell themselves about themselves are dynamic, defying reduction to any tidy formula. But the inclusion/exclusion dilemma does serve to name the key components of a dialectic.

On the one hand, America is a country that portrays itself as the land of opportunity, its people as the beneficiaries of those abundant, generous, ever-promising opportunities. Americans believe that America's exceptionality derives not only from its wealth of opportunity but from a uniquely American commitment to make its opportunities available to all, to assure its people—native and adopted—*freedom* of opportunity. This concept of freedom, however, necessarily conceals a contradiction: it must involve freedom *from* being fettered by the privileges of others, but it must also involve freedom *to acquire* privileges of one's own—and that's all right, don't think twice about whether one's own privileges won't have to imply some sort of fettering of somebody else, *sometime.*

Americans thus construct for themselves an identity that contrasts with "the Old World" where opportunities and freedoms are seen to be absent or in short supply. This faith in America as the Land of Opportunity and Freedom has been renewed and reshaped by successive waves of immigrants coming to take refuge in an ever-growing, ever-beckoning "melting pot." It was as much in the minds of the Hessian mercenaries who joined the colonists they had been hired to put down as it was in the minds of Irish refugees fleeing famine in the mid-nineteenth century or of Eastern European Jews fleeing pogroms at the century's end. No nation in the world has ever constructed so generous, so optimistic, so innocent a self-portrait as America—reigned over symbolically by a welcoming Statue of Liberty inviting the world's poor and oppressed to take shelter under her lamp of freedom.

But, for all that, the disturbing (and most often denied) truth of America has always been that opportunity rarely yields its promise easily. *Making it* in America has always been and still remains tough going. Beneath the hopeful myth that America is not only a melting pot but a limitless one, there is almost always the fear that there won't turn out to be enough in the pot for both me and the other guy. So, as if in self-protection, there has developed an American Caution, a tough, wary counterpoint to the generous American Creed. We are proud of the Creed, but we think of the Caution as a "necessity."

Yet we Americans also romanticize our tough side by calling it individualism, self-reliance, or hard-headed practicality.[66] In attractive everyday dress, it takes the form of "look out for yourself," "don't let anybody take advantage of you," and "every tub on its own bottom." Its legends and songs are about the Hunters of Kentucky, the Lion of the West, Buffalo Bill, Wyatt Earp, Teddy Roosevelt and his Rough Riders, Audie Murphy, Rocky, and Rambo.[67] At its least attractive, the American Caution expresses itself as suspicion, jealousy, and xenophobia, a denial of responsibility to worry about the harms we do to others, and a constant search for tokens of our superiority to the others we may harm, so that heedlessness of the harm will not be guilt-laden.

Racism has played an important role in reconciling the American Creed and the American Caution.[68] By dividing humanity into "Us" and "Others"—the naturally entitled and the naturally unentitled—racism permits Us to believe that We have limitless opportunities and are right to enjoy them without concern that any scarcity of opportunities for Them will encumber Our future or embarrass Our moral standing as inheritors of the Spirit of '76. To the extent that circumstances temporarily deprive Us of the full enjoyment of Our opportunities by favoring Them, We can feel aggrieved and call confidently for a return to normalcy that will restore Our traditional and rightful privileges. To impoverish the pot by giving Them a handout diminishes Our freedom of opportunity and betrays the American tradition of liberty and equality; but They cannot complain that the pot is empty when They get there, for the pot was constructed by the industry and genius of Our forebears, and They are not among the posterity who were meant to profit from its abundance.

It is not surprising, then, that the attitudes and beliefs of America's dominant culture have always been riven with the rites and stories, imaginings and rationalizations that construct race and racism in the same move. Our first candidate race, of course, was Native Americans, whose ferocity, cruelty, and treachery were rendered legendary by frontier tales, ritualized imagery, and the like. These tales had one common deletion rule: there was never any mention that *We* were taking away *Their* land and livelihood.

Africans, brought as captives to serve as slaves, were second on our racialization schedule. In no time, a long list of rituals and narratives was developed for maintaining and rejustifying them in that status— their innate lack of intelligence and initiative, their childlikeness, their sexual lust.[69] In 1699, for example, four score years after the first twenty Africans were off-loaded onto the American continent by Dutch sailors and sold as slaves at Jamestown, the House of Burgesses of Virginia refused an official request from England to enact a law facilitating the conversion of Negroes to Christianity and explained that, "for Negroes Imported hither the Gros Barbarity and rudeness of their manners, the variety and Strangeness of their Languages and the weakness and Shallowness of their minds renders it in a manner impossible to attain to any Progress in their Conversion."[70] *They* were *nothing*—reduced to not-Us, not recognizably human. Thus, the tale of the futility of trying to change the inevitable difference between black and white people was hardly original to *Plessy, Pitts,* and *Jenkins.*

The temptation to racialize Others has been evident virtually throughout the history of immigration to America, and not just where stereotypically "racial" groups, like Chinese laborers, were concerned. Few immigrant groups escaped nomination as races, and those that did were mostly Northern Europeans whose customs were already familiar. The Irish, Italians, and Eastern Europeans all suffered their season as candidate races. And when crude intelligence testing was introduced during World War I, it served principally to reinforce the would-be eugenic racializers by "showing" that immigrants from those parts of the world were natively less intelligent than *We* were—never mind that they did not have as firm a command of English or as much schooling as *We* did.

Nevertheless, most immigrants were eventually permitted to join Us by the familiar processes of assimilation. Initially viewed as threatening—threatening to Our jobs, Our clubs, Our ways, Our identity— They were kept in cultural quarantine for a suitable period of time until They demonstrated that They could become indistinguishable from Us: *ordinary* Americans. That done, they were living proofs of America's freedom and equality of opportunity, and We celebrated the American Creed by accepting them as such. Their slightly exotic origins now only served to confirm and romanticize the Creed.

But We cannot accept everybody. For even in times of the most abundant prosperity, there are commodities like *esteem* and *superiority* that need to be rationed; and when the times are less flush, material resources (which are often perceived as necessities, if only because they symbolize that their possessor has *made it* and thereby deserved a portion of America's opportunities) have to be rationed as well.[71] So the preservation of the American Creed requires that We create a category of people who are *essentially* and *immutably* different and inadmissible. They are the inferior races, virtually non-people. We construct them and maintain them as inferior by rituals of racialization and renewal designed to keep them in their place. American culture has devised an astonishingly effective system for accomplishing this kind of racialization: by segregation, by job discrimination, by material and cultural deprivation, and ultimately by criminalization and incarceration.[72]

We cannot pretend to understand exactly what ends are served by American racism toward African-Americans, partly because it has gone through numerous transformations, partly because human ends do not reveal themselves so easily. When They were Our slaves, Their racialization served obvious ends.[73] And when They became Our field hands or even Our servants, the same renewal narrative could serve for a time.[74] It has been argued that "the demise of slavery and the subsequent shift from paternalistic to competitive race relations increased the need for biological racism as a line of defense against black encroachment in areas where whites claimed prior rights and advantages."[75] There is certainly much to this. But the racialization of

African-Americans has taken many convoluted turns that economic competition alone cannot explain, as we know from the insightful studies by Cash and Woodward and Jordan and Smith,[76] and know still better from the pages and plays of William Faulkner, Langston Hughes, Lillian Hellman, Richard Wright, Robert Penn Warren, and Tennessee Williams. In our own time, race has been rejustified by elaborate (and, again, convoluted) excursions into statistical genetics—as though, even if it *were* the case that African-Americans were a fraction of a standard deviation unit down from equally schooled whites on standard intelligence tests, that would be a phenomenon of self-evident meaning,[77] or one sufficient to explain *why* IQ test scores should serve as the basis for racializing or discriminating against anybody.

For whatever reasons, the emancipation of African-Americans from slavery did not place them in the ordinary category of immigrants—Irish, Polish, Italian—but instead gave rise to a complicated socioeconomic system for reracializing them. First came Jim Crow, then the urban ghetto complex with all of its mutually reinforcing deprivations[78] narrativized as a self-punishing Hell out of Hieronymus Bosch (created, of course, by black crime and laziness and licentiousness), then "benign neglect" so long as They don't crowd Our back yard. So while white Americans in our time are, for the most part, genuinely ashamed of the institutions of slavery and overt Jim Crow in America's past, they dismiss or decline to admit today's covert Jim Crow institutions or they blame them on the victim.

Such denials feed and feed upon an intricate web of beliefs, verbalizations, and narratives, including a corpus of legal precedent and judicial interpretation. Yet the wheel turns, and from time to time we—including the Supreme Court—are able to see the unseeable, speak the unspeakable, and aspire to change what our more usual mythology declares to be natural and unchangeable. So it was for a while before and after *Brown v. Board of Education*. Let us look more closely at how that came to pass, and has now come almost to pass away.

V. On the Road: From Plessy to Brown

Between 1896 and 1995, the 100-year span on which we focus in this chapter, America and its courts were no longer concerned with slavery. Slavery had been laid to rest by the Civil War, by the Emancipation Proclamation, by the post–Civil War Amendments. African-Americans stood, in one way, in the posture of new immigrants. The great issue after abolition was whether "freed" African-Americans were indeed *free* in the same sense that all other Americans are—whether they would be permitted to become just ordinary Americans, free to partake of the beckoning opportunities that animated other Americans, that had brought the ancestors of many white Americans here as immigrants. This remained the question before the country and before the Supreme Court throughout the twentieth century.

Jim Crow answered it with a resounding negative, and the Supreme Court in *Plessy* bought Jim Crow. The *Plessy* decision can be understood as a feeble, prudential attempt to accommodate the American Creed to the American Caution at a moment when expediency was far more the American mood than idealism. *Plessy* was the culmination of a period of living with the incompatibility between the nation's cynical abandonment of Reconstruction[79] and the noble pledges of the Emancipation Proclamation and the Thirteenth, Fourteenth, and Fifteenth Amendments—America's manifestly unkept promises of an end to slavery, of equal privileges and immunities for all citizens, and of equal political rights and equal protection of the law without regard to race, color, or previous condition of servitude.[80] The Compromise of 1877 had set the tone, following that "series of famous compromises, once familiar to every schoolboy,"[81] that had sold Africans and African-Americans into slavery time and again: the compromises which (as we have seen) Justice Story found in the Constitution,[82] and the compromises of 1820 and 1850. But a Court cannot *admit* that it is making a political compromise, and even the *Plessy* Court was not so cynical as to pretend that it could find in the Thirteenth or Fourteenth Amendment a Framer's Compromise that (like Justice Story in *Prigg*) the Court could simply "enforce" without taking the responsibility for making it. So *Plessy*'s strategy was the one that we have outlined at the beginning of this chapter: profess an inability to discern that Jim Crow laws have anything to do with subordinating black people;[83] aver that any disadvantages that blacks may suffer in this Universe are natural, inevitable, and none of judges' business; and hew generally to the ever-comforting One Clear Truth that Whatever Is, is RIGHT.[84] These strategies were aided by two powerful props: the then-fashionable notion that race was a biological way of color-coding superior and inferior human beings,[85] and the dramatic death of all idealism that followed the horrors of the Civil War. As Andrew Delbanco put it neatly: "Before the war, Americans spoke of providence. After it, they spoke of luck. . . . God had been replaced by fortune, and fortune makes no moral judgments."[86]

Plessy was nominally about railroad cars, but it put the Court's stamp of approval on the notion that separation of the races was natural and unexceptionable. On this rock, Jim Crow could stand firm for more than half a century. The elaboration of public education systems featuring white and colored schools throughout the South and in some other regions was a particularly crucial step in limiting the entry of America's ex-slaves into the category of *ordinary* Americans. By consigning African-American children to separate, inferior, under-financed schools, the segregated educational establishment made it easy enough to prove that they were inferior. If black folks didn't like it, there was always crypto-police-power to enforce white superiority through tolerated mob violence, the Klan, and racist court practices.[87] And everybody knew what the conjunction of separate-but-equal meant. "Separate" was to give the Court's warrant to reality; "equal" was to wash the Court's hands symbolically of any responsibility for that reality.

It was not to be until well after World War I that the stance of America's dominant culture on the question of race, depicted as unalterable fact and canonized as constitutional law in *Plessy,* began to change. As Higham and others have noted, the isolationism and adulation of normalcy that followed the war were accompanied by a determination to keep African-Americans, like everything else, firmly in their traditional place. Their place was first reaffirmed by violence—a widespread wave of lynchings and race riots[88]—and then made inconspicuous or non-problematic in the manner of Norman Rockwell's homey *Saturday Evening Post* covers where, if African-Americans appeared at all, it was in the guise of darkies.

But around 1930 events and ideas combined to destabilize this homey vision of the world and to change precipitately the balance of the American dialectic. The 1929 Wall Street crash and a severe economic depression turned the previously-unproblematic problematic. Unemployment and hard times made poverty much less abstract, much less the invisible province of the chronically down-and-out, like black folks.

The subsequent rise of industrial unionism and New Deal activism served to reawaken the American faith that things *could change*, that the world *could be changed* by concerted human endeavor—and for the better. By the time of *Brown v. Board of Education*, there had been not only five presidential terms of New-Deal/Fair-Deal judicial appointments but five terms of New-Deal "project" thinking. The essence of this thinking was that aspiration, daring, and perseverance could reform deficient political and cultural institutions. Project thinking and the economic boom set off by World War II came together to create a confident assumption that America's prosperity would continue to expand so much that African-Americans could at last be given their share of American freedom of opportunity *without* taking anything away from whites.

And, of course, World War II became America's war against racism. Only shortly after the Depression taught Americans how precious and how perishable freedom of opportunity could be, they were exposed to the appalling spectacle of Hitler systematically destroying the freedom of opportunity of a people defined and vilified by race. As the Nazis went from economic exploitation, physical isolation, and episodic murder to relentless genocide, America increasingly took upon itself the mantle of the leader of egalitarian free societies against the monstrous evil of German racism. It retained that mantle after the war, sending one of its Supreme Court Justices, Robert H. Jackson, to be the Chief Allied Prosecutor at the Nuremberg War Crimes Tribunal. At the same time, Americans—and their Supreme Court— emerged from the war burdened with their own loads of guilt about their hypocritical mistreatment of Japanese-Americans. Both a pressure to respect the nation's wartime rhetoric decrying racism and a pressure to atone for the hypocrisy of the Japanese Relocation were bound to be in play when *Brown* presented the Court with the question of the constitutionality of separate-but-equal "white" and "colored" public schools in the early 1950s.[89]

But the Court's conception of the question was also affected by other, more subtle aspects of the cultural dialectic of the time. There was the "inward turn" in literature and theater[90] that made Americans more aware of the gripping realities of mind and more sensitive to discrepancies between words and implications, between the explicit and the implicit, between what is spelled out and what is written between the lines. There was the curious reflection of this inward turn in the public rhetoric of the New Deal and later of the war years: "The only thing we have to fear is fear itself." There was the Harlem Renaissance, a sudden rising of African-American voices in self-confident protest and pride, which burst upon the national literary consciousness in the mid-1920s and drew the attention of a widespread white reading public to the painful subjective realities of racial oppression.[91] Through the powerful images of a Langston Hughes and then of a Richard Wright, it became possible for white Americans, for the first time, to begin to comprehend in some measure what it *felt* like to be black. During World War II and the Cold War that followed, a popular rhetoric of national unity evolved that portrayed African-Americans as fighting and working for their country alongside whites. The national press began to develop "a new portrait of blacks as essentially similar to whites."[92] It began to report stories making the point that "America had expected colored people to give their lives and effort for the nation during the war, but now denied them the privilege of living in the nation as free and equal citizens."[93] The core of these narratives was not an abstract demonstration of logical contradiction but a bitter tale of betrayal; and in telling that tale, magazines like *Harper's* and *Newsweek* simultaneously understood and reinforced the growing capacity of their predominantly white readership to appreciate the experience of *being black.*

This movement in the general culture was mirrored by the Supreme Court. Contemporaneously with the emergence of the Harlem Renaissance and increasingly after 1932, the Court began to pay attention to the long-ignored phenomenon of southern state courts conniving in the lynching of African-American criminal defendants accused of violent crimes against white persons. Stereotypical "legal lynchings," like the notorious Scottsboro Cases, account for almost all of the Court's early decisions recognizing that the Due Process and Equal Protection Clauses of the Fourteenth Amendment have something to say about the *substance* and not merely the *form* of state criminal proceedings.[94] These cases—which refuse, for example, to accept a trial judge's token appointment of the entire local bar to represent defendants on trial for their life when the appointment "was little more than an expansive gesture, imposing no substantial or definite obligation upon any one" and when "the defendants did not have the aid of counsel *in any real sense,*"[95]—show the Court's earliest development of the mien of unflinching realism and acceptance of responsibility concerning African-American subordination that would later characterize its decision in *Brown*. Gone are *Plessy*'s strategies of burying the facts of bigotry and oppression beneath a feigned naiveté and portraying the results as inevitable, as nothing that judges need to have upon their consciences.[96]

The Court took stances of realism and judicial responsibility more often and in connection with a broader range of race issues between 1940 and 1954[97] (despite its queasy capitulation to expediency in upholding the discriminatory curfew and evacuation measures applied to Japanese-Americans during the war).[98] Those stances marked the unanimous opinions written by Chief Justice Vinson in the Court's 1950 cases outlawing racial segregation in state university graduate schools.[99] The 1950 cases were the leading edge of the NAACP Legal Defense Fund's litigation campaign to desegregate American education,[100] and they proved to be the precursors and immediate precedents for *Brown*. In 1954, Chief Justice Warren and a unanimous Supreme Court declared that *Plessy* could no longer command the law's respect and that "in the field of public education the doctrine of 'separate but equal' has no place."[101] *Brown* appeared to have decisively incorporated the egalitarian vision of the American Creed into the Fourteenth Amendment.

VI. On the Road Again: From Brown to Pitts and Jenkins

For a time, that vision both retained the allegiance of the Supreme Court and gained a predominant place in the nation's political and cultural imagination. As far as the public schools were concerned, the Court did not order its 1954 *Brown* decision implemented by the immediate cessation of all race-based pupil assignments but held that the lower federal courts should oversee a transition to racially nondiscriminatory school systems "with all deliberate speed."[102] At the same time, the Court itself moved rapidly to extend the rule of desegregation to all sites of public life—parks, beaches, swimming pools, and so forth.[103] When the South responded with stonewalling and violence, Dr. Martin Luther King, Jr., and other civil rights leaders took the issues to the streets. Their protest and its brutal repression in southern cities and towns galvanized egalitarian sentiment across the United States and stimulated federal legislation and executive action forbidding racial discrimination in housing, employment, public accommodations, and voting rights, as well as in education. For a generation, the Supreme Court applied the new federal legislation liberally,[104] reinvigorated older civil rights legislation,[105] and enforced the Fourteenth and Fifteenth Amendments vigilantly[106] as warrants of a commitment that racial minorities in the United States would actually enjoy equal rights and opportunities with white persons for the first time in the nation's history.

Then things changed once more, as the optimism and enthusiasm that had ushered in the 1960s began to wane. With increasing globalization (even before that word became a part of our lexicon), America seemed to be losing its long-unchallenged industrial competitive edge. The possibility that American auto manufacturing might be neither the world's best nor forever the world's most lucrative suddenly began to dawn on the scarce-believing American mind. And would the Japanese beat us out in electronics as well? With the end of the Cold War, even California's seemingly limitless defense-industry boom started to decline. All of this reminded the nation for the first time since World War II that American opportunity might *not* be ever-expanding—that America might *not* be able to welcome more faces to the table without diminishing the portions on the plates of those already seated.

The 1960s and 1970s were years when an increasing number of Americans began to feel that something economic or political or ideological was spinning out of control. The working poor, trapped at the minimum-wage level, had to work harder to make do. Meanwhile the rich, with the steady rise in equity markets and with very high payoffs in speculative investment, were becoming conspicuously much richer. America's distribution of wealth became the most unequal in the industrialized Western World. So, although the usual economic indices in those years held steady (with a few worrisome nervous tics), economic and social insecurity mounted. For the middle classes, security at the top of the fragile Jacob's ladder upward looked more alluring than ever, while the abyss threatening to open beneath their feet grew that much more terrifying.

The resulting dread—what Barbara Ehrenreich has called the fear of falling[107]—distilled selfishness and anxiety into jealousy and meanness. *People don't have the savings they "used to" or "ought to." Taxes to fill the trough for the shiftless are gobbling up our take-home pay. Government ought to get off our backs. Sure, but without it things could get a lot worse. And you move to an expensive suburb to get your child a good enough education to get into a good college, and*

then somebody else gets in ahead of him because of affirmative action.
"Affirmative action" became every politician's whipping boy because,
as President Clinton was later to put it, "there are a lot of angry white
men out there." Angry at *whom?* At the one percent of American
wealth-holders who control 39 percent of America's total household
wealth? At the political action committees that tap a portion of that
wealth to buy elections and sell public policies of their choice? At the
ever-promising, never-delivering political candidates supported by the
PACs? Well, yes but no. Topics like these didn't take hold. With the
aid of an adroit rhetorical campaign by the political right,[108] portraying "affirmative action" as "a zero-sum game in which there is a loser
for every winner and . . . the game is won and lost on the basis of
race,"[109] these angry white men had been persuaded to direct their anger at the supposed African-American (and the female) winners of the
"special privileges" that are destroying *real* Americans' freedom of
opportunity.

And *real* Americans were losing out in other and less speakable
ways as well. We lost a war in Vietnam, a war that divided America as
no war had since the Civil War. America the Almighty (*"everybody always knew we could lick hell out of all comers"*) couldn't get hold of
things, couldn't even "beat" a "backward" people. And what was
happening to public order? First a revered President was assassinated,
then his brother. And Martin Luther King, Jr. Nothing ever seemed to
get solved.[110] A Vice President was indicted, a President ousted from
office. America seemed to many to be in some sort of crazy downward
spiral. And downward still, to the worst act of terrorism in its history—committed in the name of patriotism by a perfervid American
patriot—with more than a dozen of those blown to smithereens in
Oklahoma City under six years of age.

With the erosion of our sense of American exceptionalism and
American triumphalism, the American Caution grew grimmer and
cast a longer shadow. It began to fit better—that wary attitude so well
captured in the title of Margaret Mead's anthropological account of
American culture: *And Keep Your Powder Dry.*[111] A dialogue between
the Lone Ranger and Tonto became the season's sick joke among teen-
agers:

Lone Ranger: *Tonto, I think we're surrounded.*
Tonto: *What do you mean we, white man?*

And the Supreme Court, in its decorous way, seemed to follow suit. It began deciding cases under the federal civil rights statutes in a way that consistently subordinated their objective of creating economic opportunities for African-Americans to the competing interests of whites.[112] It took to using the Equal Protection Clause to strike down race-specific governmental actions initially aimed at rectifying centuries of discrimination against African-Americans.[113] And it justified doing so with elegant paeans to color-blindness that rival *Plessy* for unworldliness.[114] In school cases, too, the Court retreated to a *Plessy*-like formalism, first reducing *Brown* to a formula[115] and then turning the formula into a departure rite by which the federal courts were to find racially-impacted ghetto schools "inevitable" and terminate desegregation efforts with desegregation unachieved.[116] Yet the Court and the country continue to pay lip service to *Brown*—and through *Brown* to the always-inspiring, egalitarian American Creed—in the very act of scuttling *Brown*'s endeavor and subordinating the Creed once again. As the well-researched report of the Harvard Project on School Desegregation recently summed it up:

"Today, *Brown*'s vision is being abandoned, but conservatives and liberals alike still treat the 1954 ruling as a source of pride. Schoolchildren commemorate *Brown*'s birthdays in ritualized celebrations of its central lesson about right's triumph over wrong. *Brown*'s promise, the children are informed, was that government would protect minority students' rights to equal opportunity in education. Meanwhile, slowly, quietly, and without the nation's comprehension, political and legal forces have converged to dismantle one of our greatest constitutional victories."[117]

And so, as a practical matter, the abandonment of *Brown*'s desegregation goal leaves large numbers of African-American children consigned to inner-city schools that are virtually all-nonwhite. It spells the exclusion of these children—and very probably their children and their children's children—from the opportunities that define what it takes to be an ordinary American today. Anyone familiar with American education knows that segregated inner-city schools are no academic match for those in predominantly white suburbs or small towns. And as technological sophistication increases the need for good education as a precondition to skilled employment—while, at the same time, the economic and cultural gap between the skilled and the unskilled increases—consignment to a ghetto school becomes a ticket to the bottom rung of the social order.

The Supreme Court's application of the Equal Protection Clause in *Bakke* and its sequels to curtail race-based compensatory affirmative-action programs[118] in higher education further compounds the African-American ghetto child's disadvantage.[119] Given the poorer quality of inner-city schools to begin with, their students do less well on standardized achievement tests. Inner-city high schools seldom offer the range of Advanced Placement (AP) and Honors courses offered by suburban high schools, and these courses often weigh heavily in the college admissions process. In addition, inner-city schools less frequently offer courses (like calculus) that are viewed as critical in imparting widely applicable conceptual skills. But, under *Bakke,* colleges have only limited ability—and are discouraged from using such abilities as they retain—to offset the competitive disadvantage suffered by ghetto schoolchildren.[120] Colleges declare that *they* are not to blame if ghetto school principals themselves have chosen not to offer AP courses. To which the principals reply that the ghetto schools need to devote their scarce resources to other priorities, particularly since there is so little hope that ghetto children will ever be able to afford a college education, even if they were well prepared for it. And this, too, is true, so far as it goes. For, as federal funding for college education gets steadily reduced, both private and public colleges and universities have shifted scholarship endowment to merit scholarships rather than need-based ones.[121] So the number of poor but qualified black students able to attend first-class colleges continues to drop,[122] while the number of white students from high schools in the well-off suburbs continues to rise.

VII. Reconciling the American Creed and the American Caution

There is an unmistakable parallel between the rhetoric that brands "affirmative action" as anathema in the political and public discourse of the 1990s[123] and the rhetoric by which the Supreme Court has justified its decisions in *Bakke* and *Adarand, Pitts* and *Jenkins.* Both rhetorics reconcile the American Creed with the American Caution in ways that make it easy to reracialize African-Americans and turn them into "not Us."

The seemingly impeccable central theme of *Bakke* and *Adarand* is that "it is the individual who is entitled to judicial protection against classifications based upon his racial or ethnic background because such distinctions impinge upon personal rights, rather than the individual only because of his membership in a particular group."[124] But underlying this theme is the supposition that no particular racial group needs constitutional protection more than any other today, though African-Americans may have needed it more in the bad old days. It follows that, in our times, Equal Protection would be offended rather than enforced by giving African-Americans a special constitutional solicitude unavailable to whites.

In like vein, the popular attack on affirmative action rests upon the premise that in today's world there is a "level playing field" on which the unfortunate discriminations of the past no longer exist. They are simply being rehashed by African-Americans to demand "special treatment." If there is such a thing today as a *racial group* standing between the self-sufficient individual and his or her destiny, that is only because race-conscious minorities believe it to be so. This is redolent of *Plessy*'s conviction that white and colored railway coaches were the same except in the eyes of over-sensitive Negroes. It permits the very concept of race-based affirmative action to be depicted as alien *both* to the hard-bitten American Caution (which scorns such hypersensitivity) and to the high-minded American Creed (which requires that individuals be permitted to compete "on the merits" with no favors given on account of immutable characteristics).

There are many subtle, implicit subtexts in the public discourse on this theme. One is that it is too much to ask that African-American inner-city children be given the educational opportunities provided by white suburbia. They and their families have not *earned* suburban privileges. Besides, white suburban schools would be *dragged down*— and those who earned a right to send their children to those schools would be deprived of an *earned privilege*—if the boundaries between city and suburbs were obliterated. The same subtexts underwrite the sanctity given to school-district lines by cases like *Pitts* and *Jenkins*. Legally, school districts are subdivisions of state government and creatures of state law; their boundaries are not immune against whatever modifications might be found necessary to effectuate rights guaranteed by the Equal Protection Clause of the federal Constitution.[125] What accounts for the *noli me tangere* quality that *Pitts* and *Jenkins* accord to school district lines is that as a matter of implicit cultural understanding they mark the boundaries of a different kind of space—the distinctive, dangerous-to-whites world of the African-American ghetto, black street culture, the urban riot, crack, and all of the other conditions that black people who *choose* to isolate themselves in metropolitan slums have *created*.[126] By walling in this racialized space and its inhabitants, people who live outside it can depersonalize the African-American inner-city child—make him or her not simply inferior but a non-person for whom there can no longer be an issue "of awakening the child to cultural values, . . . preparing him for later professional training, and . . . helping him to adjust normally to his environment."[127] Yet the Supreme Court has seen nothing problematic in treating school-district lines that have these effects as impassable boundaries to the principle of *Brown* that where the state has undertaken to give children the "opportunity of an education," such an opportunity "is a right which must be made available to all on equal terms."[128] This, in part, is why we say that the Court has not merely turned its back on *Brown* but facilitated the reracializing of African-Americans in the process.

But there is more to it than that. The Court's Equal Protection opinions also convey two distinct messages that have played a heavy part in America's end-of-the-century political and popular discourse on race. Cases like *Pitts* and *Jenkins* make it seem as if *the problem of discrimination against African-Americans that Brown set out to cure has now been fixed.* Cases like *Bakke* and *Adarand* make it seem as if *America's new race problem is that its time-honored guarantees of individual freedom are in danger of destruction by reverse discrimination against white people.* The Court thus lends legitimacy to portrayals of "affirmative action" as relentless governmental oppression of helpless whites in order to create opportunities for undeserving blacks—a portrait strikingly similar, in all its major themes, to the one that served to justify white supremacy's backlash against Reconstruction almost exactly a century earlier.

This depiction of affirmative action as being against the American grain ignores a great deal. Surely, some form of "affirmative action" was involved in our historically American practices of welcoming immigrants, of giving chronically cash-poor farm children the chance to get a near-free education at the federal-land-grant A & M colleges established after the Civil War, of creating a Tennessee Valley Authority to benefit the long-impoverished hill farms and hill towns in the South, of creating educational opportunities for veterans through the G.I. Bill following World War II as well as educational opportunities for inner-city children through the Head Start program of the 1960s. America has not been content to dismiss these chapters in its history as the mere products of economic opportunism or political pork-barreling. We do not write them off with the explanations that we opened our doors to immigrants because we needed their labor, that Lincoln finally signed the act establishing Land Grant Colleges in 1862 to consolidate his political power so that he could govern a Civil-War-torn nation, or that the TVA "bought" the South for the Democrats. On the contrary, America has taken pride in these accomplishments, has installed them as landmarks in its national heritage. Even Head Start evoked that pride, and still does.

So today's popular rejection of "affirmative action" seems to be driven not only by our end-of-the-millennium resurgence of the American Caution but by something else conjoined with it. In our view, there is a new kind of racism involved, one that has more than a single strand.

In trying to understand what is happening, we begin with the unquestionable fact that, despite the failure of *Brown* to deliver much of what it seemed to promise, there has been a steady increase in educational achievement among African-Americans since *Brown*. The black middle class has grown; black professionals and black artists participate in our culture as never before—though it can hardly be said from their testimony that the burden of Jim Crow has now been lifted or the playing field leveled.[129] A recent study suggests that despite *Bakke* and despite the difficulty African-American college students may have in financing their college education once admitted, they go on after graduation to take leadership positions in the community.[130] So even though African-Americans continue to be strikingly underrepresented in the professions and the arts, in universities, and in the upper reaches of business, a visible number of African-American individuals seem to have made it in American society, despite the subtler forms of discrimination practiced against them.

As for "the rest," that is where the trouble turns intractable. They are the "inner city blacks," stereotyped as crack users, drug pushers, deadbeat fathers who won't stick with their families or even support the babies they made out of wedlock, a third of them with jail records by age 30. All of which marks them in distinctive ways in the white American imagination. First, they are most distinctively non-Us, a totally alien Other. Second, they are dangerously non-Us: a high-crime group. And third, they are the "dregs" left behind when the hardworking, smarter African-Americans were making it into the middle class. *Alien, dangerous, shiftless.*

Thus, the new American racism takes two faces. The first face is turned against African-Americans who, with a certain assist from media-cultivated fantasy, are seen to have "made it big." It focuses on "affirmative action" as its target. Its major supporting prop is the "level playing field." Its major bogey is the "more deserving white deprived of his hard-earned chance." It is this vision that underlies the Supreme Court's decisions in *Bakke, Aderand,* and similar cases, reconceptualizing the Equal Protection Clause as a necessary instrument for protecting white people against "reverse discrimination." In this respect, the opposition to affirmative action fits the long-time mold of the American Caution.

But the second face of the new racism is far more sinister. It looks upon what it takes to be the "dregs" of the black community with scarcely disguised fear and loathing. It is a powerful force behind such police actions as the "profiling" of black motorists on the New Jersey Turnpike and the frightening killing in New York City of an unarmed black, Amadou Diallo, by a "crime squad" bent on enforcing a "zero tolerance" edict against crime. Meanwhile, close observers of the urban scene in America express increasing concern that official policies which target African-Americans for special police regulation are becoming self-fulfilling prophecies, isolating inner-city ghettos still more and turning their inhabitants more and more against the wider community.

So what can we say about the state of the American cultural dialectic on the subject of race? Like cultural dialectics everywhere, it is volatile and difficult to pin down. But one way of putting it—and we are well aware that there are others—is that we are punishing African-Americans who have made it out of the ghetto, often *just* made it, by proclaiming that they are now on an even playing field. And to that we add a second story: those who have *not* made it out are not only to blame for their failure, but they are to be regarded as irreversibly, even genetically, alien and defective: *dregs.* And by the rule of categorizing discussed in Chapter 2 in connection with how sentries behave, they must be treated as potentially dangerous.

We wish to make two points in closing: one about further complexities in the American cultural dialectic, another about the Supreme Court's place in it.

America's cultural dialectic seems remarkably, at times almost impulsively, responsive to reigning economic, political, and demographic circumstances. As with most cultures, there are repetitive cycles, which give a sort of meta-predictability to the dialectic. And as with other cultures, this country's institutional changes are often foreshadowed, even played out in advance, in its noetic space. But, above all, when things change in America, they seem to change in a peculiarly *lurching* way.

What gives American cultural change this lurching quality? It may be the very speed and scope of historical change in America since its founding. Rapid change always imposes enormous strains on a people's efforts to update and redefine their stance as a nation. And America has been in an almost constant state of change from colonial times to the present—territorially, demographically, ethnically, in economic organization. The brute fact of change—and it is both *brute* and a *fact*—can never be overlooked. It creates what our admirers like to praise as our dynamism and what critics prefer to label our "unsteadiness."

Moreover, we are a nation and a culture with multiple and often unharmonious ways of governing ourselves. The peculiar mix of centralized authority and localism that lawyers call—and some idolize—as "Our Federalism"[131] often amounts in practice to a cacophony, with voices in Washington (or Albany, or Sacramento) extolling values and endorsing policies that voices closer to home for most Americans dispute or even denounce. Determining what is the "authentic" American voice is not easy.

That may be one reason why the yin-and-yang of the American Creed and the American Caution is so tortuous, so full of clashing texts and subtexts. The Creed came into being as an expression of hope. In celebration and anticipation of immigrants escaping tyranny and oppression—and with the prospect of seemingly endless land and opportunity—it expressed a transcendent faith in freedom and betterment. But our very growth eroded those founding circumstances. Another side of us found expression in the Caution. Many historians believe that its seeds were also planted very early—whether in New England puritanism or in the other traditions that shaped our earliest conceptions of community.[132] We have never been calm about the Other. The American Creed and the American Caution have struggled in and for our national soul from the start.

Nor have we ever come to terms with their incompatibility. It has entered our cultural dialectic at all levels—local, state, and federal; executive, legislative, and judicial. Wherever it has expressed itself, it has created (to borrow from Gunnar Myrdal once again) an *American Dilemma*—race riots, a bloody Civil War, discrimination. John Higham's description of the waxing and waning of the American Creed has served us well in the preceding pages. But perhaps he has too little to say about the grimmer underside, what we have called the American Caution. America's optimistic idealism and egalitarianism and faith in progress do not simply wax and wane. They are coupled at some deep level with a wary, selfish, sometimes pitiless Caution that may be the price we pay for our sanguine, optimistic Creed. We fight a "war to save democracy" and then refuse to enter the League of Nations with those we helped save. Our Supreme Court gives us *Brown* and then backs off.

There is one insight often overlooked in what Sigmund Freud taught. We defend ourselves against our unrealistically simple hopes and wishes with counterpoint beliefs that are more convoluted than those hopes and wishes themselves. These often take the form of elaborate half-truths that we construct against the disappointment of our ideals—tortuous, self-righteous, overblown—like *Plessy*'s white lie that "separate" could be "equal," or today's white lie that the playing field is level at last for all, that affirmative action is unnecessary. Perhaps the white lies make it possible to cling to ideals, even when we do not practice them. Perhaps that's why we turn *Brown*'s anniversaries into occasions of self-congratulation. Perhaps it is why we say that *Brown* remains "good law" although the sole important territory where that law still reigns is a noetic place where we are everything we wish to be.

The Supreme Court is an inescapable player in America's cultural dialectic, and inescapably responsive to it. This point does not mean simply that, in Mr. Dooley's phrase, the Supreme Court "follows th' ilictions." Mr. Dooley's observation is as true in part—and as incomplete and unremarkable on the whole—as the Supreme Court's standing profession that it does *not* follow th' ilictions. What is quite remarkable is *how* the Court manages both to follow th' ilictions and to stand above them, to reconcile its own responsiveness to the cultural lurches of its time with a genuine ability and dedication to preserve the culture's more enduring values.

The Court's incessant efforts to effect such a reconciliation depend heavily upon—and at the same time shape—its uses of categorization and narrative and rhetorics, as we have examined them in earlier chapters and in this one. That is altogether inescapable. Our study of the process has not yielded any formulas for the "right" use of these powerful instruments of cognition and persuasion by judges (or by anybody else), and it has not been designed to do so. Our aim, rather, has been to make the instruments and their workings more visible, so that those who must use them can, if they choose, go about it a bit more consciously.

CHAPTER TEN

Reflections on a Voyage

We offer no grand conclusions. Our agenda was to make the familiar strange again, to look at law not solely as a set of characteristic practices and doctrines but also as a way of thinking—a "way of life," in Wittgenstein's famous phrase. To do this, we have focused on four activities that are common to all mental life, although they take a specialized form in legal matters: categorizing, telling stories, framing communications rhetorically, and being of one's culture. All four are as much features of the law as statute books and courtrooms; but they fade from consciousness through sheer familiarity. Our undertaking has been to bring them back.

It is impossible to think legally without legal pigeonholes. A school-desegregation order is an "interdistrict" or an "intradistrict" remedy; a biological father's bond to the child he has had with another man's wife is or is not within the "liberty" protected by the Due Process Clause; a behavior proved or admitted in court is or is not a "sale," a "contract," a "breach of contract," a "tort," a "crime." Such categorizing seems so familiar, so natural, so ordinary, so routine. But the illusion of familiarity can be deadly. There is more to legal categorizing than meets the wholly law-trained, law-habituated eye.

For even the most time-worn categories in the law—however embedded they may be in precedent, statutes, or the Constitution—grow from tangled roots nourished by everyday habits of mind and heart. They are the offspring of a culture's deeply rooted narrative and mythological practices, of its canonical tales of wrongdoing, its entrenched notions of good faith, archetypes of the "natural" family, conceptions of sanity and responsibility and just deserts. Our very notions of what constitutes a "violation" of a norm or an "extenuating circumstance" when a norm is violated are prefigured in our folklore. Even conflicts among legal principles have their counterparts in the dialectic of a culture's foundational tales—as with the perpetual dialectic between liberty and order, between Robin Hood and the Sheriff of Nottingham, between Billy Budd and Captain Vere. These conflicts are not posed or resolved by precedents and doctrinal reasoning alone, but are under the sway of culturally entrenched habits of categorizing and of storytelling. As one of us described the matter elsewhere:

> "It is probably the case that human beings forever suffer conflicts of interest, with attendant grudges, factions, coalitions, and shifting alliances. But what is interesting about these fractious phenomena is not how much they separate us but how much more often they are neutralized or forgiven or excused. [For there is an] . . . astonishing narrative human gift . . . for presenting, dramatizing, and explicating the mitigating circumstances surrounding conflict-threatening breaches in the ordinariness of life. The objective of such narrative is not to reconcile, not to legitimize, not even to excuse, but rather to explicate. . . . [N]arrativizing makes [conflict] . . . comprehensible against the background of ordinariness we take as the basic state of life. . . . To be in a viable culture is to be bound in a set of connecting stories, connecting even though the stories may not represent a consensus."[1]

Law begins, as it were, *after* narrative. It is shaped in some measure not only by the narrative claims of contending parties in litigation, not only by "findings of fact" and "rules of law" announced by judges who have heard testimony and legal argument, but by the stock of familiar categories and story types within which all people in a culture live their lives. It is shaped, too, by adversarial rhetorics. For we almost always tell our stories to convince, not simply to inform. The rhetorics of legal contention and adjudication are a sort of choreography of disputation whose permissible maneuvers are limited both by the law's established precepts of logic and procedure and by the conventions of viable narrative.

But those rhetorics also inhere in what we have called the *dialectic of culture*. Life in a culture is governed by a never-quite-resolvable tension between opposing, sometimes incompatible stances toward the world. These stances usually divide into those that are *canonical,* having to do with how things ordinarily are and should be, and those that are *imaginatively possible,* projecting how the world might be under altered circumstances. The dialectic between the two is endless, inherent in the demands of living communally, and reflects itself in law as elsewhere. Human nature feasts on the familiar, the customary, the predictable, yet also yearns for a new order of things. So while our habits become motives,[2] driving us to carry on as before, the familiar order of things can also thwart our hopes. Given what we are, we resonate to promises of the possible, to the worlds offered in novels, plays, social critiques, contrarian thoughts.

It often happens that law provides the most vivid arena in which the dialectic of culture expresses itself. In the preceding chapter we saw such an instance—a series of Supreme Court decisions dealing with issues of racial equality throughout the past century. The wrongness of *de jure* segregation perpetuated by *Plessy v. Ferguson* becomes the Trouble to be addressed by the narrative spun in *Brown v. Board of Education* a half-century later. But by the time we reach *Freeman v. Pitts* and *Missouri v. Jenkins,* another half-century on, the Trouble has become the wrongnesses created by *Brown*—schools torn from the control of their local communities, good old American freedom of opportunity denied in the name of "affirmative action," and so forth. The legal expression of this dialectic is framed in the familiar terminology of the Equal Protection Clause of the Fourteenth Amendment, but its motive power is outside the law, expressive of a deeper struggle within American culture between what has come to be called the American Creed and what we have called the American Caution, each with its categorical constructs, stories, and rhetorics.

There are many ways in which one can characterize the dialectic of any particular culture, American culture included. As was surely apparent in our wide-ranging discussion of cultures in Chapter 8, oversimplification is bound to result from identifying a *single* dialectical theme as basic or fundamental or, worse, as the *sole* theme at work in any culture. This was the fate of deMadariaga's fanciful metaphors for the French, English, and Spanish, and even of Ruth Benedict's artful account of Japan's dialectic in *The Chrysanthemum and the Sword.*[3] We do not pretend to have escaped it. For example, there has been much recent discussion—particularly from a feminist perspective—of what might be described as another American dialectic: between *rules and rights* on the one side and *relationships and care* on the other.[4] It may or may not be useful to look at the former side as an aspect (or an instrument) of the American Caution, the latter of the American Creed. But this would certainly be reductionistic. Our deeper objective in these pages has not been to sell one particular view of the dialectic of American culture, but rather to underline the importance of a dialectical dynamic in the life of any people—and to suggest that such a cultural dialectic is likely to be reflected not only in popular attitudes but in the decisions of the judiciary, whose function, after all, is to compose some harmony between the contending voices in the dialectic.

This is an exquisitely difficult function to perform, for the courts must also manage the law's own special dialectic between continuity and change. They must manage a system of ideas that protects and enshrines old, established balances, yet leaves room for the construction and justification of new ones when the times change enough. The stability of the existing order is, in some significant measure, in their keeping; but it is also a part of their job to bring into being new worlds of the possible, which they endow with the canonicity of precedent through such "landmark" decisions as *Brown v. Board of Education.* It should not be surprising that sometimes, as in the period after *Brown,* the courts recoil a long way from the new worlds they have created, while continuing to pay them homage in words that ring increasingly hollow.

In this particular instance, was it an inadequacy in the *Brown* opinion that led the Supreme Court to turn its back on *Brown* eventually? (Chief Justice Warren's opinion has been given rather poor grades in the academy, where even scholars who approve *Brown*'s result have felt obliged to write their own concurring opinions.)[5] Did the Court put itself out of business, in effect, by letting the process of desegregation drag on too long—by its acceptance of the notion that desegregation "with all deliberate speed" would be soon enough? Did it quit, in the end, when it became convinced of the inevitability of the "proposition that courts are impotent to produce significant social reform"?[6] Did the Justices respond to a changing climate of public opinion—another of those "Higham cycles"—as the Second World War receded into the past? Or was it that the Court's composition changed, and that Justices with ideologies alien to *Brown* came increasingly to dominate it? Or all of the above?

These are not questions that yield self-evident answers. But of one matter we are convinced: they can be better understood by attending not only to immediate political events but also to the ways in which a culture and its judges categorize things in the world, make sense of things by retelling them in the form of time-honored stories, and go about convincing themselves and others both how things *are* and how they *really* are.

Our professed aim of making the familiar strange again has not been motivated by a desire to promote some particular theory of jurisprudence, much less what Judge Richard Posner would call a particular brand of *constitutional theory*.[7] It has led us to examine *texts* and to suggest that they conceal some unexamined *choices,* but it has not equipped us—and could not alone equip us—to prescribe how those choices should be made. The choices ultimately need to take account of questions of value—very large questions of value—that are beyond the subject of this book.

We have our own opinions on those questions and, as a result, our own views on issues of constitutional interpretation. These could have no interest in their own right without a thorough examination of our reasons for them, so we have not set them out explicitly (whether as escutcheon or *apologia*). The reader will discern many of our views from the ways in which we so obviously disagree with the constitutional interpretations rendered by Supreme Court Justices whose opinions we have scrutinized—Chief Justice Rehnquist in *Missouri v. Jenkins,* Justice Scalia in *Michael H.,* Justice Kennedy in *Freeman v. Pitts,* Justice Story in *Prigg v. Pennsylvania,* Justice Powell in *McCleskey v. Kemp.* But while our disagreement with the results in these cases was a part of what prompted us to choose them as illustrative opinions to examine, our examination of them has not been directed toward demonstrating that the Court's *decision* in any of the cases was wrong. We have been blunt in saying why we find some of the reasoning in these opinions ill-considered, occasionally even purblind, but we have not sought to reargue the cases on the merits or to advocate different outcomes.

Rather, our aim has been to unearth concealed presuppositions, categorial pitfalls, narrative predilections, rhetorical constructions, cultural biases. We have faulted Justices for ignoring or masking choices that they put out of play simply by the way they carved their categories, told their stories, or arrayed their words, without acknowledgment of these processes. We hope our labors show that decisions which the Justices treated as logically compelled or as grounded in inexorable *givens* of law and fact were neither. But do our textual analyses point to the "right" decisions that should have been made in the cases? We do not think so.

This book is not about "right" outcomes for the law, or even about "right" paths that lawyers and judges should follow. It is about commonplace hidden pitfalls and snares that infest *every* path that any lawyer or judge *could* follow. We do not propose a particular theory of constitutional interpretation or even a protocol for judicial decisionmaking. We propose that *any* constitutional theory and *any* approach to judicial decisionmaking, of whatever stripe, would do well to take into account the kinds of cognitive activities and dilemmas discussed in the preceding chapters. Any constitutional theory, we argue, will benefit from a better sense of how the law is embedded in a culture's way of life and in the thinking processes of those who must administer and interpret and abide by the law. Without that sense, any approach to decisionmaking will be impoverished.

Our objective, then, has been to increase awareness, to intensify consciousness, about what people are doing when they "do law." We have emphasized that the framing and adjudication of legal issues necessarily rest upon *interpretation*. Results cannot be arrived at entirely by deductive, analytic reasoning or by the rules of induction, although these have their place. There always remains the "wild card" of *all* interpretation—the consideration of *context*, that ineradicable element in meaning-making. *And the deepest, most impenetrable feature of context lies in the minds and culture of those involved in fashioning an interpretation.*

To be sure, results in the law are achieved by the application of specialized legal reasoning—reasoning within and about doctrinal rules, procedural requirements, constitutional and other jurisprudential theories—and are typically articulated almost wholly in those terms. But final results are *underdetermined* by such rules, requirements, and theories. They are influenced as well by how people think, categorize, tell stories, deploy rhetorics, and make cultural sense as they go about interpreting and applying rules, requirements, and theories. And while lawyers and judges are almost notoriously conscious and critical about the rules, requirements, and theories (their *déformation professionelle,* as the French call it), they are not often mindful of the other, more basic and "familiar" processes involved in doing law. We have devoted this book to making those processes more visible—by the device of stripping them of their deadening familiarity.

That is why we have been concerned with both the imaginative worlds of great literary fiction and the ordinariness of everyday mental habits as looked at by psychologists and their kin. For Laurence Sterne's *Tristram Shandy,* Shakespeare's *Lear,* or Melville's *Moby-Dick* are not only drama but also models of how human beings envisage and interpret human plights. Kafka's *The Trial* deepens legal comprehension not because its subject is the law but because it freshens our sense of the fragility of what, seen superficially, looks very much like "ordinary life." It shakes our deeply ingrained notions of human agency, stops us dead in our tracks with respect to how things *ought* to go. It opens a vista upon the possible worlds in which our fellow mortals live; it problematizes our presumptions about the efficacy of ordinary rhetorics. Such extraordinary fictions are the means by which—to reverse the proverb we invoked earlier in the book—fish can discover water by jumping out of it.

The insights of the human sciences also help to make the familiar strange again. Studies of the foibles of categorization, of the hidden regularities of narrative structure, of our strange human ways of conveying requests or promises or excuses—these make us sharply conscious of how we manage (or fail to manage) contextual matters that are too often out of sight, out of mind. Psychologists rarely travel off to distant cultures; they take their "subjects" out of life and put them in a "lab"—a place the likes of which does not exist in real life. So if they tell us that it takes four times as many milliseconds to recognize a playing card when the suit and color do not match (like a red six of clubs) as it does to recognize an ordinary one, they may be talking literally about experimental subjects viewing trumped-up playing cards presented in the world of a high-speed tachistoscope, but what they are telling also has the power to give us a keener sense of how humans deal with the unexpected in the banality of everyday life. Their laboratory metaphors, like the anthropologist's metaphor of the Balinese cockfight or the historian's metaphor of a moment in Roman history, provide detachment from the immediate and obvious—distance, alienation, reflection, metacognition—a turn of mind which quickens us to our own thoughts and to things in the world that we seldom notice.

So, this book is not aimed at constructing constitutional theory, jurisprudential theory, or any other legal theory. It is intended instead as a *propaedeutic* to theory—including the kind of theory that practicing lawyers, as well as legal scholars, engage in.

Propaedeutic means literally "pertaining to or of the nature of preliminary instruction."[8] So in a sense, perhaps, this book is a form of *legal pedagogy.*

Yet we had better not take pedagogy for granted, legal or otherwise. It is a puzzling subject. The process of learning a first language might provide a good entry into it. Every language, viewed formally and taken out of the context of its use, has its lexicon and its syntax—the former set down in a dictionary and the latter in a "book of rules." But learning a language is learning how to *use* it appropriately, how to *do* things with language along with other people. Interestingly, we seem to gain command even of lexicon and syntax by doing things that require their use,[9] by understanding what communicating is for, what functions it serves. Happily, we seem to know how to *demand* or to *indicate* nonverbally before we ever learn how to do so in words—thanks to some innate predispositions with which we are endowed (though it is too easy to exaggerate that part of the story).[10] The crux of acquiring a first language is the opportunity to try it out in a context of use—or, to borrow a famous philosopher's phrase, to learn how to "do things with words."[11]

Law students can learn the rules of the *corpus juris* from textbooks, just as language students can learn the French syntactical *plusque-parfait* or the subtle lexical distinction between *connaître* and *savoir.* But the law, like French, is not a disembodied set of rules, independent of its uses in practice. Becoming a lawyer is learning what is involved in lawyer*ing.* And that requires more than simply knowing the doctrinal rules.

To say this is not to denigrate the classic courses in Contracts, Property, Civil Procedure, or Evidence, any more than it is to denigrate classes in French grammar. (Having the rules of French grammar available helps enormously if you aim to learn to avoid the subjunctive when you are telling your true love how dearly you cherish him or her!) Our point, rather, is that each of the traditional law-school "subjects" lives in a sea of use—in ways of categorizing, storytelling, using rhetoric, and being of your culture. *Doing* law is a way of life and of worldmaking: despite efforts to isolate its "specialness," it is not disconnected from the other ways we live life. Perhaps that is why so many contemporary efforts to bring broader "perspectives" into law schools march under hyphenated titles: "law-and-literature," "law-and-society," "law-and-anthropology," "law-and-economics," "law-and-public-policy," and so forth. Unfortunately, such hyphenated enterprises are too often curricular add-ons or isolated upper-year elective courses, or else they get shunted off into sparsely populated joint degree programs that are outside—and notoriously alien to—the mainstream of legal education.

Is it sufficient simply to *teach about* concepts like categorization, narrative, rhetorics, and culture? Is there not also some performative side to learning about such things—either in a clinical setting[12] or through simulation[13] or in some theater-like activity? We have had the heady experience of watching second- and third-year law students, after reading Aeschylus' *The Suppliants,* rewrite and stage versions of the drama as arguments for the rightness of an outcome other than the one Aeschylus wrote. Greek drama in their hands is no longer "archaic"; it often inspires brilliant narrative advocacy. And we have asked law students to write and perform a play laid in the gap of a moment (or is it a millennium?) between Genesis 22:10 (where Abraham raises the knife to slay his son, Isaac, at God's command) and Genesis 22:11 (where the Angel of God calls upon Abraham to put the knife down). Not only do they produce shockers, but they tell you afterwards that they had never fully appreciated the "openness" of "open" texts—biblical, legal, or whatever. Performative exercises may be time-consuming, and they may not be for all teachers or students. But the general consensus of those who have tried them is that they produce rich insights very different from those achieved in the big lecture class.

The dubious might ask: Don't law students have enough to do already, just learning the major elements of legal reasoning, the principles of substantive law that are indispensable to basic legal literacy (in an era of vast expansion of legal regulation), the specialized research techniques and writing conventions of legal practice (and/or scholarship), the core concepts of professional responsibility, and in addition (in many law schools now) getting a measure of introspective, hands-on clinical experience? Is it the best use of their scarce time, and of the law schools' scarce resources, to try to engage them as well in literary, psychological, cultural, and rhetorical issues? This is a thorny question, indeed. The answer will depend in part on how well one thinks law schools are actually doing with their present ways of teaching law. But we hope that this book may suggest at least some modification of the *terms* in which the question is usually put. For if we are even close to the mark about how law is interpreted and conducted in real life, it is impossible for lawyers *not* to be engaged in literary, psychological, cultural, and rhetorical issues. They will be in the thick of them—inevitably. The only questions are how *aware* they will be that they are dealing with such issues, and how *reflective* they will be about them. Is it possible, then, and is it worthwhile to make them more aware and more reflective, at the same time that the law schools strive to do (and to do better) all of the other things that law schools must do?

The dubious might also ask: What could we hope to teach law students about these things, in the last analysis? Probably nothing more—or less—than that law is a *human* exercise; that it is driven neither by immutable truths engraved in a fixed body of rules, nor by arbitrary whims and vanities. Law students know this already, just as they know that law is inevitably *interpretive* and case-by-case. But they know it in the abstract. The challenge to law schools is to help their students understand all this in the particular, in relation to the changing human condition in which they find themselves.

Analysis of Nouns and Verbs in the *Prigg,*[1] *Pitts,*[2] and *Brown*[3] Opinions

Nouns

Let us first divide the nouns relating to people and governmental entities into four categories defined by their referents. The following examples (from the *Prigg* opinion)[4] show the nature of the categories:

blacks: individuals, subclasses, or the class of persons of African descent

        for example: "a certain negro woman"
                          "Margaret Morgan"
                          "negro"; "mulatto"
                          "slaves"; "fugitive slaves"

persons: individuals, subclasses, or the class of persons generally, where neither the noun nor its context limits the reference to Africans on the one hand or to whites on the other

        for example: "a person"; "no person"
                          "the individual"
                          "a party"; "parties"
                          "fugitives from justice"
                          "disorderly and evil disposed persons"

whites: individuals, subclasses, or the class of persons not of African descent

> for example: "plaintiff in error" (Prigg)
> "Margaret Ashmore"
> "master"; "owner [of a slave]"
> "citizens of the slaveholding states"
> "person to whom labor or service may be due"; his or her "agent" or "attorney"
> "persons [who capture fugitive slaves]"

governments: political entities, their governments, organs of government, officials, agents, and so forth

> for example: "Maryland"; "the states"
> "the [non]slaveholding states"
> "the United States"
> "the general government"
> "Congress"; "State legislatures"
> "court[s]"; "judge[s]"; magistrates"; "judicial tribunals"

In the following tables and charts, **governments** are subdivided into:

> **judicial entities** [abbreviated "jud"] and
> **all other governmental entities** [abbreviated "nonjud"].

Now let's classify all of these nouns into the following nine groupings on the basis of their **syntactic use:**

subjects of active, indicative verbs of possession

The person or entity named is the subject of a verb that says that he, she, or it **has** or **possesses** something. The person or entity is thus portrayed as **agentive** and **dominant.**

> for example: "[t]he **owner** must . . . have the right to seize and repossess the slave"
> "**Congress** has the exclusive power of legislation upon the subject matter"
> "the **States** . . . possess full jurisdiction to arrest and restrain runaway slaves"

inactive possessive forms

The person or entity named is not the subject of a verb but is described as **having** or **possessing** something. Often the construction is a standard genitive, like "the remedy of **the owner.**" The person or entity is thus portrayed as **dominant,** although not necessarily agentive.[5]

for example: "[Prigg delivered Morgan and her children] into the custody and possession of **Margaret Ashmore**"
"rights of the **owner**"
"the executive authority of **the State**"
"the concurrent power of the **State Legislatures**"
"there would be a resulting authority in each of **the States**"
"the supposed wishes of **Maryland**"
"the power and duty of the **national government**"
"the power of legislation . . . is exclusive in the **national government**"
"the provisions of **Congress**"[6]
"the will of **Congress**"

indirect objects of verbs

These are nouns in the dative case and similar formulations that express the notion that something is **given to** or **taken from** the person or entity named. The person or entity is thus portrayed as having the **dominance** inherent in acquisitive capacity, but with no immediately accompanying agentivity.[7]

for example: "[the statute] saves to the **person** claiming such labor or service his right of action"
"the object of this clause was to secure to **the citizens** of the slaveholding States the complete right of title and ownership in their slaves"
"a penalty against any person who shall . . . rescue such fugitive from the **claimant**"
"a power is granted to **Congress**"
"[the] police power . . . has never been conceded to **the United States**"

subjects of active, indicative verbs other than verbs of possession

The person or entity named is the subject of a verb that says that he, she, or it **does** something. The person or entity is thus portrayed as **agentive,** although not necessarily **dominant.**

for example: "the **slave** escaped"
"**plaintiff in error** . . . caused the said negro woman to be taken and apprehended"
"**Congress** has acted"
"**Congress** has taken this very view"
"**State magistrates** may, if they choose, exercise that authority"

subjects or objects of copulas

A *copula* (or *linking verb*) is one that connects its subject to a predicate complement without expressing any action (e.g., "be," "seem," "appear"). The person or entity named as the subject or object is made a focus of attention and is given characteristics; the extent to which he, she, or it is portrayed as **agentive** or **dominant** depends upon the tenor of those characteristics; but in general copulas endow their subjects with less agentivity and dominance than do other indicative, active verbs.

for example: "the **negro woman** . . . was a **slave**"
"**plaintiff in error**, being legally constituted the **agent** and **attorney** of the said Margaret Ashmore, [did thusly]"
"every **non-slaveholding State** . . . would have been at liberty to have declared free all runaway slaves"

objects of prepositions; appositives; other nouns with mixed uses

This is a residual classification. Numerically, most of the nouns in the grouping are the objects of prepositions. Since the uses and tenors of prepositions vary widely, the person or entity named may be more or less agentive and dominant. But on the whole, the grouping reflects a level of agentivity and dominance that is intermediate between that of the groupings above and those below.

for example: "[t]here are two clauses in the Constitution on the subject of **fugitives**"
"[fugitives from justice] found in another **State** shall . . . be delivered up, to be removed to the [first] **State**"
"take him or her before any **judge** . . . residing . . . within the **State**, or before any **magistrate**"

"the national government is bound, through its
own proper **departments,** legislative, judicial,
or executive, . . . to carry into effect [etc.]"

subjects of passive verbs

The person or entity named is the subject of a verb that says that
something **is done to** him, her, or it. The person or entity is thus portrayed as **acted upon** and **dominated,** although less dramatically than
in the case of the direct object of an indicative verb.

for example: "the said **negro woman** was thereupon brought
before the said magistrate"
"such **person** or **persons** . . . shall . . . be
deemed guilty of a felony"
"**representatives** shall be apportioned among
the several states"

direct objects of indicative verbs

The person or entity named is the object of a verb that says that
some other agent **does something to** him, her, or it. The person or entity is thus portrayed as **acted upon** and **dominated** by another.

for example: "the plaintiff in error did remove, take and
carry away the said **negro woman**"
"any person who shall . . . obstruct or hinder
such **claimant,** his **agent,** or **attorney**"
"[o]ne State may require the **owner** to sue"
"the Act of 1793 . . . designated **the person**
(**the state executive**) upon whom the demand
should be made"

direct objects of infinitives, participles, or gerunds

As in the preceding grouping, the person or entity named is the object of a verb that says that some other agent or agency **does something to** him, her, or it; he, she, or it is thus portrayed as **acted upon**
and **dominated** by another. However, the action of the other agent or
agency is **abstracted** and put onto a normative plane by the casting of
the verb in non-indicative form.

for example: "[t]he owner must . . . have the right to seize
and repossess **the slave**"

"the owner of a slave is clothed with entire
  authority . . . to seize and recapture his
  slave"
"the States, in virtue of their general police
  power, possess full jurisdiction to arrest and
  restrain **runaway slaves** and remove them.
  . . . But such regulations can never be
  permitted to interfere with or to obstruct the
  just rights of the owner to reclaim his **slave**"
"a hesitation on the part of the executive
  authority of Virginia to deliver up **a fugitive**
  from justice"

The frequency counts for nouns in these subcategories and uses in
Prigg, Pitts, and *Brown* are as follows:

DISTRIBUTION OF NOUNS REFERRING TO PEOPLE OR ENTITIES IN STORY'S *PRIGG* OPINION

	blacks	people	whites	governments (nonjud/jud)
subjects of active, indicative verbs of possession	0	0	3	8 (8/0)
inactive possessive forms[8]	0	1	18	61 (55/6)
indirect objects of verbs	0	1	12	16 (13/3)
subjects of active, indicative verbs other than verbs of possession[9]	3	10	3	24 (19/5)
subjects or objects of copulas	3	1	1	8 (6/2)
objects of prepositions; appositives; other nouns with mixed uses	23	16	8	93 (73/20)
subjects of passive verbs	6	7	4	7 (6/1)
direct objects of indicative verbs[9]	9	5	4	5 (4/1)
direct objects of infinitives, participles, or gerunds[9]	16	4	0	0 (0/0)
TOTALS:	**60**	**45**	**53**	**222 (184/38)**

DISTRIBUTION OF NOUNS REFERRING TO PEOPLE OR ENTITIES IN KENNEDY'S *PITTS* OPINION

	blacks	people	whites	governments (nonjud/jud)
subjects of active, indicative verbs of possession	0	6	0	18 (10/8)
inactive possessive forms[10]	7	2	1	88 (60/28)
indirect objects of verbs	6	4	1	6 (4/2)
subjects of active, indicative verbs other than verbs of possession[11]	22	9	6	156 (74/82)
subjects or objects of copulas	12	3	1	32 (25/7)
objects of prepositions; appositives; other nouns with mixed uses	9	11	5	93 (73/20)
subjects of passive verbs	4	0	0	3 (2/1)
direct objects of indicative verbs[11]	4	4	2	9 (9/0)
direct objects of infinitives, participles, or gerunds[11]	12	20	2	8 (7/1)
TOTALS:	**76**	**59**	**18**	**413 (264/149)**

DISTRIBUTION OF NOUNS REFERRING TO PEOPLE OR ENTITIES IN WARREN'S *BROWN* OPINION

	blacks	people	whites	governments (nonjud/jud)
subjects of active, indicative verbs of possession	0	0	0	1 (1/0)
inactive possessive forms[12]	8	5	3	10 (4/6)
indirect objects of verbs	10	3	1	1 (0/1)
subjects of active, indicative verbs other than verbs of possession[13]	5	4	1	38 (8/30)
subjects or objects of copulas	9	1	0	1 (1/0)
objects of prepositions; appositives; other nouns with mixed uses	14	3	8	41 (28/13)
subjects of passive verbs	5	1	0	2 (2/0)
direct objects of indicative verbs[13]	0	0	0	1 (0/1)
direct objects of infinitives, participles, or gerunds[13]	4	3	4	0 (0/0)
TOTALS:	**55**	**20**	**17**	**95 (44/51)**

To facilitate comparison, a couple of charts may help:

Summary of Noun Uses in *Prigg, Pitts,* and *Brown*

	total frequency of nouns				
	blacks	people	whites	all humans	governments
Prigg	60	45	53	158	222
Pitts	76	59	18	153	413
Brown	55	20	17	92	95

	ratio of government entities to black persons	ratio of government entities to all humans
Prigg	3.70	1.41
Pitts	5.43	2.70
Brown	1.73	1.03

	frequency of nouns in four categories indicating **greatest agentivity/dominance**				
	blacks	people	whites	all humans	governments
Prigg	3	12	36	51	109
Pitts	35	21	8	64	268
Brown	23	12	5	40	50

	frequency of nouns in three categories indicating **least agentivity/dominance**				
	blacks	people	whites	all humans	governments
Prigg	31	16	8	55	12
Pitts	20	24	4	48	20
Brown	9	4	4	17	3

	black persons	all humans	governments
	ratio of nouns in agentive/dominant categories to nouns in non-agentive/subordinate categories adjusted so that "all humans" = 1.00		
Prigg	.10	1.00	9.80
Pitts	1.31	1.00	10.05
Brown	1.10	1.00	3.00

Verbs

Another measure of the relative agentivity and dominance of the several sorts of players in the *Prigg* and *Pitts* opinions is the frequency of use of verbs that take various human and governmental beings as their subjects. The following charts show these frequencies; again, the parallel frequencies in Chief Justice Warren's *Brown* opinion are displayed for contrast.[14]

DISTRIBUTION OF VERBS HAVING PEOPLE OR ENTITIES AS THEIR SUBJECTS IN STORY'S *PRIGG* OPINION

	blacks	people	whites	governments[15] (nonjud/jud)
Verbs with Explicit Subjects				
active verbs	9	47	48	155 (114/41)
passive verbs	9	10	2	4 (2/2)
copulas	3	2	7	11 (8/3)
total	21	59	57	170 (124/46)
Verbs with Implicit Subjects				
active verbs	0	1	9	47 (27/20)
passive verbs	0	0	0	0 (0/0)
copulas	0	0	0	0 (0/0)
total	0	1	9	47 (27/20)
All Verbs				
active verbs	9	48	57	202 (141/61)
passive verbs	9	10	2	4 (2/2)
copulas	3	2	7	11 (8/3)
total	21	60	66	217 (151/66)

302

DISTRIBUTION OF VERBS HAVING PEOPLE OR ENTITIES AS THEIR SUBJECTS IN KENNEDY'S *PITTS* OPINION

	blacks	people	whites	governments[16] (nonjud/jud)
Verbs with Explicit Subjects				
active verbs	34	21	4	393 (182/211)
passive verbs	5	1	0	13 (8/5)
copulas	12	4	1	30 (22/8)
total	51	26	5	436 (212/224)
Verbs with Implicit Subjects				
active verbs	2	0	0	66 (31/35)
passive verbs	0	0	0	0 (0/0)
copulas	0	0	0	0 (0/0)
total	2	0	0	66 (31/35)
All Verbs				
active verbs	36	21	4	459 (213/246)
passive verbs	5	1	0	13 (8/5)
copulas	12	4	1	30 (22/8)
total	53	26	5	502 (243/259)

DISTRIBUTION OF VERBS HAVING PEOPLE OR ENTITIES AS THEIR SUBJECTS IN WARREN'S *BROWN* OPINION

	blacks	people	whites	governments[17] (nonjud/jud)
Verbs with Explicit Subjects				
active verbs	25	7	4	93 (37/56)
passive verbs	7	3	0	4 (3/1)
copulas	6	1	0	2 (2/0)
total	38	11	4	99 (42/57)
Verbs with Implicit Subjects				
active verbs	7	4	0	38 (16/22)
passive verbs	0	0	0	0 (0/0)
copulas	0	0	0	0 (0/0)
total	7	4	0	38 (16/22)

All Verbs

active verbs	32	11	4	**131** (53/78)
passive verbs	7	3	0	**4** (3/1)
copulas	6	1	0	**2** (2/0)
total	45	15	4	**137** (58/79)

Again, a couple of summary charts may be useful:

Summary of Verb Uses in *Prigg*, *Pitts*, and *Brown*

	blacks	people	whites	total frequency of verbs [all verbs (active verbs)]				
				all human actors	all gov't actors	nonjud gov't actors	jud gov't actors
Prigg	21 (9)	60 (48)	66 (57)	147 (114)	217 (202)	151 (141)	66 (61)
Pitts	53 (36)	26 (21)	5 (4)	84 (61)	502 (459)	243 (213)	259 (246)
Brown	45 (32)	15 (11)	4 (4)	64 (47)	137 (131)	58 (53)	79 (78)

	ratio of government entities to black persons		ratio of government entities to all humans	
	all verbs	active verbs	all verbs	active verbs
Prigg	10.3	22.4	1.5	1.8
Pitts	9.5	12.8	6.0	7.5
Brown	3.0	4.1	2.1	2.8

Notes to Appendix

1. *Prigg v. Pennsylvania*, 16 Pet. 539, 10 L.Ed. 1060 (1842) (lead opinion by Justice Story).
2. *Freeman v. Pitts*, 503 U.S. 467, 118 L.Ed.2d 108, 112 S. Ct. 1430 (1992) (majority opinion by Justice Kennedy).
3. *Brown v. Board of Education*, 347 U.S. 483, 98 L.Ed. 873, 74 S. Ct. 686 (1954) (unanimous opinion by Chief Justice Warren).
4. To include examples from all three opinions would produce a welter and obscure the illustration of category structure.

5. A noun is not put in the **possessive** grouping (or in any of the other groupings listed in the text) if: (a) the thrust of the possessive formulation is merely indexical (that is, if it serves only to **identify** a thing by reference to the thing's owner or originator, as in phrases like "counsel for the **plaintiff in error**"; "the laws of **Maryland**"; "the Constitution of the **United States**"; "the courts of the **United States**"; "every State in the **Union**"); or (b) an adjectival form is used for a similar **identifying** purpose (as in phrases like "State law"; "State courts"; "State magistrates"). See notes 8, 10, and 12 below.

6. In context, this attribution is not merely indexical. See note 5 above.

7. Of course, there are some forms of indirect objects in English that do not have this quality of supposing an acquisitive capacity (for example, "Sam did harm to George"). But few such forms appear in the opinions we are examining.

8. This is a conservative count. It does not include either adjectival forms (category (b) in note 5 above) or indexical forms (category (a) in note 5). If those forms were added, the counts would be:

	blacks	people	whites	**governments** (nonjud/jud)
possessive nouns **and** adjectival forms	0	1	18	**94** (87/7)
possessive nouns **and** adjectival forms **and** indexical forms	0	1	19	**133** (124/9)

9. Subjects and objects of copulas are not included in this category.

10. This is a conservative count. It does not include either adjectival forms (category (b) in note 5 above) or indexical forms (category (a) in note 5). If those forms were added, the counts would be:

	blacks	people	whites	**governments** (nonjud/jud)
possessive nouns **and** adjectival forms	25	52	11	**124** (70/54)
possessive nouns **and** adjectival forms **and** indexical forms	40	64	19	**154** (96/58)

11. Subjects and objects of copulas are not included in this category.

12. This is a conservative count. It does not include either adjectival forms (category (b) in note 5 above) or indexical forms (category (a) in note 5). If those forms were added, the counts would be:

	blacks	people	whites	governments (nonjud/jud)
possessive nouns and adjectival forms	18	8	13	**41** (35/6)
possessive nouns **and** adjectival forms **and** indexical forms	18	8	13	43 (36/7)

13. Subjects and objects of copulas are not included in this category.
14. The charts include—but display separately as well as cumulatively—verbs whose subjects are **explicit** and verbs whose subjects are **implicit**.

Examples of verbs with **explicit** subjects are:
"the slave **escaped** and **fled** from Maryland"
"the plaintiff in error **did remove, take,** and **carry away** the said negro woman"
"[h]e [the owner of a runaway slave] **may not be** able **to enforce** his rights against persons who either **secrete** or **conceal,** or **withhold** the slave"
"where a claim is **made,** by the owner"
"some farther remedial redress than that which might **be administered** at the hands of the owner himself"
"every State . . . **has** the exclusive right **to prescribe** the remedies in its own judicial tribunals"
"a hesitation on the part of the executive authority of Virginia **to deliver up** a fugitive from justice"
"it [Congress] **has,** on various occasions, **exercised** powers which were necessary and proper"
"until it [the power of legislation] is **exercised** by Congress"

Examples of verbs with **implicit** subjects are:
"[f]rom this . . . judgment [below], the present writ of error **has been brought** to this court"
"[a] claim [for the delivery of a fugitive slave] is to be **made**"
"under what circumstances shall the possession of the owner, after it **is obtained,** be conclusive of his right"
"[s]o far as the judges of the courts of the United States **have been called upon to enforce** it [the Fugitive Slave Act]"
"Congress has the exclusive power of legislation upon the subject matter under the Constitution of the United States, and under the Act of the 12th of February, 1793 . . ., which **was passed** in pursuance thereof"
"it [Congress] has . . . **exercised** powers which were necessary and proper as means **to carry into effect** rights expressly given [by the Constitution]"

15. These are conservative counts. They do not include verbs whose subjects are the reified voices of governmental entities (e.g., "State legislation," "the

laws of the State," "State regulations," "the legislation of Congress," "the Act" [of 1793]); nor do they include, in the case of judicial entities, verbs that cast their subjects in the role of narrator rather than actor (e.g., "we state," "we mean," we have said [above]"). If these verbs were included, the totals would be:

	governments (nonjud/jud)
Verbs with Explicit Subjects	
active verbs	235 (170/65)
passive verbs	8 (5/3)
copulas	23 (19/4)
total	266 (194/72)
Verbs with Implicit Subjects	
active verbs	65 (30/35)
passive verbs	0 (0/0)
copulas	0 (0/0)
total	65 (30/35)
All Verbs	
active verbs	300 (200/100)
passive verbs	8 (5/3)
copulas	23 (19/4)
total	331 (224/107)

16. These are conservative counts. They do not include verbs whose subjects are the reified voices of governmental entities; nor do they include, in the case of judicial entities, verbs that cast their subjects in the role of narrator rather than actor. If these verbs were included, the totals would be:

	governments (nonjud/jud)
Verbs with Explicit Subjects	
active verbs	483 (206/277)
passive verbs	17 (9/8)
copulas	38 (27/11)
total	538 (242/296)
Verbs with Implicit Subjects	
active verbs	70 (31/39)
passive verbs	0 (0/0)
copulas	0 (0/0)
total	70 (31/39)

All Verbs

active verbs	553 (237/316)
passive verbs	17 (9/8)
copulas	38 (27/11)
total	608 (273/335)

17. These are conservative counts. They do not include verbs whose subjects are the reified voices of governmental entities; nor do they include, in the case of judicial entities, verbs that cast their subjects in the role of narrator rather than actor. If these verbs were included, the totals would be:

	governments (nonjud/jud)
Verbs with Explicit Subjects	
active verbs	123 (49/74)
passive verbs	6 (5/1)
copulas	4 (4/0)
total	133 (58/75)
Verbs with Implicit Subjects	
active verbs	39 (16/23)
passive verbs	0 (0/0)
copulas	0 (0/0)
total	39 (16/23)
All Verbs	
active verbs	162 (65/97)
passive verbs	6 (5/1)
copulas	4 (4/0)
total	172 (74/98)

Notes

1. Invitation to a Journey

1. See, e.g., Erving Goffman, *Behavior in Public Places,* New York: Free Press, 1963, pp. 98 ff.
2. We wish to acknowledge our debt to our co-teachers, Professors Peggy Cooper Davis, Nancy Morawetz, and David Richards, and to the occasional visitors who presented their ideas for discussion in the seminar: Professor Clifford Geertz of the Institute for Advanced Study, Professor Robert Gordon of the Yale Law School, Professor Lee Ross of Stanford, and Professor Richard Sherwin of the New York Law School.
3. Concerning the Russian Formalist theories, including Viktor Shklovsky's important poetics of alienation, the two main sources in English are L. T. Lemon and L. J. Reis, *Russian Formalist Criticism,* Lincoln: University of Nebraska Press, 1962; and L. Matejka and K. Pamorska (Eds.), *Readings in Russian Poetics,* Cambridge, Mass.: MIT Press, 1971. A memoirist account can be found in Viktor Borisovich Shklovsky, *A Sentimental Journey: Memoirs 1917–1922,* revised edition, Richard Sheldon trans., Ithaca, N.Y.: Cornell University Press, 1984. See also Roman Jakobson, "The Grammar of Poetry and the Poetry of Grammar," *Lingua,* 1968, *21,* 597–609.
4. Thomas Nagel, *The View from Nowhere,* New York and Oxford: Oxford University Press, 1986.
5. See, e.g., Howard Gardner, *The Mind's New Science: A History of the Cognitive Revolution,* New York: Basic Books, 1985; Jerome Bruner, Jacqueline Goodnow, and George A. Austin, *A Study of Thinking,* New York: Wiley, 1956.
6. See, e.g., the essays in Dell Hymes (Ed.), *Language in Culture and Society,* New York: Harper and Row, 1964; an excellent instance in that book is Charles O. Frake, "The Diagnosis of Disease Among the Subanun of

Mindanao." A comparable move in sociology was taken by Harold Garfinkel, *Studies in Ethnomethodology,* Englewood Cliffs, N.J.: Prentice-Hall, 1967.

7. Cf. Roman Jakobson, *Six Lectures on Sound and Meaning,* Foreword by Claude Lévi-Strauss, John Mepham trans., Cambridge, Mass.: MIT Press, 1978. The original breakthrough work was that of Roman Jakobson, G. Fant, and Morris Halle, *Preliminaries to Speech Analysis,* Cambridge, Mass.: MIT Press, 1952.

8. See Phoebe C. Ellsworth and Samuel R. Gross, "Hardening of the Attitudes: Americans' Views on the Death Penalty," *Journal of Social Issues,* 1994, *50(2),* 19–52; Samuel R. Gross, "Update: American Public Opinion on the Death Penalty—It's Getting Personal," *Cornell Law Review,* 1998, *83,* 1448–1475.

9. See William A. Schabas, *The Abolition of the Death Penalty in International Law,* 2d edition, Cambridge and New York: Cambridge University Press, 1997; *State v. Makwanyane,* 1995 (3) S.A.L.R. 391, 412–413 (C.C.) (judgment of President Chaskalson); and see Elizabeth Olson, "Good Friends Join Enemies to Criticize U.S. on Rights," *New York Times,* March 28, 1999, sec. 1, p. 9.

10. There are many approaches to studying the relations between the human sciences and the law, each with somewhat different objectives. Much of the literature is focused on (1) the causes of or responsibility for various forms of deviant or criminal behavior, (2) the nature of legal decisionmaking—particularly the subjects of jury behavior and eyewitness testimony—and (3) the fairness, effectiveness, or other effects of applying legal sanctions. A century of work on these topics has recently been reviewed and digested in a very thoughtful article by Phoebe C. Ellsworth and Robert Mauro in D. T. Gilbert, S. T. Fiske, and G. Lindzey (Eds.), *Handbook of Social Psychology,* 4th edition, New York: McGraw Hill, 1998, chap. 32. Beyond these conventional categories there are other areas of concentration in which lively research is going on—family law issues relating to child custody, the uses of psychological testing to predict forms of deviant behavior, and (a somewhat newer subject) lay persons' perceptions of justice. These topics are also reviewed in the *Handbook* just cited, in chapters by J. M. Levine and R. L. Moreland, by D. G. Pruitt, and by T. R. Tyler and H. J. Smith. We will be making use in the chapters ahead of the rather voluminous literature that these reviews cover, though we do not restrict ourselves to that literature, for our objectives are rather different from the ones that inspire most law-and-human-sciences scholarship.

11. See Anthony G. Amsterdam, "Federal Constititional Restrictions on the Punishment of Crimes of Status, Crimes of General Obnoxiousness, Crimes of Displeasing Police Officers, and the Like," *Criminal Law Bulletin,* 1967, *3(4),* 205–242, at pp. 211–215; and, e.g., *Saenz v. Roe,* 526 U.S. 489 (1999).

2. On Categories

1. See the path-breaking essay by George A. Miller, "The Magical Number 7, Plus or Minus 2: Some Limits on Our Capacity for Processing Information," *Psychological Review,* 1956, 63, 81–97.

2. Robert Oppenheimer summed it up well: "Man has a great capacity for discrimination. His potential sense of otherness is almost unlimited. Rational life begins with the selective practice of ignoring differences, failing in truth to perceive them; rational life begins with the failure to use discriminatory power in anything like its full potentiality. It lies in the selection, arrangement, and appropriate adequation to the objects of perception and thought, of limited traits, of a small residue of potential wealth." Robert Oppenheimer, "A Study of Thinking," *Sewanee Review,* 1958, 66(3), 481–489, a review of Jerome Bruner, Jacqueline Goodnow, and George A. Austin, *A Study of Thinking,* New York: Wiley, 1956. The present chapter revisits this 1956 book, which had the interesting if not altogether enviable fate of being buried by the work it subsequently provoked. For a summary of this subsequent work, see Edward E. Smith and Douglas L. Medin, *Categories and Concepts,* Cambridge, Mass.: Harvard University Press, 1981; the new Introduction to the reprinted *A Study of Thinking,* New Brunswick and Oxford: Transaction Books, 1986; and the general discussion in Jerome Bruner, *Acts of Meaning,* Cambridge, Mass.: Harvard University Press, 1990. The time seems ripe to have another go at bringing 1956's too-orderly, old-fashioned country adolescent into the brawling, postmodern city.

3. Brent Berlin and Paul Kay, *Basic Color Terms: Their Universality and Evolution,* Berkeley: University of California Press, 1969. See also Brent Berlin, D. E. Breedlove, and P. H. Raven, "General Principles of Classification and Nomenclature in Folk Biology," *American Anthropologist,* 1973, 75, 214–242.

4. This odd statistical regularity is known among linguists as "Zipf's Law" and is probably related to the fact that, given the pressure of time involved in coding and decoding speech, we shorten often-used expressions to meet the requirement that phrases in common talk should fit within a time envelope of not more than .7 second. See entry in David Crystal, *Cambridge Encyclopedia of Language,* Cambridge: Cambridge University Press, 1987, section 15, pp. 86 ff.

5. See, e.g., Shelley E. Taylor, Susan Fiske, N. L. Etcoff, and A. J. Ruderman, "The Categorical and Contextual Basis of Personal Memory and Stereotyping," *Journal of Personality and Social Psychology,* 1978, 36, 778–793. There is also a thoughtful discussion of these problems in Roger Brown, *Social Psychology: The Second Edition,* New York: Free Press, 1986, Part II, pp. 131–248.

6. See, e.g., Michael Moerman, *Talking Culture: Ethnography and Conversa-*

tion Analysis, Philadelphia: University of Pennsylvania Press, 1988, pp. 68–100.

7. See, e.g., Erving Goffman, *Gender Advertisements*, New York: Harper Colophon, 1979.

8. See, e.g., Derrick Bell, *And We Are Not Saved: The Elusive Quest for Racial Justice*, New York: Basic Books, 1987; Richard Delgado (Ed.), *Critical Race Theory: The Cutting Edge*, Philadelphia: Temple University Press, 1995.

9. The term probably owes its origin to the well-known 1979 work of Jean Francois Lyotard, published in English as *The Postmodern Condition: A Report on Knowledge*, Geoff Bennington and Brian Massumi trans., Minneapolis: University of Minnesota Press, 1984. For a more recent account of the impact of postmodernism on legal thinking, see Douglas E. Litowitz, *Postmodern Philosophy and Law: Rorty, Nietzsche, Lyotard, Derrida, Foucault*, Lawrence: University Press of Kansas, 1997. There has been a growing literature over the last several years arguing that "postmodern philosophy" has been with us virtually since the beginning of the Western philosophical tradition. A striking example is M. J. Devaney, "*Since at Least Plato . . .*," *and Other Postmodernist Myths*, Basingstoke: Macmillan, and New York: St. Martin's Press, 1997. Further discussion of the place of law in cultural analysis can be found in the essays included in Austin Sarat and Thomas R. Kearns (Eds.), *Law in the Domains of Culture*, Ann Arbor: University of Michigan Press, 1998.

10. E.g., *Oyama v. California*, 332 U.S. 633 (1948); *Loving v. Virginia*, 388 U.S. 1 (1967).

11. See, e.g., *James v. Valtierra*, 402 U.S. 137 (1971); *San Antonio Independent School District v. Rodriguez*, 411 U.S. 1 (1973).

12. See, e.g., *City of Richmond v. J. A. Croson Co.*, 488 U.S. 469 (1989); *Adarand Constructors, Inc. v. Pena*, 515 U.S. 200 (1995).

13. See, e.g., Henry Weihofen, *The Urge to Punish: New Approaches to the Problem of Mental Irresponsibility for Crime*, London: V. Gollancz, 1957.

14. See, e.g., David J. Hufford, *The Terror That Comes in the Night: An Experience-Centered Study of Supernatural Assault Traditions*, Philadelphia: University of Pennsylvania Press, 1982.

15. See *Hattori v. Peairs*, 662 So.2d 509 (La. App. 1995).

16. See *Hirabayashi v. United States*, 320 U.S. 81 (1943); *Korematsu v. United States*, 323 U.S. 214 (1944); *Ex parte Mitsuye Endo*, 323 U.S. 283 (1944).

17. See Peggy Cooper Davis and Gautam Barua, "Custodial Choices for Children at Risk: Bias, Sequentiality, and the Law," *University of Chicago Law School Roundtable*, 1995, 2, 139–159.

18. See, e.g., Daniel Kahnemann, Paul Slovic, and Amos Tversky, *Judgment under Uncertainty: Heuristics and Biases*, Cambridge: Cambridge University Press, 1982.

19. See, e.g., Guido Calabresi, "Some Thoughts on Risk Distribution in the Law of Torts," *Yale Law Journal*, 1961, 70, 499–553.

20. See Debra Friedman and Michael Hechter, "The Contribution of Rational Choice Theory to Macrosociological Research," *Sociological Theory,* 1988, 6, 201–218.

21. Irenäus Eibl-Eibesfeldt, *Ethology: The Biology of Behavior,* Erich Klinghammer trans., New York: Holt, Rinehart and Winston, 1975.

22. Gottlob Frege, "On Sense and Reference," in *Translations from the Philosophical Writings of Gottlob Frege,* Peter Geach and Max Black (Eds.), Oxford: Basil Blackwell, 1960.

23. For a thoughtful account of the transition from classical Greek "decline" theories of history to more modern "progress" theories, see John B. Bury's classic *The Idea of Progress: An Inquiry into Its Origins and Growth,* London: Greenwood, 1932. German idealist theories about the inevitability of human progress are trenchantly and amusingly discussed in Louis O. Mink, "Narrative Form as a Cognitive Instrument," in Robert H. Canary and Henry Kozicki (Eds.), *The Writing of History: Literary Form and Historical Understanding,* Madison: University of Wisconsin Press, 1978, pp. 129–149. Neo-Darwinism has always had a great appeal to social scientists given to painting history in broad strokes—as with Herbert Spencer. An interesting version of this style of evolutionary history can be found in Jerome Barkow, Leda Cosmides, and John Tooby, *The Adapted Mind: Evolutionary Psychology and the Generation of Culture,* New York and Oxford: Oxford University Press, 1992.

24. Northrop Frye, *Anatomy of Criticism: Four Essays,* Princeton: Princeton University Press, 1990.

25. And Frye himself insisted that "there is no one of critical ability who has not experienced intense and profound pleasure from something simultaneously with a low critical evaluation of what produced it" (id. at 28)—which amounts to saying that his category of "books I enjoy" fell outside his entire elaborate scheme of critical categories.

26. *Blank v. Sullivan & Cromwell,* 418 F. Supp. 1, 4 (S.D.N.Y. 1975).

27. Emile Durkheim, *The Elementary Forms of the Religious Life: A Study in Religious Sociology,* Joseph Ward Swain trans., New York: Free Press, 1965.

28. See, e.g., Sanford Levinson, "The Constitution in American Civil Religion," *Supreme Court Review,* 1979, 1979, 123–151; Thomas Grey, "The Constitution as Scripture," *Stanford Law Review,* 1984, 37, 1–25; Ronald Garet, "Comparative Normative Hermeneutics: Scripture, Literature, Constitution," *Southern California Law Review,* 1985, 58, 35–134; Robert M. Cover, "The Supreme Court, 1982 Term, Foreword: Nomos and Narrative," *Harvard Law Review,* 1983, 97, 4–68.

29. The point of the present discussion is not to revisit part II of this chapter. That section considered the functions served by categorization in general. Here we deal with the functions served by particular category systems.

30. 514 U.S. 549 (1995).

31. T. W. Adorno, Else Frenkel-Brunswik, Daniel J. Levinson, R. Nevitt San-ford, et al., *The Authoritarian Personality,* New York: Harper, 1950.

32. Claude Lévi-Strauss, *The Elementary Structures of Kinship,* James Bell et al. trans., Boston: Beacon Press, 1969.

33. See, e.g., Northrop Frye, *The Great Code: The Bible and Literature,* New York: Harcourt Brace (Harvest Book), 1982.

34. See, e.g., *Fay v. Noia,* 372 U.S. 391 (1963).

35. See, e.g., Anthony G. Amsterdam, "Criminal Prosecutions Affecting Fed-erally Guaranteed Civil Rights: Federal Removal and Habeas Corpus Juris-diction to Abort State Court Trial," *University of Pennsylvania Law Re-view,* 1965, *113,* 793–912.

36. See, e.g., Vivian Berger, "Justice Delayed or Justice Denied?—A Comment on Recent Proposals to Reform Death Penalty Habeas Corpus," *Columbia Law Review,* 1990, *90,* 1665–1714; Ronald J. Tabak and J. Mark Lane, "Judicial Activism and Legislative 'Reform' of Federal Habeas Corpus: A Critical Analysis of Recent Developments and Current Proposals," *Albany Law Review,* 1991, *55,* 1–95. The history of federal habeas corpus juris-prudence is a series of revolutionary recategorizations: in defining what it means to be "in custody in violation of the Constitution" (28 U.S.C. § 2241(c)(3)), cases like *Moore v. Dempsey,* 261 U.S. 86 (1923), and *John-son v. Zerbst,* 304 U.S. 458 (1938), recategorize "jurisdiction"; in retalia-tion, *Wainwright v. Sykes,* 433 U.S. 72 (1977), and *McCleskey v. Zant,* 499 U.S. 467 (1991), recategorize "default"; and *Teague v. Lane,* 489 U.S. 288 (1989), recategorizes Time itself.

37. Roland Barthes, *Mythologies,* New York: Hill and Wang, 1972.

38. Antonio Gramsci, *Selections from Cultural Writings,* D. Forgacs and D. Nowell-Smith (Eds.), Cambridge, Mass.: Harvard University Press, 1985.

39. See, e.g., Arthur O. Lovejoy, *The Great Chain of Being: A Study of the His-tory of an Idea* (1936), Cambridge, Mass.: Harvard University Press, 1964; Peter Brown, *The Body and Society: Men, Women, and Sexual Renuncia-tion in Early Christianity,* New York: Columbia University Press, 1988; Carlo Ginzburg, *The Night Battles: Witchcraft and Agrarian Cults in the 16th and 17th Centuries* (1966), Baltimore: Johns Hopkins University Press, 1992.

40. Thomas S. Kuhn, *The Structure of Scientific Revolutions,* 2d edition, Chi-cago: University of Chicago Press, 1970.

41. *Liverpool, New York & Philadelphia Steamship Co. v. Commissioners of Emigration,* 113 U.S. 33, 39 (1885), quoted in, e.g., *Communist Party v. Subversive Activities Control Board,* 367 U.S. 1, 71–72 (1961), and Justice Brandeis's separate opinion in *Ashwander v. Tennessee Valley Authority,* 297 U.S. 288, 341, 346–347 (1936). Numerous cases insist upon this "pol-icy of strict necessity in disposing of constitutional issues." *Rescue Army v. Municipal Court,* 331 U.S. 549, 568 (1947).

42. Jerome Bruner and Leo Postman, "On the Perception of Incongruity: A Par-

adigm," *Journal of Personality,* 1949, *18,* 206–223. If you had never seen any of the incongruous playing cards before, it took an average of 390 milliseconds to recognize one. If you had been exposed to only one before, the time needed to recognize a second one dropped to 230 milliseconds. After that, you could recognize trick cards at 84 milliseconds, on average, in contrast to the 28 milliseconds needed to recognize an ordinary playing card.

43. See George Miller, Jerome Bruner, and Leo Postman, "Familiarity of Letter Sequences and Tachistoscopic Recognition," *Journal of General Psychology,* 1954, *50,* 129–139. The research on value and perceptual recognition started with a paper by Leo Postman, Jerome Bruner, and Elliott McGinnies, "Personal Values as Selective Factors in Perception," *Journal of Abnormal and Social Psychology,* 1948, *43(2),* 142–154. It was sometimes criticized on the ground that valued things and words were more prevalent either in the world generally or in the personal worlds of the particular perceivers—in which case, the so-called "value" effect on perception could be reduced to the "frequency" effect. For our present purposes, it doesn't matter much.

44. Immanuel Kant, *Critique of Pure Reason.*

45. This view comes originally from Noam Chomsky's work. See, e.g., *Syntactic Structures,* The Hague: Mouton, 1957. Nativism has recently been re-outfitted in the tinselly but familiar raiments of latter-day "evolutionary psychology" by Steven Pinker, in *The Language Instinct: How the Mind Creates Language,* New York: William Morrow, 1994. For a well-informed critique of this approach, see Michael Tomasello, *The Cultural Origins of Human Cognition,* Cambridge, Mass.: Harvard University Press, 1999.

46. Andrew N. Meltzoff, "Understanding the Intentions of Others: Re-Enactment of Intended Acts by 18-Month-Old Children," *Developmental Psychology,* 1995, *31,* 1–16.

47. For a comprehensive account of this work, see Janet Astington, *The Child's Discovery of the Mind,* Cambridge, Mass.: Harvard University Press, 1996.

48. See, e.g., Clifford Geertz, *The Interpretation of Cultures,* New York: Basic Books, 1973, particularly chapters 2 and 3; see also Bradd Shore, *Culture in Mind,* Oxford: Oxford University Press, 1997.

49. Dan Sperber, "Learning to Pay Attention," *Times Literary Supplement,* December 27, 1996, No. 4891, pp. 14–15.

50. Eleanor Rosch, "Principles of Categorization," in Eleanor Rosch and B. B. Lloyd (Eds.), *Cognition and Categorization,* Hillsdale, N.J.: Erlbaum, 1978, pp. 27–48; George Lakoff, *Women, Fire, and Dangerous Things: What Categories Reveal about the Mind,* Chicago and London: University of Chicago Press, 1987.

51. Frank Keil, *Semantic and Conceptual Development: An Ontological Perspective,* Cambridge, Mass.: Harvard University Press, 1979; Frank Keil, "The Acquisition of Natural Kind and Artifact Terms," in W. Demopoulos

and A. Marras, *Language, Learning, and Concept Acquisition,* Norwood, N.J.: Ablex, 1986.

52. Susan Carey, *Conceptual Change in Childhood,* Cambridge, Mass.: MIT Press, 1985.

53. Richard Rorty, *Philosophy and the Mirror of Nature,* Princeton: Princeton University Press, 1980, p. 307. Rorty makes this point independently of any deep criticism of philosophical conceptions; he is talking about descriptive terms that categorize the ordinary incidents of life for the ordinary purposes of life when he says that "one is not going to find a set of necessary and sufficient conditions for goodness which will enable one to find the Good Life, resolve moral dilemmas, grade apples, or whatever. There are too many sorts of interests to answer to, too many different kinds of things to commend and too many different reasons for commending them, for such a set of necessary and sufficient conditions to be found." Id.

54. The tale told in the forty-third poem of the Kalevala says it well. Vainamoinen and his questing companions have carried off the Sampo (a miraculous mill) from the Northland and are rowing home. Wise old Vainamoinen calls to rash Lemminkainen to climb the mast, look back, and see if the horizon behind them is clear. Lemminkainen looks and reports that all is clear except that there is a little cloud in the north. Vainamoinen says, "that's no cloud; look again more closely." Lemminkainen now reports that the object in the north is a distant island, its aspens full of hawks, its birches full of speckled grouse. Vainamoinen says, "those are not birds; look closely a third time." This time Lemminkainen cries that the thing behind them, gaining on them, is a Northland warship driven by a hundred oars, its spars filled with fighting men. Vainamoinen asks for no closer examination; he tells Lemminkainen to get down and pull an oar, full speed ahead. *The Kalevala, or Poems of the Kaleva District,* Elias Lönnrot compilation; Francis Peabody Magoun, Jr. trans., Cambridge, Mass.: Harvard University Press, 1995, pp. 288–289.

55. See Chapter 3, *Michael H.,* Parts II, III, and V.

56. See Bruner, note 2 above.

57. We borrow the word from the celebrated TOTE unit imaged in George A. Miller, Eugene Galanter, and Karl H. Pribram, *Plans and the Structure of Behavior,* New York: Holt, Rinehart, and Winston, 1960.

58. See, e.g., Edwin Black, *Rhetorical Questions: Studies of Public Discourse,* Chicago and London: University of Chicago Press, 1992, pp. 21–50.

59. Frye, note 24 above.

60. Alistair Fowler, *Kinds of Literature: An Introduction to the Theory of Genres and Modes,* Cambridge, Mass.: Harvard University Press, 1982.

61. See, e.g., Jerome Bruner, "The Narrative Construction of Reality," *Critical Inquiry,* 1991, *18(1),* 1–21; Roland Barthes, "The Sequences of Actions," in *The Semiotic Challenge,* Richard Howard trans., New York: Hill and Wang, 1988, pp. 136–148, at pp. 140–142; Michael Riffaterre, *Fictional*

Truth, Baltimore and London: Johns Hopkins University Press, 1990, pp. 3–4; Erving Goffman, *Frame Analysis: An Essay on the Organization of Experience,* Cambridge, Mass.: Harvard University Press, 1974, pp. 561–562. For discussion of the power of stock stories in the law, see Richard Delgado, "Storytelling for Oppositionists and Others: A Plea for Narrative," *Michigan Law Review,* 1989, *87,* 2411–2441; Anthony G. Amsterdam, "Telling Stories and Stories About Them," *Clinical Law Review,* 1994, *1,* 9–40; and the works cited in Chapter 4, note 1.

62. The choice of story may be more or less conscious. See, for example, the following note.

63. Thomas Gilovich, "Seeing the Past in the Present: The Effect of Associations to Familiar Events on Judgments and Decisions," *Journal of Personality and Social Psychology,* 1981, *40,* 797–808. Gilovich's subjects seem to have been unaware of their own assimilation of the hypothetical foreign-policy crisis to the stories of Munich and Vietnam respectively. See id. at 806.

64. See Chapter 3, *Jenkins,* Part III, Scenes 3, 9, and 13.

65. See Birt L. Duncan, "Differential Social Perception and the Attribution of Intergroup Violence: Testing the Lower Limits of Stereotyping of Blacks," *Journal of Personality and Social Psychology,* 1976, *34,* 590–598.

66. See Chapter 6.

67. W. V. Quine, *Ontological Reality and Other Essays,* New York: Columbia University Press, 1969, pp. 125–126.

68. Metaphor, of course, provides an almost endless frontier for those seeking to extend the limits of similarity. The exploitation of metaphoric similarity is by no means limited to poetry or even to literature. While the topic of metaphor is too far-reaching to engage us here, its use in legal contexts has been examined thoughtfully in several recent studies. See particularly Steven L. Winter, "The Metaphor of Standing and the Problem of Self-Governance," *Stanford Law Review,* 1988, *40,* 1371–1516; Steven L. Winter, "Transcendental Nonsense, Metaphoric Reasoning, and the Cognitive Stakes for Law," *University of Pennsylvania Law Review,* 1989, *137,* 1105–1237; Steven L. Winter, "The Meaning of 'Under Color of' Law," *Michigan Law Review,* 1992, *91,* 323–418. Winter's work has opened a wide-ranging discussion of the role of metaphoric thinking in law.

69. [Cicero], *Rhetorica ad Herennium,* volume I of the bilingual *Cicero,* Cambridge, Mass.: Harvard University Press, 1989, with English translation by Harry Caplan, pp. 166–169 (book III, chap. iii). And see id. at 170–171: "[T]hat which, in instructing, I have, in order to give clarity and emphasis, called Craft, we shall in speaking call by the more honourable name of Strategy" (book III, chap. iv).

70. This does not mean that the person who is doing the categorizing has the function consciously in mind. To the contrary, one or more of the functions—particularly the economy function—is often served by categorizing on automatic pilot, without even being aware that one is categorizing, let

alone that one is choosing among alternative possible categories and category systems, and why.

71. Lévi-Strauss, note 32 above. His exchange theory has been brought into question by noting that, generally, the incest taboo is applied in a widely classificatory way, that many potential partners who are complete strangers to each other and whose families have no real cooperative relations are barred from marriage under the kinship exogamy rule. See George Caspar Homans and David M. Schneider, *Marriage, Authority, and Final Causes: A Study of Unilateral Cross-Cousin Marriage,* Glencoe, Ill.: Free Press, 1955.

72. Leigh B. Bienen, "Defining Incest," *Northwestern University Law Review,* 1998, 92, 1501–1640, at p. 1531.

73. Id. at 1535.

74. See id. at 1535–1537 and n. 115.

75. See id. at 1502, 1545–1562.

76. Id. at 1563–1564.

77. See id. at 1569.

78. Id. at 1568–1569.

79. Id. at 1579.

3A. Categorizing at the Supreme Court: *Missouri v. Jenkins*

1. 515 U.S. 70, 132 L.Ed.2d 63, 115 S. Ct. 2038 (1995).

2. Our *Jenkins* study will not examine any single categorizing move in depth. That would require an extended additional analysis including a detailed excavation of the sources from which the opinion draws its categories. We will reserve that kind of analysis for the second case study in this chapter. Nor will we consider how the various categorizing moves which we identify in the *Jenkins* opinion work together to support the opinion's narrative and rhetorical structure. We will not be fully prepared for analyses of that nature until Chapter 7.

3. 347 U.S. 483.

4. Id. at 495.

5. *Brown v. Board of Education,* 349 U.S. 294, 301.

6. Id.

7. *Swann v. Charlotte-Mecklenburg Board of Education,* 402 U.S. 1, 14 (1971).

8. *Griffin v. County School Board of Prince Edward County,* 377 U.S. 218, 234.

9. *Green v. County School Board of New Kent County,* 391 U.S. 430, 439.

10. *Swann,* note 7 above, at 14.

11. Chief Justice Burger authored a unanimous opinion in *Swann*—apparently designed to emulate Chief Justice Warren's celebrated feat of producing a unanimous opinion in *Brown I*—and billed it as "defining in more precise

terms than heretofore the scope of the duty of school authorities and district courts in implementing *Brown I* and the mandate to eliminate dual systems and establish unitary systems at once." 402 U.S. at 6.

12. Id. at 27.
13. Id. at 15.
14. Id. at 28.
15. Id. at 16.
16. Id. at 5.
17. Id. at 31–32.
18. Id. at 24.
19. Id. at 25–26.
20. Id. at 26.
21. 418 U.S. 717.
22. Id. at 729–730 (footnote omitted).
23. Id. at 733. The Supreme Court viewed the question posed by this decree as "whether a federal court may impose a multi-district, areawide remedy to a single district de jure segregation problem absent any finding that the other included school districts have failed to operate unitary school systems within their districts, absent any claim or finding that the boundary lines of any affected school district were established with the purpose of fostering racial segregation in public schools, absent any finding that the included districts committed acts which effected segregation within the other districts, and absent a meaningful opportunity for the included neighboring school districts to present evidence or be heard on the propriety of a multi-district remedy or on the question of constitutional violations by those neighboring districts." Id. at 721–722.
24. Id. at 743.
25. Id. at 744.
26. Id. at 744–745.
27. Id. at 745.
28. 427 U.S. 424.
29. Id. at 433 (footnote omitted).
30. Id.
31. Id. at 434.
32. Id. at 435.
33. Id. at 436, quoting *Swann*, 402 U.S. at 31–32.
34. See, e.g., *Board of Education of Oklahoma City Public Schools v. Dowell*, 498 U.S. 237, 247–248 (1991) (majority opinion of Chief Justice Rehnquist).
35. 503 U.S. 467 (1992).
36. Id. at 489.
37. The earlier appearance of the case had involved issues of attorneys' fees awarded to lawyers for the class of African-American school children. *Missouri v. Jenkins*, 491 U.S. 274 (1989).

38. A majority of the Supreme Court held that it does. *Missouri v. Jenkins*, 495 U.S. 33 (1990).

39. See, e.g., 495 U.S. at 58, 75–80.

40. The Court's decision whether or not to grant review in cases within its *certiorari* jurisdiction is completely discretionary.

41. 132 L.Ed.2d at 87, col. 2.

42. Id. at 88, col. 1.

43. Id. at 89, col. 1.

44. Id. at 89, col. 2.

45. Equipped with the background given in Parts I and II, the reader should be able to take the following tour without reading the *Jenkins* opinion itself. But we hope that you will read it, both to test our impressions of the sights against your own and to enjoy the many other sights we have no time to visit. The best way to see all the scenery would be to read the opinion through first, and then to read our tour notes with the opinion still open in front of you. It is available electronically via Westlaw or Lexis and is published in three printed versions: volume 515 of the United States Reports, beginning at page 70; volume 132 of the Lawyer's Edition of the United States Supreme Court Reports, Second Series, beginning at page 63; and volume 115 of the Supreme Court Reporter, beginning at page 2038. We will cite volume 132 of the Lawyer's Edition.

46. "What we meant in *Milliken I* by an interdistrict violation was a violation that caused segregation between adjoining districts." P. 84, col. 1.

47. Pp. 73, col. 1; 81, col. 2 and n. 4; 83, col. 1; 85, cols. 1–2.

48. P. 79, col. 2 (second brackets added).

49. See, e.g., p. 83, col. 1, saying that the purpose of the district court's remedial plan in *Jenkins* "is to attract nonminority students from outside the KCMSD. But this *inter*district goal is beyond the scope of the *intra*district violation identified by the District Court."

   The equation between "interdistrict remedy" and "interdistrict goal" or "interdistrict purpose" is built up implicitly and used to decide the case before it is explicitly acknowledged. The phrases "interdistrict relief" and "'interdistrict remedy'" are introduced in the second paragraph of the Court's substantive legal analysis (p. 79, col. 2) and are repeated frequently throughout the opinion (pp. 81, col. 2; 81, n. 4; 83, col. 2 [four times]; 84, col. 1; 86, col. 1). The phrase "interdistrict goal" is introduced a bit later (p. 81, col. 1) and repeated a couple of times (pp. 83, col. 1; 84, col. 2) before being paraphrased as "interdistrict purpose" (p. 86, col. 2). The two sets of phrases are increasingly commingled; and in col. 1 on p. 83 this process produces the holding quoted in the preceding paragraph (of this footnote). It is only thereafter, in col. 1 on p. 84, that the equation is expressly articulated and defended—rather off-handedly, as we shall discuss in the text. The opinion nowhere says anything to indicate that there is a question or an issue to be decided concerning *whether* the phrase "interdistrict remedy" includes a remedy having an "interdistrict goal"; and it downplays the possibility that the phrase might have a narrower compass. Although it quotes various sources, including the lower courts, that use terminology which would flag this possibility—"'mandatory interdistrict relief'" (p. 81, col. 2), "'mandatory interdistrict remedy'" (p. 85, col. 1), "'*mandatory* plan'" (p. 83, col. 1) and "'[V]*oluntary* interdistrict remedies'" (p. 82, col. 1)—it does not comment on them, and it limits its own use of similar qualifiers to phrases like "mandatory interdistrict redistribution of students" (p. 73, col. 1) and "mandatory interdistrict reassignment" (p. 83, col. 1).

50. P. 83, cols. 1–2 (emphasis added).

51. P. 84, cols. 1–2.

52. P. 83, col. 1.

53. The *Jenkins* majority opinion does not explain the relationship of these additional faults to its holding that the salary-increase order was erroneous. That holding seems to be supported principally if not exclusively by the reasoning which we have already examined: (A) the statement of an unqualified rule that *no interdistrict remedy is permissible without an interdistrict violation,* (B) the classification of the lower courts' findings as *no interdistrict violation,* and (C) the classification of the salary-increase order as *an interdistrict remedy.* The portions of the opinion which we consider next can be read as going to point (B) or they can be read as asserting that even if the rule stated in point (A) were not unqualified, the reasons given by the lower courts for departing from it (white flight and the present 68.3% black school population of the KCMSD) would be insufficient.

54. P. 84, col. 2.

55. P. 82, col. 1.

56. Id. It is not immediately obvious why this doctrinal rule is relevant to the issue of the proper scope of a district court's discretion to devise remedies for *de jure* segregation of the kind that was concededly at issue in *Jenkins.* (In 1984 "[t]he District Court determined that prior to 1954 'Missouri mandated segregated schools for black and white children.' . . . [and that] the KCMSD and the State had failed in their affirmative obligations to eliminate the vestiges of the State's dual school system within the KCMSD." P. 72, col. 1.) The logic seems to go as follows:

Basic rule: "The ultimate inquiry is '"whether the [constitutional violator] ha[s] complied in good faith with the desegregation decree since it was entered, and whether the vestiges of past discrimination ha[ve] been eliminated to the extent practicable."'" P. 81, col. 1.

Implied sub-rule: The presence in a school district of schools that remain "segregated" is a vestige which needs to be eliminated. See p. 81, col. 2 ("The proper response to an intradistrict violation is an intradistrict remedy . . . that serves to eliminate the racial identity of the schools within the affected school district by eliminating, as far as practicable, the vestiges of *de jure* segregation in all facets of their operations.")

Negative definition: "[I]n *Milliken I* . . ., we . . . rejected the suggestion 'that schools which have a majority of Negro students are not "desegregated" whatever the racial makeup of the school district's population. . . .' . . . '[T]he Court has consistently held that the Constitution is not violated by racial imbalance in the schools, without more' . . ." P. 82, col. 1; see also pp. 79, col. 2 – 80, col. 1.

Rule reformulated negatively: Courts crafting remedies for segregation should not undertake to eliminate racial imbalances within schools that reflect only overall racial ratios in the school district's student population.

57. P. 72, col. 2; p. 82, col. 1.
58. See the findings of the lower courts quoted in Justice Souter's dissenting opinion at pp. 125–128. What concerned the lower courts specifically was the difficulty of reducing the number of identifiably black schools in the KCMSD—25 schools having student bodies that were 90% or more African-American—by shuffling pupils around within a district that had become 68.3% African-American. Both the 90%-plus concentrations and the difficulty of alleviating them were found to have been products of *de jure* segregation because (1) Missouri had consigned African-Americans to separate and unequal schools before *Brown;* (2) after *Brown,* the State did nothing to alter attendance patterns for 30 years, until the district court in *Jenkins* ordered it to act; (3) by the time of the district court's desegregation order, the physical plant of the identifiably black schools in the KCMSD had "literally rotted," *Jenkins v. Missouri,* 672 F. Supp. 400, 411 (W.D. Mo. 1987); and (4) large numbers of white parents preferred to withdraw their children to the suburbs or to private schools rather than send them to these deteriorated facilities or face the tax bills necessary for wholesale reconstruction; so "the preponderance of black students in the [KCMSD] . . . was due to the State and KCMSD's constitutional violations, which caused white flight," *Jenkins v. Missouri,* 855 F.2d 1295, 1302 (8th Cir. 1988).
59. P. 77, col. 2 – p. 79, col. 1.
60. See text following note 40 above. "The questions shall be set out on the first page [of the petition for *certiorari*]. . . . The statement of any question presented is deemed to comprise every subsidiary question fairly included therein. Only the questions set out in the petition, or fairly included therein, will be considered by the Court." Supreme Court Rule 14.1(a).
61. P. 77, n. 3.
62. P. 77, col. 2.
63. P. 81, col. 1
64. P. 78, col. 1. This is the only aspect of the Chief Justice's reasoning that is further explained. The explanation is, however, circular: "Given that the District Court's basis for its salary order was grounded in 'improving the desegregative attractiveness of the KCMSD,' . . . we must consider the propriety of that reliance in order to resolve properly the State's challenge to

that order." Id. Whether the conclusion follows from the premise depends upon the *nature* of "the State's challenge"; and that, of course, is the question which the Chief Justice is reasoning *to* and *from* at the same time.

65. P. 78, col. 1.

66. P. 77, col. 2.

67. As Justice Souter's dissenting opinion demonstrates, Missouri knew very well how to write a Question Presented challenging the interdistrict character of the lower courts' desegregation efforts when it wanted to. It had included just such a Question Presented in a petition for certiorari at an earlier stage of the *Jenkins* litigation: "Whether a federal court, remedying an intradistrict violation . . . may . . . a) impose a duty to attract additional non-minority students to a school district, and b) require improvements to make the district schools comparable to those in surrounding districts." Missouri did not repeat that Question in its present petition for certiorari, and neither of the two Questions which it did raise in the present petition remotely resembled its earlier Question on the subject. Compare the Questions set out at pp. 114, col. 2 – 115, col. 1 with those set out at p. 115, col. 2.

68. P. 78, col. 1; p. 78, col. 2.

69. See, e.g., *Atlantic Coast Line Railroad Co. v. Powe*, 283 U.S. 401, 403–404 (1931); *Maryland v. Baltimore Radio Show, Inc.*, 338 U.S. 912 (1950) (opinion of Justice Frankfurter respecting the denial of the petition for writ of *certiorari*), approved in *Hughes Tool Co. v. Trans World Airlines Inc.*, 409 U.S. 363, 366 n. 1 (1973).

70. The authoritative discussion of this subject is Justice Frankfurter's opinion, expressing a view endorsed by a majority of the Court, in *Brown v. Allen*, 344 U.S. 443, 488 (1953).

71. To be exact, Justice Souter argues as follows: (1) Missouri's earlier certiorari petition explicitly presented the very issue that Chief Justice Rehnquist finds implicit in its present petition: whether the district court erred in ordering a set of remedies aimed to "'attract additional non-minority students to a school district.'" P. 115, col. 1. [See note 67 above.] (2) The Supreme Court granted review of other issues raised by the earlier certiorari petition but declined to review this one. P. 115, col. 1. (3) Missouri's present petition does not appear to raise the issue again. P. 115, cols. 1–2. (4) So when the school-desegregation plaintiffs designed their Supreme Court strategy following the present grant of certiorari—when they chose the portions of the record to be printed, wrote their brief, planned their oral argument, and so forth—they were entitled to expect, consistently with the Court's earlier "deliberate refusal to entertain so important an issue," that the Court would "not subsequently allow it to be raised on . . . [the Court's] own motion without saying so in advance and giving notice to a party whose interests might be adversely affected." Pp. 116, col. 2 – 117, col. 1.

72. P. 79, cols. 1–2. It is important to keep your eye on the way any piece of dis-

course *begins.* Beginnings have special communicative salience, a phenomenon that is sometimes called "primacy effect" in psychological jargon and is expressed in the folk maxim "first impressions are lasting." Beginnings also function to create meaning frames for what follows. See Michael Riffaterre, *Fictional Truth,* Baltimore and London: Johns Hopkins University Press, 1990.

73. Compare pp. 85, col. 2 – 86, col. 2, where the Chief Justice restricts the scope of *Hills v. Gautreaux* as a precedent by the traditional common-law technique of reading pronouncements in an earlier opinion as limited by the facts of the earlier case.

74. P. 79, col. 2.

75. 402 U.S. at 18.

76. Id. at 20–21.

77. Id. at 21.

78. Id.

79. Id. at 22.

80. The two sentences preceding the passage quoted by Chief Justice Rehnquist at note 74 above are: "We are concerned in these cases with the elimination of the discrimination inherent in the dual school systems, not with myriad factors of human existence which can cause discrimination in a multitude of ways on racial, religious, or ethnic grounds. The target of the cases from *Brown I* to the present was the dual school systems." (Id. at 22.) The two sentences following the passage quoted by Chief Justice Rehnquist are: "We do not reach in this case the question whether a showing that school segregation is a consequence of other types of state action, without any discriminatory action by the school authorities, is a constitutional violation requiring remedial action by a school desegregation decree. This case does not present that question and we therefore do not decide it." (Id. at 23.)

81. See text at note 36 above.

82. P. 89, col. 2.

83. The coda of the Court's discussion of the salary-increase order begins: "Nor are there limits to the duration of the District Court's involvement" and implies that the district court's inflation of the KCMSD budget has created a situation that will keep the schools dependent on court supervision forever. P. 87, cols. 1–2. The Court's discussion of the achievement-test issue concludes: "Insistence upon academic goals unrelated to the effects of legal segregation unwarrantably postpones the day when KCMSD will be able to operate on its own." P. 89, col. 1.

84. P. 89, cols. 1–2. The latter reminder is delivered in the passage found at note 82 above.

85. P. 71, col. 1 (emphasis added).

86. P. 87, cols. 1–2 (emphasis added).

87. See p. 79, cols. 1–2. The reference to *Swann* is found at notes 72–74 above.

88. P. 84, n. 6.
89. P. 88, col. 1.
90. P. 72, col. 1; p. 89, col. 1.
91. P. 72, col. 1 (second emphasis added).
92. P. 88, col. 2 (second emphasis added).
93. Cf. Michael Heim, "Logic and Intuition," in *The Metaphysics of Virtual Reality,* New York and Oxford: Oxford University Press, 1993, pp. 12–27.
94. Pp. 88–89.
95. P. 87, col. 1.
96. P. 74, col. 2.
97. P. 74, cols. 1–2 (emphasis added).
98. Pp. 74, col. 2 – 75, col. 1 (emphasis added).
99. P. 89, col. 1. This is repeated at pp. 75, col. 1; 87, col. 1.
100. P. 74, col. 2.
101. P. 77, col. 1.
102. P. 75, col. 1; see also pp. 72, col. 2; 82, col. 2; 87, cols. 1–2.
103. The categories used to describe information serve to identify "batches" of phenomena and thus to frame comparisons both within and between the batches. Suppose you have a heavy steel hoe with a five-foot handle. Do you think of it as big or small? It is a big *garden tool* but a small *piece of farm equipment.*
104. P. 72, col. 1 (emphasis added).
105. P. 77, col. 1 (emphasis added).
106. Pp. 86, col. 2 – 87, col. 1 (emphasis added).
107. P. 87, col. 2 (emphasis added).
108. P. 88, col. 1 (emphasis added).
109. P. 76, col. 1 (emphasis added). The phrase "the State's request for a determination of partial unitary status" conceals another categorization. Missouri never made a motion for a declaration of partial unitary status in the district court following the procedures set forth in *Freeman v. Pitts.* (This is why the district court made no explicit findings on various issues and why the court of appeals had to "extrapolate" the district court's conclusions.) The State simply quoted *Freeman*'s legal reasoning in opposing the district court's proposed remedial orders; it did not seek a hearing on the facts relevant to the application of *Freeman*'s reasoning to the *Jenkins* case. Cf. p. 76, col. 1: The court of appeals "concluded that the District Court implicitly had rejected the State's *Freeman* arguments in spite of the fact that it had *failed 'to articulate . . . even a conclusory rejection'* of them" (emphasis added).
110. See Arthur Conan Doyle, "Silver Blaze," in Patricia Craig (Ed.), *The Oxford Book of English Detective Stories,* Oxford and New York: Oxford University Press, 1990, pp. 6–28, at p. 22:
    "Is there any other point to which you would wish to draw my attention?"

"To the curious incident of the dog in the night-time."

"The dog did nothing in the night-time."

"That was the curious incident," remarked Sherlock Holmes.

111. P. 79, col. 2.

112. Pp. 80, col. 1; 81, col. 1; 87, col. 1.

113. "[E]ducation . . . is the very foundation of good citizenship. Today it is a principal instrument in awakening the child to cultural values, in preparing him for later professional training, and in helping him to adjust normally to his environment. In these days, it is doubtful that any child may reasonably be expected to succeed in life if he is denied the opportunity of an education. Such an opportunity, where the state has undertaken to provide it, is a right which must be made available to all on equal terms." *Brown v. Board of Education,* 347 U.S. 483, 493 (1954).

114. Id. at 494.

3B. Categorizing at the Supreme Court: *Michael H. v. Gerald D.*

1. 491 U.S. 110, 105 L.Ed.2d 91, 109 S. Ct. 2333.

2. See, e.g., Vladimir Propp, *Morphology of the Folktale* (1928), 2d edition, Laurence Scott trans., Austin: University of Texas Press, 1990. Propp proposed that all folktales have a common structure consisting of an identical sequence of operative moves ("functions").

3. A guardian *ad litem* is a person appointed by a court to protect the interests of an immature child (or other legally incompetent individual) involved in a lawsuit. For the duration of the suit, the guardian *ad litem* is responsible for performing on the child's behalf all functions that a competent adult litigant would perform for himself or herself—deciding what goals to pursue in the litigation, retaining and instructing legal counsel, and so forth.

4. A motion for summary judgment is filed before trial and asks the court to decide the case in favor of the moving party without taking evidence because there is no genuine issue of material fact to be tried and the moving party is entitled to a favorable decision as a matter of law.

5. Section 621(a) of the California Evidence Code (West Supp. 1989), as set out in 491 U.S. at 117.

6. As Justice Stevens read the record, the California courts had not held that Michael's visitation rights were extinguished *ipso facto* by the statutory bar to his claim of paternity; rather, they had denied him visitation on the ground that his continuing relationship with Victoria was not in the child's best interests. 491 U.S. at 136.

7. Id. at 113. Again, we hope that our readers will examine the text for themselves and test our analyses against their own reading. The opinion in *Michael H. v. Gerald D.* is available electronically and in three printed sources: volume 491 of the United States Reports, beginning at page 110; volume 105 of the Lawyer's Edition of the United States Supreme Court Reports,

Second Series, beginning at page 91; and volume 109 of the Supreme Court Reporter, beginning at page 2333. All of these versions display the U.S. Reports page numbers, which we will cite.

8. 491 U.S. at 113.

9. Id. at 117.

10. Id. at 118.

11. See, e.g., *Shelton v. Tucker*, 364 U.S. 479 (1960); *Griswold v. Connecticut*, 381 U.S. 479 (1965); *Papachristou v. City of Jacksonville*, 405 U.S. 156 (1972); *Globe Newspaper Co. v. Superior Court*, 457 U.S. 596 (1982).

12. See, e.g., *Meyer v. Nebraska*, 262 U.S. 390 (1923); *Pierce v. Society of Sisters*, 268 U.S. 510 (1925); *Wisconsin v. Yoder*, 406 U.S. 205 (1972).

13. 491 U.S. at 130.

14. Id. at 123 and n. 3.

15. See, e.g., Otto Rank, "The Myth of the Birth of the Hero" (1909), in *In Quest of the Hero*, Princeton: Princeton University Press, 1990, pp. 1–86; Alan Dundes, "The Hero Pattern and the Life of Jesus," in id., pp. 177–223; Lord Raglan, *The Hero: A Study in Tradition, Myth, and Drama*, London: Watts, 1949; Joseph Campbell, *The Hero with a Thousand Faces* (1949; 2d edition 1968), Princeton: Princeton University Press, 1973, pp. 318–334.

16. Edward F. Edinger, *The Eternal Drama: The Inner Meaning of Greek Mythology*, Boston and London: Shambhala, 1994, p. 54.

17. "The facts of this case are, we must hope, extraordinary." 491 U.S. at 113.

18. "[T]he surest and swiftest way to overcome our moral problems in America is by strengthening the family." Stephen Moore (Ed.), *Restoring the Dream: The Bold New Plan by House Republicans*, New York: Times Books, 1995, p. 192. "Families *are* the basis of our society. We *must* support the unified model of father, mother, and child." Dan Quayle and Diane Medved, *The American Family: Discovering the Values That Make Us Strong*, New York: HarperCollins, 1996, p. 2. Compare 491 U.S. at 123: "As we view [the precedents] . . ., they rest . . . upon the historic respect—indeed, sanctity would not be too strong a term—traditionally accorded to the relationships that develop within the unitary family."

19. See id. at 123 n. 3: "The family unit accorded traditional respect in our society, which we have referred to as the 'unitary family,' is typified, of course, by the marital family, but also includes the household of unmarried parents and their children. Perhaps the concept can be expanded even beyond this, but it will bear no resemblance to traditionally respected relationships—and will thus cease to have any constitutional significance—if it is stretched so far as to include the relationship [of Michael, Carole, and Victoria]."

20. See, e.g., Gerda Lerner, *The Creation of Patriarchy*, New York and Oxford: Oxford University Press, 1986; Martha Albertson Fineman, *The Neutered Mother, The Sexual Family, and Other Twentieth Century Tragedies*, New York: Routledge, 1995, pp. 101–176; Helen Hardacre, "The Impact of Fundamentalisms on Women, the Family, and Interpersonal Relations," in

Martin E. Marty and R. Scott Appleby (Eds.), *Fundamentalisms and Society: Reclaiming the Sciences, The Family, and Education,* Chicago and London: University of Chicago Press, 1993, pp. 129–150; Linda C. McClain, "'Irresponsible' Reproduction," *Hastings Law Journal,* 1996, 47, 339–453, particularly at pp. 385–395. The point goes beyond gender roles. In *Michael H.,* Justice Scalia configures a universe in which *conformity* and *nonconformity* appear as antipodal, inescapably conflicting elementals. 491 U.S. at 130. In such a universe, the effect of insisting that an "asserted liberty interest be rooted in history and tradition" in order to receive constitutional protection (id. at 123; see also, e.g., id. at 124, 127–128 n. 6, 131) is to make Due Process a bulwark of inherited hegemonies. Justice Scalia says this plainly in 491 U.S. at 122 n. 2: The "purpose [of the Due Process Clause] is to prevent future generations from lightly casting aside important traditional values—not to enable this Court to invent new ones."

21. See, e.g., Tony Tanner, *Adultery in the Novel: Contract and Transgression,* Baltimore: Johns Hopkins University Press, 1979. Tanner suggests that "adultery . . . forebodes the breaking of other bonds to the point of social disintegration." Id. at p. 39; see id. at pp. 85–86. This theme—reflected in stories as diverse as those of Paris and Helen (see, e.g., Euripides, *Hecuba,* particularly lines 629–650; and see Chapter 5, Part V, *Prigg*), Tennyson's *Idylls of the King,* and the Hausa folktale "The Old Woman," in Milton Rugoff (Ed.), *A Harvest of World Folk Tales,* New York: Viking Press, 1949, pp. 4–25—reinforces the specifically Euro-American view that because "marriage assures order in sexual matters, the proper inheritance of property, and the perpetuation of civilized behavior, . . . adultery must be judged a threat to both individual security and universal stability. Violate the bedroom and society wavers. Commit adultery and the great chain of being breaks a link." Donald J. Greiner, *Adultery in the American Novel: Updike, James, and Hawthorne,* Columbia: University of South Carolina Press, 1985, p. 122.

22. Early Christianity inherited a Roman tradition of symbolizing "the all-important social and political virtue of *concordia*" by "the domestic concord associated with the nuclear family" (Peter Brown, *The Body and Society: Men, Women and Sexual Renunciation in Early Christianity,* New York: Columbia University Press, 1988, p. 16) and expanded the symbol to express "the primal solidarity brought back by Christ to the universe and to the church" (id. at p. 57). It also inherited the tradition of the prophets, in which the most common metaphors for apostasy were adultery (e.g., Hosea 2:2, 2:7, 3:1, 4:13–4:14, 7:4; Jeremiah 3:1–3:20, 5:7–5:8, 9:2, 13:27, 23:10, 23:14; Ezekiel 16:32, 16:38, 23:37–23:45), whoring and harlotry (e.g., Hosea 1:2, 2:2–2:5, 3:3, 4:10–4:18, 5:3–5:4, 6:10, 9:1; Jeremiah 2:20, 3:1–3:9, 5:7, 13:27; Ezekiel 6:9, 16:15–16:41, 20:30, 23:3–23:44, 43:7–43:9), taking lovers (e.g., Hosea 2:5–2:13, 8:9; Jeremiah 2:25, 2:33, 3:1,

4:30; Ezekiel 16:33–16:37, 23:5–23:22), and lewdness (e.g., Hosea 6:9; Jeremiah 11:15, 13:27; Ezekiel 16:58, 22:9, 23:21–23:49, 24:13).

23. Propp, note 2 above, at pp. 30, 35 (functions VIII and VIIIa). Some tales, Propp found, are propelled by the external infliction of a misfortune calling for redress ("villainy"); others, by an insufficiency "realized from within" (id. at p. 35), calling for repletion ("lack"). There is a correlation, though not an exact correspondence, between these two precipitators and the positions toward adultery that Alison Sinclair identifies with the two stereotypical portrayals of the deceived husband: man of honor (villainy) and cuckold (lack). Alison Sinclair, *The Deceived Husband: A Kleinian Approach to the Literature of Infidelity,* Oxford: Oxford University Press, Clarendon Press, 1993.

24. Alfred Lord Tennyson, *Idylls of the King* (1885), "The Last Tournament," line 568. See D. H. Lawrence, *Lady Chatterley's Lover;* Sir Thomas Malory, *Le Morte D'Arthur* (1485 Caxton Text), book VIII, chap.1 – book XIX, chap. 11]; and, e.g., Edgar Allen Poe, "The Assignation"; Thomas Mann, "Little Lizzie," in *Stories of Three Decades,* H. T. Lowe-Porter trans., New York: Knopf, 1955, pp. 58–70; Tennessee Williams, *Baby Doll: The Script for the Film,* New York: New Directions, 1956. In comic genres, the stock situation is old-husband/young-wife: e.g., Giovanni Boccaccio, *The Decameron,* second day, tenth story; Geoffrey Chaucer, *The Canterbury Tales,* "The Miller's Tale," "The Merchant's Tale."

25. E.g., Charles Nodier, "Trilby" (1822), in *Smarra and Trilby,* Judith Landry trans., Sawtry: Dedalus, 1993, pp. 65–125; Nathaniel Hawthorne, *The Scarlet Letter;* Gustave Flaubert, *Madame Bovary;* Leo Tolstoy, *Anna Karenina;* Thomas Hardy, *Jude the Obscure;* Richard Kluger, *The Sheriff of Nottingham,* New York: Viking, 1992. Comic and erotic treatments of adultery, such as those in Boccaccio and the *fabliaux,* add a third variant of "lack": the marital couple's fixation on monogamy is itself an unnatural and unstable fanaticism riding for a fall. See, e.g., Boccaccio, *The Decameron,* third day, fifth and sixth stories.

26. Concerning Tristan and Iseult, see, e.g., Beroul, *The Romance of Tristan,* Alan S. Fedrick trans., London: Penguin Books, 1970; Gottfried von Strassburg, *Tristan (with The "Tristan" of Thomas),* revised edition, A. T. Hatto trans., London: Penguin Books, 1967; Sir Thomas Malory, *Le Morte D'Arthur;* Matthew Arnold, "Tristram and Iseult," in *The Poems of Matthew Arnold,* London and New York: Oxford University Press, 1913, pp. 139–161. Cf. "The Pursuit of Diarmuid and Grainne," in Tom Peete Cross and Clark Harris Slover, *Ancient Irish Tales,* New York: Barnes and Noble, 1996, pp. 370–421. Matty Grove is the common American form of the British Little Musgrave ballad. See, e.g., "Little Musgrave and Lady Barnard," in Francis James Child (Ed.), *The English and Scottish Popular Ballads* (1882–1898), New York: Cooper Square Publishers, 1965, volume

II, pp. 242–260 [Ballad no. 81]; and in Phillips Barry, Fannie Hardy Eckstorm, and Mary Winslow Smyth, *British Ballads from Maine: The Development of Popular Songs,* New Haven: Yale University Press, 1929, pp. 150–194.

27. Nathaniel Hawthorne, *The Scarlet Letter* (1850), New York: Signet Classics, 1980, p. 237. See, e.g., Judith Armstrong, *The Novel of Adultery,* New York: Barnes and Noble, 1976; Birute Ciplijauskaite, *La Mujer Insatisfecha: El Adulterio en la Novela Realista,* Barcelona: Edhasa, 1984.

28. See, e.g., Homer, *The Odyssey,* book III, lines 247–310; book XI, lines 385–456; Aeschylus, *The Choephori;* Sophocles, *Electra;* Seneca, *Agamemnon.*

29. Like that of Claudius in Shakespeare's *Hamlet.* E.g., "James Harris (The Demon Lover; The House Carpenter)," in Albert B. Friedman (Ed.), *The Viking Book of Folk Ballads of the English-Speaking World,* New York: Penguin Books, 1982, pp. 13–17; Child, note 26 above, volume IV, pp. 360–369 [Ballad no. 243]; Barry, Eckstorm and Smyth, note 26 above, pp. 304–310; "Koshchey the Deathless," in Aleksandr Afanas'ev (Coll.), *Russian Fairy Tales,* Norbert Guterman trans., New York: Pantheon Books, 1973, pp. 485–494; "The Magic Lamp," in *Classic Folk Tales from Around the World,* with an introduction by Robert Nye, London: Bracken Books, 1994, pp. 420–423, and other versions of tale type 561 in Antti Aarne, *The Types of the Folktale: A Classification and Bibliography,* 2d revision, Stith Thompson trans., Helsinki: Suomalainen Tiedeakatemia, 1964 [FF Communications No. 184], p. 204; "The Stolen Wife," in Richard Erdoes and Alfonso Ortiz (Eds.), *American Indian Myths and Legends,* New York: Pantheon Books, 1984, pp. 285–290; "The Little Finger," in Terri Hardin (Ed.), *A Treasury of American Folklore: Our Customs, Beliefs, and Traditions,* New York: Barnes and Noble, 1994, pp. 171–174; Francis Beaumont and John Fletcher, *The Maid's Tragedy;* George Chapman, *Bussy D'Ambois;* Alain Rene Le Sage, *The Bachelor of Salamanca;* Heinrich von Kleist, "The Foundling," in *The Marquise of O and Other Stories,* Martin Greenberg trans., New York: Criterion Books, 1960, pp. 229–247; Ramon del Valle-Inclan, "Sacrilege," in *Savage Acts: Four Plays,* Robert Lima trans., University Park, Pa.: Estreno, 1993, pp. 49–61; Francis Marion Crawford, "The Dead Smile," in Peter Haining (Ed.), *Irish Tales of Terror,* New York: Wings Books, 1995, pp. 202–228; G. K. Chesterton, "The Hammer of God," in *Mysteries: A Classic Collection,* with an introduction by Giles Gordon, London: Bracken Books, 1994, pp. 86–101; A. E. Coppard, "The Tiger," in id., pp. 140–149; Erskine Caldwell, *God's Little Acre,* New York: Modern Library, 1935; John O'Hara, "The Last of Haley" (1947), in *The Time Element and Other Stories,* New York: Random House, 1972, pp. 59–66; Tennessee Williams, *Orpheus Descending;* David Goodis, "Black Pudding," in Bill Pronzini and Jack Adrian (Eds.), *Hard-Boiled: An Anthology of American Crime Stories,* Oxford and New York: Oxford University Press, 1995, pp. 277–300; Michael Seidman, "Perchance to Dream," in Edward

Gorman (Ed.), *The Black Lizard Anthology of Crime Fiction,* Berkeley: Black Lizard Books, 1987, pp. 229–246; Patrick McGrath, "Blood Disease," in Chris Baldick (Ed.), *The Oxford Book of Gothic Tales,* Oxford and New York: Oxford University Press, 1992, pp. 502–518; David Drake, "The Tank Lords," in *The Military Dimension: Mark II,* Riverdale, N.Y.: Baen, 1995, pp. 217–272; Ray Bradbury, "The Electrocution," in *Quicker Than the Eye,* New York: Avon Books, 1997, pp. 55–63; the film *Ryan's Daughter* (MGM, 1970), screenplay by Robert Bolt, directed by David Lean. A homiletic version is Mason L. Weems, "God's Revenge Against Adultery" (1815), in *Three Discourses: Hymen's Recruiting Sergeant; The Drunkard's Looking Glass; God's Revenge Against Adultery,* New York: Random House, 1929, pp. 137–189, at pp. 145–166. Sanitized children's versions include "The Witch and Her Servants," in Andrew Lang (Ed.), *The Yellow Fairy Book,* New York: Dover, 1966, pp. 161–177, and "The Witch in the Stone Boat," in id., pp. 274–278. Walter Crane created a paragon of the species when he rewrote Mme. D'Aulnoy's *Le nain jaune* to conform to "the fate the wicked should expect in a fairy tale" (Iona and Peter Opie, *The Classic Fairy Tales* (1974), Oxford and New York: Oxford University Press, 1993, p. 67): the Demon Lover dies spitted on the True Bridegroom's sword. Walter Crane, illust., *The Yellow Dwarf* (1875). See Marina Warner, *From the Beast to the Blonde: On Fairy Tales and Their Tellers,* New York: Farrar, Straus, 1994, p. 253.

The crimes and punishments of Don Juan are akin to those of the Demon Lover but more complex. See, e.g., Otto Rank, *The Don Juan Legend,* David G. Winter trans., Princeton: Princeton University Press, 1975; James Mandrell, *Don Juan and the Point of Honor: Seduction, Patriarchal Society, and Literary Tradition,* University Park, Pa.: Pennsylvania State University Press, 1992; Jonathan Miller (Ed.), *Don Giovanni: Myths of Seduction and Betrayal,* Baltimore: Johns Hopkins University Press, 1991; Charles C. Russell, *The Don Juan Legend Before Mozart (With a Collection of Eighteenth Century Opera Librettos),* Ann Arbor: University of Michigan Press, 1993. The generic Demon Lover is sometimes portrayed not simply as a type but as a caste: see, e.g., Guy De Maupassant, "A Warning Note," in *Short Stories of the Tragedy and Comedy of Life,* Akron, Ohio: St. Dunstan Society, 1903, volume V, pp. 165–174; and the caste may be defined ethnically: see Calvin C. Hernton, *Sex and Racism in America,* New York: Grove Press, 1965; Winthrop D. Jordan, *White Over Black: American Attitudes Toward the Negro, 1550–1812,* New York: W. W. Norton, 1977, particularly at pp. 32–43, 150–167, 429–582; Joel Williamson, *The Crucible of Race: Black-White Relations in the American South Since Emancipation,* New York and Oxford: Oxford University Press 1984, particularly at pp. 111–135, 169–179, 306–310. (In American culture, the attribution of super-sexuality and super-lust to African-Americans now takes indirect and evocative forms, see, e.g., the film *Mandingo* (Dino De Laurentiis, 1975), book by Kyle Onstott, screenplay by Norman Wexler, directed by Richard Fleischer, more often than the traditional direct and deadpan assertions that "[t]he most distinguishing feature or characteristic of the native African, or negro, is his beastly sexual passions, which are totally uncurbed," William Patrick Calhoun, *The Caucasian and the Negro in the United States* (1902), New York: Arno Press, 1977, p. 8, and that "[t]he negro man . . . covets above all things his neighbor's maiden and his neighbor's wife," id. at p. 25; but the premise is unchanged.)

Or the wife may be made the villain. E.g., "Husband and Wife," in Afanas'ev, above, pp. 369–370; "The Peddler," in De Maupassant, above, volume V, pp. 45–55; "The Tailor's Daughter," in id., volume V, pp. 99–116; Ernest Hemingway, "The Short Happy Life of Francis Macomber," in *The Short Stories of Ernest Hemingway,* New York: Modern Library, 1938, pp. 102–136. Female villainy needs no motivation because the misogynous tradition holds that wives are naturally adulterous, e.g., R. Howard Bloch, *Medieval Misogyny and the Invention of Western Romantic Love,* Chicago and London: University of Chicago Press, 1991, particularly at pp. 13–22: "Woman, formed of flesh from the rib, remains bound by the corporeal." Id. at p. 29. See, e.g., Alexander Pope, *Moral Essays,* Epistle I, line 215 (1735); "An Adventure in Paris," in De Maupassant, above, volume IV, pp. 256–265; "Was It a Dream," in id., volume III, pp. 122–128; Husain Haddawy (Trans.), *The Arabian Nights,* New York and London: W. W. Norton, 1990, pp. 3–11 [*Prologue*].

Combinations of Villain Wife and Demon Lover produce picaresque and ironic forms. See, e.g., William Wycherley, *The Country Wife;* Arthur Conan Doyle, "The Case of Lady Sannox," in Frank D. McSherry, Martin H. Greenberg, and Charles G. Waugh (Eds.), *The Best Horror Stories of Arthur Conan Doyle,* Chicago: Academy, 1989, pp. 31–43; James M. Cain, *The Postman Always Rings Twice* (1934), New York: Vintage Books, 1992; Gabriel Garcia Marquez, *Of Love and Other Demons,* Edith Grossman trans., New York: Knopf, 1995, pp. 21–47; Karel Capek, "Proof Positive," in *Tales from Two Pockets,* Norma Comrada trans., North Haven, Conn.: Catbird Press, 1994, pp. 48–53; Cornell Woolrich, "The Corpse and the Kid," in Peter Haining (Ed.), *Great Tales of Horror,* Secaucus, N.J.: Chartwell Books, 1993, pp. 27–49; James Hannah, "Junior Jackson's Parable," in Pronzini and Adrian, above, pp. 460–473. The power of the stock plots is attested by the surprise effects achieved through subverting their expected denouement. See, e.g., "Bel Ami, or The History of a Scoundrel," in De Maupassant, above, volume VII, pp. 1–212; William Faulkner, "A Dangerous Man," in Joseph Blotner (Ed.), *Uncollected Stories of William Faulkner,* New York, Random House, 1979, pp. 575–582; Joyce Carol Oates, "Dying," in *Upon the Sweeping Flood and Other Stories,* Greenwich, Conn.: Fawcett Crest, 1972, pp. 165–185.

30. We use "eschatological" to refer to a belief that the present world order will

be replaced or radically perfected at a moment in future history. It is not, of course, unique or original to Christianity. See, e.g., Norman Cohn, *Cosmos, Chaos and the World to Come: The Ancient Roots of Apocalyptic Faith,* New Haven and London: Yale University Press, 1993. But Christian versions have been popular in the United States since colonial times, see, e.g., Robert C. Fuller, *Naming the Antichrist: The History of an American Obsession,* New York and Oxford: Oxford University Press, 1995, and were rife in the 1980s, see, e.g., Susan Harding, "Imagining the Last Days: The Politics of Apocalyptic Language," in Martin E. Marty and R. Scott Appleby (Eds.), *Accounting for Fundamentalisms: The Dynamic Character of Movements,* Chicago and London: University of Chicago Press, 1994, pp. 57–78.

31. See, e.g., Saint Augustine's *Enchiridion, or Manual to Laurentius Concerning Faith, Hope, and Charity,* chaps. 10–13.

32. See, e.g., Origen's *De Principiis,* book I, chaps. 5,3 – 5,5.

33. See, e.g., Jeffrey Burton Russell, *Satan: The Early Christian Tradition,* Ithaca, N.Y.: Cornell University Press, 1981; Jeffrey Burton Russell, *Lucifer: The Devil in the Middle Ages,* Ithaca, N.Y.: Cornell University Press, 1984; Fernando Cervantes, *The Devil in the New World: The Impact of Diabolism in New Spain,* New Haven and London: Yale University Press, 1994; Paul Ricoeur, "'Original Sin': A Study in Meaning," in *The Conflict of Interpretations: Essays in Hermeneutics,* Peter McCormick trans., Evanston, Ill.: Northwestern University Press, 1988, pp. 269–286; Andrew Delbanco, *The Death of Satan: How Americans Have Lost The Sense of Evil,* New York: Farrar, Straus (Noonday), 1996, particularly at pp. 46–51, 133–135, 175, 183–186, 197, 229–235. Origen came to grief and Augustine to grandeur trying to refute the gnostics' and the Manichaeans' versions of the first scenario without quite embracing the second. Proximity to one scenario or the other implicates one's view of Satan's domain—whether, as Robert Grant has put it succinctly, Satan rules this Age or this World. Robert M. Grant, *Gnosticism and Early Christianity,* New York: Columbia University Press, 1959, pp. 175–177.

34. Elaine Pagels, *The Origin of Satan,* New York: Random House, 1995, p. 37. See also Fuller, note 30 above; Sander L. Gilman, *Difference and Pathology: The Stereotypes of Sexuality, Race, and Madness,* Ithaca, N.Y.: Cornell University Press, 1985; Simone De Beauvoir, *The Second Sex,* H. M. Parshley trans., New York: Vintage Books, 1989, pp. xxii–xxviii; Norman Cohn, *Europe's Inner Demons: An Enquiry Inspired by the Great Witch-Hunt,* New York: Basic Books, 1975; R. Po-Chia Hsia, *The Myth of Ritual Murder: Jews and Magic in Reformation Germany,* New Haven and London: Yale University Press, 1988, p. 40 (ritual murder beliefs "created a more meaningful, coherent, alternative explanative model, that argued for the dialectical opposition between the two binary opposites of Jew/ murderer/magician and Christian/victim/ believer, between black, demonic

magic and life-giving, godly religion"); Daniel Jonah Goldhagen, *Hitler's Willing Executioners: Ordinary Germans and the Holocaust*, New York: Vintage Books, 1997, pp. 50–78.

35. Pagels, note 34 above, at p. 47.

36. Id. at p. 79.

37. Id. at p. 87.

38. Id. at p. 105; see, e.g., id. at pp. 149–178; Fuller, note 30 above. Cf. René Girard, "Generative Scapegoating," in Walter Burkert, René Girard, and Jonathan Z. Smith, *Violent Origins: Ritual Killing and Cultural Formation*, Robert G. Hammerton-Kelly (Ed.), Stanford: Stanford University Press, 1987, pp. 73–105, particularly at p. 90.

39. For example, Stephen King's *The Stand* was first published in 1978; Terry Brooks's original *Shannara* trilogy appeared between 1977 and 1985; Robert Jordan began to spin *The Wheel of Time* in 1990; the movie version of *The Omen* appeared in 1976, its third sequel in 1991.

40. Ronald Reagan, Remarks at the Annual Convention of the National Association of Evangelicals in Orlando, Florida, March 8, 1983, in *Public Papers of the Presidents: Ronald Reagan, 1983 – Book I*, Washington: G.P.O., 1984, pp. 359–364, at p. 364. We thank Simon Kinberg for insights and research leads into the rhetoric of the Reagan years.

41. President Reagan's 1984 State of the Union Address, January 25, 1984, quoted in John Kenneth White, *The New Politics of Old Values*, 2d edition, Hanover, N.H.: University Press of New England, 1990, p. 61. See also id. at pp. 60–61, 147, 151, 171. Reagan both knew his public and rallied it. During the 1980s, America's favorite TV series (*The Cosby Show*, *Family Ties* and other "warmedies") idealized the traditional marital family; audiences flocked to the box office to watch an adulterous threat to that family vilified and punished by death in *Fatal Attraction* (William J. Palmer, *The Films of the Eighties: A Social History*, Carbondale, Ill.: Southern Illinois University Press, 1993, pp. 264–265); and they flocked to the box office repeatedly to see a "new species of disaster film" featuring "the terrorist" as "[t]he new villain of the eighties" (id. at p. 114), the embodiment and symbol of "three paranoiac aspects of late-twentieth-century life—universal anxiety, the illusion of safety, [and] the fear of destabilization" (id. at p. 117). Fredric Jameson has perceived in all this an evolution of "that boring and exhausted paradigm, the gothic, where . . . a sheltered woman of some kind is terrorized and victimized by an 'evil' male"—"a class fantasy (or nightmare) in which . . . your privileges seal you off from other people, but by the same token they constitute a protective wall through which you cannot see, and behind which therefore all kinds of envious forces may be imagined in the process of assembling, plotting, preparing to give assault"—into a modern guise in which the individual victim is replaced by "the collectivity itself, the U.S. public, which now lives out the anxieties of its economic privileges and its sheltered 'exceptionalism' in a pseudo-politi-

cal version of the gothic—under the threats of stereotypical madmen and 'terrorists.' . . . And like the private version of the traditional gothic romance, they depend for their effects on the revitalization of *ethics* as a set of mental categories, and on the reinflation and artificial reinvigoration of that tired and antiquated binary opposition between virtue and vice, which the eighteenth century cleansed of its theological remnants and thoroughly sexualized before passing it on down to us.

"The modern gothic, in other words . . . depends absolutely in its central operation on the construction of *evil*. . . . Evil is here, however, the emptiest form of sheer Otherness (into which any type of social content can be poured at will)." Fredric Jameson, *Postmodernism, or, The Cultural Logic of Late Capitalism,* Durham: Duke University Press, 1991, pp. 289–290. Cf. Richard Tithecott, *Of Men and Monsters: Jeffrey Dahmer and the Construction of the Serial Killer,* Madison: University of Wisconsin Press, 1997, pp. 53–55 ("Perhaps above all, middle America sees itself as *domestic.* Harold Schechter suggests that the serial killer represents 'the savage force roaming in the dark, as the nuclear family huddles terrified inside the home,'" id. at p. 53); and see Tithecott's discussion of the image of the serial killer as the ultimate Evil Other, at, e.g., pp. 17–64, 136–150. See also Mark Edmundson, *Nightmare on Main Street: Angels, Sadomasochism, and the Culture of Gothic,* Cambridge, Mass.: Harvard University Press, 1997; Marina Warner, *No Go the Bogeyman: Scaring, Lulling, and Making Mock,* New York: Farrar, Straus, and Giroux, 1999, pp. 258–261, 382–387.

42. 1980 Republican National Platform, quoted in White, note 41 above, at p. 50. Compare Jerry Falwell's *1980 Bible Prophecy Update,* quoted by Harding, note 30 above, at p. 70: "Is there hope for our country? I think so. I believe as we trust in God and pray, as we Christians lead the battle to outlaw abortion, which is murder on demand, as we take our stand against pornography, against the drug traffic, as we take our stand against the breakdown of the traditional family in America, the promotion of homosexual marriages, as we stand up for strong national defense so that this country can survive and our children and our children's children will know the America we've known."

43. Cf. Fuller, note 30 above, at pp. 108–190. The politics of "family values" was in part a reaction against a major revolution in the nature and function of the family in Euro-American culture, a denial of the trouble perceived as lurking behind such phenomena as the increasing incidence or visibility of working mothers, divorce, legalized abortion, and overt homosexuality. See, e.g., Hardacre, note 20 above; Arlene Skolnick, "State of the Debate—Family Values: The Sequel," *The American Prospect,* May-June 1997, *32,* 86–94. Cf. George Lakoff, *Moral Politics: What Conservatives Know That Liberals Don't,* Chicago and London: University of Chicago Press, 1996.

44. Neil Forsyth, *The Old Enemy: Satan and the Combat Myth,* Princeton: Princeton University Press, 1987.

45. See note 2 above.

46. Forsyth, note 44 above, at pp. 448–451. See also Robert Mondi, "Greek Mythic Thought in the Light of the Near East," in Lowell Edmunds (Ed.), *Approaches to Greek Myth,* Baltimore and London: Johns Hopkins University Press, 1990, pp. 141–198, at pp. 177–187. The sequence remains constant in late twentieth-century desacralized versions of the cosmic combat myth such as Stephen King, *The Stand* (1978), New York: Signet, 1991.

47. Regarding Mark, Iseult, and Tristan, see the sources in notes 24 and 26 above and, e.g., Algernon Charles Swinburne, "Tristram of Lyonesse," in *The Poems of Algernon Charles Swinburne,* London: Chatto, 1911, volume IV, pp. 1–151; Edwin Arlington Robinson, *Tristram* (1927). Regarding Arthur, Guinevere and Lancelot, see, e.g., "Le Morte Arthur," in *King Arthur's Death (Morte Arthure and Le Morte Arthur),* Brian Stone trans., London: Penguin Books, 1988, pp. 183–313; Sir Thomas Malory, *Le Morte D'Arthur* (1485 Caxton Text); Tennyson, *Idylls of the King* (1885); Marion Zimmer Bradley, *The Mists of Avalon,* New York: Knopf, 1982; Parke Godwin, *Firelord* (1980), New York: Avon Books (AvonNova), 1994, and *Beloved Exile* (1984), New York: Avon Books (AvonNova), 1994; John Masefield, "The Death of Lancelot as Told by Gwenivere" (1928), in Alan Lupack (Ed.), *Modern Arthurian Literature: An Anthology of English and American Arthuriana from the Renaissance to the Present,* New York and London: Garland, 1992, pp. 443–445; Jane Yolen, "The Quiet Monk," in Mike Ashley (Ed.), *The Camelot Chronicles,* New York: Carroll and Graf, 1992, pp. 380–392.

48. See Roger Sherman Loomis, *Arthurian Tradition and Chrétien de Troyes,* New York: Columbia University Press, 1952, pp. 198–204, 214–222, 237–250, 262–266; John Matthews, *Taliesin: Shamanism and the Bardic Mysteries in Britain and Ireland,* London: Aquarian, 1991, pp. 272–273. The motif (number 322.2 in Tom Peete Cross, *Motif-Index of Early Irish Literature,* Bloomington: University of Indiana Press, 1952, p. 260) receives a wide range of treatments in Celtic myth and folktales. Compare "The Wooing of Etain," in Cross and Slover, note 26 above, at pp. 82–92, with "Cormac's Adventures in the Land of Promise," in id. at pp. 503–507, and "Young Conall of Howth," in Sean O'Sullivan (Ed.), *Folktales of Ireland,* Chicago and London: University of Chicago Press, 1968, pp. 79–97, at pp. 84–95. Cf. motifs F320 – F327* in Cross, above, at 259–260; motifs R0 – R151.3* in id. at 464–467; Stith Thompson, *Motif-Index of Folk-Literature,* Bloomington: University of Indiana Press, 1956–1957, volume 3 (1956), pp. 63–64 [Motifs F322 – F322.5], volume 4 (1957), pp. 381–395 [Motifs K1300 – K1399.5], volume 5 (1957), pp. 268–287 [Motifs R0 – R191]; Aarne, note 29 above, pp. 90–93 [Tale types 301 – 301D].

49. See Loomis, note 48 above; Jean Frappier, "Chrétien de Troyes," in Roger Sherman Loomis (Ed.), *Arthurian Literature in the Middle Ages: A Collaborative History,* Oxford: Oxford University Press, 1959, pp. 157–191, at

pp. 177–178; Patrick Sims-Williams, "The Early Welsh Arthurian Poems," in Rachel Bromwich, A. O. H. Jarman, and Brynley F. Roberts (Eds.), *The Arthur of the Welsh: The Arthurian Legend in Medieval Welsh Literature,* Cardiff: University of Wales Press, 1991, pp. 33–71, at pp. 58–61; Brynley F. Roberts, "Culhwch Ac Olwen, The Triads, Saints' Lives," in id., pp. 73–95, at p. 83; Rachel Bromwich, "First Transmission to England and France," in id., pp. 273–298, at p. 278. Like other Demon Lover figures (see Warner, note 29 above, at pp. 241–271, and, e.g., "The Incubus," in Rugoff, note 21 above, at pp. 592–595), the Otherworld Ravisher is an equivocal type: it is the very irresistibility of his appeal as "the supernatural lover—the beautiful Gandharva—who interferes with marriages" (Alwyn Rees and Brinley Rees, *Celtic Heritage: Ancient Tradition in Ireland and Wales* (1961), London: Thames and Hudson, 1994, p. 293; see generally id. at pp. 259–296) that inspires the ferocity with which he is condemned and cast out.

50. Chrétien de Troyes, "The Knight of the Cart," in *Arthurian Romances,* William W. Kibler trans., London: Penguin Books, 1991, pp. 207–294. Concerning Melwas, see the sources in note 49 above. The identification of Melwas's stronghold, Glastonbury, with the Isle of Glass (see Loomis, note 48 above, at pp. 30–31, 89 n. 21, 214–217) resonates with the Otherworld Fortress of Glass in Taliesin (see Matthews, note 48 above, at pp. 251–253).

51. Sir Thomas Malory, *Le Morte D'Arthur* (1485 Caxton Text), book XIX, chaps. 1–9.

52. Id., book V, chap. 5.

53. "Morte Arthure," in *King Arthur's Death,* note 47 above, pp. 33–168, at pp. 141–168. In this account, Mordred seizes queen and crown at the height of Arthur's victories on the continent. Compare Malory, note 51 above, books XX–XXI, where Mordred's moves—unsuccessful as to the queen—are made while Arthur is besieging Lancelot after the revelation of Lancelot and Guinevere's relationship. (The Mordred in *Morte Arthure* is the same "Modred" who, in other Arthurian tales, is Arthur's nephew or son-and-nephew by incest with Morgan le Fay.)

54. Chrétien de Troyes, note 50 above, at pp. 207–294.

55. See "Morte Arthure," in *King Arthur's Death,* note 47 above, pp. 33–168, at pp. 59–71.

56. See Snorri Sturluson, *Edda,* Anthony Faulkes trans., London: Dent (Everyman's Library), 1992, pp. 59–60, 86–88.

57. See Livy, *The Early History of Rome* [*The History of Rome from Its Foundation, Books I–V*], book I, chaps. 57–60; Ovid, *Fasti,* book II, lines 717–852; Chaucer, *The Legend of Good Women,* "The Legend of Lucrece"; William Shakespeare, *The Rape of Lucrece.*

58. See, e.g., "The Wooing of Etain," note 48 above; "Maria Morevna," in Afanas'ev, note 29 above, pp. 553–562; "The Magic Shirt," in id., pp. 110–113; "The Three Kingdoms, Copper, Silver, and Golden," in id., pp. 375–

387 (first episode, through p. 381); "The Captain and the General," in Italo Calvino, *Italian Folktales,* George Martin trans., San Diego: Harcourt Brace Jovanovich (Harvest/HBJ), 1992, pp. 645–648; "The Widow and the Brigand," in id., pp. 514–517; "The Twenty-First Night" through "The Twenty-Seventh Night," in Haddawy, note 29 above, pp. 54–66; "The Lazy Man," in Victor Montejo, *The Bird Who Cleans the World and Other Mayan Fables,* Wallace Kaufman trans., Willimantic, Conn.: Curbstone Press, 1992, pp. 106–110; "Apache Chief Punishes His Wife," in Erdoes and Ortiz, note 29 above, pp. 291–294; "Coyote Steals Another Man's Wife," in Morris Edward Opler, *Myths and Tales of the Jicarilla Apache Indians,* Lincoln: University of Nebraska Press (Bison Book), 1994, pp. 286–288; "The Running Stick," in *Classic Folk Tales from Around the World* (Nye, introduction), note 29 above, pp. 41–44; "The Wicked Girl and Her Punishment," in Paul Radin (Ed.), *African Folktales,* New York: Schocken Books, 1983, pp. 274–278. Folktales that cast Death itself as the ravisher in a Persephone/Orpheus theme have a similar structure. See, e.g., "The Children of the Dead Woman," in O'Sullivan, note 48 above, at pp. 176–179. For a comic variant, see "Old Hildebrand," in Jacob and Wilhelm Grimm, *The Complete Grimm's Fairy Tales,* Margaret Hunt trans., revised by James Stern, New York: Pantheon Books, 1972, pp. 440–444.

59. See, e.g., Robert Jordan, *The Fires of Heaven,* New York: Tom Doherty, 1993; Stephen R. Donaldson, "Reave the Just," in Martin H. Greenberg (Ed.), *After the King: Stories in Honor of J. R. R. Tolkein,* New York: Tom Doherty, 1992, pp. 1–33; "The Invisible Prince," in Lang, note 29 above, pp. 78–91. The structure is redoubled in Bram Stoker's *Dracula* (1897). In a lighter vein, it supports almost every *Popeye* cartoon episode.

60. See, e.g., L. Neil Smith, *Henry Martyn,* New York: Tom Doherty, 1989; Donald E. McQuinn, *Warrior,* New York: Ballantine Books (Del Rey), 1990; Larry Niven and Jerry Pournelle, *Footfall,* New York: Ballantine Books (Del Rey), 1990. Edgar Rice Burroughs made the structure a commonplace of adventure tales: his heroines—on two earthly continents, England, Mars, and Venus—are in an almost perpetual state of abduction. Burroughs's brand of the larger combat myth is thoughtfully examined in Richard Slotkin, *Gunfighter Nation: The Myth of the Frontier in Twentieth Century America,* New York: Harper Collins (HarperPerennial), 1993, pp. 195–211.

61. See, e.g., the film *No Down Payment* (TCF – Jerry Wald, 1957), book by John McPartland, screenplay by Phillip Yordan, directed by Martin Ritt; Albrecht Keller (Ed.), *A Hangman's Diary: Being the Journal of Master Franz Schmidt, Public Executioner of Nuremberg 1573–1617,* C. Calvert and A. W. Gruner trans., New York: Appleton, 1928, pp. 188, 210.

62. The page references in the following paragraphs are to volume 491 of the U.S. Reports.

63. Forsyth, note 44 above, at p. 95.
64. Cf. Anthony G. Amsterdam, "Telling Stories and Stories About Them," *Clinical Law Review,* 1994, *1,* 9–40, at pp. 11–13.
65. The present analysis is limited to verbs that take Michael or Gerald *individually* as their subjects. It does not include verbs whose subjects are *classes of persons* encompassing Michael or Gerald. The latter verbs show a pattern similar to the verbs displayed here but a bit more complicated.
66. Significantly, the ratio is reversed in the case of verbs predicating action by Michael and Carole together on the one hand, Gerald and Carole together on the other.
67. Delbanco, note 33 above, at p. 27.
68. Forsyth, note 44 above, at p. 4. See id. at p. 288: "By now a cluster of ideas has gathered about the words used for the adversary. . . . Satan, devil, something placed in the way [a *skandalon* or stumbling-block], opposed, opponent—all connect quite readily with 'slander' [cognate with *skandalon*] or 'false accusation, of the kind that creates scandal,' one of the primary functions of the Old Testament Satan." Michael seeks doubly to slander the marriage of Gerald and Carole: first by dishonoring it physically and then by challenging the California presumption of legitimacy designed primarily to protect "the integrity of the marital union" against embarrassing inquiries, 491 U.S. at 131; see also id. at 125.
69. Id. at 114 (emphasis added).
70. Id.
71. Id. at 113 (emphasis added).
72. Id. at 114 (emphasis added).
73. Justice Scalia later exploits the image of St. Thomas as a resort island again when he talks about "the relationship established between a married woman, her lover, and their child, during a 3-month *sojourn* in St. Thomas . . ." Id. at 123 n. 3 (emphasis added).
74. Id. at 123 n. 3 (emphasis added).
75. Job 1:7.
76. 491 U.S. at 130.
77. Although there can be no sharp analytic distinction between *the story that is being told* by a particular teller and the teller's *way of telling the story* (see Jonathan Culler, *The Pursuit of Signs: Semiotics, Literature, Deconstuction,* Ithaca, N.Y.: Cornell University Press, 1981, pp. 169–187), some narrative theorists in the Russian Formalist tradition distinguish between the *fabula* or basic plotline of a story ("a series of logically and chronologically related events that are caused or experienced by actors," Mieke Bal, *Narratology: Introduction to the Theory of Narrative,* 2d revised edition, Christine van Boheemen trans., Toronto: University of Toronto Press, 1985, p. 5) and the *sjužet* (the "*fabula* . . . presented in a certain manner," id.). That is quintessentially the difference between our focus in the preceding Parts III

and IV, which had to do with Justice Scalia's *fabula,* and the focus of the present Part V, his *sjužet.* In Part VI our focus will be his *rhetoric,* in the sense in which we develop that term in Chapter 6.   ·

78. See Chapter 2, Part V, and Chapter 4, Part III; Frank Kermode, *The Sense of an Ending: Studies in the Theory of Fiction,* New York and Oxford: Oxford University Press, 1967.

79. 491 U.S. at 118. See text at note 10 above.

80. 491 U.S. at 118–119, quoting 4 C. Markey (Ed.), California Family Law, 1987, § 60.02[1][b].

81. See, e.g., "Bricriu's Feast," in Cross and Slover, note 26 above, pp. 254–280, at pp. 256–258. Viewed rhetorically, the devices used are amplification by accumulation and by division. See, e.g., Cicero, *De Partitione Oratoria,* chap. xvi; Hermogenes, *On Types of Style,* Cecil W. Wooten trans., Chapel Hill and London: University of North Carolina Press, 1987, pp. 50–51.

82. "What Michael asserts here is a right to have himself declared the natural father *and thereby to obtain parental prerogatives.* What he must establish, therefore, is not that our society has traditionally allowed a natural father in his circumstances to establish paternity, but that it has traditionally accorded such a father parental rights, or at least has not traditionally denied them." 491 U.S. at 126.

83. See, e.g., text at notes 108–113 below.

84. "We do not accept JUSTICE BRENNAN's criticism that [our] . . . result 'squashes' the liberty that consists of 'the freedom not to conform.' . . . It seems to us that reflects the erroneous view that there is only one side to this controversy—that one disposition can expand a 'liberty' of sorts without contracting an equivalent 'liberty' on the other side. Such a happy choice is rarely available. Here, to *provide* protection to an adulterous natural father is to *deny* protection to a marital father, and vice versa. If Michael has a 'freedom not to conform' (whatever that means), Gerald must equivalently have a 'freedom to conform.' One of them will pay a price for asserting that 'freedom'" and California may choose which one. 491 U.S. at 130.

85. We have already noted some of the means by which Michael is portrayed as the aggressor: the story begins with his adulterous villainy (see text following note 62 above; cf. text at note 48 above) and casts him exclusively as a despoiler (see text at notes 65–76 above). Justice Scalia links Michael's behavior metaphorically to the "discharge [of a gun] into another person's body" (491 U.S. at 124 n.4) and analogizes it to having "begotten Victoria by rape" (id.). And there are hints that Michael has wronged Victoria and the public as well as Victoria's father and mother. The presumption of legitimacy that is the target of Michael's "challenges" (id. at 119) is described as historically rooted in "an aversion to declaring children illegitimate, . . . thereby depriving them of rights of inheritance and succession, . . . and likely making them wards of the state" (id. at 125) and in an "interest in promoting the 'peace and tranquillity of States and families'" (id.). More-

over, the statement of facts tells us that in "the first three years of her life, Victoria . . . *found herself* within a variety of quasi-family units" (id. at 114; emphasis added)—an affecting detail that is only somewhat less likely to pluck the reader's *poor child* nerve if the reader pauses to reflect that (1) this is the only passage in Justice Scalia's entire opinion that purports to describe the world through Victoria's eyes; (2) he goes out of his way to avoid describing the world through Victoria's eyes in the portion of the opinion in which he rejects her constitutional claims to preserve a relationship with Michael as well as Gerald—talking there in periphrases such as "whatever [may be] the merits of the *guardian ad litem's belief* that such an arrangement *can* be of great psychological benefit to *a* child" (id. at 130–131; emphasis added; see notes 101, 126 below); and (3) the passage about how poor Victoria "found herself" in varying social units is purporting to describe the mentation of an infant between birth and age 3.

86. "Michael *was seeking to be declared the father of Victoria.*" (491 U.S. at 118; emphasis added except on "the".) "[I]f Michael were *successful in being declared the father,* other rights would follow. . . ." (Id.; emphasis added.) "What Michael *asserts* here is a right *to have himself declared the natural father and thereby to obtain parental prerogatives.*" (Id.; emphasis added except on the last six words.) Nowhere in Justice Scalia's opinion is *Gerald* described as taking initiatives or launching offensives in this fashion. His stake in the outcome of the combat is repeatedly described as the mirror image of Michael's (see e.g., id. at 118–119, 130), but he never mirrors Michael's combativeness. The most aggressive behavior attributed to him is that he "intervened in the [legal] action [and] . . . moved for summary judgment." Id. at 115.

87. Id. at 118–119.

88. See text and notes at notes 10–17 above.

89. If the reader was not quick to ask this question on first reading, he or she would be quickened by Justice Scalia's subsequent instruction. See 491 U.S. at 131, where he treats a claim of Victoria's as follows:

"We reject, at the outset, Victoria's suggestion that her equal protection challenge must be assessed under a standard of strict scrutiny because, in denying her right to maintain a filial relationship with Michael, the State is discriminating against her on the basis of her illegitimacy. See *Gomez v. Perez.* . . . Illegitimacy is a legal construct, not a natural trait. Under California law, Victoria is not illegitimate, and she is treated in the same manner as all other legitimate children: she is entitled to maintain a filial relationship with her legal parents."

90. Id. at 126 (emphasis added except on the last six words). See also id. at 130: "Her [Victoria's] basic [due process] claim *is not* that California has erred in preventing her from establishing that Michael, not Gerald should stand as her legal father. Rather *she claims* a due process right to maintain filial relationships with both Michael and Gerald."

(Emphasis added.) Note that the last seven words in the first sentence admit that a construct is a construct—but not when attributing claims to Victoria.

91. See Chaim Perelman and Lucie Olbrechts-Tyteca, *The New Rhetoric: A Treatise on Argumentation* (1958), John Wilkinson and Purcell Weaver trans., Notre Dame and London: University of Notre Dame Press, 1971, pp. 411–459.

92. See, e.g., id. at p. 88: "That which occurs most often, the usual, the normal, is the subject of one of the most commonly used *loci,* so much so that for many people the step from what is done to what should be done, from the normal to the norm, is taken for granted."

93. On the first page of his opinion, Justice Scalia begins the project of constructing an implied natural order that can be used to portray behavior as deviant in the course of describing it. His opening sentence—"The facts of this case are, we must hope, extraordinary" (491 U.S. at 113)—is explicit about the project, although it leaves the content of the natural order to implication. The first four paragraphs of the statement of facts contain four *howevers* inserted between sentences or clauses that otherwise describe what Carole and Michael did in straightforward chronological sequence. The unstated premise of this style of narration is that there exists an invisible model for consistent behavior from which the behavior being described is observed to diverge.

94. Id. at 130 (emphasis added). The entire passage is set out in note 90 above.

95. Cf. Amsterdam, note 64 above, at pp. 21–22 and n. 76.

96. 491 U.S. at 130. See note 126 below for the way in which it is killed seven times in one sentence.

97. 491 U.S. at 131.

98. Id. at 131–132.

99. See id. at 113–116.

100. Compare Justice Scalia's refusal to abstract the facts of the case in describing Michael's claim: "the concept [of the 'unitary family'] . . . will bear no resemblance to traditionally respected relationships—and will thus cease to have any constitutional significance—if it is stretched so far as to include *the relationship established between a married woman, her lover, and their child, during a 3-month sojourn in St. Thomas, or during a subsequent 8-month period when, if he happened to be in Los Angeles, he stayed with her and the child.*" Id. at 123 n. 3 (emphasis added).

101. The only other place in the opinion in which Victoria's guardian ad litem is disaggregated from Victoria is where the disaggregation serves to deny poignancy as well as plausibility to what Justice Scalia characterizes as "the guardian ad litem's belief that such an arrangement [Victoria's maintenance of a relationship with both Gerald and Michael] can be of great psychological benefit to a child. . . ." Id. at 130–131. See note 85 above; note 126 below.

102. 491 U.S. at 124.

103. See id. at 127 ("an extant marital union that wishes to embrace the child"); id. at 129 n. 7 ("situations in which, as here, the husband and wife wish to raise her child jointly" as contrasted with situations involving "a child whom the marital parents do not wish to raise as their own"); id. at 130 ("a couple desiring to retain a child conceived within and born into their marriage"); and cf. id. ("the traditional family unit he [Gerald] and Victoria have established").

104. See id. at 129 n. 7.

105. This is not an easy feat after Justice Scalia's portrayal of Carole in his statement of the case, which emphasizes her volatility. See id. at 113–116.

106. See id. at 113 ("Carole became involved in an adulterous affair with a neighbor, Michael H."), 114 ("Carole . . . took up residence with yet another man, Scott K.").

107. See note 29 above, paragraph three, and, e.g., "Anpu and Bata," in Rugoff, note 21 above, pp. 200–208; "The Giants of Castle Treen," in id., pp. 251–255; Sue Grafton, "The Parker Shotgun," in Tony Hillerman and Rosemary Herbert (Eds.), *The Oxford Book of American Detective Stories,* New York and Oxford: Oxford University Press, 1996, pp. 639–654.

108. 491 U.S. at 121.

109. The shape of legal concepts and the Shape of Things are interwoven in Justice Scalia's presentation: consider, for example, his metaphor in id. at 110: "This is not *the stuff* of which fundamental rights qualifying as liberty interests *are made*" (emphasis added). Compare Alan W. Watts, "Western Mythology: Its Dissolution and Transformation," in Joseph Campbell (Ed.), *Myths, Dreams, and Religion,* Dallas: Spring Publications, 1992, pp. 9–25, at pp. 10–17. His paragraph describing the "California statute that is the subject of this litigation" uses the word *substantive* twice and the phrase *in substance* once. 491 U.S. at 117. Legal concepts are things that one can "objectify." Id. at 122. A legal tradition (even one discerned from the absence of case law) is something that has an "existence." Id. at 128 n. 6; see note 127 below.

110. 491 U.S. at 128–129, quoting *Lehr v. Robertson,* 463 U.S. 248, 262 (1983).

111. 491 U.S. at 129.

112. Id. (emphasis added). By building a *relationship* into the adjectives that he uses to describe a thing (here, a relationship of mirror imagery), Justice Scalia makes those relationships endemic to the thing, and he can thereafter reason from them as givens. See, e.g., his discussion of Victoria's due process claim, which opens by saying "We have never had occasion to decide whether a child has a liberty interest, *symmetrical with that of her parent,* in maintaining her filial relationship" (id. at 130; emphasis added) and ends by saying that "we find that, at best, *her claim is the obverse of Michael's* and fails for the same reason" (id. at 131; emphasis added). There is no other discussion of the relationships built into "symmetrical" or "obverse."

113. Id. at 130. In this instance, Justice Scalia offers more than the verbal figure

of *conversio* (see [Cicero], *Rhetorica ad Herennium,* book IV, chap. xiii) to establish the ontological status of the antagonistic-Double relationship. He prefaces this sentence with the observation that Justice Brennan's approach assumes that "one disposition can expand a 'liberty' of sorts without contracting an equivalent 'liberty' on the other side. *Such a happy choice is rarely available.*" 491 U.S. at 130; emphasis added. It is of the Nature of Things to resist accommodation of opposites.

114. Justice Scalia describes the claim as being that "the requirements of procedural due process prevent the State from terminating [Michael's] . . . liberty interest in the relationship with his child without affording him an opportunity to demonstrate his paternity in an evidentiary hearing." Id. at 119.

115. Id. at 120–121.

116. One of us arrived at a similar interpretation quite independent of Justice Scalia. See the discussion of *Stanley v. Illinois,* 405 U.S. 645 (1972), and cognate cases in Randy Hertz, Martin Guggenheim, and Anthony G. Amsterdam, *Trial Manual for Defense Attorneys in Juvenile Court,* Philadelphia: ALI-ABA, 1991, volume II, pp. 960–963 [§ 41.03]; and see the discussion of conclusive presumptions in id., volume II, at p. 835 [§ 35.06(e)].

117. See *Weinberger v. Salfi,* 422 U.S. 749, 770–772 (1975), explicitly distinguishing *Vlandis v. Kline,* 412 U.S. 441 (1973), along the line that Justice Scalia's *Michael H.* opinion erases; *Caban v. Mohammed,* 441 U.S. 380, 385 n. 3 (1979), explicitly characterizing *Stanley v. Illinois,* note 116 above, as a procedural due process case.

118. Justice Scalia could have accepted the characterization of the precedents as procedural due process cases restricting the permissible operation of presumptions when the presumed fact has operational consequences which differ from those of the basic fact (so that subjecting both facts to litigation and requiring the first to be "presumed" from the second has some different impact upon a party than simply substituting the second fact for the first as a matter of substantive law), but disputed Justice Brennan's attempt in 491 U.S. at 152–153 to demonstrate that this was the case with regard to the specific presumption challenged by Michael and Victoria.

119. See note 117 above and note 120 below.

120. To support his conclusion that the prior cases did not rest on procedural due process, Justice Scalia cites four law review commentators (who acknowledge that *they* are re-analyzing the case law), concurring and dissenting opinions in two of the cases, and a majority opinion in another case— *Weinberger v. Salfi,* note 117 above—that belabors the very distinction which Justice Scalia sweeps away.

121. The doctrine is most commonly stated in the formula set out in *F. S. Royster Guano Co. v. Virginia,* 253 U.S. 412, 415 (1920), which says that legislative classifications "must be reasonable, not arbitrary, and must rest upon some ground of difference having a fair and substantial relation to the object of

the legislation, so that all persons similarly circumstanced shall be treated alike."

122. See, e.g., *Smith v. Cahoon,* 283 U.S. 553 (1931); *Mayflower Farms, Inc. v. Ten Eyck,* 297 U.S. 266 (1936). It was for this reason that Justices Black and Frankfurter alike resisted the resuscitation of the doctrine in *Morey v. Doud,* 354 U.S. 457, 470–475 (1957).

123. The earliest Supreme Court cases using doctrines of procedural due process to invalidate state-created presumptions, *Bailey v. Alabama,* 219 U.S. 219 (1911), and *Morrison v. California,* 291 U.S. 82 (1934), avoided thorny Thirteenth Amendment and equal protection issues respectively; a procedural due process disposition in *Tot v. United States,* 319 U.S. 463 (1943), avoided issues like those that split the Court in *United States v. Lopez,* 514 U.S. 549 (1995). The presumption cases are simply one instance of the commonplace function of procedural due process doctrines to confine the occasions for decisive adjudication of the limits of state competence under the Constitution and assure that "questions as to the existence of constitutional power are not to be treated as raised by any controversy which may involve merely the manner of the power's exercise." Note, "The Void-for-Vagueness Doctrine in the Supreme Court," *University of Pennsylvania Law Review,* 1960, *109,* 67–116, at p. 115; see id. at pp. 109–114. Another instance is the "no evidence" cases, such as *Thompson v. Louisville,* 362 U.S. 199 (1960)—which avoided the broader issues presented by the implications of *Lambert v. California,* 355 U.S. 225 (1957), as well as those later bruited in *Robinson v. California,* 370 U.S. 660 (1962), and *Powell v. Texas,* 392 U.S. 514 (1968)—or *Schware v. Board of Bar Examiners,* 353 U.S. 232 (1957), and *Konigsberg v. State Bar,* 353 U.S. 252 (1957)—which avoided the broader issues fought out in, e.g., *In re Anastaplo,* 366 U.S. 82 (1961), and *Konigsberg v. State Bar,* 366 U.S. 36 (1961). But the same reasoning by which Justice Scalia equates conclusive presumptions with substantive rules in *Michael H.* so as to render procedural due process doctrines inapposite (491 U.S. at 120) would also equate state-court rulings of evidentiary sufficiency with state-law substantive rules so as to render the "no evidence" cases untenable: State courts have exclusive power to determine the meaning of state statutory law; therefore, any state-court decision applying a state statute to the facts of a particular case necessarily constitutes a substantive decision construing the statute to mean whatever it needs to mean in order to reach that case; therefore, there can never be a basis for the U.S. Supreme Court to find that a state-court decision rests upon "no evidence."

124. See, e.g., *Ex parte Royall,* 117 U.S. 241 (1886); *Younger v. Harris,* 401 U.S. 37 (1971); *Broadrick v. Oklahoma,* 413 U.S. 601 (1973); *In re Blodgett,* 502 U.S. 236 (1992).

125. See, e.g., 491 U.S. at 121–123, 130, 131–132.

126. The intensity of Justice Scalia's dedication to the combat mode is suggested by the massive overkill he visits on Michael's and Victoria's contentions. In the following single sentence, he denigrates or destroys one of Michael's arguments six distinct times. (Bracketed numbers and emphasis added, except on "current.")

> "Thus it is [1] *ultimately irrelevant,* [2] *even* for purposes of determining *current* social attitudes, toward [3] the *alleged* substantive right Michael asserts, that the present law in a number of States [4] *appears to* allow the natural father—including the natural father [5] *who has not established a relationship with the child*—the [6] *theoretical* power to rebut the marital presumption." (Id. at 127.)

Victoria's due process argument gets the axe seven times in six lines as follows (with the same insertions):

> "This assertion [1] *merits little discussion,* for, [2] *whatever the merits* of [3] the *guardian ad litem's* [4] *belief* that such an arrangement [5] *can* be of great psychological benefit to [6] *a* child, the claim that a state must recognize multiple fatherhood has [7] *no support* in the history or traditions of this country." (Id. at 131.)

127. Id. at 122 (emphasis added). See also id. ("[o]ur cases reflect 'continuing *insistence* upon respect for the teachings of history . . .'") (emphasis added); id. at 123 ("[t]his *insistence* that the asserted liberty interest be rooted in history and tradition is evident, as elsewhere, in our cases according constitutional protection to certain parental rights") (emphasis added); id. at 128 n. 6 (where there is "a longstanding and still extant societal tradition withholding the very right pronounced to be the subject of a liberty interest[,] . . . *the existence* of such a tradition, continuing to the present day, *refutes any possible contention* that the alleged right is 'so rooted in the traditions and conscience of our people as to be ranked as fundamental. . . .'") (emphasis added). In this last passage, the powerful noun "existence" is a reification of the negative finding described in 491 U.S. at 127: "What counts is whether the States in fact award substantive parental rights to the natural father of a child conceived within, and born into, an extant marital union that wishes to embrace the child. We are not aware of a single case, old or new, that has done so." Justice Scalia effects a similar reification through a different technique ("linger[ing] upon . . . arguments that are favorable to him, but . . . dealing with points that do not support his case . . . in as few words as possible," Hermogenes, note 81 above, at p. 47; see also Cicero, *De Oratore,* book II, chap. lxxii) in 491 U.S. at 126, where he spends seven lines describing the various laws of States that restrict standing to question a child's legitimacy (an Annotation shows "three States" with rule *A,* "one State" with rule *B,* "two States" with rule *C,* and "two States" with rule *D,* all States being named and all rules summarized), then says: "Not a single decision is set forth specifically according standing to the natural father, and 'express indications of the nonexistence of any . . . limitation' upon stand-

ing were found only 'in a few jurisdictions.'" This *only* is a counterpoint to the enumeration of previously-named-and-classified-and-described jurisdictions, which turns out, upon close inspection, to total eight.

128. Id. at 121–122 (emphasis added).

129. "Without that core textual meaning [liberty limited to physical restraint] as a limitation, defining the scope of the Due Process Clause 'has at times been a treacherous field for this Court. . . .'" Id. at 121. See id. at 122, quoting Justice White to the effect that the fact that the Court has "'ample precedent'" for expanding Due Process protection should serve as a warning *not* to do so, because whenever the judiciary "'breathe[s] still further substantive content into the Due Process Clause . . . it unavoidably preempts for itself another part of the governance of the country without express constitutional authority.'"

130. See, e.g., id. at 121–122, 127–128 n. 6.

131. "And there was war in heaven: Michael and his angels fought against the dragon; and the dragon fought and his angels." Revelation 12:7. See, e.g., Forsyth, note 44 above, at pp. 130–146, 221–257, 298–302, 348, 428–434. This is Philip Dick's *Form Destroyer*, synthesized from the dualisms of all major religions. Philip K. Dick, *A Maze of Death* (1970), New York: Vintage Books, 1994.

132. See, e.g., Forsyth, note 44 above, at pp. 266–280, 304–306, 309–383, 419, 426; Pagels, note 34 above.

133. 491 U.S. at 121, quoting *Moore v. East Cleveland,* 431 U.S. 494, 502 (1977) (plurality opinion).

134. 491 U.S. at 128 n. 6; see also id. at 122 and n. 2.

135. "We do not understand why, having rejected our focus upon the societal tradition regarding a natural father's rights vis-à-vis a child whose mother is married to another man, JUSTICE BRENNAN [in dissent] would *choose* to focus instead upon 'parenthood.'" Id. at 127 n. 6. "Though the dissent *has no basis for* the level of generality it *would select,* we do." Id. There is a "need, if arbitrary decisionmaking is to be avoided, to adopt the most specific tradition as the point of reference—or at least to announce, *as JUSTICE BRENNAN declines to do,* some other criteria for *selecting* among the innumerable relevant traditions that could be consulted. . . ." Id. at 128 n. 6. "Although assuredly having the virtue (if it be that) of leaving judges *free to decide as they think best* when the unanticipated occurs, a rule of law that binds neither by text nor by any particular, identifiable tradition is no rule of law at all." Id. "JUSTICE BRENNAN's approach *chooses* one of [two contending claims of liberty] . . . *on no apparent basis except that the unconventional is to be preferred.*" Id. at 130. Cf. id. at 124 ("'[t]hat the Court has ample precedent for the creation of new constitutional rights should not lead it to repeat the process *at will*'"). (Emphasis in all quotations in this note has been added.)

136. For the procedure of interpretation by figures, see, e.g., Erich Auerbach, *Mi-*

mesis: The Representation of Reality in Western Literature (1946), Willard R. Trask trans., Princeton: Princeton University Press, 1991, pp. 16–17, 48–49, 73–74, 116–120, 156–158, 161, 189–190, 195–202, 224–228, 231, 247, 277, 317, 323, 440, 555. In this procedure, "[t]he signifieds are given in advance," Tzvetan Todorov, "The Quest of Narrative," in *The Poetics of Prose* (1971), Richard Howard trans., Ithaca, N.Y.: Cornell University Press, 1977, pp. 120–142, at p. 127, and "[t]he translation always proceeds from the more to the less well known. . . . It is the everyday actions . . . and the ordinary objects . . . which turn out to be incomprehensible signs . . . and which need to be translated into the language of religious values," id. at pp. 125–126.

137. Consider, for example, footnote 7 in 491 U.S. at 129. The footnote begins: "JUSTICE BRENNAN chides us for . . . limiting our holding to situations in which, as here, the husband and wife wish to raise her child jointly" and ends: "It seems unfair for those who disagree with our holding to include among their criticisms that we have not extended the holding more broadly." The conceptualization here is that the plurality and the dissent are engaged, not in a reasoning process, but in a trench-by-trench struggle for contested territory. The dissent has no business criticizing the plurality's *logic;* it can only complain about (and in proportion to) the square footage that the plurality overruns. To the extent that the plurality *abstains* from capturing objectives which the dissent is presumed to be committed to defend, the dissent can have no grievance.

In the middle of the footnote, Justice Scalia makes the point that "we rest our decision not upon our independent 'balancing' of [the parties'] . . . interests, but upon the absence of any constitutionally protected right . . . in Michael's situation, as evidenced by long tradition. That tradition reflects a 'balancing' that has already been made by society itself." Michael's case is thus treated as one battle in a larger war of ideologies of constitutional interpretation, not explicitly declared on this occasion but always being fought between the Balancers and the Tradition-Upholders.

The quoted point is prefaced: "As we have sought to make clear . . . and as the dissent elsewhere *seems* to understand. . . ." This is an instance of the repeated tactic of treating Justice Brennan as either incapable of coherent reasoning or perversely motivated to corrupt it. See, e.g., id. at 122 n. 2 ("[w]e *do not understand* what JUSTICE BRENNAN has in mind by . . ."; "[n]or *do we understand* [another point quoted from the dissenting opinion]"); id. at 124 n. 4 ("JUSTICE BRENNAN insists that . . . we must look at Michael's relationship with Victoria in isolation. . . . We *cannot imagine what compels this strange procedure* of looking at the act which is assertedly the subject of a liberty interest in isolation . . ."); id. at 126 n. 5 ("[a]ccording to JUSTICE BRENNAN. . . . We *cannot grasp the concept* . . ."); id. at 127 n. 6 ("JUSTICE BRENNAN criticizes our methodology . . ."; "[t]here seems *no basis for* the contention that this methodology is 'nove[l],' . . ."; "[w]e *do not understand* why . . . JUSTICE BRENNAN would *choose to* . . ."); id. at 128 n. 6 (*"[o]ne would think* that JUSTICE BRENNAN would appreciate . . ."); id. at 130 ("We do not accept JUS-TICE BRENNAN's criticism that this result 'squashes' the liberty that consists of 'the freedom not to conform.' . . . If Michael has a 'freedom not to conform' (*whatever that means*), Gerald must equivalently have a 'freedom to conform.'"). *Ad personam* attacks on one's interlocutor are not uncommon in the opinions of divided appellate courts and are ancient weapons of the debater's arsenal, but their volume and stridency throughout Justice Scalia's *Michael H.* opinion are more consistent with a state of siege than of deliberation or even debate. See also note 135 above. (Emphasis in all quotations in this note has been added.)

138. Forsyth, note 44 above, at p. 279.

139. The defeated sorceress, witch, or succubus is due to be dragged to death at a horse's tail; see, e.g., "The Armless Maiden," in Afanas'ev, note 29 above, pp. 294–299; "The White Duck," in id., pp. 342–345; "The Merchant's Daughter and the Maidservant," in id., pp. 327–331; or burned, e.g., "Sister Alionushka, Brother Ivanushka," in id., pp. 406–410; "Hansel and Gretel," in *The Complete Grimm's Fairy Tales,* note 58 above, pp. 86–94; "The Drummer," in id., pp. 781–791; Henri Pourrat (Coll.), "The Village of the Damned," in *French Folktales,* Royall Tyler trans., New York: Pantheon Books, 1989, pp. 48–54; the vampire, impaled, see, e.g., Paul Barber, *Vampires, Burial, and Death: Folklore and Reality,* New Haven and London: Yale University Press, 1988, pp. 71–73, 158–162; Alan Ryan (Ed.), *The Penguin Book of Vampire Stories,* New York: Penguin Books, 1988; the Medusa, decapitated, see, e.g., Apollodorus, *The Library,* book II, chap. 4; Ovid, *Metamorphoses,* book IV; the Demon Lover or abductor, carved to pieces, see, e.g., text at notes 50–55 above.

140. See, e.g., Elaine Pagels, *Adam, Eve, and the Serpent,* New York: Vintage Books, 1989, pp. 98–150; Cohn, note 34 above; Jeffrey Burton Russell, *Witchcraft in the Middle Ages,* Ithaca, N.Y.: Cornell University Press, 1972; Jeffrey Burton Russell, *A History of Witchcraft: Sorcerers, Heretics, Pagans,* Ithaca, N.Y.: Cornell University Press, 1980; Jeffrey Richards, *Sex, Dissidence and Damnation: Minority Groups in the Middle Ages,* New York: Barnes and Noble, 1990; Po-Chia Hsia, note 34 above; Aldous Huxley, *The Devils of Loudun* (1952), New York: Barnes and Noble, 1996; Cervantes, note 33; Carlo Ginzburg, *The Night Battles: Witchcraft and Agrarian Cults in the Sixteenth and Seventeenth Centuries* (1966), John and Anne Tedeschi trans., Baltimore: Johns Hopkins University Press, 1992; Marion L. Starkey, *The Devil in Massachusetts: A Modern Inquiry into the Salem Witch Trials,* New York: Knopf, 1950. We refer to these sources for their consistent accounts of the portrait of the demon army that gets painted when demonification is practiced; their disagreements about the characteristics of the people demonified are immaterial for our purposes.

141. In *The Night Battles,* Carlo Ginzburg recounts the history of the benandanti, members of a fertility cult among the peasants of the Friuli in the late sixteenth and early seventeenth centuries who were converted into witches in the findings of successive inquisitors, in the imaginations of their neighbors, and eventually in their own minds, because "[t]here was no place in the theological, doctrinal and demonological theories of the dominant culture for the beliefs of the benandanti: they constituted an irrational outgrowth and therefore either had to be made to conform to those theories or be eradicated." Ginzburg, note 140 above, at p. 88. In a quintessential episode, a substantial citizen named Alessandro Marchetto reported to the Holy Office in 1621 that he had confronted a shepherd who admitted to being a benandante, and after interrogating him, "yelled at the benandante that 'he considered him to be a real witch, and in no way a benandante; that this term had no meaning, and therefore he had to be a witch.'" Id. at p. 89.

142. 491 U.S. at 122.

143. Id. at 128 n. 6. It is on this point that Justices O'Connor and Kennedy depart from Justice Scalia's opinion. See id. at 132.

144. Id. at 125.

145. Id. at 128 n. 6.

146. See, e.g., [Cicero], *Rhetorica ad Herennium,* book IV, chap. xxviii; Cicero, *Orator,* chap. xxxix; Quintilian, *Institutio Oratoria,* book VIII, chap. iv; book IX, chap. iii.

147. Justice Scalia introduces the concept of "an interest traditionally protected by our society" at page 122 of 491 U.S. Between there and the end of the opinion (at the top of page 132), he uses the words "tradition," "traditions," "traditional," or "traditionally" forty times, often with embellishments and possessives such as "rooted in history and tradition" (491 U.S. at 123), "the historic practices of our society" (id. at 124), "our traditions" (id.), "[i]n accord with our traditions" (id. at 129), and "no support in the history or traditions of this country" (id. at 131). The words "history" or "historic" appear nine times within the same ten pages; language about rootedness or deep embeddedness, six times.

148. See, e.g., [Cicero], *Rhetorica ad Herennium,* book IV, chap. liii; Quintilian, *Institutio Oratoria,* book VIII, chap. vi.

149. 491 U.S. at 123. The other rhetorical figure employed in this passage is *correctio,* which is used to "make[ ] an impression upon the hearer, for the idea when expressed by an ordinary word seems rather feebly stated, but after the speaker's amendment it is made more striking by means of the more appropriate expression." [Cicero], *Rhetorica ad Herennium,* book IV, chap. xxvi.

150. 491 U.S. at 123–124, quoting *Moore v. East Cleveland,* 431 U.S. 494, 503 (1977) (plurality opinion) (emphasis added).

151. 491 U.S. at 123. The implication is that the precedents either *establish* Michael's position or lend it no support; Justice Scalia never asks whether they

are *more* consistent with Michael's position or his own; he puts such a question out of bounds by treating legal doctrine as a *thing* having an "existence" (id. at 128 n. 6) rather than as the creature of interpretation; see notes 109 and 127 above and text and notes at notes 160–161, 190–201 below.

152. 491 U.S. at 123.

153. Id.

154. While "isolated factors" cannot serve to bring a case within constitutional protection under Justice Scalia's approach to categorization (see text at notes 167–170 below), they can serve to take it out. See footnote 3 in 491 U.S. at 123, discussed in note 100 above.

155. This passage is the one quoted in the text at note 149 above.

156. See 491 U.S. at 123–124, 128–129. Cf. Justice Scalia's characterizations quoted in the text at notes 152–153 above.

157. See Leszek Kolakowski, *The Presence of Myth,* Adam Czerniawski trans., Chicago and London: University of Chicago Press, 1989, p. 23: "[T]he values of my culture cannot be jointly implemented and kept intact. An overwhelming proportion of my acts consists of compromises in which a partial or fragmentary saving of a value occurs at the expense of saving it as a whole, and this loss is incurred in order partially to save another value. Daily life consists of such accommodations. The degree of acceptable compromise—the extent of possible abandonment of a partial actualization of a value for the sake of another value—is not clearly defined by the norms of my culture. And this indeterminacy is the greater, the greater is the potential of my culture's flowering."

158. 491 U.S. at 129 n. 7.

159. Id.

160. See Louis O. Mink, "Narrative Form as a Cognitive Instrument," in Robert H. Canary and Henry Kozicki (Eds.), *The Writing of History: Literary Form and Historical Understanding,* Madison: University of Wisconsin Press, 1978, pp. 129–149, at pp. 135–149.

161. See notes 109 and 127 above. Cf. Kenneth Burke, *A Grammar of Motives* (1945), Berkeley: University of California Press, 1969, p. 52: "The most clear-sounding of words can thus be used for the vaguest of reference, quite as we speak of 'a certain thing' when we have no particular thing in mind. And so rock-bottom a study as a treatise on the nature of substance might . . . more accurately be entitled, 'A Treatise on the Nature of I-don't-know-what.' One might thus express a state of considerable vagueness in the imposing accents of a juridic solidity."

162. 491 U.S. at 127–128 n. 6.

163. Id. at 128 n. 6.

164. Id. (emphasis added).

165. Id. at 121. See text at notes 127–131 above.

166. See text at notes 148–150 above.

167. See Mircea Eliade, *The Sacred and the Profane: The Nature of Religion* (1957), Willard R. Trask trans., San Diego and New York: Harcourt, Brace, Jovanovich (Harvest/HBJ), 1987, pp. 20–65.

168. See text at notes 153–154 above.

169. 491 U.S. at 123 (emphasis added). See Kenneth Burke, quoted in note 161 above.

170. See note 100 above.

171. Justice Scalia's first two paragraphs sharply distinguish between the spheres of law and of fact and privilege the former. The first sentence of the first paragraph is: "Under California law, a child born to a married woman living with her husband is presumed to be a child of the marriage." 491 U.S. at 113. The first sentence of the second paragraph is: "The facts of this case are, we must hope, extraordinary." Id.

    An identical juxtaposition marks the final sentences of the opinion. The next-to-last sentence is the one that we discussed in the text at note 101 above, in which Justice Scalia produces a cynical low-comedy scene starring a snoopy court-appointed guardian ad litem. 491 U.S. at 131. In the following sentence, the coda, the change of tone is dramatic: the realm of law in all its pristine purity is telegraphed to the intelligence: "Since it pursues a legitimate end by rational means, California's decision to treat Victoria differently from her parents is not a denial of equal protection." Id. at 131–132.

172. Id. at 113.

173. Id. at 114. See also, e.g., id. at 113–114 ("Gerald . . . has always held Victoria out to the world as his daughter"); id. at 114 (in St. Thomas, Michael "held Victoria out as his child"; Carole "became involved once again with Michael"); id. at 115 (Carole and Gerald now live with Victoria "and two other children since born into the marriage").

174. Id. at 116. See also id. at 119–120.

175. Id. at 130. The very notion of "family integrity" (id. at 120; see also id. at 131) presupposes an idealized state of *oneness* subject to disruption. Cf. text at notes 90–96 and 102–105 above.

176. In 491 U.S. at 118 the quoted phrases are juxtaposed to "the *immediate* benefit . . . [that Michael] *evidently* sought to obtain from that status": "visitation rights." See text at note 91 above. In Victoria's case, Justice Scalia need not reach the question "whether a child has a liberty interest, *symmetrical with that of her parent*, in maintaining her filial relationship" (491 U.S. at 130), because Victoria's "*basic claim*" is "a due process right to *maintain filial relationships with both Michael and Gerald*" (id.). Translation: eight-year-old Victoria would like to have Michael come and visit her sometime. (Emphasis in all quotations in this note has been added.)

177. E.g.: "[I]f Michael were successful in being declared the father, other rights *would follow.* . . ." Id. at 118. "All parental rights, including visitation, were *automatically* denied by denying Michael status as the father." Id. at 119. See text at notes 87–89 above. Michael's claim "derives from a funda-

mental misconception of the *nature* of the California statute." 491 U.S. at 119. See also note 109 above regarding Justice Scalia's descriptions of legal doctrine in terminology of "stuff" and "substance." (Emphasis in all quotations in this note has been added.)

178. E.g., "California law, *like nature itself,* makes *no provision* for dual fatherhood." 491 U.S. at 118. "In those circumstances in which California law allows a natural father to rebut the presumption of legitimacy of a child born to a married woman, *e.g.,* where the husband is impotent or sterile, or where the husband and wife have not been cohabiting, it is more likely that the husband already knows the child is not his, *and thus less likely that the paternity hearing will disrupt an otherwise harmonious and apparently exclusive marital relationship.*" Id. at 120 n. 1. "When the husband or wife contests the legitimacy of their child, *the stability of the marriage has already been shaken.*" Id. at 131. A striking feature of these last two examples is Justice Scalia's assumption that qualities like a "harmonious . . . marital relationship" and "the stability of the marriage" refer to a single state of affairs that is everywhere the same, always subject to the same empirical rules, and universally disruptable by (and only by) the same circumstances. "[T]his movement from actus to status involves *class* substance." Burke, note 161 above, at p. 42. (Emphasis in all quotations in this note has been added, except on "class.")

179. The tension between *loci* of quantity—emphasizing the value of what is general, normal, commonplace, and so forth—and *loci* of quality—emphasizing the value of what is unique, rare, irreplaceable, and so forth—is usefully discussed in Perelman and Olbrechts-Tyteca, note 91 above, at pp. 85–93.

180. See, e.g., 491 U.S. at 122–125, 131.

181. See, e.g., id. at 125–127.

182. See id. at 124–125.

183. See id. at 125–126; and see note 127 above.

184. 491 U.S. at 123.

185. E.g., *Pierce v. Society of Sisters,* 268 U.S. 510 (1925); *Griswold v. Connecticut,* 381 U.S. 479 (1965); *Roe v. Wade,* 410 U.S. 113 (1973).

186. *Stanley v. Illinois,* 405 U.S. 645 (1972). See also, e.g., *Santosky v. Kramer,* 455 U.S. 745, 753 (1982): "The absence of dispute [about the fundamental quality of the parent-child relationship] reflect[s] this Court's historical recognition that freedom of personal choice in matters of family life is a fundamental liberty interest protected by the Fourteenth Amendment."

187. He makes this move in two successive sentences. The first sentence simply quotes a previous plurality opinion as saying that "'[o]ur decisions establish that the Constitution protects the sanctity of the family *precisely because* the institution of the family is deeply rooted in this Nation's history and tradition.'" 491 U.S. at 123–124, quoting *Moore v. East Cleveland,* 431 U.S. 494, 503 (1977) (plurality opinion). The second sentence continues: "*Thus,*

the legal issue in the present case *reduces to* whether the relationship between persons in the situation of Michael and Victoria has been treated as a
protected family unit under the historic practices of our society, or whether
on any other basis it has been accorded special protection." 491 U.S. at 124.
(Emphasis in all quotations in this note has been added.)

188. Id. at 113.

189. Having thus established the basic locus of quantity (see note 179 above),
Justice Scalia begins immediately to exploit it. In the same paragraph he relates that "Gerald was listed as father on the birth certificate and *has always
held Victoria out to the world* as his child." 491 U.S. at 113. Subsequently
he relates that "[i]n January 1982, Carole visited Michael in St. Thomas . . .
and *[t]here* Michael held Victoria out as his child." Id. at 114. And again,
during eight months in 1983–1984, "*when Michael was not in St. Thomas*
he lived with Carole and Victoria in Carole's apartment in Los Angeles and
held Victoria out as his daughter." Id. Thus the duration of Gerald's holding-out is depicted as eternal (including, apparently, even those periods
when Carole and Victoria were living with Michael) and its scope as world-
wide; Michael's holding-out is trivialized by a verbal strategy of division.
The *coup de grace* is delivered ten pages later, in the passage we have set out
in note 100 above, where Justice Scalia says that the concept of the family
"will bear no resemblance to traditionally respected relationships—and will
thus cease to have any constitutional significance—if it is *stretched so far* as
to include the relationship established . . . *during a 3-month sojourn* in St.
Thomas, or during a subsequent 8-month period when, *if he happened to be*
in Los Angeles, he stayed with her and her child." 491 U.S. at 123 n. 3. See
also id. at 120 (Justice Scalia describes what Michael has been denied as "a
hearing on whether, *in the particular circumstances of his case,* California's
policies would be best served by giving him parental rights"). (Emphasis in
all quotations in this note has been added.)

190. Id. at 118. See text at notes 80–90 above.

191. 491 U.S. at 119.

192. Id. at 121. See also id. at 127 ("[t]hus, it is ultimately irrelevant . . ."); id.
("[w]hat counts is . . .").

193. Id. at 121. See text at notes 114–126 above.

194. 491 U.S. at 122 (emphasis added). See id. ("[o]ur cases reflect 'continual *insistence* upon . . .'"); id. at 123 (this "*insistence* . . . is *evident,* as elsewhere,
in our cases according constitutional protection to *certain* constitutional
rights"). (Emphasis in all quotations in this note has been added.)

195. Id. at 121, 123, 124. See note 151 above.

196. 491 U.S. at 120 (twice). See also id. at 126 n. 5 ("[t]o be sure . . .").

197. Id. at 123 n. 4 ("no resemblance to traditionally respected relationships");
id. at 126 ("no conceivable denial of constitutional right"); id. at 110 n. 6
("no basis for the contention"); id. at 131 ("no support in the history or traditions of this country"). Cf. id. at 130 (Victoria's claim "must fail"; it

"merits little discussion"); id. at 131 (Victoria's remaining point is "wholly without merit").

198. Id. at 124. See also id. at 128 n. 6 ("refutes any possible contention"); id. at 129 n. 7 (a point that Justice Scalia explicitly leaves undecided "is at least possible").

199. See note 137 above.

200. 491 U.S. at 129 n. 7 (a point is reserved because "it is at least possible" that it could fall outside the holding of the present case); id. at 123 n. 3 ("[p]erhaps the concept [of the unitary family] can be expanded even beyond this [the household of unmarried parents and their children given Due Process protection by the prior case law], but it will bear no resemblance to traditionally respected relationships—and will thus cease to have any constitutional significance—if it is stretched so far as to include [the facts of Michael's case]").

201. He quotes from earlier cases a statement that "although ""[i]n some circumstances the actual relationship between father and child *may suffice* to create in the unwed father parental interests comparable to those of the married father,"' "'the absence of a legal tie with the mother may *in such circumstances appropriately* place a limit on whatever substantive constitutional claims might otherwise exist.""" Id. at 129. He then goes on to say: "In accord with our traditions, *a limit is also imposed* by the circumstances [found in Michael's case]." Id. (Emphasis in all quotations in this note has been added.)

202. E.g., id. at 122 ("we have insisted not merely that the interest denominated as a 'liberty' be 'fundamental' (a concept that, in isolation, is hard to objectify), but also that it be an interest traditionally protected by our society"); id. at 122 n. 2 (the purpose of the Due Process Clause is to "prevent future generations from lightly casting aside important traditional values—not to enable this Court to invent new ones"); id. at 129 and n. 7.

203. Id. at 121.

204. Id. at 127–128 n. 6.

205. "Whatever the dominant values may be in a cultural milieu, the life of the mind cannot avoid relying on abstract values as well as concrete ones. It seems that there have always been people who attach more importance to one set of values than the other; perhaps they form characterical families. In any case their distinctive trait would not be complete neglect of values of one kind, but subordination of these values to those of the other." Perelman and Olbrechts-Tyteca, note 91 above, at p. 77.

4. On Narrative

1. There has been a good deal of recent writing about narrative in the law. See, e.g., Peter Brooks and Paul Gewirtz (Eds.), *Law's Stories: Narrative and*

Rhetoric in the Law, New Haven: Yale University Press, 1996; David Dante Troutt, "*Screws, Koon* and Routine Aberrations: The Use of Fictional Narratives in Federal Police Brutality Prosecutions," *New York University Law Review,* 1999, 74, 18–122; Graham B. Strong, "The Lawyer's Left Hand: Nonanalytical Thought in the Practice of Law," *University of Colorado Law Review,* 1998, 69, 759–798, at pp. 780–788; Leslie Feiner, "The Whole Truth: Restoring Reality to Children's Narrative in Long-Term Incest Cases," *Journal of Criminal Law and Criminology,* 1997, 87, 101–147; Symposium, "Picturing Justice: Images of Law and Lawyers in the Visual Media," *University of San Francisco Law Review,* 1996, 30, 891–1247; Linda Holdeman Edwards, "The Convergence of Analogical and Dialectic Imaginations in Legal Discourse," *Legal Studies Forum,* 1996, 20, 7–50; Neal R. Feigenson, "The Rhetoric of Torts: How Advocates Help Jurors Think About Causation, Reasonableness, and Responsibility," *Hastings Law Journal,* 1995, 47, 61–165; Randy Frances Kandel, "Power Plays: A Sociolinguistic Study of Inequality in Child Custody Mediation and a Hearsay Analog Solution," *Arizona Law Review,* 1994, 36, 879–972; Symposium, "Lawyers as Storytellers and Storytellers as Lawyers: An Interdisciplinary Symposium Exploring the Use of Storytelling in the Practice of Law," *Vermont Law Review,* 1994, 18, 565–762; Richard K. Sherwin, "Law Frames: Historical Truth and Narrative Necessity in a Criminal Case," *Stanford Law Review,* 1994, 47, 39–83; William N. Eskridge, Jr., "Gaylegal Narratives," *Stanford Law Review,* 1994, 46, 607–646; David M. Engel, "Origin Myths: Narratives of Authority, Resistance, Disability, and Law," *Law and Society Review,* 1993, 27, 785–826; Lawyering Theory Symposium, "Thinking Through the Legal Culture," *New York Law School Law Review,* 1992, 37, 1–283; Richard D. Rieke and Randall K. Stutman, *Communication in Legal Advocacy,* Columbia: University of South Carolina Press, 1990, pp. 46–50, 93–103; Thomas Ross, "The Richmond Narratives," *Texas Law Review,* 1989, 68, 381–413; Symposium, "Legal Storytelling," *Michigan Law Review,* 1989, 87, 2073–2494; Robin West, "Jurisprudence as Narrative: An Aesthetic Analysis of Modern Legal Theory," *New York University Law Review,* 1985, 60, 145–211. Cf. Alison Dundes Renteln and Alan Dundes (Eds.), *Folk Law: Essays in the Theory and Practice of Lex Non Scripta,* Madison: University of Wisconsin Press, 1995.

2. Janet Malcolm, *The Crime of Sheila McGough,* New York: Alfred A. Knopf, 1999, pp. 3–4.

3. Legal criticism shares with literary criticism the second-order "feat of making sense of the ways we try to make sense of our lives." Frank Kermode, *The Sense of an Ending: Studies in the Theory of Fiction,* New York and Oxford: Oxford University Press, 1967, p. 3.

4. It is, indeed, only when this defining state of facts is contemplated—as existing or possible—that the particular legal situation is considered to arise.

5. See Jerome Bruner, "The Narrative Construction of Reality," *Critical Inquiry,* 1991, *18(1),* 1–21; Jerome Bruner, "What Is a Narrative Fact?" *Annals of the American Academy of Political and Social Sciences,* 1998, *560,* 17–27; and also, e.g., Arthur C. Danto, *Narration and Knowledge,* New York: Columbia University Press (Morningside), 1985; Donald P. Spence, *Narrative Truth and Historical Truth: Meaning and Interpretation in Psychoanalysis,* New York: Norton, 1982. For legal applications of the insight, see, e.g., W. Lance Bennett and Martha S. Feldman, *Reconstructing Reality in the Courtroom: Justice and Judgement in American Culture,* New Brunswick, N.J.: Rutgers University Press, 1981; Nancy Pennington and Reid Hastie, "The Story Model for Juror Decision Making," in Reid Hastie (Ed.), *Inside the Juror: The Psychology of Juror Decision Making,* Cambridge: Cambridge University Press, 1993, pp. 192–221.

6. See Frederick Pollock and Frederic W. Maitland, *History of English Law Before the Time of Edward I* (1898), Cambridge: Cambridge University Press, 1968, particularly volume 2; Frederic W. Maitland, *The Forms of Action at Common Law,* London: Rothman, 1984; J. H. Baker, *An Introduction to English Legal History,* 3d edition, London: Butterworth, 1990, pp. 63–83 and 612–625. For a less technical account of the emergence of common law writs, see Arthur R. Hogue, *Origins of the Common Law,* Bloomington: Indiana University Press, 1966.

7. Classical scholars commonly observe that the citizens of Athens in the fifth century B.C. trooped back and forth between the theater, law courts, Council, and Assembly to hear alternating forms of argument about the critical dilemmas of their condition. But whether this was a matter of going to the theater when court let out or vice versa is a question of interpretation. See Jean-Pierre Vernant and Pierre Vidal-Naquet, *Myth and Tragedy in Ancient Greece,* Janet Lloyd trans., New York: Zone Books, 1990, particularly at pp. 25–39, 88–89, 185; Charles Segal, "Spectator and Listener," in Jean-Pierre Vernant (Ed.), *The Greeks,* Chicago: University of Chicago Press, 1995, pp. 184–217; Victor Bers, "Tragedy and Rhetoric," in Ian Worthington (Ed.), *Persuasion: Greek Rhetoric in Action,* London and New York: Routledge, 1994, pp. 176–195.

8. "Narrativity" is an awkward term we use to characterize either a text that is narrative or a mode of thought that turns "happenings" into a narrative form.

9. Aristotle, *Poetics.*

10. Paul Ricoeur, *Time and Narrative,* Kathleen McLaughlin and David Pellauer trans., Chicago and London: University of Chicago Press, 1984, volume 1; Paul Ricoeur, *Oneself as Another,* Kathleen Blamey trans., Chicago and London: University of Chicago Press, 1992.

11. Vincent Crapanzano, *Hermes' Dilemma and Hamlet's Desire,* Cambridge, Mass.: Harvard University Press, 1992. See also Kenneth Gergen, *The Saturated Self,* New York: Basic Books, 1992.

12. See Peggy J. Miller, *Amy, Wendy, and Beth: Learning Language in South Baltimore,* Austin: University of Texas Press, 1982.

13. Carol Fleisher Feldman, "Genres as Mental Models," in Massimo Ammaniti and Daniel Stern (Eds.), *Psychoanalysis and Development: Representations and Narratives,* New York: New York University Press, 1994. See also Victor Turner and Edward M. Bruner (Eds.), *The Anthropology of Experience,* Urbana: University of Illinois Press, 1986, particularly chapters 5, 6, and 15.

14. For a thoughtful review of the question of universals, see Bradd Shore, *Culture in Mind,* New York and Oxford: Oxford University Press, 1996.

15. Charles Fillmore, "The Case for Case," in Emmon Bach and Robert T. Harms (Eds.), *Universals in Linguistic Theory,* New York: Holt, Rinehart, and Winston, 1968, pp. 1–88; and "The Case for Case Reopened," in Peter Cole and Jerrold M. Sadock (Eds.), *Syntax and Semantics: Grammatical Relations,* New York: Academic Press, 1977, volume 8, pp. 59–81.

16. Jerome Bruner and Joan Lucariello, "Monologue as Narrative Recreation of the World," in Katherine Nelson (Ed.), *Narratives from the Crib,* Cambridge, Mass.: Harvard University Press, 1989, pp. 73–97.

17. We know of no theory that makes such a particular claim, but it is typical of the kind of evolutionary "Just-So" story currently fashionable. See, for example, Jerome Barkow, Leda Cosmides, and John Tooby, *The Adapted Mind: Evolutionary Psychology and the Generation of Culture,* New York and Oxford: Oxford University Press, 1992.

18. Merlin Donald, *Origins of the Modern Mind: Three Stages in the Evolution of Culture and Cognition,* Cambridge, Mass.: Harvard University Press, 1991.

19. Penelope Brown and Stephen C. Levinson, *Politeness: Some Universals in Language Usage,* Cambridge: Cambridge University Press, 1987.

20. Roland Barthes, *The Semiotic Challenge,* Richard Howard trans., New York: Hill and Wang, 1988; see particularly his "Introduction to the Structural Analysis of Narratives," pp. 95–135.

21. We have been unable to find this now often quoted remark in James's writings. It was told to one of us some years ago by no less a James scholar than Leon Edel.

22. See, e.g., Victor Turner, *Dramas, Fields, and Metaphors: Symbolic Action in Human Society,* Ithaca, N.Y.: Cornell University Press, 1974; Victor Turner, "Social Dramas and Stories About Them," in W. J. T. Mitchell (Ed.), *On Narrative,* Chicago and London: University of Chicago Press, 1981, pp. 137–164. Sociocultural theories often take endogenous accounts as their start-up engine, although there is usually a wide ideological gap between the two.

23. Robert M. Cover, "The Supreme Court, 1982 Term, Foreword: Nomos and Narrative," *Harvard Law Review,* 1983, *97,* 4–68.

24. James Boyd White, *Heracles' Bow*, Madison: University of Wisconsin Press, 1985.

25. Mircea Eliade, *Myth and Reality*, Willard Trask trans., New York: Harper Torchbooks, 1968, p. 11.

26. See Peter Brooks, *Reading for the Plot: Design and Intention in Narrative* (1984), Cambridge, Mass.: Harvard University Press, 1995; Peter Brooks, *Body Work: Objects of Desire in Modern Narrative*, Cambridge, Mass.: Harvard University Press, 1993.

27. Michael Toolan, commenting on Harvey Sacks, observes that "ordinary people [telling stories] have to work their way between the Scylla of the 'so what?' question (by making their stories not uninteresting) and the Charybdis of the 'I don't believe you!' reaction (by making their stories not incredible)." Michael Toolan, *Narrative: A Critical Linguistic Introduction*, London and New York: Routledge, 1988, p. 180.

28. For a particularly penetrating analysis of the relationship between "story time" and the temporal extension of the events recounted, see Paul Ricoeur, *Time and Narrative*, 3 volumes, Kathleen McLaughlin/Blamey and David Pellauer trans., Chicago and London: University of Chicago Press, 1984–1988.

29. Northrop Frye, "The Rhythms of Time," in *Myth and Metaphor: Selected Essays 1974–1988*, Charlottesville: University of Virginia Press, 1991, pp. 157–167, at p. 157.

30. See, e.g., Roger C. Schank and Robert P. Abelson, *Scripts, Plans, Goals, and Understanding: An Inquiry into Human Knowledge Structures*, Hillsdale, N.J.: Erlbaum, 1977.

31. Katherine Nelson and Janice Gruendel, "Generalized Event Representations: Basic Building Blocks of Cognitive Development," in Ann L. Brown and Michael Lamb (Eds.), *Advances in Developmental Psychology*, Hillsdale, N.J.: Erlbaum, 1981, volume 1, pp. 131–158.

32. See Schank and Abelson, note 30 above.

33. These complementary functions of narrative are epitomized by a Great Subscriber's admonitions to a Great Subverter. Teddy Roosevelt—while he was the president of the Board of Police Commissioners of New York City in 1896—reacted to a gunfight story of Stephen Crane's, *A Man and Some Others*, by urging Crane to write "another story of the frontiersman and the Mexican Greaser in which the frontiersman shall come out on top; it is more normal that way!" Robert W. Stallman, *Stephen Crane: A Biography*, New York: Braziller, 1968, p. 219.

34. See, e.g., William Labov and Joshua Waletzky, "Narrative Analysis: Oral Versions of Personal Experience," in June Helm (Ed.), *Essays on the Verbal and Visual Arts* [Proceedings of the 1966 Annual Spring Meeting of the American Ethnological Society], pp. 12–44, reprinted in *Journal of Narrative and Life History*, 1997, 7(1–4), pp. 3–38; William Labov, *Language in*

the Inner City: Studies in the Black English Vernacular, Philadelphia: University of Pennsylvania Press, 1972. Other writers on the subject have generally followed Labov's lead, though introducing important variations: e.g., Victor Turner, *From Ritual to Theater: The Human Seriousness of Play,* New York: Performing Arts Journal Press, 1982; Tzvetan Todorov, *The Poetics of Prose* (1971), Richard Howard trans., Ithaca, N.Y.: Cornell University Press, 1977; Hayden White, "The Value of Narrativity in the Representation of Reality," in W. J. T. Mitchell (Ed.), *On Narrative,* Chicago and London: University of Chicago Press, 1981, pp. 1–23, reprinted in Hayden White, *The Content of the Form: Narrative Discourse and Historical Representation* (1987), Baltimore: Johns Hopkins University Press, 1990, pp. 1–25. For an analytic critique of the general Labov-Waletzky thesis, see Jerome Bruner, "Labov and Waletzky Thirty Years On," *Journal of Narrative and Life History,* 1997, *7(1–4),* pp. 61–68.

35. See Aristotle, *Poetics,* chaps. x–xi, xviii.
36. Paul Grice, *Studies in the Way of Words,* Cambridge, Mass.: Harvard University Press, 1989. We will return to this subject in Chapter 6.
37. Hayden White, note 34 above.
38. See Hempel's classic article, first published in the *Journal of Philosophy,* 1942, *39,* and later reprinted in Patrick Gardiner (Ed.), *Theories of History: Readings from Classical and Contemporary Sources,* Glencoe, Ill.: Free Press, 1959, pp. 344–356. See also Danto, note 5 above.
39. Henry Adams, *The Education of Henry Adams,* Boston: Houghton Mifflin, 1918, p. 388.
40. See Ricoeur, note 28 above, particularly Part III (in volume 2).
41. See Chapter 5, Part IV.
42. See Chapter 3, *Jenkins,* Part III, Scene 9.
43. See Chapter 5, Parts IV and V.
44. See Nelson, note 16 above.
45. This facility is not unique to Emmy. Consider the shifts in temporal marking in the following, quite typical passage from a judicial opinion, and notice the way in which they are manipulated to posture the Court exactly where it wants to be between the historically established, immemorially venerated tradition of prudence and the ever-lurking, imminently menacing danger that threatens the Nation if its judges stray from that tradition:

> "In the field of criminal law, we '*have defined* the category of infractions that violate "fundamental fairness" very narrowly' based on the recognition that, '[b]eyond the specific guarantees enumerated in the Bill of Rights, the Due Process Clause has limited operation.' [citations omitted] The Bill of Rights *speaks* in explicit terms to many aspects of criminal procedure, and the expansion of those constitutional guarantees under the open-ended rubric of the Due Process Clause *invites* undue interference with both considered legislative judgments and the careful balance that the Constitution *strikes* between liberty and order.

As we said in *Spencer v. Texas* . . ., 'it *has never been thought* that [deci-
sions under the Due Process Clause] *establish* this Court as a rule-mak-
ing organ for the promulgation of state rules of criminal procedure.'
[additional citations omitted]"
Medina v. California, 505 U.S. 437, 443–444 (1992) (emphasis added).
Here it is not just the timeless present tense of selected verbs but the
nominalization of others ("recognition," "expansion," "interference,"
"promulgation")—another device for stopping the flow of time—that
does the work. We will return to judicial performances of this sort in Chapter 6.

46. See note 34 above.

47. See Vladimir Propp, *Morphology of the Folktale* (1928), 2d edition,
Laurence Scott trans., Austin: University of Texas Press, 1990.

48. See Aristotle, *Poetics,* chaps. xiii–xviii.

49. Andrew N. Meltzoff, "Understanding the Intentions of Others: Re-Enactment of Intended Acts by 18-Month-Old Children," *Developmental Psychology,* 1995, *31,* 1–16.

50. Carol Feldman, Jerome Bruner, David Kalmar, and Bobbi Renderer, "Plot,
Plight, and Dramatism at Three Ages," *Human Development,* 1993, *36(6),*
327–342.

51. Aristotle, *Poetics,* chap. xv.

52. Northrop Frye, *Anatomy of Criticism: Four Essays,* Princeton: Princeton
University Press, 1990, pp. 40, 167.

53. See Peter Brooks, *Reading for the Plot: Design and Intention in Narrative*
(1984), Cambridge, Mass.: Harvard University Press, 1995, particularly
pp. 90–142.

54. See note 47 above.

55. For a brilliant account of this issue, see John L. Austin's renowned article,
"A Plea for Excuses," republished in his *Philosophical Papers,* 3d edition,
Oxford and New York: Oxford University Press, 1979, pp. 175–204.

56. Kenneth Burke, *A Grammar of Motives* (1945), Berkeley: University of California Press, 1969.

57. See Jerome Bruner, *Acts of Meaning,* Cambridge, Mass.: Harvard University Press, 1990, pp. 50–51.

58. Werner Jaeger, *Paideia: The Ideals of Greek Culture,* Gilbert Highet trans.,
New York and Oxford: Oxford University Press, 1986.

59. See Amelie Oksenberg Rorty, "A Literary Postscript: Characters, Persons,
Selves, Individuals," in Amelie Oksenberg Rorty (Ed.), *The Identities of
Persons,* Berkeley: University of California Press, 1976, pp. 301–323.

60. Jaroslav Pelikan, *Mary Through the Centuries: Her Place in the History of
Culture,* New Haven: Yale University Press, 1996.

61. For a representative collection in the Oxford manner, see John Mortimer
(Ed.), *The Oxford Book of Villains,* Oxford: Oxford University Press,
1993.

62. See Jerome Bruner, *On Knowing: Essays for the Left Hand,* Cambridge, Mass.: Harvard University Press, 1962, pp. 159–165.

63. Viktor Shklovsky was a fabled literary linguist and theoretician of poetry, much known and appreciated by literary critics and academics in the Moscow of the early 1920s. His work is virtually all in Russian. Outside of Russia, he is known principally by references to him in the writings and class lectures of Roman Jakobson, who cites Shklovsky's concept of the "alienating" function of poetry in his essays on linguistic poetics in Roman Jakobson, *Selected Writings,* volumes V and VII, The Hague: Mouton, 1979 and 1985, where the name index uses the form: "Šklovskij, V. B." Shklovksy's general doctrine is that the poetic image, by estranging the beholder from the banal referent of a term, compels fresh consciousness of it.

64. *Lochner v. New York,* 198 U.S. 45, 74 (1905).

65. Id. at 76.

66. See, e.g., Aristotle, *The Art of Rhetoric,* book I, chap. ix.

67. See, e.g., Lionel Trilling, *Sincerity and Authenticity,* Cambridge, Mass.: Harvard University Press, 1972; Mikhail M. Bakhtin, *The Dialogic Imagination: Four Essays,* Caryl Emerson and Michael Holquist trans., Austin: University of Texas Press, 1990; Toolan, note 27 above.

68. Aristotle, *The Art of Rhetoric,* book II, chap. xiii.

69. See, e.g., Anthony G. Amsterdam and Randy Hertz, "An Analysis of Closing Arguments to a Jury," *New York Law School Law Review,* 1992, 37, 55–122.

70. Arthur Koestler, *The Act of Creation,* New York: Macmillan, 1964, p. 33. Koestler credits this story to Sigmund Freud, but without reference, and refers to it as "the Chamfort episode," but we have been unable to locate it in Freud's collected writings.

71. Leon Friedman (Ed.), *Argument: The Oral Argument Before the Supreme Court in Brown v. Board of Education of Topeka, 1952–55,* New York: Chelsea House, 1969, pp. 55–56.

72. See, e.g., Michael Riffaterre, *Fictional Truth,* Baltimore and London: Johns Hopkins University Press, 1990.

73. William James, *The Will to Believe,* Cambridge, Mass.: Harvard University Press, 1979. The idea of "effort after meaning" was first developed by Sir Frederic Bartlett in his landmark book, *Remembering,* Cambridge: Cambridge University Press, 1932, where he investigated the way in which memory regularizes ambiguous stories by "conventionalizing" them so as to increase their meaningfulness.

74. See Paul Veyne, *Did the Greeks Believe in Their Myths? An Essay on the Constitutive Imagination,* Paula Wissing trans., Chicago and London: University of Chicago Press, 1988.

75. See, e.g., Oswald Ducrot, *Dire et ne pas Dire: Principes de Sémantique Linguistique,* Paris: Hermann, 1972, p. 41. "The act of conveying informa-

tion . . . cannot be accomplished unless the hearer recognizes the speaker's competence and honesty to begin with, so that the information is placed from the outset beyond the alternatives of truth and falsity" (our translation).

76. E.g., Aristotle, *The Art of Rhetoric,* book III, chap. ii; Cicero, *De Oratore,* book II, chap. xxxvii; Quintilian, *Institutio Oratoria,* book I, chap. xi; book II, chap. x; book IV, chaps. i, ii; [Cicero], *Rhetorica ad Herennium,* book IV, chap. vii.

77. See Trilling, note 67 above. Trilling believed that in Anglo-American culture the ideal of sincerity arose in the sixteenth century and was eclipsed by that of authenticity in the twentieth. Authenticity now appears to be taking its lumps as a convenient instrument of hegemony: see, e.g., Regina Bendix, *In Search of Authenticity: The Formation of Folklore Studies,* Madison: University of Wisconsin Press, 1997; John Fiske, "Admissible Postmodernity: Some Remarks on Rodney King, O. J. Simpson, and Contemporary Culture," *University of San Francisco Law Review,* 1996, *30,* 917–930; and sincerity is making a bit of a comeback, at least in the world of everyday communication: see, e.g., Gerry Spence, *How To Argue and Win Every Time,* New York: St. Martin's Press, 1995, pp. 47–66.

78. Trilling, note 67 above, at pp. 57–58, 112–114. Trilling draws on Henri Peyre in characterizing the French mode and on de Tocqueville in characterizing the American. As for the English, he believes "in Hegelian terms" that "English sincerity depends upon the English class structure." Id. at p. 114. We shall return to matters of this order in Chapter 8.

79. See, e.g., Christopher P. Toumey, *Conjuring Science: Scientific Symbols and Cultural Meanings in American Life,* New Brunswick: Rutgers University Press, 1996; Steve Fuller, *Science: Concepts in Social Thought,* Minneapolis: University of Minnesota Press, 1997; Dorothy Nelkin, *Selling Science: How the Press Covers Science and Technology,* revised edition, New York: W. H. Freeman, 1995.

80. Cf. James B. Gilbert, *Redeeming Culture: American Religion in an Age of Science,* Chicago: University of Chicago Press, 1997.

81. Ronald Dworkin, *Law's Empire,* Cambridge, Mass.: Harvard University Press, 1986.

82. See the colloquy between Justice Frankfurter and John W. Davis quoted in the text at note 71 above. Whatever its doctrinal relevance—or its dramaturgical relevance in taking Davis down a peg—Frankfurter's question illustrates the sensitivity of an alert jurist to the context-dependent nature of the task of applying general rules to particular cases.

83. See, e.g., Benjamin Lee Whorf, *Language, Thought, and Reality: Selected Writings of Benjamin Lee Whorf,* John B. Carroll (Ed.), Cambridge, Mass.: MIT Press, 1956. See also Paul Kay and Willett Kempton, "What Is the Sapir-Whorf Hypothesis?" *American Anthropologist,* 1984, *86,* 65–79.

5. Narratives at Court

1. 16 Pet. 539, 10 L.Ed. 1060 (1842). We will cite the Lawyer's Edition hereafter because it is more accessible and its two-column format allows us to pinpoint text references more exactly.

2. 503 U. S. 467, 118 L.Ed.2d 108, 112 S. Ct. 1430 (1992). Again we will cite the L. Ed. text.

3. On *Prigg,* see, e.g., Paul Finkelman, "Sorting out *Prigg v. Pennsylvania,*" *Rutgers Law Journal,* 1993, 24, 605–665; Barbara Holden-Smith, "Lords of Lash, Loom, and Law: Justice Story, Slavery, and Prigg v. Pennsylvania," *Cornell Law Review,* 1993, 78, 1086–1151; Christopher L. M. Eisgruber, "Justice Story, Slavery, and the Natural Law Foundations of American Constitutionalism," *University of Chicago Law Review,* 1988, 55, 273–327; Robert M. Cover, *Justice Accused: Antislavery and the Judicial Process,* New Haven and London: Yale University Press, 1975, pp. 159–174. On *Pitts,* see, e.g., Robert L. Carter, "Public School Desegregation: A Contemporary Analysis," *St. Louis University Law Journal,* 1993, 37, 885–896; Kevin Brown, "Has the Supreme Court Allowed the Cure for De Jure Segregation to Replicate the Disease?" *Cornell Law Review,* 1992, 78, 1–83; Chris Hansen, "Are the Courts Giving Up? Current Issues in School Desegregation," *Emory Law Journal,* 1993, 42, 863–877.

4. Our colleague, Peggy Davis, has led us on this path. See Peggy Cooper Davis, "The Proverbial Woman," *Record of the Bar Association of the City of New York,* January/February 1993, 48, 7–25. For other contributions to the genre, see Thomas Ross, "The Richmond Narratives," *Texas Law Review,* 1989, 68, 381–413; Thomas Ross, "The Rhetoric of Poverty: Their Immorality, Our Helplessness," *Georgetown Law Journal,* 1991, 79, 1499–1547; Mark Kessler, "Legal Discourse and Political Intolerance: The Ideology of Clear and Present Danger," *Law and Society Review,* 1993, 27, 559–597; Elizabeth Mertz, "Consensus and Dissent in U.S. Legal Opinions: Narrative Structure and Social Voices," *Anthropological Linguistics,* Fall/Winter 1988, 30(3/4), 369–394.

5. Cf. Northrop Frye, *Anatomy of Criticism: Four Essays* (1957), Princeton: Princeton University Press, 1990, p. 109: "The critic . . . is concerned only with the . . . patterns which are actually in what he is studying, however they got there. . . . [I]n *The Mikado,* . . . back comes all [Sir James George] Frazer's apparatus, the king's son, the mock sacrifice, the analogy with the festival of Sacaea, and many other things that Gilbert knew and cared nothing about. It comes back because it is still the best way of holding an audience's attention, and the experienced dramatist knows it."

6. Barbara Herrnstein Smith, "Narrative Versions, Narrative Theories," in W. J. T. Mitchell (Ed.), *On Narrative,* Chicago and London: University of Chicago Press, 1981, pp. 209–232, at p. 216.

7. This is an aspect of what James Boyd White calls constitutive rhetoric—the

process through which "we constitute ourselves as individuals, as communities, and as cultures, whenever we speak." James Boyd White, "Rhetoric and Law: The Arts of Cultural and Communal Life," in *Heracles' Bow: Essays on the Rhetoric and Poetics of the Law,* Madison: University of Wisconsin Press, 1985, pp. 28–48, at p. 35.

8. See also Jerome Bruner, "The Narrative Construction of Reality," *Critical Inquiry,* 1991, *18(1),* 1–21; Richard K. Sherwin, "The Narrative Construction of Legal Reality," *Vermont Law Review,* 1994, *18,* 681–719. Cf. Nelson Goodman, *Ways of Worldmaking,* Indianapolis: Hackett, 1978; Nelson Goodman, *Languages of Art: An Approach to a Theory of Symbols,* 2d edition, Indianapolis: Hackett, 1976.

9. See, e.g., Mieke Bal, *Narratology: Introduction to the Theory of Narrative,* 2d revised edition, Christine van Boheemen trans., Toronto: University of Toronto Press, 1985; Wayne C. Booth, *The Rhetoric of Fiction,* 2d edition, Chicago and London: University of Chicago Press, 1983; Peter Brooks, *Reading for the Plot: Design and Intention in Narrative* (1984), Cambridge, Mass.: Harvard University Press, 1995; Lubomír Doležel, *Heterocosmica: Fiction and Possible Worlds,* Baltimore and London: Johns Hopkins University Press, 1998; Frank Kermode, *The Genesis of Secrecy: On the Interpretation of Narrative,* Cambridge, Mass.: Harvard University Press, 1979; Michael Riffaterre, *Fictional Truth,* Baltimore and London: Johns Hopkins University Press, 1990; Roland Barthes, "Introduction to the Structural Analysis of Narratives," in *The Semiotic Challenge,* Richard Howard trans., New York: Hill and Wang, 1988, pp. 95–135; Hans Blumenberg, "The Concept of Reality and the Possibility of the Novel," in Richard E. Amacher and Victor Lange (Eds.), *New Perspectives in German Literary Criticism: A Collection of Essays,* David Henry Wilson trans., Princeton: Princeton University Press, 1979, pp. 29–48; Lubomír Doležel, "Truth and Authenticity in Narrative," *Poetics Today,* 1980, *1(3),* 7–25.

10. See, e.g., Hayden White, *The Content of the Form: Narrative Discourse and Historical Representation,* Baltimore and London: Johns Hopkins University Press, 1987; Hayden White, *Metahistory: The Historical Imagination in Nineteenth-Century Europe* (1973), Baltimore and London: Johns Hopkins University Press, 1993; David William Cohen, *The Combing of History,* Chicago and London: University of Chicago Press, 1994; Ronald H. Carpenter, *History as Rhetoric: Style, Narrative, and Persuasion,* Columbia: University of South Carolina Press, 1995; Louis O. Mink, "Narrative Form as a Cognitive Instrument," in Robert H. Canary and Henry Kozicki (Eds.), *The Writing of History: Literary Form and Historical Understanding,* Madison: University of Wisconsin Press, 1978, pp. 129–149.

11. See Anthony G. Amsterdam and Randy Hertz, "An Analysis of Closing Arguments to a Jury," *New York Law School Law Review,* 1992, *37,* 55–122; Kimberle Crenshaw and Gary Peller, "Reel Time/Real Justice," *Denver University Law Review,* 1993, *70,* 283–296; Anthony G. Amsterdam,

"Thurgood Marshall's Image of the Blue-Eyed Child in *Brown*," *New York University Law Review*, 1993, *68*, 226–236; Charles Goodwin, "Professional Vision," *American Anthropologist*, 1994, *96(3)*, 606–633; Philip N. Meyer, "'Desperate for Love': Cinematic Influences Upon a Defendant's Closing Argument to a Jury," *Vermont Law Review*, 1994, *18*, 721–749; Richard K. Sherwin, "Law Frames: Historical Truth and Narrative Necessity in a Criminal Case," *Stanford Law Review*, 1994, *47*, 39–83; Anthony G. Amsterdam, "Telling Stories and Stories About Them," *Clinical Law Review*, 1994, *1*, 9–40 (hereafter cited as "Telling Stories").

12. We are concerned solely with the way in which the opinions set forth the facts of the cases. Other critics have taken the opinions to task for neglecting or misrepresenting facts in the record (see the articles cited in note 3 above), but that is not our focus except insofar as the omission of available information or the choice to depict facts in one manner rather than another possible manner has narrative implications.

13. 10 L.Ed. at 1086–1087. Prigg also abducted the woman's two children. The opinion makes only tangential mention of this, and we omit the children from the plot line. But see James Boyd White, "Lecture, Constructing a Constitution: 'Original Intention' in the Slave Cases," *Maryland Law Review*, 1987, *47*, 239–270, at p. 270.

14. 10 L.Ed. at 1087.

15. Id.

16. Id.

17. Id.

18. 10 L.Ed. at 1088.

19. Id.

20. 10 L.Ed. at 1088–1098.

21. 10 L.Ed. at 1098.

22. 118 L.Ed.2d at 122.

23. 347 U.S. 483 (1954), and 349 U.S. 294 (1955).

24. 118 L.Ed.2d at 122–123.

25. 391 U.S. 430 (1968).

26. 118 L.Ed.2d at 123.

27. Id.

28. 118 L.Ed.2d at 123–124.

29. 118 L.Ed.2d at 124.

30. Id.

31. 118 L.Ed.2d at 124–125.

32. 118 L.Ed.2d at 125.

33. 118 L.Ed.2d at 125–129.

34. 118 L.Ed.2d at 127.

35. 118 L.Ed.2d at 128.

36. 118 L.Ed.2d at 128–129.

37. 118 L.Ed.2d at 129–130.

38. 118 L.Ed.2d at 130.
39. 118 L.Ed.2d at 130–131.
40. 118 L.Ed.2d at 131–140.
41. 118 L.Ed.2d at 131.
42. 118 L.Ed.2d at 133–134.
43. See, e.g., William F. Hansen, "Odysseus and the Oar: A Folkloric Approach," in Lowell Edmunds (Ed.), *Approaches to Greek Myth,* Baltimore and London, Johns Hopkins University Press, 1990, pp. 241–272, particularly at p. 266; Mary Louise Pratt, *Toward a Speech Act Theory of Literary Discourse,* Bloomington: Indiana University Press, 1977, pp. 132–151. The display of tellability may occur in either the *abstract* or the *orientation* portion of the classic Labovian narrative sequence because whatever serves to "encapsulate the point of [a] . . . story," William Labov, *Language in the Inner City: Studies in the Black English Vernacular,* Philadelphia: University of Pennsylvania Press, 1972, p. 363, or to "orient the listener in respect to *person, place, time,* and *behavioral situation*" of a story, William Labov and Joshua Waletzky, "Narrative Analysis: Oral Versions of Personal Experience," in June Helm (Ed.), *Essays on the Verbal and Visual Arts* [Proceedings of the 1966 Annual Spring Meeting of the American Ethnological Society], pp. 12–44, at p. 32, reprinted in *Journal of Narrative and Life History,* 1997, *7(1-4),* pp. 3–38, can also be used to situate the story vis-à-vis the listener by signaling its "current relevance," Michael J. Toolan, *Narrative: A Critical Linguistic Introduction* (1988), London and New York: Routledge, 1994, pp. 163–164; see Michael Toolan, "Analyzing Conversation in Fiction: The Christmas Dinner Scene in Joyce's *Portrait of the Artist as a Young Man,*" *Poetics Today,* 1987, *8(2),* 393–416.
44. 10 L.Ed. at 1087, col. 1, para. 3, lines 1–14. Here and hereafter we shall refer the reader to columns, paragraphs, and lines whenever details of the text are crucial. The paragraph numbers treat runover paragraphs as "para. 1" in any column.
45. 10 L.Ed. at 1087, col. 1, para. 3, lines 14–21.
46. 10 L.Ed. at 1087, col. 1, para. 6, line 1 – col. 2, para. 1, line 1.
47. 10 L.Ed. at 1087, col. 1, para. 6, line 4 – col. 2, para. 1, line 21.
48. 10 L.Ed. at 1088, col. 1, para. 1, line 22.
49. 10 L.Ed. at 1088, col. 1, para. 1, lines 12–14.
50. 10 L.Ed. at 1087, col. 2, para. 4, lines 14–17.
51. The procedural summary is in 118 L.Ed.2d at 122, col. 2, para. 2 through 124, col. 1, para. 3. The statement of facts is in 118 L.Ed.2d at 124, col. 2, para. 1 through 131, col. 1, para. 1.
52. 118 L.Ed.2d at 124, col. 2, para. 1, lines 2–4.
53. 118 L.Ed.2d at 125, col. 1, para. 1, lines 13–14.
54. 118 L.Ed.2d at 125, col. 2, para. 2, line 7.
55. 118 L.Ed.2d at 122, col. 1, para. 1 through col. 2, para. 1.
56. The analyses in the Appendix are based upon the whole text of each opin-

ion, not merely the overtly narrative passages. See Amsterdam, "Telling Stories," at pp. 11–12.

57. Unless the context plainly indicates otherwise, we will hereafter use "*Prigg*" and "the *Prigg* opinion" to refer exclusively to Justice Story's opinion in *Prigg*, and we will use "*Pitts*" and "the *Pitts* opinion" to refer exclusively to Justice Kennedy's opinion in *Pitts*. We take these two opinions simply as exemplary texts for narrative analysis; for that purpose, the other opinions in each case are beyond our focus.

58. 347 U.S. 483 (1954). We use *Brown* as a comparator simply to demonstrate that it is possible to write an opinion about race and the Constitution in a very different voice from that in *Prigg* and *Pitts*, not to take the *Brown* opinion as an ideal or a norm.

59. The analytic technique used in the Appendix is inspired primarily by Halliday's approach to grammatical discourse analysis. See M. A. K. Halliday, *An Introduction to Functional Grammar*, 2d edition, London: Edward Arnold, 1994; M. A. K. Halliday, "Linguistic Function and Literary Style: An Inquiry into the Language of William Golding's *The Inheritors*," in Seymour Chatman (Ed.), *Literary Style: A Symposium*, Oxford: Oxford University Press, 1971, pp. 330–365; cf. Roger Fowler, Bob Hodge, Gunter Kress, and Tony Trew, *Language and Control*, London: Routledge and Kegan Paul, 1979.

60. We speak of the point at which the tale itself (the *fabula*) begins, not of the point at which the telling of the tale begins. For the distinction, see Amsterdam, "Telling Stories," at p. 12 and nn. 6–9.

61. We have dealt with the subject of narrative necessity in Chapter 4. To the extent that it is driven by the need to contain or redress the breach of a canonical script, the starting point of a narrative will often function both to evoke a particular script and to identify a conventional form of breach. See, e.g., Roland Barthes, "The Sequences of Actions," in *The Semiotic Challenge*, note 9 above, pp. 136–148, at pp. 138–142; Bruner, note 8 above, at pp. 11–13.

62. This is so as much in myth as in practical affairs: Tantalos serves his slaughtered son Pelops to the Gods; Pelops' son Atreus slaughters his brother Thyestes' sons and serves them to Thyestes; Thyestes' ghost adjures Thyestes' son, Aegisthus, to connive the death of Agamemnon, Atreus' son, in conspiracy with Clytemnestra, who has it in for Agamemnon for sacrificing Iphigenia; Orestes, Agamemnon's son, kills Clytemnestra along with Aegisthus and is pursued by the Furies. (Card has suggested that the problem is so vexing for immortal beings as to drive them to create mortal gods. Orson Scott Card, *Cruel Miracles*, New York: Tom Doherty Associates, 1990, pp. 231–232.) In *Reading for the Plot*, Peter Brooks develops the idea that the basic object of narrative is "to wrest beginnings and ends from the uninterrupted flow of middles, from temporality itself," Brooks, note 9 above, at p. 140; and see id. at p. 281, quoting Henry James's well-known

dictum that "'[r]eally, universally, relations stop nowhere,'" so the writer's task is to "'draw . . . the circle within which they shall happily *appear* to do so.'" One strategy is to create the familiar "binary" movement of tragedy by describing the ascent of either leg of the eternal seesaw as "the original act [that] . . . sets up an antithetical or counterbalancing movement [whose] . . . completion resolves the tragedy." Frye, note 5 above, at p. 209. You pick which leg.

63. 10 L.Ed. at 1086, col. 2, para. 2, line 1 – 1087, col. 1, para. 5, line 9. See Part II above.

64. 10 L.Ed. at 1087, col. 2, para. 1, lines 8–9.

65. 10 L.Ed. at 1088, col. 1, para. 1, lines 12–14.

66. See Mircea Eliade, *Myth and Reality* (1963), Willard R. Trask trans., New York: Harper and Row (Torchbook), 1968, particularly at pp. 5–53, 139–145, 181–184; Mircea Eliade, *The Myth of the Eternal Return* (1949), Willard R. Trask trans., Princeton: Princeton University Press, 1965 second printing [corrected], particularly at pp. 3–34, 51–92; or, for a synopsis, Mircea Eliade, "Myths and Mythical Thought," in Alexander Eliot, *The Universal Myths,* New York: Meridian, 1990, pp. 14–40, at pp. 26–29. "[I]t must not be imagined that cosmogonic and anthropogenic myths are narrated only to answer such questions as 'who are we?' and 'whence do we come?' Such myths also constitute examples to be followed whenever it is a case of *creating* something, or of restoring or regenerating a human being." Mircea Eliade, *Myths, Dreams, and Mysteries: The Encounter Between Contemporary Faiths and Archaic Realities* (1957), Philip Mairet trans., New York: Harper and Row (Torchbook), 1967, p. 161.

67. Charles Sumner (who was, incidentally, Story's pupil, Story's protégé at Harvard, and Story's Commissioner) developed such a larger narrative as the framework for his constitutional arguments against the Fugitive Slave Act. See, e.g., Charles Sumner, "Freedom National, Slavery Sectional" (August 26, 1852), in *Charles Sumner, His Complete Works,* New York: Negro Universities Press, 1969, volume III, pp. 257–366.

68. 118 L.Ed.2d at 122, col. 1, para. 1, line 1 – col. 2, para. 1, line 21.

69. No other actors appear anywhere in Kennedy's statement of the case. Cf. Part III above.

70. The tale begins: "For decades before our decision in *Brown v. Board of Education,* 347 U.S. 483 . . . (1954) (Brown I), and our mandate in *Brown v. Board of Education,* 349 U.S. 294 . . . (1955) (Brown II), which ordered school districts to desegregate with 'all deliberate speed,' DCSS was segregated by law." 118 L.Ed.2d at 122, col. 2, para. 2, line 1 – 123, col. 1, para. 1, line 4. The five words at the beginning and the five words at the end of this sentence constitute Justice Kennedy's entire tale of the Cosmos before *Brown.* His next sentence begins: "DCSS's initial response to the mandate of Brown II was . . ." 118 L.Ed.2d at 123, col. 1, para. 1, lines 4–6. After a more detailed statement of the present controversy (118 L.Ed.2d at

123, col. 1, para. 1, line 4 – 131, col. 1, para. 2, line 15), Kennedy takes up his larger tale again, once more beginning with the *Brown* decisions (118 L.Ed.2d at 131, col. 1, para. 3, line 1 – 132, col. 1, para. 1., line 3).

71. Shakespeare, for example, uses the plot structure with personalities and plights as diverse as those of *Julius Caesar, Coriolanus, Macbeth,* and *Othello.* Sophocles' Creon is a principled though over-proud ruler; Alfieri's Creon is an opportunistic schemer. (In addition to the two authors' *Antigones,* see Alfieri's *Polynices.*) Aeschylus' Agamemnon is a noble war chief slain by Clytemnestra to avenge what he believed to be the needful sacrifice of Iphigenia; Seneca and Alfieri, following Homer, make Aegisthus— driven by Thyestes' ghost—the principal in Agamemnon's murder, with Clytemnestra as a tool; but Alfieri's Agamemnon is a tragic hero haunted by the memory of dead Iphigenia, while Seneca's Agamemnon is a mere stick figure, an effigy defiled to punish Greek presumption in the sack of Troy. (In addition to the three dramatists' *Agamemnons,* see Homer, *The Odyssey,* book III, lines 193–198, 303–308; book IV, lines 512–535; book XI, lines 377–456.

72. The Conquering Hero Turned Tyrant is a subcategory of the Tyrant Tale. See note 97 below. Speaking of the broader category, Gilbert Highet notes: "[T]he ambitious ruthless tyrant [is] . . . an eternal figure. He was created in drama by the Greeks; but he was intensified into diabolism by Seneca, eagerly taken up by the Italians because their own cities produced so many of his type, and copied both from Rome and from Italy by the horrified but interested English poets." Gilbert Highet, *The Classical Tradition: Greek and Roman Influences on Western Literature,* New York and London: Oxford University Press, 1949, p. 132. Cf. Frye, note 5 above, at p. 148.

Christian Meier, following Paul Veyne, suggests that the obsessional "fear of tyranny [that] haunts tragedies from the 450s onwards" was the Greek citizens' "fear of themselves" (Christian Meier, *The Political Art of Greek Tragedy* (1988), Andrew Webber trans., Baltimore: Johns Hopkins University Press, 1993, p. 133): after the removal of power from the Areopagus, "they were afraid of being unable to sustain the pressures of citizenship, that they were going too far and becoming arrogant and willful. It was the fear of this that was embodied in the figure of the tyrant" (id. at p. 134; see also id. at p. 164). But the necessity that the old king turn tyrant and be deposed is not, of course, unique to the high classical tradition. Frye, note 5 above, at pp. 35–37, 158–160, 207–217; Joseph Campbell, *The Hero with a Thousand Faces* (1949; 2d edition 1968), Princeton: Princeton University Press, 1973, pp. 334–354; Marie-Louise von Franz, *Shadow and Evil in Fairy Tales* (1974), revised edition, Boston and London: Shambhala, 1995, pp. 25–30. See, e.g., "The Blue Light," in Jacob and Wilhelm Grimm, *The Complete Grimm's Fairy Tales,* Margaret Hunt trans., revised by James Stern, New York: Pantheon Books, 1972, pp. 530–534; "The Griffin," in id., pp. 681–688; "The Wise Wife," in Aleksandr Afanas'ev (Coll.), *Rus-*

sian Fairy Tales, Norbert Guterman trans., New York: Pantheon Books, 1973, pp. 521–528; "Forty Hares and a Princess," in Beatrice Silverman Weinreich (Ed.), *Yiddish Folktales,* Leonard Wolf trans., New York: Pantheon Books, 1988, pp. 130–135; "A Letter to God," in id., pp. 163–166; "The Land of Green Mountains," in Donald A. Mackenzie, *Scottish Wonder Tales from Myth and Legend,* Mineola, N.Y.: Dover, 1997, p. 195–224.

73. In the following summary, we'll exemplify it with these avatars: *Julius Caesar:* Shakespeare's *Julius Caesar* and Alfieri's *The Second Brutus; Agamemnon:* The *Agamemnon*s of Aeschylus, Seneca, and Alfieri; *Creon of Thebes:* The *Antigone*s of Sophocles and Alfieri; *Othello:* Shakespeare's *Othello, The Moor of Venice; Nero:* Racine's *Britannicus.*

74. Shakespeare/*Caesar,* act I, scenes 1–2; Alfieri/*Second Brutus,* act I, scene 1; Aeschylus/*Agamemnon,* lines 11–37, 520–528; Seneca/*Agamemnon,* lines 45–49, 203–207, 417–420; Alfieri/*Agamemnon,* act I, scene 1 – act I, scene 2; Sophocles/*Antigone,* lines 5–40; Alfieri/*Antigone,* act I, scenes 1–3; Shakespeare/*Othello,* act I, scene 1; Racine/*Britannicus,* act I, scenes 1–2.

75. 118 L.Ed.2d at 122, col. 1, para. 2, lines 1–6.

76. 118 L.Ed.2d at 122, col. 2, para. 1, line 1 – 123, col. 1, para. 1, line 4; 123, col. 1, para. 2, lines 1–22; 131, col. 1, para. 3, line 1 – 132, col. 1, para. 1, line 3.

77. Shakespeare/*Caesar,* act I, scene 1 [Flavius], act I, scenes 2–3 [Cassius]; Alfieri/*Second Brutus,* act I, scene 1 – act II, scene 2; Aeschylus/*Agamemnon,* lines 217–250 [the function of Detractor is initially borne by the chorus, since Clytemnestra plays the hypocrite until after Agamemnon's murder; then, having done the deed, Clytemnestra takes on the Detractor's role (lines 1372–1525)]; Seneca/*Agamemnon,* lines 162–192 [Clytemnestra], 245–259 [Aegisthus]; Alfieri/*Agamemnon,* act I, scene 1 [Aegisthus], act I, scene 2 [Clytemnestra]; Sophocles/*Antigone,* lines 20–35; Alfieri/*Antigone,* act I, scene 3; Shakespeare/*Othello,* act I, scene 1 [Iago], act I, scene 3 [Brabantio]; Racine/*Britannicus,* act I, scene 1 [Agrippina].

    Detractor's function may be divided among players: Cassius/Brutus; Ghost of Thyestes/Aegisthus/Clytemnestra; Antigone/Argeia; Iago/Brabantio.

78. 118 L.Ed.2d at 122, col. 1, para. 1, lines 1–10.

79. 118 L.Ed.2d at 123, col. 1, para. 2, line 26 – 124, col. 1, para. 1, line 5.

80. 118 L.Ed.2d at 124, col. 1, para. 2, lines 1–7.

81. Shakespeare/*Caesar,* act I, scene 2, act II, scene 3; Alfieri/*Second Brutus,* act II, scene 2; Aeschylus/*Agamemnon,* lines 156–159, 1415–1448 [Clytemnestra]; Seneca/*Agamemnon,* lines 23–61 [Aegisthus], lines 158–182 [Clytemnestra]; Alfieri/*Agamemnon,* act I, scene 1 [Aegisthus], act I, scene 2 [Clytemnestra]; Sophocles/*Antigone,* lines 20–35; Alfieri/*Antigone,* act I, scene 3; Shakespeare/*Othello,* act I, scene 1; Racine/*Britannicus,* act I, scene 1.

82. 118 L.Ed.2d at 122, col. 2, para. 2, line 1 – 123, col. 2, para. 1, line 24.

83. See 118 L.Ed.2d at 131, col. 1, para. 3, line 1 – col. 2, para. 1, line 26.

84. Shakespeare/*Caesar*, act II, scene 1; Alfieri/*Second Brutus*, act I, scene 1 [Antony], act II, scene 3 [Brutus]; Aeschylus/*Agamemnon*, lines 185–225, 529–537, 777–812; Seneca/*Agamemnon*, lines 203–210, 239–243, 260–274; Alfieri/*Agamemnon*, act I, scene 3; Sophocles/*Antigone*, lines 50–73; Alfieri/*Antigone*, act III, scene 1 [a vestigial function: Haemon's statement to Creon that Creon is not unjust and unnatural is more exhortation than praise]; Shakespeare/*Othello*, act I, scene 3; Racine/*Britannicus*, act I, scenes 1–2.

    Defender's function may be divided among players: Antony/Artemidorus; Electra/Clytemnestra/Nurse; Ismene/Haemon; Desdemona/Duke of Venice; Albina/Burrus.

85. 118 L.Ed.2d at 123, col. 1, para. 3, line 1 – col. 2, para. 1, line 3.

86. Shakespeare/*Caesar*, act I, scene 2; Alfieri/*Second Brutus*, act II, scene 3, act III, scene 2, act IV, scene 2; Aeschylus/*Agamemnon*, lines 576–584; Seneca/*Agamemnon*, lines 239–243; Alfieri/*Agamemnon*, act I, scene 3 [Electra]; Alfieri/*Antigone*, act III, scene 1; Shakespeare/*Othello*, act I, scene 3; Racine/*Britannicus*, act I, scenes 1–2 [Burrus].

    This function is omitted in Sophocles' *Antigone*, where Ismene serves as Defender and bases her defense of Creon on obligations of state rather than on any assertion of Creon's personal virtue.

87. 118 L.Ed.2d at 124, col. 2, para. 1, lines 15–20; 129, col. 2, para. 2, line 1 – 130, col. 1, para. 1, line 18; 131, col. 1, para. 3, line 6 – col. 2, para. 1, line 25; 137, col. 2, para. 2, lines 1–8; 138, col. 2, para. 1, lines 4–35; 139, col. 1, para. 3, lines 4–7.

88. "Returning schools to the control of local authorities at the earliest practicable date is essential to restore their true accountability in our governmental system." 118 L.Ed.2d at 134, col. 1, para. 2, lines 7–11.

89. Shakespeare/*Caesar*, act II, scene 1 (and, after Caesar's death, act III, scene 2); Alfieri/*Second Brutus*, act II, scene 3 – act V, scene 2; Aeschylus/*Agamemnon*, lines 800–812; Seneca/*Agamemnon*, lines 125–310; Alfieri/*Agamemnon*, act II, scene 2; Sophocles/*Antigone*, lines 29–98, 680–757; Shakespeare/*Othello*, act I, scene 3; Racine/*Britannicus*, act I, scene 2, act III, scene 3.

    In Sophocles' *Antigone*, this function is supplemented by Haemon's dialogues with Creon (lines 680–757); in Alfieri's *Antigone*, it is replaced by those dialogues (act III, scenes 1–2).

90. 118 L.Ed.2d at 123, col. 2, para. 1, line 3 – 126, col. 1, para. 1, line 15.

91. 118 L.Ed.2d at 126, col. 2, para. 2, line 1 – 128, col. 2, para. 1, line 22; 129, col. 2, para. 2, line 1 – 130, col. 1, para. 1, line 18.

92. 118 L.Ed.2d at 131, col. 1, para. 3, line 1 – 138, col. 1, para. 2, line 16.

93. 118 L.Ed.2d at 133, col. 2, para. 2, line 25 – 134, col. 1, para. 1, line 4. The sleight of hand involved in endowing *Brown* with the tragic flaw of mutually warring purposes is interesting: "We have said that the court's end pur-

pose must be to remedy the violation and in addition to restore the state and local authorities to the control of a school system that is operating in compliance with the Constitution." 118 L.Ed.2d at 133, col. 2, para. 2, lines 1–7. See Chapter 3, *Jenkins,* Part III, Scene 8.

94. Shakespeare/*Caesar,* act I, scene 2, act II, scene 2; Alfieri/*Second Brutus,* act III, scene 1 – act V, scene 2; Aeschylus/*Agamemnon,* lines 817–854, 912–929; Seneca/*Agamemnon,* lines 744–747, 784–798; Alfieri/*Agamemnon,* act II, scene 4 – act III, scene 4, act IV, scenes 3–4; Sophocles/*Antigone,* lines 165–210, 420–580, 635–757; Alfieri/*Antigone,* act II, scene 1 – act III, scene 1; Shakespeare/*Othello,* act I, scene 2 – act III, scene 4; Racine/*Britannicus,* act II, scene 1 – act III, scene 1.

95. 118 L.Ed.2d at 123, col. 1, para. 2, lines 1–13. See text at note 85 above.

96. Shakespeare/*Caesar,* act III, scene 1; Alfieri/*Second Brutus,* act V, scene 2; Aeschylus/*Agamemnon,* lines 944–1034; Seneca/*Agamemnon,* lines 798–801, 883–894; Alfieri/*Agamemnon,* act IV, scene 5 [a token gesture: Agamemnon's fate has already been sealed by Clytemnestra's determination to murder him; his arbitrary disposition of Cassandra is of little practical moment]; Sophocles/*Antigone,* lines 758–777; Alfieri/*Antigone,* act IV, scenes 2, 6; Shakespeare/*Othello,* act III, scene 4; Racine/*Britannicus,* act III, scenes 8–9.

There are many variations on the basic plot structure. For example, in *Macbeth* the accusation and defense of tyranny are almost entirely internalized (see Macbeth's soliloquies in act I, scene 3; act I, scene 7; and act II, scene 1); through a powerful inversion, Lady Macbeth indicts Macbeth for having too much of the milk of human kindness tempering his ambition (act I, scene 5). Otherwise the pattern holds: The play opens with announcements of Macbeth's ascendancy through merit (Macbeth has defeated Macdonwald and the Norweyans and is named Thane of Cawdor (act I, scene 2)); Macbeth enters (act I, scene 3), conflicted about his royal ambitions (id.); he debates with himself and Lady Macbeth whether ambition or the fear to realize it is the more unworthy (act I, scene 3; act I, scene 7; act II, scene 1); he commits decisively to ambition and therefore murder (act I, scene 7); and all else follows.

In *Titus Andronicus,* the basic plot is compressed into the first third of the first act; the rest of the play depicts the awful outcome as a Spanish Tragedy.

In Christopher Marlowe's *Edward II,* the classic structure is redoubled, with both the King and his murderer, Mortimer, cast in the conquering-hero-turned-tyrant mold. Edward II's final tyrannical moves occur in act II, scene 2 and act III, scenes 2–3; Mortimer's occur in act V, scene 4.

97. Other types of Tyrant Tales are exemplified by Seneca's *Thyestes,* Lucan's *Civil War,* Shakespeare's *Richard III,* and Alfieri's *Polynices.*

98. For a sense of the importance of starting at the right moment, compare the differing impressions conveyed by Victor Hugo's translation of 60 lines of Book I of Lucan's *Pharsalia* (the *Civil War*), Victor Hugo, "César Passe le

Rubicon," in *Oeuvres Poétiques,* Paris: Bibliothèque de la Pléiade, 1964, volume I, pp. 98–99, and by Lucan's entire text or Marlowe's translation of Book I (in Christopher Marlowe, *Complete Plays and Poems,* E. D. Pendry (Ed.), London: J. M. Dent (Everyman), 1990, pp. 487–504). Hugo's perfectly timed single-episode snapshot of the crossing of the Rubicon makes Julius Caesar a Conquering-Hero-Turned-Tyrant, whereas in Lucan and Marlowe—which treat Caesar's career panoramically—Caesar comes off as an All-Ambitious Schemer/Tyrant. (Hugo's "Buonaparte," in Hugo, *Oeuvres Poétiques,* volume I, pp. 332–335, applies the same panoramic perspective to Napoleon I with similar results.)

99. 118 L.Ed.2d at 130, col. 2, para. 2, line 30 – 131, col. 1, para. 1, line 13.
100. 118 L.Ed.2d at 136, col. 1, para. 2, line 1 – para. 3, line 12.
101. See Meier, note 72 above, at pp. 191–200.
102. Both Charles Sumner and Frederick Douglass told the tale that way. Douglass began by stating

> ". . . what is not the question. It is not whether slavery existed in the United States at the time of the adoption of the Constitution; it is not whether slaveholders took part in framing the Constitution; it is not whether those slaveholders, in their hearts, intended to secure certain advantages in that instrument for slavery; it is not whether the American Government has been wielded during seventy-two years in favour of the propagation and permanence of slavery; it is not whether a proslavery interpretation has been put upon the Constitution by the American Courts. [It is:] . . . Does the United States Constitution guarantee to any class or description of people in that country the right to enslave, or hold as property, any other class or description of people in that country? . . .
>
> ". . . It should . . . be borne in mind that the intentions of those who framed the Constitution, be they good or bad, for slavery or against slavery, are to be respected so far, and only so far, as we find those intentions stated in the Constitution. . . .
>
> ". . . [W]here would be the advantage of a written Constitution if, instead of seeking its meaning in its words, we had to seek them in the secret intentions of individuals who may have had something to do with writing the paper? What will the people of America a hundred years hence care about the intentions of the scriveners who wrote the Constitution? These men are already gone from us, and in the course of nature were expected to go. They were for a generation, but the Constitution is for ages. . . .
>
> "[Considering,] . . . then, . . . those provisions of the Constitution, which the most extravagant defenders of slavery can claim to guarantee a right of property in man [and particularly the provision in Article I, section 9 that] . . . it is said guaranteed the continuance of the African

slave trade for twenty years. . . . [L]et us suppose it did, and what follows? why, this—that this part of the Constitution, so far as the slave trade is concerned, became a dead letter more than 50 years ago, and now binds no man's conscience for the continuance of any slave trade whatever. . . . But there is still more to be said about this abolition of the slave trade. Men, at that time, both in England and in America, looked upon the slave trade as the life of slavery. The abolition of the slave trade was supposed to be the certain death of slavery. Cut off the stream, and the pond will dry up, was the common notion at that time."

Frederick Douglass, "The Constitution of the United States: Is It Pro-Slavery or Anti-Slavery?" (1860), in Philip S. Foner (Ed.), *The Life and Writings of Frederick Douglass,* New York: International Publishers, 1950, volume II, pp. 467–480, at pp. 467–473. Cf. Charles Sumner, note 67 above, volume III, at pp. 275–295, 304–305.

103. 10 L.Ed. at 1088, col. 2, para. 1, lines 16–23 (quoting Blackstone).

104. Apollodorus, *The Library,* book III, chap. 10; Hesiod, *The Catalogues of Women and Eoiae,* part 68.

105. 10 L.Ed. at 1087, col. 2, para. 1, lines 6–9.

106. 10 L.Ed. at 1088, col. 1, para. 1, lines 5–14.

107. Apollodorus, *The Library,* book III, chap. 10; Robert Graves, *The Greek Myths* (1955), London: Penguin Books, 1960 revised edition, volume 2, p. 268 [para. 159.b].

108. See Hesiod, *The Catalogues of Women and Eoiae,* part 68, lines 88–100; Euripides, *Iphigenia in Aulis,* lines 49–64; Apollodorus, *The Library,* book III, chap. 10; Thomas Bullfinch, "The Age of Fable," chap. xxvii, para. 1 (in *Bullfinch's Mythology*).

109. 10 L.Ed. at 1088, col. 1, para. 1, lines 19–22.

110. See, e.g, Euripides, *Iphigenia in Aulis,* lines 65–74. Paris had, of course, been set upon this track by Aphrodite, after gaining her favor—and incurring the wrath of Hera and Athena—by judging Aphrodite the most beautiful in the contest among the three. E.g., Homer, *The Iliad,* book XXIV, lines 30–36; Hesiod, *The Cypria,* part 1; Apollodorus, *The Library,* Epitome, chap. 3; Euripides, *The Trojan Women,* lines 921–940; Euripides, *Andromache,* lines 275–310; Ovid, *Heroides,* book V, lines 33–40, and books XVI–XVII. In *Prigg,* there may be a parallel to the judgment of Paris in Lord Mansfield's decision in *Somerset's Case,* 20 Howell St. Tr. 79 (1772), which licensed the liberation of slaves by a hospitable asylum state. See *Prigg,* 10 L.Ed. at 1087, col. 2, para. 4, line 29 – 1088, col. 1, para. 1, line 14.

111. 10 L.Ed. at 1088, col. 1, para. 3, lines 1–15.

112. Apollodorus, *The Library,* Epitome, chap. 3; Graves, note 107 above, volume 2, p. 278 [para. 160.b].

113. 10 L.Ed. at 1088, col. 1, para. 3, line 16 – col. 2, para. 2, line 24.
114. Homer, *The Iliad,* book XI, lines 160–164; Ovid, *Metamorphoses,* book XIII; Apollodorus, *The Library,* Epitome, chap. 3.
115. 10 L.Ed. at 1088, col. 2, para. 3, line 1 – 1089, col. 1, para. 1, line 15.
116. Homer, *The Iliad,* book I, lines 1–6. In Robert Fagles's translation, the passage reads:

> "Rage—Goddess, sing the rage of Peleus' son Achilles,
> murderous, doomed, that cost the Achaeans countless losses,
> hurling down to the House of Death so many sturdy souls,
> great fighters' souls, but made their bodies carrion,
> feasts for the dogs and birds,
> and the will of Zeus was moving toward its end."

Homer, *The Iliad,* Robert Fagles trans., New York: Penguin Books (Penguin Classics), 1991, p. 77. There are suggestions that Zeus contrived the Trojan War to kill off humankind. Hesiod, *The Catalogues of Women and Eoiae,* part 68, book II; see also Hesiod, *The Cypria,* part 3 [Scholiast on Homer's *Iliad* i, 5], quoted in note 141 below.
117. "It is scarcely conceivable that the slaveholding States would have been satisfied with leaving to the legislation of the non-slaveholding States a power of regulation, in the absence of that of Congress, which would or might practically amount to a power to destroy the rights of the owner." 10 L.Ed.2d at 1092, col. 2, para. 2, lines 1–7.
118. 10 L.Ed. at 1092, col. 2, para. 2, lines 20–23.
119. 118 L.Ed.2d at 134, col. 1, para. 2, lines 11–18.
120. 118 L.Ed.2d at 137, col. 2, para. 1, lines 4–13.
121. Under the fugitive-slave provisions of the 1793 Act of Congress, both federal judges and state magistrates were authorized to hear slaveowners' claims of fugitivity and to issue removal certificates. Justice Story holds that such proceedings are cases "'arising under the Constitution'" and thus "within the express delegation of judicial power given [to the federal judiciary] by [Article III of] that instrument." (10 L.Ed. at 1089, col. 2, para. 2, lines 1–12.) With regard to state magistrates, he holds only that they "may, if they choose, exercise that authority, unless prohibited by State legislation" (10 L.Ed. at 1091, col. 2, para. 2, lines 15–23); and he implies that the States are not "bound to provide means to carry into effect the duties of the national government" regarding the rendition of fugitives (10 L.Ed.2d at 1089, col. 1, para. 3, line 20 – col. 2, para. 1, line 7; see also id. at 1092, col. 1, para. 2).
122. See, e.g., Edward Shils, "Charisma, Order, and Status," in *The Constitution of Society,* Chicago and London: University of Chicago Press, 1982, pp. 119–142. The dreads of explosion and implosion—Kierkegaard's de-

spairs from infinitude and finitude—are chronicled in Kirk J. Schneider, *The Paradoxical Self: Toward an Understanding of Our Contradictory Nature,* New York: Plenum, 1990; Kirk J. Schneider, *Horror and the Holy: Wisdom-Teachings of the Monster Tale,* Chicago: Open Court, 1993.

123. *Prigg,* 10 L.Ed. at 1092, col. 1, para. 3, line 5 – col. 2, para. 2, line 7.
124. *Pitts,* 118 L.Ed.2d at 137, col. 1, para. 2, line 1 – col. 2, para. 1, line 18.
125. 118 L.Ed.2d at 127, col. 1, para. 3, lines 16–18.
126. 118 L.Ed.2d at 125, col. 2, para. 2, lines 1–2.
127. 118 L.Ed.2d at 136, col. 2, para. 1, lines 3–5.
128. 118 L.Ed.2d at 125, col. 2, para. 2, lines 6–10.
129. 118 L.Ed.2d at 128, col. 1, para. 1, lines 24–42.
130. 10 L.Ed. at 1089, col. 1, para. 1, lines 11–12.
131. 10 L.Ed. at 1089, col. 1, para. 1, lines 12–13.
132. 10 L.Ed. at 1088, col. 1, para. 3, lines 18–20.
133. 10 L.Ed. at 1091, col. 2, para. 1, lines 20–24; 1092, col. 2, para. 1, lines 7–8.
134. In *Brown,* "the movement toward free common schools" appears as the subject of one active verb (347 U.S. at 489, para. 2, line 4 – 490, para. 1, line 1); "the development [of free public schools]" appears as the subject of two active verbs (347 U.S. at 489 n. 4, lines 10–12); and "the conditions of public education" appears as the subject of two copulas (347 U.S. at 490, para. 1, lines 12–14).
135. If life is hap, struggle is silly. A "retreat into voyeurism" follows as "an expression of helplessness before the autonomy of systems." Andrew Delbanco, *The Death of Satan: How Americans Have Lost The Sense of Evil,* New York: Farrar, Straus (Noonday), 1996, p. 140. "[D]ifficult conditions become problems only when people come to see them as amenable to human action." Deborah A. Stone, "Causal Stories and the Formation of Policy Agendas," *Political Science Quarterly,* 1989, 104(2), 281–300, at p. 281. Cf. Kenneth Burke, *A Grammar of Motives* (1945), Berkeley: University of California Press, 1969, p. 17: "[O]ne may deflect attention from scenic matters by situating the motives of an act in an agent . . . or conversely, one may deflect attention from the criticism of personal motives by deriving an act or attitude not from traits of the agent but from the nature of the situation."
136. *Brown,* 347 U.S. at 493, para. 4, line 1 – 495, para. 2, line 8.
137. *Pitts,* 118 L.Ed.2d at 131, col. 1, para. 3, line 1 – 132, col. 1, para. 1, line 3.
138. "It is apparent that [school] . . . segregation has long been a nationwide problem, not merely one of sectional concern." *Brown,* 347 U.S. at 491 n. 6, lines 6–8.
139. Id. at 493, para. 3, lines 4–5. The conception is carefully constructed: "Today, education is perhaps the most important function of state and local governments. . . . It is required in the performance of our most basic public

responsibilities. . . . In these days, it is doubtful that any child may reasonably be expected to succeed in life if he is denied the opportunity for an education." Id. at 493, para. 2, lines 1–14.

140. Proof that it is no longer present can then be found in the failure of the class representatives of the African-American children to complain between 1969 and 1986. See *Pitts,* 118 L.Ed.2d at 123, col. 2, para. 2, lines 1–7; 126, col. 2, para. 1, lines 1–7; 136, col. 2, para. 1, lines 5–11. This is Justice Kennedy's version of the well-rubbed tale of the insatiate beneficiary. See Amsterdam, "Telling Stories," at p. 21 and n. 76.

141. See Hesiod, *The Cypria,* part 3 [Scholiast on Homer's *Iliad* i, 5]. In Evelyn-White's translation, the passage reads:

> "There was a time when the countless tribes of men, though wide-dispersed, oppressed the surface of the deep-bosomed earth, and Zeus saw it and had pity and in his wise heart resolved to relieve the all-nurturing earth of men by causing the great struggle of the Ilian war, that the load of death might empty the world. And so the heroes were slain in Troy, and the plan of Zeus came to pass."

Hesiod, *Homeric Hymns; Epic Cycle; Homerica,* Cambridge, Mass.: Harvard University Press, 1995, with English trans. by Hugh G. Evelyn-White, pp. 496–497. Cf. *Prigg,* 10 L.Ed. at 1088, col. 2, para. 2, lines 16–35:

> "Nay, the local legislation may be utterly inadequate to furnish the appropriate redress [to the owner of a fugitive slave] by authorizing no process *in rem,* or no specific mode of repossessing the slave. . . . The State legislation may be entirely silent on the whole subject, and its ordinary remedial process framed with different views and objects; and this may be innocently as well as designedly done, since every State is perfectly competent, and has the exclusive right to prescribe the remedies in its own judicial tribunals . . . and to deny jurisdiction over cases which its own policy and its own institutions either prohibit or discountenance."

6. On Rhetorics

1. E.g., Aristotle, *The Art of Rhetoric,* book I, chaps. i–ii; Cicero, *De Inventione,* book I, chap. v; Cicero, *Orator,* chap. xxi; Francois De Salignac De La Mothe Fénelon, *Fénelon's Dialogues on Eloquence,* Wilbur Samuel Howell trans., Princeton: Princeton University Press, 1951, pp. 61–62 [First Dialogue]; Hugh Blair, *Lectures on Rhetoric and Belles Lettres* (1819), Delmar, N.Y.: Scholars' Facsimiles and Reprints, 1993, pp. 234–237 [Lecture XXXV]; see Edwin Black, *Rhetorical Criticism: A Study in Method* (1965), Madison: University of Wisconsin Press, 1978, pp. 11–17.

2. E.g., Ivor Armstrong Richards, *The Philosophy of Rhetoric,* Oxford: Oxford University Press, 1936; Kenneth Burke, *Language as Symbolic Action: Essays on Life, Literature, and Method,* Berkeley: University of California

Press, 1966; Kenneth Burke, *A Rhetoric of Motives* (1950), Berkeley: University of California Press, 1969; Douglas Ehninger et al., "Report of the Committee on the Scope of Rhetoric and the Place of Rhetorical Studies in Higher Education," in Lloyd F. Bitzer and Edwin Black (Eds.), *The Prospect of Rhetoric*, Englewood Cliffs, N.J.: Prentice-Hall, 1971, pp. 208–219; Sonja K. Foss, *Rhetorical Criticism: Exploration and Practice*, Prospect Heights, Ill.: Waveland Press, 1989, pp. 3–8; Bernard L. Brock and Robert L. Scott, "An Introduction to Rhetorical Criticism," in Bernard L. Brock and Robert L. Scott (Eds.), *Methods of Rhetorical Criticism: A Twentieth-Century Perspective*, 2d revised edition, Detroit: Wayne State University Press, 1980, pp. 11–27, at p. 16; see also James Boyd White, *Heracles' Bow: Essays on the Rhetoric and Poetics of the Law*, Madison: University of Wisconsin Press, 1985. The modern/postmodern trend is to define rhetoric in terms of what's to be studied when "rhetoric" is studied; the classic definitions were principally concerned with what's being done when "rhetoric" is done.

3. Cf. Edwin Black, *Rhetorical Questions: Studies of Public Discourse*, Chicago and London: University of Chicago Press, 1992, p. 153: "Most rhetorical discourses can be interpreted as seeking to regulate an audience's conception of a subject and its definition of the issues attending that subject."

4. The conspiracy will often be a conspiracy of silence which perpetuates the disregard of excluded values by framing the possible subjects for action, choice, and even contemplation as though those values were nonexistent. We are not suggesting that law-talk comes into play only on occasions of actual controversy: to the contrary, it often blankets sectors of potential controversy and preempts any actual controversy by delimiting the propositions that can be asserted, questioned, or imagined in those sectors.

5. It is not a new insight that the two are cognate: "[T]he same arguments which we use in persuading others when we speak in public, we employ also when we deliberate in our own thoughts." Isocrates, *Antidosis*, in volume II of the bilingual *Isocrates*, Cambridge, Mass.: Harvard University Press, 1982 reprint, with English translation by George Norlin, pp. 326–327 [v. 256]. Advocates from Cicero to Gerry Spence have emphasized the necessity (and largely overlooked the dangers) of convincing oneself as a precondition of being convincing to others. See, e.g., Cicero, *De Oratore*, book II, chaps. xlv–xlvii; Quintilian, *Institutio Oratoria*, book VI, chap. ii; Gerry Spence, *How to Argue and Win Every Time*, New York: St. Martin's Press, 1995, pp. 47–66.

6. See Black, note 3 above, at p. 63:

"Unintentional distortion is a variation on the historic uses of secrecy and disclosure. In entering into that pact with the devil by which accuracy is exchanged for morale, the simple, pious villagers of Dachau knew only their own innocence, just as the simple, pious Mississippi gentry of an earlier time knew only the happy slave singing in the cot-

ton field. . . . Unintentional distortion is a form of disguise, but it is a disguise designed to fool oneself, to conceal something from one's own knowledge of it. Secrecy and disclosure as rhetorical forms are not employed only consciously and deliberately. . . ."
And see, e.g., Anthony R. Pratkanis and Elliot Aronson, *Age of Propaganda: The Everyday Use and Abuse of Persuasion,* New York: W. H. Freeman, 1992, pp. 123–127.

7. J. L. Austin, *How to Do Things with Words,* Cambridge, Mass.: Harvard University Press, 1962.

8. See, e.g., John R. Searle, *Speech Acts: An Essay in the Philosophy of Language,* Cambridge: Cambridge University Press, 1969; Stephen C. Levinson, *Pragmatics* (1983), Cambridge: Cambridge University Press, 1987, pp. 226–283.

9. See, e.g., Stephen E. Toulmin, *The Uses of Argument* (1958), Cambridge: Cambridge University Press, 1994.

10. We'll do so after this sentence. The sentence itself is still playing—in the double sense of being tricksy and of flaunting the excess of meaning over saying—by evoking Wittgenstein's broader claim that the only signification any utterance can have is its function as a move in the particular "language game" at hand. E.g., Ludwig Wittgenstein, *Philosophical Investigations* (1967, 3d edition), G. E. M. Anscombe trans., Oxford: Blackwell, 1995, volume I, pp. 5–27 [§§ 7–54].

11. Paul Grice, *Studies in the Way of Words,* Cambridge, Mass.: Harvard University Press, 1989.

12. Dan Sperber and Deirdre Wilson, *Relevance: Communication and Cognition,* Cambridge, Mass.: Harvard University Press, 1986. For a conceptualization of the search process in terms of frame selection, see Marvin Minsky, "Frame-System Theory," in P. N. Johnson-Laird and P. C. Wason, *Thinking: Readings in Cognitive Science* (1977), Cambridge: Cambridge University Press, 1985, pp. 355–376.

13. Stephen C. Levinson, "Activity Types and Language," *Linguistics,* 1979, *17(5–6)* [issues 219/220], 365–399.

14. Carol Berkenkotter and Thomas N. Huckin, *Genre Knowledge in Disciplinary Communication: Cognition/Culture/Power,* Mahwah, N.J.: Erlbaum, 1995, p. 6. The notion of genre as "typified rhetorical actions based in recurrent situations" is developed in Carolyn R. Miller, "Genre as Social Action," *Quarterly Journal of Speech,* 1984, *70,* 151–167, at p. 159. Basic works on speech genres are Mikhail M. Bakhtin, "The Problem of Speech Genres" (1953), in *Speech Genres and Other Late Essays,* Vern W. McGee trans., Caryl Emerson and Michael Holquist (Eds.), Austin: University of Texas Press, 1986, pp. 60–102; and William F. Hanks, "Discourse Genres in a Theory of Practice," *American Ethnologist,* 1987, *14,* 668–692.

15. Deborah Tannen, "What's in a Frame? Surface Evidence of Underlying Ex-

pectations," in Roy O. Freedle (Ed.), *New Directions in Discourse Processing* [*Advances in Discourse Processes,* volume II], Norwood, N.J.: ABLEX, 1979, pp. 137–181, at p. 144.

16. See, e.g., Grice, note 11 above, at p. 28: "There are, of course, all sorts of other maxims (aesthetic, social, or moral in character), such as 'Be polite,' that are also normally observed by participants in talk exchanges, and these may also generate nonconventional implicatures."

17. The effort may be more or less extensive. People have varying amounts of willingness and ability to extend the context by accessing information available in memory; and the funds of information available in memory will differ from person to person (including speaker and hearer) and from time to time.

18. Grice, note 11 above, at p. 28.

19. Sometimes, of course, it is that apprehension that *tells* you you're in law country.

20. After any particular piece of litigation has passed the pleading stages, there are often limitations on a party's power to shift modes of discourse. A major function of pleading rules and other procedural forms is precisely to require the parties to give early and conspicuous notice of any challenges to ordinary discourse that they intend to make. Nevertheless, litigators have a broad range of discourse options at the early stages of a litigation, and they can often find ways to keep various options open until later stages.

21. See Chapter 4, note 76 and accompanying text.

22. We may take as an example a passage in John W. Davis's 1953 oral argument to the Supreme Court in the litigation that produced the decision in *Brown v. Board of Education,* 347 U.S. 483 (1954). Davis was a legendary advocate, renowned for his clarity of expression when he wanted to be clear. He was arguing on behalf of the State of South Carolina that the Equal Protection Clause of the Fourteenth Amendment should not be construed to forbid racial segregation in the public schools. The Supreme Court had first heard argument on this issue in 1952 but had ordered it reargued the following year, so Davis must have been aware that the Justices were seriously considering putting an end to the South's longstanding dual school systems. The crescendo of his argument was this:

   "In Clarendon School District No. 1 in South Carolina, in which this case alone is concerned [*sic*], there were in the last report that got into this record something over a year or year and a half ago, 2,799 Negroes, registered Negro children of school age. There were 295 whites. . . .

   "Who is going to disturb that situation? If they were to be reassorted or commingled, who knows how that could best be done?

   "If it is done on the mathematical basis, with 30 children as a maximum, which I believe is the accepted standard in pedagogy, you would have 27 Negro children and 3 whites in one school room. Would that make the children any happier? Would they learn any more quickly.[*sic*] Would their lives be more serene?

"Children of that age are not the most considerate animals in the world, as we all know. Would the terrible psychological disaster being wrought, according to some of these witnesses [for the school-desegregation plaintiffs], to the colored child be removed if he had three white children sitting somewhere in the same school room?

"Would white children be prevented from getting a distorted idea of racial relations if they sat with 27 Negro children? I have posed that question because it is the very one that cannot be denied."

Leon Friedman (Ed.), *Argument: The Oral Argument Before the Supreme Court in Brown v. Board of Education of Topeka, 1952–55,* New York: Chelsea House, 1969, p. 215.

Is Davis making only his ostensible points that putting 27 African-American children and three white children into the same school room isn't going to improve the lot of the African-Americans or the racial attitudes of the whites? Or is he also projecting the image—deniable if he is called on it—of 27 African-American savages surrounding three helpless white victims? (Cf. David Halberstam, *The Fifties,* New York: Villard Books, 1993, p. 421: Shortly after Earl Warren arrived in Washington, "he was invited to the White House for a dinner. The President sat the new Chief Justice next to John W. Davis, then acting as chief counsel for the defendants in the segregation cases. . . . Davis, the President told Warren, 'is a great man.' . . . 'These are not bad people,' he [Eisenhower] said of the Southerners who were defending themselves in the segregation cases. 'All they are concerned about is to see that their sweet little girls are not required to sit in schools alongside some big black bucks.'")

Is Davis's apparent quip about "animals" a *double entendre?* Is his reference to the year-old state of the population figures a hint that the African-Americans are multiplying furiously and may now be even more overwhelmingly numerous? Not undeniably.

23. It is an ancient truism that "[in] any legal hearing the listener will be on the alert for signs of dissimulation." Christopher Carey, "Rhetorical Means of Persuasion," in Ian Worthington (Ed.), *Persuasion: Greek Rhetoric in Action,* London and New York: Routledge, 1994, pp. 26–45, at p. 39. That is why the classic rhetors emphasized that "a speech which is out of keeping with the man who delivers it is just as faulty as the speech which fails to suit the subject to which it should conform." Quintilian, *Institutio Oratoria,* Cambridge, Mass.: Harvard University Press, 1985–1993 reprint, with English trans. by H. E. Butler, volume I, pp. 504–505 [book III, chap. viii].

24. The trick, in Ducrot's phrase, is "to know how to say something without thereby taking the responsibility for having said it," so as to get the simultaneous benefit of "the efficacy of speech and the innocence of silence."

Oswald Ducrot, *Dire et ne pas Dire: Principes de Sémantique Linguistique,* Paris: Hermann, 1972, p. 12 (our translation). See generally id. at pp. 5–24. This, too, is ancient wisdom. See, e.g., [Cicero], *Rhetorica ad Herennium,* book I, chap. vi; Cicero, *De Oratore,* book II, chap. lxxvii.

25. Searle, note 8 above, at p. 17. See also id. at p. 18: "every possible speech act can in principle be given an exact formulation in a sentence or sentences (assuming an appropriate context of utterance). . . ."

26. Id. at p. 47.

27. Quintilian's classic statement of the point is this:

"Sometimes we shall even have to hoodwink the judge and work upon him by various artifices so that he may think that our aim is other than what it really is. For there are cases when a *proposition* may be somewhat startling: if the judge foresees this, he will shrink from it in advance, like a patient who catches sight of the surgeon's knife before the operation."

Quintilian, *Institutio Oratoria,* note 23 above, volume II, pp. 138–139 [book IV, chap. v].

28. See Anthony G. Amsterdam, "Selling a Quick Fix for Boot Hill: The Myth of Justice Delayed in Death Cases," in Austin Sarat (Ed.), *The Killing State: Capital Punishment in Law, Politics, and Culture,* New York and Oxford: Oxford University Press, 1999, pp. 148–183; Robert Rubinson, "The Polyphonic Courtroom: Expanding the Possibilities of Judicial Discourse," *Dickinson Law Review,* 1996, *101,* 1–40.

29. As in the scam immortalized by Edmund Bentley. See E. C. Bentley, "The Genuine Tabard," in Patricia Craig (Ed.), *The Oxford Book of English Detective Stories,* Oxford: Oxford University Press, 1990, pp. 87–100.

30. Consider, for example, the famous advice to prosecutors in the *Ad Herennium:* "[W]e shall examine sharply, incriminatingly, and precisely, everything that took place in the actual execution of the deed . . . so that by the enumeration of the attendant circumstances the crime may seem to be taking place and the action to unfold before our eyes." [Cicero], *Rhetorica ad Herennium,* volume I of the bilingual *Cicero,* Cambridge, Mass.: Harvard University Press, 1989 reprint, with English translation by Harry Caplan, pp. 150–151 [book II, chap. xxx]. See also Quintilian, *Institutio Oratoria,* book VI, chap. ii. Little seems to have changed in two thousand years. See Austin Sarat, "Violence, Representation, and Responsibility in Capital Trials: The View from the Jury," *Indiana Law Journal,* 1995, *70,* 1103–1135, at pp. 1122–1127. For discussion of the effects of concreteness and vividness upon data evaluation, see, e.g., Richard Nisbett and Lee Ross, *Human Inference: Strategies and Shortcomings of Social Judgment,* Englewood Cliffs, N.J.: Prentice-Hall, 1980, pp. 43–62.

31. See, e.g., Cicero, *De Partitione Oratoria,* chaps. xv–xvii; [Cicero], *Rhetorica ad Herennium,* book II, chap. xxx; Quintilian, *Institutio Oratoria,* book VIII, chap. iv; Hermogenes, *On Types of Style,* Cecil W.

Wooten trans., Chapel Hill and London: University of North Carolina Press, 1987, pp. 50–51; Chaim Perelman and Lucie Olbrechts-Tyteca, *The New Rhetoric: A Treatise on Argumentation* (1958), John Wilkinson and Purcell Weaver trans., Notre Dame and London: University of Notre Dame Press, 1971, pp. 175–176, 236.

32. *United Pilots Association v. Halecki,* 358 U.S. 613, 614 (1959).

33. *The Tungus v. Skovgaard,* 358 U.S. 588, 589 (1959).

34. See text at note 68 below. The jury had returned a verdict for the plaintiff in *Halecki* under instructions that would not have permitted such a verdict without a finding that Halecki's death *was* caused by inhaling the carbon tetrachloride fumes. That finding was immune against Supreme Court review under established procedural principles, so the qualifier "allegedly" is not merely gratuitous but disingenuous.

35. For a perceptive study of nominalization as a rhetorical device, see Tony Trew, "Theory and Ideology at Work," in Roger Fowler, Bob Hodge, Gunther Kress, and Tony Trew, *Language and Control,* London: Routledge and Kegan Paul, 1979, pp. 94–116.

36. See Arthur O. Lovejoy, *The Great Chain of Being: A Study of the History of an Idea* (1936), Cambridge, Mass.: Harvard University Press, 1964. A legal *tour de force* involving this strategy is Justice Frankfurter's opinion in *Wolf v. Colorado,* 338 U.S. 25 (1949), which flaunts its disregard of the most basic convention of twentieth-century Supreme Court opinion-writing (begin by stating the facts) to make the point that a Higher Principle Is At Stake.

37. See Chapter 3, *Michael H.,* Part VI.

38. 347 U.S. 483 (1954), and 349 U.S. 294 (1955).

39. *Freeman v. Pitts,* 503 U.S. 467, 118 L.Ed.2d 108 (1992).

40. As Perelman and Olbrechts-Tyteca observe, any argument from consistency—or what they call "the rule of justice"—"presupposes the partial identification of beings by putting them in a category"; and this operation, like any "quasi-logical argument[,] becomes possible through disregarding everything that makes the [beings or] situations different and reducing them to what makes them symmetrical." Perelman and Olbrechts-Tyteca, note 31 above, at pp. 219, 224.

41. See Chapter 3, *Jenkins,* Part III, Scenes 5–7.

42. For a good general discussion of this subject, see Ducrot, note 24 above.

43. For a good, illustrative short list, see Levinson, note 8 above, at pp. 181–184. Levinson's discussion of presupposition in general, id. at pp. 167–225, is excellent. See also Gerald Gazdar, *Pragmatics: Implicature, Presupposition, and Logical Form,* New York: Academic Press, 1979.

44. The rules of evidence applicable to much litigation include an objection to any question that "assumes a fact not in evidence" or "has no predicate." To the extent that this objection is invoked, it blocks the establishment of facts by presupposition in the testimony of witnesses. The existence of the

rule may make experienced litigators particularly sensitive to the phenomenon of presupposition. Most would twitch irritably upon hearing a question like "when did you stop using drugs?" addressed to a witness where there has been no prior testimony that the witness used drugs. But even experienced litigators seem often to miss the objection when a question like "did you manage to pull the car out of that skid?" is addressed to a witness in the absence of prior testimony that the witness *tried*. In any event, the no-predicate rule does not govern aspects of litigation other than the presentation of evidence; it does not control the form of discourse in oral arguments, briefs, or judicial opinions, for example; and it has no application in legal settings outside litigation.

45. See, e.g., Charles F. Hockett, *A Course in Modern Linguistics*, New York: Macmillan, 1958, pp. 191, 201–205.

46. See, e.g., Herbert H. Clark and Susan E. Haviland, "Comprehension and the Given-New Contract," in Roy O. Freedle (Ed.), *Discourse Production and Comprehension* [*Discourse Processes: Advances in Research and Theory*, volume I], Norwood, N.J.: ABLEX, 1977, pp. 1–40; Ellen F. Prince, "Toward a Taxonomy of Given-New Information," in Peter Cole (Ed.), *Radical Pragmatics*, New York, Academic Press, 1981, pp. 223–255; M. A. K. Halliday, *An Introduction to Functional Grammar*, 2d edition, London: Edward Arnold, 1994, pp. 295–302 [§§ 8.4–8.6].

47. See, e.g., John Lyons, *Introduction to Theoretical Linguistics*, Cambridge: Cambridge University Press, 1968, pp. 79–80; Bernard Comrie, *Aspect: An Introduction to the Study of Verbal Aspect and Related Problems*, Cambridge: Cambridge University Press, 1976, pp. 111–122. Roman Jakobson first applied the concept to syntax and semantics.

48. See Herbert H. Clark, *Arenas of Language Use*, Chicago and London: University of Chicago Press, 1992, pp. 43–45.

49. E.g., Lee Ross, Mark R. Lepper, Fritz Strack, and Julia Steinmetz, "Social Explanation and Social Expectation: Effects of Real and Hypothetical Explanations on Subjective Likelihood," *Journal of Personality and Social Psychology*, 1977, 35, 817–829. See generally Mark Snyder, "When Belief Creates Reality," in Leonard Berkowitz (Ed.), *Advances in Experimental Social Psychology*, Orlando, Fla.: Academic Press, 1984, volume 18, pp. 247–305; Nisbett and Ross, note 30 above, at pp. 183–188.

50. See Chapter 3, *Michael H.*, Part V.

51. See Chapter 3, *Michael H.*, Part VI.

52. See 491 U.S. at 124, 129 n. 7, 131–132.

53. See Chapter 3, *Jenkins*, Part III, Scene 3.

54. See Chapter 3, *Michael H.*, Parts II–III, V.

55. Aristotle, *Topica*, in *Posterior Analytics, Topica*, volume II of the bilingual *Aristotle*, Cambridge, Mass.: Harvard University Press, 1989 reprint, with English translation by E. S. Forster, pp. 354–355 [book II, chap. vi]: "Where

of necessity only one of two predicates must be true (for example, a man must have either disease or health), . . . if we have shown that one is present, we shall have shown that the other is not present. . . ."

56. *Scott v. Sandford,* 19 How. (60 U.S.) 393, 15 L.Ed. 691, 703 (1857).

57. 491 U.S. at 123.

58. See, e.g., Dorothy Holland and Naomi Quinn (Eds.), *Cultural Models in Language and Thought,* Cambridge: Cambridge University Press, 1989.

59. See, e.g., George Lakoff, *Women, Fire, and Dangerous Things: What Categories Reveal About the Mind* (1987), Chicago and London: University of Chicago Press, 1990.

60. See Chapter 5, Part VI and note 135.

61. We have noted some examples in our discussion of Justice Scalia's *Michael H.* opinion: his use of an *appearance : reality* schema to portray Michael's *real* aims (Chapter 3, *Michael H.,* Part V), his use of a *sacred : profane* schema to establish the *real* rationale of the precedents (id., Part VI), his various neoplatonist strategies for privileging the abstract (id., Part VI, Subpart Fourth), and so forth.

62. As Justice Scalia does when he ascribes his one-father-per-family rule to "nature itself." 491 U.S. at 118.

63. For example, in arguing *Brown v. Board of Education* before the Supreme Court, Thurgood Marshall used the image of African-American and white children playing together before and after school to portray desegregation as the natural state of affairs. See Anthony G. Amsterdam, "Thurgood Marshall's Image of the Blue-Eyed Child in *Brown,*" *New York University Law Review,* 1993, *68,* 226–236, at p. 236.

64. John W. Davis's counter to Thurgood Marshall's *natural-state* image in *Brown* (note 63 above) was a *civilized-state* image that depicted segregation as the condition established and accepted by generations of legal savants, laboring together in sundry conclaves to maintain the Nation. See Anthony G. Amsterdam, "Telling Stories and Stories About Them," *Clinical Law Review,* 1994, *1,* 9–40, at pp. 16–18.

65. See, e.g., Mark A. Schneider, *Culture and Enchantment,* Chicago and London: University of Chicago Press, 1993. And we for a certainty are not the first. See Aristotle, *On Sophistical Refutations,* chap. xii.

66. It is a notorious feature of rhetoric that almost every commonplace of argument "can be confronted by one that is contrary to it." Perelman and Olbrechts-Tyteca, note 31 above, at p. 85; see generally id. at pp. 83–91, 233, 289, 462; Black, note 3 above, at pp. 5–6, 52. Thus: *The more the merrier* but *Two's company, three's a crowd,* and so forth.

67. See Chapter 2.

68. See, e.g., Mieke Bal, *Narratology: Introduction to the Theory of Narrative,* 2d revised edition, Christine van Boheemen trans., Toronto: University of Toronto Press, 1985, pp. 100–117, 130–132; Mieke Bal, "On Meanings and Descriptions," in Nomi Tamir-Ghez (Ed.), *Studies in Twentieth Cen-*

tury Literature, Manhattan, Kan.: Kansas State University and University of Nebraska–Lincoln, 1981, volume 6, pp. 100–148, at pp. 134–142. For a legal application, see Anthony G. Amsterdam and Randy Hertz, "An Analysis of Closing Arguments to a Jury," *New York Law School Law Review,* 1992, *37,* 55–122, at pp. 70–75. The use of reliable and unreliable narrators to stabilize and destabilize facts is analyzed at length in Wayne C. Booth, *The Rhetoric of Fiction,* 2d edition, Chicago and London: University of Chicago Press, 1983.

69. See Tzvetan Todorov, "Narrative Transformations," in *The Poetics of Prose* (1971), Richard Howard trans., Ithaca, N.Y.: Cornell University Press, 1977, pp. 218–233; Jerome Bruner, "Two Modes of Thought," in *Actual Minds, Possible Worlds,* Cambridge, Mass.: Harvard University Press, 1986, pp. 11–43.

70. See, e.g., William Labov and David Fanshel, *Therapeutic Discourse: Psychotherapy as Conversation,* New York: Academic Press, 1977; Peggy C. Davis, "Contextual Legal Criticism: A Demonstration Exploring Hierarchy and 'Feminine' Style," *New York University Law Review,* 1991, *66,* 1635–1681; Peggy C. Davis, "Law and Lawyering: Legal Studies with an Interactive Focus," *New York Law School Law Review,* 1992, *37,* 185–207; Peggy Cooper Davis, "Performing Interpretation: A Legacy of Civil Rights Lawyering in *Brown v. Board of Education,*" in Austin Sarat (Ed.), *Race, Law, and Culture: Reflections on Brown v. Board of Education,* New York and Oxford: Oxford University Press, 1997, pp. 23–48.

71. Toulmin, note 9 above, at p. 75.

72. 408 U.S. 665 (1972).

73. *Fisher v. United States,* 425 U.S. 391 (1976); *McCray v. Illinois,* 386 U.S. 300 (1967); *United States v. Nixon,* 418 U.S. 683 (1974); *Wolff v. McDonnell,* 418 U.S. 539, 568–569 (1974).

74. 408 U.S. at 693–694 (emphasis added).

75. Id. at 691 (emphasis added).

76. Id. at 695 (emphasis added).

77. Id. at 698–699.

78. Id. at 694–695.

79. See, e.g., Frank Kermode, *The Sense of an Ending: Studies in the Theory of Fiction,* New York and Oxford: Oxford University Press, 1967; A. P. Foulkes, *Literature and Propaganda,* London and New York: Methuen, 1983; Ronald H. Carpenter, *History as Rhetoric: Style, Narrative, and Persuasion,* Columbia: University of South Carolina Press, 1995; Amsterdam and Hertz, note 68 above; Amsterdam, note 64 above.

80. See Black, note 3 above, at pp. 30–33; Amsterdam, note 64 above, at pp. 26–32; cf. Chapter 5, Part III, and the Appendix.

81. See Chapter 3, *Michael H.,* Parts III–V.

82. See Chapter 2, notes 61–65 and accompanying text. See also, e.g., Roland Barthes, "Introduction to the Structural Analysis of Narratives," in *The*

Semiotic Challenge, Richard Howard trans., New York: Hill and Wang, 1988, pp. 95–135, at p. 115, and "The Sequences of Actions," in id., pp. 136–148, at pp. 140–142; Jerome Bruner, "The Narrative Construction of Reality," *Critical Inquiry,* 1991, *18(1),* 1–21, at pp. 8–16; Richard Delgado, "Storytelling for Oppositionists and Others: A Plea for Narrative," *Michigan Law Review,* 1989, *87,* 2411–2441; Gerald P. Lopez, "Lay Lawyering," *U.C.L.A. Law Review,* 1984, *32,* 1–60.

83. See Chapter 2, Part V; Chapter 4, Parts I and III.

84. See Chapter 5, Part V.

85. See, e.g., Peter Brooks, *Reading for the Plot: Design and Intention in Narrative* (1984), Cambridge, Mass.: Harvard University Press, 1995; Jonathan Culler, *The Pursuit of Signs: Semiotics, Literature, Deconstruction,* Ithaca, N.Y.: Cornell University Press, 1981, pp. 169–187; Isolda E. Carranza, "Winning the Battle in Private Discourse: Rhetorical-Logical Operations in Storytelling," *Discourse & Society,* 1999, *10,* 509–541.

86. See, e.g., Lee Ross and Richard E. Nisbett, *The Person and the Situation: Perspectives of Social Psychology,* Philadelphia: Temple University Press, 1991, particularly at pp. 119–144; Shelley E. Taylor, "A Categorization Approach to Stereotyping," in David L. Hamilton (Ed.), *Cognitive Processes in Stereotyping and Intergroup Behavior,* Hillsdale, N.J.: Erlbaum, 1981, pp. 83–114; Galen V. Bodenhausen and Robert S. Wyer, Jr., "Effects of Stereotypes on Decision Making and Information-Processing Strategies," *Journal of Personality and Social Psychology,* 1985, *48(2),* 267–282; Susan T. Fiske, Steven L. Neuberg, Ann E. Beattie, and Sandra J. Millberg, "Category-Based and Attribute-Based Reactions to Others: Some Informational Conditions of Stereotyping and Individuating Processes," *Journal of Experimental Social Psychology,* 1987, *23,* 399–427. A classic work is Gordon W. Allport, *The Nature of Prejudice* (1954), Garden City, N.Y.: Doubleday (Anchor), 1958; for an assessment, see Thomas F. Pettigrew, "The Ultimate Attribution Error: Extending Allport's Cognitive Analysis of Prejudice," *Personality and Social Psychology Bulletin,* 1979, *5,* 461–476.

87. This was the essential insight of one of Solomon Asch's early papers. Solomon E. Asch, "Studies in the Principles of Judgments and Attitudes: II. Determination of Judgments by Group and by Ego Standards," *Journal of Abnormal and Social Psychology,* 1940, *41,* 433–465. See also Dale W. Griffin and Lee Ross, "Subjective Construal, Social Inference, and Human Misunderstanding," in Mark P. Zanna (Ed.), *Advances in Experimental Social Psychology,* New York: Academic Press, 1991, volume 24, pp. 319–359.

88. See Charles G. Lord, Donna M. Desforges, Steven Fein, Marilyn A. Pugh, and Mark R. Lepper, "Typicality Effects in Attitudes Toward Social Policies: A Concept-Mapping Approach," *Journal of Personality and Social Psychology,* 1994, *66,* 658–673.

89. See Lea S. VanderVelde, "The Gendered Origins of the *Lumley* Doctrine: Binding Men's Consciences and Women's Fidelity," *Yale Law Journal,*

1992, *101*, 775–852; Peggy Cooper Davis, "The Proverbial Woman," *Record of the Bar Association of the City of New York,* January/February 1993, *48*, 7–25.

90. See, e.g., Thomas Gilovich, "Seeing the Past in the Present: The Effect of Associations to Familiar Events on Judgments and Decisions," *Journal of Personality and Social Psychology,* 1981, *40*, 797–808.

91. See, e.g., Perelman and Olbrechts-Tyteca, note 31 above, at pp. 331–337. The power of labels is nicely captured in Quintilian's discussion of the arguments for trumping expediency with honor and vice versa:

> "[I]n such a conflict of principles it is usual to modify the names which we give them. For expediency is often ruled out by those who assert not merely that honour comes before expediency, but that nothing can be expedient that is not honourable, while others say that what we call honour is vanity, ambition and folly, as contemptible in substance as it is fair in sound."

Quintilian, *Institutio Oratoria,* note 23 above, volume I, at pp. 494–495 [book III, chap. viii]. See also the advice from the *Rhetorica ad Herennium* quoted in Chapter 2 at note 69.

92. See, e.g., Michael Choukas, *Propaganda Comes of Age,* Washington, D.C.: Public Affairs, 1965; Jacques Ellul, *Propaganda: The Formation of Men's Attitudes,* Konrad Kellen and Jean Lerner trans., New York: Vintage Books, 1973; Harold D. Lasswell, *Propaganda Technique in World War I* (1927), Cambridge, Mass.: MIT Press, 1971.

93. See, e.g., John Kenneth White, *The New Politics of Old Values,* 2d edition, Hanover, N.H.: University Press of New England, 1990.

94. See, e.g., Robert Jay Lifton, *The Nazi Doctors: Medical Killings and the Psychology of Genocide,* New York: Basic Books, 1986; Christian Pross, "Nazi Doctors, German Medicine, and Historical Truth," in George J. Annas and Michael Grodin (Eds.), *The Nazi Doctors and the Nuremberg Code: Human Rights in Human Experimentation,* New York and Oxford: Oxford University Press, 1992, pp. 32–52. Cf. Joel Kovel, *White Racism: A Psychohistory,* New York: Columbia University Press (Morningside), 1984, p. 81: "Every group which has been the object of prejudice has . . . been designated by the prejudiced group as dirty or smelly or both."

95. See, e.g., Richard Tithecott, *Of Men and Monsters: Jeffrey Dahmer and the Construction of the Serial Killer,* Madison: University of Wisconsin Press, 1997, pp. 17–43; Martha Grace Duncan, "In Slime and Darkness: The Metaphor of Filth in Criminal Justice," *Tulane Law Review,* 1994, *68*, 725–802.

96. A poll by Louis Harris found that 81% of respondents in a nationwide sample said that they would favor the adoption in their state of a proposition worded in this manner. When the respondents were then asked, "Would you still favor this proposition if it would outlaw all affirmative action programs for women and minorities?" the percentage of respondents favoring

adoption dropped to 29%. Peter Y. Harris Research Group, Inc., *A Survey of the Attitudes of a Cross-Section of American Women and Men and a Cross-Section of Voters in California on Affirmative Action, Abortion, and Other Key Issues Affecting Women and Minorities,* April 1995, pp. 1–7. See also Stanley Fish, "Op-Ed: How the Right Hijacked the Magic Words," *New York Times,* August 13, 1995, sec. 4, p. 15.

97. 481 U.S. 279 (1987).

98. 481 U.S. at 297 (emphasis added).

99. E.g., 481 U.S. at 311 ("McCleskey's argument . . . is antithetical to the fundamental role of discretion in our criminal justice system"); id. at 312 ("'would be totally alien to our notions of criminal justice'"); id. ("are an inevitable part of our criminal justice system"); id. at 313 ("discretion that is fundamental to our criminal process"); id. ("fundamental value of jury trial in our criminal justice system"); id. at 315 ("throws into serious question the principles that underlie our entire criminal justice system").

100. E.g., *Teague v. Lane,* 489 U.S. 288, 309 (1989) ("seriously undermines the principle of finality which is essential to the operation of our criminal justice system"); *Delo v. Blair,* 509 U.S. 823, 823 (1993) ("interfere with the orderly process of a state's criminal justice system"); and see *McCleskey v. Zant,* 499 U.S. 467, 491 (1991) ("Our federal system recognizes the independent power of a State to articulate societal norms through criminal law; but the power of a State to pass laws means little if the State cannot enforce them").

101. For a discussion of the process, see Michael Riffaterre, *Fictional Truth,* Baltimore and London: Johns Hopkins University Press, 1990; Michael Riffaterre, "Production of the Narrative I: Balzac's *La Paix du ménage,*" in *Text Production,* Tērese Lyons trans., New York: Columbia University Press, 1983, pp. 157–167.

102. See Chapter 3, *Jenkins,* Part III, Scene 1.

103. See Amsterdam, note 28 above.

104. See id. at 158–160.

105. Paul Ricoeur, *The Rule of Metaphor: Multi-disciplinary Studies of the Creation of Meaning in Language* (1975), Robert Czerny trans., Toronto: University of Toronto Press, 1987, p. 7. For discussion of the workings of metaphor in the law, see the references collected in note 68 to Chapter 2 of the present volume and in Amsterdam, note 64 above, at pp. 36–37 n. 163.

106. This word is a metaphor.

107. The appropriate scope of the federal habeas corpus forum has long been a hotly contested legal and political issue. See, e.g., Curtis Reitz, "Federal Habeas Corpus: Postconviction Remedy for State Prisoners," *University of Pennsylvania Law Review,* 1960, *108,* 461–532; James S. Liebman, "More than 'Slightly Retro:' The Rehnquist Court's Rout of Habeas Corpus Jurisdiction in *Teague v. Lane,*" *New York University Review of Law and Social Change,* 1990–1991, *18,* 537–635.

108. 372 U.S. 391 (1963).
109. Id. at 401 (emphasis added).
110. Id. at 400 (emphasis added).
111. Id. at 402 (emphasis added).
112. Id. at 422 (emphasis added).
113. Id. at 426 (emphasis added).
114. Id. at 403 n. 13 (emphasis added).
115. Id. at 402 (emphasis added).
116. 489 U.S. 288 (1989).
117. 499 U.S. 467 (1991).
118. 489 U.S. at 301 (emphasis added).
119. Id. at 304 (emphasis added).
120. Id. at 309 (emphasis added).
121. Id. at 311 (emphasis added).
122. Id. (emphasis added).
123. Id. at 313 (emphasis added).
124. 499 U.S. at 496 (emphasis added).
125. Id. at 491 (emphasis added).
126. Id. (emphasis added).
127. Id. at 492 (emphasis added).
128. Id. at 496 (emphasis added).
129. Id. (emphasis added).
130. *Scott v. Sandford,* 19 How. [60 U.S.] 393, 15 L.Ed. 691, 701 (twice), 706, 708 (1857) (emphasis added).
131. 15 L.Ed. at 702 (emphasis added).
132. Id. at 703 (emphasis added); see also id. at 701.
133. Id. at 702 (emphasis added).
134. 15 L.Ed. at 702 (emphasis added).
135. 15 L.Ed. at 702 (emphasis added).
136. Id. at 701 (emphasis added).
137. Id. (emphasis added).
138. 15 L.Ed. at 706 (emphasis added).
139. Id. at 702 (emphasis added).
140. Wayne C. Booth, note 68 above, at p. 149. See also Paolo Valesio, *Novantiqua: Rhetorics as a Contemporary Theory,* Bloomington: Indiana University Press, 1980, particularly at pp. 59–60.
141. James Boyd White, "Rhetoric and Law: The Arts of Cultural and Communal Life," in *Heracles' Bow,* note 2 above, pp. 28–48, at p. 34.
142. See Peggy C. Davis, "Law and Lawyering: Legal Studies with an Interactive Focus," *New York Law School Law Review,* 1992, 37, 185–207.
143. See Rubinson, note 28 above.
144. See Kathy Eden, *Hermeneutics and the Rhetorical Tradition: Chapters in the Ancient Legacy and Its Humanist Reception,* New Haven: Yale University Press, 1997; Peggy Cooper Davis, "Performing Interpretation: A Leg-

acy of Civil Rights Lawyering in *Brown v. Board of Education,*" in Austin Sarat (Ed.), *Race, Law, and Culture: Reflections on Brown v. Board of Education,* New York and Oxford: Oxford University Press, 1997, pp. 23–48.

145. See Peggy C. Davis, "Contextual Legal Criticism: A Demonstration Exploring Hierarchy and 'Feminine' Style," *New York University Law Review,* 1991, 66, 1635–1681, at p. 1681.

146. Martha Cooper, "A Feminist Looks at Critical Rhetoric," in Theresa Enos and Richard McNabb (Eds.), *Making and Unmaking the Prospects for Rhetoric,* Mahwah, N.J.: Erlbaum, 1997 [Selected Papers from the 1996 Rhetoric Society of America Conference], pp. 99–106, at pp. 104–105. See James L. Kastely, *Rethinking the Rhetorical Tradition: From Plato to Postmodernism,* New Haven: Yale University Press, 1997.

147. See Richard K. Sherwin, "A Matter of Voice and Plot: Belief and Suspicion in Legal Storytelling," *Michigan Law Review,* 1988, 87, 543–612.

7. The Rhetorics of Death

1. 481 U.S. 279, 95 L.Ed.2d 262, 107 S. Ct. 1756 (1987).

2. Warren McCleskey was put to death on September 9, 1991. One of us represented Mr. McCleskey as an attorney in the case discussed in this chapter and in other unsuccessful proceedings challenging his conviction and death sentence.

3. John C. Jeffries, Jr., *Justice Lewis F. Powell, Jr.,* New York: Charles Scribner's Sons, 1994, p. 451.

4. Id.

5. So far as Powell's biographer could make out, the "heart of the matter" for Powell in 1991 was that "[t]he death penalty should be barred, not because it was intrinsically wrong but because it could not be fairly and expeditiously enforced." Id. at 452. As we shall see, the proposition that the death penalty *can* be fairly and expeditiously enforced is the very conclusion that Justice Powell's majority opinion in *McCleskey* devotes its most strenuous rhetorical efforts to establishing.

6. See, e.g., Marvin E. Wolfgang and Marc Reidel, "Race, Judicial Discretion and the Death Penalty," *Annals of the American Academy of Political and Social Science,* 1973, 407, 119–133; Marvin E. Wolfgang and Marc Reidel, "Rape, Race, and the Death Penalty in Georgia," *American Journal of Orthopsychiatry,* 1975, 45(4), 658–668; Marvin E. Wolfgang and Bernard Cohen, *Crime and Race: Conceptions and Misconceptions,* New York: Institute of Human Relations Press, 1970, pp. 80–81.

7. 408 U.S. 238.

8. 428 U.S. 153. See also *Proffitt v. Florida,* 428 U.S. 242 (1976), and *Jurek v. Texas,* 428 U.S. 262 (1976).

9. 428 U.S. 280. See also *[Stanislaus] Roberts v. Louisiana,* 428 U.S. 325

(1976); *Green v. Oklahoma*, 428 U.S. 907 (1976); *[Harry] Roberts v. Louisiana*, 431 U.S. 633 (1977).

10. *Godfrey v. Georgia*, 446 U.S. 420, 428 (1980).

11. *Maynard v. Cartwright*, 486 U.S. 356 (1988).

12. See *Lowenfield v. Phelps*, 484 U.S. 231 (1988).

13. See *Zant v. Stephens*, 462 U.S. 862 (1983).

14. See *Pulley v. Harris*, 465 U.S. 37 (1984).

15. See, e.g., *Barclay v. Florida*, 463 U.S. 939 (1983).

16. *Lockett v. Ohio*, 438 U.S. 586, 604 (1978) (plurality opinion); see also, e.g., *Skipper v. South Carolina*, 476 U.S. 1 (1986); *Mills v. Maryland*, 486 U.S. 367 (1988).

17. See, e.g., *California v. Brown*, 479 U.S. 538 (1987); *Blystone v. Pennsylvania*, 494 U.S. 299 (1990); *Johnson v. Texas*, 509 U.S. 350 (1993).

18. E.g., *Spaziano v. Florida*, 468 U.S. 447 (1984).

19. E.g., *Coker v. Georgia*, 433 U.S. 584 (1977); *Enmund v. Florida*, 458 U.S. 782 (1982).

20. See, e.g., Laurence Alan Baughman, *Southern Rape Complex: Hundred Year Psychosis*, Atlanta: Pendulum Books, 1966; Calvin C. Hernton, *Sex and Racism in America*, Garden City, N.Y.: Doubleday, 1965; Winthrop D. Jordan, *White Over Black: American Attitudes Toward the Negro, 1550–1812*, New York: W. W. Norton, 1977.

21. These were the studies cited in note 6 above and Donald H. Partington, "The Incidence of the Death Penalty for Rape in Virginia," *Washington and Lee Law Review*, 1965, 22, 43–75. See Samuel R. Gross, "Race and Death: The Judicial Evaluation of Evidence of Discrimination in Capital Sentencing," *University of California Davis Law Review*, 1985, 18, 1275–1325, at pp. 1282–1283.

22. See, e.g., *Gardner v. Florida*, 430 U.S. 349 (1977); *Beck v. Alabama*, 447 U.S. 625 (1980); *Estelle v. Smith*, 451 U.S. 454 (1981); *Ake v. Oklahoma*, 470 U.S. 68 (1985).

23. *Turner v. Murray*, 476 U.S. 28 (1986).

24. E.g., *Coleman v. Balkcom*, 451 U.S. 949, 956 (1981) (opinion of Justice Rehnquist, dissenting from the denial of certiorari); *Alabama v. Evans*, 461 U.S. 230, 234 (1983) (concurring opinion of Chief Justice Burger); *Sullivan v. Wainwright*, 464 U.S. 109, 112 (1983) (concurring opinion of Chief Justice Burger); *Stephens v. Kemp*, 464 U.S. 1027, 1028 (1983) (opinion of Justice Powell, joined by Chief Justice Burger and Justices Rehnquist and O'Connor, dissenting); *Woodard v. Hutchins*, 464 U.S. 377 (1984) (opinion of Justice Powell speaking for five Justices).

25. Remarks of Lewis F. Powell, Jr., Associate Justice, at the Eleventh Circuit Conference in Savannah, Georgia, May 9–10, 1983. See Linda Greenhouse, "Justice Powell Assails Delay in Carrying Out Executions," *New York Times*, May 10, 1983 (late City final edition), sec. A, p. 16. Cf. Lewis F.

Powell, Jr., "Commentary: Capital Punishment," *Harvard Law Review,* 1989, *102,* 1035–1046.

26. Remarks of Lewis F. Powell, Jr., note 25 above, at p. 8. See Anthony G. Amsterdam, "*In Favorem Mortis:* The Supreme Court and Capital Punishment," *Human Rights,* Winter 1987, *14,* 14–17 and 49–60.

27. See Anthony G. Amsterdam, "Selling a Quick Fix for Boot Hill: The Myth of Justice Delayed in Death Cases," in Austin Sarat (Ed.), *The Killing State: Capital Punishment in Law, Politics, and Culture,* New York and Oxford: Oxford University Press, 1999, pp. 148–183.

28. See, e.g., *Wainwright v. Witt,* 469 U.S. 412 (1985); *Darden v. Wainwright,* 477 U.S. 168 (1986); *Stanford v. Kentucky,* 492 U.S. 361 (1989); *Walton v. Arizona,* 497 U.S. 639 (1990); *Payne v. Tennessee,* 501 U.S. 808 (1991); *Mu'min v. Virginia,* 500 U.S. 415 (1991); *Victor v. Nebraska,* 511 U.S. 1 (1994).

29. A brief filed in the Supreme Court by several of the country's preeminent criminologists and criminal-justice researchers later described the Baldus studies as "among the best empirical studies on criminal sentencing ever conducted." Brief *Amici Curiae* of Dr. Franklin M. Fisher, Dr. Richard O. Lempert, Dr. Peter W. Sperlich, Dr. Marvin E. Wolfgang, Professor Hans Zeisel, and Professor Franklin E. Zimring in Support of Petitioner Warren McCleskey, in *McCleskey v. Kemp,* No. 84-6811, at p. 3.

30. *McCleskey v. Kemp,* 753 F.2d 877, 895 (11th Cir. 1985).

31. 481 U.S. at 291 n. 7.

32. Id. at 282–283.

33. E.g., *Washington v. Davis,* 426 U.S. 229 (1976).

34. 481 U.S. at 292.

35. Id. at 292–299.

36. Id. at 299–319.

37. As in our earlier case studies, we invite you to make your own analysis of the *McCleskey* opinion before proceeding with ours, and to check our analysis against the text as you go along. The opinion in *McCleskey v. Kemp* is accessible through the electronic services and in print in volume 481 of the United States Reports, beginning at page 279; volume 95 of the Lawyer's Edition of the United States Supreme Court Reports, Second Series, beginning at page 262; and volume 107 of the Supreme Court Reporter, beginning at page 1756.

38. Randall L. Kennedy, "*McCleskey v. Kemp:* Race, Capital Punishment and the Supreme Court," *Harvard Law Review,* 1988, *101,* 1388–1443, at p. 1408.

39. This assumption is stated squarely in the opening sentence of the opinion (481 U.S. at 282–283). It is then reiterated (e.g., id. at 291 n. 7, 308–309, 312, 317–318) in various forms that retain its propositional content while progressively disembodying it. We will examine this process further in the following subpart.

40. 481 U.S. at 297.
41. Id. at 313.
42. Id. at 297.
43. Id. at 309.
44. Id. at 297. See also id. at 300–301 and n. 23, 310–311 n. 32, 319.
45. Id. at 297. See also id. at 311–312, 313, 314–315 n. 37.
46. See, e.g., *Rose v. Mitchell,* 443 U.S. 545, 554–556 (1979) ("Discrimination on account of race was the primary evil at which the Amendments adopted after the War Between the States, including the Fourteenth Amendment, were aimed. . . . Discrimination on the basis of race, odious in all aspects, is especially pernicious in the administration of justice. Selection of members of a grand jury because they are of one race and not another destroys the appearance of justice and thereby casts doubt on the integrity of the judicial process").
47. For three such professions in the year preceding *McCleskey* alone, see *Batson v. Kentucky,* 476 U.S. 79, 87–88 (1986) (opinion of the Court by Justice Powell) ("Discrimination within the judicial system is most pernicious because it is 'a stimulant to that race prejudice which is an impediment to securing to [black citizens] that equal justice which the law aims to secure to all others,'" quoting *Strauder v. West Virginia,* 100 U.S. 303, 308 (1880)); *Turner v. Murray,* 476 U.S. 28, 35–36 and n. 8 (1986) (jurors' discretion in capital sentencing "gives greater opportunity for racial prejudice to operate than is present when a jury is restricted to factfinding. This, together with the special seriousness with which we view the risk of racial prejudice influencing a capital sentencing decision, are what distinguish this case. . . ."); *Vasquez v. Hillery,* 474 U.S. 254, 262 (1986) ("[D]iscrimination on the basis of race in the selection of grand jurors 'strikes at the fundamental values of our judicial system and our society as a whole. . . .'").
48. Cf. *Brown v. Board of Education,* 347 U.S. 483, 493 (1954) ("Today, education is perhaps the most important function of state and local governments. . . . Such an opportunity, where the state has undertaken to provide it, is a right which must be made available to all on equal terms"). Similarly, Justice Powell's "opinion fails even to address the obvious counterargument [to its criminal-justice argument:] that it is precisely because the challenged conduct arises in a criminal justice setting that the Court should be *more,* not less, sensitive to any hint of racial inequality." Kennedy, note 38 above, at p. 1409. Compare the judicial pronouncements in notes 46 and 47 above.
49. 481 U.S. at 309.
50. E.g., id. at 319 ("The Constitution does not require that a State eliminate *any demonstrable disparity* that correlates with a potentially irrelevant factor in order to operate a criminal justice system that includes capital punishment. As we have stated specifically in the context of capital punishment, the Constitution does not '*plac[e] totally unrealistic conditions on its use.*'"); 315 n. 37 ("The *Gregg*-type statute *imposes unprecedented safe-*

guards in the special context of capital punishment. . . . Given these *safe-guards already inherent* in the imposition and review of capital sentences, the dissent's call for greater rationality is no less than a claim that a capital punishment system cannot be administered in accord with the Constitution. As we reiterate . . ., the requirement of heightened rationality in the imposition of capital punishment *does not "plac[e] totally unrealistic conditions on its use."*); 312 n. 35 (*"No one contends that all sentencing disparities can be eliminated. . . ."*). *Accord:* id. at 312–313, 318–319 n. 45. (Emphasis in all quotations in this note has been added.)

51. The tale was old before the Book of Job. See, e.g., *Gilgamesh* (the Sin-leqi-unninni version); "The Oak and the Reed," in *Aesop's Fables;* "The Fox and the Hedgehog," in id.; cf. "The Tortoise and the Eagle," in id. Our point is not to deride this wisdom but to observe the rhetorical techniques through which Justice Powell establishes that the present case is a fitting occasion for its exercise.

52. See Anthony G. Amsterdam, "Telling Stories and Stories About Them," *Clinical Law Review,* 1994, *1,* 9–40, at pp. 21–22 and n. 76. Justice Powell's version of the story ("McCleskey's argument . . . is antithetical to the fundamental role of discretion in our criminal justice system. Discretion in the criminal justice system offers substantial benefits to the criminal defendant" [481 U.S. at 311]) is a classic one. See "The Hart and the Vine," in *Aesop's Fables.*

53. Some skepticism might have been anticipated, if only on the ground neatly aphorized in the subtitle of Craig Haney's later article criticizing the *McCleskey* decision: Craig Haney, "The Fourteenth Amendment and Symbolic Legality: Let Them Eat Due Process," *Law and Human Behavior,* 1991, *15,* 183–204.

54. See Chapter 3, *Michael H.,* Parts II–III, V.

55. See, e.g., 481 U.S. at 319 ("Capital punishment is now the law in more than two-thirds of our States. . . . McCleskey's wide-ranging arguments . . . basically challenge the validity of capital punishment in our multiracial society"), 315 n. 37 ("the dissent's call for greater rationality is no less than a claim that a capital punishment system cannot be administered in accord with the Constitution"). *Accord,* id. at 310–311 n. 32, 313–314 n. 37.

56. See, e.g., id. at 312–313 ("in the light of [*inter alia*] . . . the fundamental value of jury trial in our criminal justice system, . . . we hold that the Baldus study does not demonstrate a constitutionally significant risk . . ."); 310–311 n. 32 ("In the individual case, a jury sentence reflects the conscience of the community as applied to the circumstances of a particular offender and offense. We reject JUSTICE BRENNAN'S contention that this important standard for assessing the constitutionality of a death penalty should be abandoned"). What Justice Brennan actually argues is not that jury sentencing in capital cases should be declared unconstitutional but that the factual showing made by McCleskey calls for invalidating death sentences imposed

under "[t]he Georgia sentencing system [which] . . . provides considerable opportunity for racial considerations, however subtle and unconscious, to influence charging and sentencing decisions." Id. at 333–334. "No guidelines govern prosecutorial decisions to seek the death penalty, and Georgia provides juries with no list of aggravating and mitigating factors, nor any standard for balancing them against one another. Once a jury identifies one aggravating factor, it has complete discretion in choosing life or death, and need not articulate its basis for selecting life imprisonment." Id. at 333. Justice Brennan concedes that the Court upheld the Georgia statute on its face in *Gregg* but says that the Baldus studies demonstrate that *Gregg* was overoptimistic in predicting that the statutory procedures would control discretion sufficiently to guard against racial discrimination in practice. ("[W]hether a State has chosen an effective combination of guidance and discretion in its capital sentencing system as a whole cannot be established in the abstract, as the Court insists on doing, but must be determined empirically, as the Baldus study has done." Id. at 334 n. 9.) Justice Brennan says that his position would not outlaw capital punishment if one accepts the premise of *Gregg* and its progeny "that it is possible to establish a system of *guided discretion* that will both permit individualized moral evaluation and prevent impermissible considerations from being taken into account." Id. at 334 n.9. In response to Justice Powell's "criticism that McCleskey has not shown how Georgia could do a better job," Justice Brennan says that "once it is established that the particular system of guided discretion chosen by a State is not achieving its intended purpose, the burden is on the *State*, not the defendant, to devise a more rational system if it wishes to continue to impose the death penalty." Id. at 334 n. 9.

Justice Powell's depiction of McCleskey's claims as challenges to "'the inestimable privilege of trial by jury'" (id. at 309)—which serves as the springboard for profuse encomia of the jury as "'the very palladium of free government'" (id. at 310 n. 31)—also ignores that much of the racial bias found by the Baldus study was located at prosecutorial decisionmaking stages rather than at jury decisionmaking stages. Justice Powell himself mentions this in describing the study (id. at 287) but then ignores it.

57. See, e.g., id. at 312 ("a capital punishment system that did not allow for discretionary acts of leniency 'would be totally alien to our notions of criminal justice'"); id. at 311 ("McCleskey's argument . . . is antithetical to the fundamental role of discretion in our criminal justice system"); id. at 314 n. 37 ("it is difficult to imagine guidelines that would produce the predictability sought by the dissent without sacrificing the discretion essential to a humane and fair system of criminal justice"). *Accord,* id. at 297, 314 n. 37 (quoted in note 59 below).

58. 481 U.S. at 297 (emphasis added).

59. E.g., id. at 314 n. 37:

"Justice Brennan [along with the three other Justices who join his dis-

sent] . . . questions *the very heart of our criminal justice system:* the traditional discretion that prosecutors and juries *necessarily must* have."
Id. at 311:

"McCleskey's argument . . . is antithetical to the *fundamental* role of
discretion in our criminal justice system. Discretion in the criminal justice system offers *substantial* benefits to the criminal defendant."
Id. at 314–315:

"McCleskey's claim . . . throws into serious question the principles that
underlie our entire criminal justice system."
(Emphasis in all quotations in this note has been added.)

60. Id. at 313.
61. Id. at 314 n. 37.
62. Id. at 313 n. 35. See also, e.g., id. at 307–308 n. 28:

"[S]entencing in state courts is generally discretionary, so a defendant's
ultimate sentence *necessarily* will vary according to the judgment of the
sentencing authority. The foregoing factors *necessarily* exist in varying
degrees throughout our criminal justice system."
Accord, id. at 312; see also id. at 297 (*"necessarily requires"*), 298 (legislatures *"necessarily* have wide discretion"), 311 ("jury's function to make the
difficult and uniquely human judgments that *defy codification* and that
'buil[d] discretion, equity, and flexibility into a legal system'"), 313 n. 35
("an *essential need* of the Anglo-American criminal justice system—to balance the desirability of a high degree of uniformity against the *necessity* for
the exercise of discretion"). (Emphasis in all quotations in this note has
been added.)

63. For a discussion of the rhetorical function of "presence," see Chaim
Perelman and Lucie Olbrechts-Tyteca, *The New Rhetoric: A Treatise on
Argumentation* (1958), John Wilkinson and Purcell Weaver trans., Notre
Dame and London: University of Notre Dame Press, 1971, pp. 115–120,
142–148, 158–163, 174–177.

64. "This case presents the question whether a complex statistical study that indicates a risk that racial considerations enter into capital sentencing determinations proves that petitioner McCleskey's capital sentence is unconstitutional under the Eighth or Fourteenth Amendment." 481 U.S. at 282–283.

65. At 481 U.S. 291 n. 7, Justice Powell says that because "the Court of Appeals
assumed that the [Baldus] study is valid and reached the constitutional issues," the Supreme Court will do the same. But, he immediately adds,
"[o]ur assumption that the Baldus study is statistically valid does not include the assumption that the study shows that racial considerations *actually* enter into any sentencing decisions in Georgia. Even a sophisticated
multiple-regression analysis such as the Baldus study can only demonstrate
a *risk* that the factor of race entered into some capital sentencing decisions
and a necessarily lesser *risk* that race entered into any particular sentencing
decision" (emphasis added except on the first "risk"). See also, e.g., 481

U.S. at 308–309 (quoted in the text at note 70 below), 312 ("*At most,* the Baldus study *indicates* a discrepancy that *appears* to correlate with race. *Apparent* disparities in sentencing are an inevitable part of our criminal justice system") (emphasis added), 317–318 ("any arbitrary variable . . . that some statistical study *indicates may* be influential in jury decisionmaking") (emphasis added).

66. See, e.g., the passages quoted in the text at notes 67 and 70 below.

67. 481 U.S. at 292–293 (emphasis added except on the first "his").

68. See id. at 293–295 (emphasis added):

> "McCleskey argues that the Baldus study compels an *inference* that his sentence rests on purposeful discrimination. McCleskey's claim that these *statistics* are sufficient *proof* of discrimination, *without regard to the facts of a particular case,* would *extend* to all capital cases in Georgia, at least where the victim was white and the defendant was black.
>
> "The Court has accepted *statistics* as *proof* of intent to discriminate in certain limited contexts. First, this Court has accepted *statistical disparities* as *proof* of an equal protection violation in the selection of the jury venire in a particular district. . . . Second, this Court has accepted *statistics in the form of multiple-regression analysis* to *prove* statutory violations under Title VII of the Civil Rights Act of 1964 [prohibiting employment discrimination]. . . .
>
> "But . . . the *application* of an *inference* drawn from *general statistics* to a *specific decision* in a trial and sentencing simply is not comparable to the *application* of an *inference* drawn from *general statistics* to a specific venire-selection or Title VII case. . . ."

69. McCleskey's Eighth Amendment claim rested principally on the theory articulated by the lead opinion in *Gregg v. Georgia,* 428 U.S. 153, 195 n. 46 (1976), that a capital sentencing "system could have standards so vague that they would fail adequately to channel the sentencing decision patterns of juries with the result that a pattern of arbitrary and capricious capital sentencing like that found unconstitutional in *Furman* could occur." Such a theory requires no showing of invidious motivation on the part of the decisionmakers involved in the case at bar. See *Maynard v. Cartwright,* 486 U.S. 356, 361–362 (1988).

70. 481 U.S. at 308–309 (emphasis added except on "prove" in the second sentence).

71. See Chapter 6 at notes 34, 68. Here the adverb is doubly unwarranted, first because McCleskey (if he wants to win his case) must be asking the Court to "accept" as the measure of an unconstitutional degree of racial prejudice only whatever "likelihood" the Court finds that the Baldus study *does* show; second, because Justice Powell himself has earlier said unequivocally that he is assuming that the Baldus study *does* show whatever likelihood it purports to show. See 481 U.S. at 291 n. 7.

72. See Chapter 6 at notes 69–71. See also, e.g., 481 U.S. at 308 (McCleskey

"argues that the Georgia capital punishment system is arbitrary and capricious in *application* . . . because racial considerations *may* influence capital sentencing decisions in Georgia" [second emphasis added]).

73. 481 U.S. at 312 (emphasis added). The second hedge is particularly glaring. In the ordinary meaning of "correlation," what the Baldus study shows is that the "discrepancy" in question (between life and death) *does* correlate with race. It would be unremarkable to use the word "appears" in describing any inference to be drawn from the correlation, but its use in describing the existence of the correlation itself is quite remarkable.

74. 481 U.S. at 291 n. 7.

75. The single exception to this rule is quoted in the text at note 107 below.

76. This is only one of the rhetorical devices used to portray Professor Baldus as an *advocate*. See, e.g., 481 U.S. at 287 n. 5 (emphasis added) ("Baldus *argued* in his testimony to the District Court that . . ." etc.).

77. See note 69 above.

78. 481 U.S. at 287 n. 5 (emphasis added). (The bracket was supplied by Justice Powell.)

79. Id. at 309 (emphasis added).

80. Id. at 310 (emphasis added). See also note 82 below.

81. Id. at 312–313.

82. See, e.g., id. at 315 n. 37 ("The *Gregg*-type statute imposes *unprecedented safeguards* in the special context of capital punishment. . . . All of these *are administered* pursuant to this Court's decisions interpreting the limits of the Eighth Amendment on the imposition of the death penalty, and all are subject to ultimate review by this Court. *These ensure a degree of care in the imposition of the sentence of death that can be described only as unique. Given* these safeguards *already inherent* in the imposition and review of capital sentences, the dissent's call for greater rationality is no less than a claim that a capital punishment system cannot be administered in accord with the Constitution"); 302–303 ("Thus, 'while some jury discretion still exists, "the discretion to be exercised *is controlled* by clear and objective standards *so as to produce* non-discriminatory application"'"); 309 n. 30 ("Nor *can* a prosecutor exercise peremptory challenges on the basis of race"); 308 ("McCleskey's sentence was imposed under Georgia sentencing procedures that *focus discretion*. . . ."); 306 ("statutory procedures *adequately channel* the sentencer's discretion"). (Emphasis in all quotations in this note has been added.)

83. The Court says it "assume[s] the [Baldus] study is valid statistically" (id. at 291 n. 7) and recites that in moderately aggravated ("mid-range") murder cases like McCleskey's, "Baldus found that 14.4% of the black-victim . . . cases received the death penalty, and 34.4% of the white-victim cases received the death penalty." Id. at 287 n. 5.

84. See id. at 311 (emphasis added): "Individual jurors bring to their delibera-

tions 'qualities of human nature and varieties of experience, the range of which is *unknown and perhaps unknowable.*' . . . The capital sentencing decision requires the individual jurors to focus their collective judgment on the *unique* characteristics of a particular criminal defendant. It is not surprising that such collective judgments often are *difficult to explain.* But the inherent lack of predictability of jury decisions does not justify their condemnation. On the contrary, it is the jury's function to make the difficult and uniquely human judgments that defy codification and that 'buil[d] discretion, equity, and flexibility into a legal system.'"

Justice Powell's rhetorical strategy of dematerializing any occurrence of racial bias in the Georgia system takes other forms as well. He dismisses McCleskey's observation that the bias demonstrated by the Baldus study is consistent with a historical pattern of discriminatory capital sentencing dating back to Georgia's Black Codes with the comment that "[a]lthough the history of racial discrimination in this country is undeniable, we cannot accept official actions taken long ago as evidence of current intent." 481 U.S. at 298 n. 20. And he deals with McCleskey's *Furman* claim by splitting it into two half-arguments—neither of which McCleskey made—and addressing each of them in isolation. Id. at 306–307 ("On the one hand, [McCleskey] . . . cannot base a constitutional claim on an argument that his case differs from other cases in which defendants *did* receive the death penalty. . . . On the other hand, . . . McCleskey cannot prove a constitutional violation by demonstrating that other defendants who may be similarly situated did *not* receive the death penalty").

85. 481 U.S. at 294.

86. Id. at 295 n. 14.

87. Id.

88. Id. at 294.

89. Id. at 295 n. 14.

90. See note 84 above. Justice Powell does not mention *Furman* or the *Furman* rule in the Equal Protection section of his opinion. In connection with the pronouncement quoted at note 89 above, he cites one of the Eighth Amendment decisions reflecting the contrapuntal *Woodson* rule.

91. See text and note at note 10 above.

92. 481 U.S. at 308.

93. "[A] State must 'narrow the class of murderers subject to capital punishment' . . . by providing 'specific and detailed guidance' to the sentencer." Id. at 303.

94. They include a requirement that the Georgia Supreme Court review death sentences to determine "whether the sentence is disproportionate to sentences imposed in generally similar murder cases. To aid the court's review, the trial judge answers a questionnaire about the trial, including detailed questions as to 'the quality of the defendant's representation [and] whether

race played a role in the trial.'" Id. at 303. Justice Powell neglects to mention that the set of trial judges' questionnaires maintained at the Georgia Supreme Court was one of the principal data sources for the Baldus study.

95. Id. at 302–303.

96. Id. at 314 n. 37. See also id. at 315 n. 37, quoted in note 82 above.

97. Id. at 305.

98. Id.

99. Id. at 306.

100. Id. at 307.

101. Id.

102. Id. at 307 n. 28.

103. See text at note 89 above.

104. See text at note 95 above.

105. 481 U.S. at 291 n. 7 (emphasis added).

106. Id. at 308 (emphasis added). See also id. at 291 n. 7: "Even a sophisticated multiple-regression analysis such as the Baldus study can only demonstrate a *risk* that the factor of race entered into some capital sentencing decisions and a necessarily lesser risk that race entered into any particular sentencing decision."

107. Id. at 313 n. 36.

108. Id. at 314–318 (emphasis added).

109. Thomas De Quincey, "On Murder Considered as One of the Fine Arts," in David Masson (Ed.), *The Collected Writings of Thomas De Quincey*, volume 13 (*Tales and Prose Phantasies*), Edinburgh: Adam and Charles Black, 1890, pp. 9–124, at p. 56.

110. See, e.g., *Gardner v. Florida*, 430 U.S. 349 (1977); *Lockett v. Ohio*, 438 U.S. 586 (1978); *Beck v. Alabama*, 447 U.S. 625 (1980); *Bullington v. Missouri*, 451 U.S. 430 (1981), and *Monge v. California*, 524 U.S. 721 (1998); *Enmund v. Florida*, 458 U.S. 782 (1982); *Turner v. Murray*, 476 U.S. 28 (1986); *Johnson v. Mississippi*, 486 U.S. 578 (1988); *California v. Ramos*, 463 U.S. 992, 998–999 (1983) (dictum) ("[t]he Court, as well as the separate opinions of a majority of the individual Justices, has recognized that the qualitative difference of death from all other punishments requires a correspondingly greater degree of scrutiny of the capital sentencing determination"). Justice Powell drew the distinction between capital and noncapital cases in his opinion for the Court in *Booth v. Maryland*, 482 U.S. 496 (1987), decided less than a month after *McCleskey*. (*Booth* has since been overruled on other grounds. *Payne v. Tennessee*, 501 U.S. 808 (1991).)

111. Compare *Hunter v. Erickson*, 393 U.S. 385, 391–392 (1969), with *James v. Valtierra*, 402 U.S. 137 (1971); and see, e.g., *Herndon v. Lowry*, 301 U.S. 242 (1937); *Shelton v. Tucker*, 364 U.S. 479 (1960); *N.A.A.C.P. v. Button*, 371 U.S. 415 (1963); *McLaughlin v. Florida*, 379 U.S. 184 (1964); *Shuttlesworth v. City of Birmingham*, 382 U.S. 87 (1965); *Ham v. South Carolina*, 409 U.S. 524 (1973); and the cases cited in note 47 above.

112. In the text, that is. His footnotes in this section of the opinion are more dubious. See Samuel R. Gross and Robert Mauro, *Death and Discrimination,* Boston: Northeastern University Press, 1989, pp. 187–188.

113. 481 U.S. at 295.

114. See the text at notes 85–89 above.

115. There are other examples in Justice Powell's opinion. His criticism of Justice Stevens's dissent is all about matter-of-degree practicalities, e.g., "it is difficult to imagine how JUSTICE STEVENS' proposal would or could operate on a case-by-case basis." 481 U.S. at 318 n. 45. On the other hand, as we have seen (at notes 70–84 above), his failure to take account of the *amount* of the "risk" shown by the Baldus study before he dismisses it on the ground that "[t]here is, of course, [always] *some* risk of racial prejudice influencing a jury's decision in a criminal case" (481 U.S. at 308 [emphasis added]) once again ignores matters of degree.

116. Yes, this sentence is rhetorical. How could it fail to be? We leave it to the reader to anatomize the species of *dissimulatio* involved (cf. Quintilian, *Institutio Oratoria,* book IX, chap. ii), together with all of the other rhetorical devices used in this chapter and throughout the book.

8. On the Dialectic of Culture

1. Alfred Kroeber, "The Super-Organic," *American Anthropologist,* 1917, *19,* 163–213.

2. Emile Durkheim, *The Elementary Forms of the Religious Life,* Joseph Ward Swain trans., New York: Collier Books, 1961.

3. Thomas S. Kuhn, *The Structure of Scientific Revolutions,* 2d edition, Chicago: University of Chicago Press, 1970.

4. Ruth Benedict, for example, in her graduate class at Columbia, devoted a lecture each year to warning students against the "anti-psychologism" implicit in Kroeber's superorganic hypothesis (but ended by telling them to get the "facts" right too!). We are indebted to Professor Ruth Heyer Young of the University of Virgina, one of Benedict's students, for this observation. She is at work on a monograph on Benedict in which she discusses Benedict's conflicts regarding psychological and institutional approaches to anthropology. For a recent, illuminating treatment of the whole subject, see Bradd Shore, *Culture in Mind,* Oxford: Oxford University Press, 1997.

5. See, e.g., Edward E. Evans-Pritchard, *The Nuer,* Oxford: Oxford University Press 1940, and *Nuer Religion,* 2d edition, Oxford: Oxford University Press, 1974. The irony of Evans-Pritchard's "institutionalism" is not that it was deficient in its interpretive reach but that it invigorated and enriched a next generation's more interpretive account of these beleaguered people of the Upper Nile. "E-P," as he was universally known, had set out a meticulous ethnology of the role of cattle in the life of these pastoralists: how they seemed to put more into their cows than they got out of them. John Ryle re-

ports that when he, as an aspiring young Oxford anthropologist, arrived in Khartoum, decades after E-P's death, his generation of fledgling anthropologists were still following the E-P-inspired interpretive rule, "Cherchez la vache!" John Ryle, "Cattle, War, and the Nilotes of High Steel," *Times Literary Supplement,* May 23, 1997, p. 10 (a review of Sharon E. Hutchinson, *Nuer Dilemmas: Coping with Money, War, and the State,* Berkeley: University of California Press, 1996).

6. This account was reported to one of us by the late Professor George Caspar Homans, who heard Evans-Pritchard tell it in a class lecture. We have been unable to find mention of it in Evans-Pritchard's writings.

7. See, e.g., James Clifford and George E. Marcus (Eds.), *Writing Culture: The Poetics and Politics of Ethnography,* Berkeley: University of California Press, 1986.

8. See, e.g., Charles O. Frake, "Struck by Speech: The Yakan Concept of Litigation," in Laura Nader (Ed.), *Law in Culture and Society,* Berkeley: University of California Press, 1997, pp. 147–167, at p. 149: "If the ethnographer claims his people do X three times a week, verification of his statement requires not simply counting occurrences of X, but also assessing the criteria for distinguishing X from all the other things people do during the week and for deciding that all the different events construed as instances of X in fact represent the 'same' activity. Information about what is the 'same' and what is 'different' can only come from the interpretations of events made by the people being studied."

9. Michel Foucault, *The Archeology of Knowledge,* A. M. Sheridan Smith trans., New York: Harper Colophon, 1972.

10. Eric Hobsbawm, "Introduction: Inventing Traditions," in Eric Hobsbawm and Terence Ranger (Eds.), *The Invention of Tradition,* Cambridge and New York: Cambridge University Press, 1983, pp. 1–14, at p. 2.

11. An instance is the transformation of Western family values in the past half-century. See Arlene Skolnick, "State of the Debate: Family Values: The Sequel," *The American Prospect,* May-June 1997, *32,* 86–94.

12. See, e.g., Claude Lévi-Strauss, *Tristes Tropiques* (1963), John Russell trans., New York: Atheneum, 1967, pp. 235–310.

13. To be sure, these records are selectively constructed and reflect the maker's interpretive stance: older chronologies were typically segmented by *reigns,* and today's employment statistics do not count "housewives" among the "employed." But even such records can serve as fact-like reference points, as *factoids,* with their limitations taken into account.

14. See Hugh Elton, *Frontiers of the Roman Empire,* Bloomington: Indiana University Press, 1996, and also Elton's more scholarly *Warfare in Roman Europe: AD 350–425,* Oxford: Oxford University Press, Clarendon Press, 1996. See also N. J. E. Austin and N. B. Rankov, *Exploratio: Military and Political Intelligence in the Roman World from the Second Punic War to the Battle of Adrianople,* New York and London: Routledge, 1995.

15. By the fourth century the Roman Army had become so ingrown that its intelligence service spent more effort reporting on the bureaucratic intrigues of Roman generals at the outposts of Empire than on probing into rebellions among the "barbarians."

16. Thomas Gladwin, *East Is a Big Bird: Navigation and Logic on Puluwat Atoll*, Cambridge, Mass.: Harvard University Press, 1970.

17. See, e.g., Paolo Freire, *Pedagogy of the Oppressed*, New York: Penguin Books, 1972; Renato Rosaldo, *Culture and Truth: The Remaking of Social Analysis*, Boston: Beacon Press, 1989.

18. See, e.g., Nancy Rule Goldberger, Mary Field Belenky, Blythe McVicker Clinchy, and Jill Mattuck Tarule, *Women's Ways of Knowing*, New York: Basic Books, 1989; Deborah Tannen, *You Just Don't Understand: Women and Men in Conversation*, New York: Morrow, 1990.

19. See, e.g., Gerald P. Lopez, *Rebellious Lawyering: One Chicano's Vision of Progressive Law Practice*, Boulder, Colo.: Westview Press, 1992; Gerald P. Lopez, "Reconceiving Civil Rights Practice: Seven Weeks in the Life of a Rebellious Collaboration," *Georgetown Law Journal*, 1989, 77, 1603–1717; James M. Doyle, "'It's the Third World Down There!': The Colonialist Vocation and American Criminal Justice," *Harvard Civil Rights–Civil Liberties Law Review*, 1992, 27, 71–126; James M. Doyle, "The Lawyers' Art: 'Representation' in Capital Cases," *Yale Journal of Law and the Humanities*, 1996, 8, 417–449; Lucie E. White, "Subordination, Rhetorical Survival Skills, and Sunday Shoes: Notes on the Hearing of Mrs. G.," *Buffalo Law Review*, 1990, 38, 1–58; Christopher P. Gilkerson, "Poverty Law Narratives: The Critical Practice and Theory of Receiving and Translating Client Stories," *Hastings Law Journal*, 1992, 43, 861–945.

20. Clifford Geertz, "Deep Play: Notes on the Balinese Cockfight," in *The Interpretation of Cultures*, New York: Basic Books, 1973, pp. 412–453, at p. 453.

21. Id. at 452.

22. See Chapter 5, particularly Parts II and III, and the Appendix.

23. See, e.g., "Affidavit of Grandison Briscoe," in Ira Berlin, Barbara J. Fields, Steven F. Miller, Joseph P. Reidy, and Leslie S. Rowland (Eds.), *Free at Last: A Documentary History of Slavery, Freedom, and the Civil War*, New York: The New Press, 1992, pp. 42–43; "Interview of Solomon Northrup," in John W. Blassingame, *Slave Testimony: Two Centuries of Letters, Speeches, Interviews, and Autobiographies*, Baton Rouge: Louisiana State University Press, 1977, pp. 288–289.

24. *Delo v. Blair*, 509 U.S. 823 (1993), at 823.

25. Robert M. Cover, "Violence and the Word," *Yale Law Journal*, 1986, 95, 1601–1629, at p. 1601. See also Austin Sarat and Thomas R. Kearns, "A Journey Through Forgetting: Toward a Jurisprudence of Violence," in Austin Sarat and Thomas R. Kearns (Eds.), *The Fate of Law*, Ann Arbor: University of Michigan Press, 1991, pp. 209–273.

26. Richard J. Evans, *Rituals of Retribution: Capital Punishment in Germany 1600–1987,* Oxford: Oxford University Press, 1996, p. 23.

27. See Clifford Geertz, "Local Knowledge: Fact and Law in Comparative Perspective," in *Local Knowledge: Further Essays in Interpretive Anthropology,* New York: Basic Books, 1983, pp. 167–234, at pp. 187–195.

28. Federal Rule of Evidence 602.

29. See Samuel R. Gross, "Expert Evidence," *Wisconsin Law Review,* 1991, *1991,* 1113–1232. It took only one notorious insanity verdict, however, to restore our basic American skeptical empiricism—selectively—on the subject of mental-state defenses advanced by criminal defendants. See Federal Rule of Evidence 704(b).

30. Salvador deMadariaga, *Englishmen, Frenchmen, Spaniards,* New York: Century, 1928.

31. George Dangerfield, *Strange Death of Liberal England: 1910–1914,* New York: Putnam, 1961.

32. Richard E. Nisbett and Dov Cohen, *Culture of Honor: The Psychology of Violence in the South,* Denver: Westview Press, 1996; see Richard E. Nisbett, "Violence and United States Regional Culture," *American Psychologist,* 1993, *48,* 441–449; Richard E. Nisbett and Dov Cohen, "Field Experiments Examining the Cult of Honor: The Role of Institutions in Perpetuating Norms About Violence," *Personality and Social Psychology Bulletin,* 1997, *23(11),* 1188–1199. Cash had earlier made a similar observation. W. J. Cash, *The Mind of the South* (1941), New York: Vintage Books, 1969, pp. 32–76.

33. See, e.g., Allison Davis, Burleigh B. Gardner, and Mary Gardner, *Deep South: A Social Anthropological Study of Caste and Class,* Chicago: University of Chicago Press, 1941.

34. Gunnar Myrdal, *An American Dilemma, Volume I: The Negro Problem and Modern Democracy* (1944), New Brunswick, N.J.: Transaction Publishers, 1996.

35. The standard source is the original edition gathered from class notes taken in Saussure's classes at Geneva by Charles Bally and Albert Sechehaye: Ferdinand de Saussure, *Cours de Linguistique Générale,* Lausanne and Paris: Payot, 1916. It was reissued by the same house (now in Paris) in 1972 and most recently in 1995. The now standard English edition was scrupulously translated by Roy Harris under the title *Course in General Linguistics,* Oxford: Oxford University Press, 1983.

36. See, e.g., Claude Lévi-Strauss, *Structural Anthropology,* Claire Jacobson and Brooke Grundfest Schoepf trans., New York: Basic Books, 1963.

37. For Lévi-Strauss's derivation of this approach from formal linguistics, see his Foreword to Roman Jakobson, *Six Lectures on Sound and Meaning,* John Mepham trans., Cambridge, Mass.: MIT Press, 1978.

38. See, e.g., Claude Lévi-Strauss, *Mythologiques* (1964–1971), John and

Doreen Weightman trans., Chicago: University of Chicago Press, in four volumes, 1983, 1990; Vladimir Propp, *Morphology of the Folktale* (1928), 2d edition, Laurence Scott trans., Austin: University of Texas Press, 1990.

39. See Chapter 6, note 66.

40. Leszek Kolakowski, *The Presence of Myth,* Adam Czerniawski trans., Chicago: University of Chicago Press, 1989, p. 23.

41. Lon Fuller, *The Morality of Law,* New Haven: Yale University Press, 1976.

42. Claims that they do are often based on the anthropologist's imposition on a culture of unifying concepts from outside. Max Gluckman's classic interpretations of Barotse law have been criticized on this ground by Paul Bohannon, who observes that "Gluckman is translating fundamentally Western ideas into Lozi [the language of the Barotse] instead of translating fundamentally Lozi ideas into English" and that by this backward translation Gluckman projects onto the Barotse his own unstated "belief in the psychic unity of mankind." Paul Bohannon, "Ethnography and Comparison in Legal Anthropology," in Nader, note 8 above, pp. 401–418, at p. 411. Bradd Shore's recent book cited in note 4 above contains an excellent discussion of cultural universals and projection of the credo of "the psychic unity of mankind" onto other cultures.

43. See text and note at note 27 above.

44. Geertz, note 27 above, at p. 205.

45. Id.

46. Id. See id. at pp. 187–195.

47. As Clifford Geertz would be the first to insist. See the concluding paragraphs of his marvelous essay on the Balinese cockfight, note 20 above, which include this passage (at p. 452): "The cockfight is not the master key to Balinese life, any more than bullfighting is to Spanish. What it says about that life is not unqualified nor even unchallenged by what other equally eloquent cultural statements say about it. But there is nothing more surprising in this than in the fact that Racine and Molière were contemporaries, or that the same people who arrange chrysanthemums cast swords."

48. Geertz, note 27 above, at p. 207.

49. Id. at p. 208.

50. Clifford Geertz, *After the Fact: Two Countries, Four Decades, One Anthropologist,* Cambridge, Mass.: Harvard University Press, 1995.

51. *Schlup v. Delo,* 513 U.S. 298, 325 (1995). The opinion cites as an example "the 'fundamental value determination of our society that it is far worse to convict an innocent man than to let a guilty man go free,'" quoting *In re Winship,* 397 U.S. 358, 370 (1970) (Justice Harlan, concurring).

52. E.g., *Boyd v. United States,* 116 U.S. 616 (1886); *Bram v. United States,* 168 U.S. 532 (1897); *Johnson v. Zerbst,* 304 U.S. 458 (1938); *Gideon v. Wainwright,* 372 U.S. 335 (1963); *Murphy v. Waterfront Commission,* 378 U.S. 52 (1964); *Miranda v. Arizona,* 384 U.S. 436 (1966).

53. See, e.g., Anthony G. Amsterdam, "The Supreme Court and the Rights of Suspects in Criminal Cases," *New York University Law Review,* 1970, *45,* 785–815.

54. *Brady v. United States,* 397 U.S. 742 (1970); *McMann v. Richardson,* 397 U.S. 759 (1970); *Parker v. North Carolina,* 397 U.S. 790 (1970); *North Carolina v. Alford,* 400 U.S. 25 (1970); *Corbitt v. New Jersey,* 439 U.S. 212 (1978); *United States v. Goodwin,* 457 U.S. 368 (1982); *Bordenkircher v. Hayes,* 434 U.S. 357 (1978); *Mabry v. Johnson,* 467 U.S. 504 (1984).

55. Herbert L. Packer, "Two Models of the Criminal Process," *University of Pennsylvania Law Review,* 1964, *113,* 1–68. See also John Griffiths, "Ideology in Criminal Procedure or a Third 'Model' of the Criminal Process," *Yale Law Journal,* 1970, *79,* 359–417.

56. Robert M. Cover, "The Supreme Court, 1982 Term, Foreword: Nomos and Narrative," *Harvard Law Review,* 1983, *97,* 4–68.

57. See Jerold S. Auerbach, *Justice Without Law?,* Oxford: Oxford University Press, 1983.

58. See Teun A. van Dijk, *Ideology: A Multidisciplinary Approach,* London: Sage, 1998.

59. See, e.g., Erving Goffman, *The Presentation of Self in Everyday Life,* New York: Doubleday (Anchor), 1959; Erving Goffman, *Interaction Ritual: Essays in Face-to-Face Behavior,* New York: Pantheon Books, 1967; Erving Goffman, *Forms of Talk,* Philadelphia: University of Pennsylvania Press, 1981; Harold Garfinkel, *Studies in Ethnomethodology,* Englewood Cliffs, N.J.: Prentice-Hall, 1967.

60. See Jerome S. Bruner and David Kalmar, "Narrative and Metanarrative in the Construction of Self," in Michel Ferrari and Robert J. Sternberg (Eds.)., *Self-Awareness: Its Nature and Development,* New York and London: Guilford Press, 1998, pp. 308–331.

61. See Ruth Benedict, *The Chrysanthemum and the Sword: Patterns of Japanese Culture,* Boston: Houghton Mifflin, 1946, particularly at pp. 219–225.

62. *Scott v. Sandford,* 19 How. 393 (1857). See Chapter 6, Part III, Subpart 4.

63. 16 Pet. 539 (1842). See Chapter 5.

64. See Michael Tomasello, *The Cultural Origins of Human Cognition,* Cambridge, Mass.: Harvard University Press, 1999, for an interesting overview of this by now well-accepted conclusion of paleoanthropological research.

65. See E. Susan Savage-Rumbaugh, Jeannine Murphy, Rose A. Sevcik, Karen E. Brakke, Shelly L. Williams, and Duane M. Rumbaugh, "Language Comprehension in Ape and Child," *Monographs of the Society for Research in Child Development,* 1993, *58(3–4)* [Serial No. 233].

66. See William Ian Miller, *Humiliation and Other Essays on Honor, Social Discomfort, and Violence,* Ithaca: Cornell University Press, 1993.

67. Andy Clark, *Being There: Putting Brain, Body, and World Together Again,* Cambridge, Mass., and London: MIT Press, 1997, p. 180.

68. Indeed, historians of nationalism now argue that the creation of national identities was brought about by a process of reifying imagined national communities through the spread of modes of dress, speech, and even selective historical memory of events like the Cawnpore Massacre, the Battle of Kosovo, Valley Forge, and the like. See, e.g., Benedict R. Anderson, *Imagined Communities: Reflections on the Origin and Spread of Nationalism,* 2d revised edition, London and New York: Verso, 1991; Anne Norton, *Reflections on Political Identity,* Baltimore: Johns Hopkins University Press, 1988; Anne Norton, *Republic of Signs: Liberal Theory and Popular American Culture,* Chicago: University of Chicago Press, 1993; Homi K. Bhabha (Ed.), *Nation and Narration,* London and New York: Routledge, 1990.

69. See Henri Bergson, *Creative Evolution,* Arthur Mitchell trans., New York: Henry Holt, 1913, pp. 272–298 [chap. IV]. "[A]n intelligence that was only intelligence, that had neither regret nor desire, whose movement was governed by the movement of its object, could not even conceive an absence or a void." Id. at pp. 282–283.

70. See, e.g., Mircea Eliade, *The Sacred and the Profane: The Nature of Religion* (1957), Willard R. Trask trans., San Diego and New York: Harcourt, Brace, Jovanovich (Harvest/HBJ), 1987; Tomoko Masuzawa, *In Search of Dreamtime: The Quest for the Origin of Religion,* Chicago and London: University of Chicago Press, 1993; and cf. Abdellah Hammoudi, *The Victim and Its Masks: An Essay on Sacrifice and Masquerade in the Maghreb,* Paula Wissing trans., Chicago and London: University of Chicago Press, 1993.

71. Cf. Tomasello, note 64 above; Marc D. Hauser, *The Evolution of Communication,* Cambridge, Mass.: MIT Press, 1996; Michael Tomasello and Josep Call, *Primate Cognition,* Oxford: Oxford University Press, 1997; Alison Jolly, *The Evolution of Primate Behavior,* New York: Macmillan, 1985; Robert A. Hinde, "Can Non-Human Primates Help Us Understand Human Behavior?," in B. B. Smuts, D. L. Cheney, R. M. Seyfarth, R. W. Wrangham, and T. T. Struhsaker (Eds.), *Primate Societies,* Chicago: University of Chicago Press, 1987, pp. 413–422.

72. Mikhail M. Bakhtin, *The Dialogic Imagination: Four Essays,* Caryl Emerson and Michael Holquist trans., Michael Holquist (Ed.), Austin: University of Texas Press, 1990.

73. See Marcel Granet, *La Pensée Chinoise,* Paris: Renaissance de Livre, 1934; Geoffrey Lloyd, "Science in Antiquity: The Greek and Chinese Cases and Their Relevance to the Problems of Culture and Cognition," in David Olson and Nancy Torrance (Eds.), *Modes of Thought: Explorations in Culture and Cognition,* Cambridge: Cambridge University Press, 1996.

74. Cf. Ann Brown, "The Development of Memory: Knowing, Knowing About Knowing, and Knowing How To Know," in H. W. Reese (Ed.), *Advances in Child Development and Behavior,* volume 10, New York: Academic Press, 1975.

75. See, e.g., Umberto Eco, Viacheslav V. Ivanov, and Monica Rector, *Carnival!,* Thomas Sebeok (Ed.), Berlin and New York: Mouton, 1984; Mikhail M. Bakhtin, *Rabelais and His World,* Helene Iswolsky trans., Cambridge, Mass.: MIT Press, 1968; E. Le Roy Ladurie, *Carnival in Romans,* Mary Feeney trans., New York: Brazilier, 1979. Compare David Aaron Murray, "The Oral Trickster," *Mythosphere,* 1999, *I,* 241–251.

76. We can accept Paul Veyne's metaphor that every society builds its own imaginative palace in the desert, and that

    "These palaces are not built in space. . . . They are the only space available. They project their own space when they arise. There is no repressed negativity around them that seeks to enter. Nothing exists, then, but what the imagination, which has brought forth the palace, has constituted."

    Paul Veyne, *Did the Greeks Believe in Their Myths? An Essay on the Constitutive Imagination,* Paula Wissing trans., Chicago: University of Chicago Press, 1988, pp. 121–122. But we think the palaces are a bit less "arbitrary and inert" (id. at 118) than Veyne does. It is their noetic space that permits them to be refurbished, sometimes even radically rebuilt, from time to time; and while we agree that this space is not something outside the palace seen, as it were, through the windows of some lofty observatory, it is a planetarium blazoned with all of the society's dreams of possible universes as well as its visions of virtual reality.

77. Often the rhetorics of possible-world advocacy are designed to defamiliarize the familiar evils they attack while conversely making the revolutionary alternatives they propose sound like canonical, everyday legitimacies. "Workers of the world unite; you have nothing to lose but your chains." The defamiliarization is the depiction of the worker's lot as bondage; once the "chains" metaphor attaches, nothing could be more natural than the call to break one's chains. For examples of the range of the phenomenon, see Nathan Leites, "Interaction: The Third International on Its Changes of Policy," in Harold D. Lasswell, Nathan Leites, and Associates, *Language of Politics: Studies in Quantitative Semantics* (1949), Cambridge, Mass.: MIT Press, 1966, pp. 298–333; Robert Wuthnow and Matthew P. Lawson, "Sources of Christian Fundamentalism in the United States," in Martin E. Marty and R. Scott Appleby (Eds.), *Accounting for Fundamentalisms: The Dynamic Character of Movements,* Chicago: University of Chicago Press, 1994, pp. 18–56; John Flowerdew, "The Discourse of Colonial Withdrawal: A Case Study in the Creation of Mythic Discourse," *Discourse & Society,* 1997, *8,* 453–477.

78. There are exceptions to this narrative order, as with mathematical and scientific conjectures, but they *are* exceptions.

79. Michael Silk, "How We Make Great Pain Bearable," *Times Literary Supplement,* April 18, 1997, p. 5 (a review of A. D. Nuttall, *Why Does Tragedy Give Pleasure?,* Oxford: Oxford University Press, Clarendon Press, 1996).

80. Id.
81. It would lead us too far afield to to inquire why, although the question is interesting. See Victor Turner, *From Ritual to Theater: The Human Seriousness of Play,* New York: Performing Arts Journal Press, 1982.
82. *Craic* is the commonly used Gaelic word for "good talk"—good-hearted but a bit ironic in highlighting human absurdity, especially one's own.
83. See, e.g., Lady Jane Francesca Wilde, "The Priest's Soul," in William Butler Yeats (Ed.), *Fairy and Folk Tales of Ireland* (1973), New York: Macmillan (Collier Books), 1986, pp. 195–199; "The Friar on Errigal," in Sean O'Sullivan (Ed.), *Folktales of Ireland,* Chicago: University of Chicago Press, 1968, pp. 144–149.
84. For a sober assessment of this unhappy series of events, see the column written by one of Ireland's most respected journalists, Fintan O'Toole, in *The Irish Times,* August 23, 1997, p. 6. Fintan O'Toole concludes his evaluation of the Father Smyth case with these words: "The most ferocious anti-clerical agitator, the most committed atheist, could never have wrought so much havoc as this ostensibly faithful servant of God."
85. For a photographic glimpse of this famous bike traffic, see Giuliano Ferrari, *Biciclette,* Reggio Emilia: Age, 1994.
86. The present Italian flag was designed and first flown in Reggio as the standard of the new Republic.
87. From an address by Bishop Francesco d'Este to the priests of the Diocese of Reggio, December 3, 1796, in Commune di Reggio Emilia, *The Two Hundredth Anniversary of the Italian Tricolour,* Reggio Emilia: CooperBanca, 1997, p. 18. For a general but rather schematized account of Reggio's history, see Massimo Pirondini, *Reggio Emilia: Guida Storico-Artistica,* Reggio Emilia: Bizzocchi, 1982. Pirondini's *Guida* also contains a useful guide to historical works on the city and *provincia*.
88. Pirondini, note 87 above, at p. 27.
89. See Nadia Caiti and Romeo Guarnieri, *La Memoria dei "Rossi": Fascismo, Resistenza, e Reconstruzione a Reggio Emilia,* Rome: Ediesse, 1996. In April 1945, the City of Reggio Emilia was awarded the Gold Medal of Valor for its role in the Resistance.
90. Joyce's famous passage describes how the threat was heard. James Joyce, *A Portrait of the Artist as a Young Man* (1916), New York: Modern Library, 1928, pp. 133–156.
91. It is of no small interest that the libertarian founders of the Cispadana Republic found it expedient to state in their proclamation to the people of Italy (October 17, 1796), "We rejoice that we are Republicans. We are not for that, less religious than you, or less firm than you in our adherence to the Catholic Church. Come then among us that you may be persuaded by your own eyes that our worship is free and unsullied." *The Two Hundredth Anniversary of the Italian Tricolour,* note 87 above, at p. 17.

9. Race, the Court, and America's Dialectic

1. Gunnar Myrdal, *An American Dilemma, Volume I: The Negro Problem and Modern Democracy* (1944), New Brunswick, N.J.: Transaction Publishers, 1996.
2. See John T. Noonan, Jr., *Persons and Masks of the Law: Cardozo, Holmes, Jefferson, and Wythe as Makers of the Masks,* New York: Farrar, Straus and Giroux, 1976.
3. See Chapter 2, Part VI, Subpart 2.
4. 163 U.S. 537 (1896).
5. Justice Harlan dissented. Justice Brewer did not participate in the case. The majority opinion, speaking for seven Justices, was written by Justice Brown.
6. 163 U.S. at 543. See also id. at 551–552.
7. Id. at 544 (emphasis added).
8. Id. at 551.
9. Id. at 550 (emphasis added).
10. Id. at 544.
11. Id. at 551.
12. 347 U.S. 483 (1954).
13. Id. at 495.
14. Id. at 492–493. See also id. at 494: "Whatever may have been the extent of psychological knowledge at the time of *Plessy v. Ferguson,* this finding [that segregation damages African-American children] is amply supported by modern authority."
15. Id. at 489 (emphasis added). See also id. at 491 (emphasis added): "American courts have . . . *labored with* the doctrine [of *Plessy v. Ferguson*] for over half a century."
16. Id. at 493 (emphasis added).
17. Id. (emphasis added).
18. Id. at 489.
19. Id. at 492–493.
20. Id. at 493.
21. Id. at 493–494.
22. 503 U.S. 467, 118 L.Ed.2d 108.
23. 515 U.S. 70, 132 L.Ed.2d 63.
24. 118 L.Ed.2d at 133.
25. 132 L.Ed.2d at 89.
26. 118 L.Ed.2d at 128; see also id. at 138; and see generally Chapter 5, Part VI.
27. 118 L.Ed.2d at 137.
28. Id. (emphasis added).
29. See Chapter 3, *Jenkins,* Part III, Scene 1.
30. "Once the racial imbalance due to the de jure violation has been remedied,

the school district is under no duty to remedy imbalance that is caused by demographic factors." *Pitts,* 118 L.Ed.2d at 136. "Where resegregation is a product not of state action but of private choices, it does not have constitutional implications." Id. at 137. See also id. at 131–132; *Jenkins,* 132 L.Ed.2d at 81–83, 87–89.

31. Regarding *Pitts,* see Chapter 5, Part V. Regarding *Jenkins,* see Chapter 3, *Jenkins,* Part III, Scene 11.

32. *Pitts,* 118 L.Ed.2d at 133. This duty is derived from the second member of the conjunction coined by *Pitts* to describe the "end purpose" of a school-desegregation case (see text at note 24 above) and is announced immediately following the coinage. By the end of the paragraph, the second member of the conjunction has completely displaced the first, and the Court is talking about "the ultimate objective" of desegregation litigation as being "to return school districts to the control of local authorities." 118 L.Ed.2d at 133–134. See also *Jenkins,* 132 L.Ed.2d at 80–81, 86–87, 89.

33. *Pitts,* 118 L.Ed.2d at 137.

34. Id. *Accord: Jenkins,* 132 L.Ed.2d at 85.

35. See Chapter 3, *Jenkins,* Part III, Scene 3. The Court's abdication of responsibility is manifested both in the result of this reasoning—to force the lower federal courts out of the desegregation business, with the bull's-eye distribution of the country's metropolitan school population permanently impacted—and in Chief Justice Rehnquist's unwillingness to acknowledge that the logic underlying it is elective. See also Chapter 3, *Jenkins,* Part III, Scene 1.

36. "[F]ederal judicial supervision of local school systems was intended as a 'temporary measure.' . . . [T]his temporary measure has lasted decades. . . ." *Pitts,* 118 L.Ed.2d at 133. *Accord: Jenkins,* 132 L.Ed.2d at 80, 89.

37. *Pitts,* 118 L.Ed.2d. at 134.

38. "[O]ur cases recognize that local autonomy of school districts is a vital national tradition . . . and that a district court must *strive* to restore state and local authorities to the control of a school system operating in compliance with the Constitition." *Jenkins,* 132 L.Ed.2d at 87 (emphasis added); see id. at 81, 89; *Pitts,* 118 L.Ed.2d at 134.

39. 391 U.S. 430, 435.

40. *Pitts,* 118 L.Ed.2d at 131. *Accord: Jenkins,* 132 L.Ed.2d at 80.

41. *Pitts,* 118 L.Ed.2d at 131.

42. See *Jenkins,* 132 L.Ed.2d at 79–86.

43. Id., 132 L.Ed.2d at 87. See also id.: "The District Court's pursuit of the goal of 'desegregative attractiveness' results in so many imponderables. . . ." See generally Chapter 3, *Jenkins,* Part III, Scene 12. As we have seen, the *Pitts* opinion rewrites *Brown*'s concern about psychological harm to African-American children as a concern for *de jure* oppression. See Chapter 5, Part VI, at notes 136–141.

44. For the story, see, e.g., Richard Kluger, *Simple Justice: The History of Brown v. Board of Education and Black America's Struggle for Equality* (1975), New York: Random House (Vintage Books), 1977, pp. 678–699.

45. See, e.g., David Halberstam, *The Fifties,* New York: Villard Books, 1993, pp. 667–690; Jack Greenberg, *Crusaders in the Courts: How a Dedicated Band of Lawyers Fought for the Civil Rights Revolution,* New York: Basic Books, 1994, pp. 228–232.

46. 358 U.S. 1 (1958).

47. This is not because *Brown* explicitly "overruled" *Plessy* in a technical sense. What *Brown* said about *Plessy* explicitly was (1) that certain "language in *Plessy* . . . is rejected"—specifically, "[a]ny language . . . contrary to [*Brown's*] . . . finding" that racial segregation "'has a detrimental effect'" upon African-American children, and that this "'impact is greater'" when the segregation "'has the sanction of the law'" because law-ordered segregation "'is usually interpreted as denoting the inferiority of the negro group,'" 347 U.S. at 494–495—and (2) that *Plessy's* "doctrine of 'separate but equal' has no place" in "the field of public education," id. at 495. However, any bar examiner would expect a competent lawyer to reason that *Plessy* had been stripped of all precedential value by the cumulative effect of these disapproving statements in the *Brown* opinion and the Supreme Court's subsequent citation of *Brown* in terse orders forbidding state-enforced racial segregation of bathing beaches, golf courses, buses, and municipal parks; see, e.g., *Mayor and City Council of Baltimore v. Dawson,* 350 U.S. 877 (1955) (per curiam); *Holmes v. Atlanta,* 350 U.S. 879 (1955) (per curiam); *Gayle v. Browder,* 352 U.S. 903 (1956) (per curiam); *New Orleans City Park Improvement Ass'n v.* Detiege, 358 U.S. 54 (1958) (per curiam); and see *Watson v. City of Memphis,* 373 U.S. 526 (1963).

48. *Pitts, Jenkins,* and similar rulings limit *Brown* to situations of *de jure* discrimination as opposed to so-called *de facto* discrimination. Cases like *McCleskey v. Kemp,* 481 U.S. 279 (1987) [see Chapter 7], *Washington v. Davis,* 426 U.S. 229 (1976), and *City of Memphis v. Greene,* 451 U.S. 100 (1981), preclude a finding of *de jure* discrimination in the absence of case-specific evidence of racial *animus* on the part of an identifiable state officer. See also, e.g., *Arlington Heights v. Metropolitan Housing Development Corp.,* 429 U.S. 252 (1977); *City of Mobile v. Bolden,* 446 U.S. 55 (1980). The upshot, essentially, is that cases of unconstitutional discrimination against racial minorities can be proved only against extremely bigoted *and* uncommonly stupid state officials. See, e.g., Alan David Freeman, "Legitimating Racial Discrimination Through Anti-Discrimination Law: A Critical Review of Supreme Court Doctrine," *Minnesota Law Review,* 1978, 62, 1049–1119. To be sure, a part of the reason why state officials today do not act out demonstrable scenarios of bigotry is that *Brown* continues to exert a restraining influence on their behavior; but we have already noted this point in the preceding paragraph.

49. "One wonders whether the majority still believes that race discrimination—or, more accurately, race discrimination against nonwhites—is a problem in our society, or even remembers that it ever was." Justice Blackmun, dissenting, in *Wards Cove Packing Co., Inc. v. Atonio*, 490 U.S. 642, 661, 662 (1989).

50. 438 U.S. 265 (1978).

51. 515 U.S. 200 (1995). See also *City of Richmond v. J. A. Croson Co.*, 488 U.S. 469 (1989); *Shaw v. Reno*, 509 U.S. 630 (1993); *Miller v. Johnson*, 515 U.S. 900 (1995).

52. John Higham, "Coda: Three Reconstructions," in John Higham (Ed.), *Civil Rights and Social Wrongs: Black-White Relations Since World War II*, University Park, Pa.: Pennsylvania State University Press, 1997, pp. 179–189. A slightly different version appears as John Higham, "America's Three Reconstructions," *New York Review of Books*, November 6, 1997, pp. 52–56. We will cite the book chapter hereafter as Higham, "Three Reconstructions."

53. Higham, "Three Reconstructions," at p. 179.

54. In the interest of compression, we omit some of the events that Higham discusses as illustrative of each of the three waves and we substitute equally illustrative events that can be described more succinctly.

55. *Slaughter-House Cases*, 16 Wall. (83 U.S.) 36 (1873). See also *United States v. Cruikshank*, 92 U.S. 542 (1876).

56. The quotations are from Higham, "Three Reconstructions," at p. 180. His reference to Myrdal is at p. 181. Higham's account of the Creed draws upon the well-known work of Gordon Wood, *The Creation of the American Republic 1776–1787*, Chapel Hill: University of North Carolina Press, 1969. Myrdal's exposition of the Creed is in Myrdal, note 1 above, at pp. 3–25.

57. Higham, "Three Reconstructions," at pp. 180–181.

58. Id. at 181.

59. Id. at 183.

60. Id. at 181. See also id. at 186.

61. Id. at 185.

62. Id. at 186.

63. Id.

64. Higham speaks of "an extraordinarily durable set of ideas that came to define a national purpose" and says that "[i]n the absence of a homogeneous ethnic identity, this compound of secular and religious ideas— . . . this amalgam of liberty, nationality and faith—was the strongest bond of unity in the new nation." Higham, "Three Reconstructions," at p. 180.

65. To avoid verbal complexities and connect our conception to Higham's and Myrdal's, we follow their convention of using "American" to refer to the United States.

66. See, e.g., Lawrence E. Mitchell, *Stacked Deck: A Story of Selfishness in America*, Philadelphia: Temple University Press, 1998.

67. See, e.g., Richard Slotkin, *Regeneration Through Violence: The Mythology of the American Frontier 1600–1860,* Middletown, Conn.: Wesleyan University Press, 1973; Richard Slotkin, *Gunfighter Nation: The Myth of the Frontier in Twentieth Century America,* New York: Harper Collins (HarperPerennial), 1993. Consider this tribute paid to former Alabama Governor George C. Wallace on the day after his death by a 65-year-old white homeowner in West Anniston: "I voted for him. Every time. I liked him standing up there in that school door, by God. . . . And the Federals had to move him. . . . He was a man, by God. He wasn't no boy." *New York Times,* September 15, 1998, sec. 1, p. A1.

68. See Myrdal, note 1 above, at pp. 88–89.

69. See, e.g., W. J. Cash, *The Mind of the South* (1941), New York: Random House (Vintage Books), 1969; Thomas F. Gossett, *Race: The History of an Idea in America,* new edition, New York and Oxford: Oxford University Press, 1997; Winthrop D. Jordan, *White Over Black: American Attitudes Toward the Negro, 1550–1812,* New York: W. W. Norton, 1977; Lillian Smith, *Killers of the Dream,* revised edition, Garden City, N.Y.: Anchor Books, 1963; Rayford W. Logan, *The Betrayal of the Negro: From Rutherford B. Hayes to Woodrow Wilson* (first published in 1954 under the title: *The Negro in American Life and Thought: The Nadir, 1877–1901*), New York: Da Capo Press, 1997; Joel Williamson, *The Crucible of Race: Black-White Relations in the American South Since Emancipation,* New York and Oxford: Oxford University Press, 1984; A. Leon Higginbotham, Jr., *Shades of Freedom: Racial Politics and Presumptions of the American Legal Process,* New York and Oxford: Oxford University Press, 1996; James M. Jones, *Prejudice and Racism,* Reading, Mass.: Addison-Wesley, 1972; Calvin C. Hernton, *Sex and Racism in America,* New York: Grove Press, 1965; Joel Kovel, *White Racism: A Psychohistory,* New York: Columbia University Press (Morningside), 1984; Toni Morrison, *Playing in the Dark: Whiteness and the Literary Imagination,* New York: Random House (Vintage Books), 1993. A standard defense of slavery, for example, was South Carolina Senator (and former Governor) James Henry Hammond's tale about how African-Americans—physically vigorous, intellectually feeble, docile, and faithful—were fitted by nature for their role as the mud-sill needed to support the South's high level of progress, civilization, and refinement. *Congressional Globe,* 35th Cong., 1st Sess., App. 68, 71 (March 4, 1858); Carol Bleser (Ed.), *Secret and Sacred: The Diaries of James Henry Hammond, A Southern Slaveholder,* New York and Oxford: Oxford University Press, 1988, pp. 272–273. Variations on the theme featured the apparatuses of biblical exegesis, moral philosophy, natural history, biological science, actuarial statistics, political theory, and humanitarianism. See, e.g., George Fitzhugh, *Cannibals All! or, Slaves Without Masters,* C. Vann Woodward (Ed.), Cambridge, Mass.: Harvard University Press, Belknap Press, 1960 [first published in 1857]; Eric L. McKitrick (Ed.), *Slavery De-*

fended: The Views of the Old South, Englewood Cliffs, N.J.: Prentice-Hall, 1963; Drew Gilpin Faust (Ed.), *The Ideology of Slavery: Proslavery Thought in the Antebellum South 1830–1860,* Baton Rouge: Louisiana State University Press, 1981.

70. Jordan, note 69 above, at p. 184. The Burgesses reported, however, that it was customary to baptize Negroes born in the colony and raise them as Christians. Id.

71. See Anthony G. Amsterdam, "Equality as an Enforceable Right: Problems and Prospects Ahead," *Proceedings of the American Philosophical Society,* 1991, *135/1,* 13–21, at pp. 19–20.

72. See, e.g., Jerome G. Miller, *Search and Destroy: African-American Males in the Criminal Justice System,* Cambridge: Cambridge University Press, 1996; Michael Tonry, *Malign Neglect: Race, Crime, and Punishment in America,* New York and Oxford: Oxford University Press, 1995.

73. See, e.g., A. Leon Higginbotham, Jr., *In the Matter of Color: Race and the American Legal Process: The Colonial Period,* New York and Oxford: Oxford University Press, 1978; Robert William Fogel, *Without Consent or Contract: The Rise and Fall of American Slavery,* New York: W. W. Norton, 1989; Kenneth M. Stampp, *The Peculiar Institution: Slavery in the Ante-Bellum South,* New York: Random House (Vintage Books), 1956; Jordan, note 69 above.

74. See, e.g., Myrdal, note 1 above, at pp. 83–110.

75. William J. Wilson, *Power, Racism, and Privilege: Race Relations in Theoretical and Sociohistorical Perspectives* (1973), New York: Free Press, 1976, p. 93.

76. For Cash, Jordan, and Smith, see note 69 above; see also C. Vann Woodward, *The Strange Career of Jim Crow,* 3d revised edition, New York: Oxford University Press, 1974.

77. It is not. The complexities of this subject are suggested by the thoughtful essays collected in Christopher Jencks and Meredith Phillips (Eds.), *The Black-White Test Score Gap,* Washington, D.C.: Brookings Institution Press, 1998; and see, e.g., Claude M. Steele and Joshua Aronson, "Stereotype Threat and the Intellectual Test Performance of African Americans," *Journal of Personality and Social Psychology,* 1995, *69,* 797–811.

78. See, e.g., William Julius Wilson, *The Truly Disadvantaged: The Inner City, the Underclass, and Public Policy,* Chicago: University of Chicago Press, 1987; William Julius Wilson, *When Work Disappears: The World of the New Urban Poor,* New York: Knopf, 1996; Jonathan Kozol, *Savage Inequalities: Children in America's Schools,* New York: Crown, 1991. Although the urban ghetto is the most striking instantiation of America's failure to undo the handicaps of economic and social disadvantage that are the legacy of slavery and Jim Crow, it is not the only site of these persisting disadvantages. "In stark, material terms . . . whites and blacks constitute two nations" within America. Melvin L. Oliver and Thomas M. Shapiro, *Black*

Wealth/White Wealth: A New Perspective on Racial Equality, New York and London: Routledge, 1995, p. 91.

79. See, e.g., Eric Foner, *Reconstruction: America's Unfinished Revolution 1863–1877,* New York: Harper and Row, 1988; Logan, note 69 above; John Hope Franklin and Alfred A. Moss, Jr., *From Slavery to Freedom: A History of African Americans,* 7th edition, New York: McGraw-Hill, 1994, pp. 220–263; Williamson, note 69 above; C. Vann Woodward, note 76 above, at pp. 31–71; C. Vann Woodward, "The Political Legacy of Reconstruction," in *The Burden of Southern History,* New York: Random House (Vintage Books), 1960, pp. 89–107.

80. See C. Vann Woodward, "Equality: The Deferred Commitment," in *The Burden of Southern History,* note 79 above, pp. 69–87.

81. Harry V. Jaffa, *Crisis of the House Divided: An Interpretation of the Issues in the Lincoln-Douglas Debates* (1959), Seattle: University of Washington Press, 1973, p. 433.

82. See Chapter 5, Parts II and IV.

83. Lawrence Friedman calls this unworldliness "the person-from-Pluto approach" and observes that it "characterizes much of the work of the Supreme Court in race cases in the years after the Civil War." Lawrence M. Friedman, "Brown in Context," in Austin Sarat (Ed.), *Race, Law, and Culture: Reflections on Brown v. Board of Education,* New York and Oxford: Oxford University Press, 1997, pp. 49–73, at p. 52.

84. Alexander Pope, *An Essay on Man,* Epistle I, line 294. Key features of this strategy parallel the essential elements of Calhoun's political philosophy: acceptance of the inevitability and unchangeability of posited human characteristics (see, e.g., John C. Calhoun, *A Disquisition on Government and A Discourse on the Constitution and Government of the United States,* Columbia: A. S. Johnston, 1851, pp. 1–7, 74, 281) sets up a need for *compromise* as the indispensable peace-keeping strategy and thus endows it with the highest moral virtue (see, e.g., id. at 63–70, 192–197).

85. Concerning the prevalence of this view at the end of the nineteenth century and the beginning of the twentieth, see, e.g., Logan, note 69 above; Gossett, note 69 above, at pp. 144–175, 253–286; August Meier and Elliott Rudwick, *From Plantation to Ghetto,* 3d edition, New York: Hill and Wang, 1976, p. 211; Woodward, note 76 above, at pp. 72–74. Racist writers of the time, some sincere and some opportunistic, mustered scientific and historical evidence as well as biblical testimony to support claims of the superiority of the "white race," see, e.g., Charles Carroll, *The Negro a Beast, or In the Image of God,* Miami: Mnemosyne, 1900; William Patrick Calhoun, *The Caucasian and the Negro in the United States* (1902), New York: Arno Press, 1977; William Benjamin Smith, *The Color Line: A Brief in Behalf of the Unborn* (1905), New York: Negro Universities Press, 1969; Robert W. Shufeldt, *The Negro: A Menace to American Civilization,* Boston: The Gorham Press, 1907; Lothrop Stoddard, *The Rising Tide of*

Color Against White World-Supremacy (1920), Westport: Negro Universities Press, 1971, and projected American and world history through the lens of racism, see, e.g., John W. Burgess, *Reconstruction and the Constitution 1866–1876,* New York: Scribner's, 1902; Madison Grant, *The Passing of the Great Race, or The Racial Basis of European History,* New York: Scribner's, 1916. Notably, D. W. Griffith's *The Birth of a Nation,* Hollywood's first feature-length film, opened in 1915. See, e.g., Fred Silva (Ed.), *Focus on The Birth of a Nation,* Englewood Cliffs, N.J.: Prentice-Hall, 1971. In all, Eric Foner's assessment seems just: "If racism contributed to the undoing of Reconstruction, by the same token Reconstruction's demise and the emergence of blacks as a disenfranchised class of dependent laborers greatly facilitated racism's further spread, until by the early twentieth century it had become more deeply embedded in the nation's culture and politics than at any time since the beginning of the antislavery crusade and perhaps in our entire history." Foner, note 79 above, at p. 604.

86. Andrew Delbanco, *The Death of Satan: How Americans Have Lost the Sense of Evil,* New York: Farrar, Straus (Noonday), 1996, pp. 138, 153.

87. See, e.g., United States Commission on Civil Rights, *Law Enforcement: A Report on Equal Protection in the South,* Washington, D.C.: G.P.O., 1965; United States Commission on Civil Rights, *Freedom to the Free: Century of Emancipation 1863–1963, A Report to the President,* Washington, D.C.: G.P.O., 1963, pp. 94–95; Leon Friedman (Ed.), *Southern Justice,* New York: Pantheon Books, 1965.

88. See, e.g., Franklin and Moss, note 79 above, at pp. 346–354; Woodward, note 76 above, at pp. 114–115.

89. See Woodward, note 76 above, at pp. 130–134; Anthony G. Amsterdam, "Thurgood Marshall's Image of the Blue-Eyed Child in *Brown,*" *New York University Law Review,* 1993, 68, 226–236.

90. See Erich Kahler, *The Inward Turn of Narrative,* Richard Winston and Clara Winston trans., Princeton: Princeton University Press, 1973.

91. See, e.g., David Levering Lewis, *When Harlem Was in Vogue* (1981), New York and Oxford: Oxford University Press, 1989; George Hutchinson, *The Harlem Renaissance in Black and White,* Cambridge, Mass.: Harvard University Press, Belknap Press, 1995; Franklin and Moss, note 79 above, at pp. 361–380.

92. Celeste Michelle Condit and John Louis Lucaites, *Crafting Equality: America's Anglo-African World,* Chicago: University of Chicago Press, 1993, p. 173.

93. Id. at 172.

94. See, e.g., *Moore v. Dempsey,* 261 U.S. 86 (1923); *Powell v. Alabama,* 287 U.S. 45 (1932); *Norris v. Alabama,* 294 U.S. 587 (1935); *Brown v. Mississippi,* 297 U.S. 278 (1936); *Chambers v. Florida,* 309 U.S. 227 (1940); *White v. Texas,* 309 U.S. 631 (1940) (per curiam), rehearing denied, 310 U.S. 530 (1940).

95. *Powell v. Alabama*, 287 U.S. 45, 56, 57 (1932) (emphasis added).

96. In *Moore v. Dempsey*, note 94 above, Justice Holmes wrote for the Court that "if the case is that the whole proceeding is a mask—that counsel, jury and judge were swept to the fatal end by an irresistible wave of public passion, and that the State Courts failed to correct the wrong, neither [theoretical] perfection in the [state] machinery for correction nor the possibility that the trial court and counsel saw no other way of avoiding an immediate outbreak of the mob can prevent this Court from securing to the petitioners their constitutional rights." 261 U.S. at 91. In *Powell v. Alabama*, note 95 above, the Court reversed the first conviction of the Scottsboro defendants on the ground that they "were not accorded the right of counsel *in any substantial sense. To decide otherwise, would simply be to ignore actualities.*" 287 U.S. at 58 (emphasis added). In the second Scottsboro case, *Norris v. Alabama*, note 94 above, the Court again reversed (or, in one case, vacated) the Alabama Supreme Court's judgments affirming the convictions, on the ground that the evidence showed that the jury commissioners had systematically excluded African-Americans from the grand and trial juries:

    "That the question [whether exclusion was practiced] is one of fact does not relieve us of the duty to determine whether in truth a federal right has been denied. When a federal right has been specially set up and claimed in a state court, it is our province to inquire not merely whether it was denied in express terms but also whether it was denied in substance and effect [and] . . . it is incumbent upon us to analyze the facts in order that the appropriate enforcement of the federal right may be assured."

    294 U.S. at 589–590. See also, e.g., *Brown v. Mississippi*, 297 U.S. 278, 286–287 (1936).

97. See, e.g., *Smith v. Allwright*, 321 U.S. 649 (1944), and *Terry v. Adams*, 345 U.S. 461 (1953) (denial of the right to vote in party primaries on the ground of race); *Shelley v. Kraemer*, 334 U.S. 1 (1948) (state judicial enforcement of racially restrictive covenants); *Brown v. Allen*, 344 U.S. 443 (1953) (federal habeas corpus review of claims of denials of due process and equal protection in state criminal proceedings).

98. *Hirabayashi v. United States*, 320 U.S. 81 (1943); *Korematsu v. United States*, 323 U.S. 214 (1944). The Court tried to make some amends in *Ex parte Mitsuye Endo*, 323 U.S. 283 (1944), but this chapter of its history is an ugly one.

99. *McLaurin v. Oklahoma State Regents*, 339 U.S. 637 (1950); *Sweatt v. Painter*, 339 U.S. 629 (1950). For example: "It may be argued that excluding [the African-American] petitioner from [the University of Texas' all-white law] . . . school is no different from excluding white students from the new law school [for Negroes]. *This contention overlooks realities.*" Id. at 634 (emphasis added).

100. See Thurgood Marshall, "An Evaluation of Recent Efforts to Achieve Ra-

cial Integration in Education Through Resort to the Courts," *Journal of Negro Education,* 1952, *21,* 316–327; Greenberg, note 45 above, at pp. 58–81.

101. *Brown v. Board of Education,* 347 U.S. 483, 495 (1954).
102. *Brown v. Board of Education,* 349 U.S. 294, 301 (1955).
103. See note 47 above.
104. See, e.g., *Heart of Atlanta Motel, Inc. v. United States,* 379 U.S. 241 (1964); *Katzenbach v. McClung,* 379 U.S. 294 (1964); *Hamm v. City of Rock Hill,* 379 U.S. 306 (1964); *Griggs v. Duke Power Co.,* 401 U.S. 424 (1971).
105. See, e.g., *United States v. Mississippi,* 380 U.S. 128 (1965); *Louisiana v. United States,* 380 U.S. 145 (1965); *United States v. Guest,* 383 U.S. 745 (1966); *United States v. Price,* 383 U.S. 787 (1966).
106. See, e.g., *Gomillion v. Lightfoot,* 364 U.S. 339 (1960); *Shelton v. Tucker,* 364 U.S. 479 (1960); *N.A.A.C.P. v. Button,* 371 U.S. 415 (1963); *Edwards v. South Carolina,* 372 U.S. 229 (1963); *Peterson v. City of Greenville,* 373 U.S. 244 (1963); *Wright v. Georgia,* 373 U.S. 284 (1963); *Anderson v. Martin,* 375 U.S. 399 (1964); *Hamilton v. Alabama,* 376 U.S. 650 (1964) (per curiam) (reversing the contempt conviction of an African-American witness who refused to answer questions when addressed by her first name); *McLaughlin v. Florida,* 379 U.S. 184 (1964); *Shuttlesworth v. City of Birmingham,* 382 U.S. 87 (1965); *Harper v. Virginia State Board of Elections,* 383 U.S. 663 (1966); *Loving v. Virginia,* 388 U.S. 1 (1967).
107. Barbara Ehrenreich, *Fear of Falling: The Inner Life of the Middle Class,* New York: Pantheon Books, 1989. See also, e.g., Katherine S. Newman, *Declining Fortunes: The Withering of the American Dream,* New York: Basic Books, 1993.
108. See, e.g., Stanley Fish, "Op-Ed: How the Right Hijacked the Magic Words," *New York Times,* August 13, 1995, sec. 4, p. 15; Susan Sturm and Lani Guinier, "The Future of Affirmative Action: Reclaiming the Innovative Ideal," *California Law Review,* 1996, *84,* 953–1036.
109. Nicholas deB. Katzenbach and Burke Marshall, "Not Color Blind: Just Blind," *New York Times Magazine,* February 22, 1998, pp. 42–45.
110. See Jules Witcover, *The Year the Dream Died: Revisiting 1968 in America,* New York: Warner Books, 1998.
111. Margaret Mead, *And Keep Your Powder Dry: An Anthropologist Looks at America,* New York: Morrow, 1942.
112. See Amsterdam, note 71 above.
113. See text and notes at notes 50–51 above. As the Court has summarized the doctrine of these cases, they hold (1) that any race-based governmental action must be subjected to a ""'"most searching examination"'"" under the constitutional principle of equal protection, *Adarand Constructors, Inc. v. Pena,* 515 U.S. 200, 223 (1995); (2) that "'[t]he standard of review under the Equal Protection Clause is not dependent on the race of those burdened or benefited by a particular classification,'" id. at 224; (3) that this standard

of review permits race-based classifications only when they are "necessary to further a compelling [governmental] interest," id. at 237, and upon a demonstration of "'the most exact connection between justification and classification,'" id. at 236; and (4) that while "government is not disqualified from acting" to eliminate the "lingering effects of racial discrimination against minority groups in this country," id. at 237, such a justification requires a convincing demonstration that any race-specific remedial program is narrowly tailored to correct some previous, factually documented, unconstitutional discrimination for which the particular governmental agency itself was responsible, *City of Richmond v. J. A. Croson Co.*, 488 U.S. 469, 498–506 (1989); *Miller v. Johnson*, 515 U.S. 900, 920–923 (1995); *Wygant v. Jackson Board of Education*, 476 U.S. 267, 274–276 (1986) (plurality opinion). The effect of these rules is to make it almost impossible to sustain race-specific governmental programs designed to increase African-American participation in the wide range of areas from which African-Americans were long excluded by a complex interplay of private discrimination and government connivance. And the Court's own application of the rules can be explained only on the theory that a majority of the Justices believe that racial discrimination against African-Americans is now an obscure, forgotten chapter in the history of the United States but that racial discrimination against white people is a clear and present danger. See, e.g., David Kairys, "Unexplainable on Grounds Other Than Race," *American University Law Review,* 1996, 45, 729–749.

114. "Reading the Equal Protection Clause to protect whites as well as blacks from racial classification is to focus upon a situation that does not and never has existed in our society." Katzenbach and Marshall, note 109 above, at p. 45.

115. See text and notes at notes 39–43 above.

116. The story of these developments between 1954 and the early 1990s is summarized in Chapter 3, *Jenkins,* Part I; the remainder of the first half of Chapter 3 and parts of Chapter 5 discuss the 1992 opinion in *Freeman v. Pitts* and the 1995 opinion in *Missouri v. Jenkins* that delineate the terms on which the federal courts are to close out school desegregation cases.

117. Gary Orfield, Susan E. Eaton, and The Harvard Project on School Desegregation, *Dismantling Desegregation: The Quiet Reversal of Brown v. Board of Education,* New York: The New Press, 1996, p. xix. For popular tellings of the tale, see Emily Yellin with David Firestone, "By Court Order, Busing Ends Where It Began," *New York Times,* September 11, 1999, sec. 1, pp. A1 and A8; Peter Applebome, "Schools See Re-emergence of 'Separate but Equal,'" *New York Times,* National Report, April 8, 1997, sec. 1, p. A10; James S. Kunen, "Nation: The End of Integration," *Time Magazine,* April 29, 1996, pp. 38–45.

118. The Supreme Court cases to date seem to leave some room for race-specific affirmative action in the admissions process for institutions of higher educa-

tion. See note 113 above. However, the United States Court of Appeals for the Fifth Circuit in the much-discussed case of *Hopwood v. Texas,* 78 F.3d 932 (5th Cir. 1996), reduced that room to uninhabitably small quarters, and the Supreme Court declined to review the Fifth Circuit's decision, 518 U.S. 1033 (1996). Such denials of review are not decisions on the merits, so the High Court's views on the issue remain uncertain.

119. See William G. Bowen and Derek Bok, *The Shape of the River: Long-Term Consequences of Considering Race in College and University Admissions,* Princeton: Princeton University Press, 1998.

120. Admissions officials are not eager to complicate their selection criteria by taking account of nonobvious characteristics that might compensate for African-American children's disadvantages—such as a handicap factor—particularly when they have to operate under the threat of *Bakke* lawsuits and the unsympathetic scrutiny of "old guard" alumni groups. State universities might attempt more imaginative approaches, such as admitting a minimum number of graduates from every high school in the state, but few are that venturesome.

121. See Michael S. McPherson and Morton Owen Schapiro, *The Student Aid Game: Meeting Need and Rewarding Talent in American Higher Education,* Princeton: Princeton University Press, 1998, pp. 116–121.

122. Id. at 37–48, 135–140.

123. See, e.g., Terry Eastland, *Ending Affirmative Action: The Case for Color-blind Justice,* New York: Basic Books, 1996; Clint Bolick, *The Affirmative Action Fraud: Can We Restore the American Civil Rights Vision?,* Washington, D.C.: Cato Institute, 1996; Jim Sleeper, *Liberal Racism,* New York: Viking Penguin, 1997; Stephan Thernstrom and Abigail Thernstrom, *America in Black and White: One Nation, Indivisible,* New York: Simon and Schuster, 1997.

124. *Regents of University of California v. Bakke,* 438 U.S. 265, 299 (1978) (opinion of Justice Powell). *Accord: Adarand Constructors, Inc. v. Pena,* 515 U.S. 200, 224–225 (1995).

125. See *Wright v. Council of City of Emporia,* 407 U.S. 451 (1972); *United States v. Scotland Neck City Board of Education,* 407 U.S. 484 (1972). If the Supreme Court concluded that school district lines had to be overridden to satisfy the promise of *Brown,* the Supremacy Clause would provide a short and decisive answer to any objection based on their supposed impermeability.

126. The verse in *Ghetto* got it exactly right: "The rich folks, they own the big City. / They down us, / For livin' the way we do. / But when you're born the child of a poor man, / You know ghetto is the only place for you." Homer Banks, Bonnie Bramlett, Delaney Bramlett, and Bettye Jean Crutcher, *Ghetto,* Irving Music Inc. (East Memphis).

127. *Brown v. Board of Education,* 347 U.S. 483, 493 (1954).

128. Id. at 492–493.

129. See, e.g., Morrison, note 69 above; Derrick Bell, _And We Are Not Saved: The Elusive Quest for Racial Justice,_ New York: Basic Books, 1987; Patricia J. Williams, _The Alchemy of Race and Rights,_ Cambridge, Mass.: Harvard University Press, 1991.

130. See Bowen and Bok, note 119 above.

131. _Younger v. Harris,_ 401 U.S. 37, 44 (1971).

132. See Rogers M. Smith, _Civic Ideals: Conflicting Visions of Citizenship in U.S. History,_ New Haven and London: Yale University Press, 1997; Eric Foner, _The Story of American Freedom,_ New York and London, W. W. Norton, 1998.

10. Reflections on a Voyage

1. Jerome Bruner, _Acts of Meaning,_ Cambridge, Mass.: Harvard University Press, 1990, pp. 95–96.

2. Gordon Willard Allport, _Pattern and Growth in Personality,_ New York: Holt, Rinehart and Winston, 1957; see particularly chapters 9 and 10, where he discusses the "transformation of motives." Recall also William James's justly famous chapter on "Habit" in his _Principles of Psychology,_ where he introduces the idea of habit-like motives.

3. See notes 30 and 61 of Chapter 8 and accompanying text.

4. See Carol Gilligan, _In a Different Voice,_ Cambridge, Mass.: Harvard University Press, 1982; Patricia Ewick and Susan Silberg, _The Common Place of Law: Stories from Everyday Life,_ Chicago: University of Chicago Press, 1998; John M. Conley and William M. O'Barr, _Rules Versus Relationships: The Ethnography of Legal Discourse,_ Chicago: University of Chicago Press, 1990.

5. See, e.g., Louis H. Pollak, "Racial Discrimination and Judicial Integrity: A Reply to Professor Wechsler," _University of Pennsylvania Law Review,_ 1959, _108,_ 1–34; Daniel Gordon, "Happy Anniversary _Brown v. Board of Education:_ In Need of a Remake after Forty Years," _Columbia Human Rights Law Review,_ 1993, _25,_ 107–129. The scholarly criticisms of the _Brown_ opinion are reviewed (and given bad grades in turn) in Lawrence M. Friedman, "Brown in Context," in Austin Sarat (Ed.), _Race, Law, and Culture: Reflections on Brown v. Board of Education,_ New York and Oxford: Oxford University Press, 1997, pp. 49–73, at pp. 49–53. For a look at some of the complexities involved in coming to terms with _Brown,_ see Morton J. Horwitz, "The Jurisprudence of _Brown_ and the Dilemmas of Liberalism," _Harvard Civil Rights–Civil Liberties Law Review,_ 1979, _14,_ 599–613.

6. Gerald N. Rosenberg, _The Hollow Hope: Can Courts Bring About Social Change?,_ Chicago and London: University of Chicago Press, 1991, p. 71. Cf. Michael J. Klarman, _"Brown,_ Racial Change, and the Civil Rights Movement," _Virginia Law Review,_ 1994, _80,_ 7–150, arguing that _Brown_ did nothing but ignite a "bizarre sequence of events" (p. 150) that slightly

speeded up "a transformation in American race relations [that] was, by mid-century, a virtual inevitability" (p. 71).

7. Richard A. Posner, "Against Constitutional Theory," *New York University Law Review,* 1998, *73,* 1–22, at p. 1: "Constitutional theory . . . is the effort to develop a generally accepted theory to guide the interpretation of the Constitution of the United States."

8. *Oxford English Dictionary,* 1971.

9. Roberta Michnik Golinkoff and Kathy Hersh-Pasek, *How Babies Talk,* New York: Dutton, 1989.

10. For the strong "nativist" explication of language acquisition, see Steven Pinker, *The Language Instinct: How the Mind Creates Language,* New York: William Morrow, 1994. For a more balanced view, see Golinkoff and Hersh-Pasek, note 9 above, and also Michael Tomasello, *The Cultural Origins of Human Cognition: An Essay,* Cambridge, Mass.: Harvard University Press, 1999.

11. J. L. Austin, *How to Do Things with Words,* Cambridge, Mass.: Harvard University Press, 1962.

12. See, e.g., Jane Harris Aiken, "Striving to Teach 'Justice, Fairness, and Morality,'" *Clinical Law Review,* 1997, *4,* 1–64.

13. See, e.g., Richard K. Neumann, Jr., "On Strategy," *Fordham Law Review,* 1990, *59,* 299–346; Edward D. Ohlbaum, "Basic Instinct: Case Theory and Courtroom Performance," *Temple Law Review,* 1993, *66,* 1–122.

Table of Cases

All cases are decisions of the Supreme Court of the United States unless otherwise indicated. The names of cases analyzed in the text are in boldface type.

Index